THE FAMILY

ALSO BY KITTY KELLEY

Jackie Oh!

Elizabeth Taylor: The Last Star

His Way: The Unauthorized Biography of Frank Sinatra

Nancy Reagan: The Unauthorized Biography

The Royals

DOUBLEDAY

NEW YORK LONDON TORONTO

SYDNEY AUCKLAND

THE
FAMILY

THE REAL STORY OF
THE BUSH DYNASTY

KITTY KELLEY

PUBLISHED BY DOUBLEDAY
a division of Random House, Inc.

DOUBLEDAY and the portrayal of an anchor with a dolphin are registered
trademarks of Random House, Inc.

Book design by Gretchen Achilles

Library of Congress Cataloging-in-Publication Data
has been applied for.

ISBN 0-385-50324-5
Copyright © 2004 by H. B. Productions, Inc.

All Rights Reserved

PRINTED IN THE UNITED STATES OF AMERICA

September 2004
FIRST EDITION

1   3   5   7   9   10   8   6   4   2

In Memoriam

William V. Kelley
(1904–2002)

Adele M. Kelley
(1916–1978)

A. Stanley Tretick
(1921–1999)

Charlie Tolchin
(1968–2003)

To my husband, John, who continues to make dreams come true

"The great enemy of the truth is very often not the lie—deliberate, continued, and dishonest—but the myth—persistent, persuasive, and unrealistic."

—JOHN FITZGERALD KENNEDY, JUNE 11, 1962,
COMMENCEMENT ADDRESS, YALE UNIVERSITY

Samuel Prescott Bush (1863–1948)
m. 6/27/1894 ───────────────────────
Flora Sheldon [first wife] (1872–1920)

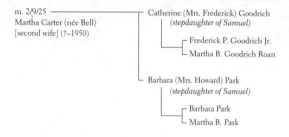

m. 2/9/25 ───────────────── Catherine (Mrs. Frederick) Goodrich
Martha Carter (née Bell)   *(stepdaughter of Samuel)*
[second wife] (?–1950)
                                       ┌─ Frederick P. Goodrich Jr.
                                       └─ Martha B. Goodrich Roan

                              Barbara (Mrs. Howard) Park
                                   (stepdaughter of Samuel)

                                       ┌─ Barbara Park
                                       └─ Martha B. Park

BUSH/WALKER/PIERCE/ROBINSON FAMILY TREE

George Herbert Walker (1874–1953)
m. 1/17/1899 ───────────────────────
Lucretia (Loulie) Wear (1874–1961)

Scott Pierce (1866–1930?)
m. 11/26/1891 ───────────────────────
Mabel Marvin (1869–1930?)

James Edgar Robinson (1868–1932)
m. 3/31/1895 ───────────────────────
Lula Dell Flickinger (1875–?)

Prescott Sheldon Bush (1895–1972)
m. 8/6/21
Dorothy Walker (1901–1992)

Robert Sheldon Bush
(1896–1900)

Mary Eleanor Bush (1897–1992)
m.
Francis Edwin House Jr. (1889–1971)

Margaret Livingston Bush (1899–1993)
m.
Stuart Holmes Clement (1895–1974)

James Smith Bush (1901–1978)
m. 1/19/29 (divorced 7/12/48)
Caroline Lowe Patterson [first wife]

    m. 8/14/48 (divorced 7/29/52)
       Janet Stewart (née Newbold) [second wife]

    m. 12/21/53 (divorced 12/4/70)
       Lois Reid Niedringhaus (née Kieffer) [third wife] (1924–)

    m. 12/4/70 Gloria Galbusera [fourth wife]

Prescott Sheldon Bush Jr. (1922–)*
George Herbert Walker Bush (1924–)*
Nancy Bush (1926–)*
Jonathan James Bush (1931–)*
William Henry Trotter Bush (1938–)*

Francis E. House III*
Flora House*
James B. House*
Timothy House (?–1992?)*

Stuart H. Clement Jr. (1920–)*
Samuel Prescott Bush Clement*
Mary Bush Clement*

Henrietta Lowe Bush (1929–1945)
Caroline (Teensie) Patterson Bush (1933?)*
Flora S. (Shelley) Bush (1935–)*

Alan Ryan (stepchild)
Nancy Ryan (stepchild)
Serena Rhinelander Stewart (1939–) (stepchild)

Jean Dula Niedringhaus (1946–) (stepchild)*
James Morrison Niedringhaus (1948?–) (stepchild)*
Mary Livingston Bush (1955–)
Samuel P. Bush II (1958–)*
Ethel Walker Bush (1959?–)*

Nancy Walker (1899–1997)

Dorothy (Doro) Walker (1901–1992)
m. 8/6/21
Prescott Sheldon Bush [see Prescott Sheldon Bush]

George Herbert Walker Jr. (1905–1977)
m. 10/29/27
Mary Carter (1905–1998)

James Wear Walker (1907–1997)
m.
Sara Mitchell O'Keefe (1916–1996)

John M. Walker Sr. (1909?–1990)
m. 11/25/39
Elsie Louise Mead (1915–)

Louis Walker (1912–2001)
m.
Grace Ballard White (1916–)

Elizabeth Walker (1929–)*
George Herbert Walker III (1931–)*
Ray Walker (1933–)*

John O'Keefe (1939–) (stepchild)
Sheila O'Keefe (1942–) (stepchild)*
Hilary Walker*

John M. Walker Jr. (1940?)*
George Mead Walker (1942?–)*
Loulie Wear Walker (1945–1955)
Elsie Mead Walker (1948?–)*
Louise Mead Walker (1954?–)
Randolph Talbot Walker (1955–)*
Marianna Walker (1956?–)

James Wear Walker II (1940–)*
Suzanne Walker (1941–)*
Dorothy (Debbie) Walker (1946–)*
Elizabeth Walker (1946–)*

Marvin Pierce (1893–1969)
m. 8/?/18
Pauline Robinson [first wife] (1896–1949)

    m. 7/3/52 Willa Gray Martin [second wife] (1911–?)

Charlotte Pierce (1894–1971)

Pauline Robinson (1896–1949)
m. 8/?/18
Marvin Pierce [see Marvin Pierce]

James E. Robinson
m.
Peggy ?

Mrs. E. C. Bonar

Mrs. E. R. Parker

Martha Pierce (1920–1999)*
James Robinson Pierce (1922–1993)*
Barbara Pierce (1925–)*
Scott Pierce (1930–)*

Jimmy Robinson

* continued on overleaf

Prescott Sheldon Bush Jr. (1922–)
m. 12/31/44
Elizabeth Louise Draper Kauffman (1922–)
- Prescott Bush III (1945–) (divorced)
- Kelsey Bush (1947–)*
- James L. Bush (1955–)*

George Herbert Walker Bush (1924–)
m. 1/6/45
Barbara Pierce (1925–)
- George Walker Bush (1946–)*
- Pauline Robinson Bush (1949–1953)
- John Ellis (Jeb) Bush (1953–)*
- Neil Mallon Bush (1955–)*
- Marvin Pierce Bush (1956–)*
- Dorothy Walker Bush (1959–)*

Nancy Bush (1926–)
m. 10/26/46
Alexander B. Ellis Jr. (1922–1989)
- Nancy Walker Ellis*
- Alexander Ellis III
- John Prescott Ellis (1953?–)*
- Josiah Wear Ellis*

Jonathan James Bush (1931–)
m.
Josephine C. Bradley (1930–)
- Jonathan James Bush Jr. (1969–)*
- William Hall Bush (1971–)*

William Henry Trotter Bush (1938–)
m. 8/15/59
Patricia Lee Redfearn (1938–)
- William Prescott Bush (1964–)*
- Louisa Bush (1970–)

Francis E. House III
m.
Patty ?
- Jeremy House (1954–)*
- Sheila House (1955–)
- Kevin House (1956–)

Flora House
m.
F. H. Fairchild
- Allmah [?] House (1958–)
- Tracy House (1960–)*
- Hillary House (1964–)*
- Christopher House (1968–)

James B. House
m. (divorced)
Margot Volya [first wife] [?]
- Christine Fairchild (1955–)

m. Vilma House [second wife]
- Henry House (1953–)
- Jeanny V. House
- S.P.B. House *
- Patrick House
- Helen House (1974–)

Timothy House (?–1992?)
m.
Joyce Hallock Ives Nichols
- Denes House
- Marika (Mary) House

Stuart H. Clement Jr. (1920–)
m.
Anne ? (1925–)
- Timothy House Jr.*

Samuel Prescott Bush Clement
m.
Harmony Twichell
- Anne Clement (1946–)*
- Jane C. Clement (1947–)
- Mary Clement (1949–)*
- Pamela Bush Clement (1954–)*
- Stuart H. Clement III (1958–)*
- Charles S.C. Clement (1968–)*

Mary Bush Clement
m.
Henry Wilde Estabrook
- Harmony Clement (1946–)*
- Margaret Clement*
- Samuel Prescott Clement*

Caroline Patterson Bush (1933–)
m. (sometime before 1959)
Wallace Hasbrouk Cole Jr. (?–2001)
- Margaret Estabrook*
- Amy Estabrook*

Flora S. (Shelley) Bush (1935–)
m. 1/17/59
John C. (Jack) Jansing
- Lucy Cole*
- Shelley Cole
- Wallace Cole III*

Jean Dula Niedringhaus (1946–) (stepchild)
m.
Robert Calhoun
- John Jansing (1965–)
- Caroline Jansing (1966–)
- Christopher Jansing (1967–)

Samuel P. Bush II (1958–)
m.
Alexandra (Max) ?
- at least one child, Lois Kieffer Calhoun*

Ethel Walker Bush (1959?–)
m.
Malcolm McAllister
- Caitlin Bush (1985–)
- James S. Bush (1987–)
- Hadley Alexander Bush (1990–)

Elizabeth Walker (1929–)
m. 1951
Reuben Holden (1918–1995)
- Grace Holden (1952–)
- Mary Holden*
- George Holden*
- Reuben Andrus Holden V*

(This generational line continues on the following page.)

BUSH/WALKER/PIERCE/ROBINSON FAMILY TREE

George Herbert Walker III (1931–)
m. 12/23/55 (divorced 10/1/62)
Sandra Elizabeth Canning (1936?–) [first wife]

    m. 7/27/68 Kimberly Collins Gedge [second wife]

    m. Carol Banta [third wife]

Ray Walker (1933–)
m. 8/7/54
Emily Allen Thompson [first wife]

    m.1/9/71? Jeanne Cowan [second wife]

Sheila O'Keefe (1942–) (stepchild)
m.
Webster B. Todd

Hilary Walker
m
Peter Gilmore

John M. Walker Jr. (1940–)
m.
[first wife?]

    m. (before March 1990) Katherine Bingham [second wife]

George Mead Walker (1942?–)
m.
Connie Hudson

Elsie Mead Walker (1948?–)
m.
Allerton W. Kilborne

Randolph Talbot Walker (1955?)
m.
Nancy Guerrieri

James Wear Walker II (1940–)
m.
Anne (Vandy) Hannan (1945–)

Suzanne Walker (1941–)
m.
Davis R. Robinson (1940–)

Dorothy (Doro) Walker (1946–)
m. 1971
Craig Stapleton

Elizabeth Walker (1946–)
m.
John W. Field Jr.

Martha Pierce (1920–1999)
m. (during early 1940s)
Walter Gelshenen Rafferty (?–1999?)

James Robinson Pierce (1922–1993)
m. 9/17/49
Margaret Dyer

Barbara Pierce (1925–)
m. 1/6/45
George Herbert Walker Bush (1924–)
   [see George Herbert Walker Bush]

Scott Pierce (1930–)
m. 1950
Janice Chamberlain

- Mary Elizabeth Walker (1956–)*
- Wendy Walker (1958?–)*
- Isabelle Walker (1960?–)*

- George H. Walker IV (1969–)
- Carter Walker (1971–)

- Christopher T. Walker (1955–)*
- Scott Holden Walker (1956–)*
- Daniel C. Walker (1960?–)*
- David E. Walker (1961?–)*
- Stephen D. Whetstone (1962–)
- Krista Whetstone (1963–)

- William Walker Todd (1965–)
- Whitney Todd (1968–)
- Jamie Todd (1970–)

- James Tucker Gilmore (1981)
- Liza Gilmore (1986–)

- John Bingham (stepson)
- Gerald Bingham (stepson)
- Charles Bingham (stepson)
- one daughter, name unknown

- Jonathan Walker (1968–)
- Dexter Walker (1972–)
- George Mead Walker (1975–)
- Jay Walker (1981–)

- Rebecca Kilborne (1985–)
- John Mercer Walker Kilborne (1989–)

- Philip Nuttle (1981–) (stepson)
- Randolph Talbot Walker Jr. (1991–)

- Loulie Berdell Walker (1972–)
- Anne White Walker (1974–)

- Christopher Champlin Robinson (1968–)
- Gracyn Walker Robinson (1971–)

- Wendy Stapleton (1974–)
- Walker Stapleton (1977–)

- John W. Field III (1970–)
- Andrew Walker Field (1974–)

- Sharon Rafferty (1943?–)*
- Kevin Rafferty (1948–)
- Pierce Rafferty
- Corinne Rafferty
- Brian Rafferty
- Gail Rafferty

- Margaret Pierce*
- Marvin Pierce II
- James R. Pierce Jr.*
- Scott Pierce III

- Kent Pierce*
- Kim Pierce
- Brett Pierce
- Derek Pierce

* continued on overleaf

Kelsey Bush (b. 8/4/47)
m. ———————————————————
Philip Nadeau

James L. Bush (b. 7/23/55)
m. ———————————————————
Susan ?

George Walker Bush (1946–)
m. 11/5/77
Laura Welch (1946–)

John Ellis (Jeb) Bush (1953–)
m. 2/23/74
Columba Garnica Gallo (1953–)

Neil Mallon Bush (1955–)
m. 7/6/80 (divorced 4/28/03)
Sharon L. Smith (1952–) [first wife]

    m. 3/6/04 Maria Andrews [second wife] ———————

Marvin Pierce Bush (1956–)
m. 6/13/81 ———————————————————
Margaret Molster (1959–)

Dorothy Walker Bush (1959–)
m. 9/1/82 (divorced 1990) ———————
William LeBlond [first husband]

    m. 6/27/92 Robert Koch (1960–) [second husband] ———

Nancy Walker Ellis
m. ———————————————————
Tom Black

Alexander Ellis III
m. ———————————————————
Robin Rand

John Prescott Ellis (1953–)
m. (divorced)
Joan Kenyon [first wife]

    m. Susan Smith Ellis [second wife] ——————————— two children

Josiah Wear Ellis
m.
Joan Corning Woodworth

Jonathan James Bush Jr. (1969–)
m. ——————————————————— three children, details unknown
Sarah ?

William Hall Bush (1971–)
m. ———————————————————
Sydney ?

William Prescott Bush (1964–)
m. ———————————————————
Lindsay Whitaker

Jeremy House (1954–)
m.
[?]

Tracy House (1960–)
m. ———————————————————
Christopher Cannon

Hillary House (1964–)
m.
Charles Sanford III

S.P.B. House Jr.
m.
Sharon?

Timothy House Jr.
m.
Anne Carey

Anne Clement (1946–)
m. ———————————————————
Charles T. Haddad (1934–)

Mary Clement (1949–)
m. ———————————————————
John E. Stein

Pamela Bush Clement (1954–)
m.
Angelo John Ianello (1953–)

Stuart H. Clement III (1958–)
m. ———————————————————
Kelly Carroll

Elizabeth Nadeau (1978–)
Kate Nadeau (1980–)
(twins) William Nadeau and Prescott Nadeau (1988–)

Sarah Bush (1983–)
Sam Bush (1985–)

(twins) Barbara Pierce Bush and Jenna Welch Bush (1981–)

George Prescott Bush (1976–)
Noelle Lucilla Bush (1977–)
John Ellis Bush Jr. (1983–)

Lauren Pierce Bush (1984–)
Pierce Mallon Bush (1986–)
Ashley Walker Bush (1989–)

Elizabeth Andrews (stepchild)
Pace Andrews (stepchild)
Thomas Andrews (stepchild)

Marshall Lloyd Bush, girl (adopted) 1986
Charles Walker Bush (adopted) 1989

Samuel Bush LeBlond (1984–)
Nancy Ellis LeBlond (1986–)

Robert David Koch (1993–)
Georgia Grace (GiGi) Koch (1996–)

Sophie Ellis Black

Alexander Ellis IV (1979–)
Christopher Ellis (1982–)
Walker Bush Ellis (1985–)

Josephine Bush
Mary Bradley Bush

Katherine Bush
Alexander Bush

Jillian Cannon (1986–)
Dylan Cannon (1989–)

Tanya Clement Haddad
Jennifer Anne Haddad
Toullo[?] Haddad
Ghassan Haddad
Elizabeth Victoria Haddad

John E. Stein Jr. (1968–) (by previous Stein marriage)
Peter Russell Clement Stein (1977–)
Anne Clement Stein (1979–)

Molly Kathleen Clement (1992–)

(This generational line continues on the following page.)

BUSH/WALKER/PIERCE/ROBINSON FAMILY TREE

Charles S.C. Clement (1968–)
m.
Kristen Wedgewood Julian

Harmony Clement (1946–) ——————————————————— Harmony Sporgberg (1975–)
m.
Steven Sporgberg

Margaret Clement
m.
Edward Green (divorced)

Samuel Prescott Clement
m.
Barbara Tutoff

Margaret Estabrook ————————————— Nicholas Stienstra (1980?–)
m. ———————————————————————————— Peter Stienstra (1991–)
Pieter Stienstra

Amy Estabrook ————————————————— Benjamin Ross (1989?–)
m. ———————————————————————————— Chelsea Bush Ross (1991–)
Philip Ross

Lucy Cole
m.
Michael Carney

Wallace Cole III ————————————————— Hadyn Cole (1986–)
m. ———————————————————————————— William Cole (1987–)
Alice Cole

Lois Kieffer Calhoun
m. ———————————————————————————— at least one daughter, Jean Baker Dwinell
James Dwinell IV

Mary Holden ————————————————————— Raphaelle Ayach (1986–)
m. ———————————————————————————— Nichole Ayach (1988–)
Jean Luc Ayach (divorced)

George Holden ———————————————————— Margaret C. Holden (1987–)
m. ———————————————————————————— John Holden (1990–)
Anne Cameron

Reuben Andrus Holden V
m.
Pamela

Mary Elizabeth Walker (1956–) ————————— Maximilian Bunzel (1981–)
m. 8/18/81 ———————————————————————— Theodore Bunzel (1986–)
Jeffrey Bunzel (1956–) ———————————————— Eli Walker Bunzel (1991–)

Wendy Walker (1958–)
m. 9/12/87
Bruce Cleveland [first husband]

    m. 8/21/91 Robert Emmet Cleary [second husband]

Isabelle Walker (1960–)
m. ———————————————————————————— three children
Bruce Klein

Christopher T. Walker (1955–)
m.
Martha

Scott Holden Walker (1956–)
m. ———————————————————————————— at least one child, born 1990, name unknown
Louise

Daniel C. Walker (1960?–) ————————————— Timothy Walker (1987–)
m. ———————————————————————————— Hannah Walker (1988–)
Leslie

David E. Walker (1961?–)
m.
Cary

Sharon Rafferty (1943–) —————————————— Rockwell Patterson
m. ———————————————————————————— Meaghan Patterson
John Patterson

Margaret Pierce ————————————————————— Jill Peters
m. ———————————————————————————— Molly Peters
Peters? ———————————————————————————— Jonathan Peters

James R. Pierce Jr.
m. ———————————————————————————————————
Dabney ?
                                                    at least one daughter, Barbara
Kent Pierce
m.
Kristen ?

CONTENTS

AUTHOR'S NOTE

I believe that the people we most admire most influence our country, so those are the lives I've chosen to examine. My subjects have included Jacqueline Kennedy Onassis, Elizabeth Taylor, Frank Sinatra, Nancy Reagan, the British monarchy, and now, the Bushes. They were not simply public figures who happened to be celebrities. When I wrote about them they were all living icons who, for better or for worse, substantially influenced our culture. I stress the word "living" because I believe in writing books about people who are alive and quite capable of defending themselves. The dead have no recourse to a biographer's unsparing revelations. *The Family*, by the nature of its scope and historical perspective, varies from that formula a bit. Prescott Bush, the scion of the Bush dynasty, is, of course, an important figure in this book. But the focus is meant to be on his son and grandson, George H.W. and George W., because they have far surpassed Prescott in political and historical importance.

Without exception, the contemporary figures I've chosen to chronicle have been reluctant and uncooperative, and in each instance I have encountered resistance as I tried to go behind the public image to the other side of the myth. As unauthorized biographies, my books have been controversial and drawn fire, even litigation on occasion, but I have never lost a lawsuit. Before publication, each book is vetted by several sets of lawyers; facts and sources are checked and rechecked and sources documented.

Still, through no fault of my own, I became a darling of the American Bar Association. In 1984, before I had written a word of his biography,

Frank Sinatra sued. He claimed that only he or someone he authorized could write about his life. After a year, he dropped the suit, and my book was published in 1986. After my biography of Nancy Reagan was published in 1991, Sinatra's lawyer, Mickey Rudin, brought suit, because he had been named as a source and objected to being thanked for his help, which he had in fact provided. He went to court and lost; he appealed, and pursued his case up to the Ninth Circuit Court of Appeals before losing again. In 1997, my book on the British royal family was published in twenty-two foreign languages, but was deemed too explosive to be published in English in the United Kingdom.

With every book I've written, I've encountered a certain amount of hesitancy on the part of potential sources, because they are understandably reluctant to talk about powerful people, either for fear of retribution or for fear of being socially ostracized. The amount of trepidation I encountered in writing this book was unprecedented, but perhaps that's what comes from writing about a sitting President whose family has a long reach. Many sources were reluctant to tell their stories on the record, and much as I dislike using unnamed sources, in some cases I had no choice. Many people who know the Bushes—friends, former employees, classmates, business associates, and even a few family members—were skittish about speaking for attribution. I heard an endless stream of excuses and apologies, some comical, others disconcerting: "You don't know that family . . . If they think I've talked to you, they'll never speak to me again." "This town is too small to rile the Bushes." "I want to live to see my grandchildren." One man said, "You can't use my name. They'll come after me. The Bushes are thugs."

"Thugs? Surely, you're kidding," I said.

"Look what they did in Florida during the 2000 recount," he answered, and then detailed the "Brooks Brothers Riot" of Republican activists who helped stop the voting in Miami by storming the canvassing board. To prove his point, the man sent records showing that many of the rioters in pin-striped suits had been paid by the Bush recount committee.

The saddest example of the fear the Bushes instill involves a family whose Jewish son was subjected to a prank by George W. Bush when both boys attended Andover. Even forty years later the family was afraid to revisit the incident and be identified. The school did not take disciplinary action. By then, George Herbert Walker Bush was a revered campus legend. The elder Bush joined the Andover board of trustees in 1963 and served until 1979, which protected his younger sons from expulsion when they both broke school rules. Jeb Bush was caught drinking and Marvin Bush was doing drugs, but unlike other students in similar situations, the Bushes were not even suspended.

In writing contemporary biography, I've become accustomed to reluctant subjects who do not want their lives depicted without being able to control the content, but the Bushes—public figures for over fifty years—have been, by far, the most reluctant. The family is obsessed with secrecy, and their potential for retaliation is great. Consequently, some people were afraid to go on the record for fear of losing their jobs, getting hit with an IRS audit, or worse. And it was fear not just of President Bush (43) but also of his father, who did all he could to close every door I opened.

On November 6, 2002, I wrote to the former President as a matter of courtesy. I said I was under contract to do a historical retrospective of his family and would appreciate an interview and the opportunity to verify certain facts. Renowned for a lifetime of writing letters, George H.W. ignored mine. Instead, he directed his aide Jean Becker to call Stephen Rubin, the publisher at Doubleday. She did that on November 11, 2002: "President Bush has asked me to say that he and his family are not going to cooperate with this book because the author wrote a book about Nancy Reagan that made Mrs. Reagan unhappy."

The President's excuse was, to put it mildly, disingenuous. For Bush 41 the only unhappy part of that book concerned the former First Lady's anecdote about him and his "girlfriend." Barbara Bush was so angry about Mrs. Reagan's revelation that she instructed Roger Kennedy, then director of the National Museum of American History, to remove a display featuring my books on Jacqueline Kennedy Onassis and Nancy Reagan from the First Ladies exhibit in the Smithsonian. Mr. Kennedy genuflected to Mrs. Bush and the display was removed.

Three months after publication of the Reagan book, George Herbert Walker Bush was President of the United States. He, too, expressed his displeasure with me in his diary, which he published in *All the Best, George Bush: My Life in Letters and Other Writings*. Bush's entry for July 25, 1991:

*Have you ever had one of those days when it just isn't too good . . .
Just one of those days when you want to say forget it. Oh, yes, the
President of Paramount that owns one of the big book companies
called in to say that Kitty Kelley wants to write a book either about
the Bushes or the Royals and he turned it down. That's nice—a
book by Kitty Kelley with everything else I've got on my mind . . . I
can't see her ever writing anything nice.*

For the record, I never proposed writing a book about the Bushes until
after the Supreme Court decision of 2000, when they became an American political dynasty, one of only two families in history to put a father
and a son in the White House. Suddenly, by fiat, they had become interesting.

After four years researching this book and interviewing nearly one
thousand people, I now understand why the former President would not
cooperate: there are many family secrets he wants to protect. From the
very beginning, he threw up every possible barrier. His prep school, Andover, refused to provide any Bush-related photographs for this book, although numerous other authors have had no difficulty in securing photo
rights from the school. The former President put his family and friends on
notice, and the George Bush Presidential Library stopped responding to
the simplest reference requests.

When I wrote to the former President's cousin George Herbert
("Bert") Walker III in St. Louis, Mr. Walker called me immediately. "It
will be such a pleasure to meet you," he said on November 4, 2002, "and
to talk to you about the family. I'll show you the house where Aunt Dotty
grew up and met Uncle Pres Bush . . . I'll be here every day of your stay,
so call me as soon as you get to St. Louis."

I made my plane reservations, but by the next day Mr. Walker had obviously been told not to cooperate. His secretary called me: "I'm so sorry,
but Mr. Walker has been unexpectedly called out of town and will not be
available during your visit." I flew to St. Louis anyway and spent several
days doing research in that lovely city. I even stopped by Stifel, Nicolaus
and Company, where George H. Walker III sits as the chairman of the
board. Not surprisingly, he was in town when I arrived but "in a meeting
all day." A few months later President Bush—George W.—appointed
Walker, his second cousin, U.S. Ambassador to Hungary.

Bert's brother, Ray Walker, joked to me at the time, "Bert had to fill out all kinds of papers, including records on all his children and his siblings and who they've made political contributions to. I was just about to donate to Ramsey Clark's Internet campaign to 'Impeach the President' but . . . I held back . . . for Bert's sake."

A trained psychiatrist, Ray Walker acknowledged the family's mania for secrecy. "They've got a lot to hide," he said during an interview on May 28, 2003. "Secrets they don't even know . . . When I was in analysis, it took me a full year just to get from my grandparents to anywhere close to myself."

Early in his administration, President George W. Bush moved to make sure that the family's personal, financial, and political secrets, particularly his and his father's, remained sealed forever. After placing his records as Governor of Texas in his father's presidential library, Bush signed an executive order on November 1, 2001, that blocks the release of all presidential documents. Until then, the National Archives had controlled the fate of White House documents, which automatically became public after twelve years. Under Bush's new rules, presidents now have the right to prevent the public from ever viewing their papers, even after they have died. Unless there is a successful court challenge to Bush's executive order, he will be able to bury the secrets of his father's direct involvement in the Iran-contra scandal as well as his own complicity in waging war on Iraq.

In the past, the Bush family has managed to protect itself from intense scrutiny by providing limited access to a select few journalists. Now that the family has become a political dynasty, the risks of exposure are far greater, and the former President is more vigilant than ever. Even with the most trusted writers he can be querulous. He directed his aide Jean Becker to reprimand the conservative writers Peter and Rochelle Schweizer after their authorized and highly favorable book, *The Bushes*, was published in April 2004:

> *I am writing you this note at the request of President Bush, No. 41.*
> *He has completed reading your book . . . he is very disappointed . . . Unfortunately, your book is filled with factual errors, innuendo, and mistaken conclusions drawn from hearsay . . .*
> *For example, you put out in a press release, and I quote, "George*

H.W. Bush was opposed to his son's plan to attack Iraq" . . . The truth is, from the very first day, President Bush, No. 41 unequivocally supported the President on the war in Iraq. He had absolutely no reservations of any kind.

As with many of Bush's responses to criticism, this one turned out to be false. In the book that George Herbert Walker Bush and Brent Scowcroft wrote, *A World Transformed*, they detailed the "incalculable human and political costs" of occupying Iraq. Further, in April 2003, after his son had taken the country to war against Iraq, the former President agonized with his friend Scowcroft. Partners in the Scowcroft Group recalled both men bemoaning the son's actions, saying that George W. Bush "was undoing a lifetime of work."

While I wrote this book, there were obstacles other than people's reluctance to talk and Bush family resistance. When I began digging for information, I ran into an extraordinary number of lost records, misplaced files, and registers that had been mysteriously destroyed by fire over the years. Documents such as bankruptcy records are inexplicably missing from federal court files; other Bush business records that should be in the public domain have disappeared. Of the fourteen requests I filed under the Freedom of Information Act, most were initially denied. Not every government agency was recalcitrant, but most stalled their responses. A Freedom of Information Act request to the State Department for a death notification of a Bush relative was denied. I requested clarification of State Department policy, citing the instructions on its Web site. The document was finally released with no explanation of the original denial. In one case I had to hire a lawyer to appeal a denial by the FBI. Here's how the process worked.

On September 18, 2001, I filed a FOIA request for information on James Smith Bush (1901–78), the black-sheep uncle of George Herbert Walker Bush. The FBI said there were no files. I appealed, knowing that James had undergone FBI clearance for his appointment to the Export-Import Bank in 1959 and for his reappointment in 1961. Four months later, on January 14, 2002, the Justice Department lawyers referred my request back to the FBI, which then managed to find the records they initially claimed not to have. Six months later, on July 24, 2002, I was informed that the files had to be processed and sent to the FBI's Office of

Public and Congressional Affairs for a "high visibility memo" to be prepared. This was explained as an administrative procedure by which public figures—President Bush (41) and President Bush (43)—were warned about the release of material. Six more months passed as the FBI returned none of my phone calls requesting information. Finally, on February 19, 2003, I hired a lawyer to appeal the delay. After receiving the lawyer's letter, the FBI released the information. By then, it had taken me two years, seventeen letters, forty-two phone calls, and one lawyer to shake loose information on a man who had been dead for twenty-five years. The Bush family has been able to hold tight to its secrets because they have been aided in many cases by Bush-appointed bureaucrats.

Not every piece of information was as hard fought, but the example illustrates the resistance I encountered in trying to fit together various pieces of the family puzzle. The Bushes are so invested in protecting their public image that they have airbrushed their family tree. Any unpleasant fact that detracts from the family's wholesome appeal or reflects negatively on their values has been deleted. Historians cannot rely on the Bush-Walker family records released by the George Bush Presidential Library. There are simply too many errors and omissions, some of which appear to be intentional. The official family tree provided by the Bush archivists does not include the two mentally retarded daughters of John M. Walker, and lists only two of James Smith Bush's wives, not all four of them; one of Ray Walker's two wives is omitted, and George Herbert Walker III is listed with only two, instead of three, wives. These might seem like trivial details until you realize that in the Bush family, divorce, particularly more than one, is considered anathema.

Sharon Bush, the ex-wife of Neil Bush, brought this home when she asked if I would have lunch with her in New York City. We agreed to meet on April 1, 2003, at a quiet restaurant. When I arrived, the Chelsea Bistro on West Twenty-third Street was empty. Minutes later Sharon scampered in, a tiny blonde in a big mink coat and high-heeled mules. She hugged her fur coat.

"My mother-in-law hates for me to wear this. She says it will make people think we're rich."

"God forbid," I said, laughing.

Sharon was accompanied by Lou Colasuonno, a partner in Westhill Partners. A former journalist, this expert publicist was determined to help a client in distress. Sharon said that the Bush family had disowned her and few lawyers in Houston would handle her divorce. She was threatening to go public with the family secrets. Over a long lunch that afternoon and on the telephone later and again the next day, Sharon poured out her anguish about "being forced" to divorce the third son of George and Barbara Bush. Sharon later acknowledged that she had married the runt of the litter.

"Neil informed me by e-mail that he was leaving me," she said. "By e-mail! After twenty-three years of marriage and three children! He's been having an affair with a woman who worked for Bar . . . The Bushes knew about the affair before I did. They even entertained the woman in their home . . . They encouraged their own son's adultery . . . What kind of family values is that?"

Her eyes filled with tears. "I've tried everything to keep my marriage together. I've begged Bar to tell Neil to come back home to us. I've broken down in front of her. 'Can't you tell him to come back to us. Please. We need him. We're a family. Please help me.' Bar has been ice-cold. She said, 'I'm sorry, Sharon. There is nothing I can do. This is between you and Neilsie.' That's what she and George call him. Neilsie. He would come back to us if she told him to. He'd do whatever she wanted. Bar runs the show. She's much stronger than my father-in-law. Much. He's really a very weak guy . . . But Bar won't help me . . .

"You'd think after all the infidelity she's had to put up with in her own marriage she'd be more sympathetic to me, but she isn't . . . She hates me because I let my daughter Lauren be a model. Bar was furious at me. She did not think that was right. She said it didn't look good. It was too glitzy—too glamorous—for the image of the family values that the Bushes were supposed to represent."

Sharon unfolded a sordid tale of the men in the Bush family and the unfortunate women who married them: her husband's use of prostitutes during his trips to Asia, his sexually transmitted disease, the extramarital affairs of Jeb Bush, and the drug use of her other brothers-in-law, including the President of the United States. She said about George W.: "He and Marvin did coke at Camp David when their father was President and not just once, either. This is a family of alcoholism, drug addiction, and even schizophrenia."

She returned again and again to the role of her rich and powerful in-laws, who, she felt, were forcing her to beg for her life. "I know you think the Bushes are such a good family, that they believe in God and all his teachings . . . I used to believe that about them, too, but I now know that they don't practice what they preach . . . They're letting Neil cut me off with only a thousand dollars a month in alimony. They're making me sell my house. I have no way to support myself. I gave up working [as a school-teacher] when I married Neil [1980] because Bush wives aren't supposed to work . . . They're supposed to raise children and do volunteer work and I did that . . . I've raised three children and contributed to every community I've lived in with Neil. That's been my whole life . . . I've worked for charity all the years of my marriage . . . Now what do I do? When I asked him how I was supposed to live on a thousand dollars a month, Neil said, 'Just get remarried.' But, Kitty, I just can't sell my body for money."

Sharon sobbed as she talked about having to move out of her home. "My father-in-law wants me to leave Houston . . . He said I'd be happier somewhere else, but if I insist on staying, he'll buy me a smaller place so I can get my last child, Ashley, through high school, then I have to sell the house and give him all the money."

The thought of living a pinched life of grocery-store coupons brought on more tears. Life as a Bush daughter-in-law had cosseted Sharon with summers in Kennebunkport and cruises through the Greek islands on the yacht of a Bush family friend. In New York City, she stayed in the penthouse of famed Yankee pitcher Roger Clemens. She socialized with Veronica Hearst. She had Billy Graham on speed dial.

When their divorce was final and Neil Bush remarried in March 2004, Sharon had managed to save her house and increase her alimony to twenty-five hundred dollars a month, but she lost the social status of being the former President's daughter-in-law. She will probably become one of the invisible wives on the family tree, no longer even a footnote to history. She has learned the hard way that there is not much room for a divorcée in the Bush family dynasty.

I, too, learned a lesson writing about this family. Some days I felt like Alice in Wonderland because what I uncovered seemed unreal and did not square with established perceptions. I began second-guessing myself, asking, "How can this be true?" I watched people cringe with fear and others fall under the spell of the family's power and wealth and influence. Then I remembered the line spoken by the actor Melvyn Douglas in the movie *Hud* about the mesmerizing power of a public image: "Little by little the country changes just by looking at the men we admire."

The country has changed quite a bit since I began writing this book and will continue to change as a result of both Bush presidencies. I hope that the research put forth in these pages will lead you to the essential truths that motivate, explain, and define the family as the American political dynasty responsible for these changes.

THE FAMILY

CHAPTER ONE

lora Sheldon Bush was fuming. Her thirteen-year-old son, Prescott, was supposed to have spent that August of 1908 at a New Jersey sports resort with a classmate and his family. Flora's husband, Samuel Prescott Bush, had sent the boy there to play tennis, while Flora, their two daughters, Mary and Margaret, their younger son, Jim, Samuel's mother, Harriet, and the family nanny were spending the month at the East Bay Lodge in Osterville, Massachusetts. But Prescott had abruptly been sent home by his friend's mother, Mrs. Dods. Flora's regal mother-in-law, Harriet Fay Bush, urged her to demand an explanation and an apology from Mrs. Dods, but Flora, whose social instincts were unerring in these matters, restrained herself. "I am not ready for that," she wrote to her husband. "I think I may hear from Mrs. D. and if so, you must forward the letter . . . for nothing has ever happened that raised my indignation more than her summary dismissal of Prescott."

A few days later Flora again mentioned her vexation: "Your mother is quite sure I ought to write Mrs. Dods. It scarcely seems right. I resent it all more than anything I have experienced."

The unexpected change in Prescott's plans upset his father, who worried that the incident might have been Prescott's fault. If so, that might affect his acceptance into St. George's School in the fall. But after hearing her son's side of the story, Flora tried to assure her husband that the youngster was not entirely to blame:

I am sorry you are disappointed in Prescott and yet I am not sur-prised. He is of course a boy of very tender years. And I sometimes

*have a feeling of great dread at sending him away to school and yet
I do feel that the strict discipline may be just the thing. He was
glad to get back to us again but he misses his sport at Osterville—
There are no tennis courts here but poor grass ones—he said if he
had his clubs he would play golf.*

The matter of Prescott's departure was finally cleared up when
Samuel telegrammed Flora that the much-maligned Mrs. Dods had indeed written to explain herself. Samuel forwarded the letter from Ohio,
and Flora was almost comforted to learn that Mrs. Dods had taken ill in
New Jersey. "It was the only excuse I could possibly have accepted," she
wrote. "Her letter was as satisfactory as anything could be + while I do not
justify the haste I at least can appreciate her anxiety to get rid of the young
company—as summer cottages are not the quiet hospitals one needs in
case of illness."

A few days later, Prescott received his golf clubs. And Samuel must
have been somewhat reassured to receive a letter from his seventy-nine-
year-old mother extolling the teenager, if not without reservation:

*I was much impressed with Prescott's appearance and manner as
he jumped out of the carriage + came to speak to me—he is a
handsome boy + a well developed figure for [illegible] growth. I
trust the time will soon come when he will—if I can use the word—
slough off the pernicious habit of fooling. If I had not seen its results in Aunt Virginia's family perhaps it would not seem to be so
fraught with danger, but with you and Flora to guard him and the
uniform discipline of a school he will doubtless find its disadvan-
tages himself. It makes friends with the boys but antagonizes the
teachers as I also know by personal experience but little can be
done except . . . protect him until he is wise enough to check it.*

Grandmother Bush was more perceptive than perhaps even she
could have realized. Her grandson's "pernicious habit of fooling" was
something that would remain with him for years. At times, the result
would be humorous; at other times, there would be serious repercussions.

Prescott could simply not be suppressed. He possessed all the precocious gifts of a firstborn son who was indulged and adored by his parents. He had inherited humor, dramatic flair, and sociability from his mother, while he exhibited his father's height, good looks, and graceful athleticism. The surprising effect of her "splendid boy" was not lost on Flora. "I have had one new experience," she wrote to her husband, "and that is the devotion of girls 18 or 19 years old to Prescott. He is having a charming time dancing with them + going swimming + indeed walking or running. Prescott + one or two boys a little older are all the boys there are + you may imagine their popularity. I shall be glad to have him away from the girls. He is very kind to me + indeed to us all—but—of course, being in such demand for any length of time might turn his head."

Even his grandmother's efforts could not rein him in, and she was someone to be reckoned with. Already widowed for nineteen years when she wrote the note analyzing Prescott, Harriet Fay Bush was born in Savannah, Georgia, of illustrious ancestors who fertilized the family tree with connections to British royalty. On occasion Mrs. Bush could be as starchy as Queen Victoria, but Flora loved her mother-in-law and fussed about the elderly woman's frailty. "I wonder how she keeps up at all," Flora wrote. "She has had so many wretched days + people tire and annoy her so very much that I have felt a number of times that it was almost too much for her."

Flora need not have worried. Behind that swansdown fan fluttered a steel magnolia who would outlast most of her relatives, including her daughter-in-law. As sturdy as the kudzu of Georgia, Harriet Fay Bush would live to be ninety-four years old.

During the summer of 1908, the Bushes were completing a two-and-a-half-story colonial-style seventeen-room home on Roxbury Road overlooking the bluff of Marble Cliff in Columbus, Ohio. They had purchased the 2.7-acre site for $12,500 the year before, and their letters were filled with details of the seven-bayed windows, five dormered bedrooms, upstairs ballroom, cedar-lined storage room, and awninged porch atop the first-floor sunroom.

"I still remember that house, and I'm ninety-five now," recalled Indiana Earl in 2001. "Of course, it was fitting for Samuel Bush to live there because he was extremely wealthy and viewed with enormous respect in the community. The Bushes' big white house sat at the top of a hill looking down on a marble quarry across the street from Sylvio Casparis's castle . . . Mr. Bush was well-to-do wealthy but not as really rich as old Mr. Casparis, who owned the Marble Cliff Quarries."

As the daughter of a prominent dry-goods merchant, Flora understood how to run a fine home and was delighted when her husband, the president of the Buckeye Steel Castings Company as well as one of the founders of the Scioto Country Club of Columbus, bought land in Grandview Heights near where her brothers and sisters were building their large homes. Flora oversaw the architectural plans for the new house and attended to the details of paying various merchants. "This bill of Sargents is a terror," she wrote. "Certainly changing those panes is pretty expensive." Her letters brimmed with eagerness to see the construction completed in time for her family to move in the fall. "We shall all be together and be so very happy," she put in one of her notes.

In an era before such modern conveniences as washing machines and dryers, Flora expressed concern for a satisfactory cellar that would be "clean and nice and serve as an excellent drying room for laundry." She acceded to her husband's love of flowers and his desire for larger gardens to accommodate more plantings, but insisted on her own way in other areas. "About the fireplace—it must be done," she wrote. "There is no doubt about it. I am willing to compromise on the red. My only choice has been a suitable brown and if that cannot be found I shall certainly never give you cause to regret the red."

As pleased as Flora was to be at Cape Cod with her children and away from the noisy builders and summer heat of the Midwest, she missed her forty-four-year-old husband, who was known to intimates by his middle name. She began each letter with loving salutations such as "My Dear Prescott" or "My Dearest Boy." Irrepressibly affectionate at the age of thirty-six, she signed off with endearments such as "Adieu, my darling Boy," "I love you my darling and am thinking of you constantly," "I love you sweetheart dearly. Don't get on too well without me," "Please miss me a little, my dearest."

Nor was she coy about her desire for the man she called "Bushy." In one letter she wrote:

I should like to have you down here fore [sic] a week after every one
has gone—+ we should lead an Adam + Eve existence—bathe and
roam about—We could have a very happy time near to nature's
heart . . . I so seldom see a person I desire for a friend. Of course it
is because you + I are so much to each other. We do not need the
others—I surely need little dear when I am sure of you—but it is
the most vital thing in the world that you stay by me.

She also wrote about her own pleasure at "bathing," especially on the
rare days she dared to ditch her petticoats, whalebone collars, and fishnet
hose. One day, she said, was absolutely perfect because "we went in without skirts or stockings and the sensation was delightful." And Flora burbled on about the children's swimming lessons: "Such progress as they are
making is truly delightful. Diving or rather jumping into the water and
swimming right off—it is fine—I would give anything to have that love for
the water or rather the faith—for I do love it—but to be without fear—
there is nothing like it."

Flora seemed quite ready to leave behind the nineteenth-century dis-
comforts of carriages and embrace the new invention of the automobile.
As she wrote to her husband, "There is only one comfortable way to get
about and that is in a motor car—such a vastly cleaner mode of travel in
this part." That was the year Henry Ford introduced his Model T, which
sold for $850.

Flushed with the good fortune of her life, Flora took nothing for
granted, especially after she had a frightening accident one morning:

A baseball flying with terrific force, having been batted 50 or 75
feet away, struck me just over the left eye. I dropped + was dazed
but soon came to my senses—Prescott white as a sheet + others
helping me up—I was able to walk over + then had applications +
things done—but I have had a horrid day—as I am lame every-
where + my poor head feels as though it was not mine. Excepting
that it hurts. It is turning a hideous green + blue. I suppose I ought
to be brave + not write you but my dear Boy I have to let you know.
It takes my breath when I realize how easily I might have been
killed or my eye put out or anything.

Days later, she wrote: "My head is getting back to its normal state again, but my eye is a hideous black + blue, but I do not suffer. I can't help feeling thankful when I think of the narrow escape."

On her last day at Osterville, she wrote that she was looking forward to returning to Ohio to see their new home: "I am still giving thanks—just think I might never have seen the bay window had the ball struck half an inch lower. I am very thankful to have gotten off so well."

By the Cape Cod summer of 1908, Flora and Samuel had been married fourteen years and had four surviving children. They had endured the death of their second child, Robert Sheldon Bush, in 1900. He was three and a half years old when he contracted scarlet fever, which he fought for six weeks until his little kidneys gave out. He was cremated and his ashes reposed in the Forest Home Cemetery in Milwaukee, Wisconsin, where the Bushes had lived for two years. They never specifically mention that sadness in the correspondence that survives. In one letter Samuel alludes to "hard things to bear" and shows he is grounded in the biblical principle that human beings grow in grace only by overcoming adversity. "We should be wonderfully happy," he wrote. "We are and we will be . . . but surely we should not care to have our lives easy. There would be no accomplishment, no development. We must meet the difficult things and by mutual help surmount them."

Long before women got the vote and feminists looked like troublemakers in lace bonnets, Samuel Bush had accepted his wife as his equal. His letters to her sound as emancipated as those John Adams wrote to Abigail in the eighteenth century:

> *You speak of the father as the governing power and very lovingly, too, but my idea is that while the father may be the governing power in some things, the mother is quite as much so in other things and that the power is a dual one and so intended by its creator and it has always been my desire to so have it and so I wish to have you on equal terms and then by mutual consideration have our marriage and love complete and fruitful of the best.*

These letters, saved by Samuel and bequeathed to his heirs, reveal a vibrant partnership between parents who loved their children abundantly and cared for their welfare, although, truth to tell, they write more of their two sons, Prescott and James, than of their two daughters, Mary and Margaret. In her letters, Flora jumps off the page in vivid color as she whirls among her various roles of caring daughter-in-law, nurturing mother, solicitous wife, and robust lover.

With her summer coming to a close, Flora made arrangements for the family to return to Ohio by train, the most comfortable means of travel in those days. "I have applied for sleeping car accomodations so that we will surely get berths . . . and have one Drawing Room."

She told her husband that their oldest child was more than ready to leave Douglas Elementary School in Columbus and start the all-boys preparatory school of St. George's in Newport, Rhode Island:

> Prescott is quite a beaux [sic] and I shall be very well satisfied to have him safely under Mr. Diman's care—the strict discipline is just the thing I agree in believing in discipline. You must be sure to arrange to go on with Prescott about the 20th as it is most necessary that you see his surroundings, meet the masters + feel satisfied about the whole.

Flora's reference is to the Reverend John Byron Diman, who founded St. George's School in 1896 and recruited Samuel Bush to serve on the school's board of trustees. She need not have worried about her husband's reaction to the school. Any parent able to spend $850 a year on tuition would have been delighted with the spectacular 350-acre campus on majestic cliffs overlooking three beaches of the Atlantic Ocean. At that time, the St. George's faculty numbered fifteen masters, and enrollment was limited to 125 boys.

"I enjoyed all the advantages of that very much indeed," Prescott recalled many years later in an oral history, describing the new world he was encountering, "with athletic fields and a beautiful gymnasium and all these things that we didn't have in the public schools . . . For that reason I think I appreciated it more than some of the boys who came there from private schools."

"St. George's was most definitely a rich boy's school," said John G. Doll, the school archivist. "We were very select, snobbish, and quite elitist then. Most of the boys were enrolled the day they were born, when their fathers sent telegrams to the headmaster to reserve their space. That all changed after the Depression.

"We had a jacket-and-tie dress code during the time Prescott Bush [1908–13] and his brother, Jim [1914–18], attended, plus a heavy emphasis on religion, with chapel once a day and twice on Sunday. The boys had to walk three miles each way to attend St. Columba's Church on Sundays. We were a big feeder into Harvard, Yale, and Princeton. Still are. We're still much smaller and more exclusive than any of the other prep schools like Exeter and Andover, but now, of course, we're coed."

Records at St. George's show Prescott Bush to have been a mammoth presence. "He was really a big man on campus," said John Doll, rattling off a stupendous record of athletics and extracurriculars, including first-squad (varsity) football, baseball, and basketball. In addition, Prescott was president of Civics Club, vice president of Red and White Council, president of Dramatic Association, leader of the Glee Club, and president of Golf Club. "He was a marvelous actor and played the lead of Sherlock Holmes in the school play," said Doll. But the biggest honor came his senior year, when he was elected head prefect. In those days, that position, the equivalent of student-body president, carried the perquisite of a private suite of rooms that consisted of a large den with a working fireplace and a small private bedroom. So Prescott must've had a very happy senior year indeed.

When Flora and Samuel received advance word that their son had been elected head prefect, they were told to say nothing until the announcement was made at school. Flora could barely contain herself. She wrote to her husband:

> *I asked Prescott if there had been any elections and he said yes— baseball and he is Captain—he said Buchanan had two votes— but he had the rest. We did not speak of the other honor—the one Mr. Griswold told us of—until just as he left he said, "Mother, I won't get that." I did not peep—nor even look wise but let it go— as I presume it is better to wait—but naturally I should like to have relieved his mind.*

Prescott entered St. George's after the sweet summer of 1908, and his graduation five years later brought him to the threshold of his life's most formative experience—Yale, class of 1917.

"For me," he said years later, "it all began with Yale." He credited the university with shaping his entire life. Certainly his career would have been different, for he met his future boss Walter Simmons, who hired Prescott for his first job, at a Yale reunion. His personal life would have been far different as well. Because of that job in St. Louis for the Simmons Hardware Company, he met the wealthy Yale family the Walkers and his future wife, Dorothy Walker. After a series of sales jobs, Prescott used his Yale connections to launch his career as an investment banker.

If it's true that, as one Yale man said, "there will always be two Yales—the Old Blues and the rest of us," Prescott Bush was an Old Blue. He made no apology to "the rest of us" for his lifelong genuflections to Yale. The school had given him everything he valued most, and he felt no need to look beyond his college ties. As far as he was concerned, he'd met the best, so he ignored the rest.

After graduation, Prescott regularly attended Yale class reunions and Whiffenpoof anniversaries. He visited New Haven and the tomb of Skull and Bones at least once—and sometimes as often as five times—a year. Whenever he could, he sang at the tables down at Mory's, the clubby Yale restaurant where the Whiffenpoofs assembled to raise their glasses and sing their songs. He was an associate fellow of Calhoun College from 1944 to 1972; a Chubb Fellow in 1958; and an associate of Saybrook College. He served as a Yale trustee. He was the first chairman of Yale's Development Board. Prescott sat on the Yale Corporation for twelve years, served as secretary of his alumni class, and was a member of the executive council. Figuratively and literally, he never left Yale.

In writing to his class on the eve of his fiftieth reunion, he reflected on the importance of the school in his life: "I am more than ever conscious of what Yale has meant to me since 1913. Wherever I found myself in war or peace, in business or politics, in sports or social life, always the fact of Yale seemed to be there. I make this acknowledgement with a grateful heart."

Prescott walked onto the New Haven campus as a Yale "legacy" of his paternal grandfather, the Reverend James Smith Bush, class of 1844, and his maternal uncle Robert E. Sheldon Jr., class of 1904. Within four years he would create his own legacy, which would open Yale's exclusive doors to several more generations of Bushes, including his four sons, his three grandsons, his two nephews, and, in 2001, his great-granddaughter:

The Yale Family Tree: Bush/Walker/Pierce

1844	*Reverend James Smith Bush (Prescott Bush's grandfather)*
1899	*Joseph W. Wear (Dorothy Walker Bush's uncle)*
1899S	*James T. Walker (Dorothy Walker Bush's uncle)*
1901	*James H. Wear (Dorothy Walker Bush's uncle)*
1902	*Arthur Y. Wear (Dorothy Walker Bush's uncle)*
1904S	*Robert E. Sheldon (Prescott Bush's uncle)*
1913x	*Francis Edwin House Jr. (married Prescott Bush's sister Mary Eleanor)*
1917	*Stuart H. Clement (married Prescott Bush's sister Margaret Livingston)*
1917	*Prescott S. Bush*
1922	*James Smith Bush (Prescott Bush's brother)*
1925	*William P. Wear (Dorothy Walker Bush's cousin)*
1927	*David D. Walker III (Dorothy Walker Bush's cousin)*
1927	*George H. Walker Jr. (Dorothy Walker Bush's brother)*
1930x	*James Wear Walker (Dorothy Walker Bush's brother, left after sophomore year)*
1931	*John M. Walker (Dorothy Walker Bush's brother)*
1936	*Louis Walker (Dorothy Walker Bush's brother)*

1940   Reuben A. Holden IV (married George H. Walker Jr.'s
        daughter, Elizabeth)

1942   Walter Rafferty (married Barbara Bush's sister, Martha
        Pierce)

1943   Stuart H. Clement Jr. (Margaret Bush Clement's son)

1943   Francis E. House III (Mary Bush House's son)

1944   Alexander B. Ellis Jr. (married George H.W. Bush's
        sister, Nancy)

1944x   Prescott S. Bush Jr. (George H.W. Bush's brother, left
        after junior year)

1948   George H.W. Bush

1953   Jonathan James Bush (George H.W. Bush's brother)

1953   George H. Walker III (George H. Walker Jr.'s son)

1955   Ray Walker (George H. Walker Jr.'s son)

1960   William Henry Trotter Bush (George H.W. Bush's
        brother)

1961   Davis R. Robinson (married Louis Walker's daughter,
        Suzanne)

1962   John M. Walker Jr. (Dorothy Walker Bush's nephew)

1968   George W. Bush

1970   Prescott Bush III (Prescott Bush Jr.'s son)

1974   Corinne Rafferty (Martha Rafferty's daughter)

1977   John P. Ellis (Nancy Bush Ellis's son)

1986   William P. Bush (William H.T. Bush's son)

2004   Barbara Bush (George W. Bush's daughter)

S = Sheffield Scientific School before it was absorbed into Yale College

x = Did not graduate

When the head prefect of St. George's arrived for his freshman year of college, he looked like a matinee idol. At six feet four, he was the second-tallest man in his class, and one of the handsomest. His hair was as dark as sealskin and parted down the middle to show what Grandmother Harriet Bush called his "noble forehead." He was a good student and majored in history, but he truly excelled in sports, particularly as a first baseman on Yale's baseball team. So important were sports in the lives of Yale men then that "Not Winning a 'Y' " was listed as one of the "Biggest Regrets of College" by the class of 1917. Prescott had won his baseball letter by his junior year. He went out for the golf team and even became a football cheerleader, all of which combined to make him one of the most admired men on campus.

"There was a sort of mystique in the old days of people who were good in sports," said Stuart Symington Jr. (Yale 1950), son of the late senator from Missouri. "My father was a superior athlete. So was Pres Bush. They were the lords of creation . . . In that era, excellence in sports was highly prized. You'd see banner headlines in *The New York Times* that Yale beat Harvard or Princeton. It mattered greatly then. In that country-club world—small, social, and cohesive—a sport played well was a gauge of competence, a badge of manhood."

In his history of the school, Brooks Mather Kelley described Yale's class of 1917 as "more interested in their games, newspapers, sports and societies than . . . the curriculum." That could have been written to describe Samuel Bush's son. Socializing was a big part of college life for Prescott, who volunteered for Interfraternity Council, Junior Prom Committee, and Class Day Committee. "To Have Made Friends" was listed by the class of 1917 as the "Most Valuable Thing Obtained from College."

Prescott began scaling Yale his first week on campus. Singing was a cherished college tradition, so he immediately joined the Yale Glee Club, the Yale Quartet, and the Yale Men's Choir. In his senior year he was selected second bass for the Whiffenpoofs. "Life is but one song," he told the *Yale Daily News*. By then, he had become known as the hottest close-harmony man Yale had seen in twenty-five years.

"Prescott loved music," said Richard D. Barrett (Yale 1953). "He was made of music. That was the core of his character—his love of singing. He was happiest when he was singing . . . and he had a wonderful booming voice, a marvelous bass that he loved using. After he left Yale, he formed a group, all Yalies, of course, called the Silver Dollar Quartet that sang for years. When they died, Prescott found us and formed another group called the Kensington Four. He craved singing and was never without song."

In a 1957 letter Prescott sent to Yale about the Silver Dollar Quartet, he said the group had been performing for thirty-five years:

> We began in 1922. For many years we made pilgrimages to Mory's to sing with the Whiffenpoofs. In the thirties we formed the Yale Glee Club Associates and planned and conducted its meetings in New York until I resigned as president, thinking a change of leadership would be helpful.
>
> We introduced many a song at Yale. They still sing many of our songs even if they have changed arrangements and tempi in some to conform with their more modern tastes.
>
> Despite interruptions such as World War II when General Spofford [Charles M. Spofford, 1924] joined Eisenhower's staff and later went to preside over NATO . . . for most of each year we still carry on at every opportunity.

Prescott reveled in group activities. He pledged Psi Upsilon fraternity and joined the College Christian Association as well as the Young Men's Christian Association of Dwight Hall. He fit easily with the 347 students of his freshman class, most of whom were white Anglo-Saxon Protestant preppies. A profile of that class emerges from their answers to a questionnaire.

The fathers of 149 students had graduated from a university, and 58 of those had graduated from Yale. More than half of the fathers had not graduated from any college. Prescott's father had graduated from Stevens Institute of Technology with a degree in engineering, so that placed Prescott in the educated minority of his class. The class of 1917 listed football as their favorite sport, Douglas Fairbanks as their favorite actor, and Maude Adams as their favorite actress. Alfred, Lord Tennyson was their favorite poet, and "Crossing the Bar" their favorite poem. Their favorite writer was Charles Dickens, their favorite novel Lorna Doone, and they said English was the most valuable subject. The person they admired most in history was Abraham Lincoln, which may account for the 227 students who listed themselves as Republicans.

The twenty-two Catholics, fifteen Methodists, ten Jews, nine Baptists, and one Buddhist in the class defined its religious diversity. Racially, there was no diversity; the entire class was Caucasian. A majority of the students said they used tobacco and alcohol, and 113 had traveled abroad by the time they arrived at Yale, but Prescott was not one of them.

When the class wrote its history shortly before graduation, they voted on those who had "Done Most for Yale" in their four years there: Harry William LeGore won with 129 votes; Prescott S. Bush placed second with 36 votes. "Most Popular" was Spencer Armstrong Pumpelly, with 174 votes; Prescott S. Bush placed fifth with 21 votes. "Most to Be Admired" was Spencer Armstrong Pumpelly, 108 votes; fourth was Prescott Bush, 30 votes. Prescott was not mentioned in the categories of "Best Natured," "Best All-Around Athlete," "Most Scholarly," "Most Brilliant," or "Most Likely to Succeed," but he did win "Most Versatile," with 70 votes.

"There's a difference, a big difference," said Stuart Symington Jr., "between going to Yale and scaling Yale. The hierarchy of Prescott Bush's Yale began with excelling in sports. With that achievement you could qualify for the next step—a fraternity, then an honor society—all a staging area for the senior societies, the final step up the ladder. The senior societies held the greatest prestige, and of them nothing mattered more than Skull and Bones. Scaling that world of Yale was more important than getting the college education or degree of Yale."

In May 1916, Prescott reached the summit; he was one of fifteen men tapped for Skull and Bones. These names—Alfred Raymond Bellinger, Prescott Sheldon Bush, Henry Sage Fenimore Cooper, Oliver Baty Cunningham, Samuel Sloan Duryee, Edward Roland Noel Harriman, Henry Porter Isham, William Ellery Sedgwick James, Harry William LeGore, Henry Neil Mallon, Albert William Olsen, John Williams Overton, Frank Parsons Shepard Jr., Kenneth Farrand Simpson, and Knight Woolley—would anchor Prescott's life, the lives of his two sisters, who would marry Yalies, and his brother, also Skull and Bones, as well as the lives of his children and his children's children. These Bonesmen became one another's best friends, confidants, colleagues, business associates, golfing partners, investors, and clients.

Skull and Bones has been called "the most powerful secret society the United States has ever known" because its members have presided at the highest realms of American business and political life. Former Bonesmen hail from some of America's most prominent families: Bundy, Coffin, Harriman, Lord, Phelps, Rockefeller, Taft, Whitney, and, of course, Bush.

A Yale student named William H. Russell started the secret organization in 1832 in an effort to create a new world order that would place the best and the brightest at the helm of society. A wealthy elitist, Russell believed that the most important decisions should only be made by those who are bred to make them, so he created an environment that would shape the characters of the men who would shape the world. He called his group the Brotherhood of Death or, more informally, the order of Skull and Bones, patterned after a secret society founded in Germany, also in 1832. Since then, Skull and Bones has maintained its "tomb"— the basement of its headquarters—on the Yale campus in a windowless house on High Street just off the Old Campus and has selected fifteen men, and later, women, too, in every junior class to be admitted to its elite ranks. These men, who automatically include the captains of the football and baseball teams, the editor of the *Yale Daily News*, the president of the student council, and the head of the Political Union, are all sworn to lifetime secrecy about their rituals and commit themselves to helping each other scale life's summits.

Within Skull and Bones, all Bonesmen are called "Knights," and members refer to the rest of the world as "Barbarians." When writing to one another, each Knight is addressed as "Pat" or "Patriarch" to signal his dominant role at life's table. In the tomb deep within the ivy-covered house, the Knights swear allegiance to each other until death renders them nothing more than skull and bones. This allegiance gives all Knights a leg up in the Barbarian world, for members are always willing to help each other with financial assistance, social entrée, and political access. The Knights also pledge a lifetime tithe to the Russell Trust Association, the corporate shell of Skull and Bones and the richest corporation in the state of Connecticut. The RTA also owns Deer Island, a forty-acre retreat on the St. Lawrence River, two miles north of Alexandria Bay, New York. On the property is a lavish clubhouse that serves as a retreat for members only.

All Knights are encouraged to "crook"—to steal something rare and valuable for the tomb, which will build up the coffers of Skull and Bones. The best crook is displayed with a plaque in the clubhouse with the crook's name, an honor all Knights seek. The competition in this area is fierce.

During Prescott's years at Yale, the United States was trying to negotiate an end to the Great War in Europe while maintaining its neutrality. Students followed the progress of the European war on large-scale maps in the university library, and Yale urged its men to train for military service in the patriotic spirit of Nathan Hale (Yale 1773), whose monument on campus, always wreathed, carries his immortal words: "I only regret that I have but one life to lose for my country."

American antiwar sentiment remained strong until May 7, 1915, when the Germans sank the *Lusitania* and 128 Americans lost their lives. Twelve months later Congress passed the National Defense Act and instituted the draft. President Woodrow Wilson campaigned for reelection with the slogan "He kept us out of war." Opposing Wilson's isolationist policies, Prescott and several other Knights formed the Republican Club at Yale to support Charles Evans Hughes of New York, the esteemed Supreme Court justice who felt that American intervention in the war was inevitable, desirable, and in fact admirable. President Wilson was able to ride antiwar sentiment to victory, but after German U-boats sank five American merchant vessels, Wilson asked Congress to declare war on Germany to keep the world "safe for democracy."

That declaration of April 6, 1917, changed the lives of Prescott Bush and many other Yale men who immediately joined the National Guard.

"At Yale I developed the thought that I really would like in the long run to get into politics, and with that in mind, I decided that I would go to law school after my graduation," Prescott said in his oral history at Columbia University. "But unhappily the war broke out . . . and I immediately went into the Army and spent a little over two years in the service, getting out in May, 1919. I was a captain of field artillery. I might say that prior to that, in 1916, during the Mexican border crisis, I entered the Connecticut National Guard as a private . . . and that training was exceedingly useful to me and to many, many other Yale men who formed the so-called Yale Battalion with four batteries of field artillery, which meant about 400 men—100 in a battery—roughly speaking."

The "Mexican border crisis" arose after the British decoded a secret telegram from the Germans. The telegram urged Mexico to declare war on the United States and promised that once America was defeated, Germany would insist on peace terms that would force the United States to return Texas, New Mexico, and Arizona south of the border. The German attempt to foment fighting within the United States was nullified with the declaration of war.

For two months in the spring of 1918, Prescott and four other Knights were dispatched to Fort Sill, Oklahoma, as members of the Army's last horse-drawn artillery unit. The unit pulled the cannons and caissons that served as ammunition carriers, and was commanded by Brigadier General Adrian S. Fleming, who placed Prescott on his personal staff because the young man continually led everyone in singing the field-artillery song: "Over hill, over dale, we have hit the dusty trail as our caissons go rolling along."

To Prescott and the other Knights of Skull and Bones, Fort Sill looked like a cornucopia for crooking, especially the Old Post Corral with its frontier relics and the Apache Cemetery that contained the grave of Geronimo, the Indian warrior who had led sensational campaigns against the white man. The chieftain had taken forty-nine scalps before the Army troops at Fort Sill finally captured him. He had escaped so many times before that he was lionized as a hero by both sides.

At the time of his death in 1909, Geronimo was the most famous Indian warrior in the world. As a result, the Apaches were afraid that white men might dig up his body and exhibit it in a traveling show or vandalize his grave, looking for gold and silver, not realizing that there would be nothing of value within because the Apaches were poor and did not bury valuables with their dead. Actually, Apaches were afraid of the dead and believed the spirits might contaminate them. They looked upon grave tampering with horror. So when the grave of a Comanche leader was desecrated, the Apaches, to prevent further tampering, spread the story that they had removed Geronimo's bones. National magazines and newspapers published stories in 1914 stating that Geronimo's remains were no longer at Fort Sill.

When the Knights of Skull and Bones arrived at the Army fort in 1918, they found all the graves unmarked and the cemetery overgrown with weeds and thorny vines. Available records failed to designate the burial site, and nine years after Geronimo's death men on the post could not recall the spot, and Apaches professed ignorance. Despite all that, the Knights claimed that they had unearthed the secret grave and had snatched Geronimo's skull in a midnight raid, along with his stirrups and a horse bit, all of which they carried back to the tomb in New Haven to be proudly displayed as the most prized of all "crooks."

These false claims proved to be another example of Prescott Bush's predilection for "pernicious . . . fooling." The actual location of the Indian chieftain's grave remained secret for many years until U.S. Master Sergeant Morris Swett, Fort Sill librarian from 1915 to 1954, shared his knowledge. He had become close to the Apaches during his many years at Fort Sill, and Nah-thle-tla, Geronimo's first cousin, had trusted Swett enough to show him the unmarked grave. Swett's story, "The Secret of Geronimo's Grave," confirmed by Apache leaders and tribal elders in Lawton, Oklahoma, was written by Paul McClung in 1964 in *The Lawton Constitution*, where it received little circulation. By then the 1918 myth of Prescott Bush and his Knights had taken hold as legend among decades of Bonesmen. The nonexistent exploit was so beguiling that F. O. Matthiessen, literary critic from Yale's class of 1923, wrote it up for a Skull and Bones history titled "Continuation of the History of Our Order for the Century Celebration, 17 June 1933":

> *From the war days also sprang the mad expedition from the School of Fire at Fort Sill, Oklahoma, that brought to the T [tomb] its most spectacular "crook," the skull of Geronimo the terrible, the Indian Chief who had taken forty-nine white scalps. An expedition in late May 1918 by members . . . planned with great caution since in the words of one of them: "Six army captains robbing a grave wouldn't look good in the papers." The stirring climax was recorded by Hellbender in the Black Book of D. 117 . . . "The ring of pick on stone and thud of earth on earth alone disturbs the peace of the prairie. An axe pried open the iron door of the tomb, and Pat. [Patriarch] Bush entered and started to dig. We dug in turn, each on relief taking a turn on the road as guards . . . Finally Pat. [Patriarch] Ellery James turned up a bridle, soon a saddle horn and rotten leathers followed, then wood and then, at the exact bottom of the small round hole, Pat. [Patriarch] James dug deep and pried*

out the trophy itself . . . we quickly closed the grave, shut the door
and sped home to Pat [Patriarch] Mallon's room, where we cleaned
the bones. Pat [Patriarch] Mallon sat on the floor liberally apply-
ing carbolic acid. The Skull was fairly clean, having only some
flesh inside and a little hair."

Many years after Prescott joined Geronimo in the happy hunting ground, this story rose up like a ghost in chains to smack the fortunes of Prescott's political son, George.

When Geronimo died, the headline in one Oklahoma paper read: "Longed to Die in Arizona Where He Waged Bloody Wars—Resisted Civilization." So in 1986, Ned Anderson, a former chairman of the San Carlos Apache Tribe in Arizona, decided to try to find the chieftain's remains and take them to Arizona. During his search, Anderson received a letter from someone who purported to be a member of Skull and Bones. "What you're seeking is not over at Fort Sill. It is in New Haven, Connecticut, on the Yale University campus. If you are interested in pursuing the matter further, I will make photographs available to you."

Anderson wrote back immediately, and the anonymous Bonesman sent him a photograph of the glass display case in the tomb containing bones, stirrups, a horse bit, and what the informant said was the skull of Geronimo "crooked" by Prescott Bush and his fellow Patriarchs. The Bonesman also included a copy of F. O. Matthiessen's document that told the story of the fictitious raid on Geronimo's grave as if it were real.

The Apache chairman retained a lawyer to retrieve the skull so that it could be reinterred with the tribe in Arizona. The Skull and Bones attorney showed up for the meeting with what appeared to be the original display case, complete with the skull, stirrups, and horse bit. Anderson mentioned that the skull didn't look exactly like the photograph he had received. The Skull and Bones attorney said he'd had it analyzed. "We found out it's not Geronimo's skull," said Endicott Peabody Davison (Yale 1945), "but the skull of a ten-year-old boy."

All negotiations fell apart when the Skull and Bones attorney demanded that, in exchange for the display case, the Apaches sign a document stipulating that the society did not have Geronimo's skull. They also had to promise never to discuss the matter. Anderson refused to sign the document. He returned to Arizona and asked his senator, John McCain, to intercede by calling George H.W. Bush, then Vice President of the United States. McCain told the Apache chairman that Bush would not take his call, but the senator had no recollection of his call many years later. The display case was returned to the tomb in New Haven, where Bonesmen to this day still erroneously refer to it as Geronimo's skull.

With America's declaration of war in 1917, Prescott headed for France, while Samuel, his civic-minded father, went to Washington, D.C., to serve as chief of the Ordnance, Small Arms, and Ammunition Section of the War Industries Board under Bernard Baruch. Described as a "Jeffersonian Democrat," Samuel Bush was a progressive who built housing for his company's employees and helped labor leaders persuade Ohio legislators to pass legislation for workers' compensation. During the war, Flora, who stayed in Ohio, had to rely on letters to communicate with her family. As she wrote to her husband:

> *Dearest,*
>
> *Yesterday brought another dear letter from Prescott + even today he must be at the front—His letters are a constant source of happiness to me—as they must be to you and I hasten always to forward them at once—I knew the news of John Overton's death [Skull and Bones, 1917] would be a trial to him. [Overton was the first of Prescott's class to die in the war.] That news came yesterday through the Associated Press and also in Prescott's letter, which shows how delayed war news necessarily is.*

Flora then refers to the front-page story in the *Ohio State Journal* that greeted her and all of Columbus on the morning of August 8, 1918. There was no byline on the story, or any indication of how the paper came by its exclusive. As a proud mother, Flora hoped that "the great epic" was true, but the realistic part of her was dubious. As she wrote to her husband: "The next mail Prescott receives will have our letter after the great news contained in Tom's letter was rec'd—He will receive a good many letters + these will fill his heart with gladness if *only* the great epic was written seriously—I hesitate to write the word *if* but to you surely I can write as I feel—and open my heart."

The *Ohio State Journal* story to which Flora skeptically referred had a headline that rang with glory:

3 HIGH MILITARY HONORS CONFERRED ON CAPT. BUSH:
For Notable Gallantry, When Leading Allied Commanders Were Endangered,
Local Man Is Awarded French, English and U.S. Crosses.

According to the anonymous reporter, a German shell had momentarily endangered the lives of three Allied leaders, General Ferdinand Foch, Sir Douglas Haig, and General John Pershing, as they were inspecting American positions. Prescott, who was guiding them about the sector on the western front, sprang forward to save their lives. In the sycophantic story, Prescott looked to be the equal of Charlemagne in valor and courage:

Suddenly Captain Bush noticed a shell coming directly for them. He shouted a warning, suddenly drew his bolo knife, stuck it up as he would a ball bat, and parried the blow, causing the shell to glance off to the right.

The three generals marveled at the exploit. Apparently they couldn't believe their eyes . . . Within 24 hours young Bush was notified of the signal recognition that was to be accorded him—the three allied commanders had recommended him for practically the highest honors within their gift.

On the following day there was a parade in Paris of soldiers to be decorated. As he was the only one to receive three honors, Captain Bush was placed at the head of the procession.

The next day the cartoonist of the *Ohio State Journal* responded with unconcealed skepticism by drawing a young boy sitting under a tree with his dog. The caption underneath the boy read:

And just as the three greatest generals in the world were passing the boy captain, he noticed with terror a German 77 flying straight for Gen. Foch, Gen. Haig and Gen. Pershing. Quick as a flash our young hero drew his bolo knife, using it as he would a ball bat knocked the deadly shell far off to the right where it exploded with-

out injury to anyone. For his notable gallantry in saving the lives of the three great generals he was awarded the cross of the legion of honor by the French government, the Victoria Cross by the English government and the Distinguished Service Cross by the American Government.

The caption above the dog's head: "Gee! I wonder if anything like that could ever truly happen to a boy!"

A week later the *Ohio State Journal*'s news story appeared on the front page of the *New Haven Journal-Courier* under a different but equally fantastic headline:

TRIPLE HONOR TO P. S. BUSH, YALE '17:

Yale Man, in Remarkable Exploit,

Averts Danger to Foch, Haig and Pershing.

Changed Course of Shell. Struck It with Bolo Knife —

England, France and America Confer Honors for Act.

It was an extraordinary tale of heroism. But within a month Flora's worst suspicions proved true. On September 5, 1918, she wrote a contrite letter to the editor of the *Ohio State Journal*, which was reprinted on the front page:

A cable received from my son, Prescott S. Bush, brings word that he has not been decorated, as published in the papers a month ago. He feels dreadfully troubled that a letter written in a spirit of fun, should have been misinterpreted. He says he is no hero and asks me to make explanation. I will appreciate your kindness in publishing this letter.

Flora Sheldon Bush
Columbus, Sept. 5

The fabrication was punctured in Ohio but not in Connecticut. The New Haven paper never retracted its report. To this day the glory story remains attached to the page of Prescott's entry in the Yale class of 1917 yearbook in the reading room of the Manuscripts and Archives division in Yale's Sterling Memorial Library.

History does not record what Grandmother Harriet Bush had to say when she learned of all these turns in her grandson's "pernicious habit of fooling."

CHAPTER TWO

As one of the seventy-three hundred millionaires in the United States in 1914, David Davis Walker was highly regarded by *The St. Louis Republic* as "a student of political conditions and current trends." At the age of seventy-four, he commandeered the front page of that newspaper with his pronouncements on race and religion. His letter to the editor published on July 22 of that year proudly endorsed segregation, eugenics, the lynch law, and the whipping post:

> *I am in favor of segregating the Negroes in all communities. I consider them more of a menace than the social evil [prostitution], and all other evils combined. I am completely in favor of the unwritten law—lynching for assaults on women, no matter whether the criminal be black or white.*
>
> *I would compel all men and women to submit to a strict physical examination by a first-class physician before permitting them to marry. For humanity's sake, I am in favor of putting to death all children who come into the world hopeless invalids or badly deformed.*
>
> *I have been a temperate man all my life, but I am bitterly opposed to these rule-or-ruin prohibition cranks. When men and women can't have a glass of beer or wine, if they want it, it's time for another civil war.*
>
> *I am in favor of a whipping-post law for every state in the Union for wife-beaters and all other petty offenders on whom jail sentences are imposed.*

Less than a hundred years later, some of D. D. Walker's fierce opinions could be glimpsed in his great-great-grandson George Walker Bush, who had become the forty-third President of the United States. Certain issues reverberated through the generations from the Roman Catholic religiosity of the great-great-grandfather to the born-again evangelism of the great-great-grandson. Both believed in the fire-and-brimstone God of retribution. On politics, the two men differed. The great-great-grandfather, a strong Democrat, believed President Woodrow Wilson had "enacted more good legislation than did the Republican Party in all its time in power since the day of Lincoln," whereas the great-great-grandson aligned himself to the hard right of the Republican Party, vehemently opposing abortion and enthusiastically endorsing the death penalty. For all his reprehensible views on race and eugenics, D. D. Walker was surprisingly emancipated toward suffragettes, and endorsed women's right to vote. In contrast, his great-great-grandson said that admitting women to Yale in 1969 "changed the social dynamic for the worse." Both strongly opinionated men might have found common ground on the restrictions of Prohibition, but one wonders if the elderly ancestor would have recommended the whipping post for his great-great-grandson, who during his drinking days was known to be verbally abusive to his wife.

Walker's screed was published in the place that had given rise to Dred Scott, the slave whose lawsuit to obtain his freedom had precipitated the Civil War. Being the crossroads between North and South, and free states and slave states, gave St. Louis a colorful but contentious history. During the Civil War, Walker was a southern sympathizer who, according to family recollections, hired someone to join the Union Army in his place. As co-founder of Ely, Walker and Company, the largest wholesaler of dry goods west of the Mississippi, he spent the war years amassing a fortune supplying goods to J. C. Penney and other similar companies, and built the biggest warehouse in St. Louis, a block-long building on Washington Street south of Tucker. He and his son George Herbert Walker, known as Bert, bought land in Kennebunkport, Maine, so the family could escape the industrial heat of Missouri summers, and he wintered in Santa Barbara, traveling to California by private train. He drove motorcars and raced horses and became a pillar of St. Louis society. By the time of his death in 1918 at the age of seventy-eight, D. D. Walker had piloted his family into the Social Register, no small feat for the penniless son of a failed farmer from Bloomington, Indiana.

Several years before he died, he started giving away money; within four years he had disposed of $300,000 ($3.6 million in 2004). His two sons, who stood to inherit his great wealth, were incensed. They went to court in St. Louis to declare their father insane and obtain a writ of prohibition against any further disbursements of his estate. Bert Walker, who testified that his father was "squandering" his money, asked the court to find him mentally incompetent and to appoint a legal guardian to manage his financial affairs. D. D. Walker then sued his sons as well as Ely, Walker and Company for money he said he was owed. After Bert's court testimony, the jury found that his seventy-year-old father "was of unsound mind." This finding was overturned by a higher court judge for technical reasons, and the matter was returned to probate court for retrial in St. Louis. D.D. appealed to the state supreme court, arguing that since he lived in California, his sanity could not be tried in Missouri. The appeal of the jurisdictional issue was pending when D.D. died on October 4, 1918, in Kennebunkport. The next day *The St. Louis Republic* reported that his two sons, George Herbert and David Davis Junior, "were too ill last night to discuss funeral arrangements."

To the very end of his life D. D. Walker believed he was a just man who gave every man a fair shake. He never acknowledged that life's playing field might have been more level for the rich and healthy than for the poor and handicapped whom he wanted killed at birth. His large grave site in Calvary Cemetery, the resting place of St. Louis Roman Catholics, attests to his sense of self-righteousness. Flocked by elaborate granite crosses, adoring cherubs, and all sorts of praying angels, David Davis Walker is buried under the words he said he lived by: "All Through His Life He Tried to Give Everyone a Square Deal."

His forty-three-year-old son, George Herbert Walker, the fifth of six children, defied his father at every turn. His anger toward the unforgiving D.D. drove Bert to the unbounded success that eventually made the Walker family the financial ballast of the Bush dynasty.

Bert Walker had attended school in England, at the behest of his ferociously religious father, who prayed he would return a priest. Instead, he came back a defiant anti-Catholic and fell in love with Lucretia "Loulie" Wear, a Presbyterian from St. Louis.

"If you marry her in a Presbyterian church, you'll go straight to hell," D. D. Walker told his son.

"I'll tell you one thing," replied Bert. "I'll go straight to hell if I don't marry her."

Bert married her out of the Catholic Church, and his father refused to attend the wedding.

Bert rejected his father's Democratic politics; he even turned his back on his own friend Franklin Roosevelt and joined the Republican Party.

D. D. Walker had boycotted the Union Pacific Railroad because he said its owner, "E. H. Harriman, was hogging all of the railroads in the country." Bert Walker went into business with Harriman.

Bert abandoned his father's dry-goods business to build his own investment empire, topping his father's fortune many times over. He, too, drove motorcars, but his were Rolls-Royces. He became the first president of the Automobile Club of Missouri. He also raced horses, but surpassed his father by buying his own stables (Log Cabin Stud) to breed champions. He served as a New York state racing commissioner. He helped found the Racquet Club in St. Louis and the Deepdale Golf Club in Great Neck, Long Island. He became president of the U.S. Golf Association and donated the three-foot silver trophy for amateur golf that became known as the Walker Cup.

Even as a young married, he lived better than most. The census of 1900 shows that when Bert was twenty-five, he and his wife and one baby had three live-in servants—a maid, a nanny, and a cook. Years later Bert outgrew St. Louis, and he moved his wife, two daughters, four sons, and four servants to a sumptuous residence in New York City. He eventually added to the size of his father's property in Kennebunkport, purchased a mansion on Long Island, New York, with marble floors, butlers, and two Rolls-Royces, and bought the ten-thousand-acre Duncannon Plantation in South Carolina, which he used for shooting parties every Thanksgiving. With his own private railroad cars, he lived like the Maharaja of Missouri.

A virtuoso wheeler-dealer, Bert Walker calibrated numbers faster than a riverboat gambler. Unhampered by business ethics, he embraced the frenzy of stock-market speculation and seized the financial advantages of short selling stocks, fee splitting, split-stock arbitrage, and buying on margin. He founded his own brokerage and ratcheted up commissions by trading on margin for securities that could then be highly leveraged. He made his fortune before insider trading became illegal. In 1929 he judged the stock market to be overpriced and sold short in the months before the crash, bolstering his riches. His business prospered so rapidly that before he was thirty, he was well known in financial circles for his ability to "make deals."

One of his "first and biggest killings" occurred when the St. Louis–San Francisco Railway Company went into receivership. Bert arranged for G. H. Walker and Company to acquire its principal subsidiary, the New Orleans, Texas, and Mexico Railway. He took commissions for negotiating the acquisition and then for selling it later at a stupendous profit.

He never let anything stand in the way of making money, and that included political principles or religious beliefs. At the age of sixty-two, he was one of the Wall Streeters publicly rapped by then-Senator Harry S. Truman for "rampaging greed" and "the larger evil of money worship." Bert flicked off the reprimand like a pesky mosquito and continued piling up large commissions from the various offices of G. H. Walker and Company in St. Louis, Clayton, and Kansas City, Missouri; Omaha, Nebraska; Waterloo, Iowa; Chicago; New York City; Philadelphia; White Plains, New York; Bridgeport, Waterbury, and Hartford, Connecticut; Springfield and Boston, Massachusetts; and Providence, Rhode Island.

Within a few years, Bert had built a financial empire that would become the family's mother lode, bankrolling the fortunes of Walker and Bush sons and sons-in-law through the generations. At various times in various offices, the following members of the Walker-Bush tribe worked for G. H. Walker and Company: George Herbert Walker Sr., George Herbert Walker Jr., George Herbert Walker III, James Wear Walker, James Smith Bush, Louis Walker, John M. Walker, Jonathan James Bush, and Ray Carter Walker.

Like a dog marking his territory, Bert Walker left his name as his imprint: the Walker Cup; Walker's Point in Maine; G. H. Walker and Company; and, not incidentally, his son George Herbert Walker Jr.

Bert became the amateur heavyweight-boxing champion of Missouri while in law school at Washington University. A man with an explosive temper, he head-butted his way through life, pummeling anyone who got in his way. "We left the holes in the ceiling in the dining room where

Mr. Walker shot at a wasp that had stung him," said Suzanne McMillan, whose family purchased Duncannon Plantation after World War II.

Burly and barrel-chested, he looked like a bull encased in a Hathaway shirt. He was not a man to be trifled with. "He was a tough old bastard," said his granddaughter Elsie Walker. "His sons hated him."

"It's true," said his youngest son, Louis Walker. "We were scared to death of him."

Louis once made the mistake of showing up for a tennis match "slightly inebriated." His father, who worshipped sports, was determined to jackhammer "a respect for the game" into the boy. To punish him for disregarding the rules of American lawn tennis, Bert sent Louis to work in the coal mines in Bradford Township, Pennsylvania, which delayed his graduation from Yale by two years. "In our family, life was based on athletics," said Louis.

Bert sent all of his sons to Yale because the men in his wife's socially prominent Presbyterian family, her brothers, had graduated from there: Joseph W. Wear (1899), James H. Wear (1901), and Arthur Y. Wear (1902). Bert felt his sons needed the best education and social entrée money could buy, but he ignored his daughters' wishes to go to Vassar, because he felt that college was unnecessary for girls. "It's not ladylike," he told them. "It will just make you hard and opinionated." After the girls graduated from Mary Institute, the elite all-girls school in St. Louis, Bert sent them to Miss Porter's School in Farmington, Connecticut, known as a finishing school for rich girls, and then to Paris for six months with their aunt so they could polish their social skills and become more valuable on the marriage market.

The two young women returned to St. Louis in the spring of 1919 because nineteen-year-old Nancy, the older, prettier, and more flamboyant of the sisters, had been selected to be First Maid to the Queen of Love and Beauty at the Veiled Prophet Ball. This was the equivalent of being named first runner-up in the Miss America pageant, the Mardi Gras carnival, and the Rose Bowl parade. "In its time, being the Veiled Prophet Ball Queen was probably the next-best thing to being crowned Queen of England," said Ann Biraben, a native of St. Louis. "And being First Maid was almost as good as being Queen."

This was the first Veiled Prophet Ball to be held since World War I, so St. Louis was gearing up for a huge social season. The entire city was swept up in the excitement of the extravaganza that lionized the young women who would make their bows to society. Everyone was invited to participate in the torchlight parade of floats and bands that preceded the invitation-only ball, and crowds lined up for six miles to watch the festivities. The society pages of both of the city's newspapers covered the teas, suppers, luncheons, and cocktail parties beforehand in breathless detail; little girls growing up in St. Louis could not be blamed for wanting nothing more in life than to be selected by the mysterious Veiled Prophet as the Queen of Love and Beauty at the ball.

Responsibilities came with the title. Following her coronation, the Veiled Prophet Queen had to give up a year of college to devote herself to the daily social obligations of her reign. No Queen ever objected enough to give up the crown, although many years later Dorothy Walker, Nancy's younger sister, said she found the entire social ritual "barbaric."

As the elder daughter of one of the city's most prominent men, Nancy Walker was a natural selection for First Maid and practically stole the spotlight from the Queen in her Paris-made gown of white tulle spangled with brilliants. No one realized then that Nancy, who looked like one of the most eligible young women in St. Louis society, was not the marrying kind. After backing out of an engagement to a minister, the stylish young woman would eventually decide that no man in the world would ever take better care of her than her father.

"She was the family's most colorful character," said Christopher Walker, who remembered his great-great-aunt as theatrical and a bit eccentric. Dorothy's children would later refer to their vivid Aunt Nancy as "Flash."

"She wore bright red lipstick no matter the occasion and big flower dresses . . . I can still see her in the back of a limousine looking like a little painted doll in a fur wrap," said Christopher Walker. "She is definite proof that the women in our family are far more interesting than the men."

Dorothy was never a Veiled Prophet Queen or even First Maid, but one little girl in St. Louis grew up wanting to be just like her anyway. "I had such a crush on Dotty," said Mary Carter. "I used to ink the back of my hand with her initials and walk up and down and up and down to her house . . . She was absolutely my hero. I worshipped her . . . She was just wonderful [at sports] and so much better than anybody else. We used to have indoor tennis, and she was so far the best of our group." Years later Mary Carter, who also graduated from Mary Institute and Miss Porter's School, married Dorothy's brother George Herbert Walker Jr., known to the family as Herbie, and became Dorothy's best friend.

Nan and Dotty, as they were known in the family, could not have been more dramatically different. Although polar opposites, they were loving sisters and good friends. Nancy was all fashion and lace and fur muffs; she enjoyed silver-service tea pourings and the luxuries of a finely appointed home. Dotty was the tomboy daughter of her sports-loving father and, like him, played to win, especially on the tennis court.

Few women in those days excelled in sports, but Dotty was a natural athlete. Her uncle Joe Wear, captain of the Davis Cup team in 1928 and 1935, told her that with a little practice, she could easily become a tennis great. As a runner-up in the first National Girls' Tennis Championship in 1918 at the Philadelphia Cricket Club, Dotty was described by the newspaper as "a rattling good tennis player." Her opponent won because "she possessed more strokes . . . and because she was the steadier of the two at critical stages of the match, but when Miss Walker has received a little more coaching there should be little to choose between them."

It was after one of her coaching sessions that eighteen-year-old Dotty bounced into the family home on Hortense Place in her ankle-length white tennis dress and was introduced to Prescott Bush, who was visiting her sister. He had stopped by to pick up opera tickets from Nancy and stayed for tea. Flora Bush's "splendid boy," who had just moved to St. Louis in the fall of 1919, had blossomed into an extraordinarily handsome twenty-four-year-old man. He was making one hundred dollars a month working for the Simmons Hardware Company, selling the Keen Kutter line of tools.

"So like Pres to have met the debutante daughters of the town's leading citizen, who just happened to belong to the St. Louis Country Club, isn't it?" said one of his relatives. The sly observation was meant to gently deride the young man as a social mountaineer. Yet St. Louis, during its social season, opened its arms to eligible young men, especially those who had served in the Great War and graduated from Yale. This particular young man, more personable than most, was not the least intimidated by the stately mansion at 12 Hortense Place, where Loulie Wear Walker's portrait dominated the drawing room. Bert Walker had commissioned

Philip Alexius de László to paint his wife because he thought the Hungarian portraitist was the natural successor to John Singer Sargent. De László catered primarily to American socialites and European royals. He painted Mrs. Walker as he had Mrs. David Bruce, Mrs. James Duke, and Mrs. Harvey Firestone—with just enough hauteur to justify the $14,000 fee ($190,150 in 2004).

Prescott Bush had met a peer in the young Dorothy Walker, at least on the tennis court, and the Walker sisters had met a charmer who just happened to share their father's passion for golf. As a member of the St. Louis Country Club, Bert Walker reigned at the top of St. Louis society, for there was no more socially prestigious or discriminating club in the city. "This is Nirvana for St. Louis," said Robert Duffy, the architectural critic for the *St. Louis Post-Dispatch*, pointing out the rolling hills of golf greens, polo fields, tennis courts, and swimming pools that made up and still make up the exquisite enclave. The property was lined with lovely multimillion-dollar mansions, but just because you bought a home on the grounds of the country club did not mean you were allowed inside. For many years the St. Louis Country Club denied membership to all Jews, Catholics, blacks, and brewers, including the fabulously wealthy Busches, the biggest name in beer.

The covenant restrictions were so exacting in St. Louis at one time that even in the richest sections of town—Kingsbury Place, Pershing Place, Hortense Place, and Westminster Place—laws mandated how many sets of lace curtains each household had to have and how often they were to be laundered. At the time Prescott Bush rang the bell on the elaborate Beaux Arts door of 12 Hortense Place, lace curtains were hanging in every window, including in "the fainting room," where trussed-up women were revived from the clutches of their corsets.

Little is known about the romantic attractions of either Prescott or Dorothy before meeting each other in St. Louis, although it's doubtful that Dorothy had had any suitors, other than the sweet attentions of Mary Carter, who was five years her junior.

As for Prescott, he could not but have noticed the large number of his class who had married when they convened at his first Yale reunion after graduation. He had already ensured the marriages of his two younger sisters by introducing them to Yale colleagues: Margaret Bush married Stuart Clement (Yale 1917), and Mary Bush married Frank E. House Jr. (Yale

1913x). (An "x" following an individual's Yale class number indicates the individual entered with that class but left early, either dropping out or graduating early.) House, according to Yale Alumni Office records, did not graduate. Prescott's younger brother, Jim, a sophomore at Yale, would never need help in getting married. To Prescott's everlasting shame (and fury), Jim Bush would marry four times, bringing further disgrace on himself and the family name with each scandalous divorce.

As for his own romantic relationships, Prescott might have been briefly engaged at Yale, if a vague recollection can be trusted, but the secondhand remembrance is scant and the details scarce.

"Years ago my first husband's great-aunt Marian Walsh Pierce told me she had once been engaged to Prescott Bush," said Peggy Adler, a newspaper researcher. "During the 1960s, we both subscribed to the New Haven Symphony, and we'd go to the New Haven Lawn Club for dinner beforehand. One night she mentioned that she had been engaged to Prescott Bush, but the name meant nothing to me at the time. She said she broke the engagement to marry Clarence 'Doc' Pierce [Yale 1909].

"Marian's brother was Richard J. Walsh, president of the John Day Publishing Company. He founded the company to publish his second wife, Pearl Buck, the American novelist who won the Nobel Prize for Literature in 1938. His first wife's name was Ruby. A New York tabloid headline on his divorce was: 'Publisher Swaps Gems.' Funny to think about how different the world might have been if Aunt Marian hadn't changed her mind and decided to marry Prescott Bush."

Prescott proposed to Dorothy in the summer of 1920, and George Herbert Walker accepted for his daughter. By then Bert had moved his family to New York City to go into business with W. Averell Harriman. Dorothy had joined the Junior League there but didn't consider New York City home. She said she didn't want to be married in Manhattan or St. Louis. Instead, she decided her wedding could only be at the place she had been born and loved the most—Kennebunkport, Maine. So she and her mother began planning for the following August. The ceremoney was to be held in St. Ann's Episcopal Church and the reception at Surf Ledge, the Walkers' summer home atop the rugged cliffs of the Atlantic Ocean.

Dorothy's seven bridesmaids, including her sister, Nancy, as maid of honor ("First Maid again, eh?"), came from the Social Register world, as did most of Prescott's ten groomsmen, six of whom were Skull and Bones men, including his brother, Jim. Dotty tried to match the wedding party by height so that Isabel Rockefeller would not tower over Henry Sage Fenimore Cooper, and Prescott, at six feet four, wouldn't look like Mr. Snow White surrounded by seven dwarfs.

BRIDESMAIDS	GROOMSMEN
Nancy Walker	James Smith Bush
Elizabeth Trotter	Frank Parsons Shepard Jr.
Hope Lincoln	Knight Woolley
Mary Keck	George Herbert Walker Jr.
Isabel Rockefeller	William Ellery Sedgwick James
Martha Pittman	John Shepley
Ruth Lionberger	Henry Sage Fenimore Cooper
	Richard Bentley
	Henry Porter Isham
	William Potter Wear

Loulie Wear Walker did most of the work on her daughter's wedding and was properly saluted by the *New York Journal American*, which described the affair as "brilliant and as perfect in details as the good taste of Mrs. G. Herbert Walker could make it."

Dorothy ecstatically told friends that she had found her prince and was looking forward to a life of happily-ever-after. She was not to be disappointed. As she wrote in a tribute many years later for Prescott's funeral, "When he stood at the altar 51 years ago and promised to 'Keep thee only unto her as long as you both shall live,' he was making a pledge to God that he never for one moment forgot, and gave his wife the most joyous life that any woman could experience."

Things could not have been happier for the young couple during their engagement. But tragedy soon interrupted their bliss. The phone rang on Saturday evening, September 4, 1920, and Prescott learned that his sparkling forty-eight-year-old mother had been tragically killed. Flora and her husband of twenty-six years were at Watch Hill, Rhode Island, with their youngest child, Jim, who was looking forward to soon being his brother's best man. Flora and Sam were belatedly celebrating their twenty-sixth wedding anniversary at Ocean House, where they had been, according to the society pages, "prominent guests for a number of summers." They had decided to take a walk along Watch Hill Road in the late afternoon. Friends passed them in a car and backed up to talk by the side of the road. Another car coming down the hill swerved quickly to avoid an accident. At that very moment, Samuel Bush left his position beside his friend's car and was followed by Flora. The driver coming down the hill slammed on his brakes but could not stop in time. Flora was killed instantly.

In her letters to her husband during the summer of 1908, Flora's reflections on the fragility of life coupled with her enthusiasm for the automobile read poignantly next to the newspaper reports of her terrible death.

The Bushes gathered sadly in Columbus, Ohio, to bury Flora a few days after the accident. They felt star-crossed by funerals and had been gathering too frequently in the last two years to bury loved ones—first Flora's father, then her sister, and now, heartbreakingly, Flora herself.

The following summer, on August 6, 1921, the Bushes and the Walkers all gathered in Kennebunkport for the wedding everyone had looked forward to with such joyous anticipation. The bride was beautiful, the groom handsome, and, despite Prohibition, the champagne flowed. Samuel Bush, looking more pensive than usual, felt lonely without his ebullient wife by his side. How happy Flora would have been to see their "splendid boy" marry into high society. Prescott was now well and truly poised to take the family name into history.

CHAPTER THREE

A down-at-the-heels banker in a po'boy cap stands on the sidewalk in the middle of morning rush hour and tries to hawk apples. A distinguished man in a black bowler strolls by and waves his walking stick.

"Well, so long," says the apple seller. "I'll see you at lunch at the Bankers Club."

The trenchant *New Yorker* cartoon captured the financial tumult of the late 1920s as the country started its slide into the Great Depression. Flappers, gangsters, and bootleggers also marked the decade, along with lynching parties and the rise of the Ku Klux Klan. With the war over, America had been celebrating, but after the crash millions had fallen into unemployment. Firms making consumer goods were forced to cut back on production because consumers stopped buying. Children danced the Charleston for pennies in front of theaters at intermission; and coal miners formed unions and went on strike. Those with industrial jobs, particularly railroad employees and clothing workers, experienced drastic wage cuts. The popularity of catalog shopping and paying on layaway had pushed the economy to its limit. So had margin buying in the stock market. During the heyday of the Jazz Age, better known as the Roaring Twenties, stock-trading records skyrocketed as Americans of modest means began speculating and buying stocks. But instead of buying with actual money, they purchased stocks with a little cash down (10 percent) and a lot of credit (90 percent). They then used the stock they'd bought as collateral for loans to buy even more stock. Bewitched by the fantasy of becoming millionaires, they gambled dangerously under the delusion that they were investing. The speculation bubble finally burst on Black Tuesday, October 29, 1929, when the stock market crashed.

During the decade preceding the crash, Prescott Bush was not much more than a traveling salesman who clung to various jobs. These jobs moved him and his young wife from St. Louis to Kingsport, Tennessee, back to St. Louis, and then to Columbus, Ohio, to work for his father for several months. Summers were spent in Kennebunkport, where Prescott and Dotty's first child, Prescott Sheldon Bush Jr., was born in 1922. When the venture with his father failed, Prescott took a job with Stedman Products near Milton, Massachusetts, where his second son, George Herbert Walker Bush, was born in 1924.

Now that Bert Walker, or "Pop," as Dorothy called her father, had a grandson named in his honor—he was immediately tagged "Little Pop" or "Poppy"—things started looking up for the Bushes, either by coincidence or by design. Prescott landed a job "to promote sales" with the U.S. Rubber Company in New York City, and in 1925 the family moved to the wealthy little town of Greenwich, Connecticut (population thirty thousand), where they bought their first home at 11 Stanwich Road. Whether the $14,000 ($148,560 in 2004) house was purchased by Dorothy or merely put in her name is unknown, but Prescott was not making much money at the time.

Dorothy was pregnant with their third child, Nancy, who was born in 1926. Bert built his daughter a one-story house on his property at Kennebunkport so that she and the children could spend every summer in Maine while Prescott was working in the city. Bert also paid for a live-in couple to cook and garden, a nurse to take care of the children and give Dotty massages, and an Irish maid named Lizzie Larkin to do the cleaning.

While much of the country was financially wobbly, Bert Walker was flying high. He cabled his partner, Averell Harriman, who was in London playing polo with the Prince of Wales:

> We closed for the horses, and payment was made last Wednesday in the sum of $225,000 [$2,092,378.65 in 2004]. At the last moment the Belmonts stated that the stable was not included and that

*they had a chance to sell it elsewhere; but I insisted that it was your
understanding and mine that it was in, and they finally ceded the
point.*

Although he had inherited $9,842.59 ($92,000 in 2004) from his
mother's estate, Prescott would recall the same period as being financially
taxing for himself and his young wife. "I know what it is to tramp the
streets all day and return to a strange hotel room in a strange city tired and
discouraged," he said years later. "Mrs. Bush and I know what it is to be
deeply in debt and to feel that we could never get out from under. Indeed
we have had some pretty difficult years together before the tide turned
and we gradually paid off our debts and began to save for the security of
our growing family."

Prescott continued selling rubber-tile flooring for another two years
until his father-in-law pulled the golden cord that transformed an itiner-
ant salesman into an investment banker. Prescott never forgot the day.

"I do remember that I left U.S. Rubber on May 1, 1926, to become
associated with W. A. Harriman and Co., which was an investment banking organization, principally owned by Averell Harriman and his brother,
Roland," he said in an oral history. "Mrs. Bush's father, G. H. Walker, was
the president of it, but Averell was the chairman, and my father-in-law
had a substantial interest in it."

Lest the interviewer assume that this professional elevation to vice
president of W. A. Harriman and Company was merely a matter of the
son-in-law also rises, Prescott emphasized his friendship with Roland
"Bunny" Harriman (Yale 1917; Skull and Bones) while acknowledging
the confidence his father-in-law had in him. "We [Averell and Roland
Harriman and G. H. Walker] talked it over and they seemed to think that
I would have some possibilities in that field that they were looking for . . .
At any rate, they offered me a job."

Going from selling rubber flooring to representing the prestigious
name of Harriman on Wall Street energized Prescott, who was thirty-one
years old when he started his new job. He joined the Round Hill Country Club in Greenwich and began playing golf with his father-in-law, who
drew him into the U.S. Golf Association, of which Bert was then president. Prescott would follow in those footsteps, serving on the executive
committee for eight years before he, too, became president.

In 1926, W. A. Harriman and Company was a brokerage firm that concentrated on foreign stocks and bonds. Through its offices in Berlin, Germany, opened in 1922, it became one of the first American investment houses to assist in rebuilding European industry after the war. As an incorporated underwriting organization, the company was prohibited from doing any type of banking. So when the Harrimans decided they wanted to start a private bank for high-net-worth clients, they turned to Roland's classmate and close friend Knight Woolley (Yale 1917; Skull and Bones), who had been a groomsman in Prescott's wedding and was godfather to his son George Herbert Walker Bush. In 1927, Woolley became general manager of the private bank known as Harriman Brothers and Company.

The two companies—W. A. Harriman and Company and Harriman Brothers and Company—made their offices in one room at 39 Broadway after the Harrimans' accountant bought six rolltop desks from a secondhand furniture dealer. "By any standards," recalled Knight Woolley, "it was all pretty crummy."

Within a few months, ferocious "powwows" began as the two groups discussed general policy. "Roland and Averell were for doing a cash business only and having no margin accounts," Woolley wrote in his memoir. "The dissenter was Bert Walker. His firm in St. Louis took margin accounts. In fact, such accounts were probably the backbone of their business."

Woolley did not know too much about the problem of margin accounts then, but he objected on the purely snobbish grounds of NOCD, code for "Not Our Class, Dear."

"At that time, Ira Haupt & Co. occupied most of a floor at 39 Broadway, the Harriman Building," Woolley wrote in a privately published memoir for his family. "On active days their customers crowded the lobby, and even the fire stairs, where they sometimes ate picnic lunches. The men's toilets were completely fouled up. They were a terrible bunch of people. If they represented typical margin account clients, I was against margin accounts."

It didn't take long for Woolley to learn that lending money to individuals for the purpose of purchasing and carrying securities was unwise and financially hazardous. That's when he butted heads with Bert, the financial buccaneer.

"One day Walker asked me to come to his office," Woolley recalled. "He was seated at his enormous flattop desk with my month-end balance sheet before him. He was jotting down some figures on a small pad as he looked up and said: 'We have a big underwriting coming along at the end of next week. I would like to clean up some of our current loans now, so we will be out of the banks for a period of about a week. I want you to liquidate at once your treasury bills, call loans and acceptances and turn the money over to us. We'll give you an I.O.U. note. I figure that your quick assets will just about do it. Later on, we'll return these funds to you.' "

Woolley immediately saw the proposition as a "dangerous dealing." He tried to keep calm and speak slowly. "I explained our obligations to our depositors and to the Federal Reserve Bank. They had our figures on file and were ready buyers of our commercial acceptances. Private banks, such as ours, in those days did not publish balance sheets, but depositors had every right to believe we handled our affairs, as did the public banks. I ended by saying to Mr. Walker that I was sorry, but that I would not do what he had ordered."

Within seconds the two men abandoned all pretense of composure. Walker, who brooked no insolence from subordinates, was red-faced and grew livid when Woolley started shouting at him. At that moment Averell Harriman walked into the room.

"Without waiting for Walker to speak, I turned to Averell and hastily outlined Walker's demand for all of Harriman Brothers' quick assets. I also reminded him of our obligations to the New York Fed as well as to our depositors . . . I concluded by saying that if Walker had his way, I intended to resign forthwith."

Harriman quickly seized control. "Knight, why don't you leave us now," he said. "I want to have a chat with Bert about this. You will hear from us later on."

Neither Harriman nor Walker ever said anything further to Woolley about the matter. "Rumor had it that a pretty vehement argument ensued," Woolley said. "Rumor also had it that they had had a series of prior disagreements. As Pres Bush . . . informed me later, it all led up to Bert's decision to retire some nine months later." The matter irrevocably settled itself—proving Woolley's fears to be correct—when margin buyers and sellers panicked, causing the stock-market crash. Over the next few months, more than a thousand banks failed. Farm prices fell, factories closed, soup kitchens opened, and breadlines formed. When people started jumping out of windows on Wall Street rather than face financial ruin, Bert Walker was comfortably ensconced at Walker's Point in Kennebunkport, nursing a bad stomach. But even he was reassessing.

Five and a half weeks after the crash he wrote a "Dear Averell" letter dated December 6, 1929:

> As I stated to you last spring I am willing to step out of the picture if doing so will best suit your book. You were good enough at that time to say an emphatic no and if that view still holds I propose that we continue as we are for another year, making certain organization changes as discussed and assigning to you such organization work as you may wish to take on . . . I should like to have Pres made an assistant to the president to handle details under my direction.

The arguments over Bert's margin buys, plus his ill health—he alluded to intestinal pain in his letters—led to his decision to resign as president of W. A. Harriman and Company. Within five months he began extricating himself from almost all the Harriman companies, except the Harriman Fifteen Corporation, the holding company Averell had created to handle his personal investments in shipping and mining. By May 1930 Bert Walker had returned to his perch as the ruling presence of G. H. Walker and Company, where he continued buying and selling on margin just as he had done before the crash. Prescott, whose close personal ties to Roland "Bunny" Harriman and Knight Woolley had become even closer, had no interest in leaving with his father-in-law.

"I heaved a long sigh of relief," said Woolley, who had won the argument about margin accounts. "The lending of money to individuals for buying and selling securities was forbidden as one of our most important unwritten rules . . . With Walker out of the way, my job was much simpler, safer and far less nerve-wracking."

But business did not improve. No one within the Harriman companies had foreseen the stock-market crash, and months later people were still reeling. By the spring of 1930, Averell Harriman had directed Prescott Bush to undertake a complete financial review of all the Harriman companies. Prescott issued a stern report calling for drastic cutbacks: the offices in Warsaw and Paris were to be closed, and the Berlin office was to be put on a budget of no more than eighteen thousand dollars a year. Other severe recommendations were made as well. "Such a retreat was personally offensive," wrote Harriman's biographer Rudy Abramson, "but Averell reluctantly agreed to it."

The aftershocks of the crash reverberated throughout the world's financial community, affecting even the biggest investment-banking houses. One of the most venerable, Brown Brothers and Company, sustained such heavy losses that it was forced to seek new capital. The Harrimans, with their inherited wealth of $70 million ($777 million in 2004), were the first approached. Conversations soon went way beyond the matter of a mere loan.

The idea of a merger between the two houses supposedly sprang from a train ride to New Haven for yet another Yale reunion. Ellery James, who worked for Brown Brothers and Company, shared a drawing room in a parlor car with Knight Woolley and Prescott Bush so they could all play cards. Idle conversation about the large number of bank mergers taking place led to further talks during the year. All concerned agreed that it made sense to combine the Harriman companies and Brown Brothers. The men who ran the companies were close friends, having known each other as Bonesmen at Yale. Robert A. Lovett (Yale 1918), a childhood friend of the Harrimans, had gone to work at Brown Brothers and Company after marrying Adele Quartley Brown, daughter of one of the senior partners. The deal was completed in a matter of weeks. The only sticking point was the name.

Justifiably proud of their illustrious reputation in financial circles, James and Thatcher Brown insisted their name be retained in the merger. Averell and Roland Harriman, who had invested over $10 million in the new partnership, were equally insistent that their name be included. Realizing the deal could fall apart over such a dispute, the Browns and the Harrimans finally agreed to put the matter before a committee composed of friends of both families. The result: Brown Brothers Harriman and Company. The news was announced December 12, 1930, on the front page of *The New York Times*.

Wall Street hailed the merger as extraordinarily good news in exceedingly bad times, especially since it was reported on the same day that the Bank of United States (no connection to the government, despite its name) closed its doors. The failure of the Bank of United States, a commercial bank with fifty-nine offices in New York, was the largest bank failure in American history at that point. So the merger of the Browns and the Harrimans was applauded on Wall Street. One financial journalist called it "a merger of financial aristocrats, a combination which unites the best of the old and new." The alliance between the two families signaled an act of faith in the economic recovery of the nation, and the news excited everyone with its promise for the future. With the Harrimans' capital, the Browns' stature, and the energy and experience of the young partners, this was clearly going to be the gold standard of investment banking.

On the morning of January 1, 1931, the day the merger took effect, Prescott Bush woke up as a full-fledged partner in a venture that seemed destined to make him rich beyond his wildest dreams. Dorothy was pregnant again and expecting their fourth child, Jonathan, in 1931, so Prescott decided to buy an eight-bedroom house to accommodate his growing family. They moved to a spacious brown Victorian house on Grove Lane situated on two acres of wooded land with a rolling lawn, a grand driveway, and a separate carriage house for "the help." Dotty financed the sale and the house remained in her name, but Prescott felt confident that he could now make sizable mortgage payments. He also joined a second country club, signing for a family membership in the Flossy Field Club so "Pressy" and "Poppy" could take swimming and tennis lessons and play field hockey. Young Nancy began piano lessons, and Dotty enrolled the two boys in the Greenwich Country Day School. The family gave thanks every Sunday at Christ Episcopal Church, where Prescott, determined to become a pillar of the community, joined the vestry. He remained on the best of terms with his father-in-law, despite Walker's resignation from W. A. Harriman and Company.

Although Dotty's father was rabidly anti-Catholic, he occasionally attended a Presbyterian church with his fervently religious wife, Loulie. "She's quite a little Bible thumper," he once said about her insistence on certain pieties, including a Sunday ban on dice games, cards, and movies. Dotty inherited her mother's fierce religiosity and began each morning by reading personal devotions to her husband and children at the breakfast table.

"These were little moral stories, three to five minutes . . . about how to live your life," said William H.T. "Bucky" Bush, Pres and Dotty's youngest son. "Every Sunday, the whole family went to church. It wasn't an option."

During the week Prescott consecrated himself to his new position within Brown Brothers Harriman. "One of my activities was to help build up deposits, to bring new clients into this firm, corporate enterprises such as the International Shoe Co., the Columbia Broadcasting Co., the Prudential Insurance Co.," said Prescott. "It required a lot of salesmanship, yes, and in the course of all this activity I became a director of a large number of American companies, including the Simmons Co. (that makes beds and bedding), the Dresser Industries Co., which is an oil well supply company, the Prudential Insurance Co., which is the second largest life insurance company, the U.S. Guaranty Insurance Co., which is a casualty company, now known as the Federal Insurance Co., Columbia Broadcasting System (radio and television), . . . the Pennsylvania Water and Power Co., and a company in New Haven called the Rockbestos Manufacturing Co. They were all in different fields."

Once he brought new clients to the firm, he explained the investment advisory service that Brown Brothers Harriman had set up. They now counseled clients for a fee instead of managing their accounts for free. It was a precursor to the way today's money-management firms work. "We set up a securities research department so that we could go more in an orderly way about advising the Harrimans, who had very substantial holdings in a great many different enterprises . . . [W]hen we'd talk to somebody who'd say, 'Look, I have half a million dollars. I don't know what to do about this market. What should I do?' we'd say, 'Well, why don't you let us do this for you? We're doing it for the Harrimans, our own partners, so and so's wife, and the children, and my own wife' and so on— 'We can do for you just what we're doing for ourselves . . .' That's how we built up the investment business."

Brown Brothers Harriman was a private investment bank for the very rich. "[An] account was hardly worth putting into this investment advisory department on a fee basis unless it could pay us a thousand dollars a year which is one half of one percent on $200,000 principal . . . I won't say we were *the* pioneers. There were already a few investment counsel firms around. But . . . we were pioneers among people of our kind."

In the spring of 1931 the German government issued a *Stillhalte*, or standstill, that froze all of the country's foreign-exchange assets. This meant no payments of any debts to foreigners.

Such a move had not been anticipated and had never been tried before by the German nation, but its banks were in crisis and its reichsmarks worthless due to overinflation. The collapse of its economy had enormous international ramifications and led to the political unrest that brought Adolf Hitler to power in 1933.

For the partners of Brown Brothers Harriman, who shouldered unlimited liability for all the firm's obligations, the German *Stillhalte* was devastating. The good ship BBH seemed in danger of capsizing under the weight of its German debts, and it faced financial ruin.

"Our new firm . . . was stuck for a total of almost $10,000,000—about the size of our capital," said Knight Woolley.

"The reserve capital accounts of some of our partners got into the red," said Prescott Bush. "In other words, the firm lost enough capital, at least on paper, so that we were below water. I was one of them."

The "red partners," including Woolley and Prescott, now owed the firm hundreds of thousands of dollars. They each took out term insurance for the amount they owed in the event they died. The firm then began selling off its German debts with a 20 percent net loss. Even so, the Harrimans still had to put up additional capital of $10 million to keep the firm solvent and strong enough to continue soliciting business.

"Averell and Roland then did a most generous thing," said Woolley. "Averell said, and I quote, 'It is perfectly ridiculous for Roland and me to try to run a banking firm with the principal working partners indebted to the firm. All of the earnings should go to the "red partners" in the same percentages they formerly had.' In other words, they would simultaneously come out of the 'red' together."

Relieved that incoming profits would first go to wipe out the deficit in their accounts, the "red partners" were still strapped for cash. "We had nothing to pay the rent or the grocer's bills," said Woolley. "At an important partners' meeting this was all fully discussed. Averell and Roland Harriman suggested that we have salaries. As the only bachelor, I was asked what I thought I could live on within reason. I said $16,000 [$197,700 in

2004]. It was then agreed that the married partners should have twice this amount, $32,000 [$395,000 in 2004]. This arrangement was to continue for many years."

For the next four years the "red partners" struggled to bring in enough business to pay off their debts. No one mentioned the firm's financial difficulties for fear of starting rumors about insolvency that would surely put them all out of business. "There may have been some people who suspected it, but we never discussed our private affairs with anybody—still don't," said Prescott Bush in an interview that remained sealed until his death. "I'm probably talking more freely to you than I ever have to anyone about this thing, hoping I'll be dead before anything happens."

The firm had recovered its financial stability by 1935, and the partners' debts were fully repaid, but Prescott did not feel financially secure for many years after that. In 1946, he refused to run for the House of Representatives because he was not yet financially independent. He had been elected moderator of the Representative Town Meeting, which was like being the unpaid Speaker of the House in Greenwich (population forty-one thousand), a position he held for seventeen years. He helped raise money for Republican presidential candidates Alf Landon in 1936 and Thomas Dewey in 1944, but it would be several years until he felt he had enough money to run for public office himself. His wife said if he hadn't had so many children in private schools and such heavy financial obligations, he would have gone into national politics earlier. She reflected wistfully: "He would have been President of the United States."

Whether it was the financial weight of being a "red partner" or natural midwestern frugality, Prescott and Dorothy lived rather simply compared with others in Greenwich who had homes with stables and swimming pools and tennis courts.

"We were well-off, but we weren't considered rich. Not by Greenwich standards," said Prescott Bush Jr. "We got an allowance of 10 cents a week growing up . . . We could buy a Good Humor for 10 cents. We used to hope we got a lucky stick because if you got a lucky stick you got another Good Humor for free."

Depression mentality ruled the household. "Mother was a stickler for saving," said Jonathan Bush. "They sold Cokes at the tennis club, but we weren't allowed to buy any there. We had to get ours at home because they were cheaper . . . And we lived in hand-me-downs. I never got a new thing to wear until I was in college."

Nancy Bush Ellis remembers "a very ordinary life" without luxuries or grand summer trips to Europe. "Father said it was too complicated to take all of us," she said. "And our house? The press tries to build up all this Greenwich estate business. But have you seen the house? It's a nice brown-shingled house. Period."

"We never felt that Dad had any kind of wealth at all," said Jonathan. "We had a cook and a maid and a chauffeur but other kids had a lot more."

Prescott junior scoffed at his brother's "pretentious" description. "To call Alec a chauffeur is the joke of all time . . . Johnny didn't know what he was talking about. George and I would get in the back of Dad's little Model A Ford and Dad would drive to the train. Then he'd get off and Alec would drive us to school. Alec was more of a gardener, really. We got a ride to school, yes, but it wasn't like Alec waited all day for Mother to say, 'Bring the car around.' "

The Model A Ford was eventually replaced by a big black Oldsmobile, but the morning ritual remained the same for the eight years the boys attended the Greenwich Country Day School. Their most vivid recollection of growing up seems to be the visceral fear they all had of their father.

"Dad was really scary," George H.W. Bush told the television interviewer David Frost. "Remember Teddy Roosevelt's 'Speak softly and carry a big stick'? My dad spoke *loudly* and carried the same big stick. He got our attention pretty quick." As an adult, George would frequently allude to his father's beatings. "He was always talking to me about how his dad beat him—actually whipped him with a strap," said Cody Shearer, a family friend who traveled with George throughout 1980. When the historian Garry Wills asked George if he ever found it hard to differ from his father, Bush was mystified. "It never occurred to me to differ. I mean, he was up here (lifts right hand as far as he can), and I was this little guy down here."

George's cousin Dr. Ray Walker, a psychiatrist, interprets George's behavior as going along to get along. "He always placated his father. Then, later on, he placated his bosses. That is how he relates—by never defining himself against authority."

Like many men of his generation, Prescott Bush believed in corporal punishment. He maintained his authority over his children with a belt, a razor strop, and even, on occasion, a squash racket.

"He was scary as hell," said Ray Walker. "He intimidated my father—he intimidated everybody . . . He was kind of distant and tall and knowing and judgmental."

Osborne Day, a classmate of George Bush's at Andover and Yale, re-called Prescott vividly. "I was certainly afraid to not be very polite to him," he said. "I guess you could say I was afraid of him. Not that I'd heard any-thing terrible about the man, but he was a serious guy, and if you were as young as I was at the time, you treated him as a serious senior person."

"If we acted disrespectfully, if we did not observe the niceties of eti-quette, he took us over his knee and whopped us with his belt," said Prescott junior. "He had a strong arm, and, boy, did we feel it . . . He was a tough Joe bastard."

"As children, we were all afraid of Dad," said Jonathan Bush. "Every one of us . . . Dad was no laughing matter."

"The boys were more scared of Dad than I was," said Nancy Bush Ellis, who added that her brothers always sent her to their father to ask for things. "I was the messenger.

"I remember one morning Pres sassed my father and he was sent away from the table. As he was going up the stairs, I don't know why, but he sassed my father again, and my father threw the newspaper, which was still folded up in three parts, at him. When Pres said, 'Ha! You missed,' my father jumped out of his chair to go for him, and I screamed, 'But he's going to kill him!' Mother said, 'No, he's not.' "

Dorothy was as tough as her husband in disciplining the children. "Oh . . . She didn't leave it up to him," said Prescott junior. "She ran the show, but if she ever needed a backup or felt that she hadn't made quite a strong enough impression on us, he would come in . . . We were scared to death of Dad when we were younger."

There was an extra reason to be scared of Prescott Bush's temper—although his children never acknowledged, even as adults, their father's drinking problem.

Their mother denied his alcoholic binges when they occurred, and told the children that they didn't actually see what they knew they saw. "It was like that phrase—What are you going to believe: What I tell you or your lying eyes?" said Charles Kelly, an investment counsel, who graduated from Yale Law School and was acquainted with the family. No warlord was more dictatorial than Dorothy Walker Bush in denying reality. She told her children that their father was simply "not feeling well," and that was that. No further discussion—ever. When Prescott was drunk or hungover, she shooed them off, saying, "Your father has been working hard and needs a little peace and quiet."

"Their father wasn't crazy about the children," said Mary Carter Walker, Dotty's childhood friend from St. Louis who had married Dotty's brother Herbie Walker. "So Dotty would sneak them up the back steps so they wouldn't bother him."

"Prescott was a handsome man who had the admiration and respect of his contemporaries," said Charles Kelly, "but it was well known that he was a major-league alcoholic."

Prescott's brother, James, was also an alcoholic. FBI files show that he was forced to resign as vice president of the First National Bank of St. Louis due to excessive drinking. He never drank on the job, but, according to the FBI files, he would miss work for several days at a time because of his secret benders. He was married four times and divorced three times, and his second wife, Janet Newbold Rhinelander Stewart, gave the FBI a sworn statement about his alcoholism. She also told her daughter that James had beaten her when drunk.

Like his brother, Prescott usually confined his drinking binges to his country clubs or places like the Hartford Club, an exclusive men's club in Connecticut.

"I was a bellboy at the Hartford Club," said Earl Balfour, "which meant we ran the elevator, the switchboard, and the hat check. Those were our main sources of income. Prescott Bush was a cheap guy who never tipped. He'd come in, go upstairs, and send down for cigars and booze. He never tipped any of the waiters or the bellboys. This went on for weeks. Finally we figured out how to exact revenge. Whenever he came in drunk and wanted to go upstairs, we'd take him in the elevator and stop about three inches from his floor. He'd step out and fall flat on his face. Just as he was going down, we'd say: 'Watch your step, sir.'"

Prescott's secret binges were considered a shameful moral failing in those unenlightened days. The genetic predisposition to alcoholism would wreak havoc with all of his children in years to come, forcing each to cope with the problem in some way. Nancy Bush married a man who became an alcoholic, and some of their children suffered severe problems of substance abuse. So did the children of George H.W. Bush. The legacy of Prescott's alcoholism became as destructive to the dynasty as denying its existence was to his immediate family. But denial was the only way Dorothy Bush could cope with this one flaw in what to her was an otherwise-perfect husband.

This secret—never mentioned or discussed within the family, let alone with outsiders—caused George to grow up with a pathological fear of personal examination, a fear that carried over into his public life. As an adult, he ran from anything that might expose the pain he had buried as a child. He was so threatened by any kind of analysis that interviewers were forewarned not to lay him on the couch with their questions.

"Is he going to get on all this psychobabble bullshit?" George asked about an interview with David Frost.

"So, this is gonna be a deal on where I'm coming from, a psychiatric layout?" George asked Gail Sheehy.

"Is it a psychoanalytical piece?" he asked Maureen Dowd, yet again revealing his obsessive desire to keep secrets and avoid self-analysis.

George learned from his mother to use perpetual motion to avoid personal scrutiny. Having inherited her father's rampaging play-to-the-death competitiveness, Dotty raised her brood to believe in the hard-charging religion of sports. The first commandment: excel as an athlete. Absolutely fearless, she pushed herself and her children to the edge of physical endurance, sometimes quite recklessly.

"We had lots of trees around our house in Greenwich, and somehow we knew she wanted us to climb every one of them," said George. "Some neighbor would see us and come to warn Mother. 'They'll be fine,' she would say. And we would hear her, and our own apprehensions would vanish. Of course, there would be scrapes and bruises . . . but it didn't seem to faze Mother or her confidence in us."

Dotty forced George, who was left-handed, to play tennis with his right hand. As a consequence, he developed a crab-like serve but became ambidextrous, which allowed him to make astonishing retrieval shots. Dotty also forced him to play golf with his right hand, which eventually made his wrists stiff and impeded his game. In baseball, he threw left-handed but batted from the right side. He admitted that if he had hit lefty, he might've been better, since his left was the controlling eye. But he didn't have the nerve to defy his commanding mother.

"Mrs. Bush had power over her children," said their friend Fitzhugh Green. "Perhaps in this matter she used it unwisely."

One day in late August at Kennebunkport, Dotty and young Pressy took their small sailboat, *Shooting Star*, into the stormy seas off the Maine coast. Even nature's whims could not dim her competitive drive. A neighbor onshore saw them taking on water and summoned Prescott senior. He and George sped off in the family motorboat, *Tom Boy*, to rescue mother and son before they capsized. Prescott junior remembers his father's fury.

"How could you, Dotty? How could you!"

Barely chastened, Dotty maintained her blind drive to win, which set the standard of excellence within the family.

"Mrs. Bush was pretty fierce about competition," recalled Jack Greenway, one of George's Andover classmates. "I think that competing with her was a rite of passage within the family . . . When it came Nancy's turn to play her [in tennis], they played so many sets at Round Hill Club in Greenwich that Mrs. Bush was taken directly to the hospital in Greenwich to be rehydrated."

More than fifty years later George recalled his mother's combative style. "I can vividly remember the bottom of my mother's feet. Yes, she played a much younger woman named Peaches Peltz in tennis back in 1935 or so. Peaches was smooth. Mum was tenacious. Mother literally wore the skin off the bottom of her feet."

The family enjoys telling the story of Dotty nine months into her first pregnancy and playing baseball at Kennebunkport. "Her last time up she hit a home run," said George, "and without missing a base (I'm told) continued right off the field to the hospital to deliver Pres."

"I had to decide early on as a daughter-in-law that you can't beat her, you have to sit back and enjoy her," said George's wife, Barbara Bush. "When I was a new bride, she beat me in paddle tennis with her right hand, then with her left."

Even in her seventies, Dotty kept up her strenuous pace. "I remember playing gin rummy with her in Greenwich when she was recuperating from a broken leg," recalled a close family friend. "She told me she suffered a fracture during the U.S. Open. Her family was watching on television, but it was a gorgeous day and she wanted to go for a walk. She couldn't get anyone to budge from the TV. So she went out by herself. She tripped and fell while climbing over a branch and broke her leg. She lay in the leaves for a couple of hours, unable to move, until a little boy came along on his bicycle. He said, 'Mrs. Bush, what are you doing lying on the ground?' She told him what had happened, and he offered to go get her family. She said, 'Oh, no. They would be very, very angry if you did that because they're watching the U.S. Open.' God forbid we should disturb anyone watching sports."

Jonathan Bush recalled the day his mother offered five dollars to any of her sons who could beat her at tennis. George, who was sixteen at the time, accepted the challenge. The children rooted for George.

"Everyone wanted him to win, and he finally did. She was at the top of her form. It was a brutal match, both of them wringing wet when they finished."

Dotty set up intrafamily competitions and graded everyone on his or her excellence in swimming, tennis, touch football, knee football, softball, tiddledywinks, checkers, fishing, golf, and indoor putting. She even set up a Ping-Pong table in the foyer of the Greenwich home, and anyone who passed through the front door was challenged.

Sports became a metaphor of life for Dotty, who judged people's characters by how they played tennis. "She had some good shots" meant she was a terrible player and a mediocre person. "He can't keep score" meant he'll never amount to much in life. "He plays the net" was high praise and marked a man for success.

Her sons, who competed for her attention, absorbed these judgments and pushed themselves to please her. She challenged them constantly—swimming matches, footraces, bridge games—and played to win at everything, never holding back.

"She loved games and thought that competition taught courage, fair play, and—I think most importantly—teamwork," said George Bush. "She taught games to us endlessly."

The "fair play" part of competition was not always observed by the children. Sometimes their desire to win trumped good sportsmanship, especially in George, who never outgrew his need to triumph, whether to please his mother or impress his father. "I hate losing," he said. "Close only counts in horseshoes and hand grenades."

During their childhood summers at Kennebunkport, George met his match in an equally competitive youngster named Bill Truesdale, who was the best sailor in the eleven-foot class of boats known as catboats, which had two sides, a bottom, a mast, and a centerboard. Bill Truesdale was the perennial winner, summer after summer, in an annual competition. One night before a big race George went down and tied a bucket to Truesdale's centerboard. The next day the boats, about fifteen of them, were towed up the Kennebunk River to the starting line offshore. The warning gun went off, and everyone put up his sail.

"There was a light breeze and Truesdale's boat barely moved," recalled Jonathan Bush. "At first he thought something was wrong with the boat, and in frustration he began to beat it with a paddle. Whack! Whack! When he got ashore he found out what George had done. He chased him for days. George would be sitting on the porch, and we'd hear 'Here comes Truesdale!' and off he'd go. That was a shout we heard all summer: 'Here comes Truesdale!' "

To the Bushes, the anecdote illustrates George's love of practical jokes. Others might see the story of sabotaging a friend's boat to deprive him of victory as something more than an adolescent caper (and, as a way of dealing with competition, something that came to fruition in George's later political campaigns). But no one would deny that the children learned from their parents to play to win.

The competitive atmosphere between the Bushes and the Walkers at Kennebunkport was often tense, sometimes terrifying. "I can remember some very earnest rock throwing up there," said Louise Mead Walker, who married John Walker, George Herbert Walker Jr.'s son. "At my own family's Sunday dinner in Dayton, whenever the men came in from golf, the question always was, 'Did you have a good game?' At Kennebunkport, the question always is, 'Did you win?' "

When George was older, his youngest brother, Bucky, was given a new ball-in-a-labyrinth game and beat George easily. Bucky went to bed proud of besting his older brother, who had been to war, married, and become a father himself. The next day George casually suggested a rematch. George won with a perfect score. Family members, in on the joke, howled with laughter. George had stayed up late perfecting his game to ambush his baby brother, who was fourteen years younger.

"My mother and father were both fierce competitors," said Prescott junior, "and it was extremely important that you compete and do the best you could [but] that you learn to be a good loser . . . In other words, to lose with dignity, even though you hated it . . . even though it made you mad as the devil, you had to maintain your composure and not throw your racket . . . or if you're in tiddledywinks, and you miss the shot that cost you the game, you couldn't throw the bowl."

And if you did?

"Well, we'd get the strap or we would spend a lot of time sitting in our rooms or something like that."

Prescott and Dotty also forbade cursing and bragging. As Mrs. Bush told an interviewer: "I just couldn't bear braggadocio."

The hell-bent prideful pursuit of winning had to always be accompanied by gracious modesty. "You could never come home and say you played well in a game," said Jonathan Bush. "You just didn't talk about yourself. Bad taste."

George Bush remembered being slapped down for arrogance when he was eight years old. He had said he thought he was off his game. "Mother jumped all over me. 'You are just learning—you don't have a game! Work harder and maybe some day you will.' "

The Bushes raised their children to win and assume their superiority as winners but to mask the assumption at all times. Enforced humility, like keeping secrets, was considered the epitome of good breeding. Chances are the Bushes might not have appreciated the perceptiveness of Mark Twain, who said, "Good breeding consists in concealing how much we think of ourselves—and how little we think of the other person."

CHAPTER FOUR

B y the 1930s the nation's railroads had become tangled in bankruptcies, unrelated to the Depression, and the U.S. Senate wanted
to know why. So the Interstate Commerce Commission started
holding hearings to investigate the complicated financial schemes that
enriched the bankers and brokers while simultaneously looting the railroads.

Leading the charge was the newly elected senator from Missouri, a
failed haberdasher named Harry S. Truman. A New Dealer from the moment of his election, Senator Truman supported all of President Roosevelt's programs to pull the country out of the Depression—the Works
Progress Administration, the Social Security Administration, the Public
Utility Holding Company Act, and the Rural Electrification Administration. Now he was determined to expose financial mismanagement of the
railroads and reform the national transportation system.

A small part of the larger problem involved the reorganization of the
Missouri Pacific system and the subsequent financing that led to its bankruptcy. This fiscal plunder, the Enron scandal of its day, fleeced employees and left directors and stockholders destitute while the wealthy
financiers and their corporate lawyers skipped out with their pockets full
of boodle. Playing a leading role in the pillage was George Herbert
Walker, who was subpoenaed to testify before Senator Truman on November 17, 1937.

Bert walked into the Senate hearing room in Washington, D.C., with
his lawyers from Cravath, de Gersdorff, Swaine, and Wood. Even in a suit
and tie, he looked like a burly boxer with a trainer and a handler on ei-

ther side, ready to remove his mouthpiece after every round and ram it back when the bell clanged. As a former amateur heavyweight champion in St. Louis, he was accustomed to pummeling brutes; the little senator in the wire-rim glasses hardly looked like a worthy adversary.

With a few polite questions, Senator Truman established that George Herbert Walker had been chairman of the board of Gulf Coast Lines when the Missouri Pacific acquired control of that company in 1925. At the time, Bert was also president of W. A. Harriman and Company, bankers for the railroad, and senior partner of G. H. Walker and Company, the brokerage firm that later sold the railroad. Bert admitted he had informed his board that the sales profit was going to W. A. Harriman and Company, but he neglected to tell them that the banking house was only a temporary receptacle for his own personal benefit.

Bert Walker testified that of the sale's $518,680.80 ($5,519,620 in 2004) net profit, he personally received $173,387.57 ($1,845,130 in 2004). An additional $72,244.84 ($768,804 in 2004) went to his brokerage firm, G. H. Walker and Company, and more moneys, in the amount of $43,346.90 ($461,283 in 2004), went to W. A. Harriman and Company, of which he was president.

The Interstate Commerce Commission characterized his various fees as "excessive compensation," but Bert's defense was that he had worked on the deal, "a protracted negotiation," for ten years without pay. "I never charged the railroad a penny of compensation," he said. "I never even charged them most of the time for my out-of-pocket expenses." Instead of taking a salary for his services, he said, he insisted on working free until it came time to sell the railroad to a big system. "I wanted the right to sell it and make the commission then."

Bert showed no shame for his stupendous profits, which, his lawyers asserted, were perfectly legal. Nor was he embarrassed when the Senate committee counsel pointed out that the gross compensation totaled more than the salaries and expenses of all the railroad's employees. Bert shrugged as if to say, "Business is business."

One month later Senator Truman stood up in the Senate to passionately attack Wall Street and the larger evil of money worship—all that George Herbert Walker represented. Truman blasted the "court and lawyer situation" in the gigantic receiverships and reorganizations that had destroyed the railroads. He specifically named Walker's law firm, "the highest of the high hats in the legal profession [who] resort to tricks that would make an ambulance chaser in a coroner's court blush with shame," and he blamed the railroads' collapse on wild rampaging greed:

> We worship money instead of honor. A billionaire, in our estima-
> tion, is much greater in these days in the eyes of the people than
> the public servant who works for public interest. It makes no differ-
> ence if the billionaire rode to wealth on the sweat of little children
> and the blood of underpaid labor . . . Wild greed along the lines I
> have been describing brought on the Depression. When investment
> bankers, so-called, continually load great transportation compa-
> nies with debt in order to sell securities to savings banks and insur-
> ance companies so they can make a commission, the well finally
> runs dry.

The senator's charges of stock juggling and other deceptions by lawyers, brokers, and bankers made the front page of *The New York Times*. The following year Truman introduced a bill to reorganize the railroads and place them under the regulation of the Interstate Commerce Commission. The bill, known as the Wheeler-Truman Act, was signed into law by President Roosevelt in 1940. Inadvertently, George Herbert Walker had helped contribute to another success for the New Deal, which he despised almost as much as the New Deal President.

"Oh, Pop hated Roosevelt," recalled his daughter Dotty. "Hated him. Roosevelt just made him see red."

That was one of many sentiments Bert Walker shared with his son-in-law. Prescott also reviled FDR and said many years after Roosevelt's death, "The only man I truly hated lies buried in Hyde Park."

"In the early days of the New Deal, the financial community was not enamored of it at all," said Prescott, "and the fact that Averell was didn't help us a damn bit at Brown Brothers Harriman. In fact, it was a little bit of a hurdle you had to take from time to time. Some big corporate client would say, 'What the hell is your partner doing down there with this red bunch of Communists and socialists? What do you mean by this?' We would laugh it off and say, 'Well, Averell feels he wants to devote some time to the national interest . . . he's become interested in trying to do something for his country, and if the President wants to use him to be Ambassador to Russia, why, fine, he's going to do it.' And he was a good Ambassador to Russia . . . He was at the very highest levels there with the Roosevelt administration."

By that time, the only Democrat left in the Bush family was Prescott's father, Samuel, who had remarried a few years after his wife's death. He advised Herbert Hoover on employment conditions in Ohio and reported to the President's Organization on Unemployment Relief. By then Samuel had sold the house he and Flora had built and moved with his new wife, Martha, to a country estate in Blacklick, Ohio. He wrote his sons a letter on May 14, 1940, and proudly shared a note he had received from the vice president of the Pennsylvania Lines West asking him to become general superintendent of the Pennsylvania Lines West of Pittsburgh:

> [It is] the only case where an officer who has left the company has been invited to return. This I have always treasured for the reason that after the departure of Mr. L. F. Loree, who was rather hostile to me because I would not yield to practices that I felt where [sic] neither honorable nor wise, is evidence of appreciation of my worth by all other officers.

Unlike Prescott's father, George Herbert Walker cared little for practices that were either honorable or wise. A prime example is his involvement in a plan to extract the last measure of profit from his investment in Silesian-American Corporation, an American company partially owned by the Harrimans that operated mines in Poland.

The investment in Silesian-American was made in 1926, seven years before Hitler was declared dictator of Germany. The acquisition became a moral problem in 1935, when Hitler instituted the Nuremberg Laws that deprived German Jews of their rights to citizenship. Untroubled by morality, Silesian-American investors kept their shares. When the Nazis invaded Poland in October 1939, they seized control of the Silesian-American mines. The American company, unable to pay its bondholders because of the Nazi takeover, declared bankruptcy. Rather than absorb the $2.4 million loss of their investment, Bert Walker and Brown Brothers Harriman decided to do business with Nazi Germany.

Since the United States allowed no direct commerce with the Nazis, Bert devised a scheme for a Swiss bank, fronting for the German owners of Silesian-American, to buy the shares of the American owners and pay off the bondholders. Unfortunately, the Swiss payment would come from ores mined in Poland with cooperation of the Nazis. Still, Bert and Brown Brothers Harriman hoped their convoluted plan would appear benign enough to get U.S. approval.

In a confidential memo, Ray Morris of Brown Brothers Harriman wrote to Roland Harriman: "We had the Silesian-American and Silesian Holding company meetings this morning, and Bert Walker came through all right, so that there was a unanimous vote in favor of accepting the proposition from the Swiss company and taking the necessary steps to put it into effect."

The U.S. government blocked the plan under Roosevelt's executive orders banning foreign transactions that might aid the Nazis. The pile-driving deal maker reconfigured the scheme for resubmission, but again it was rejected. Undeterred, Bert tried a third, and final, time; the U.S. Treasury once more slammed the door. It was against U.S. policy for companies to have any dealing with Hitler's Germany after the invasion of Poland.

The willingness of George Herbert Walker and Brown Brothers Harriman to do business with Germany was not unique in those times. Like BBH, quite a few American firms had opened offices in Berlin after World War I and were reluctant to terminate the stream of income. Others, like Sullivan and Cromwell, the New York City law firm of John Foster Dulles, who later became Secretary of State under Eisenhower, took a stand on principle.

Some time after 1935, when the Nazi persecution of Jews could no longer be denied, Dulles was confronted with a partners' revolt. As Townsend Hoopes reported in his book *The Devil and John Foster Dulles*, Dulles's law partners informed him they were prepared to resign en bloc rather than continue to do business with Hitler's Germany. Dulles protested vigorously, citing the huge loss of profits that would be incurred by giving up German transactions. The partners remained adamant. Dulles finally capitulated "in tears."

No such tearful meeting ever occurred at Brown Brothers Harriman, where Knight Woolley and Prescott Bush were the managing partners. In fact, their involvement in Union Banking Corporation from 1924 to 1942 makes them vulnerable to charges of dealing with the enemy.

Union Banking Corporation existed solely for the benefit of Fritz Thyssen, a German industrialist who had inherited an empire of steel factories, coal mines, and banks. He met Averell Harriman, the scion of the railroad magnate E. H. Harriman, during the 1920s when both were traveling in Europe. Thyssen told Harriman he was starting a bank in New York to look after his American financial interests, and he asked Harriman to serve on the board. Harriman turned the matter over to his brother, Roland, who agreed to join the directorate with a few of his partners. Thyssen's U.S. bank, a subsidiary of his Dutch bank in Rotterdam, was founded in 1924 and operated out of the Brown Brothers Harriman offices at 39 Broadway in New York City. The bank, UBC, opened an investment account with Brown Brothers Harriman, which Prescott managed, and Thyssen's bank paid investment fees to BBH. All of this was perfectly legal and quite profitable for both Thyssen and Brown Brothers Harriman for a decade. The issue became morally freighted in the 1930s when Hitler rose to power and Thyssen, an early supporter of the Third Reich, became known as "Hitler's Angel."

Still, Roland Harriman was not confronted by outraged partners. No one at Brown Brothers Harriman expressed concern that Thyssen's bank might be a Nazi front. No questions were raised about the ethics of continuing to accept fees from the man whose memoir was titled *I Paid Hitler*.

As German troops swept across Europe, absorbing Austria, bludgeoning Czechoslovakia, raping Poland, swallowing Denmark, Norway, and Sweden, grabbing Luxembourg and Belgium, invading France, and bombarding the British Isles, no one at Brown Brothers Harriman stepped forward to decry their continuing business ties with Germany.

The remunerative relationship between Fritz Thyssen and Brown Brothers Harriman continued for sixteen years. BBH's investment fees suddenly stopped coming in May 1940, when the Nazis invaded the Netherlands. On Roosevelt's executive orders, all Dutch assets in the United States were frozen, including those of UBC, Thyssen's Dutch holding company.

President Roosevelt had made no secret of his desire to bring his country into the war. In his fifteenth fireside chat to the nation, on January 6, 1941, he said, "Never before . . . has our American civilization been in such danger." He warned that the Nazis wanted "to use the resources of Europe to dominate the rest of the world." He concluded: "We must be the great arsenal of democracy."

Even the most obtuse partners of Brown Brothers Harriman had to see that it was only a matter of time before the United States would take up arms against Germany. One key partner, Averell Harriman, was living in London as minister plenipotentiary to England to expedite lend-lease aid to the British. With this in mind, and the UBC assets frozen by executive order, Knight Woolley finally wrote a letter on January 14, 1941, to the superintendent of banks of New York, expressing concern about the association of Brown Brothers Harriman with Fritz Thyssen's Union Banking Corporation:

> My partners have been giving serious consideration to withdrawing from the board. Should the United States enter the war, they feel they might be under some embarrassment because of their connection with the bank, even though we have no financial interest in the Union Banking Corporation, nor do we participate in its earnings. They act as directors merely as a matter of business courtesy.

Woolley neglected to mention the lucrative investment fees from Union Banking Corporation that BBH had enjoyed for sixteen years. The superintendent expressed full "confidence" in the BBH directors and said the department "would be gratified if these gentlemen could find it possible to remain on the Board during this period of uncertainty."

The relationship between Brown Brothers Harriman and Fritz Thyssen, who had at last disassociated himself from Hitler, became news on July 31, 1941, with a front-page story in the *New York Herald Tribune*. The headline: "Thyssen Has $3,000,000 Cash in New York Vaults." The subhead: "Union Banking Corp. May Hide Nest Egg for High Nazis He Once Backed."

The story, which named Prescott Bush as a one-share director of UBC, reprinted in full the correspondence between Knight Woolley and the New York banks superintendent. This suggests that Brown Brothers Harriman cooperated fully with the reporter in relating the history between "Mr. Harriman" and "Herr Thyssen," as the newspaper referred to the two men.

Knight Woolley's letter states that the firm's paramount concern was "embarrassment" about being publicly associated with Hitler's financier. There's no expression of moral indignation, let alone repugnance for Thyssen's previous support of the Third Reich. The concern is more for appearances as Woolley downplays the relationship between Brown Brothers Harriman and the former Nazi as merely "a matter of business courtesy."

The *New York Herald Tribune* stated: "This [relationship] took place, of course, at a time when the present world tangle could hardly have been foreseen and when such courtesies were part of the normal routine of international banking relations."

No other newspaper followed up on the story, and the issue remained dormant for many years. Only when John Loftus, a former prosecutor in the Justice Department's Nazi War Crimes Unit, decided in 1994 to look at the World War II dealings of Brown Brothers Harriman did Prescott Bush's association with Union Banking Corporation become an issue.

"If Prescott Bush were alive today," said John Loftus in 2002, "I would move to have him indicted for giving aid and comfort to the enemy in time of war."

Loftus asserted that, as the managing investment partner of his firm, Prescott Bush benefited illegally, immorally, and unfairly from the fees of a Nazi-connected company that was later seized by the U.S. Office of Alien Property.

As a former president of the Florida Holocaust Museum, Loftus is concerned with serious issues. Having left the Justice Department to investigate the extent to which U.S. intelligence agencies had recruited former Nazis, he has written extensively on the subject. But in this instance there is no evidence to support his accusation that Prescott Bush was a Nazi war accomplice.

While Prescott and his partners never stood up on the issue, Loftus mistakenly believes that UBC was an ongoing activity until 1942; it was not. All UBC assets were frozen in 1940, so it is unfair to assert that the silence of Prescott and his partners makes them complicit in the treasonous act of trading with the enemy.

As morally reprehensible as the actions of Prescott's firm might have been, it was legal to do business with UBC because it was Dutch owned. The sensational assertions that circulate on the Internet that Prescott Bush built his family fortune on the backs of Nazi victims are grossly exaggerated. No intelligence documents available from that era suggest that Prescott endorsed Nazi ideals or supported Germany's rearmament. Rather, he appears to be nothing more than a businessman very much in the mold of his father-in-law, George Herbert Walker, whose priorities—first, last, and always—were to make money.

The sounds of the war in Europe were muffled in Greenwich, Connecticut, as Pressy and Poppy were growing up. They were far more frightened of their authoritarian father than of Hitler's bombs, especially Little Pop, or Poppy, who clung to his older brother for protection from their father's fierce temper. The two boys insisted on sharing a room together, and Poppy started school a year early just to remain by his older brother's side. In those years, Prescott junior was bigger and stronger than George, despite a congenital cataract that blinded him in one eye and lameness in one leg from an injury. Although Poppy was the superior athlete, he revered his older brother because Pressy stood up to their father and actually defied him on occasion.

"Not often," said Prescott junior many years later. "Not often."

"But George never," said their brother Jonathan.

"Their father was a very austere man—cold, cold, cold," said George "Red Dog" Warren, a childhood friend. "George liked my father enormously because Dad was outgoing and friendly and very funny. That was probably the main reason George and I became such good friends. He gave me the nickname 'Red Dog,' but I can't remember why now. I do remember he came over to my house every chance he could get if my father was around."

After the Greenwich Country Day School, the boys were sent to boarding school at Phillips Andover in Massachusetts, known then as "Yale's biggest feeder." There was no question about where the sons of Prescott Bush would go to college. In those days Andover was like a miniature Yale, from its all-male enrollment to its jacket-and-tie dress code to its secret societies. Out of 215 boys in George's 1942 Andover class, 96 went to Yale.

"Andover meant more to me than Yale," George said many years later. "You had to read *War and Peace*, do your languages. You were made to study, made to think . . . The minute I walked into that place I took a giant leap ahead of many others out there in the educational system . . . I was blessed."

Known as Poppy even at school, George became part of Andover lore. He soared above his mediocre grades (C+) with an outstanding athletic record that is prominently cited in a book devoted solely to Andover sports: "Poppy Bush's play throughout the season ranked him as one of Andover's all-time soccer greats." His 1942 class yearbook listed twenty-five activities (class average was ten), including captain of baseball, captain of soccer, varsity basketball, president of senior class, and president of Greeks. The rest of his activities were boards, clubs, and societies.

The most telling citation on his list was the Johns Hopkins Prize, which was a three-hundred-dollar reward to be "divided among those students who have received no demerits for absence or tardy marks in the year." Not surprisingly, Poppy Bush was a good boy—pleasant, punctual, and respectful. Although he barely made passable grades, he handed out hymnals for daily chapel service, took up the collection plate in church, and clapped erasers for teachers after school.

"I don't know that you can judge one's life by how many entries there are in the yearbook," Bush told the Andover alumni bulletin in 1989. "What really drove me and what I loved back then was sports. The competition of athletics—I loved it . . . I wasn't a particularly good student."

No one disputes his inferior scholarship, including his roommate. "Our room during senior year at Andover saw many schoolboy intellectual bull sessions," said George "Red Dog" Warren. "Bush seldom got involved; rather, he was content to wisecrack from the sidelines. George was not an intellectual, or even intellectually curious. He was more of an achiever [a doer]."

Hart Leavitt, a Yale professor who taught English composition, nearly flunked Poppy Bush. "He just sat in the class and handed in papers . . . I had very little respect for his mentality . . . He showed no imagination or originality," said Leavitt. "In my class he was a nonentity . . . didn't contribute much. A nice guy, but that's about all. He looked like the cover on

The Preppy Handbook that came out a while ago. I didn't have much contact with him outside class."

At Andover, the basketball coach, Frank DiClementi, who had much more contact with George, raved about him. "From the first day I saw him, I knew he was something special. He came from a family with the right priorities . . . Always hustling . . . Poppy was captain of baseball and soccer, played every minute of every game, but I had to talk him into going out for basketball. He was afraid of denying another kid a place on the team . . . There was a Jewish kid nicknamed Ovie who left school when he didn't get tapped for any of the Greek societies. They talked him into coming back, and Poppy was the first to befriend him, got him to come out for baseball. One day a fly ball bounced off Ovie's head into the left fielder's glove, and Poppy congratulated him on an assist."

Due to an illness in his senior year—a staph infection in his shoulder that developed into hepatitis—George spent two weeks in Massachusetts General Hospital, and many more recuperating in bed at home. "He came very close to losing his life before they were able to get it under control," said Prescott Bush Jr. As a result, George had to repeat his senior year and spent five years, not four, at Andover.

The time off allowed Poppy to return to his prep school taller, heavier, and healthier. "He was put together, and handsome—a beautiful example of those who matured the fastest because they had the least to mature with," said William Sloane Coffin, an Andover classmate who, as Yale's chaplain during the 1960s, clashed with George over civil rights and the Vietnam War. "A lot of students that I know are a long time immature, but that's because they have a lot to mature with. Bush didn't have that much to begin with."

In a class poll, Poppy Bush did not finish first in any category, but like his brother Pressy, he placed second as the student with the "Most Faculty Drag," in recognition of "attempts to gain favor in teachers' eyes by elaborately dubious means; to pay teacher in advance with flattery for grades one hopes to get." He placed third as "Best All-Round Fellow," "Best Athlete," "Most Respected," "Most Popular," and "Handsomest." He did not make the top three for "Politician," "Ladies' Man," or "Most Likely to Succeed."

Still, he was representative of his class. In one poll by the *Phillipian*, students were asked: "Do you think studies, friendships, or athletics are the most important in the long run?" The majority chose friendships. The newspaper concluded: "The average student came to Andover with making contacts uppermost in his mind."

"Poppy Bush was very popular . . . very friendly and everybody admired him as an individual," said Henry See, another Andover classmate. "He was the kind of guy that, when you looked at him, you would say, 'I wish I was as popular as he, as bright as he.' " See credited Bush's popularity to his eagerness to be liked and his ability to please everyone. "He would have you think that you and he thought alike on issues, but when you think back, he just nodded and you thought he went along with you . . . I don't remember him ever taking a stand on anything controversial."

At Andover, teachers were called masters, classes were recitations, and nothing was more important than manhood. During weekly assemblies students were reminded: "Other schools have boys. Andover has men." Andover's motto "Non Sibi" means "Not for Self." Andover men were expected to conform to the rules. "The basic Andover code," said the *Phillipian*, "assumes every student is first and foremost a gentleman."

The epitome of Andover was Colonel Henry Lewis Stimson, Secretary of War, who was president of the academy's board of trustees and the school's most honored alumnus, having served under five presidents. Stimson was introduced by a student to the class of 1942 as the "living and vital representative of our ways and of our type of existence, who is out setting an example to the whole nation . . . living proof that the Andover Way is the way of men who guide the fortunes of nations."

On December 7, 1941, Poppy Bush was thrashing George "Red Dog" Warren in a Ping-Pong match in the clubhouse of their secret society, AUV, when they heard that the Japanese had bombed Pearl Harbor, killing 2,403 Americans. The boys dropped their paddles and dashed for their dorm. The United States was at war.

The headmaster summoned the school to assembly; the flag was raised, the national anthem played. "You men must get at attention," he said, "and stay there." The students rose to their feet as one.

The next day the student newspaper blared: "We stand as a unit against the common foe—the yellow peril of Nippon."

Andover's regimented life suddenly plunged into daily air-raid drills, first-aid classes, radio and signal courses. Students rushed to enlist, though the headmaster urged them to stay in school.

"They couldn't take us all at once," said classmate Ken Keuffel. "We wanted to volunteer. We were so patriotic."

"The attack on Pearl Harbor galvanized everybody," said Henry See. "We all wanted to serve our country. We felt like serving was our duty."

"My reaction was one of shock, almost disbelief," recalled George Bush. "I didn't fully comprehend world affairs. My interests were our undefeated soccer season just finished, basketball-baseball just coming up. Christmas vacation was only a couple of weeks away and then graduation. Then I guess that was followed by the typical American reaction that we had better do something about this. I remember the country's instant coming together for a common purpose, and my own gut feeling was the same as that of many young Americans—we wanted to fight for our country."

Poppy wrote to his parents that he planned to join those dashing young men in helmets, goggles, and leather jackets. "I made up my mind to go into the service and be a naval aviator," he said. "I knew I wanted to be a pilot. I don't know why, because I'd never flown."

His mother and father pleaded with him to stay in school and go on to Yale, saying there would be time later to serve the flag. Although two of his classmates had already enlisted, he promised his parents that he would at least wait until graduation.

His father was named the national chairman of the USO War Fund Campaign to raise money for the United Service Organizations. "We were given a goal of $32 million to raise . . . shortly after Pearl Harbor," he said. "This seemed like a staggering sum to me, but Mr. John D. Rockefeller, Jr. felt that the task was not insurmountable . . . I recall that, as we were about to start our big drive going to the office of our organization one morning and finding a letter addressed to me from Mr. Rockefeller. I opened it, and out of it fell a check for $1 million."

Prescott superseded the goal and raised $33 million ($377 million in 2004) for the USO. He was honored for his efforts in 2001 when the Prescott Bush USO Building at Camp Casey in South Korea was unveiled. His son George Herbert Walker Bush was present for the dedication ceremony.

When Poppy came home from Andover for the Christmas holidays in 1941, he attended a dance at the Round Hill Country Club in Greenwich. There he spotted a pretty brunette and asked a friend to introduce him. He and Barbara Pierce then sat out the next two dances talking, because he didn't know how to waltz. She had learned at Miss Covington's Dancing School in Rye, New York, but she only knew how to lead. "My mother would say, 'You must not be the boy every time.' But I didn't want to be left [out]. Not me. I was five feet eight at the age of twelve and already weighed 148 pounds."

Barbara was sixteen and slender by the time she met Poppy Bush. Neither had dated anyone else before nor even been romantically kissed; they came to their instantaneous attraction fresh and full of hope. Relatives remember them as two young colts chasing each other around a ring. "They were two tomboys, locking each other in closets," said George's aunt Mary Carter Walker. "They were just real tomboys."

Barbara played soccer at Ashley Hall, the girls' school she attended in Charleston, South Carolina; she also played tennis and said she could hold her breath and swim two laps underwater, all of which validated her with the rampagingly athletic Bushes. Her own mother discouraged her interest in sports as "unladylike." Pauline Robinson Pierce would have preferred a more feminine daughter, less rambunctious than the clumsy overweight youngster who was forever knocking into antique tables and breaking precious pieces of Chinese porcelain. Barbara, the third of four children, had spent most of her life as the ugly-duckling daughter of an elegant beauty. Her older sister, Martha, slim and stunningly glamorous, had made the cover of *Vogue* in 1940. Barbara, unfortunately, was built like her large-boned father. Her mother treated her like a discarded refrigerator. As a defense, she ate constantly and developed a caustic tongue.

"I thought she was really mean and sarcastic [when we were growing up]," said June Biedler, a childhood friend whom Barbara teased for having a painful stammer. This cruelty, Biedler suggested, may have been the result of having "a mother that was a little mean to her."

Unlike George, Barbara was not close to any of her siblings. She couldn't compete with her older sister, five years her senior, and she was squeezed between two brothers. Jim, the older, had behavioral problems, and Scott, the younger, had physical problems (a cyst in the bone marrow of his shoulder), which preoccupied their parents. Barbara felt deprived of their attention and affection. She compensated in scratchy ways, developing a prickly and feisty personality.

Exploring the attraction between Barbara Pierce and George Bush, Marjorie Williams wrote in *Vanity Fair*: "Most of their friends are at a loss when asked what so quickly cemented this couple. The answer often boils down to social class—that they were, as George's redoubtable mother put it, 'sensible and well-suited to each other.'"

Their so-called social class, based on nothing more than private schools and country clubs, did give them a common meeting ground, but the bonding sprang more from their own emotional needs.

They probably didn't realize when they met how much they complemented each other. Both had experienced feelings of rejection from a cold, austere parent. Barbara, who had a ruptured relationship with her mother, and George, who was not close to his father, found emotional refuge in each other. In fact, over the years Barbara reinvented herself in the image of George's mother.

"George recognized the type of person Barbara was when they first met," said his friend Fitzhugh Green. "He had seen the same characteristics in his mother: a woman of strong character and personality, direct and honest; one who cares about the outdoors and people, especially children, and is oriented to home life . . . Anyone who has met both mother and wife can see they belong in the same category."

Both George and Barbara were accustomed to corporal punishment, George from his father's leather strap and Barbara from her mother's wooden coat hanger.

Both had been exposed to the ravages of alcoholism; in an eerie coincidence, each had an alcoholic uncle named Jim whose marital breakups caused their families no end of grief and consternation. Even Barbara's most illustrious relative, her fourth cousin four times removed, Franklin Pierce, the fourteenth President of the United States (1853–57), was an alcoholic. The insidious disease with its genetic predispositions had already wrapped its tentacles around the roots of both family trees.

Politically, both came from Republican households that despised the Roosevelts; George's parents detested Franklin, while Barbara's could not abide Eleanor.

On the more elementary level of attraction, Barbara and George made each other feel special: she felt pretty for the first time in her life, and he felt adored. As his brother Jonathan said: "She was wild about him. And for George, if anyone wants to be wild about him, it's fine with him."

After the Christmas holidays, when the teenagers returned to their schools, they started corresponding. Poppy invited Barbara to his senior prom and to his graduation on June 8, 1942.

The Secretary of War, Henry Stimson, gave the commencement address, beseeching Andover's men to go to college and wait for the war to call them. He made the inevitability of battle all too real for them and their parents when he announced the deaths of four young alumni tragically lost in training maneuvers, and Andover's first casualty from combat, who was shot down while serving in the Royal Air Force. Still, some in the class of 1942 wanted to serve their country sooner rather than later, and of 215 students 68 had enlisted by the end of the year.

Following Stimson's speech, Prescott Bush asked his son if the Secretary had said anything to change his mind about enlisting.

"No, sir," said Poppy. "I'm going in."

Four days later, on his eighteenth birthday, George Herbert Walker Bush broke the parental yoke. He went to Boston and enlisted in the Navy one week after the Battle of Midway, the first decisive U.S. naval battle in which surface ships played no combat role at all. The age of the aircraft carrier had dawned. The Navy now needed pilots, and needed them fast. Bush was sworn in as a seaman second class.

"I was a scared, nervous kid," he said years later.

He had just made the first independent decision of his young life—and possibly his best.

CHAPTER FIVE

A fter the bombing of Pearl Harbor, Japan became the heart of darkness. The war metastasized from Europe to the Pacific, and benign little islands that once conjured up pretty native girls in fitted sarongs and hibiscus blossoms suddenly filled with the dead bodies of American soldiers as the Japanese bombed their way across the South Pacific, hell-bent on reaching the United States. To that end, Japan had mobilized suicide boats and human torpedoes; later it sent in kamikaze pilots who revered their Emperor as the Son of Heaven and dived to their deaths in glory while blowing up any vessel flying the Stars and Stripes. "We are prepared to lose ten million men in our war with America," said Japanese General Masaharu Homma.

Within three months of Pearl Harbor, the Japanese had captured the American islands of Guam and Wake. They had seized the Philippines, grabbed the British colony of Hong Kong, and conquered Singapore, the Dutch East Indies, the Malay Peninsula, and Burma.

There was no twenty-four-hour coverage of the carnage in those days, only newspaper and radio reports that were subjected to strict censorship. Americans did not know the full extent of the enemy's brutality until after the war. But enough news of savage death marches, beheaded soldiers, and bayoneted prisoners seeped into the Fox and Pathé newsreels shown in movie theaters each week to inflame U.S. hatred of "Nips," short for "Dai Nippon," the Japanese word for their homeland. The Land of the Rising Sun was so reviled that American citizens of Japanese ancestry living on the West Coast were rounded up and thrown into "resettlement" camps. In all, 120,000 Japanese Americans were imprisoned. The "slumbering giant," as Japan's Admiral Yamamoto had referred to the United States before Pearl Harbor, was aroused and angry.

"We must hate with every fiber of our being," exclaimed Lieutenant General Lesley J. McNair in a 1942 broadcast to all U.S. troops. "We must lust for battle, our object in life must be to kill. There need be no pangs of conscience, for our enemies have lighted the way to faster, surer, crueler killing. They were past masters. We must hurry to catch up with them if we are to survive."

Admiral William F. Halsey ordered a huge billboard, visible to passing ships in the Pacific, with his version of the Japanese short verse known as haiku:

> KILL JAPS KILL JAPS.
> KILL MORE JAPS.
> You will help to kill the yellow
> bastards if you do your job well.

Jukeboxes across America blared "Goodbye, Mama (I'm Off to Yokohama)," and schoolchildren jumped rope to the singsong racism of "I'm going to slap a dirty little Jap, I'm going to slap a dirty little Jap."

As men roared off to war, women tossed their aprons and jumped into slacks to go to work in factories. In 1942, the darkest year of the war, 2 million women picked up wrenches and assembled plane parts, giving rise to Rosie the Riveter, the national symbol of women in the workforce. The rest of the country, including schoolchildren, committed themselves to the war effort by selling war bonds, staging paper drives, and collecting scrap iron. Night baseball was canceled to save electricity. Car manufacturing was stopped to save on rubber and gasoline. Sugar, meat, and eggs were rationed and could only be purchased upon presentation of coupons from rationing books. All metal and rubber had to go to the war effort, and razor blades were supposed to be cut to one a week for each shaver. There was a shortage of hair curlers, wigs, girdles, nylon stockings, shoes, rubber diapers, hoses, bronze caskets, even flyswatters.

The rigorous prohibition on the sale of gasoline and tires forced the Walkers and Bushes to stop driving at Kennebunkport and resort to a horse-drawn wagon. The beast of burden was named Barsil. Prescott junior joked about seeing a strong resemblance between the heavy dray horse and George's girlfriend, so he called both Bar. After the horse died, the nickname stuck to the girlfriend.

During the summer of 1942, when eighteen-year-old Poppy Bush could have been splashing around the family estate in Maine, getting ready to go to Yale, he elected instead to fight what his parents called "Mr. Roosevelt's War." Standing on the platform of Penn Station in the sweltering heat of August, he waited with his father for the train that would take him to Chapel Hill, North Carolina, where he would learn how to fly torpedo bombers. Hours earlier he had kissed his mother, his brothers and sister, his aunts and uncles, and his Walker grandparents, Ganny and Gampy, good-bye. He was leaving behind his first (she would say only) girlfriend, Barbara Pierce, and his best friend, George "Red Dog" Warren, who was heading to Yale. Although Poppy had been away at boarding school for five years, he admitted feeling nervous about leaving home because "I didn't know a soul where I was going."

As the train rumbled into the station, he grabbed his duffel bag and shook his father's hand. Prescott Bush, whose boys called him "The Big One," could barely speak. With tears in his eyes, he wished his young son Godspeed.

"It was the first time I'd ever seen my dad cry," George said many years later.

Piling on board with other cadets, George, who would no longer introduce himself as Poppy, was headed for the Naval Aviation Pre-Flight School. He immediately wrote to his mother that Ted Williams of the Boston Red Sox was in his cadet class. The baseball great would go on to become what George said he had wanted to be—a Marine fighter pilot who received a commission of 2nd Lt. rather than Ensign. "The reason is they fly a lot in attack bombers—fly low and strafe as well as bomb," he wrote. "They clear the way for advancing troops. This or long range bombing appeals to me more than anything else."

George never did make it into the Marines. Instead, he spent the next ten months training at naval air stations across the country for two-month stints in Minneapolis; Corpus Christi, Texas; Fort Lauderdale, Florida; Norfolk, Virginia; and Hyannis Port, Massachusetts. He learned first to fly, and then to pilot an enormous TBM Avenger from the deck of an aircraft carrier. The Avenger could drop five-hundred-pound bombs on target.

"You cannot imagine the unnatural state flying can get you in," he wrote to his mother. "I have experienced it on several occasions already and haven't even flown blind yet. It's an utterly depressing and demoralizing feeling—much worse than getting beat at tennis. You get mentally confused and it's really terrible."

Having been forced to play sports with his right hand, George wrote with his left in a crabbed scrawl that looked like chewed toothpicks scattered higgledy-piggledy across the page. In one of his "Darling Mum" letters he apologized for his pulverized penmanship. He said the problem was that, in school, he was never taught to "write script."

He filled his letters with longing for the girl he'd left behind. Barbara, then a high-school senior, planned to go to Smith College. "She's really *the* one, Mum. I just know it . . . I only hope she doesn't give me the fluff." He wondered about his future: "Any job where I could make enough money to have the few basic things I desire would be most welcome. I often think and worry about it—I now know exactly what I want. No college, I'll have to do without, just a job anywhere with a fairly decent salary." Like other cadets, he fantasized about earning his wings and was thrilled when his mother offered to buy him a pair:

> On our blues and greens we have them embroidered right on. They are included in the price of the suit just like braid and stars, but on khakis and whites we wear the pins so—if you really do want to give me my wings that would be nice . . . Most of the ones you buy here are imitation and quite cheap $2.50 but *if you want to get me a good pair*—$10.00 I imagine you could probably get them at Brooks or some such place. If you do, make them a graduation and birthday present 'cause I'd love nothing better. Just be sure they are regulation size etc. . . . If you happen to be in Brooks or something you could look. Nothing would make me prouder than to wear a pair of wings given me by you. Maybe you could slip a GWB on the back or something.

When his mother wrote that her sister-in-law's brother George Mead had been killed in combat, George responded like a soldier. "He died the way all of us would like to die when our time comes—Mum, it's a very funny thing. I have no fear of death now. Maybe it's because I am here

safely on the ground that I say this. I do not think I will change. All hero-
ics aside, I feel, and every fellow here I'm sure feels, that the only part of
the whole thing of any worry would be the sorrow it might cause to our
families."

His mother saved all his letters. They showed how her son's small, in-
sular world had suddenly expanded because of associations with "so many
different types of fellows whose backgrounds are not like mine." Always
signing himself "Your devoted and loving Poppy" or "Ever lovingly, Pop,"
he told his mother that "the intelligent officers" like himself did not believe the "crude propaganda here. It is really sickening . . . Stuff like 'Kill
the Japs—hate—murder' and stuff like 'You are the cream of American
youth.' Some fellows swallow it all. These are the fellows many whom
[sic] are below average intelligence, 2 of my roommates, for example, get
a big kick out of hearing it . . . All the well-educated fellows know what
they are fighting for—why they are here and don't need to be 'brain-
washed' into anything." He later added. "Though I know I can never become a killer, I will never feel right until I have actually fought. Being
physically able and young enough I belong out at the front and the sooner
there, the better."

The men like George Bush who fought in World War II are called
"the greatest generation" because they went to war willingly. They saw the
job that had to be done, and they wanted to do it more than they wanted
to let the world fall under the jackboot of tyranny. They had what F. Scott
Fitzgerald called "a willingness of the heart." Many gave up the best parts
of their careers to fight, and others interrupted their educations. Few tried
to shirk service. Conscientious objectors were rare; draft dodgers were almost unheard of; and isolationists like Joseph P. Kennedy were despised.
Men with crippling infirmities tried to bluff through their physicals to
serve. Prescott Bush Jr. left Yale in 1943 to enter the Army but because of
his congenital eye cataract and a limp was turned down. So he went to
Brazil with Pan Am's Airport Development Program, which was building
antisubmarine warfare bases. Even men well past their fighting prime
rushed to take up arms: George's forty-one-year-old uncle, James Smith
Bush, entered in 1942 as an Army Air Force captain, served in Calcutta,
and was discharged three and a half years later as a lieutenant colonel
with a Bronze Star. George's mother, Dorothy Walker Bush, volunteered
for the motor corps, a group in Greenwich organized to drive people to

safety in case of a national emergency. "She knew all about carburetors and cylinders," said her daughter, Nancy.

The war blurred all class lines by putting the sons of the rich shoulder to shoulder with the sons of the poor. Tasseled loafers were exchanged for trench boots as the elite jumped into foxholes with the working class. If both survived, they emerged better men for the experience. Movie stars (Clark Gable and Jimmy Stewart), sports heroes (Joe DiMaggio and Hank Greenberg), and politicians (Henry Cabot Lodge and Franklin D. Roosevelt Jr.) slogged alongside unknown grunts, jarheads, and doughboys in America's last democratic war.

The country did not realize the convulsive transformation it was undergoing at the time, but, as William Manchester wrote later in *The Glory and the Dream*, the class structure was toppling. The deference once paid to wealth, social class, age, race, sex, and ethnic identity would be forever diminished. The elite world of Prescott Bush gave way to a more egalitarian existence for his sons. The final wallop to class entitlements came with the GI Bill of Rights, providing education and other rights for 2.3 million veterans of the war. This meant that the chimney sweep's son could go to Yale with Prescott Bush's son, a social equality that men like Prescott—and Prescott himself—initially resisted. They tried to hold tight to their previous class perquisites. But the demolished line between "us" and "them" smacked Prescott in the face on the day an Italian American from the Chickahominy district of Greenwich rang his doorbell and asked for a personal favor.

"I told him . . . I have a son named Anthony, whose IQ tested at 151 when he was nine years old, and I wanted to send him to a good prep school," recalled Albert Morano, who worked for Clare Boothe Luce, the congresswoman from Connecticut (1943–47), and later was elected to Congress himself. "Clare had promised to pay for my boy's education . . . so I went to see Prescott Bush because I heard he sent his sons to [Andover] . . .

"He [Prescott] says, 'They don't take your kind of people up at Phillips. Your son would never be able to get in that school.' I said, 'Goodbye, Mr. Bush.' He was very, very crude and rough . . . almost sarcastic. He thought I was impudent even having asked him."

In Prescott's worldview, Italians like Albert Morano were supposed to tend the gardens of the gold coast in Greenwich, and then return to their little houses in Chickahominy for sausage and pasta. To think of getting above themselves by sending their children to elite schools like Andover was, in Prescott's words, "preposterous" and "out of line." (After Prescott slammed the door on Andover, Mr. Morano enrolled his son in the Canterbury School in New Milford, Connecticut, where the young man achieved high honors. He graduated from Amherst College and Fordham Law School, compiling more higher education than any of Prescott Bush's children. Anthony A. Morano retired in 2002 as professor emeritus of law at the University of Toledo.)

"Prescott Bush was a snob, and he didn't like Italians," said Anthony Morano many years later. "He didn't like minorities . . . and our whole area [Chickahominy] was Italian, Polish, and Hungarian."

Discrimination was very much a part of the American mind-set during the war years. Even the Red Cross maintained separate containers for "white blood" and "black blood," but African Americans managed to rise above that prejudice to fight for their country. Thousands of Japanese Americans also joined the Army and took their oaths of allegiance behind the barbed wire of internment camps that had been erected to contain them when their loyalty had been questioned.

To have fought in World War II was a badge of honor. The country so revered the uniform that cheers rang out in restaurants when soldiers and sailors walked in, and military men were applauded in the streets. "As future warriors we were held in unaccustomed esteem," said Benjamin C. Bradlee, former editor of The Washington Post.

Three young naval lieutenants who did not know each other but fought in the South Pacific at the same time would become President of the United States, in no small part because each could claim service in this war: John Fitzgerald Kennedy, Richard Milhous Nixon, and George Herbert Walker Bush. Directing the European theater of operations was General Dwight D. Eisenhower, whose country would also reward him for his service with eight years in the White House. World War II was such a glorious political credential in the twentieth century that some men felt the need to manufacture a more heroic war record for themselves. Even as President, Ronald Reagan fabricated stories about being an Army photographer assigned to film the horror of the Nazi death camps. The truth is that he had never left California during the war. As a captain in the Army Air Force, he was assigned to a motion-picture unit in Hollywood, where he narrated training films and played the lead in a musical comedy about the Army.

After ten months of training, George Bush received his wings and realized his dream of becoming a Navy pilot on June 9, 1943. His father gave him a set of cuff links, which George said were his most precious possession. After the ceremony, he had a short home leave and became "secretly" engaged to Barbara, but could not keep the secret from his "beloved mum," who then told the whole family. He later chided her: "You do tell—I tell you things in the strictest confidence and you tell everyone—Aunt Margie, Mary, Ganny, Betty W. Everyone. Please don't Mum. I'd love to tell you everything always, which I have and I guess will, but I do wish you wouldn't tell everybody."

Months before, Dorothy Bush, who believed a kiss should mean eternal commitment, was horrified when she saw her daughter kissing a casual date. She shared her consternation with George, who commiserated. "I would *hate* to have Nancy a necker at heart," he wrote. "Nothing could be worse."

"Greenwich legend has it that by the time Nan Bush was eighteen, she had forty-one proposals of marriage," said her Boston friend Courtney Callahan. "She was the town beauty. Very, very flirtatious."

In his letter to his mother, George related the facts of life from his sweet and innocent vantage point:

During the summer of 1942 I kissed Barbara and am glad of it . . . I have never kissed another girl—this making myself . . . an oddity . . . since most of the boys do not stop with kissing—how terribly true that is here, more than home, but then again most of these fellows are grown men—also men with different backgrounds . . . For a kiss to mean engagement is a very beautiful idea, Mama, but it went out a while back . . .

Now for me to continue and tell you the facts of life—of the life I'm living in the 1940s . . . Pressy and I share a view which few others, very few others, even in Greenwich share. That's regarding intercourse before marriage. I would hate to find that my wife had known some other man, and it seems to me only fair to her that she be able to expect the same standards from me. Pres agrees as I said before, but not many others our age will . . . Most fellows here

[Naval Air Station, Minneapolis] . . . take sex as much as they can get. This town in particular seems full of girls (working in offices, etc.) rather attractive girls at that who after a couple of drinks would just as soon go to bed with some cadet. They are partly uniform conscious I suppose but the thing is they, as well as the cadet, have been brought up differently. They believe in satisfying any sexual urge by contact with men . . . These girls are not prostitutes, but just girls without any morals at all . . . I would be most facetious were I to deny ever having experienced said feelings. The difference is entirely in what we have been taught; not only in "what" but in "how well" we have been taught it.

George signed this letter "Much love, Pop professor 'sexology' Ph.D."

After his brief stay at home, he went to join the troops overseas. By the end of 1943 he had acquired a crew—a gunner named Leo Nadeau and a radioman–tail gunner named John Delaney. They were assigned to the USS *San Jacinto*, a carrier ship headed for the fire zone of the South Pacific. "From now on it's going to be plenty rugged duty," George wrote to his mother, "and in a way, I'm glad, 'cause I probably need the experience."

One of the few letters he wrote to his father, on November 1, 1943, was to spare "Mum . . . some unnecessary worrying." He reported that during his last flight of the day, he had hit a heavy slipstream from two previously landed bombers and couldn't fly free. He swerved, but his wheels hit the runway and as one gave way, his plane careened, falling on one wing:

Everything happened so quickly that I can't exactly remember it all. The prop hit and stopped. I was scared we'd tip over, but luckily we didn't. As soon as she stopped—I snapped off the switch, gas, and battery and leapt out and to the stern. My crewmen were scurrying out as I opened the back door. Luckily none of the three of us was injured at all. The plane is a total loss. Both wings smashed, fuselage slightly buckled, etc. etc. It gave me quite a feeling. While careening speedily and recklessly across the runway a feeling of helplessness not fear seized me. Then there flashed thru my mind the question "will we go over?"—then she stopped and I leapt.

Funny I never really was scared. After it was over I had that excited feeling in the pit of my stomach. We were terribly lucky that the ship didn't burn.

He told his father not to worry. "Nothing will happen to me. I'll just sign a report. It really was something—one of the things that make flying dangerous is the slipstream, and I really got hit bad."

After he crashed two more planes—one due to faulty gear—he began to share the news with both parents because they had insisted on knowing everything that happened. In April 1944 he wrote about a bad landing he had made, blowing out his rear tire and stopping precariously close to the catwalk. "How I hate to make a terrible landing," he wrote. "I get to worrying about it and also it's not good for the crewmen. Every day someone at least gets a tire or 2; so it's not serious, but I don't like it."

On May 23, 1944, bullets brushed his plane over Wake Island, some twenty-three hundred miles west of Pearl Harbor, and George wrote to announce that he had actually been in combat. "It is quite a feeling, Mum, to be shot at, I assure you. The nervousness which is with you before a game of some kind was extremely noticeable but no great fear thank heaven." When he returned to the squadron, he learned that his roommate was lost at sea. George cried himself to sleep that night.

"No one saw me," he wrote, "that wouldn't do."

Two months later he was forced to make a water landing and ditch his plane, which was full of bombs. He wrote that he and his crew scrambled into their raft and paddled to safety before the two-thousand-pound payload detonated. "I mean, we were just lucky we were spared," he said. They were rescued by a destroyer and returned a few days later to their carrier.

"I was scared as hell," Leo Nadeau recalled. "We had to take it into the drink, riding down with four 500-pound depth charges in the bomb bay."

The most difficult letter George ever wrote was the one he composed the day after he was shot down over Chichi-Jima, one of the Bonin Islands, five hundred miles south of Japan. On September 2, 1944, he took off with a group of planes from his squadron to bomb a Japanese radio station. His plane was hit by anti-aircraft fire as he approached his target.

He managed to complete his bombing mission, for which he received a Distinguished Flying Cross, but his two crewmates were killed. One of the deaths was particularly difficult for George to deal with. He was flying with his regular radioman, John Delaney, but he had asked Ted White, a friend of the family, if he'd like to go on this flight as the gunner. White accepted, so Leo Nadeau, the regular gunner, gave up his post. After George was rescued at sea by the USS *Finback*, an American submarine patrolling the waters for downed aviators, he wrote to his parents:

> We got hit. The cockpit filled with smoke and I told the boys in the back to get their parachutes on. They didn't answer at all, but I looked around and couldn't see Ted in the turret so I assumed he had gone below to get his chute fastened on. I headed the plane out to sea and put on the throttle so as we could get away from the land as much as possible. I am not too clear about the next parts. I told them to bail out, and then I called up the skipper and told him I was bailing out. My crewmen never acknowledged either transmission, and yet the radio gear was working—at least mine was and unless they had been hit back there theirs should have been, since we had talked not long before . . . I turned the plane up in an attitude so as to take pressure off the back hatch so the boys could get out. After that I straightened up and started to get out myself. At that time I felt certain that they had bailed out. The cockpit was full of smoke and I was choking from it. I glanced at the wings and noticed that they were on fire. I still do not know where we got hit and never will. I am now beginning to think that perhaps some of the fragments may have either killed the two in back, or possibly knocked out their communications . . . I stuck my head out first and the old wind really blew me the rest of the way out. As I left the plane my head struck the tail.

George said he saw no sign of Delaney or White after he had parachuted to safety.

"The fact that our planes didn't seem to be searching anymore showed me pretty clearly that they had not gotten out. I'm afraid I was pretty much of a sissy about it 'cause I sat in my raft and sobbed for a while. It bothers me so very much. I did tell them and when I bailed out I felt that they must have gone, and yet now I feel so terribly responsible for their fate."

He cautioned his parents not to write to Ted White's family until the government notified them. "They will probably receive the word that he is 'missing in action' so there too we will have to be tactful."

He added: "I am now fine and am in all respects ready to finish up with the squadron. I have not forgotten what has happened, but then I never shall completely forget about it; however, I am no longer as troubled by the tragic mishap as I was at first."

Disregarding his son's advice, Prescott Bush immediately contacted a friend in the Personnel Department of the Navy for a report on the White case. The young man's father, Edwin "Ted" White, had graduated from Yale, which is how Prescott knew the family. White's son, Lieutenant Junior Grade William G. "Ted" White, also graduated from Yale, class of 1942, and was a member of Skull and Bones. As soon as Prescott received the Navy's report, he sent it with his own two-page letter to Ted White's mother:

> I feel very sad indeed, Ann, to write such a letter for I know what the feelings of yourself and your husband must be. Your son was such a wonderful lad and I am so glad that my boy knew him. His letters spoke so highly of him previous to this disaster; and also, of course, his letters written on the submarine, are just heart-breaking. Our boy is a very sensitive, gentle fellow, and I am fearful that this incident will have hurt him very deeply.
>
> This is the third plane that Pop lost . . . I wish they would send him home now . . . I will write you later on enclosing exact excerpts from his letter.

A few days later Prescott sent a copy of George's long and anguished letter to the Whites, and begged them to keep it confidential. Sadly, there was no similar letter from Prescott to the family of the other lost crewman, John Delaney, who was the youngest of seven children in Providence, Rhode Island. His mother had died when he was two, and his father when he was seven. John had been raised by his six older sisters. At the age of eighteen, he spent the only money he had ever earned to get his teeth fixed so that he could pass the Navy physical and go to war. He never had a chance to go to Yale.

The families were told later that one other parachute was seen bailing out from the plane about three thousand feet over the water. Unfortunately, the chute never opened. Both of George's crewmen, after being reported missing in action for a year and a day, were presumed dead.

George remained aboard the submarine for thirty days while it completed its war patrol; after R&R in Hawaii, he was entitled to rotate home, but he elected to return to his squadron, where very little was said about what had happened over Chichi-Jima.

"He came into the ready room and sat down next to me," said Chester Mierzejewski, the turret gunner for the squadron commander's plane, who was especially close to John Delaney. "[George] knew I saw the whole thing. He said, 'Ski, I'm sure those two men were dead. I called them on the radio three times. They were dead.'

"When he told me they were dead, I couldn't prove they weren't. He seemed distraught. He was trying to assure me he did the best he could. I'm thinking what am I going to say to him. I have to give him the benefit of the doubt."

George's regular gunner, also close to Delaney, avoided the painful subject. "We had plenty of chances to talk about it," said Leo Nadeau. "It's just that I didn't want to talk about it and I don't think he ever wanted to talk about it . . . When he came back aboard ship, he wasn't a very happy man, and I wasn't a very happy man, either, because I'd lost a real good friend. That radioman had been trained with me right from day one. And, of course, I knew Delaney a heck of a lot better than I knew Bush, because we lived together—we were both enlisted men. The loss . . . and the mere fact that I had been that close to going, just bothered me . . . I never wanted to question George, because I never wanted him to have any idea that I doubted what happened. I never wanted him to get that feeling."

George flew fifty-eight missions before his honorable discharge in December 1944, an admirable record for one of the Navy's youngest pilots. He returned home a war hero.

No one ever questioned his actions about bailing out over Chichi-

Jima until he ran for President in 1992 and berated his opponent, Bill Clinton, for avoiding military service. By then many in George's squadron had died, but Chester Mierzejewski, the eyewitness to that flight in 1944, took issue with what he saw as discrepancies in George's story. Mierzejewski said he was disturbed after hearing George say on television—during the 1992 campaign—that he had nearly died when his plane was shot because his wings caught on fire and the cockpit erupted in flames.

Mierzejewski wrote to George that these recollections were "entirely different from my recall of the incident . . . I would not want someone who is not for your candidacy to stand up in public and dispute what you say."

George, who was known as a constant and compulsive correspondent, writing notes to everyone he had ever met, never answered Mierzejewski's letter. Months later, the turret gunner went public with his recollections in the *New York Post*, disputing the assertion that there were two parachutes. Mierzejewski maintained that only one man got out of the plane and that was the pilot. "I was hoping I would see some other parachutes," he said. "I never did. I saw the plane go down. I knew the guys were still in it. It was a helpless feeling."

He again contradicted George's claim about the plane and the cockpit being on fire. Mierzejewski, who won a Distinguished Flying Cross, was a hundred feet away from George's plane at the time and was able to see into the cockpit. He said he remembered only "a puff of smoke" that quickly dissipated. "This guy is just not telling the truth," he said. "His plane was never on fire," and "no smoke came out of his cockpit when he opened his canopy to bail out."

Others on the same bombing mission had different recollections. Milton Moore, who was George's wingman and the pilot of Mierzejewski's plane, made the same bombing run after George. "He got hit and went on in, smoking," Moore said. "I pulled up to him, then he lost power and I went sailing by." Don Melvin, the squadron commander, speculated that a shell must have hit an oil line on George's plane. "You could have seen the smoke for 100 miles," he recalled.

Smoke is a critical issue in this story. If a pilot's plane was not on fire, he was trained to make a water landing in order to put his crew in a better position for rescue. George had not done that. He bailed instead.

"I think he could have saved those lives, if they were alive," said

Mierzejewski. "I don't know that they were, but at least they had a chance if he had attempted a water landing."

Mierzejewski's account appeared in the newspaper under a blaring headline: "War Buddy Disputes Bush Bailout Tale." George was incensed by the implication that his youthful panic had caused the death of his crewmen. He immediately released the intelligence report of the 1944 mission to rebut the gunner's story. Reporters followed up, interviewing the few surviving members of his VT-51 squadron for their recollections. There was no rush to judgment on the part of anyone who served with George Bush, only a reluctance to return to the war to replay that tragic incident. Some expressed regret, disappointment, and sadness over the loss of George's crew, but each accepted the finality of the judgment George had made and the actions that ensued in the cyclone of war.

"I don't know . . . until you've been there, you can't . . . you know you've got conjecture a mile long," said Legare R. Hole, a pilot who was executive officer of George's squadron.

"We were just hurt," said Wendell Tomes, a radioman and tail gunner in the squadron. "Delaney got killed, and I don't think he had a chance to bail out, to come out safely. I was hurt by it because he was a good friend of mine, a good friend of everybody on the ship . . . At the time I'd have preferred [that George make a water landing] but he had to make the decision. He was as scared as the rest of us, so he had to do what he thought best."

By the time George returned to his ship in November 1944, U.S. planes had bombed Berlin, the Marines had established footholds in the Marshalls and Marianas in the Pacific, and General Douglas MacArthur had returned to the Philippines after the United States inflicted heavy damage on the Japanese at the Battle of the Philippine Sea.

At home, Franklin Roosevelt was running for an unprecedented fourth term as President with Harry S. Truman as his running mate. This was too much for rabid Roosevelt haters like the Walkers and Bushes, who threw themselves into the Republican campaign of their friend Thomas Dewey, the forty-two-year-old prosecuting attorney of New York.

George wrote, "I think most feel FDR will win, but then most of the people I know around here [officers] seem to be Dewey voters. The south-ern boys will support Roosevelt. The ones I've talked with seem to think he's some sort of a god—I don't believe they look too closely at what the New Deal administration has done or has not done."

Despite FDR's declining health, the sixty-two-year-old President was the most experienced politician in U.S. history, and the country felt safer with him at the helm than with his opponent, who kept haranguing about the dangers of Communism. With Russia as a U.S. ally against Hitler in 1944, Dewey's Red-baiting didn't make sense. Roosevelt won with 54 per-cent of the vote.

"I know how discouraged you must be," George wrote to his parents, "and I feel the same way. My knowledge of the campaign etc. is not ex-tensive but from all reports it was not a pleasant one."

When President Roosevelt died on April 12, 1945, Prescott wrote to his friend Samuel Merrifield Bemiss in Richmond, Virginia:

> The death of the President has been no doubt a source of much dis-cussion in Richmond—or has it? I have been amazed at the lack of interest in it here, or in Pinehurst, or on the trains, or in New Haven. Aside from surprise, no emotion have I seen, and I have sought it out. I hesitate to express my true thoughts concerning his passing for my respect for the office is very great—but my respect for F.D.R. as the occupant was sorely lacking. But we need not go into that, I suppose. I am not worried about Truman at all; in fact, I think he will do an acceptable job, take good advice, use his cab-inet well, work closely with Congress, and make good appoint-ments. I have no fears on the international front. I think Churchill and Stalin had the "high sign" on F.D.R. but will not have it on Truman because Truman will lean on his State Department and Senate very heavily.

In November 1944, the thought of four more years of Roosevelt had thrown the Bushes into a torpor of depression, but by Christmas their spir-its had begun to soar as they looked forward to the weddings of their two oldest sons. Prescott seemed especially impressed that his namesake son was marrying an admiral's daughter. In a letter to Averell Harriman he wrote:

You may be interested to know that our son, Prescott, Jr., is to marry
a young lady named Betty Lou Kauffman, daughter of Vice Admi-
ral Kauffman, Commander of Destroyers in the Pacific, and one of
the top men in the Nimitz organization. This young lady is a very
lovely person and we are perfectly delighted over the engagement.
We have never met the Admiral, who I understand has a very fine
record in the Navy, but we have met Mrs. Kauffman and the
daughter.

There was no such letter from Prescott extolling George's fiancée, Barbara Pierce, whose father had not yet worked his way to the top of the corporate ladder at McCall Corporation. At the time Marvin Pierce was only a company vice president, which was not as prestigious as the admiralty. His wife, Pauline Pierce, the daughter of an Ohio Supreme Court justice, was every inch the snob that Prescott Bush was. She felt that her daughter should be marrying better, if for no other reason than to enhance Pauline's position in the Garden Club of America. (In a letter to a friend, Marvin described his wife's garden club as "an association of the snottiest outfits engaged in that sort of work." Yet he understood how much his wife loved having her picture appear in the New York society pages whenever she won a medal in the international flower show, especially for her expertise in pollinating lilies.) Pauline spent her husband's modest income as if they were rich, and rarely paid her bills, which forced him into continual debt. At one point the family's liabilities were so dire that Marvin had to take a $100,000 loan ($1.05 million in 2004) from his McCall's stock. That loan took him years to repay.

When Barbara was growing up, Rye was a Social Register community of affluent families in Westchester County, but the Pierces were neither Social Register nor affluent. Pauline Pierce, who wanted very much to be part of "society," scrambled to keep up, but she was never asked to join the Junior League and her daughters were never chosen to be debutantes. She dismissed the Bushes as a nice enough family, but not as nice (that is, wealthy) as she'd like, and she pronounced George singularly unimpressive, especially when she compared him with Walter Rafferty, the Marine captain whom her pretty daughter, Martha, had married.

"Father appreciated George," said Barbara. "Mother did not."

Still, Pauline insisted that Barbara have a proper Christmas wedding with eight attendants in emerald green satin and matching satin shoes, an extravagance almost unheard of during war-rationing years. After a year and a half at Smith, Barbara had dropped out of college, where classmates remember her daydreaming through classes and doodling her name in notebooks as "Mrs. George Herbert Walker Bush." She returned home to help her mother plan the wedding and the reception for three hundred guests at the Apawamis Country Club. Pauline ordered engraved invitations for December 17, 1944, but Barbara had to scratch out that date and write in a new one when George did not get home until December 24. That social faux pas only further exasperated his future mother-in-law.

At the last minute, George's seventy-year-old grandmother, Loulie Walker, was unable to attend the wedding. She had been thrown from a horse and broken her hip. Pauline Pierce could hardly believe someone that age would still be horseback riding.

On January 6, 1945, Barbara appeared in a long white satin gown and a veil of rose point lace that belonged to Dorothy Walker Bush. She walked down the aisle of the Rye Presbyterian Church on her father's arm to marry Lieutenant Junior Grade George Herbert Walker Bush, who stood at the altar in his Navy dress blues, complete with his mother's gift of gold wings and his father's cuff links.

The young couple, who had met as teenagers and found refuge in each other, were overjoyed to be starting a new life together. They could hardly wait to get away from home and their overbearing parents, particularly her imperious mother and his magisterial father.

CHAPTER SIX

rescott Bush wanted to make sure that Yale knew his boy was coming. With the largest freshman class enrolled to date—1,172 men
in 1945, including 800 veterans on the GI Bill—Prescott didn't
want George to get lost in the shuffle. So he wrote a letter to Charles Seymour, president of the university, on October 11, 1945, and suggested
they have lunch the next day. At the time Prescott was a member of the
Yale Corporation, which is to the university what the College of Cardinals
is to the Vatican. So his "Dear Charlie" letter packed a punch:

> I called your office this morning and in your absence left word with
> your secretary that I hoped very much that you could have lunch at
> Mory's at one thirty with Brig. Gen. Charles M. Spofford (Yale
> 1924), and myself tomorrow. Chuck and my son, George, who has
> just gotten out of the Navy after more than three years of service in
> naval aviation, are going to play golf in the morning at the Yale
> golf course, and I have set one thirty so as to be sure we will not
> keep you waiting.

Just to make sure that the university president got the point, Prescott
added: "I will also bring my son, George, to lunch. He left Andover in
June 1942 and went directly in the Navy on his eighteenth birthday. Now,
at twenty-one and a half years, he is married and entering Yale on November 1st in the special school for return[ing] servicemen."

Not only was Prescott a member of the revered Yale Corporation, but
he served on every committee that had to do with the securing and ex-

penditure of funds. In addition, he had undertaken the university's $80 million expansion drive. So he was not a man to be ignored by the university's president. Despite the last-minute invitation, Seymour joined Prescott and his party for lunch the next day. (Research in the Yale archives shows that no other incoming freshman in that class was accorded such preferential treatment.) George Herbert Walker Bush was off to a roaring start.

Even twenty-eight years after his graduation from Yale, Prescott continued to be a huge presence on campus. "You could not *not* meet Prescott Bush if you stayed at Yale at all," said the former English professor George de Forest Lord. "He often was coming to sing with the Whiffenpoofs. He was very enthusiastic about the college, dedicated, and clearly influenced by the Yale milieu and Yale spirit, an old-fashioned Yale man—a gentleman."

If Prescott was a big dog on the Yale campus, George was a little puppy who slipped his leash, wagged his tail, and ran in all directions. By the time he graduated two and a half years later (he went to school year-round with no breaks to achieve this accelerated schedule) with a bachelor's degree in economics, and a minor in sociology, Poppy Bush, as he had resumed calling himself after the Navy, had gobbled all that Yale had to offer—socially, scholastically, and athletically.

He tried to emulate all of his father's achievements but fell short around the piano. "Poppy couldn't sing worth a damn—no pitch, bad voice, and completely tone-deaf," said a family friend. "When he tried to sing, dogs went deaf. Pres's other kids had great voices. Pres junior and Johnny and Bucky were all Whiffenpoofs at Yale, and Nancy starred in some of her college musicals. In fact, she and her father composed most of the songs for *Raisin' the Deuce*, her Vassar Soph Party show. Thank God, Pop was a good athlete. Otherwise, Prescott might've put him up for adoption."

"Anybody that's interested in Bush has got to focus on that wonderful combination of scholar-athlete that he proved to be," said former Ohio Congressman Thomas "Lud" Ashley, a Yale classmate and one of George's best friends. "In fact, he wasn't anything particularly special . . . but he was special in that he was a good student and an even better athlete, I'd say. Baseball and soccer. He went out for soccer, and by the end of the first week he was on the varsity soccer team. He was a very gifted athlete."

The postwar years at Yale were unusual because the campus was crowded with veterans on the GI Bill, many of whom were married and in a hurry to get their degree. A college diploma meant a good job, and these men wanted to get out and make a living, so they wasted no time on campus fripperies or the bright sparkles of youth. They hunkered down to studying, made good grades, and became the hardest-working, most serious students that colleges had ever seen. The Yale Class Book of 1948 noted: "An interesting change [on campus] was the size of the Dean's Lists which went up in much greater proportion than the size of the student body." *The New York Times* reported the trend in colleges across the country: "The GIs are hogging the honor rolls and the Dean's lists."

And that included George Herbert Walker Bush. Despite his lackluster grades at Andover, he surprised everyone by placing in the top 10 percent of his college class and graduating Phi Beta Kappa. He also won the Francis Gordon Brown Prize, which is awarded to the member of the junior class who most closely approaches the standard of intellectual ability, character, capacity for leadership, and service to the university set by the Yale alumnus Francis Gordon Brown. "I think in practice the prize is awarded to an athlete who has a reasonably good grade point average," said Geoffrey Kabaservice, a Yale historian.

George, a two-letter man, qualified on both scores. Batting right and throwing left, he was a natural first baseman who tried to play like his idol, Lou Gehrig. "Nothing flashy, no hot-dogging, the ideal sportsman," George said of the Yankees' legendary first baseman. "He could field, hit, hit-with-power, and come through in the clutch."

When George was named captain of the 1948 baseball team, the *Yale Daily News* said: "He is generally considered as one of the flashiest fielding first basemen in collegiate circles." His teammates agreed. "The key thing about Poppy, as everyone called him, was that he was so sure-gloved," said Frank "Junie" O'Brien. "All the infielders knew that if they threw the ball anywhere near him, he was going to pull it in."

George was not as impressive at bat. Known as "Good Glove, No Hit," he had a .239 batting average in 1947; the next year he raised it to

.264, but he was never good enough to be scouted by the pros like Frank Quinn, a pitcher on the team, who was signed by the Red Sox for a fifty-thousand-dollar bonus. George helped Yale win the NCAA Eastern Championships in the first two years of the College World Series—1947 and 1948—but Yale lost both series in the finals.

George's Uncle Herbie, who idolized his nephew and held him up as a model to his two sons, attended every baseball game George played from the middle of February to the end of June. The entire Bush-Walker family turned out on June 5, 1948, for the big Princeton game in New Haven, and the Bambino himself presented the typescript of his autobiography, *The Babe Ruth Story*, to the captain of the Yale baseball team for the Yale library.

"When Ruth turned the manuscript over to me, his hand trembled and his voice could barely be heard," George recalled in his autobiography. "It was obvious that he was dying of cancer; but some of the young, free-spirited 'Babe' was still there, very much alive. 'You know,' he said, winking, 'when you write a book like this, you can't put *everything* in it.' The ceremony was one of his last public appearances."

A young reporter ran out on the field. "I was on the radio and saw this happening, so I ran over with my mic in hand and got a short interview," recalled Stan Ross (class of 1951). "Ruth was an impressive man, a giant, but all I can really remember now is that he ate five hot dogs while we were standing there. And who would have known then that this weak-hitting first baseman [George Bush] would have become anything later in life."

The Babe proclaimed Yale Field, once an apple orchard, the finest playing surface he had ever seen. He sat through six innings, with Yale ahead 9–1, before he left the ballpark. Yale beat Princeton 14–2 that day; two months later Babe Ruth was dead.

George joined everything at Yale: the 1946 Budget Drive, the Undergraduate Athletic Association, the Undergraduate Board of Deacons, the Interfraternity Council, and the Triennial Committee. He belonged to the Torch Honor Society and Delta Kappa Epsilon fraternity and was the last man tapped for Skull and Bones. This was the society's signal that he would be the leader of his class based on the biblical precept "So the last shall be first, and the first last: for many are called, but few chosen" (Matthew 20:16).

"Poppy was always running for office," said Harry Finkenstaedt (class of 1948). "He was a self-styled big wheel on campus and that's about the best I can say for him . . . We were in the same fraternity and I remember a group of us were in the lobby of DKE. Someone said, 'Did you know that Poppy's going to be the next president of DKE. He's running for office.' I said, 'Well, that's the trouble with Poppy. He's always running for office.' After the group broke up, someone said, 'Do you know who that woman was standing with us? That was Barbara Bush.' So a few days later when I saw her, I said, 'I probably hurt you by saying that about Poppy.' She said, 'Well, I must admit, it was a bane.' I thought, 'What the heck is a bane?' It was the first and last time I ever heard that expression.

"I've known Bush since Yale but I'm afraid I'm not much of a fan . . . He was just a friendly guy in a hurry . . . kind of a hand-shaking hustler type . . . always campaigning for something."

George was definitely running a fast track at Yale, in part because of his desire to graduate quickly. He received college course credit for his three years in the Navy and started university at the age most students graduate. He became a father during his freshman year when Barbara, who gained sixty pounds in that pregnancy, gave birth to their first son, George Walker Bush, on July 6, 1946.

The Connecticut birth certificate shows that Barbara, twenty-one, was in labor for seven hours. She is listed as "white" and "housewife," which fairly describes the life she reported to the *Smith Alumnae Quarterly* when she wrote of herself: "I play tennis, do volunteer work and admire George Bush." At the time, she and George and Georgie, as they called their new baby, shared a house in New Haven with two other families and a large black standard poodle named Turbo. Other than a part-time job in the Yale Co-op to pay for her cigarettes, Barbara played bridge, went to the movies, and audited a course in furniture and silver. After the baby was born, she stayed home and took care of him when she was not taking him to his father's baseball games.

Even with the added responsibility of fatherhood, George maintained his frantic pace, entertaining constantly and traveling with the Yale baseball team for all their out-of-town games.

He wrote to his good friend FitzGerald "Gerry" Bemiss that Barbara was the perfect wife for such a whirling dervish:

She lives quite frankly for Georgie and myself. She is wholly un-selfish, beautifully tolerant of my weaknesses and idiosyncrasies, and ready to faithfully follow any course I choose . . . Her devotion overcomes me and I must often stop in my mad whirl around college, etc. to see if I am considering her at all.

Having grown up watching his father pull the golden cords of his Skull and Bones connections, George knew that induction into the secret society was the ultimate honor for a Yale undergraduate. As a legacy son of a renowned Bonesman, and the nephew of the moneyed Bonesman George Herbert Walker Jr. (Uncle Herbie), he seemed to be a shoo-in. After all, the Russell Trust Association—the corporate shell for Skull and Bones—listed its address at the New York City offices of Brown Brothers Harriman, and its funds were invested by Uncle Herbie at G. H. Walker and Company. But there was still a niggling doubt. As Sinclair Lewis (Yale 1908) wrote of Skull and Bones: "Some good men always carried away scars. And the finality and exclusiveness of the choosing created and would continue to create a faint and enduring fault line in the Yale brotherhood."

In Greenwich the Bushes and their friends sat by the phone, worrying and waiting. "I remember when George Bush was tapped for Skull and Bones," said Joseph Verner Reed Jr., who was ten years old at the time. Prescott and Dorothy Bush frequently wintered with the Reeds in Hobe Sound, the exclusive Florida enclave developed by Reed's father and ruled by Reed's mother. "We were all sitting anxiously by the telephone at my mother's house waiting for the news . . . It was a big excitement. And we raised a glass of orange juice to his success."

George had run hard for his tap, which he received on May 15, 1947, from Charles S. Whitehouse, who went on to a career with the Central Intelligence Agency. The CIA attracted such a high percentage of Bonesmen, skilled at keeping secrets, that they called the agency "the home office."

On that spring night in 1947, George met the men who would become some of his closest lifelong friends: Thomas William Ludlow Ashley, Lucius Horatio Biglow Jr., John Erwin Caulkins, William Judkins Clark, William James Connelly Jr., George Cook III, David Charles

Grimes, Richard Elwood Jenkins, Richard Gerstle Mack, Thomas Wilder Moseley, George Harold Pfau Jr., Samuel Sloane Walker Jr., Howard Sayre Weaver, and Valleau Wilkie Jr.

Meeting on Thursday and Sunday nights, the Bonesmen began their initiation rite by lying in a coffin and reciting their sexual history in a ritual known as "CB," or "connubial bliss."

"The first time you review your sex life . . . We went all the way around among the fifteen," said Lucius Biglow Jr., a retired Seattle attorney. "That way you get everybody committed to a certain extent. So when we came around to round two, you knew where you stood . . . It was a gradual way of bonding and building confidence."

Round two was sharing their "LH," or "life history," which was a three-hour recitation of their dreams, shames, and traumas. Short of any future psychotherapy sessions, that time spent in the tomb was probably the first and last time these men ever openly shared so much of themselves. It bound them together for life. "In Skull and Bones we all stand together," said William Connelly Jr. (class of 1945). "Fifteen brothers under the skin. [It is] the greatest allegiance in the world."

When George's turn came to give his "LH," he climbed into the coffin and related the most searing experience of his life, sobbing as he told the Bonesmen about getting shot down over Chichi-Jima and losing his crew, especially his friend Ted White, who had also been a Bonesman, class of 1942.

"It tore him up, real anguish," said Lud Ashley. "It was so fresh in his mind. He had a real friendship with this man . . . [He] was heartbroken. He had gone over it in his mind a hundred thousand times and concluded he couldn't have done anything . . . He didn't feel guilty about anything that happened on the plane . . . But the incident was a source of real grief to him."

The men who had fought in the war understood the two things an officer must do to lead men—care for their welfare and show physical courage. They agonized for George, who in bailing out that day felt that he had done neither. "[W]hat really anguished him was the fact that it was either he gets out or he goes in, you know, with whatever's left behind him," Ashley told the writer David Robb in an unpublished interview. "[T]hat was really a matter that still hurt him greatly at that time. He couldn't really talk about it for any length of time without choking up. The thing that just drove him to distraction was the fact that he was the only one that got out.

"It was good for him to be able to talk to people who reassured him . . . but he did come back to it. But it was an absolutely impossible situation. He knew that but he kept saying, 'I keep wondering if there wasn't something I could have done.' "

More than fifty years later some Bonesmen still recalled the details of George's harrowing flight. "He took it to heart when he was shot down," said Frank O'Brien in 2003. "I don't think he ever got over it. Well, of course he's over it, but I don't think it's ever far from his thoughts, even today."

An aura of mystery surrounds Skull and Bones, even for those who ridicule its gothic rituals and morbid arcana, including the society's mantra: "The Hangman equals Death / the Devil equals Death / Death equals Death." The society's secret rituals take place in the inner sanctum of the tomb, which is referred to as "T" or "322." The society took that number as its symbol because the Greek orator Demosthenes died in 322 B.C., and, according to legend, Eulogia, the goddess of eloquence, ascended into heaven and did not return until 1832, when she took up residence with Skull and Bones.

Each Knight is given a cryptonym, which the society will call him for the rest of his life. Some receive traditional Skull and Bones code names like "Magog" (for the Knight who is the most sexually experienced); "Gog" (for the least sexually experienced); "Long Devil" (for the tallest man); and "Little Devil" (for the shortest).

George embraced the Skull and Bones concept of being the best of the best, and later let that elitism influence some of his political decisions. To his detriment he used membership in the secret society as a validation of being a "good man" and made several of his political appointments based on nothing more than a Yale degree and membership in Skull and Bones. To George H.W. Bush's way of thinking, all Bonesmen were superior to other men. As President, when he sought a mentor for making military decisions, especially about using force in the Gulf War, he emulated a master Bonesman, Henry Lewis Stimson, who was Secretary of War under Roosevelt and head of Andover when George was a student.

Unlike his father, George never became a huge or looming presence at Yale, but he clung to Skull and Bones for the rest of his life. He never let a year pass after graduation without sending a check to the RTA. Until 1966, those checks (he always sent ten dollars) were written to the Russell Trust Association. In June 1966, the "King" of each class (last man tapped) received a "Personal and Confidential" letter from "Pat" (Patriarch) M. Malcolm Baldridge, president of RTA, announcing that Skull and Bones "was most fortunate to recently receive a favorable decision from the Internal Revenue Service exempting from income tax all gifts, and donations made to RTA, Inc."

As the "King" of his class, George was to personally contact his club mates, "inform them fully of this favorable development, and in this manner hopefully raise the entire level of giving to RTA."

Baldridge spelled out why Skull and Bones needed more funds:

1. Expenses of running and maintaining the "T" have been constantly increasing.

2. With more scholarship knights, RTA has found it necessary to relieve the incoming club of certain expenses formerly assumed, such as meals and operating expenses of the "T."

3. We would like to set up a revolving loan fund for members of RTA who need help in pursuing graduate studies. These loans would be interest-free with the stipulation that the loan would be repaid as rapidly as possible, once the individual develops earning power as a result of his graduate training. We have had numerous requests for such loans that we are now not able to satisfy.

He closed by saying, "If you have any questions our Treasurer, Herbie Walker, will be glad to hear from you."

George dutifully contacted all his Bonesmen and sent them a copy of Baldridge's letter "to encourage you in your affluence to do what you can for RTA." He wrote:

The letter explains better than I could the new tax-exempt set up and I can only add my sacred words of encouragement that you participate to the fullest.

Send them stocks, bonds, or even cash; but the big thing is, send
something in so D-146 will be second to none.

He signed the letter, "Yours in 322, GB."

Later some of those same Bonesmen wrote to George asking for contributions to their Yale class reunion, but George would not contribute.
He cared less about Yale than he did about Skull and Bones.

In 1970 William F. Buckley Jr. (class of 1946) asked George if he
would agree to run with him for the Yale Corporation. "George said no
on the grounds that he had lost interest in Yale," Buckley told Geoffrey
Kabaservice. "He said that when the students were revolting in 1970 he
was giving a speech at a college in which most of the students were indi-
gent and were grateful for the education they received and that he considered that the behavior of undergraduates at Yale resulted in the
forfeiture of primary alumni interest."

Even when Lud Ashley, one of his closest friends, asked him in June
1970 to contribute to their class-reunion gift, George refused. Their class
had hoped to raise $1 million for Yale but turned in only $475,000. Afterward George wrote to Ashley: "The figures aren't as bad as U thot—
thus I'll still do nothing for a while yet. RTA. Si!! '48 or 45W, No." ("W,"
for "war," indicated those classes that entered Yale on the accelerated program.)

Shortly before he graduated, George wrote to Gerry Bemiss about his future: "My mind is in a turmoil. I want to do something of value and yet I
have to and want to make money . . . So where does that leave me . . ."

He knew that the family's financial mother lode was his to be mined
if he wanted:

> *I could work for Herby Walker in St. Louis—G. H. Walker & Co.*
> *investments etc. . . . but the people I'd be doing business with in the*
> *investment business, I know to some degree now. I am not sure I*
> *want to capitalize completely on the benefits I received at birth—*
> *that is on the benefits of my social position . . . doing well merely*
> *because I have had the opportunity to attend the same debut par-*
> *ties as some of my customers does not appeal to me.*

George didn't know what he wanted to do with his life, but, as he wrote to his friend, he knew what he didn't want to do, and that was to be "a straphanger" like his father, commuting to a job in the city every morning and returning home to the suburbs every night. "I was looking for a different kind of life, something challenging, outside the established mold. I couldn't see myself being happy commuting into work, then back home, five days a week." He later admitted he had to get out of Greenwich. "I didn't want to live in the suburbs and be 'Pres Bush's boy.' "

Making money was crucial to George. As he wrote to his friend Gerry Bemiss, he had gone through Yale on the GI Bill, was married, and had one child. "After Georgie goes through 3 squares every day, one's wallet becomes thin and worn." Assumptions to the contrary, George Herbert Walker Bush did not come from extraordinary wealth. Comfortably prosperous, his family was not of unlimited means and could not subsidize him. As young marrieds, George and Barbara rented apartments in which they had to share bathrooms with other renters as well as refrigerator space. Unlike some of his friends, George had no trust fund to sustain his financial future. He certainly had rich relatives on his mother's side of the family, but his father had only recently recovered from years of indebtedness to Brown Brothers Harriman. Although Prescott served on several corporate boards Columbia Broadcasting System, Procter & Gamble, Pennsylvania Water and Power Company, the Prudential Insurance Company of America, Simmons Company, United States Guarantee Company, Vanadium Corporation of America—directors did not collect large fees in those days. Prescott told his children he was in no financial position to subsidize them beyond their college educations. Upon graduation, they were on their own.

"Dad believed in the old Ben Franklin copybook maxims when it came to earning, saving and spending . . . [M]y brothers Pres, John and Buck, my sister Nancy, and I—all grew up understanding that life isn't an open-ended checking account," George wrote in his memoir *Looking Forward*. "From an early age we knew that if an illness or something really serious occurred, our folks would be there to help, but once we left home, we'd make it on our own, in business or whatever we entered in later life."

What Prescott Bush did provide, though, were the golden cords of his invaluable personal connections, and on these he did not stint. Prescott junior had been the first to benefit from his father's advantageous friendships when he was given a job with Pan American Airways in South America. That employment opportunity came thanks to his father's close relationship with Juan Trippe, Pan American's founder and chairman, and with Samuel F. Pryor Jr., a Republican Party official who lived in Greenwich and served on the Pan Am board with Prescott senior. Besides sharing the same politics, the three men frequently played golf together.

When George needed to find a job, his father set up an interview with Procter & Gamble, but they turned George down. "No soap," he reported to his father. So Prescott suggested he contact H. Neil Mallon, who was Skull and Bones with Prescott at Yale (class of 1917). Having never married until the age of sixty-nine, Mallon had lavished enough time on the Bush children to become their beloved "Uncle Neil." They looked forward to his visits from Ohio because he always brought out the best in their father, who was not gruff and dour around him. For George especially, Neil Mallon became a surrogate father who was warm and outgoing and gave George the attention he craved. "He taught me everything I knew in life," George wrote to the Mallon family after Neil died, "including how to throw a baseball." The family found the part about the baseball particularly poignant because it was not Neil Mallon who played varsity baseball at Yale but Prescott Bush.

In 1929, Prescott had brought Neil Mallon to the attention of Bert Walker when W. A. Harriman and Company purchased the Dresser Company, based in Bradford, Pennsylvania, and needed to find a president to run it.

"Neil was the bright young man of our class at that time," Prescott recalled in his oral history. "He'd made tremendous headway as vice-president of U.S. Can Co. twelve years out of college . . . so we brought Neil in . . . and he was made president of the company. I went on the board of the Dresser Co. at that time and remained on it for 25 years.

"During those years we developed the Dresser Co. [into Dresser Industries] by acquiring other properties . . . I was Neil Mallon's chief advisor and consultant in connection with every move that he made with that business during that period."

So when George called "Uncle Neil" for job advice, Mallon sat down and shared his visions of the future: he told George that because of the growing need for energy in the United States, oil and gas exploration would become the twentieth century's new frontier. He explained that since the war, Dresser had been diversifying into products like oil derricks, blowers, drill bits, and refractories, and was exploring new oil and gas markets around the globe. At the time, Dresser was the largest oil-equipment company in the world.

"What you need to do is head out to Texas and those oil fields," Neil Mallon said. "That's the place for ambitious young people these days."

He then offered George an opportunity to learn the business from the bottom up as a trainee for IDECO (International Derrick and Equipment Company), a Dresser subsidiary in Odessa, Texas, at three hundred dollars a month. According to George's recollection in his autobiography, Mallon said, "There's not much salary, but if you want to learn the oil business, it's a start." George neglected to mention the pot of gold that "Uncle Neil" had promised him at the end of the rainbow.

According to his brother Prescott junior, Neil Mallon had told George before he started at Dresser: "You'll have a chance to run the company someday."

So it was off to the black oil fields of West Texas for George Bush, who drove the new red Studebaker his parents had given him as a graduation present. The money they had saved on his tuition, thanks to the GI Bill, almost covered the cost of the $1,525.50 car.

"There wasn't anything subtle or complicated about [our move to Texas]," George admitted at the time. "We . . . just wanted to make a lot of money quick." Later he would portray the move away from home as a great act of independence. Some people, such as the historian Garry Wills, saw it as nothing more than George relocating "to work for his father."

Barbara had been elated when George told her they would be moving to Texas. "You know, George never asks anything . . . He makes up *our* mind . . . but I was excited about a whole new world. I'd never left—the farthest—well, I went to Ohio, I guess. We just didn't travel much in my family. So I'd never met a Texan."

Like George, she wanted to get away from their families. "George's mother was a formidable and strong woman, and so was my mother," she told the writer Peggy Noonan, "and we wanted to get out from under the parental gaze, be on our own." Barely communicating with her own mother at the time, Barbara was allowing her take-charge mother-in-law to run her life. She didn't even try to object. "How could I? Dorothy Bush was the most competitive human being on the face of the earth." While Barbara was intimidated by George's mother, she was terrified of his father and did not understand his stern sense of humor. Once, while visiting her in-laws in Greenwich, Barbara said she had to leave to visit her parents in Rye. Without smiling, Prescott joked: "Did we give you permission to visit those strangers?" Barbara burst into tears.

When she heard her father-in-law yell at her son, young Georgie, for pulling the dog's tail, Barbara hid. "I backed in my room and thought, 'The kid is on his own.'"

"His father was scary," she said many years later. "He was six feet four, very successful businessman. At the time we met, he was just becoming a little famous 'cause he was the first head of the USO. But I remember sitting in a house . . . and he said to me, 'Did I ever tell you you could smoke?' And I was so taken aback by that, and I said, 'Well, did I marry you?' And he burst out laughing, and we were friends from then on."

The few trips that Barbara did make to Rye to see her parents were just as difficult for George as they were for her. "Once when George and I were visiting after we were married, Mother asked him not to go to the bathroom at night because he woke her up when he flushed the toilet. George, already inventive at the age of twenty-something, went out the window!"

Barbara, who emulated Dorothy Walker Bush as the model of motherhood, was determined to make her own large family. "All our children were planned," she told the writer Gail Sheehy. "By me!" Shortly after George graduated from Yale, she became pregnant again, but miscarried, and grew quite despondent. George wrote to his mother: "I know that her disappointment over this miscarriage was large. As I told you before we are both sort of hoping that we will have another child before too long. She thinks about it a lot. And foolishly worries too much. I don't like to have her upset."

George headed to Odessa the day after he returned from the College World Series in Kalamazoo, Michigan. He sent Barbara and Georgie to

Kennebunkport for two months until he found them a place to live. He said the first apartment was "on the wrong side of the tracks," requiring them to move three times in the next four months. Eventually they found an apartment where they did not have to share a bathroom with strangers. George had called Barbara in August, and after flying twelve hours in a prop plane, she and George had arrived in Odessa, where it was hot, dry, and gritty with sand. The town was segregated by Jim Crow—blacks on one side, whites on the other. Oil was life in this boom-or-bust town, which boomed from fifteen thousand people to over forty-two thousand during the decade from 1940 to 1950. The flares of unwanted natural gas being burned off the rigs lit up the night skies above Odessa. The first time Barbara smelled the gaseous fumes she evacuated their two-room apartment in the middle of the night. "When I was young and went to Texas," she admitted many years later, "I thought Texans were barbarians."

George's parents visited the couple in January 1949, when Prescott flew to Texas on a Dresser inspection trip and Dotty joined him on the company plane. They all posed for a picture in front of the plane, and that photo captures a fleeting but telling moment. Prescott looks like the prosperous investment banker he was in a suit, tie, white shirt, pocket handkerchief, and black homburg. Tall, distinguished, and commanding, he has one hand in his pocket and the other entwined through his wife's arm—one unit indivisible. George, looking boyish in a flannel shirt and windbreaker, stands on the other side of his mother, affectionately close, holding his two-and-a-half-year-old son, Georgie, who is wearing his first pair of cowboy boots. There is no physical space between any of them. Barbara, who is off to the side of George, is tethered to the group only by holding on to her son's little hand. There is physical space between her and her husband's family, as if she's strangely disembodied and separate from their intimate grouping, not yet a part of the unit.

When George and Barbara finally moved away, they tried to stay away. They were transferred from Odessa in April 1949 to Huntington Park, California, where George went to work as a laborer on an assembly line for Pacific Pumps, a Dresser subsidiary. He elected to join the United Steelworkers of America and, as he wrote to a friend, became "a dues paying CIO steelworker." Barbara was again pregnant when they received word on September 23, 1949, that her fifty-three-year-old mother had been killed in a freak car accident. The story was reported on the front page of *The New York Times*:

AUTO CRASH KILLS PUBLISHER'S WIFE
AS HE REACHES FOR SPILLING CUP

Marvin Pierce was driving to the Rye railroad station when Pauline placed a cup of coffee on the seat between them. He saw it tipping and reached over to stop the hot liquid from spilling on his wife; the car swerved, hit the shoulder of the road, plunged one hundred feet down an embankment, and crashed into a tree and a stone wall. Striking the windshield, Pauline fractured her skull and was killed instantly.

Her relationship with Barbara, always fractious, had not improved after Barbara's marriage to George. "I think my mother thought Barbara was still nineteen years old and living in the house," said Barbara's brother Scott in 2001. "The truth of the matter is my mother died so soon thereafter that there was no resolution of that."

Barbara decided not to go home for her mother's funeral, although her brother Jim and his wife, who had just been married, interrupted their honeymoon to come home for the service. Barbara implied later that she could not afford the expense of traveling to Rye. "Contrary to popular belief," she said, "it would have been an enormous [financial] strain. My father would have had to pay for my trip." Yet the week before she had traveled to Cleveland for her brother Jimmy's wedding. Years later a Bush niece was asked to explain why Barbara would not go to her mother's funeral. Elsie Walker responded carefully: "I don't think she had the easiest of relationships with her mother."

George, too, was strangely casual about the catastrophe. On October 21, 1949, he wrote to his friend Gerry Bemiss, but only toward the end of the letter did he offhandedly mention his mother-in-law's death, incorrectly describing the accident:

Did you know Bar's mother was killed in an auto accident 3 weeks ago while driving Mr. Pierce to the station?

Our life here is socially non-existent but we are happy, very much so. Best to you and drop me a line—Pop.

When Barbara gave birth three months later, she and George named their little girl after Barbara's mother, Pauline Robinson, and called her Robin. Blessedly, they did not know that within three years this blond, blue-eyed baby would bring them to their darkest days.

CHAPTER SEVEN

On October 26, 1946, Prescott and Dorothy gathered all the Bushes and Walkers together for the wedding of their only daughter, Nancy (the "necker"), and Alexander "Sandy" Ellis Jr. at St. Paul's of Glenville, a Catholic church in Greenwich.

Many people observed that in marrying the tall, dark, and handsome Ellis, Nancy had chosen a man much like her father, except that Ellis was Catholic. Yale class of 1944, he had served in Europe during World War II from February 1943 to January 1946 and fought at the Battle of the Bulge, earning a Purple Heart and a Bronze Star. At Yale, he was a member of George Bush's fraternity, DKE, and Skull and Bones. For ushers at his wedding Ellis, a progressive Republican in the mold of his future father-in-law, chose, besides George "Poppy" Bush, John Lindsay, who met his future wife at the wedding and who later was mayor of New York City (1966–73); James Buckley, who became senator from New York (1971–77) before he was appointed by Reagan to the federal bench in 1985; and John Chafee, who became Secretary of the Navy under Nixon (1969–72) and then senator from Rhode Island (1976–99).

Prescott and Dorothy were now in their fifties with two children still to raise. In high school when his sister married, Jonathan Bush, fourteen, had entered Hotchkiss in 1945. His father frequently drove up to the school in Lakeville, Connecticut, to watch him play baseball and perform in school plays. Still at home in Greenwich was William Henry Trotter Bush, known as Bucky, who was born in 1938, when Dotty was thirty-seven years old. Bucky did not start Hotchkiss until 1952. With sixteen years separating their first child from their last, Prescott and Dotty practically raised Bucky as an only child.

"Dotty and Pres seemed to love being parents," recalled Bob DeVecchi, who graduated from Yale a year after Jonathan Bush. "I remember when I was married to Flossie Sloan from Greenwich and we were in Washington while I was in the Foreign Service sometime around 1957. We lived in a tiny little house in Georgetown and had just had our first child. We met Prescott and Dorothy Bush, who lived in the neighborhood, and on several occasions Dotty would call us and say, 'Now, why don't you children go out and have a nice quiet dinner or go to a movie and have an evening to yourselves. We're home alone tonight and we have no children or grandchildren around so we'd love to babysit for you' . . . We would take our little girl, Maggie, or Chopsie, as we called her, over in a baby carriage, and she would spend the evening with the Bushes, who were then in their sixties."

As his children were growing up in Greenwich, Prescott Bush became involved in local politics and built his reputation over seventeen years as moderator of the Representative Town Meeting. By 1950, he had established himself as a pillar of the community, and when Greenwich was suggested as a possible site for the newly created United Nations, he knew exactly what to do.

Prescott had already declared himself on the issue, but people wanted to see how he would handle the raging factions. As moderator of the RTM, he had usually managed to get his way, including the 1937 resolution he had passed protesting FDR's proposed packing of the Supreme Court. But the UN issue had roiled the town into a fury and become a matter of national interest.

"That was a famous meeting," recalled John F. Sullivan in his oral history for the Greenwich Public Library. "They called it 'When they were bringing the camels to Greenwich.' That was the argument about the United Nations."

Big cities like Philadelphia, Atlantic City, Chicago, and San Francisco and even the Black Hills of South Dakota were competing furiously with New York City for the privilege of providing the United Nations with a tax-free home. But Prescott Bush was encouraging the small town of Greenwich (population fifty-five thousand) to decline the honor.

"It was probably the most well attended meeting we ever had," said Sullivan. "Everyone turned out. The room was so packed people had to sit on the floor."

Prescott gaveled the meeting to order, and, adhering to Robert's Rules of Order, he listened politely to all divergent points of view, provided he was properly addressed as "Mr. Chairman." Then Josephine Evaristo jumped up and demanded the floor. Barely five feet tall, the feisty little Democrat, who represented the working-class area of Chickahominy, acted as if she were as tall and commanding as the patrician moderator himself. Unlike everyone else around Prescott, including his own family, she was not intimidated by him.

He smiled patronizingly as she began blasting the snooty Republicans in town who objected to bringing foreigners into their midst.

"Why are you against the UN coming here, you woodchucks?" she bellowed. "You let us have the incinerator."

The roly-poly firebrand knew how to raise the hackles of the predominantly Republican town meeting. She never stopped hammering on the issue of the town incinerator, although it had been ten years since Prescott had "recommended" it be placed in her district. At the time she had objected strenuously and encouraged her constituency to sue. Even after losing the case in court, she continued ranting about the injustice of Greenwich's rich toward the poor. "The Republicans can do anything they want in this town," she fumed. Every winter she grumbled loudly about the snow being removed on Grove Lane, where Bush lived, days before the Italians and Hungarians and Poles in Chickahominy ever saw a snowplow.

At that time there was a divisive gap between the rich Protestants of Greenwich, who lived in "the backcountry," and the working-class Catholics, who lived "in town." Mrs. Evaristo, who worked three jobs to support her large family and taught English at night to the immigrant Italians, frequently rolled into the weekly RTM meetings in dungarees and a baseball cap. She was from "the town" and was not a friend of Prescott's.

When she launched into her bombast about the incinerator, he quickly gaveled her out of order, called for the question, and marshaled a voice vote on whether Greenwich should be home to the United Nations. The resolution, which he had favored, passed by a 2-to-1 margin—110

votes for, 55 against. That evening, Prescott sent a telegram to Clare
Boothe Luce, the congresswoman from Greenwich:

> *Resolved, that it is the sense of the meeting that, while the residents*
> *of Greenwich are desirous of obtaining world peace through the*
> *United Nations Organization, the Town of Greenwich should op-*
> *pose the placing of the capitol of the United Nations Organization*
> *in or adjacent to Greenwich.*

By 1950, Prescott had mastered the intricacies of parliamentary procedure, and, as he recalled in his oral history, he had learned a great deal
about local government. "All during those years, I was an active practicing Republican. I worked hard for [Alf] Landon in 1936, when he got
clobbered so badly [by FDR]. I used to raise money for Bob Taft when he
was running in Ohio. I did the same for Tom Dewey when he was a nominee in '44 [he lost to FDR] and '48 [he lost to Harry Truman]. And in
1947 I was asked by the state chairman of our party if I would become
chairman of the Connecticut Republican Finance Committee, whose
duty it was to finance the party in the state of Connecticut, and I did."

In the summer of 1949, Connecticut Republicans were scrambling
around for a gubernatorial candidate to contest the statehouse as well as
someone to run against U.S. Senator William Benton, who had been
named to succeed Senator Raymond Baldwin upon Baldwin's resignation
to accept a Connecticut judgeship. The term for Benton's seat expired in
1953, so whoever won it would have to run again two years later. During
a dinner of the state central committee, Harold Mitchell, state chairman
of the Republican Party, asked Prescott if he had ever considered running
for public office.

He said that he had not. "I live in the wrong part of the state," Prescott
recalled saying. "Greenwich is known upstate as a commuter town. It
would be hard for them to swallow a Greenwichite at the state level for
Governor or Senator. I'm a commuter. I'm an international banker."

Prescott had also been approached about running for Congress in
1946, when Clare Boothe Luce retired from the House of Representatives, but his partners at Brown Brothers Harriman discouraged him.

"Look, if this was the Senate we'd back you," said Roland Harriman,
"but we need you more here than the House needs you."

Prescott didn't argue. He later said, "I was not financially independent enough to be comfortable about my family's future." Prescott noted that his children's schools were very expensive and that they and Dotty would have had to make great sacrifices if he'd run. "We would have eaten all right. But I felt it would have been quite a sacrifice . . . It would have been a big come-down for me, financially, at that time."

By 1950, though, Prescott had received an inheritance of $55,779 ($393,500 in 2004) from his father's estate. When Samuel P. Bush died at his home, Ealy Farms, in Blacklick, Ohio, on February 8, 1948, the news was reported on the front page of the *Ohio State Journal* with a large photograph above the fold, a newspaper's most prominent placement:

S. P. BUSH, RETIRED BUSINESS,
CIVIL LEADER, SUCCUMBS AT 84

With his inheritance, plus the blessing of his partners at Brown Brothers Harriman, Prescott was ready to run.

"What should I do?" he asked Harold Mitchell.

"You've got to get around the state and make yourself known, especially to groups that are apt to be convention delegates. The convention is 680 members, and these are the town political leaders and legislators in the state legislature. You've got to get around and meet these people. I think I can help you with some speaking engagements, but I can't promise you anything definite."

Prescott consulted his Yale classmate Harry Luce, the editor and founder of *Time*, who indicated that he, too, might like to go for the GOP nomination. "Harry, I guess, like myself, had always had sort of a hankering for this thing, and so I said, 'My gosh, Harry, you'd be a much better man for this than I, and I'll back you.' "

Prescott arranged for Harry Luce to sit down with the state Republican chairman, who told the illustrious editor that although he lived in Ridgefield, Connecticut, he was more identified with New York City. He needed to spend more time in Connecticut and less at *Time* magazine. Luce bolted. He called Prescott the next day. "I can't divorce myself from *Time* to that extent, not possibly." So the field was open.

The next day Ted Yudain, the editor of *Greenwich Time*, wrote a front-page story saying that Prescott was not a declared candidate but "may be available" for the nomination. A few weeks later Yudain wrote another front-page story: "Bush to Toss Hat in Ring for Senate Early Next Week."

"Ted Yudain was a powerhouse in Connecticut, and he 'made' Prescott Bush by convincing the upstate GOP that the moderator of the RTM in Greenwich was a big deal," said Lowell Weicker, who served as Connecticut's governor (1991–95), U.S. senator (1971–89), and member of the House of Representatives (1969–71). "Check the record and you'll see that Ted practically drop-kicked Prescott over the goalposts with his press coverage."

The record proves Weicker to be right. The editor of *Greenwich Time* became Prescott's unofficial campaign manager and major political adviser. He traveled with him throughout the state in advance of the June convention in 1950 to introduce him to political leaders. He then reported those travels in his newspaper—glowingly:

> *"Bush, until recently GOP State Finance Chairman, started from scratch with little support. Campaigning all over the state since early April, he has become one of the strongest candidates in the field." (May 22, 1950)*

> *"Party leaders here reported enthusiastic state-wide response to Bush's pre-convention campaign and it was evident that many leaders feel Bush will be one of the best campaigners and strongest candidates on the GOP ticket this summer." (June 9, 1950)*

Then Vivien Kellems stepped forward to oppose Prescott. She had first opposed Clare Boothe Luce for the GOP nomination to Congress in 1942 because, she said, she didn't want a "penthouse liberal" carrying the party's banner. One of Luce's biographers described Kellems, a wealthy industrialist whose company manufactured grips to pull cables through conduits, as "a lady of reactionary opinions . . . [who] was the darling of the National Association of Manufacturers." Prescott Bush described her in his oral history as "a wicked little woman" and "just the meanest." He later edited his comments for public consumption; he substituted "difficult" for "wicked" and drew a line through his characterization of her as "just the meanest."

For several uncomfortable weeks she drew Prescott into a bitter intra-party struggle, but Ted Yudain encouraged him to forge ahead, saying that the GOP delegates would never give the nomination to someone as controversial as Kellems. Close to the convention *Greenwich Time* ran a banner headline across the front page: "Bush Seen Certain for GOP Senatorial Nomination; Will Stand Against Sen. Benton."

Prescott appeared at the Republican state convention on June 15, 1950, in a straw hat and performed with his singing group, the Silver Dollar Quartet.

The barbershop quartet, all former presidents of the Yale Glee Club, had been formed in 1922. Their song "Silver Dollar" was published in 1939, and they sang it every time they performed:

> *You can roll a silver dollar down a line in the ground, and it'll*
> *roll because it is round.*
> *A woman never knows what a good man she's got until she turns*
> *him down.*

Picking up his guitar at that GOP convention, Prescott also sang in a booming bass: "I'm Going to Raise the Deuce When I Get Loose in Town." At fifty-five, he was still as hammy as a twelve-dollar Smithfield, but the delegates applauded his corny songs. Cheering wildly, they gave him the GOP nomination. Prescott, tall and tan, was now ready to run.

"But he was just as green as a pepper then," recalled Raymond K. Price (Yale 1950). "I was in my senior year when Bert Walker [son of George Herbert "Herbie" Walker] asked me to help out in the campaign. I was very involved in the Yale Political Union, and I was a natural to recruit for a Republican. I then recruited six other classmates, and for two or three days a week we each worked for Prescott during the last six weeks of the campaign, doing what I call 'Bushing.' We traveled with the candidate throughout the state and helped beat the bushes for Bush.

"He was a delight and quite a gentleman, but I do remember when he was taken in to visit a voter in a mobile home, he was at a loss for words. He looked around the little trailer and said, 'Well, no matter how humble there's no place like home.' He meant it as a compliment, but the voter was quite offended."

"I always thought Pres did a very good job of mingling with the ordinary guy," said John Alsop, a former member of the Connecticut House of Representatives whose family pedigree reached back to President James Monroe, "but he really didn't understand them very well. He'd just never been one."

Even his son Prescott junior agreed. "My father . . . had been a little stiff and a little awkward in [that] campaign . . . [H]e didn't quite relate to people as warmly as he could."

Hoping to attract voters from the opposition party, Prescott campaigned in Democratic strongholds. In one he was harangued by his RTM nemesis.

"Now all of a sudden you're a lover of labor," bellowed Josephine Evaristo. "Mr. Bush, I'm just talking about the members of my family that caddied for you. You never even paid them on time, and you never gave them a tip. So since when now have you become a lover of labor?" She recalled that "the house near came down with claps" after her outburst. "I never forgot when my brothers were caddy kids and he never paid them right away and he never tipped them. And the kids hated him. They really did . . . because he was cheap."

"I'm not a millionaire," Prescott told reporters. "I have a high earning power, but I never did have any capital." He estimated that if he were elected to the Senate, which paid $12,500 a year, plus a $2,500 tax-free retirement fund, he would suffer a 75 percent cut in his income of $60,000, the equivalent of $463,690 in 2004. He said his principles demanded that he make the economic sacrifice. "Why should I continue to lead a business life when I know that there are much more important things than that?"

Prescott had received a strategy briefing from U.S. Senator Ralph O. Brewster, chairman of the Republican Senatorial Campaign Committee, who told the political neophyte that the GOP policy was to concentrate all fire on Truman's Secretary of State, Dean Acheson. Acheson was to be blamed for the undeclared war in Korea and, according to the political columnist Marquis Childs, "for practically everything unpleasant that has happened since V-J day."

Bush bristled because he and Acheson (Yale 1915) served on the Yale Corporation together.

"I don't think you can make that sort of case," he told Brewster. "How do you know that Acheson is entirely to blame? What proof do you have?"

"We have all the proof we need," Brewster said.

Prescott eagerly adopted the issues of "Korea, communism, confusion and corruption." He enthusiastically charged the Truman administration with "shameful bungling," saying that American soldiers were dying in Korea because of the President's "policy of no policy that got us into an unnecessary bloody and costly war in the Far East." He personally savaged the President for leaving the United States "defenseless," and said, "None of us should shirk in the slightest way the terrible responsibility of helping provide whatever is necessary to maintain and support American troops." But he couldn't bring himself to criticize a Yale man.

Instead of citing Acheson by name, he demanded that Washington officials "tell us the full facts as to the seriousness of the war situation. I am afraid we are not yet being told how serious is the danger of what America may expect."

Everywhere Prescott went, he handed out pictures of his family, including his wife, his five children, two daughters-in-law, one son-in-law, and three of his six grandchildren. On the back of each photo, he had written: "Because I want to work for my family's future happiness and yours—I ask you to vote for me on November 7." By the end of the campaign, he had distributed eight thousand of these photographs at political rallies, filling stations, and hot-dog stands.

In 1950 there was one television station in Connecticut, WNHC-TV in New Haven, and only 90,000 sets in a state of 570,409 households. But Prescott, who was a director of the Columbia Broadcasting System, understood the penetrating power of the new medium. William S. Paley, the president and chairman of CBS, had convinced Prescott that televisions would rule the future, so he purchased as much television ad time as his campaign could afford, and programmed his spots to run before and after football games and during the World Series. His opponent, a former advertising executive at Benton and Bowles, also ran campaign commercials on TV and set up small kiosks with rear-projection screens in shopping centers and on street corners to continuously play those ads.

In November the polls showed Bush and Benton running neck and neck. But that changed on the Sunday night before the Tuesday election, when Drew Pearson broadcast his election predictions on his influential national radio show:

In Connecticut, some very unfair Communist charges have been made against Senator Brien McMahon and William Benton, despite which they have not retaliated. In fact, they have not even mentioned that Benton's opponent, Prescott Bush, who is Finance Chairman of the Birth Control League, and I predict that fair campaigning will pay dividends, and Senators McMahon and Benton will be elected.

Pearson had just dropped a megaton bomb. Prescott was living—and running for office—in a predominantly Catholic state where birth control was still illegal. Connecticut's draconian law, established in 1879, stated that any person who used any drug to prevent conception could be fined no less than fifty dollars and imprisoned for no fewer than sixty days. Anyone "who assists, abets, councils, causes, hires or commands another to commit any offense may be prosecuted and punished as if he were the principal offender."

Pearson's allegation presented Prescott with a politician's worst dilemma: to tell the truth and lose, or to lie and tough it out. Sidestepping a profile in courage, Prescott grabbed the lie. He denied that he was ever a part of the Birth Control League, which had merged with similar organizations in 1942 to become Planned Parenthood. His wife, already proficient at denying reality, staunchly supported him.

The telephones in Connecticut started ringing like rattlebones. "No, no, it's not true," said Dorothy Bush. "Of course, it's not true. He's never been on the Birth Control League at all."

Recalling the incident sixteen years later, both Bushes clung firmly to their original denials. "The cards were handed out at noon in [Catholic] churches saying 'Listen to the broadcast tonight at 6,' " recalled Dorothy Bush. "It was Sunday night . . . if it had happened the week before so you could do anything about it—but it was just that very day, 6 o'clock."

"I'd forgotten the exact sequence but that was it," said her husband. "The state then . . . [was] probably about 55 percent Catholic population with all the Italian derivation people, and Polish is very heavy, and the Catholic Church is very dominant here, and the archbishop was death on this birth control thing. They fought repeal every time it came up in the legislature and we never did get rid of that prohibition until [1965]."

Despite their vehement and righteous denials, Dorothy and Prescott had in fact been early and active supporters of Margaret Sanger, the founder of the American birth-control movement, and they joined their friends Nancy Carnegie Rockefeller and Elizabeth Hyde Brownell in supporting the goals of family planning. Drew Pearson had a copy of the letter Mrs. Sanger had sent to thousands of friends and supporters on January 8, 1947, announcing Planned Parenthood's first national fundraising effort. The goal was to raise $2 million and integrate Planned Parenthood into the health and welfare services of the country. Margaret Sanger had signed the letter as honorary chairman. Listed at the top of her letterhead as treasurer: Prescott S. Bush.

Pearson had pierced the bull's-eye with his 1950 predictions for Connecticut. Prescott lost to William Benton in an agonizingly close race by one-tenth of 1 percent, and he never forgave Drew Pearson: "His smear actually cost me the election in the opinion of every politician in the state of Connecticut because I only lost by 1,000 votes when they cast 862,000."

Thirty years later Dorothy Bush was still claiming that the columnist had lied. "Pres lost that race purely through a dirty trick," she told Alexander Cockburn for *Rolling Stone*.

The vote was so close in 1950 that the Republicans called for a statewide recount but were forced to drop their petition a week later because of "insufficient evidence" of voter irregularities. The seat was crucial to the control of the U.S. Senate: with Benton the winner, the Democrats had a 49–47 advantage.

George felt guilty for not helping his father campaign. In a letter to Gerry Bemiss he wrote: "The only thing I feel real badly about is that I did nothing, absolutely nothing, towards helping Dad in his campaign. We felt terribly about the outcome after the way Dad worked at it. I do feel that he made a lot of friends though and I think he will be hard to beat if he runs again in 1952."

A couple weeks later John Alsop wrote to a Margaret Sanger supporter saying that the word in Connecticut's Republican circles was that Prescott Bush "was beaten on account of his activities with" Planned Parenthood and that "it will probably have a frightening effect on other Republican politicians."

Still, the party regulars encouraged Prescott to capitalize on his new name recognition so he would be in position to run again in 1952. Having taken a leave from Brown Brothers Harriman to campaign, he now returned to his job and resumed his role as moderator of the RTM. But he traveled throughout Connecticut on the weekends to make speeches and attend political rallies. "During the interim he worked hard building support around the state for renomination," said Prescott junior.

In his speeches, Prescott bashed the Truman administration for "the mess in Washington," and anytime he could pillory FDR he reached a full-throated rant. He called for the abolition of the Reconstruction Finance Corporation, a program Roosevelt had expanded to provide government loans for construction projects.

"It's a feeding station for political vultures," Prescott thundered to the Women's Republican Club of Hartford, Connecticut. "Formed during a world-wide depression to meet a national emergency, the RFC served a useful purpose in the reconstruction of a badly shaken economy. But in recent years, it has been used to reconstruct . . . businesses that might bring profit to those with access to the White House . . . Undeserving borrowers, grafters and corrupt politicians have been able to get the use of our money to finance bowling alleys, beauty parlors, racetracks, resort hotels and liquor companies. In return for this generosity with the people's money, stenographers get mink coats, presidential aides vacation in luxurious resort hotels, and clerks who know the ropes suddenly become corporation executives at high salaries."

Prescott on the stump rivaled Elmer Gantry at the pulpit, and Ted Yudain reported every thunderous statement. On November 9, 1951, *Greenwich Time* carried a small item headlined "Prescott Bush Off for Europe; To Visit 'Ike.' "

The Bushes had been planning a monthlong vacation in Europe to visit England, France, and Germany with their Greenwich friends Mr. and Mrs. Samuel Meek. Since they would be in Paris for several days, Prescott decided he should meet General Dwight D. Eisenhower, the supreme Allied commander of Europe in charge of NATO. Throughout the summer and fall of 1951, GOP grandees had been making pilgrimages to Eisenhower's headquarters to try to persuade him to run for President in 1952. Prescott, who had been a strong Taft supporter, switched allegiance and jumped into the long line of Ike suppliants that included Thomas Dewey, Herbert Brownell, Lucius Clay, John Foster Dulles, and

Henry Cabot Lodge, all pleading with the general to be their standard-bearer. Prescott asked William S. Paley to provide an introduction, so the CBS president wrote to Eisenhower on November 9, 1951, and mentioned Bush's hopes to visit him at his headquarters.

The two men met on November 20, and on December 3 Eisenhower wrote to Paley: "I have already seen Prescott Bush. We had a very nice chat about ten days ago. I liked him very much." By then Prescott's letter to Ted Yudain had become the basis for yet another front-page story in *Greenwich Time*: "Bush Believes Gen. Ike Available for '52; Call Must Be Compelling."

Yudain quoted Prescott's letter in full:

It is my firm opinion that the General is a Republican and always has been. It is equally clear in my mind that he is a man with a tremendous sense of duty and that he will have to feel compelled by that sense very strongly if he is to consider the acceptance of the Republican nomination. I am convinced he would accept no other. Still the "call" will have to be unmistakably clear.

I had a very interesting talk alone with General Eisenhower at SHAPE [Supreme Headquarters Allied Powers Europe]. More than anything else, I was impressed with his humility and modesty. He is, of course, fully absorbed with his immediate responsibilities and consumed with the thought that his work in Western Europe is of paramount importance. He discussed this briefly but concisely and clearly.

His register of callers, which I signed and glanced through in the waiting room, was full of familiar names of prominent political figures from America. He is aware of the clamor for him.

I suggested that perhaps the sorry condition of our government at home might be even a more important challenge than the defense of Western Europe, since the latter was heavily dependent upon a strong, clean and wholesome administration of our domestic affairs, and that corruption from within had been proven over the centuries as great a danger as aggression from without. And I felt that the long tenure of power by the Democrats, with the resultant decline in morality, had caused a loss of respect for government on federal, state and local levels.

Someone said that when he returned home recently, General Ike "slammed the door wide open." Maybe so. But my guess is that through the door must come a more compelling call to duty than he has ever had. If so, he will heed it.

Obviously, I asked no embarrassing or leading questions respecting the General's intentions. The conclusions I have drawn are all my own.

When Prescott returned home, he resumed his speech making. He decided to spend every weekend up to the Republican convention in May stumping the state. His zeal to get the 1952 Senate nomination finally trumped his reluctance to criticize a Yale man, and now he pounded Dean Acheson for being soft on Communism. In each town, Bush addressed breathless Republicans, who were praying for Eisenhower to accept their nomination.

"When I talked to the General in France," Prescott said, "he told me about his political affiliation. 'Of course I'm a Republican. Everybody knows that.' " Even though those words contradict his printed letter, he used them at every stop to receive a standing ovation.

In 1950, Prescott mastered the first lesson in politics: name recognition. In 1952, he felt all he had to do was show the delegates how well known and worthy he was and the nomination would be his. Unfortunately, he hadn't read the part in the political playbook about the boys in the back room.

The Republican governor of the state, John Davis Lodge, decided that Prescott was not dynamic enough to win, so Lodge threw his support to William A. Purtell, a gregarious Catholic from Hartford whose region and religion were major assets in Connecticut.

"In state politics the governor commands an enormous amount of influence because he controls the patronage," said Prescott Bush Jr., "and as a result he was able to swing enough votes to Purtell to defeat my father . . . At that point [my father] said, 'Well, that's it. I've given it two chances and the party thinks somebody else can do it better. So I'm through.' "

The convention loss was a humbling experience for a proud man, and Prescott limped home thoroughly demoralized. He'd run and lost twice and didn't want to do it again. In mid-June 1952, he went back to work at Brown Brothers. In July, he threw his support behind Purtell, and even held a reception for him in Greenwich.

That summer the rising star of Connecticut politics was the state's senior senator, Brien McMahon, a dazzlingly articulate Irish Catholic who had graduated from Yale Law School. He had announced his candidacy for President with the campaign slogan "The Man Is McMahon." His platform sought to ensure world peace through the fear of atomic weapons. His promising campaign capsized when he was diagnosed with cancer. He withdrew his candidacy, but the Connecticut delegates to the Democratic National Convention still nominated him as their choice for President on July 27, 1952. The following morning Senator McMahon fell into a coma. The next day he died.

His death became national political news because suddenly the control of the U.S. Senate pivoted on the two seats from Connecticut. Governor Lodge appointed William Purtell to hold the McMahon seat until Connecticut's Republicans could nominate a candidate. With Purtell's temporary appointment, the Republicans in the U.S. Senate now had forty-eight votes, bringing them to a tie with the Democrats.

Party leaders believed the GOP's best chances of wresting Senate control from the Democrats turned on the two seats in Connecticut, which had the best chance of going Republican with Eisenhower at the top of the ticket.

Prescott was licking his wounds at his vacation home on Fishers Island when the GOP delegation arrived. "About seven of them," he recalled. "They [came] to beg me to stand for nomination. I said, 'Listen fellows, I've had it. I've destroyed all my files. I'm not going around that state again with my hat in my hand.' "

As he wrote to his friend Sam Bemiss on August 5, 1952: "It is not my intention to make any effort for the . . . nomination . . . but if [it] should come to me I believe I should accept and work very hard for a victory which looks possible in Connecticut this time."

Prescott junior remembers the state chairman telling his father, "We'll do everything we can to make sure you win."

"My father said, 'Look fellows, I went flat out to get the nomination at the last convention and was rejected.' He said, 'I felt I was owed that after the 1950 race when I was a novice. But if you will deliver the nomination—I'm not going to work for the nomination—but if you deliver the nomination then I will be glad to run and I'll work as hard as I know how . . . I don't know what's different between me now and in May, nothing is changed, I'm the same person.' "

The national committeeman patiently explained that events had changed, not people, and with Eisenhower as the nominee the Republicans could sweep the state in 1952, and four years later, when Prescott would be running again. "You're lucky you didn't get it in 1950," Meade Alcorn said. Out of earshot he muttered, "The stupid bastard can't lose this one unless, of course, he shits in his damn straw hat."

Some party leaders had grown tired of Prescott's plodding speeches and his barbershop-quartet gigs. As *The Bridgeport Telegram* noted, "Republicans don't think of him as a world-beater in the field of oratory and . . . he might not be as strong a campaigner as another . . . he's more like an old comfortable shoe."

Prescott considered what the party leaders had to offer. "I thought it over pretty carefully, and all of the old thoughts came back to me, do you see, resurgence of interest, and I suddenly realized: well, my God, maybe I will be a U.S. Senator yet."

En route to the convention in September, the "old comfortable shoe" nearly tripped on the sharp stiletto of Clare Boothe Luce, who swooped in at the last minute and decided she would like to be nominated for Brien McMahon's seat. The former congresswoman and playwright was a bombastic, colorful speaker who roused Republicans when she called Truman's Democrats "lynch-loving Bourbons, economic spoonies, political bubble-heads and wampum and boodle boys." Now with a flip of her elegant wrist, she dismissed Prescott as "Wall Street Bush," saying, "He's a good loser, and he's getting better at it all the time."

"Clare was just determined that she wanted to be the senator," said Prescott Bush Jr., "and so she and her husband, Harry Luce, launched her campaign to defeat my father."

Recalled Prescott senior, "She hired a big ballroom at the Bond Hotel [in Hartford] the night before the convention and held open house for all the delegates. They all went and ate her food and drank her beverages and had a gay old time. And I didn't have any headquarters. I stood out in the lobby of the Bond Hotel and shook hands with everybody that came and went and talked with them. But I was not concerned because I felt that . . . we were going to get it on the first ballot."

Prescott enjoyed a close friendship with Harry Luce, but he was wary of Harry's wife. "I've always been a little frightened of Clare, because I don't deal easily with women who are severe or terribly determined . . . I've always been afraid of women who are pithy and sharp and sarcastic at times and that sort of thing . . . I've always been trained, and trained myself, to be deferential to them, and I don't know how to deal with them when they respond differently." (As a senator, Prescott opposed the Equal Rights Amendment, which was approved by the U.S. Senate in 1953, barring laws discriminating against women because of their sex. "I am for preferred rights for women, always have been and always will be," he said.)

As the party leaders had promised, Prescott got the nomination for the remainder of McMahon's four-year term. His opponent was the popular congressman from Hartford, Abraham A. Ribicoff, described by *Time* magazine as "the best Democratic vote-getter in the state." When Averell Harriman came to Connecticut to endorse Ribicoff, Prescott became incensed.

"I regard him [Harriman] as unqualified for public service because of his surrender to the left wing of the Democratic party," he said of his former business partner. "His political thinking and judgement have changed completely since he ceased active participation in our firm years ago to enter government."

Prescott junior and his wife, Betty Lou, who had moved to Greenwich in 1950, spent their weekends campaigning, while George H. Walker Jr., "Uncle Herbie," served as his brother-in-law's major fundraiser. From Texas, George sent a fifty-dollar check with a note to his Uncle Herbie: "Your efforts on Dad's behalf are terrific . . . I am attaching a small donation—its size in no way reflects my interest, for I find myself thinking all the time about things up there in Conn.—Dad just has to win this time."

Nancy Bush Ellis, who lived in Boston, came to Connecticut with her daughter, Nandy, and posed for a campaign picture holding a sign: "Win with Bush!" From his dormitory at Yale, Jonathan called frequently to compare figures on the statewide polls. At Hotchkiss, Bucky was too young to understand the importance of this race to his father.

The first thing Prescott did for his third attempt at public office was to hire an Irish Catholic campaign manager named Elmer Ryan.

"Do you think that my being a Protestant and not a Catholic is apt to affect me in this 1952 election?" he asked.

"Oh, no, Pres, don't worry about that," said Ryan. "We just look upon a Protestant as a Catholic who flunked his Latin."

Driving around the state with the Bushes, the campaign manager noticed the billboards that said: "You're Better Off with Ribicoff."

"I wish we could develop something to offset that slogan: 'You're better off with Ribicoff.' That's pretty good."

Dotty spoke up from the front seat: "You're in a jam with Abraham." Ryan laughed, and the next day Prescott used the phrase. "Don't believe that sign that says you're better off with Ribicoff," he said in a speech. "The fact is you'll be in a jam with Abraham."

As he recalled the "unhappy" incident years later, some people misinterpreted his remarks. "So I was faced with the charge of being anti-Semitic right away. I remember the editor of my paper [Ted Yudain] and his brother [Bernie Yudain], both of whom were of Jewish persuasion, came to see me at the house as soon as this all appeared in the papers, and they had telephone calls from Hartford, 'What about Bush, is he anti-Semitic?'

". . . I told them exactly what had happened . . . They were perfectly satisfied with it. Well, it was one of those things that was here today and gone tomorrow because it was obviously not designed to be anti-Semitic. If I'd wanted to be anti-Semitic I'd have attacked it in a mighty different way than that . . . There wasn't any thought of anti-Semitism in it. None at all. I would be too stupid to do a thing like that."

The morning after his "jam with Abraham" remark, Prescott delivered a fighting-mad breakfast speech to 180 people, and Ted Yudain gave him the front page of *Greenwich Time* to defend himself by accusing the Democrats of "smears that make me anti-Semitic." He then said that Ribicoff liked to pose for pictures with servicemen because he "sat out World War II in Hartford." Prescott's campaign brochures carried a picture of him standing with his son George in his naval uniform, under which was written: "In World War I Pres Bush served under fire in the Meuse-Argonne offensive and rose from private to Captain of Artillery.

Here he is with son George, World War II Navy pilot who survived being shot down twice in the Pacific."

Prescott was exonerated from the charges of anti-Semitism by his hometown paper, *Greenwich Time*, as well as by *The Harvard Crimson*. Reporting the charges on November 1, 1952, Michael J. Halberstam wrote: "Ribicoff's backers are incensed because of what they term Bush's anti-Semitic innuendos; he constantly refers to his opponent as 'Abraham' or 'Abe Ribicoff.' The charge is at best a tenuous one."

Emboldened by editorial endorsements from *The New York Times* and the *Herald Tribune*, Prescott accused President Truman of "dropping the match that lit the fires of war in Korea." After refusing to release his personal-income figures, he lashed the members of the administration for misusing taxpayers' money and described them as an "evil gang of left wingers." He made a major speech calling for "a spiritual and moral reawakening." All of these elements would surface fifty years later in the political campaigns of his grandson George W. Bush.

Prescott knew that his biggest campaign asset was the beloved Dwight D. Eisenhower. So when the general came to Connecticut, Prescott made sure he accompanied Eisenhower to New Haven and introduced him at Yale. More than six thousand people braved an unseasonable snowstorm that day to hear Ike denounce his rival, Adlai Stevenson. The *Yale Daily News* reported a few boos as Prescott stepped forward in his raccoon coat, waving his arms and acting as the general's cheerleader. On Election Day, New Haven, which had not gone Republican since 1924, gave its heart to Stevenson by more than six thousand votes.

Shortly before the election, Senator Joe McCarthy, the red-meat Republican from Wisconsin, arrived in Connecticut to campaign for the GOP ticket. The bellicose solon's crusade against Communists packed the Kline Memorial Hall in Bridgeport, where he held up a beefy hand claiming to have the names of one hundred Communists in the State Department. Prescott had wanted to boycott the rally, but the state's Republican leaders insisted that he and Senator Purtell attend.

"I never saw such a wild bunch of monkeys in any meeting that I've ever attended," Prescott recalled. "We were seated on the stage, both

Purtell and myself, and also two or three others who were invited to speak before McCarthy spoke.

The national committeeman and the Connecticut state chairman welcomed McCarthy warmly. Then it was Prescott's turn to speak.

"I went out on the stage with my knees shaking considerably and I said that I was very glad to welcome a Republican Senator to our state and that we had many reasons to admire Joe McCarthy. In some ways he was a very unusual man. At least he had done one very unusual thing—he had created a new word in the English language, which is 'McCarthyism.' With that everybody screamed with delight.

"Then I said, 'But I must in all candor say that some of us, while we admire his objectives in his fight against Communism, we have very considerable reservations sometimes concerning the methods which he employs.' With that the roof went off with boos and hisses and catcalls and 'Throw him out.' But I finished my remarks with one or two innocuous sentences and sat down. They booed and screamed at me. Joe McCarthy got up from across the stage and walked over and shook hands with me. I was taken aback by this very friendly gesture in view of all the booing going on . . . He said, 'I want you to have dinner with me after this show's over' . . . I said, 'Fine, Senator, I'll be delighted.' "

The national committeeman James C. Shannon publicly rebuked Bush for his "reservations," and *The Hartford Courant* reported the story with the headline "GOPs Boo Bush's Anti-smear Stand." Vivien Kellems, who also attended the McCarthy rally, declared Prescott's behavior outrageously stupid. She said, "Mr. Prescott Bush rather pathetically committed political suicide and erased himself from the political scene." However, *The Manchester Herald* commended Prescott's courage and said, whether it was foolhardy or not, "Bush has reserved a corner of Bush he knows he can live with. And in our observation of the political game, that kind of thing has never really turned out to be weakness."

The Eisenhower landslide swept Bush and Purtell to victory in November, giving Connecticut its first two Republican senators in twenty years. Bush defeated Ribicoff by 28,960 votes, but Ribicoff pulled more votes than his party's presidential contender, which laid the foundation for his political future as governor, cabinet member, and U.S. senator. Although Bush trailed Eisenhower by 51,547 votes, he had won the unexpired term of Brien McMahon, which meant that he became a senator as soon as his election was certified, making him the state's senior senator. Purtell, who beat Senator Benton, became the junior senator, and could not be seated until January 3, when the new Congress convened.

Before leaving for Washington, D.C., Prescott convened the Representative Town Meeting to turn over his gavel. "I feel like a small boy who had asked for a small toy at Christmas, and came down stairs and found a Cadillac," he said. "It is not my privilege to own a [real] Cadillac but . . . I hope to drive my political Cadillac well."

That evening, in a letter to Whitney Griswold, the president of Yale University, Prescott confided his fear of the future: "I find myself now rather trembling with apprehension as I face this new life. Maybe, however, it will be like a ballgame, the nervousness wearing off after the first few plays. Believe me I welcome your prayers and your hopes for me. If I fail, it will not be for lack of trying hard."

Prescott said he intended to continue his service on the Yale Corporation, which would bring him to New Haven at least once a month. Then he addressed a subject of particular concern: "I would like you to sit down with me sometime alone and explain why it was that the Yale faculty was not with us in this election. I noted that the Harvard faculty was with us. This should be purely an impersonal conversation. I feel that I really need a better understanding of the point of view of that wonderful faculty regarding politics."

The next day he packed his straw hat and headed for Washington.

CHAPTER EIGHT

arbara had not noticed the bruises on her little girl's arms and legs, but she was puzzled by Robin's continuing listlessness and wondered why she seemed to have so little energy. "It seemed wrong for her to be that exhausted . . . She had been a normal three-year-old, and suddenly her schedule for the day was to lie down someplace."

Weeks before, on February 11, 1953, Barbara had given birth to the Bushes' third child, John Ellis Bush, known as Jebby, and the baby was already eating more than his three-year-old sister, who only picked at her food. So Barbara made an appointment for Robin to see the family's pediatrician. Dr. Dorothy Wyvell examined the youngster, asked about the black-and-blue contusions, and took a blood test. She told Barbara to take the little girl home and come back in the afternoon with George to discuss the test results.

Robin had been born in Compton, California, and after a year in the state the Bushes moved to Texas. They lived in Odessa for six months, and then moved to Midland, where George and his neighbor John Overbey, an oil and gas lease broker, conceived the idea of starting their own oil-exploration business. They wanted to create a company to purchase mineral rights next to properties that were being drilled for oil.

Typically, large oil companies bought up leases at a fixed price to explore for minerals. The landowners retained royalties, which entitled them to a percentage of the oil found on their properties. An independent company, such as Bush-Overbey, would buy a percentage of the landowners' royalties; if oil was found, the landowner got his royalty, and the independent company got whatever royalty it had negotiated with the landowner. If the independent company dug a dry well, the company lost its investment, but the landowner was protected by rental fees from the independent company as well as the big oil company. George Bush described this high-risk business as speculating in royalty percentages.

In a rush to get rich, George told Neil Mallon about his plans to leave and start this new business with John Overbey. Neil, who had given George his start at Dresser with the expectation that he would one day run the company, encouraged him to go out on his own. Mallon even took the time to explain how to structure and finance an independent oil company. George knew that he would need a minimum of $1 million to get started, so he turned to the family's financier, Herbie Walker. Using the designated high-risk portion of assets he invested for a group of large British trust funds, Uncle Herbie provided $350,000 in capital. Eugene Meyer, the owner of *The Washington Post* and a client of Brown Brothers Harriman, provided $100,000, half of which was in the name of his son-in-law, Philip L. Graham. John Overbey recalled that Prescott Bush provided another $50,000—a fact George never mentioned to biographers. The omission suggests his reluctance to be seen as anything less than a "self-made" success.

"Most big investors were in the East," George said, "so we spent as much time scouring the big cities for funds as we did the farmlands for oil rights."

Bush-Overbey was not selling a tangible product, simply a speculation in oil leases and mineral rights. Their real business was providing a tax shelter for their wealthy investors. As George explained it: "To get money, we'd have to attract investors outside the business, people willing to take a risk on an oil venture. If we struck oil, our investors would get a percentage of the income, depending on the amount of their investment; if the well proved dry, they could write off their losses."

He traveled constantly to woo Uncle Herbie's rich East Coast contacts and throughout Texas researching courthouses for land records. He happened to be in the Ector County courthouse, twenty miles from Midland, when Barbara called to say that they had an emergency appointment with Robin's pediatrician that afternoon.

Dr. Wyvell greeted the Bushes with tears in her eyes. She sat them down and said their child had leukemia, a cancer that floods the bloodstream with millions of abnormal white blood cells.

"Robin has the highest white blood cell count I've ever seen," the doctor said.

"Well, let's do something," said George. "What do we do?"

"George, you can't do anything about leukemia."

"There's nothing you can't do something about," George insisted.

"There is no cure for leukemia," said Dr. Wyvell. "I advise you to let nature take its course. Spare yourself the agony of treatment for this is an advanced case."

In 1953, nearly every child diagnosed with leukemia died within six months. Dr. Wyvell gave Robin three weeks.

"The doctor gave us the best advice anyone could have given, which, of course, we didn't take," recalled Barbara many years later. "She said, 'Number one, don't tell anyone. Number two, don't treat her. You should take her home; make life as easy as possible for her' . . . George said, 'No way.' He immediately dropped me home, went straight over to my friend Liz Fowler's house, and said, 'Liz, please go down and see Barbara. The doctor says Robin has leukemia.' So we broke the first rule before we got going. When he got home later that day, he called his uncle, who worked at Sloan-Kettering hospital in New York."

Dr. John M. Walker, the brother of George's mother, Dorothy, had joined Memorial Sloan-Kettering in 1952 as a clinical assistant in surgery. Acknowledged as the best athlete in his exceedingly athletic family, he had played championship football, baseball, squash, and golf. Then he was struck with polio in 1950 and lost most of the use of his limbs, eventually becoming bound to a wheelchair.

George was forever grateful to his Uncle John for using his influence to get Robin admitted to Sloan-Kettering for the experimental cancer treatments that extended her life a few months. "I hated the chemotherapy, for her, but it was very good for us," said Barbara. "We had a chance to work out, to tell her we loved her."

Years later, when George became President and was in a position to do something significant for his uncle, he nominated Dr. Walker's son John M. Walker Jr. to a federal judgeship, appointing him to the U.S. Court of Appeals for the Second Circuit. "It's the least I can do for someone whose father did so much for me," George told one of his White House lawyers. "Besides, Johnny's as well qualified as anyone else for the position."

In addition to his own handicap, Dr. Walker had two daughters born with Down syndrome. His most important influence on George was giving him sensitivity to the needs of the disabled that he might not otherwise have developed. For most of his life George remained insensitive to the imperative of racial justice and had a consistently less than admirable record on civil rights. He did, however, become a champion for the disabled. His admiration for his uncle, who had been crippled at the height of his career, led George to his finest hour as President: on July 26, 1990, he signed the Americans with Disabilities Act, only three weeks before his Uncle John, then eighty-one, died of complications from an aneurysm.

Not all members of the Bush family were quite so sensitive to the issue. When the ADA bill was first introduced in Congress in the late 1980s, George was Vice President under Ronald Reagan. His younger brother Jonathan, named after Dr. Walker, happened to be visiting Washington during a Senate debate on the legislation, first proposed by Connecticut Senator Lowell Weicker, who had graduated from Yale with Jonathan in 1953. That evening Jonathan returned to New York City to attend his first board meeting of *American Heritage*, the magazine then owned by his father's good friend Samuel P. Reed. The meeting was held in a private dining room of the Knickerbocker Club, where the younger Bush was introduced to the board of directors. Everyone applauded as he stood to say a few words.

"Well, I've just come up from Washington, where I was listening to Teddy Kennedy make a speech for the crips," he said, using a pejorative term for "cripples."

There was a moment of stunned silence until the editor Byron Dobell spoke up, reprimanding Jonathan for mocking the disabled. "Even if you think that, you should not say it," Dobell said.

After the meeting, one of the directors approached the editor.

"Boy, that was something—speaking up like that to the brother of the Vice President of the United States."

"It never crossed my mind to let it pass," said Dobell. "I thought what he said was preposterous, and for grown men to sit around and not say anything would have been even more preposterous."

George might have remained as unenlightened as his brother had it not been for John Walker's intervention on behalf of his dying daughter. As he wrote to his friend Paul Dorsey:

He was a great cancer surgeon . . . a strong purposeful man. I told him of our local doc's advice and he said, "You have no choice— none at all—you must treat this child. You must do all you can to keep her alive." And he went on to tell me of the strides in the field and of the importance of hope. So we treated her and we watched her die before our eyes, but we also saw the wonders of remission and the dedication of the nurses and doctors, and we saw progress and we knew his advice was right. Six months later when it was all over—I thought back with gratitude for this sensible advice—it was tough on Barbara—I guess the toughest assignment a mother could have—for she was there for the bone marrow tests—the ordeals of blood. Someone had to look into Robin's eyes and give her comfort and love and somehow, Paul, I didn't have the guts.

The day after George's conversation with Dr. Walker, the Bushes flew Robin to New York City to begin the experimental treatments. For the next six months she was, in the words of Epictetus, "a little spirit bearing up a corpse."

Years later Barbara would remember the plane ride from Texas, because up to that point she had had a history of getting airsick. "But the first time we took Robin to New York, I got on and off the plane and didn't get sick. Robin needed me, and I wasn't thinking about myself. I haven't been airsick since."

Barbara left her six-year-old boy, Georgie, and her newborn baby, Jeb, in the care of neighbors while she poured herself into shepherding her daughter through the harrowing miasma of bone-marrow biopsies, blood transfusions, and chemotherapy. In New York City, she stayed with Ganny and Gampy Walker in their sumptuous Sutton Place penthouse, only a few blocks from Sloan-Kettering. Eventually George's mother sent a nurse to Midland to take care of George and his two sons, who moved back into their own small home on West Ohio Street. Barbara spent months in New York, concentrating solely on her young daughter. She knew Robin was going to die; she was too much of a realist not to accept that fact. But there was also the hope for the occasional remission, a temporary respite from the rampaging cancer that was devouring the little girl's cells. Barbara threw all she had toward that fleeting incentive, and from time to time she was rewarded. On one occasion, Robin felt well enough to be taken out of the hospital to Sutton Place to visit her great-grandparents for a day. Another time she went to Greenwich to see her grandparents. Barbara also took the little girl home to Midland for a few weeks, but Robin hemorrhaged there and had to be flown back to New York. Her last trip out of the hospital was to Kennebunkport, in the summer, where she saw her brothers.

During the time of Robin's illness Bush-Overbey was making only a modest profit, but George's silk carpet ride into the oil business had drawn the attention of Hugh and Bill Liedtke, two slow-talking, quick-thinking lawyers from Tulsa, Oklahoma, who specialized in forming oil partnerships. They had offices down the hall from the Bush-Overbey Oil Development Company in the Midland National Bank building, and the four men and their families soon became friends and began socializing regularly.

"There wasn't much else to do in Midland then but get together for barbecues," recalled Hugh Liedtke. At that time, the small dust bowl of a town had a population of twenty-five thousand people, a few churches, a lot of saloons, one movie theater, and one brothel.

"George put that whorehouse to good use when Dresser decided to have a board meeting in Midland," recalled Stephen Thayer, Neil Mallon's stepson. "George had to make the arrangements for the board, and there was no hotel in Midland high-rent enough for that group at the time, so he rented the whorehouse, where the board and their wives stayed for a week."

In 1953, Bush, Overbey, and the Liedtke brothers decided to merge their businesses and create an oil company that they named after the Mexican revolutionary Emiliano Zapata. "There was a Zapata movie playing at the time, starring Marlon Brando," recalled Liedtke. "We needed a name, something that would pique people's curiosity, and we thought that sounded pretty good."

First they formed Zapata Petroleum; a year later they created Zapata Offshore Company. After George severed his business relations with them, the Liedtkes merged the original Zapata into South Penn Oil Company. With the help of J. Paul Getty, one of the firm's largest stockholders, Hugh Liedtke engineered a friendly takeover that became Pennzoil. He would later acquire Getty Oil Company, sue Texaco into bankruptcy, and refuse to settle with the bankruptcy lawyers until 1987, when he convinced a jury that Texaco should pay Pennzoil $3 billion. George had indeed found himself one tough business partner. Liedtke was so tough he would eventually even butt heads with George's great benefactor, Uncle Herbie.

In the beginning, the decision was made that each side of the partnership would be responsible for raising $500,000. So, once again, knowing that Uncle Herbie would never deny him anything, George tapped the family bank for his share. Herbie Walker was so besotted with his nephew that for the first twenty years of George's marriage, he and Barbara repeatedly vacationed with Herbie and his wife, Mary, with Uncle Herbie always paying the way.

George Herbert Walker Jr. revered his namesake nephew to the point that it made his own sons uncomfortable. "I was annoyed by all the energy George was receiving that should have gone to my brother," said Ray Walker, a psychiatrist and the youngest of Herbie's three children. "Hero worship of someone outside himself was very much a part of my father's makeup. First it was George. Then, when Dad owned the Mets [1960–77], it was Tom Seaver. Dad had an unlived life. He latched on to George because they both believed in money and power as the priorities in life.

"I remember my Yale roommate, Bob Gow, who ran Zapata for a while, telling me how Dad would call George all the time, and George would hold the phone away from his ear so he wouldn't have to listen to Dad drone on and on and on. He'd just say, 'Yes, yes, yes.' But that's the kind of guy George is. He's ingratiating and likable . . . It's impossible not to like him . . . but he's definitely a yes-man. Dad loved that."

Herbie Walker realized that George's principal role as a partner in Zapata was to be a pipeline to capital, so the investment banker raised $1.3 million for his nephew to start up his new venture. That sum included investments from the Rockefellers and the Astors. Uncle Herbie, who also made money from these transactions, would continue to be George's golden goose throughout his business career. In 1990, *The New Republic* placed the cumulative amount he had raised for George's various oil ventures over the years at $7 million.

The Liedtkes had their own access to big money through their father, who was chief counsel to Gulf Oil. George's original partner, John Overbey, unfortunately did not have a money spout in his family, so he was eased out of the partnership when George and his uncle created an entity called Walker-Bush Corporation, which became the owner of Bush-Overbey.

Zapata Petroleum plunged $850,000 of the original investment into a single oil field, and to everyone's amazement the gamble paid off. The oil came gushing in. As Bill Liedtke told the *Houston Business Journal* in 1999: "We drilled 130 wells and never had a dry hole."

During their daughter's illness, while George was flying back and forth from Texas to New York on the private planes of his rich oil friends, Barbara became a maternal martinet, laying down the law to her children, her husband, her friends, her relatives, and even her formidable mother-in-law. "I wouldn't let George junior play with Robin because she bruised so easily," Barbara said. "In fact, I kept the kids apart almost that whole time. We didn't tell Georgie, because we thought he was too young to know [that his sister was dying]. Actually, I was afraid he would tell Robin and I didn't want her to know. I was very firm at the time and, I suspect, rather tough. I made up my mind that she was going to be happy. If anybody cried in Robin's hospital room, I'd ask them gently to please leave the room. Poor George. It just killed him. I'd have to say, 'If you cry, you can't stay.' " She said that her husband and his mother were the worst offenders. "They were just too softhearted."

Barbara was forced many times to reexamine her decision not to tell her oldest son about his sister's terminal illness. "I don't know if that was right or wrong," she told *The Washington Post* in 1999. "I mean I really don't but I know he [Georgie] said to me several times, 'You know, why didn't you tell me?' Well, it wouldn't have made a difference . . . [And besides] we thought he was too young to cope with it."

Barbara was implacably strong during Robin's illness, whereas George was emotionally fragile. So much so that his good friend Lud Ashley stepped in as a kind of surrogate to support Barbara, visiting Robin on a regular basis and looking in on the little girl at night when Barbara had returned to the Walkers' penthouse to sleep.

Raising money for his new oil venture brought George to New York frequently, and he always joined Barbara at the hospital, but the pitiful sight of his little daughter enveloped in tubes and so weak she could not even lift her hand to wipe her runny nose was sometimes more than he could bear. Despite his best intentions, George frequently broke down when he walked into his daughter's room, and Barbara would make him leave until he could pull himself together.

"Poor George had the most dreadful time and could hardly stand to see her get a blood transfusion," Barbara wrote in her memoir. "He would say that he had to go to the men's room. We used to laugh and wonder if Robin thought he had the weakest bladder in the world. Not true. He just had the most tender heart."

Only twenty-eight years old, Barbara had no one to turn to during this time. Her husband was traveling constantly for his new business venture. Her mother, from whom she had been estranged, was dead. Her father, now president of McCall Corporation, had remarried and was immersed in his new life. Many of her Texas friends had withdrawn from her, fearing, as many people do, such close proximity to cancer and death. She was not close to either of her brothers, and her older sister, Martha Rafferty, who frequently donated blood used for Robin's many transfusions, was busy raising her own large family. Barbara found her greatest comfort in the company of the distressed and ailing who were all around her, and she bonded with other mothers in the hospital who were also overseeing the last days of their dying children.

The prickly part of her personality softened in the hospital. The raw toughness that could ruffle country-club sensibilities came through as firm resolve to the no-nonsense nurses. Barbara related well to the medical staff and placed all her confidence in their recommendations. When they suggested a risky operation to arrest the internal bleeding caused by the drugs Robin had been given, Barbara, who could not reach her husband, made the decision to go ahead, despite Dr. Walker's advice to the contrary. She was hoping against hope that the surgery would buy Robin more time, but the little girl never came out of the operation. "One minute she was there, and the next she was gone," Barbara wrote in her memoir. "I truly felt her soul go out of that beautiful little body . . . [and never] felt the presence of God more strongly than at that moment."

On the evening of October 11, 1953, George was en route to Manhattan when his daughter fell into a coma. Two months shy of her fourth birthday, she slipped away shortly after he arrived at the hospital. The next day he and Barbara went to Rye to play golf with her father.

"It was the first day we'd been out," said Barbara. "We just got up and went out. Played golf. Didn't tell anyone. I later thought that if people had seen us, they would have said, 'Why are those people doing that?' We just wanted to get away."

That day *Greenwich Time* carried Robin's obituary and said a private memorial service would be held at Christ Church Chapel. There was no funeral because the Bushes decided to leave their daughter's organs to the scientists at Sloan-Kettering. Dorothy Bush and Lud Ashley later buried her in the Bush family plot in Greenwich, Connecticut, but George and Barbara did not attend.

Yet, from the day Robin died, she remained a part of the family. Barbara put her portrait, a gift commissioned by Dorothy Walker Bush, above the living-room mantel, and whenever she was asked how many children she had, she always included Robin in the count. This unnerved some of her friends, who didn't know what to say or how to react in the face of such a tragedy. Barbara said she resented people for not mentioning Robin or for acting as if she had never existed. She vowed to have another daughter as soon as she could, and she kept getting pregnant until she did. Neil was born in 1955; Marvin in 1956. Finally, in 1959, after a miscarriage, Dorothy Walker Bush arrived, and Barbara, thirty-four, stopped having children.

It was many years before she or George could talk about their little girl's death without crying, but the day finally came when Barbara could say, "I now look back at Robin as a blessing."

During the long months of Robin's hospitalization, Barbara's strength emerged as never before, as did George's frailty. But after their daughter died, the marital dynamic changed. Stripped to the emotional bone, Barbara fell to pieces. She cried constantly and tried to retreat into solitary sadness. George, who now functioned better than he had during his daughter's excruciating illness, rallied his wife. It was his turn to carry them through the worst ordeal parents can endure, and he continually distracted her with friends and activities. Still, Barbara's hair turned white, she ground her teeth at night, and she smoked two packs of cigarettes a day. A heavy, mourning matron took possession of the large-boned body where once had lived an athletic young woman.

"He wouldn't let me be alone," she recalled many years later. "He held me in his arms, and he made me share it, and accept that his sorrow was as great as my own. He simply wouldn't allow my grief to divide us . . . push us apart, which is what happens so often where there is a loss like that."

Barbara frequently spoke of "other people who could not survive such a trauma without a divorce." The truth is that no matter what marital strain she would endure as George's wife, she never had to worry about the dissolution of her marriage. She had married a mommy's man who was constitutionally incapable of doing anything that would dishonor his mother, and to Dorothy and Prescott Bush the one abomination that even God could not forgive was divorce.

Divorce was so repugnant to them that they actually shunned Prescott's brother, James, when he left his first wife, Caroline Patterson, after nineteen years of marriage. They had three children, one of whom was killed in 1915 in the car James was driving.

James Bush left his first family to marry an elegant New York socialite named Janet Newbold Rhinelander Stewart, who had two children by two previous marriages. Exquisitely beautiful, Mrs. Stewart was on the same "Ten Best-Dressed Women" list as the Duchess of Windsor, and she wore pearls the size of eggs. She, too, came from a moneyed background but was far too glamorous for the midwestern likes of Prescott and Dorothy Bush. Rigorous in their rectitude, they refused to accept her as James's legitimate wife. They never forgave him for leaving a woman whose "good family" was distantly related to the National Cash Register fortune. Divorce left no room for redemption with Prescott and Dorothy, and their children grew up very much aware that their parents had barred their uncle from their home because of his marital mistake. "They never spoke to him," recalled Nancy Bush Ellis.

"It's true," said Serena Stewart, James Bush's stepdaughter, who lived with him and her mother in St. Louis for the duration of their four-year marriage. "We never saw Prescott and his wife during that time. They never visited or called or wrote. Nothing."

The cold shunning of their uncle was a powerful example for the five Bush children. While some of them, particularly Nancy and George, would eventually embark on long, serious extramarital affairs of their own—Nancy with the historian Arthur Schlesinger Jr., and George with his secretary Jennifer Fitzgerald—they would never sever their marriages. By the time George entered politics, he had developed the compartmentalized mentality of a Mafia don who keeps home and hearth separate from work and play. He infused that Mafia mind-set with a touch of Molière, who said, "It is public scandal that offends; to sin in secret is no sin at all." George and Barbara understood and respected each other's boundaries. Hers was home, where she reigned as the mother of his children; his was work, where he did what he did without threatening his wife's security or social standing. Although George was not referring to sexual dalliances when he wrote to his friend Paul Dorsey in 1967, he did indicate how he segmented his personal and professional lives: "Because I keep my business and politics separate from my home life—usually that is. She [Barbara] is not informed on issues and intrigue—perhaps this is selfish on my part but we have a close, close relationship with the kids, et al, and I just want to have that oasis of privacy."

In the fall of 1953, as Robin's days were drawing to an end, Prescott Bush asked Barbara to accompany him to the Putnam Cemetery in Greenwich to see the small family plot he had purchased on a shady hillside. Next to a freshly planted dogwood tree he had had erected a modest granite headstone that said "BUSH." As Barbara and her father-in-law paced off the site, she was genuinely touched. "That darling man bought that lot so Robin would have a place to rest."

Barbara remembered the fifty-eight-year-old senator looking disapprovingly at some of the elaborate death mansions on top of the hill.

"I knew old so-and-so," he said. "He certainly thought highly of himself, didn't he, Bar?"

Prescott had no way of knowing then that his own tombstone would one day draw the same kind of unflattering observation, for he would be laid to rest nineteen years later under a pile of the most grandiose nouns his widow could bestow. After selecting a black-onyx gravestone rimmed with never-tarnish bronze, Dorothy, the family's mythmaker, directed the following be inscribed in large raised never-tarnish bronze letters:

PRESCOTT S. BUSH

1895–1972

UNITED STATES SENATOR 1952–1963

LEADER, ATHLETE, SINGER, SOLDIER, BANKER, STATESMAN,

CHURCHMAN, COMPANION, FRIEND, FATHER,

HUSBAND EXTRAORDINARY.

After Robin's burial in 1953, the Bush family plot would welcome Prescott (1972), Dorothy (1992), and Prescott's brother, James (1978), who by then had left his third wife for another woman and alienated himself from almost everyone in the Bush family. His granite stone is shoved toward the bottom of the plot, barely noticeable in the grass, which is how the family treated him during his disgraceful last years. His death was "a great relief to all of us," George admitted to the State Department official who shipped James Bush's body home from the Philippines, where he died destitute in a veterans hospital. His uncle's alcoholism, plus his many marriages and divorces, had embarrassed George and the family for years.

There was more than just embarrassment to George's disdain. He wanted to keep hidden that his Uncle Jim, late in life, had embezzled $750,000; such a revelation could be politically damaging to George's aspirations for high office. "No one in the family knew all the details of what happened," Serena Stewart said. "I talked to Jim's daughter, Shelley Bush Jansing, about it and she confirmed the embezzlement—we both knew the amount—but we didn't know—and still don't—how he did it and how he got away with it . . . Only George knows all those details and he would never tell anyone, not even Shelley . . . My mother, Jim Bush's second wife, knew that he had embezzled three-quarters of a million dollars after the end of his third marriage [1970] and fled the country . . . By then he had been in banking for years and had been a director of the Export-Import Bank [1959–63] . . . so I guess he knew how to move money around." A friend of Jim's fourth and final wife said: "The money that Jim ran off with supposedly was Rockefeller money from accounts that Jim was handling as an investment manager."

Like his brother, Prescott, James Smith Bush had seemed blessed by fate. He followed his brother to Yale, where he, too, was Skull and Bones. Upon graduation Jim embarked on a career in investment banking. He married Caroline Patterson of Dayton, Ohio, became a managing partner in G. H. Walker and Company, and served in World War II as a lieutenant colonel in the Army Air Corps, winning a Bronze Star. During home leave in 1945, he was driving on Long Island with his wife and their fifteen-year-old daughter, Henrietta, when a truck struck their car. His daughter was killed instantly, and he was seriously injured. The driver of the truck was charged with recklessness. A year later Jim Bush, who began drinking heavily after the accident, lost his job as vice president of the First National Bank of St. Louis.

Despite problems with alcohol, Bush belonged to the society set in St. Louis, where he was "well and fondly thought of by people in my parents' social circle," said Stuart Symington Jr.

As president of the Yale Club of St. Louis, Bush was active in the community and appointed to various boards, including the board of curators of the University of Missouri, an appointment he received from the governor. "I remember when Jim was the Veiled Prophet at the Veiled Prophet Ball," said Serena Stewart. "That was as high society as society ever got in St. Louis."

Bush had married Serena's mother, Janet, a month after he divorced his first wife in 1948. He became Janet Stewart's third husband, which for Prescott and Dorothy was two husbands too many. Prescott did not speak to his brother again until Janet divorced Jim in 1952.

By the time he married his third wife, Lois Kieffer Niedringhaus, in 1953, and six years later when he received his presidential appointment to the Export-Import Bank, Jim had returned to the good graces of Prescott and Dorothy, who spent time with the couple and their three children in later years. Prescott, despite his own periodic bouts of heavy drinking, had no tolerance for his brother's alcoholism. In 1970 Jim told Lois, the mother of three of his five children, that he was leaving her for another woman. On the day of their divorce, December 4, 1970, he married a woman named Gloria Hodsoll Galbusera, and they left for Italy.

They stayed in Milan for six months until he left her, taking her money and fleeing to the Philippines. He died there in 1978, blind, drunk, and broke.

No one in the family has ever explained what happened to the misappropriated $750,000, and Jim Bush's offense never became public. Several pages of his FBI files have been redacted, and his State Department files have been destroyed. The two embassy officials who dealt with Bush in his last months confirmed that there had "been some sort of scandal" but did not know exact details. As director of the CIA, George Bush was able to keep his uncle's crime and his squalid last years in the Philippines a secret from everyone, including his children. Prescott disinherited Jim with a codicil to his will in 1971, a year before he died. In place of a bequest to his brother, Prescott left three thousand dollars apiece to his brother's three children with Lois Kieffer Niedringhaus. George directed the State Department to send his uncle's remains to the Bush family plot in Greenwich.

The last Bush to be buried in Prescott's plot would be his widow. Her modest granite stone looks very unassuming alongside her husband's large imposing stone and strongly suggests that this pile-driving woman lived in her husband's huge shadow. Dorothy Walker Bush had basked in Prescott's reflected glory and even in death did all she could to burnish his image. She left instructions upon her death that she be laid to rest next to him the way she had lived. So her marker simply reads:

HIS ADORING WIFE
DOROTHY WALKER BUSH
1901–1992

Following Robin's memorial service in Greenwich, the Bushes raced back to Midland to tell their son Georgie about his sister. He was in the second grade at Sam Houston Elementary School, and he saw his parents drive up to the school in their green Oldsmobile. He scampered outside to greet them, fully expecting to see Robin.

"I remember looking in the car and thinking I saw Robin in the back," George W. Bush told *The Washington Post Magazine* in 1989. "I thought I saw her, but she wasn't there."

He had known she was sick, but he had no idea she was dying. When they told him in the car that she was gone, he couldn't understand why they had kept it a secret from him. "Why didn't you tell me?" he asked them. He repeated the question for many years. As his mother later said, "You have to remember that children grieve . . . [and] he felt cheated."

When George H.W.'s youngest brother, Bucky, sixteen, visited Midland, he was surprised by young George W.'s reaction to his sister's death. "He was really struck with it," said Bucky Bush. "He was hurt by it, almost as if somebody had taken something away from him that he had cherished very, very dearly . . . he was that young and had that kind of an adult reaction to losing a sibling."

At this point, Prescott Bush could have stepped in to play a comforting role in George W.'s life because Prescott also had lost a sibling when he was Georgie's age, but, unfortunately, there was no closeness between grandfather and grandson, and Texas was too far away from Connecticut for regular visits.

"It [the death of his sister] certainly had an impact on him," recalled Randall Roden, a childhood friend of George W.'s from Midland. "I know that he suffered as a result of it in trying to sort those things out."

One night not long after Robin's death, little George was allowed to spend the night with his friend at the Rodens' home, but he kept waking up with nightmares. Finally Barbara arrived to take her son home, and explained to his confused friend about Robin's death.

"It was a profound and formative experience," Roden recalled. "I don't remember having a conversation about it—what does it feel like that your sister died? But I certainly remember the event, and I remember the period afterward and that there was enormous sorrow and there was this sense in the aftermath of something bad having happened."

Seeing his mother racked with grief every day propelled young George into trying to make her happy, to do anything to alleviate her pain. His father was still traveling constantly, working to build his new business, and that left his mother alone at home for days on end with her children. Of the two boys, only Georgie was old enough to truly understand what had happened.

"Mother's reaction was to envelop herself totally around me," he later told friends. "She kind of smothered me and then recognized that it was the wrong thing to do."

He became, according to his mother, "my little man." He told jokes to make her laugh, constantly performed stunts to distract her from her sadness. His cousin Elsie Walker Kilbourne, who lost one of her own sisters, said, "You look around and see your parents suffering so deeply and try to be cheerful and funny, and you end up becoming a bit of a clown."

Barbara later admitted that she had leaned too heavily on her young son. She didn't realize what she was doing to him until she heard him one day tell a friend that he couldn't come out because he had to stay inside and play with his mother, who was lonely. "I was thinking, 'Well, I'm being there for him,' " she said. "But the truth was he was being there for me."

Having given up some of his carefree childhood to his emotionally needy parents, especially his grieving mother, young George would overcompensate years later. Forsaking his role as the responsible firstborn son, he would chase his adolescence well into adulthood. Yet at the age of forty, he would put the lie to F. Scott Fitzgerald's famous dictum that there are no second acts in American lives. For George W., his sister's death would remain a defining experience, not just establishing the powerful bond with his mother, but also affecting how he dealt with the world. Life would become a party, full of humor, driven by chance, shaded by fatalism. Even as a teenager, young George told his friends, "You think your life is so good and everything is perfect; then something like this happens and nothing is the same."

CHAPTER NINE

Hollywood could not have cast a more impressive-looking U.S. senator than Prescott S. Bush. Tall and elegant in pinstripes, monogrammed shirts, and silk pocket squares, he looked like Jay Gatsby had dressed him. In autumn, he favored glen-plaid suits; in summer, two-tone shoes. For black tie, patent-leather slippers and a paisley silk cummerbund.

"I remember him wearing green linen slacks at the Chevy Chase Club," said Nancy "Bitsy" Folger, whose father, Neil H. McElroy, was Secretary of Defense under Eisenhower.

"I remember spectator shoes, gold cuff links, silk hankies—the works," said Marian Javits, wife of New York's Senator Jacob Javits.

"Today he'd probably be on the cover of *Gentlemen's Quarterly*," said Ellen Proxmire, wife of Wisconsin's Senator William Proxmire.

With his year-round country-club tan, Prescott Bush looked as dashing as Clark Gable in *Gone With the Wind*. Aswim in a sea of shiny blue polyester suits, white Dacron shirts, and string ties, Prescott stood out in "the world's most exclusive club" like a Rolls-Royce in a Studebaker showroom.

No one looked more like he belonged in the Senate than this very lucky investment banker from the Nutmeg State. Upon his arrival in Washington in November 1952, Prescott assumed the role of the senior senator from his state because he was filling Senator McMahon's unexpired term. His committee assignments included Banking and Currency as well as Public Works.

As sure-footed as he appeared on the surface, Prescott took a pratfall in January 1953, when he signed on as one of sixty-three co-sponsors of the Bricker Amendment. The legislation, introduced to curtail the treaty-making powers of the President, appealed to conservatives who were still haunted by Roosevelt's deal making at the 1945 Yalta conference. They believed that a sick and doddering FDR had carved up the world with Stalin while Winston Churchill, bloated with brandy, nodded off. Bricker's ardent supporters included the Liberty League, Daughters of the American Revolution, the American Medical Association, the Committee for Constitutional Government, the *Chicago Tribune*—all of whom presented petitions signed by over a half-million Americans.

As a son of the establishment, Prescott Bush didn't think twice about co-sponsoring the amendment, especially when he saw the opposition: the League of Women Voters, the Americans for Democratic Action, *The New York Times*, *The Washington Post*, the American Bar Association's Section on International and Comparative Law, the American Association for the United Nations, and Eleanor Roosevelt. Anything that Mrs. Roosevelt was for, Prescott was against, until he found out that Eisenhower was also opposed.

"I'm so sick of this I could scream," the President was quoted as telling his cabinet. "The whole damn thing is senseless and plain damaging to the prestige of the United States. We talk about the French not being able to govern themselves—and we sit here wrestling with a Bricker amendment."

Once the President's opposition became known, Prescott reevaluated his stand. In those days either a senator was an Eisenhower man or he wasn't, and when Connecticut newspapers started tweaking Bush for disloyalty to the President who had gotten him elected, he quickly reversed himself. Just as quickly the White House rewarded him with a seat on the President's Commission on Foreign Economic Policy, which meant frequent trips abroad to research policies of international trade, at taxpayers' expense. When the showdown on the Bricker Amendment came on February 26, 1954, Prescott was safely back in the fold to help the administration win a tough battle by one scant vote.

By then, the Bushes had settled into their new life in Washington. Prescott had never been happier, and Dotty thrived on being able to share her husband's work. She visited his office frequently, and on occasion helped out with the mail. She became a daily visitor to the Senate gallery

and mastered legislative issues, particularly those pertaining to Connecticut. She wrote her children long newsy letters about her exciting life in
the nation's capital. "It's wonderful with a Republican in the White
House for the first time in twenty years," she wrote. She quoted her father
in her relief to be rid of "those awful Roosevelts" and "that Terrible Truman." She made Washington sound like a little Paris on the Potomac, an
international gathering place for the good and the great. She confided
chatty personal details of the famous people she and the senator met at
embassy balls, Georgetown dinners, garden parties, congressional teas,
lectures, gallery openings, and White House receptions:

> *I went to play badminton at Mrs. Hugh D. Auchincloss's with
> Martha Krock, wife of Arthur Krock of the* New York Times, *and
> several other girls. Mrs. Auchincloss is the mother of "Jackie"
> Kennedy, wife of the nice young Senator from Massachusetts, who
> has been laid up so long with a bad back. I was delighted to hear
> from her that after this last operation, in which they removed a
> great deal of pin from his spine, that he seems to be recovering
> rapidly.*

Her husband's political mentor, Ted Yudain, asked her to write a similar letter that he could publish in *Greenwich Time* and distribute as a
weekly column to other newspapers throughout the state. "I agreed only
because he said it would help Pres," Dotty recalled years later. And help
Pres it did, greatly warming up his frosty image for his constituents. Her
column, signed Mrs. Prescott Bush, appeared regularly as a society-page
feature titled "Washington Life as Seen by a Senator's Wife."

Ordinarily, she wrote with a honey gloss, especially about her husband ("Every personal contact with that man increases my respect for
him, if such a thing is possible") and her grandchildren ("The feel of
those little pairs of arms around my neck meant more to me than any diamond necklace ever could"). A devout, even adamant Christian who
grew up going to Presbyterian church three times every Sunday, Dotty infused her columns with her religiosity. She frequently quoted from the
Bible as well as the prayers and incantations she liked best from the many
church services and spiritual lectures she attended: "When I saw John
Foster Dulles, our Secretary of State, just named 'Man of the Year' by

Time magazine, with his truly modest bearing, passing the bread and wine, I was reminded of Christ's words: 'He that would be great among you, let him become your servant.' "

Believing that everyone should pray at least twice a day, Dotty was incensed when the Supreme Court ruled that school prayer was unconstitutional:

The six judges who concurred in that decision seem to completely ignore the fact that we are a nation founded under God. The first thing the Pilgrim Fathers did when they landed on the bleak Massachusetts coast was to kneel and give thanks to God.

This country was founded so that its citizens could be free to practice religion—freedom of, not from religion.

Are we going to weaken our country by denying our children their rightful heritage?

She was equally forthright about her strong partisan views. In one column she dismissed the Soviet General Secretary, Nikita Khrushchev, as "a double-dealer" and demanded to know: "How do the leaders of a law-revering nation, with high moral standards, deal with the Russian leaders who have no regard at all for the truth?"

She also voiced her dismay at "the official support given to the exchange of Cuban rebels when nothing is being done for American citizens imprisoned in China."

In another column, she chastised the Senate for taking too long to confirm President Eisenhower's appointments:

When our boys were little, one item on their report card read, "Claims no more than his fair share of time and attention," abbreviated in our family to "claims no more." Well, the Senate Committees have certainly been getting a good fat minus in "claims no more," especially where Presidential appointments have been concerned.

She adored Eisenhower and wrote emotionally when he appeared at the Republican Women's National Convention after suffering a heart attack:

Television makes him look so pale, that it was a joy to see him in the flesh, and see for ourselves how ruddy and vigorous he looks.

It was a very moving moment. All the women clapped and screamed and waved, but the really touching thing was that after he had spoken, there was hardly a dry eye around me, and I'm not ashamed to say that my handkerchief was in use, too. There is just something so big and fine and noble about that man.

She lambasted Senator Wayne Morse, the Republican turned Democrat from Oregon, for opposing Clare Boothe Luce to be Ambassador to Brazil. As the senior senator from her state, Prescott had escorted Mrs. Luce into the hearing and made a robust statement of support for her in front of the Foreign Relations Committee. Immediately, Senator Morse objected to her 1944 campaign statement charging that President Roosevelt was "the only American President that ever lied us into war." Lighting cigarette after cigarette, Mrs. Luce conceded that her language had been "most intemperate." Morse maintained that such language disqualified her from diplomacy. She fingered the fur piece on her lap and kept taking her glasses on and off. After several hours of wrangling, she departed for New York. She was overwhelmingly confirmed days later, with only eleven Democrats voting against her.

Responding to reporters' queries, she said she was delighted to be the new Ambassador. Then she added: "My difficulty, of course, goes some years back and begins when Senator Wayne Morse of Oregon was kicked in the head by a horse."

Within the hour, Morse claimed the floor of the Senate for a point of personal privilege. "Not so soon did I expect that those of us who voted against Clare Boothe Luce would be proven so right," he said. "I am not surprised that this slanderer that the Senate confirmed just a few minutes ago would make this kind of statement . . . I will pray for God's guidance for this lady so she will be more stable in the performance of her duties than she was when she issued that statement this afternoon."

The Senate listened tensely as several members who had voted for her confirmation now expressed regret for having done so. Three days later Mrs. Luce went to Washington to meet with President Eisenhower, who accepted her decision to quit.

Prescott Bush issued a statement saying he deeply regretted the necessity for her resignation, but Dotty Bush was not so politic:

> [T]he appointment of Mrs. Luce would have been so acceptable to the Brazilians and it seems a pity that her talents cannot be used because of one man's vindictiveness. Last week's performance by Senator Morse in his attack on Mrs. Luce did a real disservice to his country as I feel sure Clare Boothe Luce would have done a marvelous job for us in Rio. Oh my! Washington! Why we don't all have ulcers, as we seem to leap from one fight into another.

Dotty considered wasting time a sin, which is how she described the "inordinate number" of congressional committee hearings that cabinet members have to endure:

> They place an unbearable burden upon the departmental heads of government. Why couldn't a new system be worked out? Why couldn't every Representative and every Senator on every committee on the Hill having to do with defense, send his questions in writing, and then the Secretary could appear for as many days as necessary to answer all the questions? In this way, all the duplications would at least be done away with.

When Congress proposed a 50 percent pay raise for itself, her husband objected. "I don't think that anybody who wants to make money ought to be a Senator or a Congressman," Prescott said. "I look upon this job as a service job like the ministry, like teaching; and, if you want to make money, if you want to be in business for profit, then don't be a Senator or a Congressman."

Prescott, who made $12,500 as a senator, had given up his seven paid directorships in publicly owned companies when he took office. He continued to receive a handsome partnership income from Brown Brothers Harriman, which was allowed in those days. Other senators received income from their law firms or their businesses back home.

Prescott did support a pay increase for federal judges because they had to give up all outside income, but he tried to block the raise for members of Congress. His Connecticut colleague, William Purtell, objected. Purtell asked Bush if one of the tests in Congress should be acquired or inherited wealth, both of which Prescott had by that time, and whether members of Congress with growing families should be required to choose between "providing for their loved ones" and "serving their constituents."

Prescott retorted that many in Congress never had it so good and many were not worth what they were currently getting paid. "The mere fact that one man says he can't make ends meet doesn't indicate we should raise the pay 50 percent," he said.

Revering the Senate as a public trust, he genuinely felt that the office should be above mere money, but he did not recognize, or at least acknowledge, that such high-mindedness was much easier to maintain with a continuing flow of cash from Brown Brothers Harriman, plus the large inheritance that his wife received (put in trust for her children) upon the 1953 death of her father.

Prescott enjoyed every bit of decorum that accompanied his position, and demanded the perquisites of his high office. He insisted that his grandchildren call him "Senator," according to the recollections of Jeb Bush. Prescott's sister Margie Clement, who lived in New Haven, was encouraged to fly the American flag whenever he visited. "I lived a couple of houses down on Bishop Road," said Michael Lynch, the registrar of vital statistics in New Haven, "and everybody always knew when Mrs. Clement was expecting company. She would put out a small American flag—I don't think it was even three by five—when Prescott arrived. They didn't put out the flag on any other occasion."

Prescott expected the same kind of respect from his Senate colleagues. During a 1953 debate on interest rates for government bonds, Senator Albert Gore, Democrat of Tennessee, caught himself calling Senator Bush "the gentleman from Connecticut," which is the way House members address each other. In the Senate, the rules call for members to address each other as "the distinguished Senator."

Gore immediately apologized, saying it was his first Senate speech after a long career in the House and that he had lapsed inadvertently. He assured the Senate that while he considered Prescott a gentleman, he also regarded him as a distinguished senator. Prescott accepted his apology with a forgiving smile. Such civility was not evident forty-seven years later when Prescott's grandson battled Gore's son for the presidency.

Nor was Lyndon Johnson so courteous. The Texas senator once interrupted Prescott on the floor of the Senate in a debate over trade. Prescott tried to assert his right to continue talking when Johnson insisted he stop his "bush league" debate so he could proceed with Senate business. Harry McPherson, who worked for Johnson at the time, recalled the incident as coming close to violating the Senate rules of civility. "I remember I was sitting in the well of the Senate and my head snapping back as Johnson said that. You know you're not supposed to speak directly about another member that way. Prescott Bush continued gamely to make his point, but I think he was trying to call attention to the inappropriateness of what Johnson had said."

On another occasion Louisiana's Democratic Senator Russell Long took vigorous exception to something Prescott said on the floor of the Senate. "They frequently disagreed," recalled Hamilton Richardson, Long's legislative assistant, "and I think Senator Long got a little carried away in his comments about Senator Bush, although I don't remember the exact issue . . . What I do remember is Senator Bush getting up and saying that Senator Long's conduct reminded him of the Roman Emperor who made his horse Consul of Rome. 'Only in that case, unlike with Senator Long, the Emperor appointed the whole horse.'"

Many Senate aides remember Prescott Bush as a formidable man of patrician carriage who fawned over his betters, charmed his peers, and was utterly unapproachable to underlings.

"During the 1950s there were no restaurants on the Hill, so you'd see everyone eating in the cafeteria," said Bobby Wood, an aide to Alabama's Democratic Senator Lister Hill. "Most senators ate there with their staffs while a few, only a few, preferred eating in the senators' private dining room in the Capitol. Prescott Bush was one of the few who never ate in the cafeteria with the help. In fact, he didn't even like being on the same elevator with us. He'd always take the 'Senators Only' elevator."

"I remember him as a dark and scowling man," said Frank Valeo, a former staff member on the Senate Foreign Relations Committee, "but exceptionally well dressed."

"He looked more like a senator than any senator I've ever met," said William Hildenbrand, the former secretary of the Senate. "He would never come on the Senate floor unless looking impeccable. He was the kind of guy who probably put out the garbage in pressed pajamas, or wore

black tie to bed. He carried himself with all the confidence of an aristocrat."

"God, he was a stickler for the details of etiquette and doing things
just so," recalled Pat Holt, former chief of staff for the Senate Foreign Relations Committee. "I remember meeting up with him on a foreign trip
in Guatemala at a social function one night. He was an enthusiastic golfer
and had asked the attaché to arrange a golf game. The attaché apparently
invited five people to play. Bush took him aside and said, 'I used to be
president of the U.S. Golf Association, and I must tell you that serious
golfers do not play in parties of five. We play only in foursomes.' "

During the floor debate on pay raises, Dotty watched intently from
the gallery as the Senate defeated her husband's amendment and then,
over his objections, passed the pay increase he opposed that gave senators
$22,500 a year. "I knew Pres was going to speak against such a substantial
raise," she wrote in her column. "His point of view was not popular in the
Senate, but when the final vote came there were 24 others who voted with
him. I suffer with him, but am always just especially a little more proud
of him when he takes an unpopular stand, because, in his heart, he feels
that that is best for the country."

Temperamentally, the Bushes were in perfect harmony with the
Eisenhower era of Republican grandees—moderate men with an international perspective who believed in human rights. They didn't realize it
at the time, but they were in the final evolutionary turn of the Republican Party to the right, and soon their kind of politics would be doomed.
Within the next two decades the liberal Republicanism of Jacob Javits
(New York), Clifford Case (New Jersey), Leverett Saltonstall (Massachusetts), John Sherman Cooper (Kentucky), George Aiken (Vermont),
Thomas Kuchel (California), and Margaret Chase Smith (Maine) would
be extinct. By the time the grandsons of Prescott Bush—George W. Bush
and Jeb Bush—ran for public office, they would be practicing an extreme
brand of Republican politics that bore no resemblance to the moderate
views of their grandfather.

"I'm so glad Pres is gone and doesn't have to bear the shame of his
right-wing grandson's lies to the country," said Betsy Trippe DeVecchi in
July 2003. "Prescott was such an honorable man he never would've lied
or been unprincipled the way George W. Bush has been in dragging us
to war in Iraq."

The only daughter of Juan Trippe, the founder of Pan American Airways, Betsy Trippe DeVecchi grew up in Greenwich with the Bush children in the 1940s and was a close friend of Jonathan Bush, who was called Johnny Jim. "Prescott taught me to play tennis on the Rockefellers' indoor court," she said. "He was a lovely man, and his wife, Dotty, was so warm and gracious. Once they drove me up to Hotchkiss to see Johnny Jim in a play . . . Pres sat on the board of my father's company. They shared the same Republican politics. Both were big friends of Wendell Wilkie and Tom Dewey and, of course, President Eisenhower."

Prescott was the type of man Dwight Eisenhower admired: a wealthy investment banker who had married above himself. In addition, Prescott played expert golf, which is why he was occasionally called by the White House to join the President's foursome at Burning Tree Club in Maryland. As the former president of the U.S. Golf Association, Prescott saw to it that they installed a putting green on the White House grounds because, as he told the Greenwich Rotary Club, Ike needed the practice.

"Many of you might get some comfort to know that the President also struggles with his game, particularly his putting," Prescott said. "An uncomfortable nervousness reaches him and this reaction happens on two-foot putts. I recently said to him, 'I know what the matter is with your putting, Mr. President. It is simply terror.' "

Ike then told Prescott that he had tried twenty-two different putters in eight months to improve his game. As Prescott told the story, he grinned, knowing he was the better golfer. "The President," he said, "still has something to gain in the putting department."

The Bushes felt comfortable with the sixty-two-year-old President and the political philosophy he had borrowed from Abraham Lincoln:

> The legitimate object of government is to do for a community of people, whatever they need to have done, but can not do at all, or can not, so well do, for themselves—in their separate, and individual capacities.
>
> In all that the people can individually do as well for themselves, government ought not to interfere.

Prescott and Dotty admired Eisenhower's political moderation, although others described Ike's agenda as nothing more than a list of steps he refrained from taking. Perhaps, as suggested by *The New Republic*, that was the key to his overwhelming popularity: "The public loves Ike. The less he does the more they love him. That, probably, is the secret. Here is a man who doesn't rock the boat."

During the early part of his administration, Eisenhower's reluctance to "rock the boat" nearly capsized the ship of state. Throughout his political career, he refused to take a public stand against Senator Joe McCarthy and his rampaging anti-Communist campaign. A famous Herblock cartoon in *The Washington Post* depicts a confrontation between the two men in the Oval Office: Grinning fiendishly, an apelike McCarthy stands with a blood-covered meat cleaver in his hand while Eisenhower draws a feather sword. Like a bewigged fop in a Gilbert and Sullivan operetta, Eisenhower protests, "Have a care, Sir."

Even Herblock's punishing ridicule could not move Eisenhower to oppose the Wisconsin senator, who had been whipping up the nation's fears about Communists creeping into the government. In the wake of the USSR's exploding the hydrogen bomb, the investigation into Hollywood's writers, actors, and directors by the House Un-American Activities Committee, and the spy trial and execution of Julius and Ethel Rosenberg, McCarthy's Red-baiting fulminations had thrown the country into a frenzy. He had called President Truman and his Secretary of State, Dean Acheson, "the Pied Pipers of the Politburo." He even accused the revered former secretary of state George C. Marshall of being "a man steeped in falsehood." Still, Eisenhower would not speak up. When his advisers pleaded with him to oppose McCarthy, Ike refused. "I just will not," he said. "I refuse to get into the gutter with that guy."

Heedlessly, McCarthy continued swinging his meat cleaver at the military, the State Department, and the CIA. He threatened the Voice of America for filling its libraries with the works of "Red" writers. He terrorized academia, the media, and the federal bureaucracy. He thundered about "security risks," "subversives," "fifth columnists," and the "Red menace." He fomented opposition to Eisenhower's appointments of some of the most respected men in the country, including Harvard's president James B. Conant to be High Commissioner in Germany and U.S. Army General Walter Bedell Smith to be Undersecretary of State. He even went so far as to accuse the President himself of sending "perfumed notes" to friendly powers who were profiting from "blood trade" with Red China. Still, Eisenhower said nothing.

McCarthy's polls soared so high that few people had the courage to oppose him. One who did step forward was the freshman senator from Maine, Margaret Chase Smith, who made her "Declaration of Conscience" in 1950 after McCarthy's reckless speech in West Virginia in which he ferociously attacked "205 card carrying" Communists in the State Department. Without mentioning him by name, she said that the deliberative body of the U.S. Senate had "been debased to the level of a forum of hate and character assassination sheltered by the shield of congressional immunity." She concluded her fifteen-minute address by saying, "I do not want to see the Republican Party ride to political victory on the Four Horsemen of Calumny—fear, ignorance, bigotry and smear."

McCarthy scornfully denounced her and the six senators who supported her declaration as "Snow White and her Six Dwarfs." Another Senate critic was J. William Fulbright of Arkansas, whom McCarthy ridiculed so often as "Senator Half Bright" that bushels of mail so addressed were delivered regularly to Fulbright's office.

After the Eisenhower landslide swept Republicans to victory in both houses of Congress, McCarthy became chairman of the Permanent Subcommittee on Investigations of the Senate Committee on Governmental Affairs. When it came time to vote on a $214,000 appropriation for his committee—a defeat would have disbanded the committee and effectively ended McCarthy's reign of terror—the Senate caved. Even its most resolute members rolled over for McCarthy, including John F. Kennedy of Massachusetts, Lyndon B. Johnson of Texas, Hubert H. Humphrey of Minnesota, Estes Kefauver of Tennessee, Mike Mansfield of Montana, Warren Magnuson of Washington, Richard Russell of Georgia, Herbert Lehman of New York, and Margaret Chase Smith of Maine. Following suit was Prescott Bush. Only Fulbright of Arkansas had the courage to vote against the appropriation. As he wrote to his Oxford tutor:

> I fear for the future. McCarthy is an unscrupulous demagogue with many of the characteristics of Hitler . . . He has come upon the scene just as television is becoming a powerful medium, and we do not know how to evaluate his influence. To me he is completely

*revolting from every point of view, but I cannot deny that he seems
to have a very substantial following.*

Once his committee was funded, McCarthy launched an investigation into Communism in the U.S. military. He held hearings and hectored witnesses, brandishing doctored photographs and forged letters to
"prove" that the Army had promoted Communists. When he savaged a
decorated Army general and declared him unfit to wear the uniform, even
Eisenhower was outraged, although not enough to go public. Instead, the
President secretly gave the Army the go-ahead to draw up a list of countercharges against McCarthy, who had been blackmailing the military to
get preferential treatment for one of his aides who had been drafted. The
televised hearings became known as the Army-McCarthy smearings, a
muddy slugfest that riveted 30 million viewers in May 1954.

Under camera lights for thirty-six days McCarthy's outrageous conduct so embarrassed the Senate that within weeks a member of his own
party introduced a resolution to censure him "for conduct unbecoming a
member of the United States Senate."

Prescott, who had once decried McCarthy's tactics, now worried
about his own reelection chances in a predominantly Catholic state that
was a bastion of McCarthy support. To dodge the bullet of a censure vote,
Prescott proposed a twenty-three-point code of fair practices for committee proceedings, claiming that if such a code had been in place the "unpleasant spectacle" of the Army-McCarthy hearings could have been
avoided. He received some positive press coverage in Connecticut for his
proposal to restore congressional fair play, but one paper, *The Bridgeport
Post*, took notice of his "reluctance to tangle personally with Senator Mc-
Carthy." In Washington, D.C., Prescott's proposed code was as ineffectual
as Eisenhower's feather sword.

Traveling the state, Prescott canvassed his political advisers about
what he should do, especially after his Senate colleague William Purtell
announced that he would vote for McCarthy. When reporters asked
Prescott how he would vote, he deliberated:

*I will limit myself to saying this: Senator McCarthy's stated objec-
tive is to fight Communism. I share that objective, as do all good
Americans. But, in the past I have frequently expressed reservations*

about the methods he has employed. Nothing in the hearings to date has caused me to dismiss those reservations. On the contrary, they have been reinforced.

In the weeks leading up to the censure vote, McCarthy mounted his own defense by lashing out at the Senate as a "lynch party" hell-bent on destroying his anti-Communist campaign. One of his biggest supporters was the conservative writer and Bonesman William F. Buckley Jr., who wrote, "McCarthyism . . . is a movement around which men of good will and stern morality can close ranks." Prescott, who sought to be included in such ranks, reworked his code of fair practices and offered it again as an alternative to avoid censure. The next day's *St. Louis Post-Dispatch* reported his proposal under the headline "Watered-Down Substitute for M'Carthy Censure Move Offered in Senate."

After burying Prescott's proposal in committee, the Senate moved to reconvene after the November elections to consider the motion for censure. Dotty returned to her perch in the gallery to watch the proceedings and reported the palpable strain that gripped everyone:

To me this whole session seems very sad. There is a certain suspicion and caution amongst the wives in the Gallery which never existed before, some not even speaking to others. I do hope by the time January comes along all this will have blown over, or our Senate Ladies' Day will be ruined . . . Perhaps I am unduly sensitive to tenseness, but to me all week the atmosphere in the gallery was most unpleasant.

"Prescott had worried about that censure vote for weeks," recalled Bernie Yudain, a former editor of *Greenwich Time* and the brother of Ted Yudain, the newspaperman who was Prescott's political mentor. "He knew that he could be signing his political death warrant if he voted to censure McCarthy. I was in Washington at the time, and he called me up and asked me to come to his office. He opened a cupboard jammed from floor to ceiling with mail. Thousands of letters from McCarthy supporters in Connecticut, all threatening him if he voted against their man.

"Pres talked about how much he loved being a senator, and how it had enlarged his life. He said he would never have gotten to know Por-

tuguese workers and Italian stonemasons in Chickahominy or the Irish
Catholics in Brack City, if he had not been Connecticut's senator. He
wanted to keep his position, but he also wanted to do the right thing and
vote his conscience."

By December 1, 1954, Prescott had finally made up his mind. He arrived at the Senate and stood to make a floor speech, his voice shaking
with emotion:

> *Mr. President, all my life I have looked upon membership in the
> United States Senate as the greatest office to which one could as-
> pire. Even as a schoolboy, I acquired a respect for the Senate that
> has stayed with me through the years . . .*
>
> *Like other Senators, I had necessarily observed the junior Sena-
> tor from Wisconsin, and had more than once expressed reservations
> concerning his methods, while endorsing always his stated objec-
> tives of combating communism at home and abroad.*

He said he had to vote to censure because the honor of the Senate was at
stake, and failure to rebuke McCarthy would be a victory for Communism. "For he has caused dangerous divisions among the American people because of his attitude," said Prescott, "and the attitude he has
encouraged among his followers, that there can be no honest differences
of opinion with him. Either you must follow Senator McCarthy blindly;
not daring to express any doubts or disagreements about any of his actions;
or in his eyes you must be a Communist, a Communist sympathizer, or a
fool who has been duped by the Communist line."

Prescott Bush Jr. remembered that when his father finally made his
decision, he was told that his political career was over. "[The] then Republican county chairman Bill Brennan warned that it would cost him
the election in 1956."

The senator later said he deeply regretted the necessity of incurring
the acute dislike of so many of his constituents but he had reached his
conviction after careful analysis of the issues and could not be persuaded
to alter it.

On December 2, 1954, the Senate voted 67–22 to censure Joe Mc-
Carthy, and the next day Prescott received a note from J. William Fulbright, his best friend in the Senate, congratulating him on his stand.

"This morning I read your speech in the Congressional Record and I think it was excellent," Fulbright wrote. "I can well appreciate that, under the circumstances in Connecticut and especially with your colleague voting the other way, you were in a very difficult spot. It took a lot of courage and you deserve full credit for adopting such a statesman-like position."

Prescott was so thrilled by the positive reactions he received that he decided to announce his plans to seek reelection. "He was insufferable about that vote and bragged constantly about his great opposition to McCarthy, which, as I recall, was a long time coming," said Dotty's nephew Dr. Ray Walker. "I can still hear him going on and on about how great he was standing up to 'all those Catholics in Bridgeport.'"

In a burst of bonhomie Prescott invited all the state's political reporters to a private lunch at the Hartford Club. He told them he was in the city to pay his respects to the new governor, Abe Ribicoff:

> I wrote the governor-elect shortly after the election congratulating him on his victory and inviting him to feel free to call upon me for any assistance which he considers I may give in state problems in Washington. I also suggested that if it were the governor-elect's pleasure that he invite me to visit with him when next I had an opportunity to be in Hartford. I received a most gracious reply and it is in response to his cordial invitation that we are meeting at his home on Bloomfield Avenue.

It was fitting that Prescott visit Governor-elect Ribicoff at his home rather than invite him to the Hartford Club. "That was a very exclusive club in those days, and very, very anti-Semitic," said the governor's son, Peter Ribicoff. "No Jewish person ever set foot in that club until my father was elected governor. The inaugural luncheon for the incoming and outgoing governors was always held there.

"My father went in 1954, but when he was reelected governor in 1958, he told the Hartford Club that he was aware of their restrictive policies, and since he hadn't heard of any Jewish person being inside the club since he was last there, he thought it best that the inaugural luncheon be held in one of the local hotels."

Sensitivity to restrictive covenants eluded Prescott Bush, who, like many of his generation, belonged to private clubs that admitted whites only and discriminated against Jews, women, and people of color. He also owned houses in Greenwich, Connecticut, and Hobe Sound, Florida, towns that carried restrictive covenants (contracts stated that homes could not be sold to black people). His dear friend Samuel Merrifield Bemiss believed in segregation, as did his best friend in the Senate, J. William Fulbright, who voted against every civil rights bill without apology. So Prescott seemed an unlikely choice to lead the charge for the Republicans on civil rights, but as chairman of the platform committee for the 1956 GOP convention, he pushed for a stronger plank than the Democrats. He supported federal fair-employment practices that outlawed discrimination; he proposed ending the filibuster; he declared himself against the poll tax; he urged the party to publicly applaud the Supreme Court decision in *Brown* v. *Board of Education* barring racial segregation in public schools.

He received a "My dear Pres" letter on June 22, 1954, from his friend Samuel Bemiss:

> [F]or heaven's sake soft pedal the Republican Party's accomplishments with the assistance of the NAACP . . . The Supreme Court is still a New Deal court and to us represents a philosophy, which we regard with profound misgivings . . . History seems to indicate that decent and dignified segregation is a natural condition which has prevailed among peoples and animals since the Garden of Eden.

The worst thing in the world, Bemiss warned Bush, would be "a return of a New Deal government dominated by the Roosevelts and their standard of morality."

In the end, Prescott did not get all that he sought in the civil rights plank, because Eisenhower drew his feather sword and deferred to the GOP's southern delegates. But by then Connecticut's senior senator had laid down an admirable marker of principle and tolerance that would severely challenge his political son, George Herbert Walker Bush, in the years to come.

CHAPTER TEN

Prescott cared greatly about his public image. When he edited his oral history for Columbia University, he changed one of his quotes from "and by God" to "and by gosh," because he did not want to be perceived as someone who invoked the name of God outside of prayer. His concern for appearances also prompted him to issue a press release when, after winning his Senate seat, he resigned his corporate directorships: "Though reluctant to give up these associations of many years' standing, I am anxious to free myself entirely of obligations, which I cannot fulfill. I also want no possible conflict of interest with my duties as a United States Senator."

As obsessed as he was with his own image, Prescott was obtuse about what constituted proper behavior for other politicians. He certainly did not understand the ramifications of slush funds when it came to keeping the public's trust. The unreported money collected by politicians became an issue in 1952 when Richard Nixon's secret fund of eighteen thousand dollars was exposed. Although the fund was technically legal at the time, the Democrats jumped on the issue and made it look unethical. The public outcry threatened Nixon's place on the GOP ticket, especially when Eisenhower did not fly to his defense. The Republican National Committee purchased a half hour of television time for seventy-five thousand dollars so that Nixon could refute the charges.

"My fellow Americans," he began, "I come before you tonight as a candidate for the Vice Presidency and as a man whose honesty and integrity has been questioned." He then described the purpose of the fund and how it worked. He said the money was used solely for campaign expenses. In laying out his meager financial status, Nixon said that his wife could not afford a mink coat, only "a respectable Republican cloth coat." He denied accepting gifts of any kind, except for a black-and-white puppy from a campaign supporter in Texas. His daughter Tricia had named the puppy Checkers, and Nixon said he would not send it back. He praised Eisenhower and vowed to work hard for the Republican ticket. He asked viewers to support him by sending telegrams to the Republican National Committee. The RNC was soon flooded with over 1 million calls and wires.

Prescott Bush was one of the first to telegram his support:

No fair-minded person who heard Senator Nixon bare his heart and soul to the American people Tuesday night could fail to hold him in high respect.

I have felt all along that the charges against Dick Nixon were a dirty smear attempt to hurt him and the Republican ticket. I doubt that either party can ever hope to put up a better citizen for high public office than Senator Nixon.

I believe the efforts to smear Dick Nixon will boomerang in his favor. Nixon is absolutely honest, fearless, and courageous. I'm proud of him.

Prescott, who believed in keeping certain matters secret, told reporters that he saw "no particular advantage" in forcing congressmen and high government officials to list all their sources of income. "The country has gotten along for 150 years without forcing men in public office to expose their private financial lives," he said.

This view, which ran contrary to the Corrupt Practices Act, brought him troublesome publicity in 1955 when he, too, established a slush fund—more than twice the size of Nixon's.

Newspaper reports of the time indicate that Prescott was facing political opposition. The right wing resented his vote to censure Joe McCarthy. He had not been invited to the huge McCarthy rally that one thousand people attended in Connecticut in 1955, and his absence was noted, prompting speculation that conservative Republicans might try to challenge him in the 1956 election. Determined to hold on to his Senate seat, Prescott established his fund to hire the number-one public-relations specialist in the state and to launch a series of semimonthly television talk shows in which he, Prescott, would be the star.

Prescott's fund, which violated Connecticut's election laws, was not reported to the secretary of the Senate or to the Republican State Central Committee. Six Wall Street bankers, including two of his brothers-in-law, bankrolled it. Each man made a personal contribution and agreed to approach others to do the same. Confidential letters were sent out over the signature of John B. Gates of Greenwich, who was listed as treasurer of the appeal. Below Gates's signature were the names of George H. "Herbie" Walker Jr., also of Greenwich; James W. Walker; Lindsay Bradford; Gerrold Bryce; Thomas McCance (Brown Brothers Harriman); and Roland Harriman (Brown Brothers Harriman).

The story of "Bush's slush fund" first surfaced in Connecticut in the *Bridgeport Herald* but became national news when the syndicated columnist Drew Pearson picked it up—Prescott's second run-in with Pearson.

Despite his animosity toward the columnist, Prescott took Pearson's call in 1955. The call was about the slush fund. Prescott explained that the money came from contributors who supported his political point of view. "I have never had a single one of them ask me for special favors," he said. "They are the kind of people who are willing to contribute to get the kind of government in Washington they believe in."

After writing that Prescott had committed a "criminal offense" by not reporting his fund, the columnist quoted him as saying that his friends gave him money because they agreed with his stable fiscal policy. Pearson examined Prescott's voting record and determined that the senator's votes concurred with the views of his big contributors on many more than financial matters. The conclusion was that Prescott was just another sleazy politician in debt to special interests.

The *Waterbury Republican* editorialized in his favor:

> In the case of a man of Sen. Bush's high-mindedness and integrity it is natural to believe that the "private" fund is the frank and harmless arrangement that he represents it to be. But the abuses to which such funds could lend themselves are glaring. If there are public men who can be bought, here plainly is a formula for making the purchase.

The *St. Louis Post-Dispatch* editorialized against him and the "bland self-justification" Prescott used to defend his slush fund. "Funds like this are usually secret, or at least poorly publicized, until some enterprising newsman digs them out. Thus they violate the spirit of corrupt practices legislation which is meant to expose political contributions to public view." The newspaper upbraided men like Nixon and Prescott Bush for "selling a piece of their position, standing and influence as members of the United States Senate—and doing so even if none of the contributors to the fund receives a direct and personal favor in exchange."

The unethical charge stung, because Prescott considered himself more honorable than most. Besides, he protested lamely, other senators had set up similar funds. He concluded that Drew Pearson had singled him out because he, Prescott, was above reproach. "I think Pearson deliberately picks out people—and I hope this doesn't sound immodest—but I think from time to time he does pick out people where he thinks they're immune, where their reputation is so good that it'll be news to attack him."

Prescott continued his rant against Pearson years later in his oral history:

> He twisted the thing around that it was a slush fund, you see, that people were going to buy favor with Senator Bush by making these personal contributions for his use . . . Just like the Nixon fund, where they crucified Nixon. I never personally felt there was anything wrong with the Nixon fund. It was a thoroughly clean proposition, done by people who believed in him at that time and wanted to promote his candidacy for the Vice-Presidency . . . They believed him to be a useful man and a helpful man . . . so they were willing to make these contributions for his campaign.

Luckily for Prescott, Pearson's column was only carried in two Connecticut newspapers, so there was no fertile ground for a scandal. Prescott simply contacted both newspapers and refuted the charges, and the story soon died. He continued using his slush fund to finance his public-relations man, Charles Keats. One of the publicist's assignments was to draft an endorsement letter for Prescott from President Eisenhower; the letter was to be released to Connecticut's media during the summer congressional recess, when Prescott would be traveling around the state to shore up reelection support.

In later years Bush biographers would write about the close personal friendship between Senator Bush and President Eisenhower, an impression conveyed by the Bush family and bolstered by a June 20, 1957, front-page photograph in *The New York Times* of the two men playing golf. The day before that game with Japanese Prime Minister Nobusuke Kishi, Prescott bragged about being Ike's favorite golf partner and estimated he played with the President at least a dozen times at Burning Tree in Ike's first term. Records in the Eisenhower Library indicate the two men played golf seven times in eight years. Those occasional games, plumped by the burnished recollections Dotty Bush gave to writers (and members of the Bush family), created a vivid picture of fraternity. Dotty genuinely believed that her husband was nothing short of essential to Eisenhower's personal and political success. In fact, she promulgated the myth that Prescott had convinced Ike to run for President in 1952 when, in fact, he had simply been one of many peripheral supplicants.

Research into the Eisenhower archives in Abilene, Kansas, indicates that the relationship between Prescott Bush and Dwight Eisenhower was, if not one-sided, certainly lopsided, with Prescott the ardent pursuer and Ike the gracious recipient. The letters and memos show that Prescott was like an adoring fan at the stage door waiting for Ike, ever the star, to sign an autograph. Prescott's various invitations—for the President to be his guest at the Alfalfa Club's annual dinner, to visit him in Gettysburg— were graciously acknowledged but always politely declined. "The documents do indicate that the relationship probably meant more to Senator Bush than to President Eisenhower," said Sydney Soderberg, a historian at Kansas Wesleyan University.

Having once fallen out of the chorus line over the Bricker Amendment, Prescott did not want to get out of step again with the administration. He suffered no ramification over his political difference, other than his own psychic discomfort. As soon as he found out Eisenhower opposed the amendment, he changed his position to be in accord. Prescott, who owned a big black standard poodle, could easily have posed with his dog in front of the White House and been asked the question "Which one is the President's poodle?"

Prescott went out of his way to befriend Sherman Adams, the former governor of New Hampshire, who was Eisenhower's chief of staff. Adams quickly became his conduit to the President.

When Prescott requested a letter of endorsement from Eisenhower in August 1955, he sent Adams a draft that was so self-serving even Prescott seemed embarrassed:

> Dear Sherm,
>
> This is purely a suggestion which I did not write and which makes me blush. Anything along this line would be wonderful to have.
>
> Pres Bush

The last paragraph of the five-paragraph letter was effusive in the extreme:

> Wherever you go, I want you to give the people of Connecticut my best wishes. From personal observation, I can assure them that you are my idea of what a United States Senator should be and that they are fortunate in having you represent them.

Adams sent Prescott's grandiloquent draft to Bryce Harlow, a White House speechwriter, who toned it down considerably for the President's signature. The final endorsement commended Prescott for his "effective and loyal support in the United States Senate" and "with my warmest appreciation" congratulated him on a job well done.

Prescott released the letter to Connecticut's newspapers, which published it as front-page news: "President Praises Bush for His Loyalty, Support" (*Greenwich Time*); "Pres. Gives Support to Sen. Bush, Calls him 'Loyal friend, Advocate' " (*Hartford Courant*). But the continuing publicity that Charles Keats had envisioned from Ike's endorsement was soon drowned in the waves of Hurricane Connie and, five days later, Hurricane Diane.

"Those two hurricanes hit Connecticut in August 1955 and knocked the state into total disaster," recalled Herman Wolf, a former aide to Governor Abe Ribicoff. "While the entire Atlantic coast from North Carolina through Massachusetts was affected, Connecticut suffered the most. We lost seventy-seven lives, and the flooding destroyed homes, farms, businesses, roads, shores, and utilities, causing over $350 million in property damage.

"We were still reeling from the first hurricane when we got hit by the second. The governor was at a governors' conference in West Virginia and couldn't get back that day so the lieutenant governor and a couple of the governor's top aides moved into the state armory in Hartford to try to cope with the catastrophe.

"We worked around the clock, taking calls and making calls. About two in the morning, I felt a tap on my shoulder. I turned around and looked up and up and up. There was Prescott Bush, all six feet four inches of him, standing there. In a very quiet voice, he said, 'Herman, what can I do to help?'

"I didn't have time to converse, even with a United States senator. So I just shouted, 'Get us some helicopters so we can survey the damage at dawn.' That's all he had to hear. He turned around and left. I don't know where he went. I don't know who he called, but at dawn there were two helicopters from the federal government ready to fly us around the state.

"For my money—and I'm a Democrat who worked for Abe Ribicoff—Prescott Bush was a fine gentleman. In fact, he was the best of the Bushes. After him, the blood thinned as it went down the line. His son George Herbert Walker Bush wasn't much to look up to, and then, God help us, we got George's son George Walker Bush, and the less said there, the better."

Prescott threw himself into the flood-recovery crisis for Connecticut, touring the state to talk to the victims and survey the damage. He introduced legislation for federal flood insurance so that property owners and small-business men would be protected from financial ruin. He also submitted additional bills to increase Federal Housing Authority mortgage insurance for repair or replacement of damaged homes; to provide for rent-free accommodations for certain needy disaster victims; to provide temporary housing for disaster relief; to authorize construction of flood-control reservoirs; and to increase emergency-relief highway funds.

For all this he drew approving editorials from various newspapers. *The Hartford Courant* pronounced him a man far different from (and better than) the one elected four years earlier:

When Senator Bush first appeared on the scene he was dismissed as an agreeable outsider who, after a prosperous career in business, wished to dabble in politics. Since he has been in the Senate he has grown visibly on the job, until he has taken on a stature that already ranks him high in the world's most powerful legislative chamber.

Just when Prescott thought he might have seen the last of Drew Pearson, the muckraking columnist targeted him again. This time the issue was the Harris-Fulbright Bill to deregulate the gas industry. Pearson predicted that Prescott Bush would vote in favor of the bill in order to enrich his son George.

George, like all Texas oilmen, supported the scheme. When oil lobbyists started pressuring him to secure his father's vote, he called Prescott to discuss the legislation. George claimed that deregulation would encourage more independent producers to explore for natural gas, which would increase the supply and thus ultimately lower prices. Prescott, who maintained that prices would skyrocket with deregulation, was unimpressed by his son's argument. He told George that the majority of people in his state lived in large urban centers and could not afford to pay the high prices that would result from deregulation.

Senator Paul Douglas, the liberal Democrat from Illinois, charged that the bill was nothing less than a conspiracy by big oil and gas companies to reap obscene profits at the expense of the nation's urban masses, many of whom were absolutely dependent on natural gas for heating and cooking. Prescott agreed.

When George couldn't convince his father, he sought out his friend Paxton Howard to make the case. Howard, an attorney for Shell Oil Company in Midland, Texas, and an unregistered lobbyist, agreed to visit Hobe Sound during Prescott's vacation and talk to him.

Howard was later subpoenaed to testify before the Senate special committee investigating lobbying efforts in support of Harris-Fulbright. Under oath, he admitted he had received a five-thousand-dollar bonus from Shell for trying to get Prescott and two other senators to change their votes.

"Senator Bush's son, George, lives in Midland, and he is a friend of mine," Howard testified. "George was very much for the gas bill—George wanted his father to get the facts on this bill—George was particularly anxious that I contact the Senator and lay the case before him. So I told him that I would be happy to do it if he would just arrange for the time. So he did, and I talked to the Senator about an hour."

"Was it not just the reverse," one senator asked, "that George was not so interested in trying to have his father influenced as you were?"

"Naturally, I was interested in the Senator, but the matter of Senator Bush arose from George Bush . . . He initiated it, and there would be no reason for it otherwise."

Prescott listened to the lawyer his son had sent, but Paxton Howard did not change the senator's mind. George refused to give up. He flew to Washington, where he told his father that he had been threatened. He claimed he was being hit with severe pressure to turn his father around. "Calls were then made to my former boss, Neil Mallon, at the Dresser Company," said George. "The head of Phillips Petroleum, K. S. (Boots) Adams, told Neil that 'if Prescott Bush doesn't vote for this bill, you can forget selling any more Dresser equipment to Phillips, and you can tell George Bush to forget his offshore drilling business.' "

George told his father: "I think you ought to know about these things."

Prescott brushed the words aside. "Don't you believe them. They'll never put you out of business. They wouldn't dare, because this would be the worst possible mistake they could make. This will not affect you at all. I'm going to vote against the bill because on the whole I think that's in the best interest of my state as well as the United States to vote against this bill. But don't you worry about it, and if there's any after effects from it, just tell me about them, and we'll take care of that."

By coincidence, Prescott was scheduled to play golf with the President later in the week. He told Eisenhower everything that George had told him. Eisenhower wrote in his diary on February 11, 1956, that he had heard the head of a big oil company who had once supported Prescott "announced that never again would he support such a fellow and referred to him in indecent language."

By this time, two other senators had stepped forward to report they had been offered bribes from the oil industry in an attempt to influence their votes. That led to the Senate committee investigation. But despite the controversy, the Harris-Fulbright Bill passed the Senate and was sent

to the President for his signature. Although Eisenhower had initially favored the legislation, he now hesitated. Cabinet minutes from February
13, 1956, indicate his concern about signing the contentious bill into law:

> *The President asked whether any President had ever signed a bill*
> *while the Senate was investigating its passage. He thought that*
> *any good bill ought to be passed without having a terrible stench*
> *connected with it . . . He then cited a story he had heard of oil in-*
> *dustry people blatantly bragging of how they had fixed Sen. Bush,*
> *because of his opposition, by taking a tremendous amount of busi-*
> *ness away from his son. The President then noted how the*
> *American people, even though erroneously, hold the President re-*
> *sponsible for everything.*

In the end, Eisenhower realized that most voters live in large urban
areas and if he signed a bill tainted by charges of bribery, the Democrats
would exploit the issue during the campaign. So he vetoed the Harris-
Fulbright Bill, and there was not enough support in the Senate to over-
ride the presidential veto.

On this issue, Prescott voted principle over purse. The negative effect
on a member of his own family did not change his decision. Unfortunately, the father's political template would never become the son's.
When George Bush entered politics eight years later, he showed he was
influenced much more by his mother's upbringing than by his father's:
his only priority was to win. Unlike his father, George needed to be liked
by everyone rather than respected. That left no room for taking an unpopular stand, even if it meant doing the right thing for his constituents.

Not everyone considered Prescott Bush a man of principle. In fact,
his 1956 opponent for reelection, Thomas J. Dodd, called him a "liar."
Dodd, a two-term congressman from West Hartford, was a man of stature
in his own right. After graduating from Yale Law School, he became an
FBI agent, then a federal attorney. He served as chief of counsel for the
prosecution of Nazi war criminals at Nuremberg, for which he received a
presidential citation, the U.S. Medal of Freedom, and the Czechoslova-
kian Order of the White Lion.

During the 1956 campaign, he became exasperated hearing Prescott
rattle off his legislative accomplishments on behalf of flood control, a cru-

cial issue for the state, as well as veterans' benefits. Prescott pompously named each one of the bills after himself—"the Bush-McCormack Amendment," "the Bush-Long Amendment," "the Bush-Lehman Amendment," "the Bush-Pastore Bill."

Dodd was further aggravated by the Bush campaign brochure that featured a photo of Prescott sitting next to the President, so close their shoulders touched, and watching Eisenhower sign a piece of paper. The headline: "President Eisenhower Signs a Senator Bush Bill."

During their first debate in Canaan, Connecticut, Dodd exploded when Prescott referred to a flood-prevention act as "the Bush-McCormack Act."

"Senator Bush is not telling the truth to this audience. There is no such thing as the Bush-McCormack Act. There's just no such thing."

Dodd's charge—although not true—threw Prescott into a swivet. He maintained control but admitted later how difficult it was for him. "Our campaign in Connecticut was a pretty rough and tough . . . I'm not disposed to get into personalities in campaigns, and have always tried to avoid them but Dodd was a very difficult opponent, and made it very difficult for me to hold my temper and keep my equilibrium."

Dodd kept charging that Prescott overstated his importance. "There has been a deliberate misrepresentation of the record in efforts to convince the voters that Sen. Bush co-authored popular legislation when the true record shows all too clearly that he had little or nothing to do with it," said the congressman.

Prescott felt that his honor had been besmirched, so he bought television time to prove that the Bush-McCormack Act was not the fraud that Dodd had claimed. He went on the air with statements from half a dozen prominent Democrats, including Senators Herbert Lehman and John F. Kennedy, to verify that he had worked on legislation dealing with flood insurance and hurricane protection. "We made this all very clear," said Prescott later, "and it put Mr. Dodd in quite a bad hole. But to me this illustrates the rashness of this man. He's willing to make very reckless charges and very reckless statements, and I formed the opinion then, which I haven't changed since, that he's a very unreliable sort of person . . . It was a ruthless, stupid thing for him to do, when he knew damn well, really, that there was a Bush-McCormack Act."

Dodd had blasted Prescott for naming four acts of legislation after himself. He had been right about three of the so-called Bush acts. Prescott took issue with the fourth, the only one that legitimately belonged under his name. The Connecticut race attracted national attention in 1956 because the seat was crucial to whether Republicans would take back control of the Senate. The Democrats presented Dodd as "the Man from Main Street, not Wall Street," and the Republicans presented Bush as "the President's Man." As Prescott recalled, each of them jockeyed to be the common man:

> *Dodd would make a remark like this . . . "Well, of course, Senator Bush seems to have a lot of time to play golf. I can't afford to play golf" . . . which would by inference say that Bush is a wealthy fellow that hasn't got much to do, whereas I'm the poor struggling fellow that has to work all the time . . . Somebody asked him what his hobby was and he said, "Horseback riding." So when I got up I said, "Well, I congratulate my opponent. I've never been able to afford a horse."*

Dodd was the only Democrat in Connecticut's congressional delegation. Even then he did not enjoy the full support of his colleagues in the House of Representatives. Representative Lud Ashley, a Democrat from Ohio overlooking Prescott's own struggle with alcohol, wrote to his good friend George Bush: "I've got my fingers crossed for your Dad. Dodd is a real phony—which I've known ever since he got drunk on a New England–bound train. He was a disgrace, and I hope that he gets the beating he deserves."

Polls predicted a close Senate race. After Labor Day, Prescott rented an apartment in Hartford, where he and Dotty lived for two months so they could campaign easily around the state. She had taken elocution lessons in Washington, and a class in public speaking to prepare herself. She memorized her speeches about "peace, prosperity and progress" until she could stand up and talk for twenty minutes without notes and sound extemporaneously fresh. The campaign provided her with a car, a driver, and her own hectic schedule. While her husband covered the big cities, she handled ladies' teas and small-town luncheons. They both made hand-shaking tours in every county in Connecticut. In fact, with the exception of George and Barbara, the entire Bush family—aunts, uncles, in-laws, children, grandchildren—turned out in full force to campaign.

This time around, Prescott left his straw hat at home: no banjos, no barbershop quartets. As the *New York Journal American* noted, "No more gimmicks and stunts."

He stood tall on civil rights and lambasted the southern Democrats in the Senate, particularly the senior senator from Mississippi, James Eastland. He charged that Democrats talk one way in the North and another way in the South. He accused the Democratic standard-bearer of "hollow promises" and "deceptive words" on racial relations.

"Adlai [Stevenson] and the Democrats in the North, including my own opponent, know in their hearts their promises [on civil rights] don't ring true as long as the Senior Senator from Mississippi must be their party's choice as chairman of the Senate Judiciary Committee . . . A vote against me is a vote for Jim Eastland. Nothing will happen on civil rights in the way of necessary legislation if the Republicans do not control Congress." He added that the Democrats offered nothing but a return to the New Deal, which "was a complete failure."

Prescott went to New York to campaign for the attorney general, Jacob Javits, telling crowds: "We need men like Jack Javits in the Senate to help the Eisenhower Republicans like [New York] Senator [Irving] Ives and myself who have been working for civil rights legislation and the removal of harsh and discriminating provisions of the McCarran-Walter Immigration Act."

Prescott was stalwart on civil rights. "He was one of the few who was with us on the crucial votes in 1956," said Howard Shuman, former administrative assistant to Senator Paul Douglas. "Prescott was a progressive Republican, far and away better than his son George or his grandson George W."

There is no question that Prescott stood up on the cutting issue of his day, something George would never do. When George ran for the U.S. Senate from Texas, he opposed the civil rights bill of 1964. He also supported restrictive covenants and tried to scuttle the fair-housing bill in 1968 before he voted for it. The rest of his political career reflected only the most opportunistic stands on racial matters, so unlike his father.

During the 1956 campaign, the Republicans sent their heaviest artillery into Connecticut to help Prescott: Vice President Richard Nixon, House Minority Leader Joseph Martin, former Governor Thomas Dewey, and Senator Clifford Case of New Jersey all visited the state. In October, the Democrats, who had sent no one to help Tom Dodd, practically conceded the state.

On Election Day, Prescott and Dotty returned to Greenwich to vote, and that evening they awaited the returns in the newspaper offices of *Greenwich Time*. In 1956, the owner of the paper, Constance Johnson Beech, had sold the paper to a group of seven local investors, which included Prescott and some of his slush-fund contributors. That same year, not too surprisingly, *Greenwich Time* endorsed one of its owners as a "senator of stature" who "deserves a full, six-year term of his own."

On election night Bush and his family watched as a campaign worker, chalk in one hand and a much-used cloth in the other, stood on a chair in front of a big blackboard, rapidly writing the figures shouted from newsmen on the telephones, keeping a vigil on the voting machines around the state.

Within an hour of the polls closing in Connecticut, it became apparent that the Republicans were winning the U.S. Senate seat, all seats in the House of Representatives, plus most of the seats in the state's House. John M. Bailey, the Democrats' Connecticut state chairman, was stunned. "President Eisenhower has broader coattails than we thought he had," he said. By 9:00 p.m., the Eisenhower landslide had become a political avalanche that buried almost all of Connecticut's Democrats, including Tom Dodd. Prescott had more than quadrupled his 1952 plurality, racking up a 131,000 margin of victory and winning seven out of eight counties. By 9:50 p.m., Dodd had conceded. He sent a telegram to Bush at his home in Greenwich: "Congratulations on your victory. My very best wishes for a happy and successful term in the United States Senate."

Tom Dodd would run again for the Senate two years later against William Purtell and win. He served with Prescott in the U.S. Senate until Prescott's retirement in 1963. During those years that they represented the state together, neither man could put aside the 1956 campaign long enough to become friends. Their relationship remained civil, but barely so.

The man from Wall Street never forgot being called a "liar" by the man from Main Street, and he retaliated ten years later in his oral history by characterizing Dodd as someone who had "assumed the likeness of Joe McCarthy in his speeches." Prescott claimed that the Connecticut intelligentsia didn't like Dodd and that they feared him. "They felt that he represented something that was spiritually offensive to them, that he was a threat to intellectual freedom, and so I'm satisfied in that election, 1956, the intellectual community, the universities, went rather heavily for me."

Prescott recorded those words, knowing they would not be published during his lifetime but would become part of the historical record that would live long after all the principals had died. His oral history also suggests that his condemnation of Dodd was based on nothing more than Prescott's friendship with Whitney Griswold, the president of Yale.

"In 1952, he [Griswold] told me he'd voted against me," said Prescott, "but in 1956, he voted for me, and enthusiastically." Prescott surmised that Griswold's enthusiasm sprang from Prescott's censure of Joe McCarthy, plus Prescott's opposition to loyalty oaths for college professors. He believed that those two stands swung the intellectual community over to his side.

Prescott accused Tom Dodd of being "distinctly pro-McCarthy," although the public record shows that Dodd campaigned vigorously on behalf of Connecticut Senator Brien McMahon against Joe McCarthy's efforts to unseat him in 1950. Despite Dodd's ardent anti-Communism, he resisted the overly zealous Red-baiting of the Cold War epitomized by the thuggish tactics of Joe McCarthy. Prescott's indictment of him as a McCarthyite seems unjust, suggesting the lingering resentment of a tough political campaign. Prescott's "how dare he" attitude might have clouded his judgment because the record indicates that Bush's anti-Communism was just as ferocious as Dodd's. In fact, the two men held similar views. Both took strong positions on defending freedom in West Berlin; both signed a petition opposing the seating of Communist China in the United Nations. Both spoke out against Communism in Latin America, and Fidel Castro in Cuba. In fact, Prescott predicted in 1961 that the Cuban dictator would be overthrown "within six months."

Both men were anti-Communist in their foreign policy views, but neither believed, like some in the 1950s, that Communism was a domestic threat within the United States.

In February 1960, according to FBI documents, Prescott denounced the U.S. Air Force for suggesting in its manual that Communists had infiltrated the National Council of Churches. "The claim is outrageous," he said, "and the Secretary of Defense [Thomas S. Gates] should be criticized for his irresponsibility."

The day after Prescott's denunciation of Gates he began receiving letters and telegrams of protest. His secretary quickly called the FBI and asked for information to substantiate his position. Documents show that she was told the FBI files were confidential and that she should check with the Senate Internal Security Subcommittee or the House Un-American Activities Committee. A memo of the call was sent to the director, J. Edgar Hoover, who penned a note of approval: "Right. The Senator got himself into this position and will have to get himself out."

Hoover later received a letter from the mustachioed movie star Adolphe Menjou, one of the bureau's "special correspondents" (that is, informants):

I was astounded to read that Sen. Prescott Bush of Connecticut had attacked the writer of the Air Force Manual with regard to Subversion in the Clergy. I wrote to the Senator enclosing material clearly showing that the Communists had not overlooked the Clergy in their efforts to hoodwink the American public. I could not believe that a United States Senator in 1960 could have been so naïve.

Hoover responded to "Dear Adolphe":

With regard to your inquiry, Senator Bush has not spoken to me personally about this matter but has written me just recently about getting together. I am unable to make satisfactory arrangements to do so at this time because of out of town commitments.

Hoover's response to "Dear Adolphe" basically told the actor that the FBI would not be of any help to Prescott Bush. At that time the National

Council of Churches was a target of the rabid right in part because the NCC was active in the civil rights movement in the South. In 1947, Menjou had named names of alleged Communists in Hollywood before HUAC and, in 1958, he joined the John Birch Society.

Two months after Hoover's letter, Prescott's office called the FBI again to obtain information concerning the Communist connections, if any, of three organizations: the National Association for the Advancement of Colored People; the Industrial Areas Foundation, whose director was Saul Alinsky; and the Progress Development Corporation in Princeton, New Jersey.

According to the FBI documents, Bush's office "wondered if any of these organizations had been cited by the Attorney General. He said he had checked a list of cited organizations dated 1954 and did not note these organizations as being listed. He said that, in addition, he desired any information which we could make available concerning the organizations."

The FBI obviously considered Prescott too liberal to be worth helping and rudely suggested again that he consult the records of the House Un-American Activities Committee and the Senate Internal Security Subcommittee. On the memorandum is a note wondering "why the Senator's office would make this kind of inquiry concerning the NAACP, in view of the fact it [Communist infiltration] is so well known."

By 1960, the NAACP had begun portraying itself as the anti-Communist alternative on civil rights. However, at times since its founding in 1909, the organization had been allied with American Communists on racial issues—hence the "everybody knows" tone of the FBI memo. Saul Alinsky was not a Communist but a labor liberal involved in organizing poor black neighborhoods in Chicago around issues of education, housing, and employment. The Progress Development Corporation in Princeton was involved in building desegregated housing in Illinois.

The record shows that on the crucial matters of his day—civil rights and McCarthyism—Prescott Bush was a man of principle who came down on the morally right side. Unlike his son George Herbert Walker Bush, and later his grandson George Walker Bush, Prescott did not sell out on principle for political gain. He recollected in his oral history that he paid a price: "Herbert Brownell, who had been in the [Eisenhower]

Cabinet as Attorney General, . . . said, 'Well you know, Pres, some of those fellows didn't want you to be re-elected. They didn't think you were the kind of Republican that they wanted.' "

Prescott told Brownell how Senate Minority Leader William F. Knowland, a Republican from California, had come to Connecticut to campaign in 1956. Knowland, a conservative who was constantly at odds with Eisenhower, made two speeches in the state. "In both cases, I introduced him," said Prescott, "but he never mentioned my name during his speeches and I was the candidate for re-election and the one introducing him. He mentioned the congressman in each of those districts who was running for reelection but never mentioned my name."

"Well, that's further evidence of just what I'm saying," said Brownell. "I don't think they really wanted you to win."

Prescott finally understood that he was not conservative enough for the Republican Party, then swinging to the right. Yet *The Milford Citizen* thought so highly of Prescott that the paper ran an editorial suggesting he replace Richard Nixon as Eisenhower's running mate in 1956: "We believe the Republican Party has no man in its ranks better qualified to serve as Vice President of the United States than Sen. Bush, and we hope a vigorous effort will be made to have him nominated for that potential vital position."

Prescott lived long enough to see his former opponent go down in ignominy. Targeted by Drew Pearson for senatorial malfeasance, Thomas Dodd took a daily pounding from the columnist in 1966 after four members of his Senate staff had leaked personal letters about his financial dealings. The relentless publicity forced the Senate to investigate the matter, and in 1967 Dodd was censured for using political funds for his personal benefit. The 92–5 vote was an overwhelming rebuke by his colleagues. He was defeated for reelection in 1970 and died at the age of sixty-three in 1971, a year before Prescott.

Dodd's financial misconduct led the Senate to enact laws governing the use of political funds for private use, which, fortunately for Richard Nixon and Prescott Bush, had not existed during their slush-fund years.

Publicly, Prescott managed to show restraint over Dodd's disgrace, perhaps mindful of the saying "There but for the grace of God go I." However, his son George, who was in the House of Representatives at the time, showed no such decorum. He gleefully denounced his father's opponent to colleagues. In a letter dated April 8, 1967, almost three months before the Senate censure of Dodd, George Bush, then a congressman, wrote to a friend, defending political fund-raisers:

> As to the Dirksen Banquet—a party needs money to run: it's that simple—no thing for Dirksen, just dough for the party . . . I don't agree that fundraising dinners are corrupt—directly or indirectly. If you Tom Dodd it and add on to the house or send the kids somewhere on the proceeds—that is a horse of a different shade.

Years later George Bush published his letter without a care toward the unseemly comment deriding Tom Dodd. By then, George had achieved his life's dream and established himself in political circles as "the world's nicest guy."

CHAPTER ELEVEN

All of the Bush children relished their father's position as a United States senator. They each basked in the reflected prestige and took on a bit of his luster as their own. Some did so more than others.

Prescott junior, the firstborn, who returned home from Brazil in 1948, became his father's unpaid political consultant and trusted confidant. Pressy, or P2, as the family also called him, drove his father, P1, to speaking engagements around the state on the weekends, when they would discuss issues and plan strategy. Sometimes they were joined by Prescott junior's young son, Prescott III, a.k.a. P3.

At one point, Prescott junior seemed headed for his own career in politics. An insurance broker with Johnson and Higgins in New York City, P2 commuted to and from Greenwich every day exactly as his father had done. He was elected to the Republican Town Committee and represented his district at the Representative Town Meeting, which his father had moderated for seventeen years. He headed the Red Cross Flood Relief Drive in 1955 and was reelected the next year as chairman of the Greenwich chapter of the American Red Cross. Active in Christ Church like his father, P2 became chairman of the Greenwich Boy Scout Camp and Conservation Fund Drive. At the age of thirty-five, he was nominated Man of the Year by the Greenwich Junior Chamber of Commerce. He also succeeded his father as president of the Greenwich Country Club.

Everything seemed in place for a political ascension, but it never happened.

"If you're from out of town and you visit P2 in Greenwich," said a

Bush family friend, "he and his wife will drag you to the country club to see his oil portrait, which is prominently featured on the wall with other presidents of the Greenwich Country Club, including P1 . . . It's kind of sad, really, that Prescott junior never got beyond that country-club mentality."

As a politico, P2 was strictly a behind-the-scenes player. He became his father's henchman, particularly when P1 wanted to prevent Albert Morano from returning to the House of Representatives. Morano was a Republican and part of Connecticut's delegation, but his brashness irritated Prescott. When the Democrats swept Connecticut in 1958, Morano lost his seat. He attempted to run again but claimed that the Bushes stepped in to stop him. There is some evidence to suggest he may not have been hallucinating.

"My father had said to me, 'If Morano ever takes his foot off the base, let's make sure he never gets back on,' " Prescott junior revealed in his oral history for the Greenwich Library.

P2 was always eager to do his father's bidding, and his father felt the Italian-American congressman had gotten "above himself" on many occasions, but none more so than the time Morano had asked Prescott to help his son, Anthony, get into Andover.

Neither man ever forgot the confrontation, and Morano never forgave. "I don't know whether his name was originally B-U-S-C-H, but his demeanor was German. Blustery," Morano said many years later. "He [Prescott] always walked around town with a walking . . . you know, with a stick that the generals use . . . Baton . . . He walked around Greenwich with a baton and leggings and all that stuff . . . And his wife used to go around campaigning. I used to feel sorry for her because he'd yell at her, 'Where is my coat?' and 'Get my coat.' And swear at her, too. A lot of people heard that, so his disposition was mean. He had no charm, no nothing."

Morano, in a three-way race for the primary to recapture his seat, felt he could win because the other two candidates were "white Anglo-Saxon Protestants," and "those two would have split the vote . . . I would have won easily."

Instead, Morano lost after one of his opponents, Frederick Pope Jr., withdrew and the Bushes threw their support to the other man, Abner W. Sibal. Morano blamed Prescott for his defeat, accusing the senator of offering to recommend Pope for a federal judgeship so he would withdraw from the race. Morano also insisted that money had been paid to the Bridgeport delegation to vote for the Bush candidate. Morano went public with his accusations. "I had it all printed in the paper," he said, "and they [the Bushes] never challenged me."

Bernie Yudain, a columnist for *Greenwich Time*, covered the race and knew all the principals. "I never saw a dollar change hands," he said, "but it is fair to say that that [buying off the Bridgeport delegation] was certainly the perception in political circles at that time . . . I don't think many people got that delegation for free."

"It's hearsay, but it's what my father believed and what he told us," recalled Anthony Morano many years later. "He lost and Bush blocked [him]. I don't know exactly how Bush did it . . . Prescott Bush did not like my father."

The same man who championed civil rights as a political concept in the U.S. Senate turned on his Italian American colleague in Connecticut with all the meanness and spite of class discrimination. Prescott's admirable stand for equality shattered when put to the test of treating Albert Morano as a peer. But Morano refused to be intimidated by his so-called betters. In 1960, when Prescott announced that he would seek reelection in 1962, Morano announced that he would challenge Prescott for the nomination. He said, "The Republican party in Connecticut has as its top official a U.S. Senator who projects a reactionary image of a party seemingly indifferent to the aspirations and hopes of the people."

One of Morano's major supporters was Lowell Weicker, who later represented Connecticut in the House of Representatives and the U.S. Senate and was elected the state's governor. Weicker recognized the conflict between Bush and Morano as a classic struggle between the haves and the have-nots.

"Morano got screwed," said Weicker. "He was a good man, and he didn't deserve the treatment he got . . . The Bush family did not think that he was—quote—'representative'—unquote—of Fairfield County, and Fairfield County is the gold coast of Connecticut . . . I had supported Morano, and this did not enhance my standing with the Bush family. Matter of fact, my own political ambitions had to be put on the back burner for a while because of my support for Morano."

In that campaign, the Bushes acted as a family, with Prescott junior following his father's lead. Whatever values they espoused were not consistent with their political maneuverings. They went out of their way to vanquish an opponent whose major failing, in their eyes, was that he was upwardly mobile.

By 1958 the state of Connecticut had gone Democratic; it was almost impossible for any Republican to get elected for quite a while. Prescott junior did not attempt to run for public office until many years later, in 1982, when he tried to take the Republican Senate nomination away from the incumbent, Lowell Weicker. At that point, Pressy's brother George was Vice President under Ronald Reagan, and George did to his brother what P1 and P2 had done to Morano—poleaxed him. Behind the scenes George forced Prescott junior to withdraw his candidacy after six months and support the Republican incumbent rather than divide the party further. George sledgehammered his brother exactly as his father had once done—without fingerprints—but George didn't act in time to save the Bushes from the embarrassment of one of their own.

Before George had managed to remove his brother from the political battle, Prescott junior had been asked a question at a meeting of the Greenwich Republican Women's Club about the influx of illegal immigrants into the community. He said, "I'm sure there are people in Greenwich who are glad [the immigrants] are here, because they wouldn't have someone to help in the house without them."

The comment was reported in *Greenwich Time*, which contacted Prescott junior's campaign manager, who jumped in to do damage control. "That just doesn't sound like Pres Bush—it sounds like somebody who's not in touch," said Jack Murphy. "I just don't think he would've said that."

Prescott junior admitted being totally out of touch. "I made the statement," he said, "but it was a joke, really, with a bunch of these ladies. I was just kidding them. One of these gals asked about the thing, and I said it jokingly . . . There are a lot of these Mexicans, Colombians working in just about every community around the state . . . the illegal immigrants . . . it's a serious problem. I'm very concerned with it, I really am."

Democrats and Republicans jumped on Prescott junior with both feet. They stomped him for the initial gaffe and again for his strained explanation. "If Mr. Bush's comments are accurate," said his Democratic opponent's campaign manager, Jeffrey Lichtman, "they're just another indication that Republican millionaires have a different view of the world. Their ancestors got off the boats so long ago that they've forgotten the reasons that brought all those Pilgrims here in the first place." Prescott junior bowed out of the race several weeks later.

During her father's eleven years in the Senate, Nancy Bush Ellis lived in Massachusetts with her husband and their four children. But Nancy frequently visited her parents in Washington and acted as their hostess for dinner parties at the F Street Club. To be the offspring of a U.S. senator in those Eisenhower days of white gloves and brass spittoons was to experience certain deference, and, according to one of her Vassar classmates, "no one enjoyed being deferred to more than Nan Bush."

Nan came to Washington to meet the first American astronaut, Commander Alan B. Shepard, to attend Gridiron shows, to lunch at the Sulgrave Club, to mingle at White House receptions. She socialized with senators and ambassadors and Supreme Court justices. Politically, though, she was a liberal Democrat, more influenced by the politics of her lover, the historian Arthur Schlesinger Jr., than those of her father. For many years, she admits, "I was out in what George calls 'deep left.' "

"Nan is the political maverick in the family, if there is one," said her brother Prescott junior.

Her intimacy with Schlesinger led to a close friendship with John F. Kennedy. When Nan's daughter, Nandy, visited Prescott and Dorothy in Washington, the little girl was excited to learn that her grandparents had been invited to the Kennedy White House.

"Oh, Gampy," she said, "please dance with Jackie."

The next morning at breakfast Prescott reported to his granddaughter that he had done exactly as she had instructed.

After the Bay of Pigs invasion in April 1961, Nancy Bush Ellis supported Eleanor Roosevelt's suggestion to send something to Cuba as an apology for U.S. policy. Her father, still in the Senate, blamed President Kennedy for the "fiasco" and blasted his "left-wing advisers." Her brothers agreed, and could not believe their sister had aligned herself with Eleanor Roosevelt, whom the entire Bush family despised. Nancy recalled that during a family visit to Connecticut, her brothers "jumped all over me . . . And Dad said, 'If your sister has driven all the way down here for this, the least you can do is not pick on her.' I was almost trembling in tears. I was right on for Mrs. Roosevelt."

Prescott expressed himself on the Bay of Pigs in a letter to Mrs. Allen Dulles shortly after her husband died:

> I recall in the summer of 1961, after the ill-fated Bay of Pigs affair, you were away and we called Allen [CIA director] to come for supper, and he accepted. That afternoon he called and asked if he could bring a friend and he brought John McCone, whom we had known well but had not thought of as a particular friend of Allen's. But Allen broke the ice promptly, and said, in good spirit, that he wanted us to meet his successor. The announcement came the next day.
>
> We tried to make a pleasant evening of it, but I was rather sick at heart, and angry too, for it was the Kennedys that brought about the fiasco. And here they were making Allen seem to be the goat, which he wasn't and did not deserve. I have never forgiven them.

A political activist, Nancy Bush Ellis served as the co-chair of the New England section of the NAACP Legal Defense and Educational Fund and did volunteer work with the Boston United South End Settlement House, the New England Medical Center, the Boston Symphony, and the Massachusetts Audubon Society. She continued in this vein even after her brother George became a Republican congressman. A 1968 memo in the Lyndon Baines Johnson Presidential Library from the President's press secretary states: "Bush's sister, incidentally, is a Democrat. She said she was for the President [LBJ] and wished her brother, George, had become a Democrat when he moved to Texas."

Once George entered national politics, Nancy pared down her Democratic involvements. She continued raising money for the NAACP Legal Defense and Educational Fund, but she became stridently supportive of her brother, which baffled her liberal friends, her Democratic neighbors, and even some of her more moderate relatives. "I've learned over the years to stay off the subject of Big George and his hard-right politics," said a cousin, "and never ever to mention the dismaying policies of Little George."

Of all of Prescott's children, Jonathan was the one who most loved to perform. This would have been a definite asset in politics, but like Prescott Bush Jr., he had a tin ear for political sensitivities and was not much given to compromise. After his father had championed the civil rights bill of 1957, Jonathan made the front page of *Variety* with plans for an off-Broadway production that was perceived as racist. The headline in the show-business trade daily read: "Jonathan Bush Would Revive Minstrel Era."

After mentioning that his father was Senator Prescott Bush, the story reported Jonathan's intention to produce an "authentic" period show that would include "some Negro talent along with the blackface components."

The story concluded:

> *Minstrel shows fell out of vogue because of their datedness and hateful racial stereotypes of "Mr. Bones" but even when latter-day Elks, Moose and kindred groups assay amateur minstrelsy there has cropped up periodic objection from the NAACP for reasons of "stereotype," "Uncle Tomism," and the like.*

The negative publicity forced Jonathan to shelve his plans. On top of that was the sting of *Variety*'s curt dismissal of his career as a performer. The paper alluded to his unfulfilled "Ray Bolger ambitions," saying that "he was formerly a professional dancer." Jonathan thought of himself more as a full-fledged actor. Following his 1953 graduation from Yale, where he had been a Whiffenpoof like his father, he served in the military, then moved to New York City, where he attempted to support himself in the performing arts.

"I don't think he ever got any further than being a dime-store Santa Claus," joked one of his Yale roommates, "but at least he tried."

A former song-and-dance man, Jonathan had starred in prep-school plays at Hotchkiss. His mother was dazzled by his ability. Watching him perform several years later in *Bus Stop* at the Southern Playhouse, Dorothy Bush shared her maternal pride in one of her columns. "No Broadway show ever held me more spellbound," she wrote, "and I must confess I got a great thrill out of seeing Jon give a true to life characterization of Bo Decker." When Jonathan landed the role of Will Parker in an off-Broadway production of *Oklahoma*, *The New York Times* reviewed him as "a first rate hayseed."

Unfortunately, Jonathan's talents could not support his tastes. "He wanted the Walker lifestyle," said one of his Yale roommates, "and make no mistake, the Walkers felt they were every bit as important as the Bushes. After all, *they* had the money. Not the Bushes."

Making money was the first commandment of both families, and Jonathan struggled with his decision to forgo finance for the stage. In the end, the money ruled, and so, according to his roommate, the family took him in. In 1960, Jonathan joined G. H. Walker and Company. He was the only Bush, aside from his uncle James Smith Bush, to be listed in the Social Register. Jonathan joined the River Club in New York City and lived what his brother George called "the luxe life."

"Too bad in a sense," said his cousin Ray Walker, "because Johnny has the capacity to see the truth and tell the truth, more so than anyone else in the family."

With a master's in business administration from New York University, Jonathan eventually opened his own financial firm. With the Walkers' moneyed contacts, he stepped into the shoes of Uncle Herbie and became the family's financier. Jonathan would do for little George and his oil ventures what Uncle Herbie had done for big George. When Junior started a small oil company, Arbusto, in Midland, Texas, he turned to his uncle, who brought him some of the most powerful businessmen in America as his initial investors. Partnership documents show that George W. relied extensively on his uncle's ties to raise seed money. In later years, Jonathan also shook the money tree for all of his brother's political campaigns as well as those of his nephews.

"Being the adult child of a U.S. senator, especially in the 1950s, when politics was not so polarized, was a great luxury," said Ymelda Chavez Dixon, whose father, Dennis Chavez, was a New Mexico senator from 1935 to 1962. "You were invited everywhere . . . The velvet cords got lifted, the stanchions were moved and the 'Do Not Enter' signs taken down. You were swept into the corridors of power along with your parents. Suddenly the names you only saw on the front pages of *The Washington Post* and *The New York Times* were your dinner partners. You danced with diplomats, cabinet members, and Supreme Court justices. You listened to the Secretary of Defense debate the Secretary of State over coffee. You inhaled this closeness to power like an aphrodisiac, and before you knew it, you had come down with what they call Potomac Fever—and that, as you know, is incurable."

All of Prescott's children were affected by this political malady, but none more so than George, who was bewitched by his father's new life and visited Washington every chance he got. Dorothy sent her newspaper columns to all her children, and her weekly reports of Georgetown dinner parties, embassy balls, and White House soirees made Washington, D.C., look like the crossroads of the world, especially to her son and daughter-in-law stuck in the sandpile of Midland, Texas. When George read about his father playing golf with the President of the United States, meeting prime ministers, introducing legislation on the floor of the Senate, and debating foreign policy with heads of state, he decided that he, too, wanted the same kind of life. After one of his visits to Washington in 1959, when he met the commander of the Atlantic Fleet and listened to his mother converse in French with a UN diplomat, he returned to Midland and told his friend C. Fred Chambers: "I don't know if I want to be a politician, but I'd like to hold office, like my father. That's what I'd like to do with my life."

George seemed impressed by the aura surrounding a U.S. senator and the respect accorded to those who held high office. He was taken more with the power than with the ideological desire to serve. In later years, he would claim that he wanted "to give something back in the way of public service to the nation," but his cousin suspected that what George really wanted was a position of importance that would give him the respect his father enjoyed. George talked about it with his Uncle Herbie, and they agreed on what was most important to them in life.

"I still remember a dinner when they said that people in politics are the most important people in society," said George's cousin Ray Walker, "and that people in business are the second most important . . . They couldn't come up with a third. Power and money . . . That's all that mattered to them. I was so disgusted. I got up and left the room."

Neither George nor his uncle noticed Ray's departure. Nor would they have understood why Ray felt dismayed that they did not value anyone but politicians and financiers. "I tried to do the family thing [work for G. H. Walker and Company] for five years," said Ray, "but then I couldn't take it anymore. I quit, went back to school, entered medicine, and became a psychiatrist . . . I always say that my family drove me into psychiatry."

Becoming what his father had become became George's goal in life. First financial success; then politics. He needed no other focus beyond scaling Mount Prescott. Eventually he would achieve both, but, according to many who knew him, he would never feel that he had lived up to his father's accomplishments. "Even after he became President of the United States, he felt diminished by his old man," said a deputy assistant from the first Bush White House. "Maybe it was because he knew he'd only made it to the White House on Reagan's coattails. Whatever it was, we all knew, or I should say we all sensed from what he'd said, that he felt he hadn't risen to the level of his dad." George's own son George Walker Bush would never suffer the same crisis of confidence.

Big George began his serious ascent toward financial success from 1955 to 1959, running Zapata Offshore Company as a subsidiary of Zapata Oil. Based in Midland, the offshore company drilled wells on contract in the Gulf of Mexico. George's Uncle Herbie, a major stockholder and a member of the board of directors, sold the bonds that paid for Zapata's mobile deepwater drilling rigs, each of which cost approximately $3.5 million to build. George paid himself a salary of $30,000 ($192,000 in 2004) a year and oversaw all the company's operations from sales to contracts. He negotiated with oil companies to lease Zapata equipment, which, he explained in a letter to his stockholders, brought the company revenue whether or not they struck oil. His biggest responsibility during those years was chasing money.

As the financial cartographer, Uncle Herbie drew the treasure map that led George to rich investors. These investors needed the large tax write-offs that risky oil investments provided. They did not need George's company to succeed; they simply needed to like him and trust him enough to invest their money with him. For both sides, it was a no-lose situation, and George filled his end of the bargain admirably. He made an excellent first impression on all these men and usually came away with their financial commitment. He followed up each visit with a personal letter, a habit instilled in him early by his father. Zapata Offshore started with a $1.5 million stock offering. Among the stockholders were most of George's Skull and Bones class from Yale.

The company invested in the technology of R. G. LeTourneau, who invented a mobile three-legged drilling barge. Zapata Offshore was Le-Tourneau's first customer, and the barge was christened *The Scorpion* on March 20, 1956, in a ceremony in Galveston that George attended with Barbara and their nine-year-old son, Georgie. That summer George's youngest brother, Bucky, arrived in Midland with his prep-school class-mate Fay Vincent, later to become commissioner of Major League Base-ball. Bucky, the Bush "baby," stood six feet five and weighed 280 pounds; Vincent was about the same size. Both had played football at Hotchkiss and upon their graduation came to work for George as "roughnecks," lay-ing pipes in the oil fields. In Midland, they got their first exposure to hard work, hot sun, and redneck Texans.

Fay Vincent recalled the summer as his passage into manhood. "I got a crash course in racism," he said, "and it was life-changing . . . It was my first trip to the South. The landmark Supreme Court case *Brown* v. *Board of Education* had been decided in 1954, and as a result 'separate but equal' was no longer lawful. But in 1956 in Texas, separate and unequal remained the guiding principle in the oil fields. There were no blacks in those fields; no black roughnecks, no black suppliers, vendors, or driv-ers . . ."

By the end of its first fiscal year, Zapata Offshore reported earnings of $325,779 ($2.3 million in 2004); by 1957, the company had increased its earnings to $776,345 ($5.1 million in 2004). The following year the com-pany lost $524,440 ($3.4 million in 2004) but recouped its losses the next year. George did not have the stomach for the high-stakes risk of offshore drilling. "I'd be a nervous wreck every time I'd hear about a hurricane out there [the Caribbean or the Gulf of Mexico]," he said. The constant worry of placing a $3.5 million drilling barge into stormy waters exacer-bated bleeding ulcers that would plague him the rest of his life.

George thought the treasure of the oil business lay in foreign offshore drilling, whereas Hugh Liedtke saw the future in mergers and acquisi-tions. In 1959 they agreed, amicably, to separate their ventures, and George decided to move his family and Zapata Offshore to Houston to be closer to the Gulf of Mexico.

"Hugh was a different kind of guy [from George]," recalled Hoyt Tay-lor, a Zapata engineer from 1954 to 1972. "Hugh's a guy that wants to make money. George Bush don't really give a damn. I mean, yeah, being successful is important to him. He definitely wanted to make enough money that his family could live well and provide education and all that. But as far as pilin' up a big pile, George didn't give a damn. It didn't interest him . . .

"He was real conservative about his spending . . . [but] . . . he set good examples. Just the little things. Like he bought his own stamps. He didn't run his damn personal mail through the company's stamp machine. Hell, I used to sign his expense accounts, and when he went to New York, he [put in] for 250 bucks or some silly thing, and I said, 'Hell, there ain't no way you could go to New York City for $250' . . . He said, 'That's all the time I spent on company business; the rest of the time was my own damn business so sign this son of a gun and shut up' . . .

"He drove an old two-door Plymouth automobile that was kind of a disgrace, and I drove a damn Buick Limited, and I stayed nervous for fear that he'd decide that I hadn't ought to be driving that big damned old car, but he's the kind of guy that when times were boomin' he's liable to get on you a little bit about being loose with the company money . . . and yet when the boom was off and times was tough, he'd tell you go get you some damn money and gather some of those customers up and take 'em out and entertain 'em."

What some admired as George's Yankee frugality, others saw as mean stinginess. When he was on the GI Bill at Yale as a young married, he insisted his wife get a job to pay for her cigarettes. So Barbara worked at the Yale Co-op to finance her cigarette habit. Dotsie Wheeler Adams, another young bride on campus, recalled that when Barbara brought home some old books she had bought at a secondhand store, George told her she would have to return them because they couldn't afford to keep them. Kenneth Raynor, the golf pro at Kennebunkport's Cape Arundel Golf Club, recalled George Bush as the kind of guy who "loves to look for [free] balls. We'll be playing along and all of a sudden he disappears. We find him reaching down into the water to rescue a golf ball" that someone has lost. George constantly pleaded poor; in a 1952 letter to Neil Mallon, he wrote: "Bar is urging me to take her to Dallas sometime this fall for a Christmas shopping trip. My check book keeps insisting that we not make this trip." The Bush family maid, Otha Taylor, recalled the day that Barbara had let her go home an hour early. The next day Barbara nervously pulled her aside. "Mr. Bush came in last night and he was saying you weren't there . . . 'Where's Otha? She's supposed to stay here until her hour is up, regardless if she has anything to do or not.' " Mrs. Taylor was angry at the elder Bush, and told her brother, "He's a really mean man. He was telling his wife not to let me go."

George's penuriousness exacerbated the financial anxiety that Barbara developed as a child. After attending Rye Country Day School for a couple of years, she was pulled out during the Depression and sent to public schools. She grew up with a spendthrift mother whose bedside drawer was always filled with unpaid bills. As she told Donnie Radcliffe of *The Washington Post*, when she wanted to buy a coat, her mother would caution, "Now, don't go to Best & Co. when you buy that coat, go over to Lord and Taylor's because I owe Best." Barbara's paternal grandfather, Scott Pierce, had come from a wealthy family but lost his fortune in the 1890s, which forced his son, Marvin, to work his way through college. "My grandfather never recovered," Barbara said. "He sold insurance in Dayton, Ohio . . . Daddy and his sister, my aunt Charlotte, supported Grandfather and Grandmother Pierce financially for years." Barbara's mother, Pauline, was not pleased with her reduced circumstances and constantly criticized the elder Pierces. Although Barbara's family lived comfortably and even had domestic help, finances were strained because of the medical problems of her youngest brother. Barbara remembered her mother always talking about "when her ship came in."

In her own life, Barbara tended to look at things through the door marked "Unaffordable." She said that when George was traveling for Zapata Offshore to Kuwait, Venezuela, Mexico, Brunei, and Trinidad, "we couldn't afford for me to go to those places with him." George told her she couldn't go to Kennebunkport every summer because they "couldn't afford it"—although he went. She shopped for Christmas presents on seasonal sales; she cut up Christmas cards to make gift tags; and she stashed her half-price booty from discount stores in a closet for the holidays.

George swore that he came from "a comfortable but not wealthy" background because he grew up with so many people who were wealthier. His poor-mouthing sounded comical to some of his employees, who joked about him as "a penny pincher" but gave him high marks as a boss.

"Hell, you just don't meet a finer person," said Hoyt Taylor. "Everyone around there that worked for him thought that he was a first-class guy . . . There was one or two or three that wound up getting the ax, but

funny thing was that even those—most of 'em, not all, but most—
remained friends . . . Some guys kind of get a little greedy and [when] this
[one] guy did, George fired him. He didn't ask somebody else to do it for
him, either. He'll tell you that you're gone . . . I'll tell you that if you
ever . . . received one of George Bush's ass-eatin's, you'll understand that,
because he can do it, very politely and usin' a lot of those damn twelve-
cylinder words out of Yale . . . but, anyhow, you can walk right under the
bottom of that door when you leave."

Moving from Midland to Houston in the summer of 1959 required
logistical planning by the Bushes because they were transporting a business, building a house, and expecting a baby. They decided to send
Georgie, who was now thirteen, to Scotland for the month of August to
visit the son of James Gammell, one of Zapata Petroleum's biggest investors. The Bushes parked their other three children—Jeb, six, Neil,
four, and Marvin, three—plus the family dog, Nicky, with a babysitter in
Midland. "At least we weren't put in a kennel," Jeb joked years later when
asked why his parents were constantly leaving the children with neighbors
and friends and babysitters. At that time, George and Barbara moved
themselves into an apartment in Houston for four months to await the arrival of Dorothy Walker "Doro" Bush, born August 18, 1959. The proud
father wrote to friends in Midland: "You can imagine how thrilled we are
to have a baby girl in the family. Barbara came home yesterday and the
boys all gathered around and looked over the new baby with great concern. She looks just like all the others."

The Bushes' new home at 5525 Briar Drive in the Broad Oaks housing development of Houston was built to their specifications on 1.2 acres
and, although legally unenforceable, carried a restrictive racial covenant
that stated: "No part of the property in the said Addition shall ever be sold,
leased, or rented to, or occupied by any person other than of the Caucasian race, except in the servants' quarters."

These restrictive covenants, attached to both the properties that the
Bushes bought and sold between 1955 and 1966, were common in Texas,
although ruled illegal by the U.S. Supreme Court in 1948. As late as
1986, the Justice Department had to force the county clerk of Harris
County in Houston to include a disclaimer on every certified real-estate
record that such racial covenants were "invalid and unenforceable under
Federal Law."

As George was settling into a racially restrictive area in the South, his father was in the North needling Democrats for filibustering against civil rights. During the 1960 presidential campaign Prescott was part of the GOP "truth squad" that chased across the country "cleaning up" the "inaccuracies" of John F. Kennedy. During a special Senate session in August, Prescott sent a telegram to Kennedy in Hyannis Port, heckling him about his absences from the Senate floor:

> It is now 11 p.m. and your Democratic colleague [Senator Russell Long of Louisiana] still filibusters after eight hours. We are anxious to vote on Medicare.
>
> It is hot and sultry here. Won't you please, as an experienced sailor, grasp the tiller and steer us to the "new frontier." This is the time for greatness.
>
> Kindest regards.

Two months later Richard Nixon's running mate, Henry Cabot Lodge, predicted a Negro would be named to the cabinet if the Vice President were elected President. As a member of the "truth squad," Prescott quickly stepped forward to clarify the matter: "I think Mr. Lodge perhaps overstepped the bounds of propriety . . . He doesn't name cabinet members and he knows that. He later qualified his statement to say he meant qualified Negroes would be considered for appointment."

Prescott campaigned doggedly and devotedly for the Nixon-Lodge ticket, and his wife was even more partisan. "They are the team for the times," Dorothy told women's clubs throughout Connecticut. "Senator Kennedy, who has missed 331 Senate roll calls, excluding the times he was ill, has generated an appeal similar to Frank Sinatra among teenagers . . . The American people are too sensible to turn the election for President into a popularity contest . . . John F. Kennedy is a very ambitious young man who has neglected his work (by missing Senate votes) not only to fill his ambition, but the ambition of his father as well . . . It is fearful to think that a man of wealth can set out to gain an office and let it be bought for him." Dorothy might have been shocked to hear people say the very same thing about her grandson during the 2000 presidential campaign.

ABOVE LEFT George Herbert Walker (1874–1953), known as Bert, was the father of Dorothy Walker, the grandfather of George Herbert Walker Bush, forty-first President, and the great-grandfather of George Walker Bush, forty-third President. In 1900, Bert Walker founded G. H. Walker and Company, the source of the family's wealth.

ABOVE RIGHT Lucretia "Loulie" Wear Walker (1874–1961) in Palm Beach, Florida, early 1900s. When the devoutly religious Presbyterian married Bert Walker in 1899, his Roman Catholic father, D. D. Walker, refused to attend the wedding. Loulie, who did not like the name Lucretia, was the mother of Dorothy Walker Bush.

RIGHT Samuel Prescott Bush (1863–1948), a year before he died. He graduated from Stevens Institute of Technology in Hoboken, New Jersey, in 1884, with a degree in engineering. Later he moved to Columbus, Ohio and became president of the Buckeye Steel Castings Company (1905–27). He married Flora Sheldon and had five children: Prescott, Robert, Mary, Margaret, and James.

LEFT Dorothy Walker Bush and Prescott Sheldon Bush (1895–1972). They married on August 6, 1921, four years after Prescott graduated from Yale. They had five children, Prescott Sheldon junior, George Herbert Walker, Nancy, Jonathan James, and William Henry Trotter, and lived in Greenwich, Connecticut, where Prescott became moderator of the Representative Town Meeting in 1935. He ran for the U.S. Senate in 1950, was elected in 1952, and served until January 1963, when he retired.

RIGHT James S. Bush (1901–78) and his new bride, Janet Rhinelander Stewart (he was her third husband; she was his second wife), leaving Christ Methodist Church in New York City after their wedding in 1948. The marriage lasted four years. Janet, listed among the ten best-dressed women in the world, was the daughter of Fleming Newbold, president of the *Washington Star*. Jim Bush left his first wife, Caroline Patterson of the National Cash Register family, to marry Stewart. His older brother, Prescott, did not speak to him for several years. Jim Bush, the family black sheep, would marry twice again before his mysterious death in the Philippines.

MIDDLE RIGHT Pauline Robinson Pierce (1896–1949), mother of Barbara Bush, married Marvin Pierce following their graduation from Miami University in Ohio. A great beauty, she lived above her means, which forced her husband to go into debt to support her lifestyle. She died in a car accident. Her husband remarried. Barbara Bush, who did not attend her mother's funeral, named her first daughter Robin, after Pauline Robinson.

BELOW Marvin Pierce and family in Rye, New York, circa World War II. Left to right: Scott (b. 1930); Marvin; Jim (1922–93); Martha Pierce Rafferty (1920–99) with her daughter, Sharon Rafferty; and Barbara Pierce (b. 1925). Marvin (1893–1969) was born in Sharpsville, Pennsylvania. He was a star athlete in college and received graduate degrees from MIT in civil engineering and from Harvard in architectural engineering. He was president of McCall Corporation from 1946 to 1958.

ABOVE The wedding of George Herbert Walker
"Poppy" Bush and Barbara "Bar" Pierce in Rye, New
York, on January 6, 1945. From left: Jonathan Bush,
Nancy Bush, George (home from the Navy), Barbara,
Prescott, Dorothy, Prescott junior, and his wife,
Elizabeth, and William Henry Trotter Bush, known as
Bucky. Barbara, who said she married the first man
who kissed her, became closer to his family than she
was to her own.

RIGHT Nancy Bush Ellis, George H.W. Bush's only
sister, born in 1926. She graduated from Vassar, class
of 1946, and married Alexander "Sandy" Ellis Jr. (Yale
1944). She was a liberal Democrat and had an affair
with the Kennedy historian Arthur Schlesinger Jr.
Ellis was active in raising money for the NAACP.
When her brother ran for President in 1988, she
became a Republican to vote for him.

ABOVE LEFT Prescott S. Bush (class of 1917), known as Pres or Doc, prepped at St. George's School in Newport, Rhode Island. At six feet four, he was figuratively and literally a big man on campus at Yale. He played sports, lettering in golf and baseball, sang with the Whiffenpoofs, and joined Skull and Bones, leaving an illustrious record that paved the way for his sons. He served on the Yale Corporation and remained involved with Yale throughout his life.

ABOVE MIDDLE George Herbert Walker Bush (class of 1948) finished Yale in three years on the accelerated program for returning veterans of World War II. He graduated Phi Beta Kappa with a degree in economics. An outstanding first baseman for the Yale team, he joined Skull and Bones and was president of his fraternity, DKE.

ABOVE RIGHT The Skull and Bones roster from the class of 1948. The secret society, founded in 1832, became the most important part of Yale for George Herbert Walker Bush, whose best friends and financial backers in his political races were Bonesmen.

Edward Williamson Andrews Jr., Thomas William Ludlow Ashley, Lucius Horatio Biglow Jr., George Herbert Walker Bush, John Erwin Caulkins, William Judkins Clark, William James Connelly Jr., George Cook III, Endicott Peabody Davison, David Charles Grimes, Richard Elwood Jenkins, Donald Loyal Leavenworth, Richard Gerstle Mack, Thomas Wilder Moseley, Frank O'Brien Jr., Philip O'Brien Jr., George Harold Pfau Jr., Samuel Sloane Walker Jr., Howard Sayre Weaver, Valleau Wilkie Jr.

LEFT Babe Ruth, two months before he died in 1948, presents his book *The Babe Ruth Story* to Yale's baseball captain, George Herbert Walker Bush, for the Yale library. Like his father, George played first base on the Yale team, where he was known as "All Glove, No Hit."

LEFT George Walker Bush (class of 1968) was born in New Haven during his father's first year and was admitted as a Yale "legacy" in 1964. He did not achieve the distinctions of his father or grandfather, but he became president of his fraternity, DKE, and joined Skull and Bones. Unlike his grandfather, George wanted nothing to do with Yale upon his graduation.

BELOW George W. Bush's transcript from Yale, where he graduated near the bottom of his class. When he received an honorary degree from the university in 2001, he said, "And to the C students, I say, you, too, can be President of the United States."

C.E.D. Scores	Verbal	Math.	Engl.	Math.	Biol	Span-4	Pred.	R/C		Yale Son: 1948
	566	640	532	684	581	670	71	114/238		

Year	1964-1965	1965-66	1966-1967	1967-1968
	183 Lawrence	1355 Dav	1325 DC	1285 DC

YALE ACTIVITIES RECORD

1964-1965	1965-66	1966-1967	1967-1968
Davenport Football	Davenport Football	Davenport Football	Davenport Tackle Football Captain
Freshman Baseball		Davenport Touch Football	
		Rugby Club	
	Davenport Social Comm (Armour Council)	Dav Soc Comm (Armour Council)	Davenport Armour Council
	Delta Kappa Epsilon	Delta Kapp. Epsilon	
			Skull & Bones
	Davenport "B" Basketball	Davenport "B" Basketball Capt.	Davenport "A" Basketball
	Davenport Baseball	DC Baseball	

YALE UNIVERSITY NEW HAVEN CONN.

Mr. George Walker Bush
5000 Longmont Apt. 8
Houston, Texas 77027

School: YALE COLLEGE Class 1968
Major: History Birthdate 7/6/46
Degree: B.A. Date Awarded 6/10/68
Admitted from: Phillips Academy, Andover, Mass.

Course and No.	Jan.	June	Course and No.	Jan.	June	Course and No.	Jan.	June
1964-1965			**1966-1967**			**1967-1968**		
English 15	76	76	American Studies 59a	71	—	History 39a	HP	
Philosophy 10a	75	—	Anthropology 25	80	85	History 85-1	HP	HP
Political Science 21a	73	—	City Planning 10a	75	—	History 89	SAT	HP
Science II Geology	75	—	History 35a	80	—	Japanese 22	Cred	HP —
Spanish 40	76	75	History 54a	70	—	Political Science 48	P	P
Philosophy 15b	—	88	Classical Civil. 23b	—	78	History 36b	—	P
Science II Astronomy	—	69	History 35b	—	84	History 56b	—	HP
Political Science 13b	—	71	History 54b	—	76			
			Philosophy 38b	—	78			
1965-66								
Economics 10	71	72						
History 32a, 32b	71	71						
History 58a, 58b	76	84						
Sociology 55a	70	—						
Spanish 41	71	80						
History 63h	—	88						

Year	1964-1965			1965-66			1966-67			Cum. Index	1967-68			Final					Departmental Examination	
Term	Jan.	June	Year	Jan.	June	Year	Jan.	June	Year		Jan.	June	Year		Jan.	June	Year	Final		
Average	75	75	75	74	80	77	79	81	80	77									Pass	✓
Percentile	23	22	21																High Pass	
Credits			18		10			10			10	40							Superior	
Degree Credits			9		10			10											Failure	
Ranking Scholar																				
Dean's List																				

LEFT President Dwight D. Eisenhower and Senator Prescott Bush in 1956. Prescott ran this photo in his reelection campaign against Democratic Representative Thomas Dodd under the heading "President Eisenhower Signs a Senator Bush Bill."

RIGHT Senator Prescott Bush, representing Connecticut, known then as the Hat State, adjusts a straw Panama he gave to Vice President Richard Nixon on May 6, 1953, after a weekly lunch of freshman Republicans in the U.S. Senate. Bush, who favored jaunty brown-and-white spectator shoes and plaid double-breasted blazers, was known as one of the best-dressed men in the Senate.

LEFT Planned Parenthood fund-raising letter of January 8, 1947, lists Prescott S. Bush as treasurer of Margaret Sanger's first national fund-raising drive. At that time, contraception was against the law in Connecticut, and the state had a large Catholic constituency. In 1950, during Prescott's first race for the U.S. Senate, the syndicated columnist Drew Pearson accused Bush of being a member of Planned Parenthood. Bush lost and accused Pearson of spreading the lie that cost him elected office. This fund-raising letter proved Pearson right.

ABOVE The New England Conference of Senators, June 26, 1958. Seated left to right: Henry S. Bridges (R-NH), John O. Pastore (D-RI), Prescott S. Bush (R-CT), and Theodore F. Green (D-RI). Standing left to right: Norris H. Cotton (R-NH), Ralph E. Flanders (R-VT), George D. Aiken (R-VT), Leverett Saltonstall (R-MA), and John F. Kennedy (D-MA). The day after this photo, Kennedy made a speech criticizing the administration's handling of a crisis in Lebanon: "The fact remains that the American people have no clear and consistent understanding of why we are there, what we are going to do, or what we hope to accomplish . . . We are confronted once again with armed conflict in the Middle East because we have developed no alternative to armed conflict."

ABOVE The gravestones of Prescott S. Bush and his wife, Dorothy Walker Bush, in Putnam Cemetery, Greenwich, Connecticut. Dorothy selected the never-tarnish bronze marker for the senator: "Leader, Athlete, Singer, Soldier, Banker, Statesman, Churchman, Companion, Friend, Father, Husband Extraordinary." Her stone, laid twenty years later, identifies her simply as "His Adoring Wife."

LEFT George H.W. Bush and Eisenhower. Bush had been chairman of the Eisenhower-Nixon campaign in Midland, Texas, in 1952 and 1956. Calling on his father's friendship with the President, Bush sought Eisenhower's endorsement for his failed Senate race in 1964 and for his successful congressional race in 1966.

ABOVE LEFT President Richard Nixon shaking hands with George Herbert Walker Bush. As a one-term congressman, Bush angled to become Nixon's running mate in 1968. After Bush gave up his House seat to fight a second losing campaign for the Senate in Texas in 1970, Nixon launched him on his career as a presidential appointee. Bush said about his first political mentor: "[H]e appointed me to the United Nations and he saw me as a man with prospects in the Republican Party."

ABOVE RIGHT Secretary of State Henry Kissinger discussed policy with George H.W. Bush, U.S. liaison to China, 1975. Bush recorded his dislike of Kissinger in his diaries, citing his imperious manner and arrogance.

ABOVE George Herbert Walker Bush became UN Ambassador on February 26, 1971, and served for twenty-three months. This appointment resurrected his public career after he lost the 1970 Senate race in Texas, his second attempt at winning a statewide office.

LEFT Appointed by President Nixon to put out the fire of Watergate, George Bush was chairman of the Republican National Committee from January 1973 to September 1974. At the RNC, he hired Lee Atwater and Karl Rove and began building the political network that would carry him and his son to the White House.

Prescott fired off telegrams to Nixon throughout the 1960 campaign, supporting his position on the islands of Quemoy and Matsu and denigrating Kennedy's "irresponsible adventures" into foreign affairs, especially Cuba, which Prescott said had "come with ill grace from a member of the Senate Foreign Relations Committee." Tsk-tsking his colleague, Prescott concluded: "Senator Kennedy has been slighting his homework, due probably to his poor attendance record at committee meetings."

Shortly before Election Day, Prescott wired Nixon and predicted: "Connecticut will give you pleasant surprise early Tuesday night."

Instead, the state flabbergasted Prescott and disappointed Nixon by going for Kennedy. Adding to Prescott's discomfort was the public drubbing he was receiving from Albert Morano, who, now out of Congress, threatened to run against him so that Connecticut could have a senator "who cares for all the people, not just a few." Prescott never deigned to respond to Morano's charges, but on December 30, 1960, he announced that he would run for reelection in 1962. At the time, he was not looking forward to returning to Washington, where the Democrats now controlled the White House as well as the Senate and the House of Representatives. In a handwritten letter to Nixon after the election, Prescott wrote:

Dear Dick:

As the smoke clears, I send you this word of my continued admiration and respect. Washington will not seem the same to me after eight years service there with you, and in an administration for which I had no other feeling than pride and respect.

I had hoped we could continue in the same climate with you presiding. I could gladly have given my best to support your programs.

You had conducted yourself with courage, decency, and great ability, thus earning the continued admiration of those, including myself, who have been privileged to support your campaign vigorously.

With warm personal regards, I am
Sincerely,
Pres Bush

Two weeks later Prescott sent a letter to President-elect Kennedy, albeit not handwritten or as heartfelt as his letter to Nixon but still collegial:

> *Dear Jack:*
>
> *I congratulate you upon your brilliant campaign for the nomination and election. I trust that you may be given strength to do your utmost for our country. You have proven yourself an extremely able man, better suited for the Presidency than any of the aspirants who opposed you for the nomination.*
>
> *I shall try to be helpful whenever I can, especially in matters affecting our National Security, Defense and foreign policy.*

In January 1961, Dorothy attended the joint session of the Senate and the House after the Electoral College ballots were officially counted and Richard Nixon proclaimed that John Kennedy was elected President of the United States. "This was an unusual situation," she wrote in her column, "the first time in 100 years that the vanquished candidate has had to announce the election of his opponent."

Dorothy would not live long enough to see history repeat itself in the year 2000, when the incumbent Vice President, Al Gore, had to announce the election, decided by the Supreme Court, of his opponent—Dorothy's grandson George Walker Bush.

During the 1960 presidential campaign Governor Abe Ribicoff had done such a spectacular job turning out Connecticut's vote for JFK that the President tapped the governor to become Secretary of Health, Education, and Welfare.

"Abe went to Washington—in fact he lived a few houses from Prescott and Dorothy Bush in Georgetown," said former Ribicoff aide Herman Wolf, "but after a couple of years he got restless with the bureaucracy and decided to resign and run for the Senate."

Galvanized by the specter of having to run against the popular governor in a state that now had more registered Democrats than Republicans, Prescott reached out to the Ribicoff constituency.

The Connecticut Jewish Ledger of March 1, 1962, ran an exclusive with the headline: "Bush to Add Rider to Foreign Aid Bill Striking at Saudi Arabian Bias." The story stated that the 1951 Dhahran Air Base agreement, coming up for lease renewal, gave the Saudis the right to reject any American they considered unacceptable. The principal use of this section of the agreement was the exclusion of American Jews from service at Dhahran. Prescott said, "In any new agreement with Saudi Arabia, we should make it unequivocally clear that we insist there be no restrictions because of religion, race or ethnic background of any member of the American personnel assigned to Dhahran . . . This is the time for us to assert our principles, to express our repugnance for discrimination and to demand equality for all citizens in any foreign agreement."

Two months later Prescott endeared himself to Connecticut's Catholics by opposing the Eisenhower administration on federal aid to parochial schools. "As a matter of law," he said, "I am convinced that the Supreme Court's decisions allow room for aid to these schools and that federal loans would come well within the permissible constitutional limits."

Always responsive to his constituents, Prescott now worked overtime, responding to every letter and phone call that came into his office. When he received a complaint about "off-color" plays staged at the Westport Playhouse that were scheduled to tour South America as part of a cultural exchange program, he protested on the Senate floor.

"I am most concerned about two plays—The Zoo Story by Edward Albee and Miss Julie by August Strindberg—that have been described to me as filthy," he said. He demanded "some control" over plays performed by American acting companies in foreign countries, even if they were not sponsored by the government, and suggested he would introduce legislation that would set up a federal review board. Prescott's outrage was triggered by a letter from the director of the Department of Overseas Union Churches of the National Council of Churches of Christ in the United States. The director, who lived in Stamford, Connecticut, had asked: "How many Latin American viewers will be able to see through the filth to some abstract and artistic integrity? Why should we expect any people to respect us when we glorify prostitutes and homosexuals and gangsters under the guise of entertainment?"

Forty years later, when asked about Prescott Bush's censure of his play, the Pulitzer Prize–winning playwright Edward Albee responded:

I've gotten very used to Republican anti-intellectual and anti-creative posturing, and general congressional misbehavior in the form of such things as The House Un-American Activities Committee and the Army-McCarthy hearings.

The interesting thing about Senator Prescott Bush's condemnation of "The Zoo Story" was the height of objectivity which his ignorance of the piece gave him. I'm also grateful that he put me in the company of Strindberg. I wonder if he had read "Miss Julie" either.

I don't want to get too much into my continuing and growing dismay with the Bush family beyond saying that democracy is fragile and that many people surrounding the present president [George Walker Bush] seem less concerned with the democratic process than I.

When the 1962 polls indicated that Ribicoff would defeat Bush by 10 percent, Prescott called upon former President Eisenhower for help. Vacationing in Palm Desert, California, Eisenhower responded with a note: ". . . certainly want to do anything appropriate, and that in the opinion of the experts will be helpful, to aid in your campaign. The Republican Party needs more statesmen of the capacity and qualifications you have so ably demonstrated."

Taking this as a yes, Prescott wired back and asked Ike to appear at a political rally in Hartford on October 13, 1962:

I understand that you will be on your way to Boston to appear there the next day. As you know I shall be engaged in a difficult campaign for re-election since it is contemplated that Secretary of HEW, Abraham Ribicoff, former governor of Connecticut is now planning to run for the Senate against me.

I can think of no single thing which would be [sic] fortify me and the rest of the candidates on the Republican ticket as having you present on that date for this meeting. I have cleared this with Senator Barry Goldwater, chairman of the Senatorial Campaign Committee and also Bill Miller, National Chairman. Both give it their blessing and both will concur in the hope that you can be with us in Hartford.

I am most anxious about this and do hope you can fit it into
your plans.

> *With respect and warm regards, I am sincerely yours,*
> *Prescott Bush, USS*

Eisenhower's response had to leave Prescott feeling slightly whip-sawed. Nine months before the scheduled event, Ike said he was "uncertain" about his plans:

> *May we leave the whole matter in abeyance for the time being (and*
> *will you go ahead with your own plans as though I could not be*
> *present). When I get back East, I shall have a talk with Bill Miller*
> *to determine exactly what he wants me to do in the campaign, and*
> *what I can, without the expenditure of too much time and energy*
> *(and opposition from Mamie) do to accommodate his suggestions.*

On his sixty-seventh birthday, May 15, 1962, a few weeks before the GOP convention in Connecticut, Prescott made a momentous decision. After conferring with his wife and his doctor, he called party leaders together in Hartford the next day and announced in a choking voice that he would not be a candidate for reelection.

"The vigorous seven-day work week of the past few months has convinced me that I do not have the strength and vigor needed to do full justice to the duties of the campaign ahead nor to the responsibilities involved in serving six years in the Senate, most of which would be in my seventies," he said. "The advice of my physician has strongly reinforced my decision."

The announcement shocked the political press corps in the state and eased the way for Ribicoff's election. Despite early polls showing Ribicoff's lead, most Connecticut newspapers had given Prescott an even chance of winning reelection, but no one thought it would be an easy campaign, especially without Eisenhower's coattails.

"A lot of people felt Bush bowed out rather than get beaten by Ribicoff," said Herman Wolf many years later, "but I honestly think Bush would've won that election. The people of Connecticut were not all that happy with Abe for leaving them in 1960 to join JFK's cabinet."

In her first column after her husband's surprise announcement, Dorothy Bush wrote that she was grateful for his decision to retire: "Dizzy spells at the end of days spent on the road followed by sleep-destroying nervous pains in the stomach from worry over whether or not he would have the physical strength necessary to get through the six months and six years ahead, was the warning."

What she didn't write about was her concern that the pressure of running for reelection would trigger Prescott's drinking, which Dotty never admitted was alcoholism. To her, alcoholism was not a disease but a moral failing, and that was not something she could accept in the husband she adored.

"We both knew that once the convention had taken place, the Senator would have to keep going, even if he died in his tracks," she wrote. "After these warnings, suppose he collapsed in the middle of the campaign? What a weapon to hand an opponent!"

"No," she concluded. "The chance must be given to nominate a younger, more vigorous candidate whose strength is not in question."

Prescott always regretted his decision. "As I look back on it," he said four years later, "I think it was a mistake. The information we had at that time, about the prospects for the election, were very favorable . . . A public opinion poll which we had showed that I probably would beat anybody they [the Democrats] could put up. So as I look back, having not been happy in retirement for four years, or nearly four years now, and watching the scene down there with great interest . . . I often wish I had gone to a hospital and rested up for about 4 or 5 days or a week, and I've often wished my doctor had said to me, 'Now, listen—don't make any decision now. You're in a terrible state of mind. Go over to the Greenwich Hospital and rest for a week, and then I'll talk to you.' But no, she said, 'You'd be a fool if you ran.' I remember her language. But I was in a state of exhaustion, frankly, and that's no time to make an important decision. So I do regret it . . . I've been awfully sorry, many times, that I made that decision."

Prescott's consolation prize came in June 1962, when he received an honorary degree from his beloved Yale along with the pianist Arthur Rubinstein, former Secretary of State Dean Acheson, and President John F. Kennedy. The President, Harvard class of 1940, rocked the house when he underscored Harvard's scholarship and Yale's social status. "It could be said that now I have the best of both worlds," said Kennedy, "a Harvard education and a Yale degree."

George had flown to New Haven to watch his father be honored by his alma mater. As usual, he had left Barbara and the children behind in Texas. During those years of their marriage he traveled at will while Barbara stayed home. He frequently went to New York City on business, and then stayed to play. He flew to St. Louis so often that he became a member of the St. Louis Country Club, and he regularly visited his parents in Washington, D.C., whereas his housebound wife once went for four years without seeing her in-laws. Nor did George ever miss a summer in Kennebunkport, if only to fly in for a few days to see his Uncle Herbie. Barbara and the children only made it to Maine every other year because, she claimed, they couldn't afford the expense of the trip as a family. When they could, she drove the children in the family car and George flew.

From the very beginning, the Bushes' marriage was run to accommodate George. Part of that equation was the mentality of Barbara's generation, which believed that wives should stay home, raise children, and keep house. The other part of the dynamic was Barbara herself. "In a marriage where one is so willing to take on responsibility and the other is so willing to keep the bathrooms clean, that's the way you get treated," she said.

She knew that she had married a man who wanted a wife exactly like his mother, so she tried to emulate her mother-in-law at every turn. "Barbara worshipped Dotty, and she said she tried to pattern her life on her," said Mary Carter Walker, who was married to Uncle Herbie.

Barbara dyed her white hair for many years because her mother-in-law asked her to. Dotty thought Barbara would look better for George, but every time Barbara went swimming, her brown hair turned green. Then one day she stopped trying to make herself look better. "George Bush never noticed," she said almost bitterly. "So why had I gone through those years of agony?"

George needed his wife to be as adoring as his mother had been, and he let Barbara know whenever she missed the mark. "I remember George said to me once when we were first married, 'You know, you ridiculed me in public, Bar, and I wish you wouldn't do that,'" she recalled. "Well, it was just a dumb thing, but he was dead right, and I never did it again." (Years later, when he called her "a blimp" on television, she absorbed the insult with a smile and told reporters that her husband had a wonderful sense of humor. Proving the power of parental example, George W. Bush made a similar remark to reporters years later, describing his wife, Laura, as "a lump.")

Barbara was a great mother for boys—tough, athletic, and disciplined—but while she shared the same unyielding grit as her mother-in-law, she lacked Dorothy's soft touch. "My grandmother [was] an unbelievable person," said George W. Bush, "one of the most gentle, kind souls I've ever met. I wouldn't necessarily describe Mother . . . as a gentle soul."

With her husband gone most of the time, Barbara had to take her pleasure in her children. As Donnie Radcliffe noted, "She was highly organized. Her cupboards were stocked, her children's scrapbooks up-to-date, her thank-you notes always in the mail. She methodically sewed nametags in her children's clothes and cooked commendable spaghetti. She never missed a meeting with the teachers and never played bridge. Her housekeeping matched her mind: no clutter."

"She always made me feel like a slob," said her Texas friend Marion Chambers.

Still, it wasn't easy for Barbara, as she admitted years later. "I had moments where I was jealous of attractive young women, out in a man's world. I would think, well, George is off on a trip doing all these exciting things and I'm sitting home with these absolutely brilliant children, who say one thing a week of interest."

Barbara longed to have more of her husband's time and attention. When she broached the subject of needing some verbal demonstration of tenderness, George brushed her off. "You shouldn't have to tell that. You see it. You know it."

By the time they moved to Houston, Barbara knew that her husband was steering their life in another direction. She had seen him sprawled on the floor watching the 1960 political conventions on television. "I'm going to be up there one of these days," he told her. "Just wait."

Barbara didn't doubt him for a minute, and she soon shared her confidence with the rest of the family. "I remember when we were sitting in Nancy Walker's house in Kennebunkport," recalled Mary Carter Walker. "There were about five ladies and they said, 'How would you ever like to be First Lady?' And we went around . . . And then we came to Barbara and she said, 'I'd like it, because, you know, I'm going to be First Lady sometime.' "

She had to start at the bottom of the political ladder. A few years after her last child was born, her husband announced that he was going to run for chairman of the Republican Party of Harris County. Given the number of Republicans in Houston who did not belong to the John Birch Society at the time, George Bush might just as well have announced that he was going to shoot polar bear in the Gulf of Mexico.

CHAPTER TWELVE

Texans say the difference between Midland and Houston is the difference between no riches and nouveaux riches. Midland is where you go to strike oil, and Houston is where you go after the first gusher. In Midland, the Bushes were Presbyterians. In Houston, they became Episcopalians, considered by some a step up the liturgical ladder. Moving from Midland to Houston also meant a brand-new house with seven bedrooms, a third-floor sauna, an exercise room, a swimming pool, and a long driveway, plus live-in help for Barbara and private schooling (the Kinkaid School) for Georgie, which put him on the fast track to Andover. For big George, the move meant a bigger political playground—meaner and muddier.

By 1959, Houston, like Dallas, had become a hotbed of extremism. The nation's sixth-largest city had become a stronghold of the John Birch Society, a rabid anti-Communist right-wing organization founded by Robert Welch and bankrolled by the Texas oil billionaire H. L. Hunt, who sponsored the vitriolic radio program *Lifeline* that aired in forty-two states. Over the next ten years, the John Birch objectives were to abolish the graduated income tax, repeal Social Security, end busing for the purpose of school integration, dissolve U.S. membership in the United Nations, and nullify the treaty that gave the Panama Canal to Panama.

The Birchers publicly castigated President Eisenhower, CIA Director Allen Dulles, and Chief Justice Earl Warren as "dedicated conscious agents of the Communist conspiracy." They contended that the Council on Foreign Relations, for many years led by David Rockefeller, was an elite international cabal that sought to establish world tyranny. In Dallas,

Birchers spat on Adlai Stevenson, the U.S. Ambassador to the United Nations, and heckled Vice President Lyndon Johnson. In Houston, they tried to take over the Republican Party of Harris County, until GOP locals sent up a flare. The locals wanted someone sensible who could expand the party and still keep it safe for the conservative senator from Arizona, Barry Goldwater, to be the standard-bearer in 1964. George Bush felt he was the right man for the job. "I am a 100 percent Goldwater man," he said.

He wrote to his friend and fellow Bonesman Representative Lud Ashley, an Adlai Stevenson Democrat from Ohio, that he was running for the unexpired term (one year) of chairman of the Harris County GOP.

"I think I'll win," he wrote. His friend would come to realize that George was never paralyzed by the difference between certitude and certainty. "I'm not used to losing," Bush told reporters in 1964.

George was so unknown in Houston then that the newspaper ran someone else's picture over his name when he announced his candidacy. George called the editor to complain and sent him a personal photograph, which the paper published after he won an overwhelming victory—by default. He became the Republican chairman of Harris County in 1962 when his opponent Russell Pryor withdrew. As county chairman, he immediately launched an aggressive lawsuit to force legislative reapportionment in Texas to get a winnable district for the Republicans.

For the first time since Reconstruction, the Texas GOP felt emboldened to make such a demand and challenge Democratic dominance. The historic comeback of the Texas Republican Party had begun in the fall of 1960, when the people of the state were given the chance—legitimately—to vote twice in the same election for Lyndon Johnson, who appeared on the ballot both as John F. Kennedy's running mate and, for added insurance, as a candidate for reelection to the U.S. Senate. This maddened Republicans. Dorothy Bush, who was campaigning vigorously in Greenwich for Richard Nixon and Henry Cabot Lodge, fumed that "Senator Johnson is the forgotten man . . . so unsure of the election he had a special law passed so he could run for senator again as well as vice president just in case he should lose."

LBJ won his Senate seat by defeating John G. Tower, a pint-size professor of political science from Southern Methodist University. Johnson also won the vice presidency and carried the state for Kennedy. When LBJ resigned from the Senate, Tower jumped back in the race. This was the only good news to come out of the 1960 election as far as Prescott Bush was concerned. As he wrote to Tower: "I am . . . delighted to hear that you are once more in the race. I can think of nothing more beneficial to Texas than your victory. I have a strong feeling that you will make an excellent United States Senator. I admire your courage and your whole approach to politics."

In the special election required by Texas law, Tower won the LBJ seat and became the first Republican since Reconstruction sent to the Senate from a southern state. His election marked an epic turn in Texas politics that would lead to Republican supremacy within forty years.

The one big city that Richard Nixon carried in 1960 was Houston, a fact not lost on the ambitious new chairman of the Harris County GOP. Within three months of his election to his minor post, George Bush started talking about becoming the next Republican senator from Texas. He felt he was the best man to take on the venerable Ralph Yarborough, whom George considered "far too liberal."

George was encouraged in this fantasy by his family and friends, who believed, as he did, that anyone who met him would vote for him. "If you can get enough exposure," Lud Ashley wrote, "if enough people get to know you personally or via television—you'll get elected."

Almost forty, George had reached peak handsomeness, a fact frequently mentioned in the state's small-town newspapers. "He could very well be cast into a movie role of his true life story," said the *Austin American-Statesman*. "He looks like a U.S. Senator," said *The Kingsville Record*. "The candidate is a handsome man, handsome in a way that appeals to men as well as women," said the *Refugio County Press*.

In addition to his good looks, George was blessed with indefatigable energy, inexhaustible financial resources, and an efficient campaign organization. "He is by all odds the classiest Republican ever to flash on the Texas scene," wrote the political columnists Rowland Evans and Robert Novak.

After George conferred with his father and friends, he decided in 1962 to announce a run for the Senate the next year. He was convinced he would win in 1964 on the coattails of Barry Goldwater, whom he admired as much as his father had admired Eisenhower. "Goldwater is the best chance we have," George said. He gave a copy of Goldwater's manifesto, *The Conscience of a Conservative*, to his son Georgie, a student at Andover.

Georgie's roommate, John Kidde, was surprised to see the book lying on Bush's desk. "What the hell is this?" he said. "We didn't have any time to read anything extracurricular. If we did, you would read a novel. But George seemed honestly interested in the book. He said his parents had asked him to read it. I remember him telling me what Goldwater stood for."

At the time George Herbert Walker Bush decided to run for the Senate, New York Governor Nelson Rockefeller, who had divorced his wife in 1961, was the leading GOP contender for President. He was far ahead of everyone else in the polls, including Goldwater, until May 4, 1963, when the governor announced that he was going to remarry. The press then reported that he had been having an affair with his new wife, Margaretta Fitler "Happy" Murphy, when both were married to others. She gave up custody of her four children to marry Rockefeller, and the scandal whip-lashed the country.

The Hudson River Presbytery immediately censured the prelate who had married Governor Rockefeller and Mrs. Murphy as a "disturber of the peace," and in Chicago the Young Adults for Rockefeller for President quickly disbanded. The following month Prescott Bush, who had previously supported Rockefeller for national office and urged Nixon to pick him as his running mate in 1960 over Henry Cabot Lodge, now assailed the governor in a speech to the graduating class of Rosemary Hall, an all-girls high school in Greenwich and the sister school of Choate.

"Have we come to the point in our life as a nation when the governor of a great state—one who perhaps aspires to be nominated for President of the United States—can desert a good wife, divorce her, then persuade a young mother of four youngsters to abandon her husband and their four children and marry the governor?

"Have we come to the point where one of the two great political parties will confer upon such a one its highest honor and greatest responsibility? I venture to hope not.

"What would Abraham Lincoln think of such a chain of events? Have our standards shifted so much that the American people will approve such a chain of events? I venture to hope not."

Prescott said that whether Rockefeller's actions were appropriate would depend on educators, opinion makers, and religious leaders. Then he added: "It will depend on whether our people are ready to say 'phooey' to the sanctity of the American home and the American family.

"Are we ready to say goodbye to the solemn pledge 'to have and to hold until death do us part'? Young ladies, I hope not, for your sake."

The next day Prescott elaborated on his fulmination by telling reporters that Rockefeller should "publicly withdraw" from presidential contention. "The Governor's actions are a matter of great disappointment, for I have always been for Mr. Rockefeller, and consider him a very able, versatile man, one I have always respected and held in high esteem. But we can't overlook this chain of events and I think people should speak out honestly on the question."

Prescott stopped short of endorsing Barry Goldwater to help his son's campaign in Texas, but the political impact of his blast was not lost on the Republican National Committee's George Hinman, a close political associate of Rockefeller's. Hinman knew that George Bush could not survive politically in Texas if his father, already perceived by conservatives as far too liberal, had supported Rockefeller in any way. In this instance, Prescott was able to combine a little politics with a lot of outrage over divorce. Hinman was not convinced.

"I always have some question about people who pass harsh moral judgments on other people's lives and situations they know nothing about," said Hinman. "In former Senator Bush's case it's clear that the motivation is a good deal more political than moral. It's too bad the young ladies before whom he defamed the Governor could not have been aware of the political motivation behind this intemperate attack."

Prescott said he had been inundated with telegrams and letters showing "overwhelming approval" of his criticism. George, too, received letters commending his father, including one from Rockefeller's foe William F. Buckley Jr., editor in chief of *National Review*: "I wrote your father, by the way, to congratulate him on his courage in making the statement about Governor Rockefeller . . . I hope he hasn't suffered from it."

Several months later Texas newspapers would report that Prescott Bush, former U.S. senator from Connecticut and father of the GOP candidate for Senate, had been named as a defense adviser to Barry Goldwater's Peace Through Preparedness Committee.

Prescott might not have been so censorious about Governor Rocke-feller's marriage and divorce had he known what a New York attorney says he knew about Prescott's son George's extramarital dalliances.

According to the attorney, at the time Prescott was preaching Bush family values to New York's governor, George Bush was having an affair with an Italian beauty named Rosemarie [last name deleted for privacy rea-sons], whom he had met on one of his numerous business trips. Rosemarie told the attorney that the couple shared an apartment in New York City and that George promised to get a divorce and marry her. He changed his mind in the fall of 1964 and broke off the relationship, but he agreed to pay the last three months of the year lease on their apartment. Rosemarie sought legal counsel, thinking she might have recourse for breach of promise.

"According to my records, she came to see me at 11 a.m. on Sep-tember 21, 1964, at our law firm in the Chrysler Building," recalled the attorney, then a junior partner with Upham and Meeker. "She was quite upset, very emotional . . . I'd never heard of George Bush at that time, but being a New Yorker I certainly knew who his father, Prescott Bush, was.

"As I recall, Rosemarie said she was from a noble Italian family— Rome, I think—and that she would never have entered into an adulter-ous relationship if George had not promised to leave his wife and marry her. She said she could not return home because of the shame. She was very emotional . . . I got the impression that she and Bush not only lived together in Manhattan when he was here but that he squired her around to social events and they were very much a couple in public around the city. She told me he even put his name on the apartment directory which made her think she might have grounds for a common law marriage . . . You've got to remember that this was in 1964 when only the most afflu-ent people were flying. Planes were luxury travel then . . . So it would've been fairly easy for George Bush to have lived two lives then—one as a married man in Houston and quite another one in New York City . . . He was not the only married businessman to have such an arrangement.

The attorney was impressed by the lovely Rosemarie and believed her story. "I still remember Rosemarie's dark hair and dark eyes," he said many years later. "She was extremely attractive, lively and volatile. She had met one of the senior partners of my law firm at a party and in a weak moment when she said she needed a lawyer, he suggested she consult with me. Even if we had handled that kind of work, which we didn't, she did not have a legal case and I had to tell her so . . . I felt bad because she was so emotionally distraught . . . I never saw her again."

According to plan, George announced his candidacy for the Senate in September 1963, and by the end of the next month he and his family had begun to feel confident about his impending success. His father wrote to his good friend Samuel Bemiss in Richmond, Virginia: "Poppy looks to be fairly sure of the Republican nomination in Texas and Senator Tower told me . . . he thought he would win the election."

Cheered by Prescott's news, Bemiss, a conservative southern Democrat who met the Bushes while summering at Kennebunkport, sent a campaign contribution to George and mentioned his son Gerry's campaign for the Virginia Senate: "The important issues seem . . . the poll tax and hatred of the Kennedys. We want to retain the poll tax [to keep poor blacks from registering to vote] but would be glad to see the Kennedys go back to Ireland."

George took a similar stand in his own campaign. He ran hard against civil rights during a time when antiblack violence had inflamed passions throughout the South and the North. In June 1963, President Kennedy addressed the nation in a heartfelt appeal on behalf of civil rights as a moral cause. In one of the best speeches of his life, the President called upon the country to honor its finest traditions:

> *We are confronted primarily with a moral issue. It is as old as the scriptures and is as clear as the American Constitution. The heart of the question is whether all Americans are to be afforded equal rights and equal opportunities . . . One hundred years of delay have passed since President Lincoln freed the slaves, yet their heirs, their grandsons, are not fully free. They are not yet freed from the bonds of injustice. They are not yet freed from social and economic oppression. And this Nation, for all its hopes and all its boasts, will not be fully free until all its citizens are free . . . Now the time has come for this Nation to fulfill its promise . . . the fires of frustration and discord are burning in every city, North and South, where legal remedies are not at hand . . . A great change is at hand, and our task, our obligation, is to make that revolution, that change, peaceful and constructive for all . . . Next week I shall ask the Congress of the United States to act, to make a commitment it has not*

fully made in this century to the proposition that race has no place
in American life or law.

The day after the President's speech Medgar Evers, a black activist
from Mississippi and a World War II veteran of the D-day invasion, was
assassinated by a rifle shot in the back as he walked toward his wife and
children.

Against that tragic background, on June 19, 1963, the President sent
to Congress the most far-reaching civil rights bill in the country's history.
To demonstrate a mandate for the legislation, Martin Luther King Jr. led
250,000 people to Washington, D.C., that summer. He stood at the feet
of Abraham Lincoln at the memorial of the Great Emancipator and filled
the air with the incandescent rhetoric of his "I Have a Dream" speech.

"As television beamed the image of this extraordinary gathering across
the border oceans," King later recalled, "everyone who believed in man's
capacity to better himself had a moment of inspiration and confidence in
the future of the human race."

Campaigning in Texas, George Bush ignored Martin Luther King Jr.
and vigorously opposed President Kennedy and his civil rights bill at every
turn.

"I am against the Civil Rights bill on the grounds that it transcends
civil rights and violates the constitutional rights of all the people," Bush
said. "Job opportunity, education and fair play will help alleviate in-
equities. Sweeping federal legislation will fail.

"I am opposed to the public accommodation section. I still favor the
problem being handled by moral persuasion at the local level."

Determined to campaign in each of Texas's 247 counties, George in-
veighed against the civil rights bill at every stop. He also charged that "a
liberal left-wing radical like Ralph Yarborough," the state's senior senator,
would be the first in line to vote for it.

"I think most Texans share my opposition to this legislation," Bush
told five hundred women at the Dallas Country Club, which was restricted to whites only. "And Yarborough's consistent voting record shows
utter disregard for the wishes of his constituents."

Yarborough, like George's father, had voted for the Civil Rights Act of
1957. In fact, Prescott had supported the strongest (unpassable) version of
the 1957 civil rights bill; he also supported the 1960 Civil Rights Act, and

he supported every civil rights amendment offered to any bill in 1961 and 1962—and even put forth several such amendments himself. Yet there is nothing in documents released to date that indicates Prescott's personal views concerning his son's lack of commitment to civil rights in 1964 or his campaign tactics. In later years, George's mother expressed her dismay and disapproval, but in 1964 there is nothing to suggest that his father showed any concern or offered any advice. Whenever Prescott mentions the campaign in a letter, he simply says he is excited about the prospect of George's winning. When George loses, his father says "the lad" has nothing to be ashamed of.

Prescott was a Republican who presumably could hold his nose and support Republicans of many stripes, his own son included, just as Democrats for years had supported southerners with opposing views. While Prescott attacked southern Democrats in public when civil rights bills rolled around, the rest of the time he managed to maintain strong friendships with Senator William Fulbright of Arkansas and Samuel Bemiss of Virginia, both of whom held racist views.

On November 22, 1963, George and Barbara headed for Tyler, Texas (population thirty-five thousand), where he was scheduled for a luncheon speech to the Kiwanis Club, a group of one hundred men, meeting at the Blackstone Hotel.

"I remember it was a beautiful fall day," recalled Aubrey Irby, the former Kiwanis vice president. "George had just started to give his speech when Smitty, the head bellhop, tapped me on the shoulder to say that President Kennedy had been shot. I gave the news to the president of the club, Wendell Cherry, and he leaned over to tell George that wires from Dallas confirmed President Kennedy had been assassinated.

"George stopped his speech and told the audience what had happened. 'In view of the President's death,' he said, 'I consider it inappropriate to continue with a political speech at this time. Thank you very much for your attention.' Then he sat down.

"I thought that was rather magnanimous of him to say and then to sit down, but I'm a Republican, of course, and I was all for George Bush. Kennedy, who was bigger than life then, represented extremely opposite views from Bush on everything."

The luncheon meeting adjourned, and George hurried across the street to meet Barbara at the beauty salon for their scheduled flight to Dallas. Before leaving the city, George called the FBI in Houston. Files obtained under the Freedom of Information Act document George's 1:45 p.m. call to the Houston field office: "Bush stated that he wanted to be kept confidential but wanted to furnish hearsay that he recalled hearing in recent days . . . He stated that one James Milton Parrott has been talking of killing the President when he comes to Houston."

The man George turned in was an unemployed twenty-four-year-old who had been honorably discharged from the Air Force upon the recommendation of a psychiatrist. He was also a John Bircher who had vigorously opposed George during Bush's campaign for GOP chairman of Harris County. During his interview with the FBI, Parrott said he was a member of the Texas Young Republicans and had been active in picketing members of the Kennedy administration but that he had not threatened the President's life.

Years later, when he was running for President, George would claim that he never made the call. Documents were then produced that refreshed his memory. He also claimed that he did not remember where he was the day John F. Kennedy was killed—"somewhere in Texas," he said. George Bush is possibly the only person on the planet who did not recall his whereabouts on that day, although his wife clearly remembered their being in Tyler. She said that at the time of the assassination she was writing a letter in the beauty salon and that they left shortly after hearing the news. They flew to Dallas en route to Houston, and in Dallas they had to circle Love Field several times while the second presidential plane was taking off to return to Washington, D.C.

"The rumors are flying about that horrid assassin," Barbara wrote in her letter. "We are hoping that it is not some far right nut, but a 'commie' nut. You understand that we know they are both nuts, but just hope that it is not a Texan and not an American at all."

George and the three other candidates vying for the GOP Senate nomination suspended campaigning for several weeks but resumed after the first of the year.

On January 1, 1964, George issued a campaign biography that trumpeted his military career: "He was shot down in combat, during action which added the Distinguished Flying Cross to his three Air Medals." Ten years earlier, perhaps with an eye to his political future, George had written to the Navy requesting the three Air Medals on the basis of the number of missions he had flown in the Pacific theater during World War II. The Navy confirmed from records that George had indeed flown the requisite number of missions and awarded him his three Air Medals. Legare Hole, a pilot in George's unit, explained that Bush's medal count had been held down during the war by the policy of his outfit's commanding officer: "I think you got Air Medals for every five strikes you went on . . . our group, and this was the skipper's decision, I presume, along with the air group commander, didn't award anything of that nature, it was strictly on the merits of the mission."

By June 1964, George had won the primary runoff, and in July he went to the GOP convention in San Francisco as a Goldwater delegate. His father also attended the convention as an alternate delegate from Connecticut, secretly leaning toward the moderate William Scranton, governor of Pennsylvania. Afterward Prescott wrote to his friend Sam Bemiss and asked him to come to Kennebunkport: "I want to tell you about our trip to SF for the convention. It was especially interesting, as Pop was there with his Texas delegation and quite it's [sic] hero because of his recent primary victory. The corps of Texas news men think our George has a good chance to win in Nov. Wouldn't that be sumpin'?"

When President Johnson signed the civil rights bill into law in July 1964, George continued wrapping himself in the mantle of states' rights, which was conservative code for no federal intervention on racial matters. "The new civil rights act was passed to protect 14 percent of the people," George said. "I'm also worried about the other 86 percent." At every campaign stop he thumped Senator Yarborough for voting for the bill. "There is nothing more challenging to a conservative than to run against this man," George said. "I am for the great traditions of this state and those of the Senate itself, and it irks my soul to see a man turn his back on his own people."

"That was a vicious campaign," recalled Alex Dickie Jr., an aide to Yarborough. "Bush tried to make Ralph look like a nigger lover . . . Bush played that racial card over and over and appealed to the lowest common denominator in people. He did it then and he has never stopped."

To some people, Bush's opposition to the civil rights bill put him in league with segregationists. Like them, George said he would "hate to see" the Constitution "trampled on in the process of trying to solve Civil

Rights problems." He said he drew support for his views from the strong showing of the blatantly racist governor of Alabama, George Wallace, in the Democratic primaries. "This indicates to me that there must be general concern from many responsible people over the Civil Rights bill from all over the nation."

Charles Sargent Caldwell, a Senate aide to Yarborough, felt the political repercussions of his boss's vote for the legislation. "George Bush attacked us for that vote practically every time he made a speech . . . Bush's people—he had lots of surrogates, of course—would never make a speech on behalf of the Republican candidates that they didn't bring up Ralph voting for this Civil Rights Act."

By the summer of 1964 George Bush had become convinced that he was going to win. He had collected the endorsements of twenty Texas newspapers, including both Dallas papers, both papers in Fort Worth, and *The Houston Chronicle*. When he formed a statewide organization of Democrats for Bush, even President Johnson started to worry.

"Now the problem we've got is getting Yarborough to beat this attractive young boy, Bush," the President told the union leader Walter Reuther. "And he [Yarborough] ought to quit fighting with [Governor John] Connally and every Democrat . . . The only ones he ought to cuss is Republicans . . . They'll wind up having Tower in the Senate and having Bush in the Senate. That's the way they're going. Of course, Yarborough is a very weak candidate. Civil rights and union labor and the Negro thing is not the way to get elected in a state that elects Connally by 72 percent . . . He's handicapped in that state. Now he wouldn't be handicapped in Michigan or New York, but he's handicapped in Texas."

The Democratic Party in Texas was divided into conservatives like the popular Governor John Connally, moderates like President Lyndon Johnson, and liberals like Senator Yarborough, who was a minority in his own party and known to be quarrelsome.

George Bush figured that anyone as disputatious as Yarborough could not possibly win. The boy who had grown up needing to be liked by everyone was now a forty-year-old man who believed his likability was invincible. "Ralph Yarborough is unpopular in the State," George wrote Lud Ashley, "and even though the President comes from Texas, I think there will be many people who will want to see Yarborough bumped off."

Tough, seasoned, and twenty years older, the senator dismissed George as a pretty-boy pip-squeak who was bankrolled by rich Texas racists. Although Yarborough's campaign was disorganized and underfinanced, he hammered away at his opponent as a rich carpetbagger who belonged "to all them fat Houston clubs." When George was questioned about his memberships in the Bayou Club, the Ramada Club, and the Houston Country Club—all whites-only clubs—he said he had no problem with belonging. "I always believe people should associate with their friends in things like that." Yarborough jabbed him as a "Connecticut Yankee," and George shot back: "I'd rather be from Connecticut and for Texas than from Texas and for Walter Reuther."

George ridiculed Yarborough for voting for medical care for the aged. He compared the bill to a federal program to air-condition ship holds for apes and baboons, dubbing it "medical air for the caged."

He blasted Yarborough for supporting such "left-wing federal spending programs" as the Rural Electrification Administration. Yarborough scoffed that George "wouldn't know a cotton boll from a corn shuck" and was "plumb dumb" to level "so un-Texan a blow at the farmers and ranchers of Texas" by suggesting the elimination of the REA.

George derided Yarborough's support for the War on Poverty with a reference to the "sun tan" project of the 1930s, the Civilian Conservation Corps, which George said had failed miserably, although the CCC had built many parks and kept youths from running the streets jobless during the height of the Depression.

"Bush wanted to keep the jam up top," said Alex Dickie Jr., "whereas Yarborough wanted to put the jam on the bottom shelf for the little people." The senator supported federal aid to education, medical care for the aged, social justice, rights of working men and women, conservation, farm supports, rural electrification, and community development, all of which George opposed.

Having twisted to the far right of his father, George, as head of the Harris County GOP, had portrayed himself as a conservative who could get along with John Birchers on an individual basis. He said that the Republican Party should not be a refuge for segregationists, and yet his effort to bring Negroes into the party was to start a separate GOP organization for them. His good friend Lud Ashley, a Democrat, wrote to him in 1964: "You're so much better than Goldwater, Tower and that wing of the party, both ideologically and as an intelligent human being that there's just no contest."

Despite Ashley's personal endorsement, there is nothing to show that George Bush was better than what he was espousing. Winning was everything to him. "I like to win," he told the Associated Press. "Like to succeed. I feel goaded on by competition."

He later expressed regret at running so far to the right in 1964, yet he ran against civil rights again in 1966 in his first congressional race, and when he did vote for open housing in 1968, he seemed to do so in spite of himself—because black GIs expected it, not because it was the right thing to do. Having supported two Eisenhower campaigns (1952 and 1956) and Nixon's effort in 1960, George clearly planned to stay a Republican, but during 1964 he did not advertise the fact.

Yarborough taunted him for launching a $2 million campaign and littering the landscape with billboards of himself that barely mentioned the word "Republican." George countered with allegations that the senator had accepted fifty thousand dollars in a brown paper bag from the Texas fertilizer king Billie Sol Estes, who was in prison for mail fraud and conspiracy.

At rallies Yarborough read from Bush's campaign material showing that Zapata Offshore drilled for oil in Kuwait, the Persian Gulf, Borneo, and Trinidad. "Every producing oil well drilled in foreign countries by American companies means more cheap foreign oil in American ports, fewer acres of Texas land under oil and gas lease, less income to Texas farmers and ranchers," said Yarborough. "The issue is clear-cut in this campaign—a Democratic senator who is fighting for the life of the free enterprise system as exemplified by the independent oil and gas producers in Texas, and a Republican candidate who is the contractual driller for the international oil cartel."

In the oil fields of East Texas, "Smilin' Raff," as Yarborough was known, asked crowds if they were ready to vote "for a carpetbagger from Connecticut who is drilling oil for the Sheikh of Kuwait."

Slipping in the polls every week, Yarborough kept on slugging. "Let's show the world that old Senator Bush can't send Little Georgie down here to buy a Senate seat," he told his supporters. He zinged the pretty boy's "big ole Daddy" as "out to buy hisself a seat in the United States Senate" so many times that Prescott Bush finally responded with a letter:

"George Bush's Daddy did not *send* him to Texas. He chose to go 16 years ago and we have been very proud and happy that Texans have taken him to their hearts."

From afar Prescott enjoyed the rough-and-tumble of his son's campaign and did whatever he could to help him. But the father's style was as different from the son's as were their politics. Somehow Prescott had managed to transcend the limits of his conservative background when he ran for office, whereas George seemed to have regressed. His 1964 campaign was opposed to everything his father represented: civil rights, the Nuclear Test Ban Treaty, open housing, Medicare. George called Medicare "socialized medicine" and Martin Luther King Jr. "a militant."

"George Bush is certainly not his father's image in my view," said Charles Sargent Caldwell, a staff assistant of Yarborough from 1957 to 1970. "I can recall Prescott Bush being in the Senate of the United States. He was there when I was there, and I recall him as among that vanishing breed of progressive-minded Republicans . . . George Bush . . . is much more conservative. He was affected by his move to Texas . . . There was no doubt about the fact that if you were going to enter the GOP and become active in it in a place like Odessa or Midland, you were dealing with a bunch of folks who were really very, very conservative . . . you could be considered a moderate in Midland, Texas, and you would still be to the right of virtually anybody running for office in Massachusetts . . . That's just the kind of country [it] was."

In Texas, George had landed on a planet that could not support life as a progressive Republican. So he acclimated himself (some say too easily) to the conservative redneck terrain. At the time Senator Goldwater advocated using "small tactical nuclear weapons" to defoliate the jungles in South Vietnam, George also proclaimed his support for restricted use of nuclear weapons, if "militarily prudent." He then bashed Yarborough for supporting the Nuclear Test Ban Treaty.

"Lawd almighty," exclaimed Yarborough. "Bush doesn't believe in clean air, doesn't believe in keeping out all the strontium 90 and all the chemicals that pollute the atmosphere, that create cancer in babies, create leukemia, make sterile men and women."

Immediately George's finance manager, Martin Allday, suggested he counterpunch with the story of Robin's leukemia. "I said, 'George, you can turn this to your advantage.' " But George, according to Allday, said the family tragedy was out of bounds.

Perhaps this rare example of restraint accounted for George's assessment of himself during that campaign. In his 1987 autobiography, *Looking Forward*, he wrote: "Just as people listening to a candidate running his first race learn something about the candidate, the candidate learns something about himself. I found out that jugular politics—going for the opposition's throat—wasn't my style."

By then he had obviously forgotten his conversation a few weeks after the 1964 campaign with John Stevens, his Episcopal minister in Houston. Stevens recalled George's saying, "You know, John, I took some of the far right positions to get elected. I hope I never do it again. I regret it."

Yet jugular politics would be repeated so often in future campaigns that it became a pattern. George would always repent after caving in to his baser instincts, or what Yarborough called his "meanness to little people." George's need to win was so great that he would do whatever was necessary to get elected while at the same time hiding behind a carefully crafted image of niceness. Throughout the 1964 campaign he distributed pictures of himself surrounded by his wife, his dog, and all of his children. He used his son Georgie, eighteen, to tape a thirty-second TV spot in Spanish to appeal to Mexican Americans in the Rio Grande.

During that summer, young George worked in his father's campaign, looking up phone numbers, delivering signs, and compiling briefing books on all the counties in Texas. Before he left for college in September, he drove the Bush Bandwagon Bus for a whistle-stop tour of fifty cities, including the tiny towns of Paris, Honey Grove, Bells, Electra, Henrietta, Quanah, Tahoka, Dimmitt, Big Spring, Snyder, Floydada, O'Donnell, Lamesa, Odessa, and Midland.

At every stop, young George jumped off the bus with his parents and scooted around town to draw a crowd for his father.

"I remember him well," said Don Dangerfield, a retired fireman in Odessa, then an activist against racial segregation. "That boy knew he was going places, touring the white side of town like there was never going to be any doubt about it, just because of who he was."

Big George spoke on courthouse squares, in parks, at receptions, barbecues, ice-cream socials, picnics, livestock auctions, factory workers' lunch hours, and "come to Jesus" meetings. The Bush Bluebonnets, a group of pretty young women who wore big blue hats while they distributed Bush buttons and brochures, and the Black Mountain Boys, whom George introduced at every stop as "four Church of Christ lads from Abilene," accompanied George and Barbara on the bus trip. The "lads," an old-fashioned term George had picked up from his father, sang their cowboy rendition of "The sun's gonna shine in the Senate some day, George Bush is gonna chase them liberals away." Huge, happy, clapping, stomping crowds at every stop convinced the Bushes of certain victory.

Barry Goldwater made two appearances in the state with George, as did Richard Nixon, again to stupendous crowds. Particularly buoyed by Nixon's visit, George wrote to thank him:

> It helped immeasurably. You really got under Ralph's skin and he kept going around after this visit saying, "I really am effective" and "my colleagues really do like me." In fact, he ran in a few left-wing colleagues to prove his point. Your visit was great and all of us here appreciate it. It was a terrific help in fund raising.

"We're going to win," George told his supporters in the middle of October. "I can feel it. I can just feel it." Yarborough had slipped so far in the polls that *The Houston Chronicle* headlined the front page with the news: "Yarborough, Bush Even." *Newsweek* predicted victory: "Insiders like Bush in a squeaker." Even the *Yale Daily News* weighed in: "George Bush is young, energetic, and very conservative, and a victory over liberal incumbent Ralph Yarborough would make him a power in the GOP. And a victory is quite likely." The Democrats in Harris County were so worried they fired off a telegram to the President in the White House:

> IN VIEW OF THE UNBELIEVABLE NUMBER OF DEMOCRATS WHO ARE CONSIDERING VOTING FOR GEORGE BUSH WE CONSIDER IT IMPERATIVE THAT YOU MAKE AN APPEARANCE IN HOUSTON BETWEEN NOW AND ELECTION DAY TO SUPPORT THE CANDIDACY OF OUR GOOD DEMOCRATIC SENATOR RALPH YARBOROUGH

The President flew to Texas to campaign for Yarborough, but by Election Day the Bush team had become so certain of victory that they

changed their party site from the campaign headquarters to the largest hotel ballroom in Houston simply to accommodate the crush of well-wishers
who wanted to celebrate George's win. Prescott and Dorothy flew in from
Connecticut with their son Jonathan. Young George flew home from his
freshman year at Yale to be with his family for the grand occasion. The
ballroom of the Hotel America had been stuffed with balloons for the celebration.

"At 7:01 p.m. as we were pulling into the parking lot of the hotel for
our victory party, the radio announcer cancelled it," recalled young
George. " 'In the race for U.S. Senate in Texas, Senator Ralph Yarborough has defeated George Bush.' "

Dejectedly, young George assumed the job of posting the election returns for the growing crowds. By 9:00 p.m., it was painfully obvious to
everyone that President Johnson had won the greatest landslide victory in
thirty years of American politics. He swept forty-four states and the District of Columbia, practically drowning Goldwater, who conceded before
midnight. The Johnson tidal wave also swept Ralph Yarborough into office with 1,463,958 votes to 1,134,337 votes for George Bush.

Standing in the hotel ballroom, George was thunderstruck by his loss.
He circled the room, shaking hands and thanking volunteers for their
hard work. He smiled gamely and tried to hold back his tears as he conceded defeat and congratulated his opponent. "He beat me fair and
square," he said, his voice trembling. "I have been trying to think whom
we could blame for this and regretfully conclude that the only one I can
blame is myself." Toward the end of the evening, campaign workers spotted young George W. in tears.

Later his stunned father met with reporters. "I just don't know how it
happened," said George. "I don't understand it. I guess I have a lot to
learn about politics . . . The straight party lever hurt me and with a Texan
on the ballot that hurt me. I understand we were beaten very badly in minority precincts but . . ."

Yarborough was jubilant, especially when President Johnson dropped
by his headquarters to offer congratulations. The President addressed
campaign workers: "Thank you for not handicapping us for another six
years with another Republican senator."

The senator later described the campaign as "one of the vilest in history." He said he knew his vote for the civil rights bill might have cost him

votes. "I knew that only 38 percent of the people of Texas approved it and that was risky. I voted for the long-range best interest of Texas. I wouldn't be true to myself if I didn't." He received 98.5 percent of the state's black vote in 1964, the first year there was no poll tax—which greatly hindered poor voters, that is black voters, from voting—in federal elections in Texas. He then tore in to his opponent and said George Bush "ought to pack up his baggage and go back where he came from."

At that point, *The Houston Post*, which had made no endorsement in the race, suddenly made up its mind. In an editorial titled "Snide Statement," the paper wrote:

> *We found it difficult to decide before the election whether Sen. Ralph Yarborough or Houston's George Bush would make the better senator. However, Yarborough made it easy for us—and others—to decide who looked better after the election.*
>
> *The bigger man is George Bush, who took a bitter defeat gracefully. Bush, in his concession speech, said he had nobody to blame but himself. "He [Yarborough] beat me fair and square and I wish him success," Bush said.*
>
> *And Yarborough, the big winner? He issued a snide statement to the effect that Bush ought to pack his bags and leave the state. We'd like to point out to Ralph that Texas needs more men like George Bush, regardless of affiliation.*
>
> *Yarborough won bigger than many thought he would. But he comes out of it a smaller man than his opponent. And he lost something that should be important, even to a politician—respect.*

Samuel Bemiss, who like George opposed the Civil Rights Act, sent condolences to "My dear Pres" on November 4, 1964:

> *Poppy reflected honour and credit on his family and friends. . . . He has lost nothing and gained much.*

Prescott responded to "Dear Sambo": "It was just too much, the updraft of the LBJ vote and the down pull of the Goldwater Miller team. Our lad was hurt by both altho he polled more votes than any Rep. ever polled in Texas, including Ike."

George's father, at age sixty-nine, was struggling to adjust to his own precipitous political retirement. He also wrote to Bemiss: "I miss the Senate. I can't get over it. There was a full life."

Prescott never adjusted. Writing to his Yale classmates for their fiftieth reunion, he admitted how much he continued to miss the Senate:

> *I miss its excitement, its pressures and its privileges, particularly the privilege of service to my party and to the people of the State I have come to love. But . . . I believe I am [finally] getting more philosophical about my dilemma. Life has been too good to me to permit fretfulness in the closing years. After all, I have always believed in retirement at 65 or 68, so I really should never complain about a decision, which was my own, as I approached 68.*

Shortly after leaving the Senate, Prescott was unceremoniously dropped from the Social Register.

George, meanwhile, was devastated by his own loss. "The only time I remember his being very, very down was when he was beaten for the [Senate]," said Mary Carter Walker. "When he came . . . to visit us, I never saw anyone as depressed as he was. But he got over it after a few days. Got out on the golf course and got over it."

Actually, it took George much longer to recover from his staggering defeat than his Aunt Mary realized. When he finally limped back into his office, he started writing letters to his supporters. He promised Richard Nixon he would stay active in the party, admitting that it was "hard to concentrate [on business] after the intensity of the Senate campaign." He thanked President Eisenhower for his endorsement and apologized for losing. "I think the greatest thing ever to happen to my father, in a very eventful life, was his service in the United States Senate. Perhaps it was overly ambitious of me to think that I might be there, too."

Seven months after the 1964 Senate race, George was still smarting over his loss when he wrote to Lud Ashley: "I've recovered, well almost, from Nov."

Young George had returned to Yale, where 70 percent of the campus had supported Lyndon Johnson. The *Yale Daily News* reported that of the twenty-two alumni running for public office, all but four had won; the four losers, Republicans all, included George Herbert Walker Bush, who "was expected to present a stiff challenge to Yarborough, but was trounced in Johnson's two-to-one landslide."

Young George did not mention his father's defeat to any of his four roommates. One of them, Clay Johnson, kept looking for signs of despondency, but said he saw none.

Years later George W. would claim that after the election, he ran into the Yale chaplain William Sloane Coffin on campus and introduced himself. Coffin, according to George, said, "Oh, yes. I know your father. Frankly, he was beaten by a better man." George claimed that this incident engendered his lifelong distrust of easterners and began to shape his political thinking. "What angered me was the way such people at Yale felt so intellectually superior and so righteous. They thought they had all the answers. They thought they could create a government that could solve all our problems for us."

The first time George mentioned the incident with Coffin to anyone was when he was being interviewed by *Texas Monthly* in 1994, thirty years after it had allegedly occurred. Running for governor of Texas, George may have felt he needed to country-boy his Ivy League credentials. His story was repeated by *The Washington Post* in 1999, which carried a denial from Coffin that was heavily offset by a quote from Barbara Bush: "You talk about a shattering blow. Not only to George, but shattering to us. And it was a very awful thing for a chaplain to say to a freshman at college, particularly if he might have wanted to have seen him in church. I'm not sure that George W. ever put his foot again [in the school chapel]."

Yet Barbara Bush, known for holding grudges, did not mention this "shattering blow" in her memoir. Nor did George himself deem the life-changing event worth mentioning in his autobiography. Both omissions tend to cast some doubt on the credibility of the story.

"I don't recall any conversation with George W. Bush at Yale, and I certainly don't remember my saying anything so cruel, even in jest," said William Sloane Coffin many years later. By then George's story had been printed in *The Hartford Courant* and *The New York Times*. "After so many people mentioned the story George was telling, I wrote to him and said I had a hard time imagining my saying with utmost seriousness that his father had been beaten by a better man. But if George was telling the story, I had to believe him, and so I asked him to forgive what neither of us understood."

George scribbled a short note in reply: "I believe my recollection is correct. But I also know time passes, and I bear no ill will."

To those who know William Sloane Coffin, an avowed human rights activist, the story seems preposterous. To those who know George W. Bush the story seems improbable. Not one of his dorm mates interviewed many years later recalled his mentioning the incident at the time it supposedly occurred. Yet no one wanted to publicly challenge his credibility.

Coffin was a man of immense stature at Yale when he was chaplain. In the forefront of civil rights, he had been arrested in 1961 on the first Freedom Ride in Montgomery, Alabama. A champion of civil disobedience, he also became a national figure in the antiwar movement. Gratuitous cruelty was not part of his character.

"I can maybe—and I stress maybe—see George running into the Rev on campus and feeling that he [Coffin] wasn't all that sympathetic to George senior's loss," said one Yale man in George's class, "but that's only because Reverend Coffin was known to be for civil rights and against the war in Vietnam, in total contrast to George's father, who opposed civil rights and supported the war."

In the ensuing years, William Sloane Coffin and George Herbert Walker Bush would become ideological foes, and perhaps the younger George, who always picked up the cudgels for his father, allowed his general animosity to form a specific recollection—one that would resonate in the state where he was seeking office.

By the time George W. Bush told his Reverend Coffin story in 1994, he had entered the political arena in which truth was frequently the first casualty. In 1964, such a story about an illustrious liberal chaplain would not have been accepted. Thirty years later, in a more conservative climate, the story might seem almost plausible.

As far as George Herbert Walker Bush had strayed from his father's political principles, his firstborn son, George Walker Bush, had begun to stray even further.

CHAPTER THIRTEEN

The lawsuit George lodged as chairman of the Harris County Republican Party rocketed to the U.S. Supreme Court, and in 1964 their ruling of "one man, one vote" fell back in his lap like a bowl of rich cream. The ruling required the city of Houston, previously one congressional district, to be divided into three. One of the new districts—the seventh—was predominantly rich, white, and Republican: that was the district George wanted to represent in Congress. A poll he commissioned showed that a Republican could easily win there, so he announced his candidacy for the 1966 congressional race. He said he was "a man who will owe his allegiance and his vote only to his constituents." Not a difficult position to take, because most of his constituents were just like him.

This time George took no chances. He knew he needed to get elected to public office if he was ever to become President, so he resigned his position at Zapata to devote all his energy to political campaigning. He hired an advertising executive from J. Walter Thompson in New York City to orchestrate his media. He brought Richard Nixon to Houston to launch the campaign, he persuaded House Minority Leader Gerald Ford to raise money, and he sought another endorsement from President Eisenhower.

He wrote to Ike:

There is no incumbent and it is a district that I carried 57% to 42% in the Senate race in 1964. My opponent is a conservative Democrat . . . but I feel I can beat him.

I hate to impose on my Father's friendship with you once again,
but if it would be possible to endorse the enclosed picture as sug-
gested below, I would appreciate it.

George explained that the picture was for "a Negro friend, Mr. Jesse Johnson, who is working for me . . . The Negro vote could be the difference in
our race and since I'm running against an ex–district attorney, I feel that
we will have an excellent chance to pick up a good percentage of the Negro vote."

The number of black voters in his district was comparatively small,
but it was a voting bloc George wanted. To soften his oft-stated opposition
to civil rights, he followed the suggestion of his masseur, an African American named Bobby Moore, and sponsored an all-girls Negro softball team
called "the George Bush All Stars." He wrote in his campaign brochure
as a partial explanation for the sponsorship: "Organized athletics is a wonderful answer to juvenile delinquency."

His opponent, Frank Briscoe, accused him of pandering to black voters, but George deflected the charge. "I think the day is past when we can
afford to have a white district," he said. "I will not attempt to appeal to the
white backlash. I am in step with the 60's."

Always hyperactive, George swung into overdrive, spinning around
the district like a hamster on a wheel. He worked feverishly, out every day
at sunrise, going door-to-door, shaking hands, telling people he cared, but
as one writer covering that campaign noted, "about what was never made
clear." Still, George was doing exactly what his highly paid Madison Avenue adman, Harry Treleaven, had told him to do: establish a likable public image. In a campaign memo, Treleaven had written: "Bush . . . must
be shown as a man who's working his heart out to win." As always, what
was important to George—and what he assumed was important to everyone else—was image. Substance was of relatively little value, as was any
sort of vision, moral code, or core beliefs. What mattered was winning—
and being perceived as a winner.

His opponent looked so reactionary that George appeared moderate.
Like George, Frank Briscoe opposed any kind of civil rights legislation,
but Briscoe also firmly embraced the John Birch Society, which George
had finally repudiated. After his first campaign, George said he was
ashamed that he had not done so sooner. Segregated public accommo-

dations were still common then in East Texas and not unheard of in Houston. Yet both men opposed government interference that might end such racist restrictions. George claimed that legislation was not necessary to ensure open housing for all. "There are wonderful alternatives in the field of housing that will help all persons attain home ownership," he said vaguely.

He took out a full-page ad in *Forward Times*, the black weekly; a photograph showed him with white shirtsleeves rolled up, tie loosened, and his jacket slung over his shoulder—a direct steal from his telegenic Yale contemporary John Lindsay, the mayor of New York City. The message accompanying George's photo:

Vote for the Man Who Really Cares About the Things That Are Worrying You These Days. Elect GEORGE BUSH to Congress and Watch the Action.

His slick television ads, his substantial financial backing, plus his name recognition from the 1964 Senate race gave him a resounding (58 percent to 42 percent) victory in November 1966. George Bush had won his first election. But in the end, his appeal to the black community did not work. He did not carry the black vote in his district, something he did not understand. "It was both puzzling and frustrating," he wrote in his autobiography. "Running for Congress, I talked about the possibility of [breaking the Democratic Party's grip on black voters] with a longtime friend . . . who chaired the United Negro College Fund when I headed the UNCF drive on the Yale campus in 1948."

This recollection is typical of George H.W. Bush. Not only does it show the way he rewrites history to fit his convenient view, but it also allows him to find it "puzzling and frustrating" that a Republican who opposed open housing would not find support from black voters. The fact is that George had never "headed" a United Negro College Fund drive at Yale. There *was* no United Negro College Fund on the campus in 1948. Rather, he worked on the school's annual budget drive, a charity project that allotted 18 percent of the drive's twenty-five-thousand-dollar goal to the United Negro College Fund, a far remove from directly raising money for private black colleges. The national office of the United Negro

College Fund said its archives show no record of George Herbert Walker Bush being affiliated with them at any time during his entire Yale career.

"Uh . . . maybe he got himself confused with his younger brother Johnny," joked a friend. "Johnny is a member of the Executive Committee of the United Negro College Fund and a former board chairman. Or his father, Prescott, who worked to raise funds for private Negro colleges back in 1952 when he was state chairman of the United Negro College Fund in Connecticut."

In later years of campaigning and public life, when George needed to embrace civil rights, he would cite his volunteer work at Yale. He further exaggerated his dubious claim on behalf of the United Negro College Fund so many times that it did not just become real to historians and biographers; it became real to George. When he was asked in 1988 how he could in good conscience portray himself as a candidate for black Americans when the Reagan administration had watered down civil rights for eight years, he sat silently and never objected. Maureen Dowd wrote in *The New York Times* that he looked genuinely hurt by the question. "But," George said, "I helped found the Yale chapter of the United Negro College Fund."

George's 1966 victory meant yet another move for the Bushes because, unlike some congressional wives, Barbara did not want to stay in their home district while her husband went to Washington, D.C. She knew this congressional seat was the first step toward what George really wanted, and she fully intended to go along for the ride. Young George W. was still attending Yale at this time, so the move did not affect him, but fourteen-year-old Jeb wanted to remain in Houston with his friends and finish ninth grade. (Jeb was relatively used to being parentless. He had spent the first nine months of his life with neighbors while his mother lived in New York City attending to his dying sister. In the ensuing years his father was mostly a fleeting presence. If George wasn't traveling on business, he was campaigning. "Even when we were growing up in Houston," Jeb admitted later, "Dad wasn't home at night to play catch. Mom was always the one to hand out the goodies and the discipline. In a sense, it was a matriarchal family . . . He was hardly around.")

Barbara asked the Houston oil attorney Baine Kerr whether Jeb could live with the Kerrs during the year. Farming him out to friends was better than her staying in Texas, separated from her husband, whom she rarely saw. When the Kerrs agreed, Barbara and Jeb were both ecstatic.

The Bushes bought a house in Spring Valley, a restricted residential area within the district with real-estate covenants that forbade sales to blacks and Jews. Still, the move to Washington did not promote the family togetherness that Barbara had envisioned. "George went home [to Houston] every week that first term [1967–69]," she recalled. "But the children and I could go only during school vacations."

Eleven-year-old Neil had been diagnosed with dyslexia in the second grade, and Barbara knew he needed special education. She decided to enroll him and his younger brother, Marvin, in St. Albans, the exclusive Episcopal boys' school in Washington, D.C. Her daughter, Doro, or Dordie, as she was sometimes called, went to National Cathedral, the companion school for girls.

"I worked for GB that first term," said Virginia Stanley "Ginny" Douglas. "Everyone in the congressional office called him GB. We were a great big family . . . He and Bar pulled people into their lives . . . GB was constantly building relationships. Constantly . . . Johnny and Bucky Bush were in the office a lot. They called GB 'Poppy,' his growing-up name . . . My fiancé, later my husband, and I took Neil and Marvin to a lot of baseball games with the Washington Senators, and we took Doro ice-skating. We saw a lot of the younger kids.

"GB had a hilarious sense of humor. I remember a wig salesman came into the office selling falls and hairpieces. GB put on a fall with long flowing curls. He tore down the hallway to show Congressman James R. Grover, a Republican from New York who spoke with Long Island lockjaw. GB came back in the office and said, 'Well, Grover didn't like it. The man has no sense of humor.' "

As soon as George was elected in 1966, his father began working his connections to get him a prime committee assignment. As always, Prescott started at the top. He called Wilbur Mills, the chairman of the House Ways and Means Committee, the most powerful committee in the House of Representatives. No freshman congressman had been assigned to this committee since 1904, because Ways and Means was the preserve of seasoned men with expertise in tax law, especially those whose reelections were guaranteed. "Why waste satin on stand-ins?" reasoned the prag-matic chairman.

Prescott knew that a seat on Ways and Means was a leg up in con-gressional life, much like Andover and Yale in real life. So he prevailed on his friendship with Mills to make an exception for George. The chair-man, a Democrat, said that the House Minority Leader Gerald Ford made all the committee assignments for Republicans, but Prescott, know-ing how to flatter a powerful man, said that Jerry Ford would agree to whatever Wilbur Mills wanted.

George got his seat, but he never admitted his father's intercession. Rather, in a letter to one friend, he ascribed the assignment to serendip-ity: "I hope you approved of my committee assignment. Let's face it. There's a lot of luck involved in this, and I was at the right place at the right time. But no matter how you skin it, it's a real good break for a fresh-man Congressman to be on the Ways and Means Committee." (The Bushes rarely acknowledge that privilege and position often account for their success; it is the reason, years later, George W. could run for Presi-dent as an "outsider," never publicly admitting that being the son of a for-mer President might have helped elevate his political standing.)

Barbara Bush pushed the self-made man myth as much as anyone in the family. She did not blink when she answered the television inter-viewer David Frost's question about Prescott helping his political son. "He never did," she said with a straight face. "Nor did his father ever make a phone call for George, which I read fairly often. Never."

Amassing wealth—or as the Bushes put it, "securing our future"—became their first priority, and each man declared his financial success an independent achievement. Even Prescott denied the realities of his fam-ily background and the stature of his father as one of the leading indus-trialists of his day. "[This] was consistent with perpetuating the myth of the self-made man," wrote the historian Herbert Parmet, authorized bi-ographer of George Herbert Walker Bush.

George, too, insisted that he had earned his fortune on his own, and never acknowledged that he had relied on his father and his uncle George Herbert Walker II for the thousands of dollars he needed in 1951 to start Bush-Overbey, the high-risk Texas oil venture that eventually led to his success with Zapata.

Before leaving Texas, George sold all his shares in Zapata and publicly declared his net worth with the clerk of the House of Representatives: $1,287,701 ($7,380,434 in 2004). At the time such full financial disclosure was unusual and quite admirable. George was the only member of the Texas delegation to make a voluntary statement of his assets, including a list of all his stocks. (Tax records and financial disclosure forms over the years indicate that he did not raise his net worth until 1992, when he finally retired from public service, joined the Carlyle Group, and began charging $80,000 for speeches and public appearances. By the age of eighty, in 2004, George Herbert Walker Bush was worth an estimated $20 million.)

He arrived in Washington as a freshman congressman in the minority party, which meant he was among the lowest forms of political plant life, but having declared himself a staunch supporter of the war in Vietnam, he felt he was part of the moral majority. "I will back the President no matter what weapons we use in Southeast Asia," he said after Lyndon Johnson escalated the war. "I am for our position in Vietnam and opposed to those who want to pull out and hand Southeast Asia to the Communist aggressors."

As his close friend James A. Baker III said: "George respects authority. Has deep respect for authority." That respect—which his relationship with his father, and later with Richard Nixon and Ronald Reagan, showed him almost powerless to overcome—plus his conventional mind-set put him at odds with William Sloane Coffin, the charismatic Yale chaplain who believed that American involvement in Vietnam was so legally wrong and morally repugnant that he counseled young men to resist the draft. Flabbergasted, George could not accept Coffin's actions, which he characterized as "provoking lawlessness." George was correct in such a description, for until Coffin tested the legal concept of civil disobedience, there was no protection in this country for expressing dissent—there was only arrest.

The day before the march on the Pentagon, October 20, 1967, Coffin arrived in Washington accompanied by 250 antiwar protesters, including America's beloved pediatrician Benjamin Spock, the writer Norman Mailer, and the poet Robert Lowell. The potent mix of religion, fame, and Ivy League prestige drew mass-media coverage to their staged drama on the steps of the Justice Department. Before going inside to deliver a bag containing 994 draft cards collected at antiwar rallies that week, Coffin made a speech.

"We cannot shield them," he said. "We can only expose ourselves as they have done. We hereby counsel these young men to continue in their refusal to serve in the armed forces as long as the war in Vietnam continues, and we pledge ourselves to aid and abet them in all the ways we can. This means that if they are now arrested for failing to comply with a law that violates their consciences, we, too, must be arrested for in the sight of the law we are now as guilty as they."

To their disappointment Coffin and the men with him were not arrested, which unsettled their critics, including Kingman Brewster Jr., the president of Yale. Besieged by calls from outraged alumni, Brewster addressed the controversy kicked up by his chaplain at Yale's Parents Day Assembly a week later. He read a letter written by a freshman to the *Yale Daily News* that he felt represented the majority of the student body:

> *Such a drastic choice as civil disobedience must be an individual one, as one suffers the consequences alone. One cannot allow himself to be sucked into the frenzy of a mass sign-in. One must be absolutely sure that he is not only opposed to the War in principle but is also willing to suffer years of imprisonment, a certain degree of public shame, and a specter that will follow him until he dies . . .*
>
> *I truly admire those who are fortunate enough to have made up their minds as to how far they are willing to carry their dissent, or their approval. But I defend my right to be undecided—to carry my indecision right up to the day of my induction, if necessary. I will not sign an agreement, which I do not intend to carry out.*

Yale's president made clear his disapproval of the chaplain's pronouncements and actions, but then he said:

> *Would Yale be a better place if the Chaplain were not free to pursue his own convictions, including the preaching and practice of non-violent disobedience of a law he feels he could not in conscience obey? I think not . . . Even though I disagree with the*

234 / KITTY KELLEY

Chaplain's position on draft resistance, and in this instance de-
plore his style, I feel that the quality of the Yale educational expe-
rience and the Yale atmosphere has gained greatly from his
presence . . . his personal verve and social action . . . So I not only
find it easy to condone what I disapprove . . . but I am also sure
that your sons will look back upon Yale in 1967 as a better place
to have lived and learned because of the controversies, including
the draft resistance controversy, which so tax the patience of so
many of their elders.

The Old Blues rose up in arms. Within twenty-four hours George got a letter from his Uncle Herbie (Yale 1927), who had received the Yale Medal, the highest award of the Yale Alumni Board, for raising over $2 million for his alma mater:

Just so you will be completely up to date on the Coffin affair. I am
sending you the full release that was given out in New Haven Sat-
urday on Brewster's statement . . . I don't know how you feel about
it, but most of us here think Brewster's statement leaves much to be
desired.

Jonathan Bush (Yale 1953), who was working for G. H. Walker and Company, registered his disapproval in a letter to Kingman Brewster:

I agree with you that Yale is more important to the country than
ever and that Yale is in effect training tomorrow's leaders. I do not
like to think that tomorrow's leaders are being influenced by unpa-
triotic acts on the part of the university faculty.

I am sure you have received many complaints about William
Coffin. I do not want to belabor the subject but I wish to add my
protest also. Every time his name is mentioned in the paper, that
of Yale is mentioned with him. I believe that is sad for our great in-
stitution.

George, too, was irate. He fired off a letter on his congressional stationery to the executive secretary of the Yale Development Board about
Brewster's speech. "The first part [disapproving of the chaplain] I liked,"

he wrote. "The second part [defending the chaplain] I didn't." That was basically the extent of his analysis and the extent of his attempt to understand Brewster's defense of his chaplain's right to freedom of speech.

In a letter to a Houston constituent, George wrote:

The case of Reverend Coffin troubles me very much. I have discussed it with the Justice Department and as a member of the Yale Development Board, I am planning to protest to the President of Yale this weekend. The Justice Department simply tells me that they are "studying the matter" and also that they are waiting for a Supreme Court decision on the whole question of draft cards very soon. You are absolutely right about the lack of law enforcement in this area, and I have protested and will continue to protest. Those who stormed the Pentagon and deliberately broke the law were given minimal fines and for all intent and purposes were turned loose. This was totally wrong.

Getting no satisfaction from the Justice Department, George turned to the House Un-American Activities Committee, notorious for Communist witch-hunting, and received a three-page report dated November 7, 1967, on Dr. Benjamin Spock. Years later George stipulated that the HUAC report—which he included with the papers he donated to his presidential library—be sealed.

When he arrived in New Haven for Yale's board meeting, George came armed with legal research showing that Coffin may have violated a statute of the District of Columbia code pertaining to selective service, which would also put him in violation of the U.S. Criminal Code. George reported back to his Houston constituent: "I did have a talk with Yale's President Kingman Brewster. In fact, it turned out to be a full-scale debate with him before 80 members of the Yale Development Board."

A "full-scale debate" is a rather inflated description of the one respectful question George posed, later acknowledged by Yale's director of operations and development:

It was a great treat for us to have you with us. Everyone around here is still talking about your superb question from the floor about civil disobedience and the Chaplain. In bringing up the

*subject in the way you did you made a significant contribution
to the success of the whole weekend and for that we are most appreciative.*

Continuing his vendetta against Yale's chaplain, George wrote to another constituent. He described the fifty thousand people who marched
on the Pentagon as a "pitiful demonstration":

*As a Yale graduate and a member of the Yale Development Board,
I have protested these actions . . . The Justice Department tells me
they are not sure Coffin has violated the law, but I have two specific references which I am confident he has violated. It is a disgrace to my University and, more important, to our country. I will
do what I can.*

Mounting pressure finally forced the Justice Department to act. The
FBI arrested Spock and Coffin with three other activists for receiving draft
cards from those who refused to serve in Vietnam. Known as "the Boston
Five," the men were indicted for conspiracy to aid and abet draft resistance, a felony for which, if convicted, they could receive ten years in
prison and be fined ten thousand dollars. Their trial in Boston, which
came to be known as "the Spock Trial," began May 20, 1968, at the height
of the war.

Bracketed by the assassinations of Martin Luther King (April 4, 1968)
and Robert F. Kennedy (June 6, 1968), the trial focused on the concept
of civil disobedience, in particular on those protesters who believed that
the massacre of the Vietnamese was an absolute evil. Yet the court barred
all testimony that questioned the legality of the Vietnam War, and the
moral point of the protesters was overshadowed by the continuing escalation of the war itself. In the end, four of the five men were found guilty,
including Spock and Coffin, and sentenced to two years in prison. They
appealed and the convictions were overturned in 1969. The government
did not take further action. Faculty and students at Yale paid more than
half of Coffin's legal fees.

As his university was being battered like a ship in the winds of a hurricane, George Walker Bush, a senior in 1967, made his debut in *The*

New York Times. While the father was defending his country's right to bomb Southeast Asia, the son was defending his fraternity's right to "brand" its pledges.

"It's only a cigarette burn," George W. said. "There's no scarring mark physically or mentally."

Triggered by an exposé in the *Yale Daily News* about fraternity hazing, accusations arose that George's fraternity, Delta Kappa Epsilon, engaged in "sadistic and obscene" initiation procedures. "The charge that has caused the most controversy on the Yale campus is that DKE applied a 'hot branding iron' to the small of the back of its 40 new members," reported *The New York Times*.

"I can't understand how the authors of [that] article can assume that Yale has to be so haughty not to allow this type of pledging to go on at Yale," said George. As the fraternity's former president, he said the branding was done with a hot coat hanger. "It's insignificant," he said. "Totally insignificant." He claimed Yale's fraternities had the least severe initiations in the country, adding that Texas fraternities used cattle prods.

In the twelfth cycle of the Vietnamese calendar, 1967 was the Year of the Goat, but for Americans it was the year of death. More U.S. soldiers died in combat that year than in all the war's previous years. By the end of 1967, more than 480,000 American troops had been sent to Southeast Asia, more than in the Korean War at its peak. Already American involvement in the Vietnam War had lasted longer than in World War II, and the weekly bomb tonnage dropped on North Vietnam had exceeded that of all the World War II tonnage dropped on Germany. Antiwar demonstrations in the United States, once filled with long-haired lefties out of the antinuke movement, became more mainstream as the middle-class mothers of the ten thousand expatriates who had fled to Canada took to the streets. In December 1967, President Johnson announced a traditional Christmas cease-fire and grounded the B-52s while he visited the troops in Cam Ranh Bay.

Congressman George Bush also took advantage of the lull to visit Southeast Asia. He left Houston the day after Christmas for sixteen days in Vietnam, Laos, and Thailand. Upon his return, he issued a statement of rah-rah optimism, expressing "an overwhelming sense of pride in my country." He did not realize that he had been bamboozled by the military promise of "light at the end of the tunnel." Nor did he recognize the trap of open-ended conflict that would ensnare even more American troops. Rather, he reported "in every aspect of the war—political, economic and military—I saw or heard evidence of progress." He urged patience on the part of the United States. "The losses the enemy is taking are heavy, and the Viet Cong are gradually losing their grip on the people in the countryside. These factors will ultimately force them to quit."

Two weeks later the enemy that was supposedly "losing their grip" launched an offensive during Tet, the Buddhist lunar holiday. With more than eighty thousand North Vietnamese troops, they attacked every major city and most of the provincial capitals. The Vietcong had now pushed the battle from the jungles to the cities, and though they suffered huge losses, they gained a psychological and political victory with the element of surprise. The Tet Offensive turned the American attitude toward the war, especially after the respected CBS newsman Walter Cronkite reported on his trip to view the aftermath of the attacks.

Highly critical of U.S. officials, Cronkite contradicted official statements on the war's progress. He criticized American leaders for their foolish optimism and advised immediate negotiation, "not as victors, but as an honorable people who lived up to their pledge to defend democracy, and did the best they could." (Negotiations would start and stop until the Paris Peace Accords went into effect in January 1973, and U.S. troops were withdrawn. South Vietnam soldiered on until Saigon fell to the Communists in 1975 and the country was reunited. The loss of American lives exceeded fifty-eight thousand.)

On March 31, 1968, President Lyndon Johnson announced that he would not seek reelection. "If I've lost Walter Cronkite," the President confided to friends, "I've lost the country."

The President was pushed to his decision by Democratic Senator Eugene J. McCarthy of Minnesota, who stunned the country by nearly toppling the President in the New Hampshire primary. McCarthy's showing (41 percent to 49 percent for LBJ) was considered an enormous victory for the antiwar movement.

"When Johnson made the announcement that he was not going to run for President," recalled Mark Soler (Yale 1968), "the bells of Harkness Tower, the main carillon on campus, started ringing. There was incredible jubilation all over."

The country's view might have been changing, but George Herbert Walker Bush remained stubbornly committed to the war, even when family and friends tried to dissuade him. As early as 1954 his father had opposed sending "ground troops into the swamplands of Indochina." Prescott had said then, "If our military support is needed over there, I believe it should be limited to sea and air forces." Ten years later he said that escalation of the war had lost the United States the good opinion of the world.

"There's hardly any section of the world . . . which is enthusiastically behind our position in Southeast Asia . . . and this hurts. This makes it more difficult for the President to implement his policy . . . It's a lot more comfortable to have world opinion with you on any major foreign policy issue than it is to be suspect, or to enjoy the disapproval of a large section of [the] world."

Still, George remained a hawk. He believed that the Tet offensive was not a military setback for U.S. forces, and that only campus liberals believed that South Vietnam would not triumph over the north. He wrote to Richard Gerstle Mack, a fellow Bonesman, on Easter Sunday, 1968:

> I just don't buy that this is an immoral war on our part. If you want to argue that all war is immoral—fine; but this selectivity and this blind willingness to emphasize the weaknesses of the South Vietnam government while totally overlooking the terror of the VC and the past slaughters by Ho and the boys I can't buy . . .
>
> The thing that amazes me often is the arrogance and total lack of compassion on the part of some doves who suggest that those who don't want to turn tail and quit really don't want the war to end . . . These smart critics are immune to the repeated abuses, the sheer terror and torture of the VC.

Four years later, in 1972, George was forced to reassess his condemnation of war protesters for their "arrogance" and "lack of compassion." His son Jeb, then eighteen, had pulled a low lottery number in the draft—number twenty-six—and he told his parents that he was thinking of becoming a conscientious objector. As Barbara Bush recounted to the UPI in 1984, "George said, 'Whatever you decide, I will do. I will back you 100 percent.' " But the family was spared its crisis. The draft for Vietnam ended one day before Jeb, who had already passed his physical, might have been called. When Jeb ran for governor of Florida years later, he disputed his mother's recollection.

Although he had not been needed for his second-born son at the height of the Vietnam War, Congressman Bush had been able to pull the golden cords of his connections for his eldest son, who enlisted in the Texas Air National Guard on May 27, 1968. At a time when 350 Americans were dying in combat every week, George W. was twelve days away from losing his student deferment from the draft. He had taken the Air Force pilot-aptitude test and scored only 25 percent—the lowest acceptable grade—but because he had the powerful intercession of Ben Barnes, the Speaker of the Texas House of Representatives, George W. was allowed to jump over the year-and-a-half waiting list of 150 names and be admitted to the Guard. He was given one of the last two slots for pilots, was sworn in as an airman on the day he applied, and became a second lieutenant without ever going to Officers' Training School. On his application, he specifically checked the box that read: "Do *not* volunteer for overseas service."

The last time such magic occurred Cinderella's fairy godmother had waved a wand over a pumpkin and said, "Bippity bobbity boo." Colonel Walter B. "Buck" Staudt, commander of the Texas Air National Guard, said almost as much when asked to explain the preferential treatment for George Walker Bush: "He said he wanted to fly just like his daddy."

The son described his thought process to a Texas interviewer twenty years later: "I'm saying to myself, 'What do I want to do?' I think I don't want to be an infantry guy as a private in Vietnam. What I do decide to want to do is learn to fly."

This attitude was typical of the Bushes. They accept the privileges that their status confers on them without question. They do not acknowledge their privileges or relate them to others' lack of same. Consequently,

George W. as President could vehemently oppose affirmative action as some kind of "quota" and not see his acceptance to Yale and his easy entrée into the National Guard as any sort of equivalent.

Of course, young George was not the only son saved from Vietnam by a powerful father. A report by *Congressional Quarterly* showed that of the 234 sons of senators and congressmen who came of age during the war, only 28 went to Vietnam, and of that group, only 19 saw combat—a stark testament to rank and privilege.

The Vietnam War dominated the era, but President Johnson and Congress had other issues to deal with as well. The last vestige of legal discrimination was put to the test in the spring of 1968, shortly after the assassination of Martin Luther King and the riots that inflamed the inner cities. The House of Representatives scheduled a vote on the Federal Fair Housing Act, which prohibited discrimination in the sale, rental, and financing of housing. The bill had passed the Senate, narrowly avoiding a filibuster, and President Johnson wanted his signature in place as the capstone of his legacy.

Having campaigned against civil rights in 1964, and against open housing in 1966, George Bush was expected to oppose the Fair Housing Act in 1968. But he received a letter from a young constituent who had worked for him for two summers as an intern. The young man, Charles G. "Chase" Untermeyer, who was from Houston and had graduated from Harvard in 1968, took it upon himself to advise the congressman to seek his better angels. He recommended that George vote for open housing as the right thing to do. He quoted Edmund Burke's definition of a legislator's function in a free society: "Your representative owes you not only his industry, but his judgment; and he betrays instead of serves you, if he sacrifices it to your opinion."

George thought so highly of Untermeyer that when the young man received his Navy commission, the congressman recommended him as an aide to Rear Admiral Draper L. Kauffman, commander of the U.S. naval forces in the Philippines. Admiral Kauffman just happened to be the brother-in-law of Prescott Bush Jr.

By April 1968, George knew that he would have no opposition for reelection. His Houston district was so safe that the Democrats didn't even bother putting up a token candidate. He could easily vote for open housing without facing political consequences. So he dashed off a quick response to Untermeyer:

> I am most grateful for your "unsolicited views" on open housing . . .
> I'll vote for the bill on final passage—have misgivings—giant political misgivings—also constitutional—also I know it won't solve much . . . but . . . in my heart I know you're right on the symbolism of open housing . . . This will be my character builder and friend antagonizer—and your letter helped me decide.

Initially, on the procedural vote, George tried to scuttle the bill and send it to conference, which was an attempt to stall passage, weaken the legislation, and kick it back to the Senate, where it would surely be defeated on a filibuster the second time around. In a newsletter to his constituents, he said that he had tried to sabotage the bill as written because of "certain legal concerns." When that attempt failed, the House called for a vote on the bill itself, and George found his voice.

The next day he wrote to Untermeyer:

> Charlie-me-boy:
> . . . Yesterday I voted for the Civil Rights bill. Today, I am being fitted for my lead underwear. And Sunday, I go back to Houston.

Although George had served in a segregated Navy, belonged to whites-only clubs, and lived in houses with restrictive covenants, he was not totally blind to the disproportionate number of poor black men serving in Vietnam while the white sons of privilege, including his own, stayed home. The disparity between America's privileged whites and poor blacks was never as cruel or as clear as it was in the rice paddies of Southeast Asia.

When George returned to Houston for a town meeting, he recalled his trip to Vietnam. "I chatted with many Negro soldiers there," he said. "They were fighting, and some were dying, for the ideals of this Country; some talked about coming back to get married and to start their lives over.

"Somehow it seems fundamental that this guy should have a hope. A hope that if he saves some money, and if he wants to break out of a ghetto, and if he is a good character and if he meets every requirement of purchases—the door will not be slammed solely because he is a Negro, or because he speaks with a Mexican accent."

George told friends that the meeting started "with catcalls and boos" and ended with "a standing ovation."

Unaccustomed to any criticism, he was stung days later by the negative mail he received. For a man who thrived on adulation, even a slight rebuke was a body blow. He referred continually to "the venom and vitriol" he experienced. He wrote to one friend about the "seething hatred—the epithets—the real chicken shit stuff in spades—to our [office] girls: 'You must be a nigger or a Chinaman'—and on and on—and the county crowd disowning me and denouncing me and wondering if they could 'still continue to support me'—and . . . the snubs by legislative candidates who were wanting my support and fawning all over me a couple months ago."

He wrote to another friend about "the hundreds of letters I have gotten . . . boy does the hatred surface . . . most of the mail has been highly critical . . . emotional and mean."

As the years passed, George tended to recall his stand for open housing as if it were accompanied by a haunting trumpet that signaled some lone act of stupendous bravery instead of a rare attempt to do the right thing—and suffer no political repercussions. He had been one of nine Texas congressmen to vote for the bill, but he frequently forgot to mention the other eight. After interviewing both George and Barbara Bush in 1988, Gail Sheehy wrote: "As a congressman in 1968 he was the only member of the Texas delegation to vote for open housing." The writer said she didn't think to verify the vote of the Texas delegation, because she assumed the Bushes had been telling the truth. "I should have known better," she said.

By that time the man who had magnified his college involvement with the United Negro College Fund had slipped onto the dangerous shoals of exaggeration and the lies of omission. He emerged years later with an aggrandized view of himself that was as distorted as a fun-house mirror. When the time came to build his presidential library in College Station, Texas, he approved in the monument to himself an exhibit that crowned him with the laurels of integrity.

The display is titled "A Profile in Courage," from the title of John F. Kennedy's Pulitzer Prize–winning book about men who stood up for principle at great political cost. Visitors to the library read the following about a young Texas congressman:

> In 1968 Congressman Bush voted for the Open Housing Bill, which prohibited discrimination in housing and property right. The America of those years was still in turmoil over Civil Rights and Bush's position on this issue was not well received among his conservative constituency in Houston. Local opponents believed that passage of the bill would lead to "government control of private property."
>
> After the vote hate mail from segregationists poured into his Texas office. George Bush met his critics head on. Appearing before a hostile crowd in the Memorial West section of his district he calmly but firmly staked out his philosophical ground, reminding the audience that African Americans and Hispanics were at that very moment under enemy fire in Vietnam, serving their country. Discrimination against these men, here at home, just was not right. "Somehow," he concluded, "it seems fundamental that a man should not have a door slammed in his face because of race or color."
>
> After a moment of silence, the audience rose to their feet clapping and cheering; the young congressman had won the day.

After only eighteen months in the House of Representatives, George became frustrated with his role as a lowly congressman. He and his father decided he was ready for national office: he wanted to be Vice President of the United States. Together father and son mounted a campaign to persuade Richard Nixon to make George his running mate in 1968. Helping launch this long-shot campaign was his father's good friend Rowland Evans, whose political column with Robert Novak was syndicated by *The Washington Post*. Two months before the Republican convention Evans and Novak's June 5, 1968, column was headlined: "Young Texas Congressman Bush Gets Nixon Look as Running Mate."

"Evangelist Billy Graham, a keen judge of political talent, recently transmitted to his friend Richard M. Nixon an unusual suggestion: Rep.

George Bush of Texas for Vice President," wrote the columnists. "This possibility is based on Bush's television style, regarded by Dr. Graham as among the best of current practicing politicians. Nixon has been particularly impressed by spontaneous comments from newsmen covering his campaign that Bush was the sole redeeming feature of the otherwise dismal television spectacular by Republican Congressmen early this year."

Seizing on the national publicity, George and his father devised a campaign to impress Nixon with George's influence in the corporate worlds of business and finance, the mother lode of political fund-raising. Prescott again called in his political and social IOUs, and within days Nixon received letters from thirty-five of the most important Republicans in the country beseeching him to select George Bush as his Vice President. Some of the names on Prescott's list included George Champion, chairman of the Chase Manhattan Bank; Donald B. Lourie, chairman of the Quaker Oats Company; Daniel C. Searle, president of G. D. Searle and Company; Walter Hoving, chairman of the board, Tiffany and Company; and John E. Bierwirth, chairman of the board, National Distillers and Chemical Corporation. Other corporate giants included Overseas National Airways; Pennzoil United, Incorporated; Northwest Bancorporation; Hanes Corporation; J. P. Stevens and Company; First National City Bank of New York; and, of course, the Bush family's standbys: Brown Brothers Harriman and G. H. Walker and Company.

Files in the Bush Presidential Library reveal a concerted effort on the part of George and his family to push him forward as Vice President. All of George's biggest Texas supporters weighed in as well, including W. S. Farish III, president of W. S. Farish and Company, and H. Neil Mallon, chairman of Dresser Industries. Mallon's letter to Nixon said: "Billy Graham is reported to have said that George Bush is the best on TV he has ever seen. I agree . . . You need him on the ticket."

When George received a letter from his friend Louis F. "Bo" Polk Jr., vice president of finance for General Mills—who wrote that he was "pumping for Bush for Vice President as hard as I can. With your good looks and humor and my brains and ability as a lover to back you up, there would be no stopping you"—George responded: "Don't just sit there mouthing platitudinous statements. Get in there and write Nixon a fiery letter."

Prescott shrewdly advised his son to contact Thomas Dewey, the former governor of New York, who had lost the presidency in 1948 to "Give 'Em Hell" Harry Truman but still remained a power within the Republican Party. Dewey, a close friend of Prescott's, presided over a secret coordinating committee to advise Nixon on a running mate. Dewey and George Champion made sure that the committee interviewed George Bush.

George went to the GOP convention in August full of hope that he might be chosen. He did not realize until much later that Nixon had discarded him early on because he was too inexperienced in government and had never won statewide office. After the riots of April 1968 in D.C., Baltimore, Chicago, Trenton, Cincinnati, Newark, Detroit, and Boston, Nixon said he needed someone who understood the cities, and he narrowed his choices to mayors and governors, but no one expected him to choose the man who had nominated him for President in Miami Beach. Stunning everyone, including his closest advisers, Nixon announced his running mate was to be Maryland's Governor Spiro T. "Ted" Agnew.

Prescott immediately wrote to Governor Dewey:

I fear, Tom, that Nixon has made a serious error here. He had a chance to do something smart, to give the ticket a lift, and he cast it aside. I can't figure out why, when you were down to the last three names, any one of which would have been a better choice. I am sure Agnew is a good man. But to the press and the independents it seems like a pointless choice, or perhaps better, a wasted opportunity. And many seem to think it is worse than that . . . just a gesture to the Wallace South. If that pays off, I fear Dick will "lose on the peanut what he makes on the banana," as the Italian fruit vendor said.

Three days later, Dewey responded to his old friend:

George has made such a fine impression in Washington and, indeed, on all the members of the Coordinating Committee where he appeared, that my expressed views about him for Vice President came from conviction and admiration. I was not alone in this I may say and I was in good company . . . I think there was simply a feeling that he had not been in public office long enough. Every-

*thing else was favorable and I am sure that he can look forward to
a distinguished career with no limit on his future.*

George was thrilled to read Dewey's letter. He wrote to him immediately:

I am most appreciative of [your] interest and help.

*The wine was a little heady—getting even considered for this
post, but I do feel that the efforts made on my behalf were made
with taste and in such a way as not to disrupt what I consider are
many fine relationships in the Congress.*

*Thanks ever so much for your interest in this Silky Sullivan long
shot. [Silky Sullivan, a racing term for a horse that makes a big run
from far back, was named for the horse that once made up forty-one
lengths to win a race.] Though we finished out of the money, it was
a great big plus for me, and I am indebted to you for your interest.*

When George responded to his friend Bob Connery, he wrote:

*We did have a little somewhat abortive run for the vice-presidency.
When I saw Nixon in San Diego last week he confirmed that he
gave it very serious consideration, but decided against it because
of my short service in the House. I hope the ticket does well and I
feel that Agnew, off to a shaky start, has only one way to go and
that's up.*

Privately George referred to Nixon's choice of the Greek American
Agnew as "Zorba, the Veep."

Although Nixon had chosen the governor of Maryland to be his running
mate, he was so impressed by George's corporate clout that he made
the young man his protégé.

From his father George had learned well the art of influence. He saw
firsthand how it could fashion a successful political career. Like his father,
he, too, would pull the family's golden cords for each of his sons so that
they could achieve financial independence. Then they, too, would insist
they had made their millions on their own and that they had won election
to high public office independent of the family's dynastic assets.

During his 1968 campaign to be the vice presidential nominee, George carved time out of his frenetic schedule in June to attend his eldest son's graduation from Yale, which was two full days of festivities. But George could only spare a couple of hours, and he stayed just long enough to see his son receive his diploma. Young George spent the rest of the time with friends.

"He hung out with my family for most of the two days," said his Texas roommate, Clay Johnson. "I remember as his dad left, he made some comment about [wishing his] dad didn't have these other obligations. 'I wish . . . it would have been great if my dad could have been here during the whole time.'

"It wasn't said in passing," said Johnson. "Everybody wants their family there sharing with them . . . He's very aware of the toll that public service takes on the family members."

"My father died in 1986," recalled Roland "Bowly" Betts, George W.'s fraternity brother and close friend. "George told [my family] a story about how after he graduated from Yale, he wrote my father a letter, thanking him for being his father-in-absentia. Nobody's closer to their father than George, but his father was . . . busy. And he [George] just started bawling. Of course, then I'm bawling, and my wife is bawling, and soon all of us [my two daughters and George] are bawling."

On his son's graduation day, Congressman Bush had issued a press release denouncing the Poor People's March on Washington and their encampment on the Mall known as Resurrection City. He had written to the Reverend Ralph David Abernathy, who led a ragtag army to the nation's capital in a mule-drawn covered wagon to petition the government. Abernathy's mission was to lobby Congress for a $2.50 minimum wage, 1 million federal jobs, and a guaranteed income. George said he was "disturbed by the powder keg atmosphere" of the assembled poor. His press release thundered: "This Congress will not buy threats."

To his cousin Ray Walker, Uncle Herbie's son, such a reaction on George's part was in keeping with the Bush family's grandiose sense of entitlement.

"Does anyone from that family understand what it is to be poor? No," he said. "And the bigger question is: Do they understand their own ignorance?" Ray Walker included the Walkers as well as the Bushes in his disapproval, saying that both families lacked genuine empathy for those less fortunate.

Congressman Bush was not interested in getting to Yale in time to hear the speech of Dick Gregory, the black comedian and social activist. Gregory had arrived on the eighteenth day of a thirty-two-day fast to protest the war in Vietnam. He was unshaven, and his eyes were bloodshot. But he said he came to give Yale graduates an insight into what it was like to be Negro in America:

> Think about going to buy a pack of cigarettes. You put your money in the machine, but nothing happens. You put more money in, and still nothing happens. You did what you were supposed to do, but nothing happened. So you kick the machine and you kick it again, but still nothing happens. It's frustrating as hell. That cigarette machine owes you a pack of cigarettes, but it doesn't deliver.

The class of 1968 gave the comedian a standing ovation. Years later, when he wrote his political memoir, George W. Bush remembered Gregory's speech. "It was a different perspective," Bush said, "and it made a lasting impression."

His father's preoccupation at that time was to punish those who kicked the cigarette machine by inciting arson, looting, and violence during the 1968 riots. Bush introduced legislation to remove from federal employment anyone convicted of unlawful acts in connection with civil disorders. His bill went nowhere in Congress, but the publicity he received in Texas reinforced his hard-rock credentials as a law-and-order conservative who reflected the views of his constituency.

En route to the graduation ceremony at Yale, Congressman George Bush bypassed the Prescott S. Bush Mall, a sixty-unit low-rent housing project for senior citizens in New Haven that had been named in honor of his father. As a senator, Prescott had helped launch one of the most comprehensive programs of urban development in America and was honored for his interest in slum clearance and urban renewal. "In the beginning, when we were pioneers, my job as Mayor of New Haven was lonely and filled with frustration," said Richard C. Lee at the dedication ceremony. "There was one voice, however, that was always heard, and it was the voice and vote of the senior senator from Connecticut." Rents for the Bush development, including heat and hot water, started at forty-five dollars a month.

On that particular day in 1968 the difference between Prescott Bush and his political son could be measured in the miles that separated the muddy covered wagon in Resurrection City from the shiny black limousine speeding through the slums of New Haven to the lush oasis of Yale.

CHAPTER FOURTEEN

George W. Bush was determined to go to Yale. His family's long line of Old Blues stretched back four generations to his great-great-grandfather the Reverend James Smith Bush (class of 1844). His grandfather Prescott, whose devotion to the school never flagged, was known on campus as the senator from Yale. As a member of the Yale Corporation for twelve years, an associate fellow of Yale's Calhoun College, and a member of the Yale Development Board, Prescott could easily tug his old school ties to get his grandson admitted if George really wanted to go.

"George, Yale is not a choice; it is a commitment. Do you know what that means?"

"I think so, Senator," said the grandson, who was not allowed to address his grandfather in any other manner. "It means sticking with something no matter what."

Prescott pointed to the young man's breakfast plate. "It is the difference," he said, "between ham and eggs. The chicken is involved. The pig is committed."

Prescott liked to express himself in folksy ways. When he resigned from the Yale Development Board a few years later, he was asked if he would like to serve on an advisory committee. He wrote to Yale's president Kingman Brewster:

I felt like the old colored preacher who was retiring at age 70 after 45 years with this same congregation, and in making his farewell prayer he said: "Oh Lawd . . . thou knowest that I have

served thee long and to the best of my ability, thou knowest of my
love for thee, and thou knowest that, even retired, I shall want to
do all I can to help thy people here, but only, Oh Lawd, in an ad-
visory capacity."

After visiting his grandfather, young George returned to Andover and talked to the dean. He was told that his mediocre grades probably would not meet Yale's stringent requirements. The dean suggested that George list two other choices for college. George wrote down: "(1) Yale, (2) Yale, (3) Yale." As a backup, he applied to the University of Texas, but only because the dean insisted. George's prep-school record, which he has never allowed to be released, was problematical, and not simply for less than stellar grades. During his years at Andover—1961 to 1964—he plastered a large Confederate flag on the wall of his room, which made the black students there feel distinctly unwelcome. Such blatant racism was tolerated by the school, especially from the son of George Herbert Walker Bush, one of Andover's most esteemed alumni.

"George senior was a huge legend at Andover," said Genevieve "Gene" Young, a New York editor who served on the Andover board with Bush. "He was known as a rock—that's the Andover speak for a really big man on campus."

George Herbert Walker Bush, who was on the Andover board of trustees from 1963 until 1979, had to intercede with the school on more than one occasion for his errant sons. Jeb was required to repeat the ninth grade when he entered Andover from the Kinkaid School in 1967. He later violated the zero-tolerance ban on alcohol and was suspended, but after his father's intercession he was allowed to stay on. When Jeb graduated in 1971, his father handed out the class diplomas. Jeb's brother Marvin entered Andover in 1971, and he, too, had to repeat the ninth grade. The next year Marvin and several friends were caught doing drugs. The friends were expelled, but again Daddy Bush interceded. He pleaded his son's case so effectively that Marvin was allowed to finish his sophomore year. Instead of expulsion, Marvin was given an "honorary transfer" that enabled him to enter Woodberry Forest in Orange, Virginia, in 1973, and finish his last two years of high school.

Young George was admitted to Andover in 1961 as a tenth grader—what the school then called a "lower middle." He entered with his younger cousin Kevin Rafferty, the son of Barbara's sister, Martha; an older cousin, Prescott S. Bush III, P3, the son of Prescott Bush Jr., was already in attendance, proving that Andover was the family's adolescent way station. From the moment George arrived, he struggled to survive. He labored to pass the basic diploma requirements: four years of English and expository writing; three years of math and a foreign language with no English spoken in class; one and a half years of science and history; one year of religion and one of art or music; plus four electives, from Russian to anthropology. Although 110 students in his class of 290 made the honor roll, George never did. He ended up graduating near the bottom of his class.

"George's grades were the same as mine—a bare-bones C," said J. Milburn "Kim" Jessup. "We passed by only a prayer and a whisker, but both of us got into Yale because we were legacies of our Yalie fathers."

Time magazine had cited Phillips Academy in Andover, Massachusetts, as "the nation's best prep school." For a public-school kid from Midland, Texas, who did not know his way around grammar and had never met a dictionary, Andover was academic boot camp.

"It was cold and distant and difficult," George admitted years later. "Hard, hard, hard . . . In every way, it was a long way from home . . . Forlorn is the best word to describe my sense of the place and my initial attitude . . . My feelings of loneliness eased pretty quickly, though, as I made friends fast. The studies came slower. Andover was hard, and I was behind."

George's first English assignment was to write an essay about an emotional experience. He chose his sister's death. He struggled to find the right words. He wanted to write "and the tears ran down my cheeks," but he had already used the word "tears" several times. So he turned to the thesaurus his mother had given him when he left home. He searched for another word for "tears." He wrote: "And the lacerates ran down my cheeks."

The essay was returned to him with a big red zero. Scrawled across the top were the words: "DISGRACEFUL. See me immediately." George was so scared, he asked friends, "How am I going to last a week?"

Years later he told the "lacerates" story to illustrate how poorly prepared he was for the rigors of Andover. Neither his previous education nor his home life had fostered any kind of appreciation for learning. He did not realize that most fifteen-year-olds of his social and educational level would have known the difference between "tears" as a noun and "tears" as a verb.

"In those days, Texas boys who got shipped off to school were usually in trouble with their parents," George wrote in his autobiography. "In my case, Andover was a family tradition; my parents wanted me to learn not only the academics but also how to thrive on my own."

George senior had loved Andover. He felt the school's rigorous discipline—the strict dress code of jacket and tie and daily chapel—was exactly what his unruly son needed. Big George also knew that Andover was the only prayer little George had of getting into Yale, and for the Bush family Yale was the ultimate ticket-punch.

Barbara was heartsick when her firstborn left for school. She had come to rely on him for companionship because her husband was rarely home. The dependent nature of the mother-son relationship showed itself on the day in the 1960s when Barbara had a miscarriage and young George drove her to the hospital because his father, as always, was traveling.

Halfway there, Barbara said, "I don't think I'll be able to get out of the car."

"I'll take you to the emergency room, don't worry," said her son.

As Barbara recalled the incident, Georgie picked her up at the hospital the next day. "He talked to me in the car and he said, 'Don't you think we ought to talk about this before you have more children?'"

When Georgie left for Andover, Barbara felt as if she were losing her best friend. "Every day I walked down the driveway to meet the mailman to see if he had written. I was homesick . . . Finally, the mailman, John Taylor, rang the doorbell and thrust a letter into my hands with a big smile on his face. He knew how much I missed Georgie. Fortunately, he didn't hang around to see me open the letter. It started out, 'Last weekend was the greatest in my life' . . . I burst into tears . . . Our boy had the best weekend of his life without us."

In the beginning George and his friends were miserable at Andover. His Texas roommate, Clay Johnson, said that he spent his first six months trying to figure out how, without totally disgracing his family, he could get kicked out so he could go back home. "We were in way over our heads in a foreign land," he said. "We found we had to struggle just to catch up with everybody else . . . George, who is upbeat and energetic and a can-do guy, was challenged as much as the rest of us."

"Oh, God," said Kim Jessup. "Andover was awful. It was like going to college when you were fourteen years old. Actually, the school was so tough that college was easy. After four years at Andover, I was able to sail through my first year at Yale . . . but I still hated Andover. We were not allowed to live in adolescence there. We couldn't be boys. We were supposed to be 'men' who were to become leaders. The Andover motto: Serve others and promote yourself. You became a product of prep-school arrogance because they inculcate you with the belief that you are born to a purpose beyond other people. This produces bizarre behavior on the part of high-WASP types like myself and some elevated Catholics, which is about all there was at Andover in those days.

"Funny, but we thought we were a diverse group because not all of us were rich. We knew there was a plumber's son in our class and a few scholarship students, which, I suppose, was the prep-school definition of diversity at that time. Not everyone had a bunch of Roman numerals after his name, but there were guys who talked about their 'summer place' and their 'winter place' as if they moved into different estates with each season. We certainly weren't a class of celebrity kids. There were no big-name sons of movie stars or statesmen or tycoons. We didn't pay attention to anyone's father then, but our parents did, which is probably why I knew the names of Glenn Greenberg, son of the baseball great Hank Greenberg; Didi Pei, son of the architect I. M. Pei; and Torbert Macdonald, the godson of John F. Kennedy. Torby was probably the biggest deal in a way because JFK was President at the time."

Not even a close personal relationship with the President of the United States could bestow a sense of security at Andover. "I felt strange because I came from a working-class town in Massachusetts," said Torbert Macdonald, whose father was a congressman and one of the President's best friends. "Georgie, which is what I called him then, felt strange, too, because he was a kid from West Texas and a real outsider in that snooty northeastern prep-school environment. He was not a patrician at all. The two of us felt pretty alienated . . . and now that I read some of the confessions of the rest of our class online, I realize that almost everyone felt that way, but at the time I only knew how I felt and how Georgie felt."

Diversity within George's class of 290 was limited to two African Americans, one Puerto Rican, one Asian, and no more than twenty Jews. "There was a definite Jewish quota," said Eric Wallach, "but then no serious Jew would have gone to Andover in those days . . . It was Babbitt land. White bread, Protestant, country club, upper Episcopalian. The school was so out of touch that they held a service for Jews on Sunday. [Jewish Sabbath is Saturday.] I was immensely toughened by the experience of going there, but I hated it. We clocked in for everything. The place was run on martinet time."

Many from the class of 1964 recalled Andover as austere, dismal, and dispiriting. "Not very many people were happy to be there," said Peter Pfeifle. "There was a great deal of cynicism and unfriendliness in the air, people putting people down. It was like an old-fashioned English boys' school where you were watched all the time and weren't having much fun overall."

Enter George W. Bush, the brash up-your-nose and in-your-face prankster. "He used his audacity and chutzpah to entertain us," said Torbert Macdonald. "He was gregarious, verging on goofiness. Very sarcastic but without malice. He did not mind being the butt of a joke as long as people laughed. He needed an appreciative audience. He did not have a lot of respect for authority, so he was not afraid to mouth off. We called him 'The Lip' . . . He was also known as the Bombastic Bushkin . . . There was a small party everywhere he went.

"Georgie cared mightily about getting on with the jocks because they were the only cool guys on campus. He roomed with John Kidde because John was a football star. You have to understand how important sports were to us in those days. Georgie wasn't a jock like his father, so he ingratiated himself with the jocks as if the association would confer a kind of jock status . . . and I guess it did in a way, because Georgie was popular."

Upon graduation George W. Bush had not racked up the page of yearbook honors that his father had earned. Nor was Georgie voted "Most Likely to Succeed," "Best Liked," or "Ladies' Man," but he did place second as "Big Man on Campus," and he came in third for "Wit."

Andover stressed athletics as part of its regimen. "Sports was mandatory," recalled Conway "Doc" Downing. "There were seventeen teams and you had to go out for everything whether you were good or not— basketball, baseball, football, rugby, winter track, spring track, lacrosse, wrestling, swimming, hockey, skiing, crew, rifle, sailing—you name it. Georgie and I played junior varsity basketball together and spent a lot of time warming the bench. He could only dribble with his right hand, so he was useless on the court and I wasn't much better. The only time he ever started in a game was when a regular got sick and the coach put George in. He only lasted about a minute and a half before he lost his temper and smashed the ball in a guy's face. The coach yanked him, and that was the end of ole George's basketball career . . . As a baseball player, he wasn't much better. Unlike his father, George always seemed to have his foot in the bucket . . . and football . . . well, forget it.

"Since he couldn't be a jock, George became head cheerleader so he could sit on the Athletic Advisory Board, which was comprised of all the team captains. Being a jock or associating with jocks was the only way to be accepted at Andover. The only way."

Head cheerleader was considered a leadership position at Andover, but it was not something George bragged about back home. "Uh . . . no," said one childhood friend with a laugh. "Going to an all-boy school was already suspect enough. Back home they called Andover 'Bend over.' " Randall Roden, another friend from Midland, who went to Andover, said: "They would've had a field day with George had they known he was head cheerleader. In Texas a cheerleader is a girl with big hair, a twirly skirt, and pretty legs."

When Barbara Bush visited Andover to attend a game, she helped her son lead the cheers. "She was the original soccer mom," said Kim Jessup. "She came to a varsity game on the same weekend my mother was visiting. It was three games before the end of the season and George was a cheerleader. The stands were filled and there's George and his mama on the megaphone and she's yelling the cheers alongside him. My mother, who I'll admit was quite the snob, was horrified. She said Barbara Bush was a loudmouthed boor. Thoroughly uncouth."

Unable to live up to his father's legacy as one of Andover's most out-standing athletes, George played his own kind of sports. "Pig ball was one of his favorite games," recalled Jessup. "You'd huddle, throw the football as high as you could, and call out a guy's name as 'pig.' Then you forgot about the football and beat the hell out of the pig. It was a dumb-ass game, but bullyboys like George loved it . . . He also loved stickball, which is baseball played with a broomstick and a tennis ball and funny hats. George made himself the High Commissioner of Stickball, which was a joke job. He organized campus teams into a league and gave all the teams dirty names like 'Crotch Rots.' He named one team 'Trojans' so we'd all cheer for condoms and 'Nads,' so we would all yell 'Go Nads.' Everyone associates George with stickball at Andover, but to me he is the epitome of pig ball . . .

"Just par for a bullyboy who happened to become President of the United States. My roommate poured gasoline on a guy, and my roommate ended up being head of St. Mark's. Maybe it's all part of prep-school bullying . . . We could pummel each other, but God help us if we ever struck a teacher. Legend has it that Humphrey Bogart got expelled from Andover for 'incontrollably high spirits' be-cause he threw a master into Rabbit's Pond. None of us, not even George, would've had the balls to do that . . . we would've been too scared."

Fistfights were kept to a minimum, despite the high level of teenage testosterone. "It must have been all those hard-time athletics, plus we were convinced that they put saltpeter in our food," said Torbert Mac-donald. "I only remember one incident of violence and that was when we got the news of President Kennedy's assassination. I was devastated be-cause I knew what it would do to my father. Everyone was stunned. The only guy in our class who was insensitive and started taunting me was Dick Wolf. He never got his degree from Andover, but he managed to be-come a success as the executive producer of *Law and Order* on NBC-TV. He was a real shithead—nasty and mean—and I remember smashing my arm into his big fat gut when he started in about Kennedy minutes after the assassination."

On that afternoon, November 22, 1963, the Andover swimming coach, Reagh Wetmore, reacted by immediately calling his broker. The chorus instructor, William Schneider, called off practice by hanging a sign on his door: "I don't feel like singing." Randy Hobler, one of George's classmates, wrote in his diary: "President Kennedy assassinated in Dallas, Texas today during parade. Everybody here at school shocked. Free cut from English 'cause of it . . . still can't believe what happened to Kennedy. Horrible." Classes were canceled, and the flag on campus was lowered to half-staff.

The class of 1964 had watched a dizzying swirl of history: Roger Maris hitting his sixty-first home run on October 1, 1961; John Glenn's three-orbit space mission in Mercury *Friendship* on February 20, 1962; the Cuban missile crisis eight months later; Martin Luther King's "Letter from a Birmingham Jail" in April 1963; and the U.S. arrival of the mop-top Beatles in February 1964.

"If I had to come up with one sweet memory of Andover, it would be the last three weeks in May," said Kim Jessup, "because the weather was finally warm then and the pressure of finals was off. But the last May before graduation was hell because of George's damned drinking."

Alcohol was absolutely forbidden on or off campus, but the High Commissioner of Stickball had figured out a way to beat the system. He had designed an official stickball membership card that seemed to carry the imprimatur of Andover. He distributed the cards and said they could double as fake IDs. In Gothic script, the card stated: "Officially Certified Andover Stickball League Identification Credential." There was room for the team name, the boy's Social Security number, and all the requisite information of a driver's license. At the bottom, the card carried the signature of the High Commissioner, who had given himself the nickname "Tweeds Bush," after the political legend Boss Tweed. George also included the signatures of the "League Psychiatrist," "Chief Umpire," and "Official Scribe."

"People took the cards and started slipping off campus to go to Boston so they could drink and get drunk," said Kim Jessup. "All of the class was drinking heavily by senior year, except for me and my roommate, who were so straight we didn't go off campus. We were dummies. A few weeks prior to graduation we got cornered in the gym by the trainer and forced to give up the names of seniors who had been drinking. I got hazed for the last three weeks of school, and George retaliated later by taking me off the DKE rolls at Yale."

Having made it through Andover without flunking, George felt he had earned the right to go to Yale. Despite what Andover officially called his "unremarkable" record, and an SAT score of 1206, he became the beneficiary of his family's connections. He was accepted at Yale with the class of 1968, and he made no apologies for his good fortune. In fact, he bridled at the "intellectual arrogance" of those who denigrated him as a legacy kid. He told his classmate Robert Birge that what irritated him most about "Ivy League liberals" was their sense of guilt about being born to privilege. As an Andover graduate and a member of an established Yale family, George W. Bush headed for New Haven, where his peers perceived him as part of the ruling class on campus.

"The school was still pretty preppy then," said Richard Lee Williams, "and there wasn't much of a public-school presence . . . Everyone knew that George had a bunch of blood relatives who had paved the way for him to get in . . . That was well known . . . and, of course, he was from Andover." That Andover was the *ne plus ultra* of prep schools did not have to be explained.

"The conspicuous Bush at Yale at that time was Prescott," said David Roe (Yale 1969), who had graduated from Andover. "George being related to Prescott was a big deal."

"George's father was a nobody then," said Christopher Byron (Yale 1968), "but everyone knew his grandfather had been the senator from Connecticut. Prescott was huge at Yale. So George had a name behind him when he arrived, but there were much bigger names on that campus. Anybody who showed up in New Haven with the name Sterling was much more important . . . Every third building on the Yale campus is the Sterling this or the Sterling that. Sterling was definitely a good name to have then . . . There are no Bush buildings on campus—no Bush library, no Bush chapel, no Bush towers. Still, the fact that George was a prep-school graduate and came from a big Yale family counted for a lot in those days."

"Preppy culture really ruled then," said Ron Rosenbaum (Yale 1968). "I was a Jewish kid from a public school, and for me going to Yale was like entering an alien culture."

When the class of 1968 arrived on the Old Campus, where they lived their freshman year, they were addressed by the president of Yale. "We were told that we thousand men, and I emphasize men, had been chosen by Yale to basically lead the country," recalled one member of the class. "And we were privileged to be there. It was a great honor and we ought to allow Yale to educate us so that we would be ready to lead."

Such were the expectations for the class of 1968. Yet none of them anticipated that years after graduation they would be considered one of Yale's most outstanding classes. Every class at Yale has its stars, but this particular class seemed to produce a cornucopia of success that touched almost every facet of American society. Performing above and beyond expectations, the class of 1968 produced a Pulitzer Prize–winning author (Daniel H. Yergin), a famous Hollywood director (Oliver Stone), a Rhodes scholar and Deputy Secretary of State (Strobe Talbott), an Olympic swimmer (Don Schollander), governors (Anthony "Tony" Knowles and George W. Bush), ambassadors (Derek Shearer and Clark T. Randt Jr.), and, in 2000, the forty-third President of the United States.

"We're all still scratching our heads about George," said Ken White (Yale 1968 and DKE) in 2003. "Especially those of us who were in the fraternity with him. He just was the last guy you'd ever expect to see in the White House . . . Maybe Strobe Talbott or John Kerry, who was a couple of years ahead of us, even Joe Lieberman, who was the class of 1964. But not George. Not ever. My wife remembers him roaring drunk one night at a DKE party without a date doing the Alligator; that was some sort of dance back then when you fell to the floor on all fours and started rolling around. It's hard to see a guy like that holding down the highest office in the land."

George had pledged Delta Kappa Epsilon in his sophomore year, and "the drinking jock house," as the fraternity was known, became the center of his collegiate universe. At that time only 15 percent of the student body took part in fraternity life, and fewer than four hundred out of George's class of one thousand chose to go through rush.

"Only a small fraction of the university cared about fraternities," said David Roe, "but George was part of that dying subculture."

"Fraternities were definitely on the decline by the time George and I joined Deke," said Joseph Howerton (Yale 1968), "because they were fairly expensive on a campus where almost 50 percent of the students were on some kind of financial aid. Dekes had to pay four hundred dollars a year in social fees, plus you had to eat there at least once a week. We lived in Davenport College our last three years, but we went to the Deke house to drink and party on the weekends . . . It was like a private club . . . we brought in terrific bands for dances after football games . . . and the camaraderie was great."

For those big football weekends George frequently invited Cathryn Lee Wolfman, his Houston girlfriend. "It was the pre-coed days, so if you were lucky, you'd see your girlfriend every other weekend," said Roland "Bowly" Betts (Yale 1968). "Cathy was around. I used to see her at Deke."

During Christmas break of his junior year, George bought Cathryn a diamond ring at Neiman Marcus. He was determined to marry his beautiful blond fiancée his senior year and live off campus, exactly as his father had done. "Cathryn was the pick of the litter," said Doug Hannah, George's friend from Houston who had accompanied him to choose the ring. "George was really headstrong, and I think that was his thinking there. If George was a trophy hunter and that was his goal, that might have been what he was going for."

Their engagement was announced on the society page of *The Houston Chronicle*—"Congressman's Son to Wed Cathy Wolfman"—where it was noted that Cathryn's stepfather owned a fashionable women's clothing store. "That was the part that rankled Barbara," said Cody Shearer, a former journalist and onetime close family friend. "She couldn't abide the fact that Cathryn's stepfather was Jewish . . . 'There'll be no Jews in our family,' she said."

Cathryn Wolfman reflected on her relationship with George many years later with nothing but fondness. "My experience with the entire Bush family was wonderful," she said. "George and I met through mutual friends when we were eighteen and parted company when we were twenty. During that time I attended Rice University in Houston, while George was at Yale in New Haven. For the most part, we saw each other only while on vacation from school. We had a lot of fun together, along with our friends in Houston, and led quite privileged, sheltered, and innocent lives."

"We planned to marry the summer before our senior year, and I intended to transfer to Connecticut College. Sometime in the spring of 1967, George called to postpone the wedding. We continued to date through the following year, but went our separate ways after graduating from college in 1968. George returned to Houston from New Haven, and I left for a new job in Washington, D.C."

When he asked her to spend another summer with the family at Kennebunkport, the popular Rice coed demurred, and George was dumbfounded. "I don't want to go to Maine, George," she said. "And I don't think this is going to work out." She slipped the engagement ring off her finger and handed it to him.

"I remember a serious discussion in which I said that I wouldn't be going on the family's vacation in Maine and that we should call off our engagement," Cathryn said years later. "Our relationship had gradually cooled during our senior year in college . . . and we had made no specific plans to marry . . . The conversation breaking our engagement was a hard one, and I'm sure we were both upset by it. But I don't remember any tears or angry exchanges . . . We saw each other again several weeks later when he came to Washington, D.C., to visit his parents. We saw a lot of each other during the week he was in town, but it became clear in my mind that there truly was no future in the relationship . . . We saw each other only once thereafter, several years later, at a party in Houston, and we spoke just briefly."

George said nothing to his friends at Yale about Cathryn breaking their engagement, other than that his plans had changed.

"It wasn't that George was hugely popular at Yale," said Ken White. "He wasn't the stud jock that everyone liked. But he did have a bad-boy swagger that's appealing to other guys. He smoked unfiltered Lucky Strikes to be macho."

Part of machismo is never looking weak, especially in front of other males, and whenever George was challenged, his hair-trigger temper flared. "As freshmen on the Old Campus . . . one of the things we would do was throw the football as hard as we could at each other, stand about ten yards away," said Peter Markle (Yale 1968). "And I spotted George and I threw it at him and he wasn't ready. He was so mad. He picked up the football, must have come at me a hundred miles an hour. I ducked. But he had a capacity to get mad . . . He had a tough side to him . . . He was very competitive."

Another classmate remembered a similar run-in. "It was an argument over a parking space," said Kurt Barnes (Yale 1968). "He won. He got the space and I chalked it up to the fact that in Texas they must learn to drive straight in, and in the East we learn to back in."

Some who lived in Davenport College with George gave his swagger a wide berth. "He lived upstairs from me two years running," said George Sullivan (Yale 1968). "I did not know him well—by choice. He was a frat boy. I was not. I was proud of it. And he was proud of being a frat boy . . . Enough said."

Being members of Delta Kappa Epsilon meant the world to George and his roommates, most of whom had gone to Andover. "George was a slam dunk for Deke," said Charles Marshall (Yale 1967). "We had to take him because he was a legacy. You never turn down a legacy, especially when the legacy was once president of the fraternity like Daddy Bush was in 1947.

"George was sort of an ordinary guy for our fraternity because he wasn't an outstanding athlete like Calvin Hill [Yale 1969] or Paul Jones [1968]; he certainly wasn't an ass man, because George could barely get a date in college. He came from Andover with a lot of influence [friends], so I guess he'd made a big name for himself in a small pond. I thought he was just another rich preppy brat with a big-time Yale grandfather behind him . . . As pledge master, I was prepared to whip his butt. He kind of surprised me when he didn't wimp out . . . Then he really surprised me when he got himself elected president of the fraternity in his junior year. Being president of DKE takes you to the first pew at Yale. I can't remember when a Deke president wasn't tapped for Bones. Without that, George might not have made it into Bones, even with all his family muscle."

The tap from Skull and Bones came to George on the last Thursday night of April 1967, when the tower clock struck eight. He was not the last man tapped like his father, an honor reserved for the most outstanding member of the class, but he became part of the most diverse group ever to be tapped up to that point. For the first time in its history Skull and Bones had opened its Waspy gates to African Americans (one), Muslims (one), and Jews (two): Roy Leslie Austin, Robert Richards Birge, Christopher Walworth Brown, George Walker Bush, Kenneth Saul Cohen, Rex W.F. Cowdry, Donald Etra, G. Gregory Gallico III, Robert Karl Guthrie, Britton Ward Kolar, Robert Davis McCallum Jr., Muhammad Ahmed Saleh, Thomas Carlton Schmidt, Donald Arthur Schollander, and Brinkley Stimpson Thorne.

Each of these men had distinguished himself in some activity at Yale—intellectual, athletic, or social. George's distinction was, unquestionably, social. Years later many who lived with him in Davenport College were forced to reexamine their cherished belief that hard work triumphs over all. Some sounded cynical as they reappraised the rewards of meritocracy over aristocracy, and a bit of resentment seeped into their recollections of the young man who had skipped studying in favor of socializing and yet ended up with the most powerful job in the world.

"It's not that anyone is jealous," said Ken White, "because we're all at the peak of our careers and doing quite well. It's just that George . . . from what we knew of him then . . . doesn't seem to be the . . . a . . . well . . . the best-equipped person to be President of the United States."

"He never seemed to care about studying," recalled Thomas Wik (Yale 1968).

"I do not consider him a well-educated man at all," said Richard Hunter (Yale 1969).

"He put me off because he just didn't seem like he was working very hard in school," said John Gorman (Yale 1968). "He would appear in the morning like he'd partied all night . . . He viewed himself as a Texan and did not want to be considered part of the eastern establishment at Yale . . . so he went out of his way to act . . . crude . . . It's quite amazing that someone you held in low esteem later becomes President."

The stories of George's alcoholic escapades at Yale traveled the Andover network. At Harvard, Torbert Macdonald listened sadly to the tales of his old friend, whose politics were as out of sync with the times as his fraternity carousing. "Poor Georgie," said Macdonald. "He couldn't even relate to women unless he was loaded . . . There were just too many stories of him turning up dead drunk on dates."

"Most of the preppies, I'm one, but most of the prep-school crowd hung out in those fraternities," said Carter Wiseman (Yale 1968), "and their major goal in life was to get drunk as often as possible."

Drinking, especially at the Deke house, was accepted as a given at Yale, and by 1966 drugs had been thrown into the mix. "Marijuana was already on campus by then," said Christopher Byron. "Next came drugs of all kinds. They were everywhere."

In 1967 the Yale Daily News said an article in the New York Post had charged that marijuana was being concealed in the tomb of Skull and

Bones. In those days such a story was considered shocking enough to be newsworthy. Harder drugs soon followed, with cocaine becoming the most popular drug on campus. One member of the class of 1968 admitted years later selling cocaine to George W. Bush during their time at Yale. He confided his part of the drug transaction to the writer Erica Jong in 2001; he confirmed that drug buy in 2002 with the caveat of confidentiality.

"You cannot use my name," he said, "because we're talking about a felony offense . . . Besides, it was many, many years ago and this guy is now President of the United States."

Another man, at Yale's graduate school (MFA 1965), recalled "doing coke" with George, but would not allow his recollections to be used on the record for fear of retribution. This man, independently wealthy and living on the West Coast, said he did not feel right about "blowing George's cover because I was doing the same thing." A confirmed Democrat, he admitted he could not stand George's Republican politics but said he liked him as a person. "Besides," he added, "I don't need the fallout from our recreational drug use at this point in my life."

Years later, George's sister-in-law Sharon Bush alleged that W. had snorted cocaine with one of his brothers at Camp David during the time their father was President of the United States. "Not once," she said, "but many times."

George never denied buying, selling, or using illegal drugs. In 1999 he swore to key political supporters that he had never used "hard drugs," by which he meant that he had never shot up heroin. When he was accused of being born with a silver spoon up his nose, he admitted to "youthful mistakes." Running for national office, he carefully crafted his response to fall within the federal guidelines for public officials. "As I understand it," he told The Dallas Morning News in 1999, "the current FBI form asks the question, 'Did somebody use drugs within the last seven years?' and I will be glad to answer that question, and the answer is 'No.'" He refused to answer any more questions.

"Hell, it's not George's substance abuse that bothers me as much as his lack of substance," said Tom Wilner (Yale 1966 and DKE). "That he coasted on his family name is understandable. Lots of guys do that. But Georgie, as we called him then, has absolutely no intellectual curiosity about anything. He wasn't interested in ideas or books or causes. He didn't travel; he didn't read the newspapers; he didn't watch the news; he didn't even go to movies . . . How anyone ever got out of Yale without developing some interest in the world besides booze and sports stuns me. This guy has no concept of complex issues . . . He's a simpleminded zealot and—God help us all—he's now the guy with his finger on the button."

Yale had not been an easy ride for young George, even as an Andover graduate, a fraternity man, and a member of Skull and Bones. Ordinarily, those credentials would have allowed him to rule the campus, but as George told one of his Yale advisers, he felt his childhood in Texas set him apart socially from the more polished easterners who had similar résumés. He felt he was looked down upon by "snobs" and "elitists." He also felt alienated on the liberal campus, because of his father's conservative politics. In fact, he came to despise what he called "arrogant liberal intellectuals."

"George was definitely not on the popular side of the war issue, but he stood his ground," said Robert J. Dieter, a Yale roommate for four years. "Saying someone was conservative back then almost had a moral sting. I remember him coming back to the room and telling me that someone had been in his face about his father's position. There was a certain arrogance that the left conveyed back then. It was hurtful."

As a result, George spent most of his time carousing at the DKE house. Some classmates remember him as a "hard-drinking good-time guy" and "a jock sniffer" who "loved to raise hell." Russ Walker, a friend from Oklahoma City, recalled returning from a party with George one night when the inebriated Bush dropped to the ground and started rolling in the middle of the street. "He literally rolled back to the dorm," said Walker. "It was raucous teenage stuff that perhaps he grew out of later rather than sooner."

George's drinking occasionally brought him to the attention of law enforcement. In November 1967 he was arrested for pulling down a goalpost at Princeton while celebrating a Yale football victory. "The game ended and we all poured out and George was on the goalpost," recalled Clay Johnson. "We tore that sucker down and the campus police said, 'You all are coming with us.' So we went marching over to the campus police station and they said, 'You've got ten minutes to get out of town.' "

The year before, George had been caught with friends stealing a

Christmas wreath from a store door in New Haven to hang on the front door of the fraternity house. He was arrested for disorderly conduct, but the charges were dropped.

His third arrest occurred eight years after graduation, in the summer of 1976, for driving under the influence in Kennebunkport.

Despite memorable drinking bouts with his DKE brothers, George said he could hardly wait to leave Yale and its "intellectual snobbery." Once he left, he never looked back. He would not attend class reunions; he would not contribute money; he would not share reminiscences in the alumni magazine. The fourth-generation legacy student would have nothing to do with Yale.

"There was a liberal orthodoxy that pervaded Yale, and if you challenged that, it wasn't that you had a point of view but that you were dumb," recalled Collister "Terry" Johnson Jr., another of George's roommates.

George did not realize it at the time, but his class was one sweep in front of the dustpan. The class of 1968 was the last legacy class in which the sons of alumni were almost automatically accepted, thereby rewarding those with the most advantages. After 1968, admissions to Yale were to be based on merit. No more preferences for private schools; no more Social Register requirements. No more quotas for Jews.

The year after George's graduation the freshman class had more students from public and parochial schools than private schools for the first time in Yale's history. Women were admitted ("That's when Yale really started going down hill," said George W. without a trace of humor); the Reserve Officers' Training Corps was banished from campus; the dress code of jackets and ties was abolished. Fraternities, which the class yearbook described as a "benign irrelevancy," soon disappeared, and even the secret societies lost some of their allure as more and more students began turning down taps, even from Skull and Bones.

Upon graduation, George was eager to sever all relations with Yale, except for a few friendships with his fraternity brothers. He dismissed everyone else as "liberal pussies." His animus toward the college was such that he did not submit more than his name and a post office box for his twenty-fifth reunion class book. In a letter his father commended him for his attitude: "Thank God, George, you got the best from Yale, but you retained a fundamental conviction that a lot of good happens for America south and west of Woolsey Hall," one of the main student centers on the Yale campus.

During the next decade, George's best friend from DKE, Bowly Betts, intervened to mend the frayed school ties.

"Bowly is a bazillionaire from New York City—he developed Chelsea Piers—and he sits on the Yale Development Board," said a fraternity brother. "He got Richard Levin, the president of Yale, together with Georgie right after the inauguration in Washington, and helped engineer Bush's honorary degree during the first year of his presidency. That's how Bowly got Georgie to drop his hard-on against the school."

As part of his rapprochement with Yale, George invited the class of 1968 to the White House on May 29, 2003, for a picnic before their thirty-fifth reunion in New Haven.

Garry Trudeau (Yale 1970) skewered the event with a week of *Doonesbury* strips. In one scene, he drew the President as an empty-headed Roman centurion welcoming "all my classmates" to the White House: "Even the hippie snobs who used to sit around having heavy, boring talks about Vietnam. But especially the guys I came of age with, who always had my back—my college roomies. Stinky! Gopher! Kegger! Droopy! You're the Best!"

"Can you believe our rush chairman invaded *Iraq*?" bleats a drunken Old Blue in another day's strip. Informed that his fraternity brothers have arrived at the White House, the President in imperial headgear tells an aide, "Cordon them off. I'll be right there."

In the next day's strip, the class representative commends the five hundred members of the class who have shown up with their wives. "I know coming here posed a dilemma for some of you. On the one hand, it's very exciting to be invited to the White House . . . On the other hand, Junior here, has done more harm to our economy, environment and standing in the world than any president in memory! Talk about a TOUGH call. Ha. Ha. Ha. But seriously . . ."

"Have him sent to Asia Minor," snaps the centurion headgear.

"Done sire," says the centurion's gofer.

Trudeau had captured the turmoil surrounding the evening and the soul-searching many experienced upon receiving their invitations. More than a few members of the class stayed away in private protest against the war in Iraq. Others accepted, despite their opposition.

"I'm a member of the Yale class of '68 who won't be attending the reunion event at the White House because of revulsion toward Bush's policies," said Jacques Leslie. "The war in Iraq was unwarranted and promoted deceptively, his environmental policies are disastrous, and his attack on legal rights and constitutional rights is frightening. I would not be able to shake his hand without showing hostility."

Another classmate, who met Deng Xiaoping during a visit to China, said he had shaken the hand of the "Butcher of Tiananmen Square," so shaking George Bush's hand couldn't take him any lower.

"There's enough spirit of '68-ness, you might say, still in me to be disturbed by the rush to 'kiss the ass of the ruling class' (as they used to say)," said Ron Rosenbaum. "Indeed, one of the reasons I think the invitation is distasteful is that it will inevitably be spun as the final surrender of the spirit of '68 to the establishment."

Mark Soler said he stayed away from the White House part of the reunion because he profoundly disapproved of George W. Bush's presidency. "When we were in college, we thought we would change things for the better when it came time for our generation to step forward," he said. "We thought nobody among us could ever make the mistake of getting stuck in a ground war with no exit strategy and no clearly defined goals. We thought that would be impossible because we, the class of 1968, had learned the lessons of Vietnam . . . Now look what's happening in Iraq . . . and to think it was brought on by one of our own . . . Supposedly George was a history major; he should have learned at the very least that 'the past is prologue.' "

Reports of the White House picnic dominated the weekend reunion in New Haven. "I don't know what shocked me more," said one member of the class. "Seeing George Bush as President of the United States, or Peter Akwai as a woman. I'm still reeling."

Stories were swapped about the man many considered least likely to become President, and how he greeted classmates he had once disdained, even shaking hands with a woman he had once known as a man.

"You might remember me as Peter when we left Yale," Petra Leilani Akwai said as she passed through the receiving line. Since their college days together Peter, now Petra, had undergone a sex-change operation. The President, who had undergone his own transformation during that time, did not blink.

"Now you've come back as yourself," he said.

His response surprised some of his classmates. They had assumed the born-again President would be censorious toward a transsexual. Instead, George appeared at ease in a situation that others found slightly uncomfortable.

Listening to his classmates discuss their dinner at the White House, for which each had been charged $150, Mark Soler inquired about the fascinating presidential discussions he had missed. He was sorely disappointed. He heard that the leader of the free world had walked around patting several prosperous stomachs and chiding his classmates for being overweight when he was holding his own at 191 pounds.

"He claims he's nearly six feet," said one.

"Right. More like five ten on tiptoes."

One classmate patted Soler on the shoulder. "You missed nothing," he said. "I spent five minutes talking to the guy, and it was just like talking to a Sears repairman."

George, who had graduated with a C average, waited thirty-five years before he returned to Yale. When he did, he was President of the United States. Even then, he had to be lured with an honorary degree, something his father and his grandfather had also received. However, in George's case, 208 members of the Yale faculty had signed a petition protesting the honor to such "a mediocre man." George knew that 84 percent of the student body had voted against him in the election of 2000, but rather than resume his old rant at the "snobs" and "elitists," he tried to charm them.

He began by congratulating the parents of the graduating class. "It's a great day for your wallets," he said. The audience rippled with laughter, knowing that he was paying thirty-three thousand dollars a year in tuition for his daughter Barbara, class of 2004.

Although he had acknowledged his past arrests, the subject of his run-ins with the law was still sensitive enough that White House speechwriters deleted a joke from his original text that read: "It's great to return to New Haven. My car was followed all the way from the airport by a long line of police cars with slowly rotating lights. It was just like being an undergraduate again."

He addressed the graduates, emphasizing the importance of their college degrees and the lifetime of privilege conferred by Yale. "You have to be a Yale graduate to be President," he quipped, "and you had to have lost the Yale vote to Ralph Nader."

He appeared not to notice that some graduates had painted a white "5–4" on their tasseled caps, a reference to the Supreme Court decision of 2000 that had ended the Florida recount and put him in the White House.

He saluted the graduates and their college accomplishment. "To those of you who received honors, awards, and distinction, I say, 'Well done.' And to the C students, I say, you, too, can be President of the United States."

The applause fell short of a rousing ovation.

CHAPTER FIFTEEN

arbara Bush jumped out of the family station wagon in her bare feet and yelled hello to William Millburn, the black doorman, who grinned from ear to ear.

"I just loved it that Mrs. Bush would walk into St. Albans without her shoes on," he said. He chuckled as he recalled the incident and shook his head. "No other St. Albans mother would ever have done something like that—come racing into the school in bare feet—but Mrs. Bush was real friendly and down-to-earth when she was dropping off stuff for her boys. Most of the other parents had a real get-away-from-me decorum to them. But not Mrs. Bush. She didn't have no somebody airs, at least not in those days . . . She was a little on the heavy side of all the mothers, but she was my favorite . . . She liked that we were taking care of her boys."

Barbara had been so relieved when Neil and Marvin were admitted to the prestigious Episcopal school in Washington, D.C., that she marked the day in her diary, January 3, 1967, in big capital letters: "BOYS AC-CEPTED AT ST. ALBANS."

"It's my recollection that she boarded those boys because they needed to have some kind of male father image in their lives," said John Claiborne Davis, the assistant headmaster. "Their own father just wasn't around much, being a congressman and all. That wasn't unusual for St. Albans parents. Our elite clientele was military and political and diplomatic, and these busy people needed to board their sons, especially when they were traveling or entertaining a lot like the Bushes. We boarded their sons during the week to give the boys discipline, but if their parents were in town, we allowed them to go home on the weekends."

The assistant headmaster discussed the young sons of St. Albans's "elite clientele" as if they were dogs that needed a kennel, but his views about Congressman George Bush being an absentee parent were borne out by others on the faculty.

"The Bushes were not parents who ran up to the school all the time, and he, the father, certainly was never around," said Stanley Willis, the former head of admissions. "He was a distant figure in their lives."

"I have no memory of the Bushes ever being around the school," said Howard Means, a former English teacher. "I taught Neil, who was an average kid. He tried very hard and got frustrated over his learning problems, but he was one of the nicest kids I ever had in class. I've never figured out his parents, but Neil was sweet."

George was not the only parent missing from the children's lives at that time. Barbara, too, was remembered by the mother of one of her daughter's best friends as being detached and spending more time on Washington's social whirl than on her children.

"My daughter Carey was in the fourth grade with Doro Bush, or Dordie, as she was called by the kids at National Cathedral School for Girls in Washington," recalled Marjorie Perloff, then an associate professor of English at Catholic University. "The girls were close friends in 1968, and from what I saw of Dordie, I would say that Barbara Bush was less than the devoted mother who spent lots of time with her children, supervising their games, their meals, and their homework . . . I know that is the Hallmark-card image of Mrs. Bush now, but when I knew her in 1968, she was hardly around . . . Behind the public image of Barbara Bush is the reality of a rich woman whom many of us recall as seeming to enjoy her dogs more than her children, a woman who rarely smiled.

"As a professor, I could arrange my classes so as to be home by 4:00 p.m. or so, when Carey and her sister came home . . . Dordie Bush, who was much younger than her four brothers, seemed to be largely on her own, a classic poor little rich girl. She was very sweet and shy and had difficulty with her schoolwork. Sometimes, when she came over to play with Carey, I would help her with her homework, and she often came over to use our *World Book Encyclopedia*. I recall once asking, 'Dordie, don't you have an encyclopedia at your house?' The answer was no. And I must confess that when I drove Dordie home and the maid opened the door, she revealed a house that looked singularly devoid of books. Barbara Bush's fabled literacy project, it seems, didn't begin at home."

The New Yorker's Brendan Gill, who once visited the family compound at Kennebunkport, told a similar story about the Bushes and their disinterest in books. The writer, an insomniac, tried to find something to read late at night. After investigating the entire mansion, he could find only one book: *The Fart Book.*

Years later, when Barbara needed to be affiliated with a public cause, she embraced literacy and filled her bedroom bookshelves with books. Having one son, George, who had reading problems, and another son, Neil, who was dyslexic, she realized that being able to read was the basis of education. She later established a foundation dedicated to family literacy.

As fourth graders, Doro Bush and her little friend frequently spent the night at each other's houses, but, according to Carey's mother, both girls preferred the Perloffs' house. "Most evenings the only person at home at the Bushes' was the maid, as the live-in housekeeper who took care of the children and did most of the household chores was then called. It was the maid (or maids) who cleaned, cooked, did the laundry, and ordered groceries on the phone . . .

"Not that Barbara Bush wasn't sometimes at home. Whereas most stay-at-home mothers from National Cathedral School for Girls played golf or tennis at the country club, went to countless lunches and charity affairs, played bridge, and shopped, Mrs. Bush, Carey recalls, preferred to shut herself up in her third-floor sewing room, doing needlepoint. At Christmas, each of Dordie's friends received a pincushion with her name on it, embroidered by Barbara Bush.

"But, as Carey remembers it, Dordie's mother never spent a moment with the girls when they were playing at her house, never inquired about homework, and Carey never sat down to a family dinner . . . The Bushes were out almost every night—at cocktail parties, dinners, receptions, charity balls, political events. Dinner, under these circumstances, was prepared by the maid and served to the girls in the family room. Barbara was often out of town for a number of days, accompanying George on his professional trips. As for George, he was pretty much the Invisible Man in Dordie's life."

On the move constantly, George flew to Houston every other week-end, and during the week in Washington he and Barbara went out almost every night. "They went to everything—dinner parties, diplomatic recep-tions, embassy balls—everything," said Ymelda Dixon, a society colum-nist for the *Washington Star*. "That's how I got to know them."

Betty Beale, the doyenne of Washington's society columnists during the 1960s, developed such a close friendship with the Bushes that she would be invited to visit them all over the world. "I stayed with them in China, visited them in New York, and, of course, at Kennebunkport," she said. "They were very social and cared very much about being in Wash-ington society."

In addition to socializing, George accepted every speaking engage-ment that came his way. In 1968, he was asked to be a Chubb Fellow at Yale, an honor that had been bestowed on his father. The fellowship in-volved spending a few days on campus, lecturing, attending classes and seminars, and meeting with students.

"I remember when he arrived because some breathless aide came running into my office," said the Yale chaplain William Sloane Coffin. " 'Congressman Bush wants to exercise. He wants to play squash.'

" 'Okay,' I said. 'Bring him on.' George was always a good athlete, but I was lucky enough to know my way around a squash court. The word spread quickly on campus that the right would square off against the left on Court 2. We soon drew a big crowd."

The reverend's antiwar politics were as well known to Yale students as Bush's pro-war support of Richard Nixon. Both men played as if more were at stake than a squash game.

"I beat him three in a row," recalled Coffin. "He insisted we play more. So we did. I beat him again. But he wouldn't call it a game. He was so competitive. Ferociously competitive. He wanted to play until he won. By then, we were hogging the court. So I suggested we play the next day. He gritted his teeth and said no. He insisted we keep going. So we did. That time I kicked a little ass and it felt good."

George was just as driven about running for political office. After making a little squeak as a first-term congressman when he tried to snag the vice presidential nomination, he now wanted to make a great big noise. He was determined to run against Ralph Yarborough again in the 1970 election.

"Don't do it, George," said his father. "Stay where you are. There's a great life to be had in the House. You've got an important committee assignment and the respect and friendship of the most powerful chairman on the hill."

When Prescott visited George in Washington, he accompanied him to the Hill. "I can't think of anything that has pleased George more in years," Barbara wrote to her father, Marvin Pierce, a few months before he died. "Dad Bush came to visit the Ways and Means Committee and the chairman [Wilbur Mills] invited him to sit with the committee. George tells me that this is the first time he has seen this happen since he's been here . . . Then his dad visited the House floor and everyone showed such great pleasure in seeing him again and one and all came to greet him. George was thrilled."

Prescott tried to counsel his son on certain political realities. He said that George now occupied a safe Republican seat in a state where the ratio of Democrats to Republicans was three to one. "Look at the numbers," Prescott said. "Texas is still a Democratic state. Even conservative Yellow Dog Democrats don't vote for Republicans."

George thought otherwise. "They'll vote for me," he said, "especially over Ralph Yarborough."

His father grew exasperated. "You've only been in the House a short time, and you've already introduced important legislation. Imagine what you could accomplish in a few years."

George's main interest in Congress was population control. Like his father, he supported Planned Parenthood, and he advocated family planning as a way to protect a woman's health and to combat poverty. In those days, family-planning advocates spoke openly of contraception, and legal abortion was the goal of many, including George Herbert Walker Bush. "My distinct recollection at that point in history is that George was a 'choice' person," said former Republican Representative John Buchanan of Alabama, using the word for abortion rights.

"He was most definitely pro-choice—then," said former Democratic Representative James H. Scheuer of New York. "He was my minority [Republican] man on the Select Committee on Population and was very supportive until he became Reagan's VP. Then he had to adopt Reagan's backward position and refute family planning and become pro-life. After that, when George would see me in the hall of the House of Representatives, he'd say, 'Jim, don't break my cover.' And I never did—until now. George was a nice guy. He couldn't have continued supporting family planning and still made the national ticket. So he made a political choice."

"George and Barbara were very active in Planned Parenthood from the time I knew them at Yale in the 1940s," said Franny Taft, who had married the grandson of President William Howard Taft. Franny's husband, Seth, was a nephew of Ohio's Senator Robert A. Taft, known as Mr. Republican. "We worked like crazy then to make birth-control advice available, and you have to remember in those days birth control was still illegal in Massachusetts and Connecticut. That's when Barbara and George were progressive. Then they moved to Texas and became right-wingers."

George joined Representative Scheuer to introduce the Family Planning Services and Population Research Act, which became law in 1970 and, under Title X, the only federal program solely dedicated to family planning and reproductive health. In 1988, under Ronald Reagan, a gag rule was imposed on Title X clinics, prohibiting them from providing abortion counseling, which George had once supported. While in Congress, George was so committed to providing contraceptives for all who wanted and needed them that Wilbur Mills called him "Rubbers."

For weeks George had resisted his father's rationale about the 1970 Senate race. "I know I can beat Yarborough this time," he said. "I can just feel it. Last time [1964] he rode in on Lyndon's coattails. This time he's more vulnerable." George explained that his campaign would be well financed because President Nixon wanted him to run and had promised him White House support. In addition, his friend John Tower, the Republican senator from Texas, was in charge of the Republican Senatorial Campaign Committee, so even more money would come his way. As for giving up his safe House seat, George told his father that if he lost the race, Nixon had promised him "a high post" in the administration. "I really think this is my time," George said. He later explained his ambition to an interviewer: "I want to score and then be captain, get promoted and then be boss, achieve something and then get elected to something else." To him life was a series of successes in which he would always wind up on top. There was never any sense of ideological purpose. It was only about winning.

George decided to seek the counsel of the best politician in Texas, then in retirement at his ranch on the Pedernales River. As a Republican congressman, he had won a favorable nod from Lyndon Johnson by skipping Nixon's inaugural festivities in January 1969 to be at Andrews Air Force Base to say good-bye to the Johnsons as they left Washington.

"LBJ was mighty impressed that Bush had shown up that day to pay his respects," said the former Johnson aide Harry McPherson. George's presence made the absence of Texas Senator Ralph Yarborough even more conspicuous. His courtesy to the former President led to an invitation to visit the LBJ ranch in Stonewall, Texas, which he and Barbara eagerly accepted.

Months later, as George tried to make up his mind about the 1970 Senate race, he called Johnson's office, hoping he might prevail upon the former President to remain neutral in the race. George asked if he could visit the ranch again on a political matter. He was granted a fifteen-minute audience on condition that the meeting be kept confidential.

"I got right to the point," George recalled to friends. "I said, 'Mr. President, I've still got a decision to make and I'd like your advice. My House seat is secure—no opposition last time—and I've got a position on Ways and Means.' "

Johnson said he had heard the rumors that George was thinking about running for Yarborough's seat. Sensing that George might be seeking his support, the former President said he was a Democrat and would always support the Democratic candidate.

"I don't mind taking risks," George said, "but in a few more terms I'll have seniority on a powerful committee. I'm just not sure it's a gamble I should take, whether it's really worth it."

Johnson looked George in the eye and spoke slowly and deliberately. "Son. I've served in the House." Pause. "And I've been privileged to serve in the Senate, too." Longer pause. "And they're both good places to serve. So I wouldn't begin to advise you what to do, except to say this—that the difference between being a member of the Senate and a member of the House is the difference between chicken salad and chicken shit." Long pause. "Do I make my point?"

Johnson had insisted the meeting be kept confidential lest Texas Democrats think he was advising a potential Republican candidate about challenging the Democratic incumbent. Bush wanted the meeting publicized because he knew it would boost his status among the conservative Democrats he was wooing. He held a press conference on May 28, 1969, and—surprise, surprise—for some reason Sarah McClendon of the Mc-Clendon News Service just happened to ask if he had talked to President Johnson about the Senate race in Texas. George said that they had discussed it at the ranch: "But I have no feeling regarding his involvement in this matter. I would say that since this subject has come up—I would like the record clearly to show that there was a question asked about this. Because he is in one party and I'm in another, it would be clearly unlikely that he would ever be able to be for me."

Peggy Simpson of the Associated Press followed up: "How come you met with President Johnson? Did you ask for the meeting? What did you learn?" George allowed how he had learned a great deal.

He jumped on the phone minutes later and called the LBJ ranch. Speaking to the presidential aide Tom Johnson, George said he was "very concerned" about his press conference. "I am worried that some of the reporters will try to read something into my visit that was not intended. I am particularly concerned that they will believe that the President might not want to support Senator Yarborough and would do something to aid me in a way to hit back at Senator Yarborough."

The aide dutifully took notes on what George was saying. In his memo to the President, Johnson wrote:

> The Congressman said that this matter was very much on his conscience and on his mind and that he wanted you to know that he had not tried to use you in any way. In fact, he said he thought that he had handled the visit very discreetly and had said nothing to anybody about it. He said, of course, that he had asked for the invitation and that . . . the question of the Senate race had not even been discussed.

The next day George wrote a disingenuous letter to the President, a seasoned pro in the deceptive art of leaking to the press. George enclosed a transcript of the question-and-answer session he had held with Mc-Clendon and Simpson, saying: "Their questions came out of the blue and in retrospect, it might have been better had I said 'no comment.' However, at the time I thought such an answer might only invite further and possibly incorrect speculation."

On January 13, 1970, George decided on chicken salad: he announced his candidacy for the Senate. "We've polled it to death, we've talked it all out, and now I've determined that this is the thing for me to try to do," he said. "I recognize that it's going to be a long, tough 10 months, but I am convinced that I can win this race."

"It was a long shot," said his brother Jonathan, "but he wanted to get into position to run for President."

George immediately sent application cards to all black and Hispanic residents who had not yet registered to vote. He urged them to fill in the cards. "Once registered, you can then vote in any party's primary, as we do not register by party in Texas." His letter, written on congressional letterhead, noted that it was not printed at the government's expense.

George began his campaign by soldering himself to Richard Nixon. He supported Nixon's continuation of the war in Vietnam; he endorsed Nixon's nomination of Judge G. Harrold Carswell for the Supreme Court, despite the judge's racist opinions; he even offered up his eldest son, then in flight school in Georgia, as an escort for Nixon's daughter Tricia.

Nixon reciprocated by giving George $106,000 in illegal campaign contributions. This money came from a secret campaign slush fund called "Operation Townhouse." Ledger sheets in the National Archives show at least half of these contributions—$55,000—were in cash and not reported as required by law. Operation Townhouse was a secret channel of contributions from wealthy Republicans to Nixon's favorite candidates in fifteen states. George received $10,000 from W. Clement Stone, a Chicago millionaire, in four checks. Only $2,500 was reported on Bush's campaign financial report; Henry Ford II sent George $9,500 through Operation Townhouse, but Bush's campaign financial report listed only $2,500 as having been contributed by Ford. Yet George signed a sworn statement that he had reported "all gifts and loans of money or other things of value received by me."

A memo from the presidential aide Tom Johnson in the Lyndon Baines Johnson Presidential Library indicates that Senator John Tower was also taking good care of George:

Mr. President:
You may be interested in the following:

1. *Senator Tower is in charge of the Republican Campaign.*

2. *Senator Tower has allocated almost twice as much money to Congressman Bush as any other of the candidates.*

3. *Congressman Bush has received $72,879.00. The next highest is Ralph Smith of Illinois. ($37,204.00)*

With money raining down on him, George had no financial worries, but after May 1970 his real problem became his opponent. Ralph Yarborough had been defeated in the Democratic primary by a rich, conservative former congressman named Lloyd M. Bentsen Jr. A George Bush clone, Bentsen had the added advantage of being secretly backed by John Connally, the popular governor of Texas, as well as by former President Johnson.

George panicked. He wrote to Harry Dent, the White House political operative, to request fifteen minutes of Nixon's time: "Harry. There is no way to over-emphasize now the importance of 'Bush getting things done,' etc. . . . I wanted Bentsen to win. He has."

Naively, and incorrectly, Bush added that Bentsen's win was "a plus" because:

1) there will be a real liberal backlash and 2) the vote will be small—nothing on the ballot in any race for the liberals to turn out for.

He cited John Kenneth Galbraith's letter to *The Texas Observer* in which the Kennedy Democrat had urged Texas liberals to vote for Bush and to defeat Bentsen. Galbraith's logic was that as prospective senators, both men were equally bad. But "a Bentsen victory will tighten the hold of conservatives on the Texas Democratic Party, force the rest of us to contend with them nationally, and leave the state with the worst of all choices—a choice between two conservative parties."

Nixon, too, knew there was not a dime's worth of difference between Bush and Bentsen. As White House Chief of Staff H. R. "Bob" Haldeman wrote in his campaign report before the elections, "Make note have already won one—Texas." Haldeman explained that view in a note to then–White House speechwriter William Safire, who was composing last-minute campaign commercials for Nixon. Haldeman proposed that the message should say, "Vote for a man who will work for and with the President, not a man who will work against the President." But he cautioned that this message "should not be used in places like Texas where the opponent (Bentsen) would be working for the President, too."

George had more than a Senate race at stake in 1970. If he won and swept Texas with more than a million votes from Democrats, Republicans, and Independents, he was in the best position to replace Spiro Agnew and become Nixon's running mate in 1972. Agnew had been unable to carry his own state of Maryland in 1968 and was already vulnerable. "This I knew from Prescott Bush," recalled the syndicated columnist Charles Bartlett. "He and Nixon were very close and Nixon had told Pres that he'd love to run with his son . . . George had a real fire in those days . . . All he had to do to get on the national ticket was win big in Texas."

On election night, W., who had devoted himself full-time to his father's campaign after F-14 flight school at Ellington Air Force Base, prepared to celebrate what his parents had assured him would be a victorious evening. Prescott and Dorothy Bush had come from their winter home in Hobe Sound, Florida, to witness the expected entry of the second Bush generation into the U.S. Senate. Champagne flutes were standing on silver trays in the Bush suite at Houston's Shamrock Hotel as close friends and campaign aides gathered to watch the returns.

Young Doro sat next to her father on the couch as George turned on the TV to CBS. Twelve minutes into the broadcast the election was over. Walter Cronkite said his computers called the race for Bentsen by 200,000 votes.

Doro, then in the fifth grade, started crying. "I'll be the only girl in my class whose father doesn't have a job," she whimpered. George W. and Marvin broke down. Barbara, too, shook with sobs, and Neil and Jeb collapsed in tears. George hugged them all and said everything would be all right. But the family knew that he had just lost what he wanted most in life—a chance to become President.

"He was shattered by the loss," said his aide Jack Steel. "He said it was just the end of everything."

"It was sort of like being on a train going 180 miles an hour and hitting a brick wall," said Pete Roussel, Bush's congressional press secretary. "We were so deflated."

George confessed his agony the next day. "I had but one goal, a single purpose," he wrote to a friend. "This loss has sent me to the depths."

A few days later he rallied enough to write to the major-league baseball player Carl Warwick: "My main balloon has burst—we didn't win the pennant. But today it's clear that the world will keep turning. Tuesday night with those great kids in tears I wasn't a bit sure."

Barbara was inconsolable. "When I called her up after the loss, she couldn't stop crying," recalled George's sister, Nancy Ellis. A year later Barbara was still upset. She told Jerry Tallmer of the *New York Post* how much harder it was to lose the race for the Senate a second time. "George took it hard too but better than me. Men are so much braver. I still don't like it. I hate to think about it. I get so angry."

Young George got very drunk on election night. He admitted later he had never seen his father sink as low as he did with that defeat. Big George confided his despair to his old friend James A. Baker III and said that he was going to get out of politics. He told his financial chairman, Robert Mosbacher, "I feel like Custer."

In truth, George's public life looked as though it was over. Unable to get himself elected to statewide office, despite two campaigns and several million dollars, he had failed the first test of a politician. Nixon planned to dust off his obligation to George by appointing him head of the Small Business Administration or else giving him a White House staff position with no specific duties. In his view, George H.W. Bush no longer had a political future.

"I feel like I saved his public career," said George's friend Charles Bartlett, the Pulitzer Prize–winning journalist, "and I'm quite proud of it . . . The day after the election when George was wiped out by Bentsen, I called Doug Bailey, a brilliant political consultant. The two of us sat down for lunch at the Federal City Club, and tried to think of a way to keep this bright young man on the political horizon . . . In those days George was one of the most attractive, energetic young men in either party. He had real fire then . . . and idealism. He lost it in later years, I think, but then I thought he was worth saving and so did Doug. We figured if he took a government job, he'd be buried in the bureaucracy and never heard from again. We knew that Nixon wasn't about to give him much more after the debacle in Texas. What we didn't know was that Nixon was secretly courting John Connally, the Democratic governor of Texas, to join his cabinet as Secretary of the Treasury; Connally was the guy who backed Bentsen to beat Bush, so that tells you how much Nixon thought of Bush at that point . . . Doug and I came up with the UN as the best way to keep George politically alive . . .

"I reached him at his campaign headquarters and he was still pretty shattered . . . I told him our plan, which didn't go down too well at first. Barbara later told me it didn't go down at all. 'We hated the UN in Texas,' she said. 'Always hated the UN.' She reminded me that George had campaigned against the United Nations. I looked it up later and saw that George had said the UN 'has largely been a failure in preserving freedom.' At the time I told George to come to Washington right away and we'd have dinner with Bob Finch, a Nixon aide, who could push the plan to the President. I explained to George that there was no better way for him to stay in public life than to become the U.S. Ambassador to the United Nations."

Over dinner Bartlett briefed Bush on how to play his longest and strongest suit—his high-society connections. With keen political insight, the journalist pointed out that Nixon had not been adequately represented by the previous UN Ambassador, Charles Yost, a Democrat who publicly opposed the administration's position on Vietnam. Plus, Nixon had always felt like a gargoyle on the cathedral of New York society. He would want to have someone as socially acceptable as George Herbert Walker Bush doing his bidding at the United Nations, entertaining recalcitrant diplomats, and selling Nixon's political gospel to the great and the good of Manhattan's media.

"George got into it right away," recalled Bartlett. "The next day he called the White House and went in to make his pitch. After the President offered him some insignificant position, George said he'd rather have the UN because he felt that he could make friends for Nixon in a way that no one else could. At the same time, his unswerving loyalty would enable him to represent U.S. foreign policy the way Nixon wanted it represented. The President listened, and asked him to step outside for forty-five minutes. Nixon then summoned Haldeman and called Henry Kissinger [National Security Adviser] . . . and . . . forty-five minutes later he gave George the UN."

It was a masterstroke on the part of Bartlett and Bailey because that appointment eventually led to a series of other appointments that elevated George Bush on to the national scene. At the time, though, the appointment was considered a blatant payoff for a political loser. *The New York Times* howled about putting someone with no qualifications into such a "highly important position" that had once been held by such illustrious people as Edward Stettinius, Henry Cabot Lodge, Adlai Stevenson, and Arthur J. Goldberg. The *Washington Star* lamented that a forty-seven-year-old "lame duck congressman with little experience in foreign affairs and less in diplomacy" would be given the nation's highest ambassadorial post. The newspaper speculated that the only possible reason for such folly could be Nixon's hope to blow life into Bush's political future: "He could be trying to fill in the blanks in the handsome young Texan's qualifications for national office with a crash education in foreign affairs and by providing the national exposure that will make the name George Bush a household word by 1972."

Privately, the Secretary of State was horrified. "He's a lightweight," said William P. Rogers. Henry Kissinger agreed. He dismissed George as "soft," "not sophisticated," and "rather weak." Of course, this made him ideal for the end run that Kissinger and Nixon had in mind for recognizing Red China. But even George's closest friends were flabbergasted by his appointment.

"What the fuck do you know about foreign policy?" exclaimed Lud Ashley.

"Ask me that in 10 days," said George, who had regained his breezy self-confidence. He said he would "cram" for whatever he needed to know to pass his Senate confirmation hearings and then emerge as an instant Foreign Service officer who was, in his flyboy slang, "good to go."

The UN appointment had revived George's moribund career. In addition, he acquired the title of Ambassador, plus a seat in Nixon's cabinet; a salary of $42,500; a wonderful new residence in New York City (a nine-bedroom apartment in the Waldorf Towers that cost $55,000 a year); a staff of one hundred and eleven people, including a chauffeur, a chef, hotel maids and housekeepers, and full catering services; and an entertainment budget of $30,000 to do what he did best—give parties. Even Bush's official biographer, Herbert Parmet, acknowledged that "his self-proclaimed credentials for taking on the UN job came down to loyalty, personality and the ability to mingle in the right circles."

Unfortunately, George never mastered the foreign policy requirements of the job.

"He was an embarrassment," said Sydney M. "Terry" Cone III, counsel to Cleary, Gottlieb, Steen, and Hamilton, and the director of New York Law School. "I'm a member of the Council on Foreign Relations, and I had lunch with him when he was the UN Ambassador. I was appalled. The man knew nothing. Absolutely nothing. It was my opinion that he had no concept of the world; no understanding of foreign policy. He was obviously a political appointee that Nixon had to do something for . . . I was ashamed that such a man was representing our country in the United Nations at a time when we needed someone of intelligence and stature. George Bush was only a meeter and a greeter."

In his own diary, George appeared more preoccupied with personalities than policies. On March 20, 1971, he wrote that he had attended the funeral of Thomas Dewey with New York's Senator Jacob Javits:

> Javits is amazingly selfish. He handed a big envelope to the driver and told him while we were in the church to take the envelope to the Westbury Hotel. The driver looked slightly panicked, recognizing that in this long motorcade he couldn't possibly do that and get back into line. When he explained this to Javits, he was slightly perturbed. This is very much like the time Javits raised hell with the people handling the baggage in Mexico when we were there on an antiparliamentary trip. He was pushy and not very pleasant.

On the same day George wrote about his Yale classmate New York Mayor John Lindsay: "John seems so darned arrogant and removed. It's almost as if he were competitive or living on stage . . . it seems very peculiar . . . He is a very difficult, funny guy . . . very hard for me to read."

George wrote the same thing about Ross Perot when he came to plead for prisoners of war: "Ross Perot is a difficult fellow to figure out. He has always been very friendly to me . . . but he is a very complicated man."

In his diary from April 5, 1971, George described Secretary-General U Thant: "He sat there friendly but impassive. He is a difficult fellow to read—always tremendously polite to me, always very friendly, but showing lots of reserve."

On April 19, 1971, George wrote: "Kissinger is a warm guy with a good sense of humor. He keeps telling me, 'You are the President's man.' He is much more communicative with me than Bill Rogers [Secretary of State]."

On June 12, 1971, he blasted Democratic Senator Ted Kennedy of Massachusetts:

> Teddy Kennedy made a speech on the floor of the Senate . . . in which he said that Nixon wanted to prolong the end of the war until 1972 for political purposes to help get re-elected. To me this was one of the crassest, cruelest statements I had ever heard. When I gave a speech to the Andover Chamber of Commerce with a good press conference beforehand, I denounced the statement as cruel and mean. I can understand debate on the war, but I cannot understand somebody making a statement like that and yet the press let Teddy get away with it. They simply don't jump him out as they would somebody else. It was irresponsibility at its worst, and yet he wasn't damaged a bit by it, I am sure.

He complained about the social whirl:

> We are going to have to cut down on some of these useless evenings. Tonight it was the Stuttgart Ballet. Actually, it was great fun, but it didn't help the job any, it didn't help the President any, and it didn't help my ulcers any. I am very tired. I have never seen a job where there is such constant activity. There are so many things to do. There is one appointment after the other.

George could not bear to miss a party, even if he had to arrive late and improperly dressed. "I saw a bit of him at the UN when the last Taiwanese representative would invite George to dinner—that was during the days the Republicans were being good to us [the Taiwanese]," said Gene Young. "George tore into the dinner in his sailing clothes—rain gear and

Top-Siders—and spent the whole night talking . . . he sounded like a Yale sophomore—yak, yak, yak . . . He wouldn't stop talking . . . It was just yak, yak, yak . . . saying the most vapid things."

George and Barbara entertained constantly. They hosted big cere-monial parties at least once a week and seated dinners almost every other night. They took diplomats to Greenwich for tea parties with George's parents in their new home on Pheasant Lane. Others they took to Shea Stadium to watch the Mets play, always sitting in his Uncle Herbie's box. As one of three principal owners of the baseball team, Herbie had access to the choicest seats.

One issue that George frequently mentioned in his diary was relocat-ing the UN outside of New York City. When his father was moderator of the Representative Town Meeting in Greenwich in 1946, Prescott had maneuvered to keep the UN out of Connecticut and establish its head-quarters in the Turtle Bay area of Manhattan. In 1971, George wrote:

> New York, it seems to me, is the absolute "worst" place where it could be in the United States. The press gives a distorted view of America, the problems of the city give a distorted picture of Amer-ica, and all in all if one were starting from scratch, it should not be here . . .
>
> The Host Country problems are beginning to bug me . . . The crazy JDL [Jewish Defense League] let loose a bunch of frogs and mice which terrified the people in the building. Today the South African Consulate was bombed by black extremists. New York is a miserable place to have the UN. This is heretical to say in the Mis-sion, but it is true.

On October 25, 1971, the UN voted to recognize Red China and give the People's Republic of China the seat occupied by Taiwan, or Nation-alist China. George had vowed in his Senate campaigns if that were to happen, he would advocate U.S. withdrawal from the United Nations. Now, as Nixon's Ambassador, he had to argue for "dual representation" and plead for two seats: one in the Security Council, for Communist China, and one in the General Assembly for Taiwan. He had lobbied hard among the 129 missions for support and had thought he had enough delegates committed to the U.S. policy. But on the final count, he lost

59–55, with 15 countries abstaining. He took the defeat as a personal rebuke and said he was disgusted by the anti-American sentiments. "For some delegates—who literally danced in the aisles when the vote was announced—Taiwan wasn't really the issue," George said. "Kicking Uncle Sam was."

When the Taiwanese Ambassador, Liu Chiegh, walked out of the hall with his delegation for the last time, George leaped up and caught him before he reached the door. Putting an arm around the man's shoulder, George apologized for what had happened. Ambassador Chiegh said he felt betrayed by the organization his country had helped found and supported over the years. He also said he felt let down by the U.S. government. So did George, who had been barred from all foreign policy deliberations by the White House, the National Security Council, and the State Department. He was especially embarrassed on the occasion of the UN vote because Kissinger was in Beijing making arrangements for Nixon's trip to China.

For George the most enjoyable part of being U.S. Ambassador to the UN was talking with his father as a peer rather than a pupil. They discussed Vietnam, civil unrest, and the turbulence on campuses, especially at Yale. Although Prescott was opposed to expanding the war in Southeast Asia and the bombing of Cambodia and Laos, he became exercised when Yale's Calhoun College extended an invitation to Daniel Ellsberg to meet with students. Ellsberg had been accused of theft and conspiracy in disclosing to *The New York Times* the Pentagon Papers, a seven-thousand-page top-secret Department of Defense history of the U.S. involvement in the Vietnam War from 1945 to 1971. Prescott did not approve of lending Yale's prestige to a man who, he felt, had broken the law by making public classified information. "I can hardly think of anyone who is less deserving of such an honor," Prescott wrote to Calhoun Master R.W.B. Lewis. In protest, Prescott resigned as associate fellow of Calhoun College, a position he had held for twenty-eight years.

By that time the former senator was battling the ravages of pipe smoking and binge drinking, which had finally compromised his health at the age of seventy-seven. For months he had been plagued with a racking cough that, in the spring, was diagnosed as lung cancer.

"It was during this time that he called me," Joyce Clifford Burland remembered. "He said, 'I want to see you for lunch.' We met in New York

City and talked about how much we loved singing. My former husband [Richard Barrett] and I and Wesley Oler had been part of the Kensington Four, a singing group that Pres assembled in Washington when his other singing partners had died. He was desolate when he lost them. We met every month to sing and share our passion for music. We did this for years. We even traveled to Hobe Sound when he was there in the winter. Pres taught us all the songs and arrangements he had used with the Silver Dollar Quartet. I was the only woman he had ever sung with, and I felt so proud that he thought I was good enough to be included. Although he was thirty years older than we were, there was no generational difference. When you were singing with Prescott, you were connected to his core . . . I absolutely adored the man . . . I would have laid down in traffic for him.

"After our lunch, we were walking down the street and he said that he had brought me something. 'I want you to have my Whiffenpoof medallion,' he said, placing it in my hands.

"I protested that something that precious belonged to his son Johnny Bush or someone else in his family. But Pres insisted. 'No,' he said. 'I want you to have it.' Six months later he was dead. I realize now that he was saying good-bye and at the same time sparing me the sad burden of knowing he was dying. That's the kind of man he was. Edwardian in the best sense of the word. He observed certain proprieties, and one was courage in the face of adversity."

Several months before he died, Prescott altered his will with a few codicils. He left intact his $20,000 bequest to Yale for the Alumni Fund, but he reduced his bequest to Skull and Bones (RTA Incorporated) from $2,500 to $1,000. He also reduced his bequest to the Episcopal Church Foundation of New York City from $10,000 to $2,500. He remembered his private secretary in the U.S. Senate, Margaret Pace Harvey, and his administrative aide, David S. Clarke, with $5,000 each. But he was so angry at his brother James Smith Bush for divorcing his third wife, Lois Kieffer Niedringhaus, and running off with another woman that he disinherited him. Instead, Prescott left $3,000 apiece to the three children Jim had had with Niedringhaus. He left $140,000 to each of his own children, and the rest of his $3.5 million estate to his wife, Dorothy, with investments "to provide adequately for her maintenance, support, welfare and comfort."

Prescott appointed two of his sons, Prescott junior and Jonathan

James, to be his executors and stipulated that they serve "without fee or compensation." He stated that they must employ the investment services of Brown Brothers Harriman and Company for the first five years after his death.

Lest George feel slighted, Prescott stated that he had appointed his second son an alternate executor, "soley because of his remote residence and in order to simplify the administration of my estate and of the trust."

In the fall of 1972 Prescott entered Memorial Sloan-Kettering hospital for tests. "I have deep worry about him," George wrote in his diary. "He seems instantly old, unlike his old self in many ways."

Dorothy Bush moved into the Ambassador's residence at the Waldorf-Astoria and spent every day at her husband's bedside. After he complained of several restless nights, she told his doctors she longed to spend a night with him because she felt he would rest better. They agreed and she slept in his room. The next day, October 8, 1972, he died peacefully. He was seventy-seven years old.

Flags throughout Connecticut were lowered to half-staff on the day of his funeral, and wires poured in from the White House, the Senate, and the House of Representatives. Dorothy instructed her family not to wear black. "Bright colors only," she said. "This is to be a joyous celebration of your father's life." She told them they were not to sit with her in Christ Church. "I want everyone to see you sitting with your lovely families because that is a public tribute to your father." She insisted that the grandsons be pallbearers and join her in the front pew. She asked the Westminster Choir College of New Jersey to come to Connecticut to sing. She informed the Reverend Bradford Hastings that he was to read the eulogy she had written.

The governor of Connecticut arrived with Connecticut Senator Lowell Weicker and Representative Stewart B. McKinney, New York City's Mayor John Lindsay, Yale's President Kingman Brewster, Averell Harriman, and all the partners of Brown Brothers Harriman. Everyone crowded into the small Episcopal church in Greenwich to hear "a tribute to Prescott Bush from the one who knew him best and loved him the most."

Dotty's eulogy, lovingly sentimental, enshrined her husband and extolled their marriage: "When he stood at the altar 51 years ago and promised to 'Keep thee only unto her as long as you both shall live,' he was making a pledge to God that he never for one moment forgot, and gave his wife the most joyous life that any woman could experience."

Prescott Sheldon Bush was laid to rest in Putnam Cemetery, where a small American flag adorned his tombstone.

That evening George wrote in his diary: "My father, my mentor, my hero died."

CHAPTER SIXTEEN

"I am angry that so many sons of the powerful and well-placed . . . managed to wangle slots in Reserve and National Guard units . . . Of the many tragedies of Vietnam, this raw class discrimination strikes me as the most damaging to the ideal that all Americans are created equal."

—COLIN L. POWELL,
My American Journey, 1995

George Herbert Walker Bush vigorously supported sending other men's sons to Vietnam, but not his own. In 1968 he made sure his firstborn would not be drafted. He did this with one telephone call to Sidney Adger, a Houston businessman and Bush family friend. Adger called Ben Barnes, the Speaker of the Texas House of Representatives, and Barnes called the head of the Texas National Guard, Brigadier General James Rose. Rose called the commanding officer of the unit, Lieutenant Colonel Buck Staudt.

In February 1968 young George, a senior at Yale, took an Air Force officers test. "I was not prepared to shoot my eardrum out with a shotgun in order to get a deferment," he said. "Nor was I willing to go to Canada. So I chose to better myself by learning how to fly airplanes." He scored the lowest possible passing grade on pilot aptitude. Yet, because of his father's influence, he was accepted into the Air National Guard. "They took me because they could sense I would be one of the great pilots of all time," he told *The Houston Chronicle*. He also said he "just happened" to get the coveted slot twelve days before he was eligible to be drafted. "I think they needed pilots."

"That is so disingenuous," said Mark Soler. "You didn't just happen into the Guard in those days or fall upon a slot in the Reserves. You had to sign up early because it took months and months to get in; then you had to wait until there was an opening. At that time there was a national waiting list of 100,000. The waiting was agony. Unless, of course, you had someone to pull strings for you . . . I didn't have that kind of pull. I had to wait to get into the Reserves, which is how I ended up not being drafted. I never considered that I served in the military in any way that was especially patriotic . . . I had to go weekends for six years, but it was a way of not being drafted. To say otherwise is willful denial. When we graduated from Yale in 1968, if you didn't get into the Reserve or the Guard, or get a deferment, or become a conscientious objector, or go to Canada, then you were headed for downtown Da Nang."

George enlisted in the Texas Air National Guard on May 27, 1968, and became a member of the 147th Fighter Group, known as "the Champagne Unit," because it included the sons of Lloyd Bentsen, John Connally, and several Dallas Cowboys. George pledged to perform two years of active service, plus four years of reserve duty, which meant he was obligated to fly one weekend a month and spend two weeks at military camp every summer.

The unsettling parts of this scenario begin with his father's lie that he did not use his influence to get his son a berth in the National Guard, followed by his son's claim that he did not join simply to avoid the draft. "Hell, no," George W. told *Texas Monthly* in 1994. "Do you think I'm going to admit that . . . I just wanted to fly jets." He admitted he had no desire "to be an infantry guy as a private in Vietnam." But he denied trying to avoid combat. "One could argue that I was trying to avoid being an infantryman," he told *The New York Times* in 1999, "but my attitude was I'm taking the first opportunity to become a pilot and jumped on that and did my time."

The Bush family lies, sometimes called "misstatements" by Bush family spokesmen, made aspects of George W. Bush's military record open to question later on, particularly the last two years, when he flew sporadically. According to one set of records, he was all but unaccounted for. Those documents, released in 2000, showed no record by any National Guard unit that George W. Bush ever showed up between May 1972 and May 1973 for scheduled weekend flights, summer military training, or the periodic drills required of part-time Guardsmen. Four years later, in February 2004, after a spate of criticism, the White House released a document indicating the Guard had given George credit for sufficient hours to fulfill his duty during the questionable period of May 27, 1972, to May 26, 1973. The 2004 document raised questions about the previously released record, which showed no Guard credit for May 1972 through May 1973. Equally puzzling, if George did fly all his required hours, is why his superiors in Texas did not fill out a required evaluation form. They maintained they had not seen him on base and thought he was still in Alabama.

Retired First Lieutenant Robert A. Rogers, an eleven-year veteran of the Air National Guard, said the document released in 2004 showing George W.'s intermittent Guard service from October 1972 through May 1973 is not a National Guard document. Rather, the document is an "ARF [Air Reserve Force] Statement of Points Earned." The 2004 document released by the White House is like the document released in 2000 by the Bush campaign that supposedly showed George W. had performed duty from the end of May through July 1973. These two documents show Air Reserve Force credits, which are not given for active service and were not accepted by the Texas Air National Guard.

"The lack of punishment for his misconduct represents the crowning achievement of a military career distinguished only by favoritism," said Rogers. "Bush had a solid record up to April 17, 1972. In fact, he was a poster boy for the Texas National Guard because of who his father was. But then he disappeared. He did not attend any unit he was supposed to from April 17, 1972, through May 28, 1974. He just walked away. As a result, he got 'ARFed,' which is what we call the penalty applied by the Air Reserve Force for nonattendance. Bush was subjected to disciplinary action and slapped with six additional months in which he was eligible to be called up to active duty in the Army . . . That's a big thing in time of war. As a result of that disciplinary action, he did not receive his honorable discharge from the Air Reserve Force until November 1974. Had he not been delinquent, he would have been honorably discharged in May 1974, six years after his enlistment."

George W. was finally released from the Reserves in November 1974, six years and six months after he had joined the National Guard. His six-month penalty was never reported by the press, but no one real-

ized then that he would one day be sending American forces into combat to do what he would not do: become cannon fodder. By the time he
was in line to run for national office, his medical records from the military had been sealed for privacy reasons, and the Bush family lies had
hardened enough to provide the rock of credibility he needed to send
U.S. troops into war.

In 1968 registering for the draft was mandatory for all males eighteen
years old. Being subject to the draft was a duty that healthy young men
with no deferment had to bear. At that time such service usually meant a
tour in Vietnam. This accounted for the high number of antiwar demonstrations on college campuses.

"I guess guys like George didn't have to worry because they knew they
were never going to have to fight," said Mark Soler.

George's fraternity brother and later his business partner Roland Betts
said that George faced a different kind of pressure. "He felt in order not
to derail his father's political career he had to be in military service of
some kind."

Members of the Yale class of 1968 were surprised when George said
he didn't remember any antiwar disturbances on campus. "I know that's
what he claimed, and God knows the guy did a lot of drinking in college,
but he just couldn't have been that drunk," said Christopher Byron. "Vietnam was the terror of our lives . . . There was an antiwar march or antiwar meeting or protest at least once a week at Yale . . . and every time
Reverend Coffin opened his mouth there were camera crews crawling all
over that campus."

Others in the class of 1968, including Mark Soler, share similar recollections. "All we ever talked about at Yale then was school, sex, and the
war in Vietnam," he said, "and not always in that order."

After graduating from Yale in June 1968, George reported to Ellington Air Force Base in Houston, and then took his six weeks of basic airman training at Lackland Air Force Base in San Antonio. Upon
completing it in September 1968, he was commissioned a second lieutenant. He returned to Ellington, where the Texas Air National Guard
staged a special ceremony so that Congressman Bush could be pho-

tographed pinning second-lieutenant bars on his son. "That's how they do things," said Brigadier General John Scribner, director of the Texas Military Forces Museum in Austin, "play it up big, especially since he was a congressman's son. That was important to the Guard."

George received his commission without ever attending Officers' Training School. "I've never heard of that," said Tom Hail, a historian for the Texas National Guard. "Generally they did that for doctors only, mostly because they needed flight surgeons." Normally such a commission required eight full semesters (four years) of college ROTC courses or eighteen months of military service or the completion of Air Force Officer Candidate School.

With his commission in hand, George went on inactive duty in September 1968 to work in the political campaign of his father's friend Representative Edward Gurney, the Republican candidate for U.S. Senate from Florida. Jimmy Allison, the media strategist who had helped the senior Bush get elected to Congress and had worked for him against Ralph Yarborough, was going to run a similar campaign for Gurney against LeRoy Collins, the former governor of Florida.

"The race was getting so much attention we decided we needed a press plane and someone to take care of reporters," recalled James L. Martin, then Gurney's top aide. "That's when Jimmy said young George Bush was available."

"Telephone calls were exchanged," said Pete Barr, another campaign media strategist, "and young George came to Orlando . . . to sheepdog the press . . . He always said he was the pillow-toter."

The "pillow" was essential equipment for the candidate. Gurney, who fought in World War II, had suffered a bullet wound to the spine and needed to sit on a soft feather cushion, which George dutifully carried for him. The wound made campaigning arduous, so Gurney periodically retired to his home in Winter Haven to rest. George whiled away the time with Pete Barr.

"We would play a lot of tennis and drink a lot of beer," said Barr, "and talk a lot of politics."

Gurney's opponent, LeRoy Collins, had been the first elected politician in the South to declare publicly that segregation was "unfair and morally wrong." Ed Gurney hammered him the same way George Bush had hammered Ralph Yarborough. Gurney branded Collins "Liberal

LeRoy," distributed photographs of him meeting with Martin Luther King, and bashed him as a radical, an agitator, and a race mixer.

Gurney won by 300,000 votes. Political analysts recognized that he had sailed into office on the jet stream of Nixon's "Southern Strategy," a thinly disguised appeal to white bigotry.

Second Lieutenant Bush witnessed the noxious efficacy of stirring racial hatred, which, unfortunately, became a hallmark of his family's future campaigns. His father's presidential campaign in 1988 used a vicious race commercial to win, as did George's 2000 primary campaign in South Carolina. The end result for both Bushes was victory at the expense of decency.

Many years after the Gurney campaign, a curious circle of history drew George W. Bush near the legendary Florida governor he had worked so hard to defeat. On December 10, 2000, George, then governor of Texas, watched the Florida recount begin that would determine his presidency. The hand count commenced in the LeRoy Collins Public Library in Tallahassee, where Governor Collins's retort to a rabid segregationist was inscribed on the wall: "I don't have to get re-elected, but I do have to live with myself."

Ed Gurney's victory in 1968 had made him Florida's first Republican senator since the Civil War and given George Herbert Walker Bush renewed hope that he could win the Senate seat in Texas in 1970.

After the Gurney campaign, Second Lieutenant Bush returned to full-time active duty in the National Guard. He was assigned to flight school at Moody Air Force Base in Valdosta, Georgia, where he learned to fly the T-38 Talon.

"I gave then-Lieutenant Bush two of his check rides, including his final instrument and navigation flight check," said Jim Wilkes. "He was an excellent pilot and so graded."

George received his silver wings in December 1969 and returned to Ellington, where he trained to fly the missile-armed supersonic F-102 Delta Dart jet fighter called the Voodoo. Retired Colonel Maurice H. Udell, who instructed him, was impressed by his attitude. "He had his boots shined, his uniform pressed, his hair cut, and he said, 'Yes, sir' and 'No, sir,' " he recalled. "I would rank him in the top 5 percent of pilots I knew. And in the thinking department, he was in the top 1 percent. He was very capable and tough as a boot."

On March 24, 1970, the Guard issued a press release to the Houston papers praising their "first hometown student" as an exemplary citizen soldier: "George Walker Bush is one member of the younger generation who doesn't get his kicks from pot or hashish or speed. Oh, he gets high, all right, but not from narcotics . . . As far as kicks are concerned, Lt. Bush gets his from the roaring afterburner of the F-102."

Three months later the Guard issued another press release when George graduated from training school. The press office included a photo of George with his father and a photo of Congressman Bush shaking hands with the commanding officer, Buck Staudt. Another press release followed in July 1970, when George completed a successful deployment to Tyndall Air Force Base Florida and fired a missile from his F-102. On Election Day in November 1970 before the polls closed, the Guard issued yet another press release to announce the promotions of George W. Bush and Lloyd Bentsen III to first lieutenant even as the elder Bentsen was defeating the elder Bush.

Throughout that year George had worked on his father's campaign for Senate. Shortly after his dad's bitter defeat, George and his Yale classmate Don Ensenat applied to University of Texas Law School. Neither was accepted, although Ensenat eventually became a lawyer. Page Keeton, then dean of the Law School, wrote to one of the people who had recommended George. Without a sterling academic record to emphasize, the writer had stressed George's immense likability, which left the dean unimpressed: "I am sure young Mr. Bush has all the many amiable qualities you describe, and so will find a place at one of many fine institutions around the country. But not at the University of Texas."

His mother recalled her son's first big rejection as slightly unnerving. "I think that got under his skin a bit," Barbara said, "because I don't think he was used to not doing what he wanted to do."

Without graduate school or a full-time job, George idled his days around the pool of the Chateaux Dijon, the expensive apartment complex he had moved to in Houston.

Finally his father, who had gotten him every job he had ever had, stepped in again. This time big George called Robert H. Gow, who had been an officer of Zapata Offshore when George was running the company. Gow, who was a member of Yale's class of 1955 and of Skull and Bones and a roommate of George's cousin Ray Walker, had left Zapata to start Stratford of Texas, an agricultural conglomerate. As a favor to George senior, Gow hired young George as a management trainee.

"We weren't looking for someone," Gow told *The Washington Post* in 1999, "but I thought this would be a talented guy we should hire, and he was available."

George joked about his new job to friends. "I'm now wearing a suit and tie and selling chicken shit," he said.

When he wasn't traveling for the company, he was sitting in the boss's office.

"George liked to talk," said Gow. "He was searching for what to do. He was constantly wanting to talk about what to do with his life."

He lasted nine months before he quit in boredom. "I didn't mind the chicken shit," George said, "just the suit and tie."

For a while in 1971 he flirted with the idea of running for the state legislature, but he changed his mind.

"He may have decided he wasn't ready," said Don Ensenat. "The role model he saw in his father was that you go out and make a name for yourself outside the political arena first." The Texas Legislature, which meets only 140 days every two years, is not considered full-time employment, so candidates are expected to be established members of the community when they run.

George remained unemployed for several months and lived off his trust fund—the $10,000 left in the educational trust set up by his paternal grandparents. He put in haphazard hours with the Guard, but not enough to meet his requirements. By April 1972, he was lagging behind. That same month the Air Force began executing random drug tests, which meant that any pilot or mechanic could be requested on the spot to submit to urinalysis, blood tests, or examination of the nasal passages. On April 17, 1972, George W. Bush made his last recorded flight before disappearing from the official records until October 1972.

By then the psychedelic sixties had spun into the seventies, affecting even the military. Few families, including the Bushes and their relatives—the Walkers and the Ellises—went untouched by the influence of drugs, whether marijuana, amphetamines, or cocaine.

Jeb Bush, an Andover student in those days, described himself as a "cynical little turd at a cynical little school" who smoked pot and inhaled.

Josiah Wear Ellis, known to his friends as Joey, snorted cocaine regu-

302 / KITTY KELLEY

larly at Colorado College. "I was living on the top floor of the house where Joey Ellis and the child of a noted member of the Federal judiciary would come to buy their coke," said Bill Penrose, who also attended Colorado College. "He was a cocky, smug guy, utterly indifferent to people less well off than him. Joey was totally into the Bush thing. 'We're-in-charge-and-we-should-be. We're entitled.' "

Joey Ellis's brother John does not deny the family's struggle with drug abuse. "We all got hit," John told Beverly Jackson of the National Institute on Drug Abuse. "Our family suffered terribly." John Ellis, the son of Nancy Bush Ellis and a first cousin of the Bushes, admitted going into Hazelton in 1988 for drug rehabilitation. He later tried to launch a magazine called *Fix* as a support tool for people trying to conquer their addictions.

Beginning in the 1970s, the Bushes, like other families, coped with the drug scourge and the cross-addiction of alcohol. As recently as 2003, one of W.'s younger brothers, Marvin, was getting illegal prescriptions from a Virginia dentist named Denis Peper for narcotic substances. Peper told a close friend that he wrote "off the books" prescriptions for Marvin. The dentist's license was suspended on October 17, 2003, by the Commonwealth of Virginia.

"The Ellis family and the Bush family have had serious problems with booze," said Marylouise Oates, a writer and Democratic activist. "I remember when John Ellis called to say he couldn't come to my wedding because he was going into Hazelden. He was taking Antabuse and still drinking then . . . I'll bet George W. went to Hazelden, too, but I can't prove it."

While there is no indication that George W. Bush was institutionalized for substance abuse, legitimate speculation arose after he failed to show up in 1972 for his annual physical with the National Guard and was suspended from flying. This raised the question of whether he had been reported for drug abuse and, if so, whether he had been disciplined or treated.

Such information would be contained in the report of the Flight Inquiry Board, which routinely conducts an official review of the reasons for suspension and then determines appropriate action. The report of the Flight Inquiry Board is missing from the military records of George W. Bush that were released under the Freedom of Information Act in 2000 and from the records released by the White House in 2004. After two records' releases, the report of the Flight Inquiry Board is still missing.

"Bush's 'failure to accomplish annual medical examination,' as the record states, could not have been either casual or accidental," said retired First Lieutenant Robert Rogers. "There is circumstantial evidence pointing to substance abuse by Bush during this period . . . Is it unreasonable to raise the possibility that he was suspended from flying as a direct or indirect consequence of substance abuse? It might be if there was no way for Bush to prove his innocence. But George W. Bush can readily defend himself, if he so chooses, simply by voluntarily releasing his complete military records, which he has refused to do."

Bill L. Burkett, a retired state plans officer with the Texas National Guard, claimed that in 1997 the Texas National Guard Archives had been "scrubbed" by order of then-Governor Bush's staff to protect the governor. Burkett said he was present when certain members of Bush's staff contacted the Guard. One he specifically identified was Dan Bartlett, then the governor's liaison to the Texas National Guard. Burkett said that after Bartlett's call to Major General Daniel James III, the documents were shredded. James was the adjutant general for the state of Texas at the time and denied Burkett's allegation. On June 3, 2002, James was appointed national director of the Air National Guard by President George W. Bush.

In the spring of 1972, George W. embarked on what he would later describe as his "nomadic years." Seeing him adrift, his father stepped in again to get him another job with Jimmy Allison, who was running Republican Winton "Red" Blount's campaign for Senate in Alabama against Democratic Senator John Sparkman.

In his UN diary George senior mentioned Blount, a multimillionaire builder who had resigned as Nixon's Postmaster General to run for office. "I like him," George wrote. "He is strong—a real man."

After George senior called Jimmy Allison, young George was hired in May 1972 for nine hundred dollars a month to work in what was considered an impossible campaign against an unbeatable incumbent. After Blount announced his candidacy, one Alabama columnist noted, "It's as good a time as any to go over Niagara in a barrel."

Republicans were still a rare species in the South. "At that time in Alabama, people would spit on you if you were a Republican," recalled Nee Bear, one of several women George dated during the Blount campaign. Even President Nixon, a fellow Republican, would not step forward to support his Postmaster General. "Sparkman was a leading senator," Red Blount recalled, "and the President needed his support."

George's job was to monitor the polls, but he kept the bad news to himself. On Election Day, his roommate, Devere McLennan, was preparing for a victory-night party. "That's when George explained to me we weren't going to win," he said.

It was a monumental loss. "Red got 36 percent of the vote, compared to 72 percent for Richard Nixon," George recalled. "The ticket splitting was phenomenal."

Those who worked with George at that time remember him as an affable social drinker who acted much younger than his twenty-six years. They recall that he liked to drink beer and Jim Beam whiskey, and to eat fistfuls of peanuts, and Executive burgers, at the Cloverdale Grill in Birmingham. They also say George liked to sneak out back for a joint of marijuana or into the bathroom for a line of cocaine. The newspapers in Birmingham for that year carried many stories about the scourge of cocaine from Vietnam and China, much of it imported by the French.

George, according to the recollections of others, tended to show up late every day for work, "around noon," come into the office, prop his cowboy boots on a desk, and start bragging about how much he had drunk the night before.

Red Blount's nephew C. Murphy Archibald, an attorney in Charlotte, North Carolina, remembered George telling stories about how the New Haven police always let him go, after he told them his name, when they stopped him "all the time" for driving drunk as a student at Yale in the 1960s. Bush told this story—"what seemed like a hundred times"—to others working in the campaign, said Archibald.

"He would laugh uproariously as though there was something funny about this. To me, that was pretty memorable, because here he is, a number of years out of college, talking about this to people he doesn't know. He just struck me as a guy who really had an idea of himself as very much a child of privilege, that he wasn't operating by the same rules."

During the Blount campaign, George spent a great deal of time with

"Blount's Belles," a group of young Republican women and Montgomery debutantes who worked for the campaign. Red Blount's son, Tom, at the time an architect in Montgomery, recalled his encounter with Bush: "He was an attractive person, kind of a 'frat boy,' " Tom said. "I didn't like him."

Tom recalled thinking to himself, "This guy thinks he is such a cuntsman, God's gift to women. He was all duded up in his cowboy boots. It was sort of annoying seeing all these people who thought they were hot shit just because they were from Texas."

Behind his back they called George "the Texas soufflé," because, as Archibald said, "he was all puffed up and full of hot air."

As "campaign coordinator," his official title in the newspapers, Bush was supposed to stay in phone contact with campaign managers in Alabama's sixty-seven counties and handle the distribution of all campaign materials. These materials included a pamphlet accusing Blount's opponent, Sparkman, of being soft on race. The material also included a doctored tape from a radio debate distorting Sparkman's position on busing, making him look as if he favored forced busing. Such a position in the Deep South at that time was political suicide. Sparkman was forced to deny a series of false charges linking him to George McGovern, the 1972 Democratic presidential candidate tainted as a "liberal." The race-baiting tactics would be repeated years later when George joined forces with Lee Atwater to run his father's campaign in 1988, which featured the Willie Horton ads, and again when George ran against John McCain in the South Carolina primary.

As an "obligated reservist" in 1972, George was required to continue his duty in the National Guard no matter where he was living. Weeks after he moved to Alabama, he applied for transfer from Texas to an Air Reserve squadron in Montgomery, but his application was rejected. The Alabama outfit did not fly and did no drills. "We met just one weeknight a month," said the commanding officer Lieutenant Colonel Reese R. Bricken. "We were only a postal unit. We had no airplanes. We had no pilots. We had no nothing."

This left George without a Guard unit in Montgomery. So he did nothing for May, June, July, and August of 1972. "He should have commuted back to Houston to perform his duty," said Robert Rogers. "That's what other Guardsmen did in the same situation."

Bush knew he could not fly again until he took a physical, so he requested a nonflying transfer of duties for September, October, and November 1972 to the 187th Tactical Reconnaissance Group in Montgomery. Permission was granted, and he was ordered to report to Lieutenant Colonel William Turnipseed. But George never showed up. Neither Colonel Turnipseed nor his administrative officer, Lieutenant Colonel Kenneth Lott, remembered First Lieutenant Bush.

"Had he reported in, I would have had some recollection and I do not," Turnipseed told *The Boston Globe*. "I had been in Texas, done my flight training there. If we had a first lieutenant from Texas, I would have remembered."

The Texas Air National Guard assumed that George was reporting in Alabama. In an annual evaluation report for May 1972 through April 1973, one of his supervising officers, Lieutenant Colonel William D. Harris Jr., wrote: "Lt. Bush has not been observed at this unit during the period of this report." He noted that Bush "had cleared this base on 15, May 1972, and has been performing equivalent training in a non-flying role with the 187th Tac Recon Gp at Dannelly ANG base, Alabama." Bush's second supervising officer in Texas, Lieutenant Colonel Jerry B. Killian, wrote: "I concur with the comments of the reporting official." The Alabama National Guard has no documents pertaining to George W. Bush and no reports of him ever performing his Guard duty.

After the Blount debacle, George returned to Houston, and a few weeks later he flew to Washington, D.C., to spend the Christmas holidays with his family. He was twenty-six years old. During that time he went out drinking with his favorite brother, sixteen-year-old Marvin. Driving home that evening, George smashed into several garbage cans before making his way into the driveway. He swaggered into the house with the bravado of someone who had drunk too much, and there was his father, sober and unsmiling.

"You want to go mano a mano right here?" George junior challenged.

Some have suggested this incident symbolized young George's defensiveness in the presence of his far more successful father. George shrugged it off years later. "It was probably the result of two stiff bourbons," he said. "Nothing more."

Friends of the senior Bushes say their frustration with the carousing of their eldest son was no secret. "I remember the old man saying he didn't ever think young George would get it together," said Cody Shearer. "He talked about it all the time."

"I covered the Popster [George H. W. Bush] in Houston and have known him since 1970," said the journalist John Mashek. "He was always shaking his head in despair over what to do about George junior."

At the time of the "mano a mano" incident, his father's concern was over the lack of judgment that had prompted George to take his underage brother out drinking and to drive home under the influence of alcohol.

Once again George Herbert Walker Bush picked up the telephone. This time he called John L. White, formerly with the Houston Oilers. Ambassador Bush said that he wanted his son to perform community service with Project PULL (Professional United Leadership League), a mentoring program for inner-city youth started by White and his teammate Ernie "Big Cat" Ladd.

"John knew George Bush's father very well," said White's widow, Otho Raye White. "They wanted to build his [son's] character at the time."

George Herbert Walker Bush, who was on the PULL board, thanked John White a year later by using his influence to get PULL additional funding from Congress. An internal memo in the Gerald R. Ford Library to the Honorable George Bush dated August 16, 1974, states:

> We have arranged for John White to receive some new guidelines and assistance from the National office.
>
> New LEAA [Law Enforcement Alliance of America] legislation pending before the House and Senate Conference Committee will include direct funding authority for youth offenders and PULL related programs.
>
> Will keep you advised.
>
> John Calhoun, Staff Assistant to the President

Young George reported for work in January 1973 at PULL headquarters: a warehouse on McGowen Street in Houston's tough Third Ward. "His dad and John White brought him right to the black belt," said Ladd. "Any white guy that showed up on McGowen was gonna get caught in some tough situations. You better be able to handle yourself."

The PULL program offered kids up to seventeen years of age sports, crafts, field trips, free snacks, rap sessions, tutoring for those who had been expelled, and big-name mentors from the athletic, entertainment, business, and political worlds. The summer after George senior negotiated a "conditional release" from Andover rather than expulsion for Marvin, he sent him to Houston to join George at PULL. The bad Bush brothers were the only two white boys in the place.

"They stood out like a sore thumb," said Muriel Simmons Henderson, one of PULL's senior counselors. "John White was a good friend of their father. He told us that the father wanted George W. to see the other side of life. He asked John if he would put him in there."

Ernie Ladd recalled young George as "a super, super guy . . . If he was a stinker, I'd say he was a stinker. But everybody loved him so much. He had a way with people . . . They didn't want him to leave."

George stayed only seven months at PULL before he announced he had been accepted at Harvard Business School. On September 5, 1973, he requested his discharge from the Texas Air National Guard to go to graduate school. Having served five years, four months, and five days toward his six-year obligation, he received an honorable discharge. He would receive a second honorable discharge from the Air Force Reserve in November 1974 at the end of his six-month penalty.

When George arrived at Harvard to join the class of 1975, his father was running the Republican National Committee for Richard Nixon at the height of Watergate. George, who espoused his father's politics, found himself in a hostile political environment where Nixon was considered the Antichrist.

"Cambridge was a miserable place then to be a Republican," recalled George's aunt Nan Bush Ellis, who lived in Massachusetts, a state known as a Democratic stronghold. In the environs of the town that surrounded Harvard, only four hundred people were registered Republicans. George spent many weekends with his aunt and her family outside of Boston, lambasting Harvard's "smug guilt-ridden affected liberals."

"I remember seeing Georgie at the Harvard Business School," said Torbert Macdonald, his classmate from Andover, "but he looked so lost and forlorn I didn't have the heart to say hello."

Most of the class of 1975 at the B-school knew they were headed for Wall Street, but not George. "He was trying to figure out what to do with his life," said his classmate Al Hubbard. "He was there to get prepared, but he didn't know for what."

Other classmates were not quite as generous in assessing George's aptitude. "He was remarkably inarticulate," said Steve Arbeit. "God, so inarticulate it was frightening. The reason I say that he is dumber than dumb is not that I saw his test scores or his grades; it's the comments he made in the classes we had together that scared me . . . He was totally unimpressive in an atmosphere where you were judged completely on your class participation.

"There's always a layer of kids who are in the school because their parents are somebody. It's almost a legacy sort of thing. Most of them acted like everybody else, except for George, who would not say hello to someone like me if we passed in the hall . . . I'm not the same social class. My father is not chairman of something . . . So unlike most of the people who try to pretend you-don't-know-who-my-dad-is type of thing, George was the opposite."

Ruth Owades, chairman of Calyx and Corolla, a flower catalog company, and a member of George's class, remembered people pointing him out. "At a place like Harvard Business School, you always knew who the sons or daughters of famous people were—but mostly the sons. And then there were the rest of us."

Alf Nucifora, another classmate, recalled George as a "nonentity with a rich boy's attitude who obviously got into school because of the divine right of kings . . . You did not see a great future for this man. There's no way that any sane individual could ever have made such a prediction."

During his first year George came to the attention of Yoshi Tsurumi when the macroeconomics professor announced his plan to show the film *The Grapes of Wrath*, based on John Steinbeck's book about the Great Depression. "I wanted to give the class a visual reference for poverty and a sense of historical empathy," Tsurumi explained. "George Bush came up to me and said, 'Why are you going to show us that Commie movie?'

"I laughed because I thought he was kidding, but he wasn't. After we viewed the film, I called on him to discuss the Depression and how he thought it affected people. He said, 'Look. People are poor because they are lazy.' A number of the students pounced on him and demanded that he support his statement with facts and statistics. He quickly backed down because he could not sustain his broadside."

Professor Tsurumi continued: "His strong prejudices soon set him apart from the rest of the students. This has nothing to do with politics, because most business students are conservative, but they are not inhumane or unprincipled. Unlike most of the others in class, George Bush came across as totally lacking compassion, with no sense of history, completely devoid of social responsibility, and unconcerned with the welfare of others. Even among Republicans his kind was rare. He had no shame about his views, and that's when the rest of the class started treating him like a clown—not someone funny, but someone whose views were not worthy of consideration . . . I did not judge him to be stupid, just spoiled and undisciplined . . . I gave him a 'low pass.' Of the one hundred students in that class, George Bush was in the bottom 10 percent. He was so abysmal that I once asked him how he ever got accepted in the first place. He said, 'I had lots of help.' I laughed, and then inquired about his military service. He said he had been in the Texas National Guard. I said he was very lucky not to have had to go to Vietnam. He said, 'My dad fixed it so that I got into the Guard. I got an early discharge to come here.' "

From the eight hundred people in the class of 1975, George stood out, and not because of who his father was. "I don't remember if he was one of the Texans who had Aggie horns on the front of his big American-made car—most of them did—but I can still see him in his cowboy boots and leather flight jacket walking into macroeconomics," recalled one classmate. "He sat in the back of the class, chewing tobacco and spitting it into a dirty paper cup . . . He was one red-assed Texan who made sure he was in your Yankee face and up your New England nose."

CHAPTER SEVENTEEN

"I would pay to do this job," Barbara told the reporter from the *New York Post*. She twirled around the State Room of the Waldorf-Astoria, pointing out the paintings on loan from the Whitney Museum. "That's a Bellows, a Sargent . . . and you did notice the two Gilbert Stuarts? In our own rotunda. You did get that. Didn't you?" She reeled off all the parties she had attended as the wife of the U.S. Ambassador to the United Nations.

"Of course we went to the wedding," she said, referring to the White House nuptials of Tricia Nixon in the Rose Garden. "Then last week we had a reception of about 50 late one afternoon. African ambassadors of five nations came to meet 12 black college presidents and their wives who are going to spend six weeks in Africa. And we took six people from the Japanese embassy . . . to Greenwich . . . Before that we had a seated dinner of 36. And we had six Mets over yesterday . . . They had lunch with George at the UN and came over here in the afternoon."

Barbara loved the social whirl and never wanted it to end. But after President Nixon was reelected, in 1972, he called for the resignations of all political appointees. George had made twenty-eight major speeches during the campaign, so he was assured another position in the administration, but he didn't know what it would be.

"If it's the Republican National Committee, promise me you won't take it," Barbara said as he was leaving to meet with the President. "Anything but the R.N.C."

The last thing Barbara wanted was to descend from her lofty perch as an Ambassador's wife and chase around the rubber-chicken circuit as the wife of a party hack. Having spent twelve months dealing with diplomats at the United Nations, George fancied himself an expert in foreign policy, and he longed to be named Secretary of State or, at the very least, Deputy Secretary. In a letter to the President promoting himself as a diplomat, George said: "I have been dealing happily, and I hope effectively, with the top international leadership."

The President, who described George as "a total Nixon man," had other ideas. While cursing "Ivy League bastards," Nixon knew George to be one Ivy Leaguer he could count on for slavish loyalty. "Eliminate the politicians," he told his chief of staff, "except George Bush. He'll do anything for the cause." H. R. Haldeman agreed. "[George] takes our line beautifully." On November 20, 1972, the President invited George to Camp David and offered him the chairmanship of the Republican National Committee. George accepted on the spot.

The next day, after talking to Barbara, he wrote to the President:

Frankly, your choice for me came as quite a surprise particularly to Barbara. The rarefied atmosphere of international affairs plus the friendships in New York and the Cabinet seem threatened to her. She is convinced that all our friends in Congress, in public life, in God knows where—will say, "George screwed it up at the U.N. and the President has loyally found a suitable spot." Candidly, there will be some of this. But—here's my answer—Your first choice was the Republican National Committee. I will do it!

Previous George H.W. Bush biographers, all handpicked and approved by Bush, have written that George "very reluctantly" accepted the "unenviable job" as if he were a servant beholden to his master. "It was to be . . . a sacrifice on the altar of loyalty," wrote Nicholas King. "It was . . . more of a political albatross," wrote Herbert Parmet. "It was . . . like being made Captain of the Titanic," wrote Fitzhugh Green.

Not so. George might have indicated such feelings after Watergate became an international scandal and forced Nixon's resignation, but at the time he was offered the Republican National Committee, he did not hesitate. Not for one second. He knew that a President was made by a hundred thousand chicken dinners and a million handshakes in small towns across America. According to unpublished entries in his diary, he saw the RNC as an important stepping-stone. Not only was he serving the President he admired; he was meeting the people he needed to know in order to make another tilt at national office. Looking toward 1976, George knew that being on a first-name basis with Republican National Committeemen, precinct chairmen, and major fund-raisers was crucial if he was to position himself for the presidency.

William J. Clark (Yale 1945W), who was in Skull and Bones with George, outlined the strategy he was to follow in a "Dear Poppy" letter dated January 31, 1973:

> *Tactics: The first step is to name Bush as Chairman of the Republican Party, fresh from his prestigious assignment at the U.N. For two years Bush travels around the country meeting every state and county chairman, establishing his credentials, charming the big money amateurs, and setting up a lot of debts during the '74 campaign for later collection.*

George's position at the Republican National Committee did nothing for the social aspirations of his wife, and Barbara did not hide her disappointment from the President. The writer Gore Vidal recalled a conversation with his friend Murray Kempton shortly after one of the journalist's periodic lunches with Richard Nixon. Kempton had mentioned George Bush, and according to Vidal, Nixon had responded: "Total light-weight. Nothing there—sort of person you appoint to things—but now that Barbara, she's something else again! She's really vindictive!" Vidal characterized the comment as "the highest Nixonian compliment."

George had countered his wife's objections about leaving the UN to return to Washington, D.C. "You can't turn a president down," he told her. Barbara had to know that her husband would have wrapped himself in a feather boa and tramped through Times Square in high heels before he would have said no to Richard Nixon.

Yet George frankly acknowledged in a letter to his sons that he did not have the President's complete confidence because he was one of those "Ivy League bastards":

> *The President's hang-up on Ivy League is two-fold. The first relates to issues. He sees the Ivy League type as the Kennedy liberal*

Kingman Brewster on the war—arrogant, self-assured, soft profes-
sors moving the country left. Soft on Communism in the past—
soft on socialistic programs at home—fighting him at every
turn—close to the editors that hate him. In this issue context he
equates Ivy League with anti-conservatism and certainly anti-
Nixon.

Secondly I believe there is a rather insecure social kind of hang-
up. Ivy League connotes privilege and softness in a tea sipping,
martini drinking, tennis playing sense. There's an enormous hang-
up here that comes through an awful lot. I feel it personally. It
stings but it doesn't bleed . . . But I must confess that I am con-
vinced that deep in his heart he feels I'm soft, not tough enough,
not willing to do the "gut job" that his political instincts have
taught him must be done.

A month after George's appointment was announced, G. Gordon
Liddy and James W. McCord were convicted of breaking into the Democratic Party headquarters in the Watergate and illegally wiretapping
the premises. A week later the Senate established the Select Committee
on Presidential Campaign Activities to be chaired by Sam Ervin, a Democrat from North Carolina. Televised hearings were to begin in May
1973.

George, an inveterate diarist, kept an RNC diary like the one he had
kept at the UN and would keep in China and later as Vice President. He
tried to dictate his thoughts into a tape recorder every day and gave the
tapes to his secretary to transcribe. His diaries may have lacked the felic-
ity of Samuel Pepys, the seventeenth-century British Admiralty officer
whose diaries set the historical standard for delicious bons mots on the
ways of court, but George's unpublished comments provide a contemporaneous account of feelings that he later tried to deny. In one diary entry
(March 13, 1974), he acknowledged his ability to squirm in and out of du-
plicity: "I have been calling them as I see them, so far. Bending, stretching a little here or there, insisting that things that I don't want to put my
name on have the White House name on them, not mine."

From his diary it is clear that when George took over the Republican
National Committee, he believed in President Nixon's innocence. In

fact, George was about the last Republican in Washington to finally recognize the President's complicity.

On April 17, 1973, George seemed slightly concerned about "the grubby Watergate matter" because people were mailing in their RNC membership cards, saying they no longer desired to belong to the party. But he never faltered in his belief in Richard Nixon. He met with the Republican leadership, who recommended that he tell the President to waive executive privilege so that his White House counsel, John Dean, could testify before the Senate Watergate Committee. George requested a meeting with the President to relay the information: "I told him that his overall great record was being obscured by this mess . . . The President was cool, thoroughly understands the problem and that talk did much to reassure me that the matter will be cleared up."

On July 11, 1973, it was revealed that Senator Lowell Weicker, a member of the Watergate Committee, had received money during his 1970 campaign from Operation Townhouse, the Nixon slush fund set up to funnel cash to Republican candidates.

The day after the story appeared, George called Weicker to tell him that he, too, had received funds from Operation Townhouse for his failed Texas Senate campaign. According to Weicker, Bush asked whether he should burn the record of all the Townhouse transactions. Weicker had received $6,000, all of which he had reported. Bush had received $106,000, of which only $66,000 had been reported. "George wanted to burn all the pay-outs," said Weicker. "Not just his own."

Weicker, who lived in Alexandria, Virginia, next to John Dean, had been warned that the illegal campaign contribution might be used against him if he continued speaking out against the administration. Weicker wondered if Bush's phone call on July 12, 1973, might be a ploy to sabotage him.

"[George's question about burning the list] was a very peculiar question, coming as it did not long after I had requested publicly that the special prosecutor's office investigate the Townhouse fund," Weicker recalled. "Destroying potential evidence is a criminal offense. It came to mind that the call might be an attempt to set me up, and I wondered if Bush was taping it. My response would have been the same whether he was or he wasn't.

" 'Until now,' I said, 'Watergate has been a scandal of the Nixon reelection committee. You burn that list and you're making it a scandal of the entire Republican Party.' "

George later denied that he had suggested burning the records. Weicker stood by his recollection. "I know what he said. That is one conversation, shall we say, that was burned in my mind."

The Nixon White House had reason to fear Lowell Weicker. "He was a Republican who spoke out about the wrongfulness of their actions," said Sam Dash, chief counsel to the select committee. "He was, to use the Nixon term at the time, 'off the reservation.' Without Lowell Weicker we would never have had John Dean's testimony, because, according to the immunity statute, I needed a two-third's vote of the committee. If it had just been three Democrats against three Republicans, I could never have given Dean immunity, but Weicker gave me his vote. This enabled us to get Dean's testimony. Without that, there would have been no case."

Richard Nixon wrote in his memoirs that during one of their early meetings, George had expressed concern about the ever-widening Watergate scandal. As always, George's concerns were practical rather than moral. "He privately pleaded for some action that would get us off the defensive." George found that "action" on July 24, 1973, the day after the Senate Watergate Committee served the President with a subpoena ordering him to turn over the White House tapes. George managed to temporarily derail the committee's investigation of the President by spearheading a campaign against the committee's top investigator, Carmine Bellino.

At a hastily called press conference, George produced affidavits from three private investigators—one was dead, and the other two had been convicted of illegal wiretapping—alleging that Bellino, through an intermediary, had attempted to hire them in 1960 to bug the Washington hotel where Nixon had been preparing for his television debates with John F. Kennedy, for whom Bellino had been working as a campaign aide.

Bush said he believed that Nixon's hotel suite had been illegally wiretapped before his 1960 debates and that if true, such bugging could very well have affected the outcome of the 1960 presidential election. "The Nixon-Kennedy election was a real cliff hanger," said Bush, "and the debates bore heavily on the outcome . . . I cannot and do not vouch for the veracity of the statements contained in these affidavits but . . ."

THE FAMILY / 317

Bush's charges detonated an outcry from twenty-two Republicans, who signed a petition calling for an investigation of the allegations against Bellino. Senator Ervin appointed three members of the Senate Watergate Committee to look into the charges, and Sam Dash appointed the committee's assistant chief counsel, David Dorsen, to oversee the investigation.

"It was a frame-up," said Dash, now a professor of law at Georgetown University. "We were all angry about it. We thought Bellino was a man of great integrity, and we thought the charges against him were an effort by people who thought they could harm the integrity of the committee by harming its chief investigator. Both Sam Ervin and I believed then that this was a Nixon dirty trick—an effort by the Republicans to put us off the track from doing the work of the committee."

Bellino denied Bush's charges and accused him of slander and defamation. "Mr. Bush has attempted to distract me from carrying out what I consider one of the most important assignments of my life," he said at the time.

The investigation of Bush's charges lasted two and a half months before Bellino was cleared. After calling him "an honorable and faithful public servant," Senator Ervin announced, "There was not a scintilla of competent or credible evidence . . . to sustain the charges against Bellino."

The committee lawyers admitted that the investigation into Bush's charges had indeed slowed them down. "It hurt us a lot," Bellino said shortly before his death. "I think it was a terrible thing that George Bush did. His charges were absolutely false. Bush was doing the bidding of the White House. His real reason was to disrupt my work because I had all the financial records of H. R. Haldeman, John Ehrlichman and Charles Colson. In fact, there were some things that have never come out. But once you had that smoking gun with Alexander Butterfield admitting to Nixon's bugging the White House—that was enough to proceed on.

"Still Bush could have destroyed the case completely if Butterfield hadn't come along . . . Without that they [the committee] would have given up. The Republicans didn't want the investigation to continue for a long time."

George Bush never apologized to Carmine Bellino before he died in 1990. Years later, when asked about Bush's charges against Bellino, Sam

Dash sighed. "Carmine Bellino was one of the finest financial investigators in the country. His integrity was beyond reproach . . . I guess the best that can be said of George Bush at the time was that he was vulnerable. He didn't do enough checking himself, and he allowed himself to be used."

Bush's "dirty trick" bought the White House some time in 1973, but not enough to avoid scandal. On October 10, Spiro Agnew resigned as Vice President for accepting cash payments from Maryland businessmen in the White House. Bush met with the President a few days later and expressed his support for Agnew. George said that he and Barbara planned to call upon the former Vice President, whom they personally liked and respected:

> *I said I might be criticized for this but I felt affection for the man. The President indicated I did just the right thing and he told me he himself had bought Agnew his Cabinet chair ($600) . . . Nixon talked at some length . . . on the Agnew matter saying that he was caught up in something that had been a way of life in Maryland, and others had done it for a long long time and that if the same spotlight was put on other public figures that was put on Agnew those figures would not measure up (paraphrase).*

George was eager to show Richard Nixon how loyal he was:

> *I also told the President that I had been urged . . . to run for Governor of Texas but that I had decided not to do it now. I felt there was a chance for a Republican to win and it would be important but I felt that my leaving might inadvertently increase the speculation that I had no confidence in the administration—it might add an air of instability . . . The President agreed that it would be good to stay on the job.*

Even after most of the Republican establishment accepted the inevitability of the President's guilt, George remained committed to Nixon and continued sending out "Support the President" information from the Republican National Committee. One Republican senator called to complain that the party should remain separate from the presidency. "I made the distinction that I was speaking out against Watergate," said George, "but we weren't going to separate from the President."

His fealty toward Nixon produced several snipes at Henry Kissinger, whom George felt had leapfrogged to prominence on the back of a beleaguered President. A diary entry from October 13, 1973, reads: "I also couldn't help but think of the irony when Kissinger got the Nobel Peace Prize. Here was Nixon taking all the flack [sic] on the war, Kissinger executing his policies, and Henry walking away with a coveted honor."

Kissinger's "high-handed" tactics and his "enormous ego problem" continued to annoy George. On November 30, 1973, he wrote: "I am troubled by the fact that Kissinger gets the Nobel Prize. Kissinger gets credit for the Middle East and the President gets credit for bombing Hanoi and no credit for the Middle East."

Finally, on December 3, 1973, George shared his indignation with the President:

> I mentioned the fact that I did not appreciate the comment that Kissinger had made when he was in China. I told the President that although Al Haig had explained the matter to me I still wasn't happy because it is Nixon's bombing but it's Kissinger's Nobel Prize. It's the President standing down the Russians but it's Kissinger's Middle East peace . . . I said that Haig had told me that he had fired off a cable to Kissinger asking about what Kissinger had meant when he said that no matter who is President the policy will go on. Kissinger came back and said he had been misquoted. The President looked knowingly at me on all of this, indicating that we both know where the support really lies. It all brought home to me that a President weakened by a scandal must indeed put up with certain things he never would put up with if he were not in that shape.

As much as Nixon said he despised Ivy Leaguers, he selected one to continue the short life of his second term. After Agnew resigned, the President nominated House Minority Leader Gerald R. Ford (Yale Law School 1941) to take his place. It was the first use of the Twenty-fifth Amendment, which had been added to the Constitution in 1967 after President Kennedy's assassination to provide procedures for promptly filling the vacancy of Vice President or President. Ford was sworn in on December 6, 1973.

By January 1974 George's diary had recorded the President's growing agitation over the impeachment inquiry by the House Judiciary Committee. He considered stepping forward to say, "Impeach me or get off my back." He sent George to the Republican leadership to see what they thought. George reported back, and Nixon dropped the idea. He told George: "We will be in for a tough two or three months."

Again eager to show his unwavering devotion, George told the President how he was responding to criticisms against the administration: "I told him how I had answered some of the questions—that my kids were not being drafted, that nobody was shooting at George as a jet pilot. [George was attending Harvard Business School.] He [the President] seemed interested in how I was handling some of the issues."

George groused about the "unfair" treatment Nixon was getting from the press and took a shot at the Kennedys, who he felt "always got a free pass": "They talk about the bombing of Cambodia, but there is no mention of JFK and the Bay of Pigs."

George's need for the President's approval comes through in his diary: "Al Haig told me that the President felt I was doing a good job . . . Rose Mary Woods [Nixon's secretary] said the same thing."

George continued to be in awe of Nixon, even as evidence of corruption piled up, pointing to the President's illegal abuse of power. When experts determined one of the tapes in Nixon's possession had been deliberately erased five times, showing an eighteen-and-a-half-minute gap, George jumped to his defense. "That deletion or whatever it was has nothing to do with the President," he said. He accepted all of Nixon's shifting explanations without question.

On April 5, 1974, George recorded in his diary that he had visited the President in the White House:

> The desk was as clean as ever—shined—certain unreality about all of that at least compared to the way I do work and most everybody else does. There is never a scrap of paper on that desk except for a file or two in a very orderly fashion. I would say this is a positive thing in the President's case—ordered, neat, tidy, ready for decision, etc.

During the spring of 1974, Dean Burch, formerly chairman of the Federal Communications Commission, had been brought to the White House as counselor to the President and liaison between the White House and the Republican National Committee. He and George had the unpleasant task of telling the President about party defections and Republicans who would not step forward to support him. Again George recorded Nixon's reactions with admiration: "He recognized people were trying to get him or pile on but he remained very cool. His responses were manly and there was no anger. Frankly if things had gotten that screwed up as they were . . . I would have been inclined to blame me or Burch or somebody. But he didn't do this at all."

George recalled his reaction to one particularly difficult meeting in which the President had been told about the number of Republican candidates who did not want him to campaign for them:

> *My distinct feeling in being with the President to whom I feel loyalty and indebtedness but never very close on a personal basis—my distinct feeling at the end of this meeting was that I had left a real man. With all the problems that he had it is a sad thing when every chicken shit politician across the country can be joined by many of the Nixon haters in the press to put the worst possible cast on things.*

George berated the media: "The press doesn't understand this. It's all very easy for them. You slam a guy. You carve him up. You do your thing. You get the story and the headline. But they don't understand this question of loyalty, the question of what's fair, what's right."

On July 24, 1974, the Supreme Court ruled 8–0 that the President did not have "absolute authority" to control material that had been subpoenaed. He was ordered to turn over the tapes. Among the shocking revelations on the transcripts was the "smoking gun" tape—a conversation recorded on June 23, 1972, in which Nixon told Haldeman to block the FBI's investigation of the Watergate break-in, which had occurred six days earlier.

At that point Senator Barry Goldwater told George that the President did not have the votes in the Senate to survive an impeachment by the House. By then almost everyone, except George, had accepted the inevitable. On August 6, 1974, Nixon held his last cabinet meeting, which George recorded in his diary:

> *My heart went totally out to him even though I felt deeply betrayed by his lie of the day before. [He is referring to the "smoking gun" tape, which had become public.] The man is amoral. He has a different sense than the rest of people. He came up the hard way. He hung tough. He hunkered down, he stonewalled. He became President of the United States and a damn good one in many ways, but now it had all caught up with him. All the people he hated—Ivy League, press, establishment, Democrats, privileged—all of this ended up biting him and bringing him down.*

Al Haig told George on August 7, 1974, that the President would announce his intention to resign the next day. Only then did George write a letter calling for just such a resignation:

> *Dear Mr. President:*
> *It is my considered judgment that you should now resign. I expect in your lonely embattled position this would seem to you as an act of disloyalty from one you have supported and helped in so many ways . . . [G]iven the impact of the latest development, and it will be a lasting one, I now feel that resignation is best for the country, best for this President. I believe this view is held by most Republican leaders across the country. This letter is much more difficult because of the gratitude I will always feel toward you.*

He had his letter delivered to the White House hours before the President went on television to announce his resignation. To some stalwarts George looked like he had dismounted his white horse long enough to kick the corpse before it was dragged out of town. By the time he called for the President's resignation, his letter looked almost gratuitous, as if it were nothing more than a breathless dash for the history books. "I wanted to be fair," George told Roy Reed of *The New York Times*, "but I didn't want to step in it and track it into the living room."

George exonerated himself in his diary:

I don't want to pile on. I don't want to add to the woes of the Pres-
ident. I don't want to increase the agony of his family. And yet I
want to make damn clear the lie is something we can't support . . .
I suppose when it is written one can establish that perhaps I should
have done more, but I am not made up to walk on the body of a
man whom I don't love but whom I respect for his accomplish-
ments.

Again he scorched the media:

The incivility of the press had been a disturbing and paralyzing
kind of thing over the last few months. And now it continues, that
blood lust, the talons sharpened and clutched, ready to charge in
there and grab the carrion of this President . . . Nixon's enemies can
now gloat because they have proved he is what they said he is. No
credit, no compassion, no healing, simply the meat-grinder at work.

He told friends he was relieved his father had not lived through the
Watergate scandal. "I'm really glad Dad is not alive. It would have killed
him to see this happen. He thought we were the party of virtue and all
bosses were Democrats."

In the last Nixon cabinet meeting as reconstructed by Henry
Kissinger, George was described as "petty and insensitive," bowing and
scraping like a "courtier" to improve his own position, concerned with
himself rather than his country.

Gerald Ford was sworn in as President on August 9, 1974, after Nixon
had left the White House in a helicopter. To the end the former President
refused to accept disgrace. His parting gesture was to stand at the top of
the steps with his arms outstretched and his fingers extended in Vs for victory. His bizarre ear-to-ear grin exuded sheer defiance.

George did not wait twenty-four hours before making his lunge for
the vice presidency:

We have had a lot of press calls about Ford picking me for Vice
President. [Rep.] Bill Steiger [R-WI] called and said that he and
Martha Griffiths [D-MI] had decided that I was the guy. . . . Mary

Matthews in [Rep.] Barber Conable's office said that Barber [R-NY] had said that's what it should be. Jerry Pettis [R-CA] said that he and many are undertaking it. The press are hypothecating [sic].

Ford had announced that he would poll Republicans in and out of government for their recommendations. Telegrams were sent by the RNC, specifying that preferences be wired back to the chairman—none other than George H.W. Bush—which may or may not have skewed the results: 255 for Bush and 181 for Rockefeller. No one else was close.

On August 9, 1974, George recorded in his diary: "Suspense mounting again. Deep down inside I think maybe it should work this time. I have that inner feeling that it will finally abort. I sure hope not. Another defeat in this line is going to be tough but then again it is awful egotistical to think I should be selected."

After previous attempts to get himself on the national ticket, George had become proficient in self-promotion. In 1968 he had bombarded Nixon with letters from America's financial establishment. This time he went for the Republican heartland, and President Ford was inundated with letters from congressmen, state legislators, governors, and mayors.

On August 12, 1974, the new President summoned George to the White House to ask his views about the vice presidency.

"I am in a peculiar position," said George, "because I know that my name has been considered."

The President nodded. "I am getting strong recommendations on it," he said.

"Well, if it would be agreeable with you and it doesn't seem to be putting on the hard-sell, I'll give you my credentials as well as shortcomings and then try to be somewhat objective."

George jumped in:

I went through the resume—Phi Beta Kappa economics, Yale, East and West, successful in business, Ways and Means, finances in order, knowing the business community, press relations, politics, U.N. We talked about all of these and I told him I thought he had to get his own mark on foreign policy, and I thought that there would be times when it would be good to have his total man—

*namely his Vice President going on these foreign trips and I felt I
could do that well.*

George left the White House feeling quite optimistic, as he recorded in
his diary: "For the first time I have the feeling that it might work about the
Vice Presidency."

On August 20, 1974, he was in Kennebunkport watching television
and waiting for the President to enter the East Room of the White House
to make his announcement. The phone rang. The White House operator
asked him to hold for the President. Ford came on the line to tell him that
he was about to introduce Nelson A. Rockefeller as his Vice President and
wanted George to know beforehand. Crushed, George managed to offer
Ford his total support.

Within minutes a reporter arrived at the family compound and
walked over to Bush.

"You don't appear to be too upset," he said.

George responded tersely. "You can't see what's on the inside."

Furious about not being selected, he resolved to resign from the
RNC. "He thought he had it," recalled Eddie Mahe Jr., political director
of the RNC. "He said they could shove the RNC job."

George spent the next day writing letters to his friends. In a note to
Lud Ashley, he wrote: "Yesterday was a real downer. I guess I had let my
hopes soar unrealistically but today perspective is coming back and I realize I was lucky to be in the game at all."

He also wrote to James A. Baker III:

Dear Bake—

*Yesterday was an enormous personal disappointment. For valid
reasons we made the finals (valid reason I mean a lot of Hill, RNC,
& letter support) and so the defeat was more intense—*

*But that was yesterday. Today and tomorrow will be different for
I see now, clearly, what it means to have really close friends—more
clearly than ever before in my life.*

As a consolation prize, Ford offered George any assignment he
wanted. George recorded in his diary that he met with the President on
August 22, 1974, to discuss the matter: "The President indicated that the

decision on the VP had been very close. 'You should have been very com-plimented by the support.' "

Ford, a kindly man, obviously wanted to soften the blow for George. Private papers in the Ford Presidential Library indicate that the President had decided on Nelson Rockefeller from the beginning. George never was a contender, except in the press and in his own mind.

The President offered to make George Ambassador to the Court of St. James, the most prestigious post in the Foreign Service: "He won-dered if it was substantive enough—so did I. We talked about the money. I told him I had lost a lot of money and didn't know if I could afford it."

The President then offered the second-most-prestigious post—Ambassador to France, but George passed because he could not speak French.

"I don't have any languages, either," Ford said comfortingly.

Finally they touched on China, and George, who had not discussed the decision with his wife, said he wanted to succeed David K.E. Bruce as head of the U.S. mission in Peking, now Beijing. Ford was surprised because there was no ambassadorial status to the appointment and not much social life, but he agreed to the assignment. George wrote in his di-ary: "I told [the President] that I wanted to do more in foreign affairs in the future . . . I indicated that way down the line, maybe 1980, if I stayed involved in foreign affairs, I conceivably could qualify for Secretary of State. [He] seemed to agree."

Profiling the new chief of mission to the People's Republic of China in *The New York Times*, Christopher Lydon wrote, "In the career of George Bush it seems that nothing succeeds like failure." George never forgave the journalist for accusing him of failing upward.

In the first entry to his Peking diary George questioned his motives for leaving Washington:

> *Am I running away from something? . . . Am I taking the easy way out? The answer I think is "no" . . . I think it is an important as-signment. It is what I want to do. It is what I told the President I want to do, and . . . I think it is right—at least for now . . . I think in this assignment there is an enormous opportunity of building*

credentials in foreign policy, credentials that not many Republicans will have.

Professionally the appointment to China would enhance George's credentials, but personally it would discombobulate his thirty-year marriage, send his wife packing for three months, prompt her to burn her love letters, and eventually lead to her severe depression.

"It wasn't just another woman," said someone close to the situation, discussing the wedge that had come between George and Barbara. "It was a woman who came to exert enormous influence over George for many, many years . . . She became in essence his other wife . . . his office wife."

George had never been a compulsive womanizer with one-night stands or flameout affairs. Rather, he maintained a few flirtatious relationships, which his wife had tolerated because he never humiliated her. He chose his other involvements very carefully (usually out of town) so as not to threaten his marriage. Then along came Jennifer Fitzgerald, who started out as his secretary and became so much more.

"George met her when she was working for Dean Burch," said Roy Elson, former administrative assistant to Democratic Senator Carl Hayden of Arizona. "Dean was Barry Goldwater's man at the Republican National Committee; then Dean went to the White House under Nixon and stayed with Ford until the end of 1974. Jennifer was his personal assistant . . . I knew her very well and there's no question in my mind what her relationship was with George Bush but that's because of what Dean confirmed . . . and why shouldn't I have believed Dean? He was my best friend until the day he died . . . we went to college together and later roomed together in Washington, D.C."

Jennifer Ann Isobel Patteson-Knight Fitzgerald was forty-two years old and divorced when she walked into the Oval Office on November 30, 1974. As she waited to have her farewell photo taken with President Ford, she toyed with the long string of pearls wrapped around her neck. The door opened just as she broke the strand, but not her stride. Short, blond, and pretty, she smiled, and let the broken pearls dangle as she posed with the President, who also smiled. She was leaving in a few days for the People's Republic of China to become personal assistant to the chief of the mission, and George Bush could hardly wait.

"I am looking forward to Jennifer Fitzgerald coming over to be my secretary," he wrote on October 21, 1974, the first entry of his China diary. He had told friends that she would be his "buffer" with the State Department, someone loyal to him and not looking for State Department advancement. "I don't know what particular skills she brought to the job," recalled one member of the U.S. mission. "She certainly couldn't type."

In those days Peking was a remote outpost seven thousand miles from Washington, D.C. It might as well have been 7 million miles. Mail took one week to be delivered through the State Department's diplomatic pouch and six weeks by postal service. Peking had no television, no English radio, no English movies, no English newspapers or magazines. Telephone calls cost sixteen dollars for the first three minutes. Adding to the feeling of isolation was what George described as China's "underlying hatred of foreigners."

Barbara suddenly decided to leave Peking before Jennifer's arrival, saying she wanted to spend Thanksgiving and Christmas with the children, first in Washington and then in Houston, where Jeb was living with his new bride. Barbara would not return to China until the next year.

Her departure rankled George for several reasons, not least of which was having to pay for her ticket. There were only two flights a week in and out of Peking in those days, and because Barbara had not made plans, she asked whether she could fly home on the White House plane with Henry Kissinger after his diplomatic visit. He had arrived in November for five days with his official entourage, his wife, and his children.

George wrote in his diary:

> Barbara boarded the plane with the Kissinger group and headed off for the first Christmas we will be apart in 30 years . . . [T]he day of the departure they told me there was a little flap in the States about Kissinger's kids and wife and that the press was insisting that they pay. And [Kissinger's aide] thought it would be better if I paid. So I, a little sore about it, wrote out a check for sixteen hundred dollars to the U.S. Air Force and said, "Now you tell them I paid in advance" for . . . the first-class trip.

Described by his friends as "extraordinarily frugal," and by his aides as "downright cheap," George badgered the State Department for weeks to be reimbursed for the sixteen hundred dollars. He resented having to pay for Barbara's first-class fare. He had had a similar experience as UN ambassador when he was sent to Europe for an orientation tour. First-class tickets had been provided for him and his top aide, but if Barbara insisted on accompanying him he was required to pay for her. "There was lots of teasing about how we would go," she recalled. "George said he would send me back messages from first-class to coach, or maybe I could come up and visit first-class once in a while." In the end, George refused to pay for her to fly first-class. Instead, he traded in the government paid tickets, and, as Barbara recalled, "We all flew coach class."

In China, George also would not pay for flying the family dog, C. Fred, to Kennebunkport for the family's annual vacation. As he noted in his diary: "Hassle over C. Fred. He now cannot go as extra baggage but rather as a separate package at baggage rates—$9 a pound, times $28 a dog, plus $12 a cage equals 9x40=$360 one way. Sorry, he stays here!"

Barbara's sixteen-hundred-dollar ride on the Kissinger plane continued to annoy George four months later, when he saw a magazine with a photograph of the Kennedy children scampering toward Marine One as it landed with the President at JFK's home in Middleburg, Virginia. George wrote in his diary: "I wondered whether the reporters were swarming around in those days to see who was paying for the helicopter."

Jennifer Fitzgerald arrived in Peking on December 5, 1974, and the next day she and George left for twelve days in Honolulu for the Chief of Missions Conference. His diary noted some State Department business and concluded with his reflections at the end of the trip:

> *Spent the last two days out of that Sheraton Waikiki madhouse and in the 4999 Kahala apartment—just lovely . . . Checked out the bathhouse again . . . Totally relaxing. Someday I will write a book on massage I have had ranging all the way from Bobby Moore and Harry Carmen at the UN to the steam baths of Egypt and Tokyo. I must confess the Tokyo treatment is the best. Walking the back, total use of knees, combination of knees and oil, the back becoming a giant slope does wonders for the sacroiliac, and a little something for the morale too. Massage parlors in the U.S. have ru-*

*ined the image of a real massage. It is a crying shame. Flew back
to Peking on Iran Airlines. Jennifer and I alone in first class.*

George's seventy-three-year-old mother had become concerned
enough about Barbara's departure to make her own arrangements to visit
her son over the Christmas holidays. Sensing a possible crisis in his life,
Dorothy Walker Bush and her sister-in-law Margie Clement (Prescott's
seventy-five-year-old sister) stayed with him for three weeks. They arrived
on December 18, 1974.

George's mother remained the most important woman in his life, and
the day before her arrival he wrote about her impending visit with breathless anticipation: "Mother arrives tomorrow. I have that kind of high
school excitement—first vacation feeling."

Dotty Bush understood her son's driving ambition. She knew how
much he needed to play a role on the world stage, and she wanted Barbara to look the part of an important man's wife. Dotty had urged her
daughter-in-law to try to improve her matronly appearance. She did this
kindly by suggesting that Barbara might feel better with a little more exercise. She then remarked how pretty Barbara had looked as a brunette,
adding that George looked quite boyish for a grown man. That's when
Barbara got the message and started dyeing her white hair so she wouldn't
look so much older than her husband.

In his mind George had slotted his wife into the mother-of-my-
children category, a ranking of respect that was bracketed in steel. Like a
Mafia don, he kept the wife category separate from the category of other
women. While his attentions strayed over the years, his family commitment remained solid. That was Barbara's insurance policy—knowing she
would never be divorced—but in 1974 that was not enough.

"I don't think there was much going on in that marriage by then," recalled Nadine Eckhardt, who was married to Democratic Representative
Bob Eckhardt of Texas. "We saw a lot of them in the days when George
and Bob served in Congress together.

"I have given lots of thought to the duality of people like the Bushes.
All of us have male and female in us; some more, some less. George and
Barbara married young and had those kids when the hormones were
working well. By the time I met them George was very 'femme.' Slim and
silly and a hopeless flirt. In my book I say he was cute and we were at-

tracted to each other. It was sort of like when you're attracted to a gay guy and you know nothing's going to happen so you just forget about it and be friends."

Another congressional wife who observed the Bush marriage was Marian Javits, the widow of the late senator from New York Jacob Javits. "George needed more hugging and touching," she said. "Passion was a need for him that was probably part of his great ambition . . . We visited them in China and while I do not understand Barbara, I do know she adored George. Pure love . . . I think she saw that her biggest strength was to imitate his mother, almost become his mother . . . Barbara let herself look the way she did on purpose. If George had wanted her to look any other way, she would have. Believe me . . . I know this as a wife . . . I think with Barbara her kids made up for everything."

In later years other women would comment on the way Barbara "mothered" her husband. "I was working at CBS-TV when I first met the Bushes," recalled Carol Ross Joynt. "He came into the Green Room with a gray-haired woman who I thought was his mother. Someone told me she was his wife, and I became fascinated by their dynamic because they were not a matched pair . . . He engaged women immediately. He's not a lecher, but he makes eye contact with sexual energy. He's polite and does not behave improperly—he's no Bill Clinton—but the sexual message is there. She [Barbara] is oblivious to it all. She's supremely confident and in charge of him like a mother overseeing her child. It's clear that she's the one in the relationship who totally wears the pants . . . and it's also clear that he relies on her."

Roberta Hornig Draper, whose husband was the U.S. Consul General in Jerusalem, met the Bushes when they visited Israel. "Barbara seemed to wet-nurse George like a little boy. She brushed the dandruff off his shoulders, she straightened his tie, and she was always pushing him along the way. She didn't tie his shoes or wipe his runny nose, but you get the idea."

"I can tell you that when I met Barbara Bush in China she was most sensitive to the plight of an unhappy marriage," said the writer Phyllis Theroux. "My then-husband had taken the first group of American businessmen to China—the head of Cargill and Westinghouse and Manufacturers Hanover Trust and John Deere—all big guns . . . Our marriage was in deep trouble at the time, and I don't know how Barbara Bush figured this out, but she knew I wasn't happy. I was married to a very ambitious young man and there were strains . . . She said to me, 'You know there are times when you really just have to sort of take a backseat and realize that your husband is in a phase in his life where you're just not going to have a lot of time with him. But believe me, it will get better.'

"I remember being so grateful to her for those words that I impulsively grabbed her hand and kissed it. She was probably a little taken back by that but she was not overcome. She didn't go 'ooh' and 'aah' and she didn't put her arms around me. She just accepted it . . . She obviously knew what she was talking about when it came to unhappiness within a marriage."

By the time Barbara returned to China in 1975, after three months away, she had decided to fill her hyperactive husband's life with a continual flow of visitors to occupy his attention—congressional tours, American businessmen, visiting diplomats, personal friends, and family. George noted his wife's effort in his diary: "Bar is knocking herself out for these guests and I do hope they appreciate it. She is marvelous at showing people around and all of that."

On April 30, 1975, George and Barbara were attending a reception at the Netherlands' embassy when they received word that Saigon had fallen. Later George recalled the evening:

The Vietcong were there. Three little guys about four feet high that rushed happily out of the room. The Vietcong and the North Vietnamese embassies are bedecked in flags and having understandable celebrations. Firecrackers . . . It is a rather sad thing and you can sense the hostility and certainly the tension when I walk by certain groups at these receptions . . . The whole aftermath of Vietnam making me slightly sick.

Four of the five Bush children arrived in Peking in June 1975. Twenty-two-year-old Jeb stayed in Houston, where he held a job with the Texas Commerce Bank. To his parents' great consternation, he had recently married a young Mexican woman named Columba Garnica Gallo, who did not speak English. George had just graduated from Harvard Business School; Neil, twenty, was an undergraduate at Tulane; Marvin, nineteen, was about to enter the University of Virginia (thanks to the intercession of the Bemiss family); and Doro was about to turn sixteen. Since most of the family was together for the first time in years, Doro decided to celebrate her birthday by finally getting baptized, which George noted in his diary:

> What an experience. Baptism in Communist China . . . The Chinese wonder why we were doing it. Bar explained that we wanted the family together and hadn't been able to do it [before this] . . . We were happy the Chinese agreed to do it after they consulted in a meeting . . . A very special day, an occasion.

During that visit the family also celebrated young George's twenty-ninth birthday, which his father noted in his diary on July 6, 1975: "He is off to Midland, starting a little later in life than I did, but nevertheless starting out on what I hope will be a challenging new life for him. He is able. If he gets his teeth into something semi-permanent or permanent, he will do just fine."

Weeks before, George had expressed concern over his son's future. "He talked about young George to me on occasion," said Gene Theroux, a Washington, D.C., attorney who headed the National Council on U.S.-China Trade. "He didn't think his son was headed in the right direction then to ever amount to much." The elder Bush had met Sandy Randt Jr., who graduated from Yale in George's class. Bemoaning young George's footloose life, his father said, "Will he ever get his act together?" This was a family refrain for many years.

The nonstop stream of houseguests provided constant distraction, and so many requests for visas that the State Department complained George was doing too much entertaining.

"There wasn't anything else for him to do," said the administrative officer of the U.S. mission. "Our [U.S.] embassy was in Taipei and Kissinger was on top of that, so George didn't have a thing to do but maintain an American presence in Peking . . . Ambassador Bruce had paved the way and he was the best choice to be our first representative after recognizing China because he was our most illustrious diplomat. The Chinese would've taken exception if we had sent anyone with less prestige than David Bruce . . . George was a good replacement because by then the

Chinese revered Richard Nixon, and they knew that George, as chairman of the Republican National Committee, had been Nixon's man, so they felt they were getting the President's right hand when George arrived. You needed to tell the Chinese that they had someone powerful in the U.S. compound, otherwise they would lose face. Because of George's close relationship with Nixon he looked powerful to the Chinese. They didn't care about Watergate. They tape-record people all the time, so that was no big deal. Breaking into offices to steal papers was routine to them, and lying was all in a day's work, so Watergate was not a detriment to George in China.

"Although it was a nothing job and George had nothing to do but eat and drink and play Ping-Pong, he did it well. He was not at all like David Bruce, who was a grandee and would not attend diplomatic receptions because, as head of the liaison office, he would have had to stand in line behind the Palestine Liberation Organization and David Bruce was simply not going to do that. Nor was Bruce about to socialize with a bunch of tacky second-rate diplomats at a Nigerian festival or the thirtieth anniversary of the liberation of Czechoslovakia, but the Bushes loved those sorts of things and went to every reception they could. Bruce was a Brahmin; George was just a schmoozer . . . We would never have thought of calling Mr. Bruce anything but Mr. Ambassador, whereas everyone called George by his first name . . . The Chinese let us know in no uncertain terms that George was not considered an Ambassador. They said his title from the UN was simply a courtesy moniker without diplomatic weight. They called him 'Busher' and did not accommodate him like they did Ambassador Bruce. They never said no. But if we'd ask if 'Busher' could see the Chairman, the Chinese would say, 'Not convenient right now.' Never no."

George would not be permitted to meet Chairman Mao Tse-tung until President Ford visited China in December 1975. By then, George had packed his bags and was ready to go home.

He had started growing restless in the spring of 1975. After six months, China had lost its exotic appeal, national-day celebrations had grown stale, and his political juices had started percolating. Always restless for the next appointment that might put him closer to becoming President, George rarely lasted more than a year in any of his jobs. There was never enough time for him to make a substantive contribution, other than acquiring an impressive credential. He wrote to his friend Nicholas Brady, chairman of Wall Street's Dillon, Read: "I'm sitting out here trying to figure out what to do with my life."

His boredom seemed to communicate itself to members of the Andover board of trustees, who were perplexed by his obsession with parietals—the rules governing dormitory visits by the opposite sex. "He seemed to have an unhealthy interest in parietals," recalled Gene Young, an Andover board member. "Parietals—that's what his main concern was when he was in Beijing. I mean, messages would float in from him about parietals . . . Probably one of his sons had gotten into trouble in an earlier time, but it struck us all as a funny thing for an Ambassador to China to be worried about."

George began to consider his political career. He noted in his diary:

Giving a little thought to possibly running for governor of Texas. I have time to think this out. The plan might be to go home after the elections in '76, settle down in Houston in a rather flexible business thing, shoot for the governorship in '78, though it might be extremely difficult to win. Should I win it, it would be an excellent position again for national politics, and should I lose, it would be a nice way to get statewide politics out of my system once and for all. I hate to undertake another losing campaign and I am a little out of touch with what it all means down there, but I can get a little quiet work done on the situation.

George would not have to face another losing campaign. On November 1, 1975, he received a wire from Henry Kissinger marked "Secret sensitive exclusively eyes only":

The President is planning to announce some major personnel shifts on Monday, November 3 . . . The President asks that you consent to his nominating you as the new Director of the Central Intelligence Agency . . . Regretfully, we have only the most limited time before the announcement and the President would therefore appreciate a most urgent response.

"Oh, no, George," said Barbara with tears in her eyes.

Congressional hearings had exposed the CIA's felonious misdeeds—secret drug testing on human beings, spying on U.S. citizens, and assassination plots against foreign leaders. But after fourteen months in China, George was ready to leave. He wired Kissinger immediately and accepted:

Henry, you did not know my father. The President did. My dad inculcated into his sons a set of values that have served me well. In my own short public life, one of these values quite simply is that one should serve his country and his president. And so if this is what the President wants me to do the answer is a firm "yes." In all candor I would not have selected this controversial position if the decision had been mine, but I serve at the pleasure of our president and I do not believe in complicating his already enormously difficult job.

George asked that prior to the public announcement his mother and his five children be called and told the following:

The president has asked us to leave China. He wants me to head the CIA. I said yes. This new job will be full of turmoil and controversy and Mum and I know that it will not make things easy for you. Some of your friends simply won't understand. There is ugliness and turmoil swirling around the agency obscuring its fundamental importance to our country. I feel I must try to help. I hope you understand. Soon we can talk it over. Love.

CHAPTER EIGHTEEN

Prescott S. Bush III was the elder son of George H.W. Bush's older brother, Prescott Jr. Prescott III, or P3, as his family called him, liked to regale friends with wild tales of trolling through the Lower East Side bars of Canal Street in New York City. One friend recalled: "He used to tell us crazy stories of hanging out with black hookers, who were shooting up noca crystalline, and one hooker in particular, who was pregnant. She sat on a bar stool and squeezed milk from her breasts into an arc which Prescott tried to catch in his mouth."

The namesake grandson of Senator Prescott Bush had not followed his family's trajectory to the pot of gold at the end of the rainbow. He had made it from Andover through Yale (class of 1970), and in the tradition of all Bush men he even married well, albeit briefly. The young woman had come from what the Bushes called "a good family"—a socially recognized family with money. She was acceptable on all counts, save one: she was a Democrat. When she mailed her wedding invitations, she made sure each envelope carried a stamp that bore the picture of a Democratic President. "Just a subtle little rebellion," recalled one of her bridesmaids. The invitations to Greenwich arrived with the jaunty image of FDR, condemned by the Bushes' country-club set as a traitor to his class.

Shortly after the wedding the newlyweds traveled to Europe intending to live in Greece, but once there Prescott went out for a walk one afternoon and never returned to the marital bed. The intimacy required of marriage, plus the weight of his family's impossible expectations, came crashing down on him. P3 could no longer cope. He wandered through

Europe for a while and stayed with relatives in Switzerland while his parents flew to his young wife's side and helped her return to the United States.

"He stayed with us for a while," said a cousin, "but then his family called because they were concerned and they were looking for him, which absolutely scared him stiff. He had a thing about the family not finding him. I don't know what the basis of that was, because Prescott junior and his wife are both very kind people, but whatever had shifted in their son was directed to hiding from his family."

A discreet divorce ensued on the grounds of abandonment, and the young bride never saw Prescott S. Bush III again. He was later diagnosed with schizophrenia.

"I met him years after that and he said he had been institutionalized for a long time. He talked a lot about it. He appeared to be heavily medicated, but he was a sweet guy, although obviously odd and highly eccentric. We all hung out in Florida with mutual friends, and then got together in New York for a while. We even visited his parents in Greenwich, but I got the feeling that they just wished he'd go away," said a friend. "His father was a harrumphy type of guy, and he considered Pressy an embarrassment, because, of course, Pressy had the family name . . . but he obviously wasn't going anywhere with it—he wasn't going to be a senator like his grandfather or even president of the Greenwich Country Club like his father—so his parents acted like they didn't want to have much to do with him."

By January 27, 1976, Prescott S. Bush III had moved to a scabby apartment in the East Village of Manhattan. "He hadn't been in touch with his family for many years, and he didn't pay attention to the news. He told us he was sitting in a coffee shop with his roommates, who claimed to be part of the Weathermen Underground movement. I'm sure Pressy wasn't involved in any of their revolutionary actions—planting bombs in government buildings and blowing up town houses and the like . . . Pressy's refuge was bird-watching and reading Greek and studying the literature he had read at Yale . . . But he said he happened to see a newspaper lying on the floor and he noticed on the front page that his uncle George Herbert Walker Bush had just been made head of the CIA . . . Pressy kicked the paper under the table because he didn't think it would be a good idea for the Weathermen to know that he was related to the head of the CIA."

The relationship would not have done George Bush any good either. His confirmation process had been contentious. Both Democrats and Republicans had objected to him as being too partial, too political, and too partisan. Imagine the outcry had those senators learned that George's nephew was living with members of a covert terrorist organization whose stated goal was inciting armed revolution to topple the U.S. government.

At the same time President Ford submitted George's nomination, he forced Nelson Rockefeller to announce that he would not seek reelection as Vice President in 1976. Rockefeller's politics were too liberal for the right wing of the Republican Party, and Ford wanted to be reelected without opposition within the GOP. When the President was asked if being the director of the CIA would eliminate George as a possible running mate, Ford said that George would be very much in the running. The President's response triggered another barrage of brickbats. The *Washington Star* editorialized, "Nice Man, Wrong Job," saying that George did not meet the Rockefeller CIA Commission recommendation for "persons with judgment, courage and independence to resist improper pressure and importuning." *The Baltimore Sun* said, "Who will believe in the independence of a former national party chairman?" *The Wall Street Journal* dismissed George as "just another upward-striving office seeker."

George's nomination looked insane to most Democrats and some sane Republicans. Republican Senator William V. Roth of Delaware and Republican Representative James M. Collins of Texas wrote to the President and begged him to reconsider. Collins, a Texas colleague of George's, praised him, saying he was "as fine as any man in Washington," but added, "He is not the right man for the CIA . . . As the former Chairman of the National Republican Committee he is a partisan voice . . . They [Democrats] are going to crucify him on this job and Senator Church will lead the procession."

Senator Frank Church of Idaho, the chairman of the Senate Intelligence Committee, did not disappoint. The Democrat blasted George as "the poorest choice possible." Church stated that an ambitious politician like Bush should not be put in control of the government's intelligence agencies. As CIA director, George would also be director of Central Intelligence, which meant he would be the President's coordinator for the country's entire intelligence apparatus and oversee the intelligence activities of every federal agency, including the Federal Bureau of Investigation, National Security Agency, Defense Intelligence Agency, National Reconnaissance Office, National Imagery and Mapping Agency, and diplomatic intelligence at the State Department. Church charged that the White House was using George's appointment to further his political ambitions. Democratic Senator Thomas McIntyre of New Hampshire declared the nomination "an insensitive affront to the American people."

Senator Church argued that the position of CIA director was too important to be a "political parking spot" for an ambitious politician. The agency needed a director who was independent of political pressure when advising the President, rather than one who hoped to be the President's running mate. George, who was transparently ambitious, had never demonstrated political independence. He argued that he had recommended resignation to President Nixon, but as Democratic Senator Patrick Leahy of Vermont noted, that recommendation came quite late in the day.

During George's two days of hearings before the Senate Armed Services Committee, he would not withdraw from consideration as Vice President, which inflamed resistance on both sides of the aisle and caused David Cohen, president of Common Cause, to withhold his endorsement: "A CIA head who is ready to consider high elective office less than one year after his appointment will be perceived to service the short-term political needs of a sitting president rather than the duties of the agency and the best interests of the nation."

Senator Church offered to mute his opposition if George would remove himself from political consideration in 1976. George refused, adding, "To my knowledge no one in the history of the Republic has been asked to renounce his political birthright as the price of confirmation for any office." Democratic Senator Stuart Symington of Missouri urged him to change his position and promise that if confirmed, he would stay on the job for at least two years. George, who had never come this close to the vice presidency before, would not budge. "If I was offered the nomination," he said, "I can't tell you I wouldn't accept it."

Even so, the Senate committee voted 12–4 to confirm George as director of the CIA. But three of the four members voting against him signed a minority report, stating:

> *Rightly or wrongly, the public will be understandably suspicious of the potential for political abuse of the agency by a director who once chaired one of the major political parties. We cannot, and should not, ignore this public reaction, for it can undermine the rebuilding of confidence so necessary if the CIA is to fulfill its proper role.*
>
> *We are also concerned that Mr. Bush's nomination sets a precedent of political appointments to a post that should be completely insulated from political considerations.*

After the President read the minority report, he sensed trouble for full confirmation. He drafted a letter to the chairman of the committee, stating in part: "If Ambassador Bush is confirmed by the Senate as Director of Central Intelligence, I will not consider him as my Vice Presidential running mate in 1976."

President Ford called George in to approve the letter, and George asked the President to say that it was his idea to forfeit political consideration in 1976, not the President's. Ford, who had granted Rockefeller this courtesy when he forced him to not seek reelection as Vice President, now did the same for George. The President added to his letter of December 18, 1975: "He and I had discussed this in detail. In fact, he urged that I make this decision. This says something about the man and about his desire to do this job for the Nation."

"That was about the shortest-lived campaign for V.P. in history," Barbara wrote to a society columnist at the *Washington Star*.

George, who later wondered if he had not played into a wily scheme by Ford to deprive him of the vice presidency, was confirmed by the Senate (64–27) on January 27, 1976.

As a precondition to accepting the President's appointment, George had insisted on bringing Jennifer Fitzgerald with him to the CIA as his confidential assistant. A memo in the Ford Presidential Library dated November 23, 1975, indicated that his demand was to be met: "Please advise me as soon as you have completed office space arrangements for George Bush and Miss Fitzgerald. JOM [John O. Marsh, White House lawyer] has maintained close contact with Bush and wants to give him the details of whatever accommodations are set up."

George was sworn in by Justice Potter Stewart (Yale 1937), a close family friend whose wife, Andy, was Barbara Bush's best friend. George invited five hundred people to attend his swearing-in ceremony. After the oath, the President accompanied him into the main building of the CIA to greet about one thousand employees who could not attend the swearing-in ceremony because of the presence of the press.

Being named CIA director finally gave George what he had always wanted: a real seat at the table. He had been begging for "cabinet status" ever since he was appointed UN Ambassador. He had been allowed to attend a few meetings then and later as chairman of the National Republican Committee, but now he was finally entitled to a regular place within the cabinet, as well as on the National Security Council. Just sitting in the dugout with the varsity seemed to be enough for George.

"The guy never said a word during NSC meetings," recalled Roger Molander, who received his Ph.D. in engineering science and nuclear engineering from the University of California at Berkeley. Molander's principal area of responsibility in the NSC was strategic nuclear-arms control, and he observed George on a regular basis. "He was a total cipher. He came into the NSC meetings, sat down, and never said a word. Nothing. No proposals. No rebuttals. No initiatives. Nothing. I was there from the end of Nixon [1972], all of Ford [1976], and through Carter [1980], and I can tell you that George Bush was not even a bit player in any of those meetings. Ever. The most memorable dynamic was between the big brains of Henry Kissinger and James Schlesinger . . . Bush was a nonentity."

While George did not impress the President's counselors, he wowed the CIA's beleaguered bureaucrats. "He was perfect for the agency," said Osborne Day (Yale 1943). "I'd retired from the CIA by the time George took over, but I've known him and his family for years, and I can tell you the guys in the Outfit [the insiders' term for the CIA] loved him . . . He was temperamentally suited for the job, more so than most of the damn fools the White House sent over. First of all, George already knew a lot of the fellows there. After all, he had gone to Yale, and Yale has always been the agency's biggest feeder . . . In my Yale class alone there were thirty-five guys in the agency."

The late Robin Winks, author of *Cloak and Gown*, an examination of Ivy League predominance in U.S. intelligence work, said that the Office of Strategic Services and the CIA wanted "young men with high grades, a sense of grace, with previous knowledge of Europe . . . and ease with themselves, a certain healthy self-respect and independent means . . . Oh, yes, and good social connections." He said that Yale was a great place to look for such characteristics, which is also why people said that OSS stood for "Oh So Social."

Professor Winks said most Ivy Leaguers (Harvard, Yale, Princeton, Dartmouth, Cornell, Penn, Brown, and Columbia) met the elite qualifications for intelligence work, but Yale had an advantage, because of its system of residential colleges, plus its secret societies, particularly Skull and Bones. For many years Yale contributed more men to "the Outfit" than any other Ivy League school. In fact, the Yale University library was once used as an overseas cover for an intelligence operation run by the OSS, and most of the mythic spy figures, from James Jesus Angleton to Richard McGarrah Helms, were Yalies. But in the wake of the Church hearings, both Angleton and Helms were driven from the agency.

"You can understand why George fit in so well at the CIA," said Osborne Day, "when you understand that he was one of them . . . and they loved him."

George approached every job he ever had with the exuberance of a carney barker. At the CIA, he knew he was supposed to restore agency morale. He began with a media offensive to try to make the CIA more palatable to the public. Within his first two weeks on the job he scheduled editorial conferences in New York City and Washington, D.C., with *The New York Times*, the *Daily News*, *The Wall Street Journal*, *Newsweek*, *Time*, the *Washington Star*, and *Women's Wear Daily*.

A CIA memo from the *Time* luncheon on February 23, 1976, indicated that the magazine had submitted a story for agency approval. When the agency objected, *Time* canceled the story. The CIA information specialist Angus Thuermer briefed George on the matter:

> *Murray Gart [acting editorial director] is the one who cancelled—*
> *when we gave him the implications of the story—a piece about*

CIA Chiefs of Stations: 'twas to have been a little series of thumb-nail sketches. Horrible. We have been able to help Time on a corporate basis, as it were, when their businessmen junkets around the world have taken place. Gart was terribly concerned about the businessmen's security in the Middle East, for example. Our people kept alert.

A cozy relationship had existed for many years between news organizations and the CIA, which had once used reporters as secret agents. The agency also had sent employees abroad under the cover of being accredited to American news organizations. These revelations roiled newsrooms as journalists felt their credibility had been compromised. George urged the news organizations to "bury the past" and keep the names of their reporter-spies secret.

When William S. Paley, the chairman of CBS, invited George for lunch on February 4, 1976, he did so as a courtesy to his friendship with George's late father. Prescott had helped financially structure the company when he was at Brown Brothers Harriman and served on the CBS board for many years. The luncheon, supposed to be a lovefest, quickly turned into a slugfest when George was challenged about the CIA policy of using American reporters as spies. He tried to play down the seriousness of a journalist's serving two masters and stressed that the agency would keep the names secret. The CBS anchorman Walter Cronkite objected.

"The names should be put on the table for the protection of those not guilty of such behavior," he said.

Sensing the outrage—and knowing how important it was, personally and professionally, to keep the media on his side—George returned to the agency, where CIA lawyers quickly retooled the policy. The next day George announced that the CIA would no longer hire newsmen working for American publications to do undercover work; nor would the agency recruit clergy to help gather intelligence: "It is the agency policy not to divulge the names of cooperating Americans. In this regard the CIA will not make public now or in the future the names of any cooperating journalists or churchmen."

George said he did not think using reporters and clergymen for spy purposes was improper but he did recognize the unique position of religion and press freedom in the Constitution. He said the new CIA ban was simply "to avoid any appearance of improper use by the agency."

A few days later George, still working the media, appeared on *Meet the Press* and talked about the role of the CIA in the nation's security. Watching him was the singer Frank Sinatra, who decided he would offer his services to the agency. Sinatra told his television producer, Paul W. Keyes, to arrange a meeting for him with the director. George was intrigued by Sinatra's proposition and agreed to fly to New York City the next day. He invited the singer and his producer for drinks at his brother's apartment in Gracie Square. He then called Jonathan.

"Are you ready for some guests, including Frank Sinatra, in your apartment at 6:30 p.m.?"

George had hoped to keep his meeting with Sinatra out of the press because he did not want to deal with the political consequences of socializing with a man known to be connected to organized crime. Sinatra had introduced John F. Kennedy to Judith Campbell Exner. She had testified before the Church Intelligence Committee that Sinatra also had introduced her to the Chicago mobster Sam Giancana. Her sexual adventures with all three men established a direct link between the White House and the Mafia. She later would claim to have carried messages from Kennedy to Giancana to assassinate Fidel Castro. In light of these gangland ties, the director of the CIA might have thought twice before meeting with Frank Sinatra, but George could hardly wait to meet the Mafia's favorite movie star.

George showed up early at his brother's apartment on February 23, 1976, accompanied not by Barbara but by Jennifer Fitzgerald. They had flown together from Washington to New York City on a government plane.

"It was a great evening," recalled Jonathan Bush. "Sinatra made a very sincere and generous offer to help the CIA in any way possible. He said he was always flying around the world and meeting with people like the Shah of Iran and eating dinner with Prince Philip and socializing with the royal family of Great Britain. He emphasized time and again that his services were available and that he wanted to do his part for his country . . . I thought it was kind of nice of Frank Sinatra. He was very natural and I was spellbound."

The sixty-one-year-old singer talked about his childhood in Hoboken,

New Jersey, and spoke with great feeling about his family and his love of children and his love of country.

"We all feel that way," said George.

When Sinatra offered again to put his personal contacts to work for the good of the United States, George tried to be humorous. "There is some special work you could do for us in Australia, Frank."

Luckily for George, the singer, known for his violent temper, laughed at the allusion to his much-publicized concert tour. Sinatra had lacerated Australia's press as "a bunch of bums and parasites who have never done an honest day's work in their life." He called the men "a bunch of fags" and the women "buck-and-a-half hookers." His coarse comments caused such an uproar that the country's 114 unions went on strike, and the stagehands, waiters, and transport workers refused to work for him, forcing Sinatra to cancel his tour.

Over drinks that evening the singer dazzled the Bush brothers, who were enthralled to be in his presence. "We felt like applauding after he left," Jonathan said. "We had a big laugh about it and then we all got smashed."

Up to that point, George's closest contact with Hollywood had been Jerry Weintraub, the producer. They had become friends when Weintraub married the singer Jane Morgan, who grew up in Kennebunkport, not far from the Bushes' summer retreat. The producer became George's staunchest supporter in Hollywood, where he entertained the Bushes at dinner parties and raised thousands of dollars for George's various political campaigns, and later for those of young George.

From the outside George Herbert Walker Bush looked as straight as a rep tie, but over the years he had tiptoed outside the confines of his regimented world to walk on the wild side. "He liked to sneak out here to make the rounds with Jerry and hang out with movie stars," said a well-known screenwriter. Years later, Weintraub was dubbed by *Spy* magazine as George Bush's "most embarrassing friend." George called him "Mr. Hollywood."

George was equally entranced with being director of the CIA. "It's the most exciting job I've had to date," he told friends. He signed personal letters "Head Spook." Like a little boy with a Halloween costume, he even tested agency disguises by wearing a red-haired wig, false nose, and thick glasses to conduct an official meeting. "He got a big kick out of that," said Osborne Day.

George monitored all media references to the agency and did not hesitate to request secret files. According to CIA memos released under the Freedom of Information Act, he seemed especially curious about information pertaining to the assassination of John F. Kennedy.

In one memo, dated September 15, 1976, he asked his deputy director to look into the news accounts that linked Lee Harvey Oswald's assailant, Jack Ruby, to the mobster Santos Trafficante. Bush wrote: "A recent Jack Anderson story referred to a November 1963 CIA cable, the subject matter of which had some UK journalist observing Jack Ruby visiting Trafficante in jail (in Cuba). Is there such a cable? If so, I would like to see it."

In a memo dated September 9, 1976, George asked about another Jack Anderson column that said CIA records showed the former CIA Director John McCone had briefed Lyndon Johnson about the JFK assassination and suggested that "the Cubans may have been behind the assassination." George wrote in the margin of the column: "Is this true?"

A few days later he received a five-page CIA memorandum that disputed the allegations.

Still another memo, dated October 4, 1976, concerned an article saying that contrary to sworn testimony by Richard Helms, there was a CIA document that indicated a low-level CIA official had once considered using Oswald as a source of intelligence information about the Soviet Union. George wrote: "Will this cause problems for Helms?"

Years later, when George became President of the United States, he would deny making any attempt to review the agency files on the JFK assassination. When he made this claim, he did not realize that the agency would release eighteen documents "in full" and "in part" that showed he had indeed, as CIA director, requested information—not once but several times—on a wide range of questions surrounding the Kennedy assassination.

As CIA director, George testified before Congress fifty-one times during his 355-day tenure. By then he had perfected the "bending" and "stretching" of truth that he had first noted in his RNC diary. George was as smooth as an eel slithering through oil. His lies on behalf of the CIA ranged from outright falsehoods and adamant denials to obfuscations and evasive omissions.

He dragged his feet in providing information to Justice Department prosecutors in their case against Richard Helms, who had lied to Congress about the CIA's role in the 1973 military coup in Chile.

He covered up the CIA's lies to Congress about Cuban involvement in Angola, and he denied the CIA had planted false propaganda in the U.S. press about the Soviets in Angola.

He pushed the Justice Department to prosecute the *Washington Post* reporter Bob Woodward for publishing the first account of CIA electronic surveillance of government representatives in Micronesia. Bush maintained that Woodward had violated the Signals Intelligence Act, which makes it a felony to publish any classified information. Yet Bush withheld the CIA files that would have proved the agency's involvement. So the Justice Department dropped the case against the journalist.

He refused to cooperate with the investigation into the Washington, D.C., bombing of the car of the former Chilean Ambassador to the United States, Orlando Letelier, that killed Letelier and Ronni Moffitt, a colleague from the Institute of Policy Studies. The murder was directed by Chilean dictator Augusto Pinochet's secret service, and the CIA knew that two of the assassins were in the United States at the time of the bombing. Needing to cover up the CIA's involvement with the Chilean secret service, George directed the agency to leak the story that the bombing was the work not of the obvious suspects but of leftists looking to create a martyr for their cause.

"Look, I'm appalled by that bombing," George told Justice Department lawyers. "Obviously we can't allow people to come right here into the capital and kill foreign diplomats and American citizens like this. It would be a hideous precedent. So as director, I want to help you. As an American citizen I want to help. But as director I also know that the Agency can't help in a lot of situations like this. We've got some problems." George then turned to the CIA's general counsel. "Tell them what our problems are."

When George took his oath of office, he swore to uphold the laws of the country, which as of February 1976 included Executive Order 11905, known as the assassination ban: "No employee of the U.S. Government shall engage in or conspire to engage in political assassination."

In an interesting confluence of history, the assassination ban was re-laxed in 2001 by his son George W. Bush, then President, who authorized the agency to seek the death of Osama bin Laden and members of Al Qaeda after the terrorist attacks on the World Trade Center and the Pentagon. In 2002 President Bush also said he was prepared to rescind the ban in order to assassinate Saddam Hussein.

As director of the CIA, George Herbert Walker Bush never appeared at any congressional hearing or intelligence briefing without at least three agency experts. "I had serious contact with him when he was CIA director because I was the point man for the Senate Foreign Relations Committee staff for dealing with the intelligence community," said Pat Holt. "We were George and Pat in those days. He came up to talk to the chairman and the ranking Republican member and me when he wanted covert action. In contrast to his predecessor [William Colby], who always came alone, George always brought people with him . . . But he was more forthcoming than most, and I found him right up there in the top rank of CIA directors whom it was easiest to get along with . . . But he was certainly not in the top rank of CIA directors like Colby and Helms who were informed and knowledgeable. Those guys were in a class by themselves. Both had come out of OSS and into the CIA . . . real pros. George was hardly a pro."

George confirmed his amateur status as "Head Spook" when he flew from Washington, D.C., to Los Angeles and bounded off the plane with Representative Barry Goldwater's suitcase, leaving his own behind. The Associated Press reported the "mix up" and wondered if the CIA director felt the same embarrassment a spy feels when he loses his underwear.

When testifying before Congress, George would make an opening statement to the committee, and then introduce an agency expert to address the substantive questions. He would prearrange for one of his staff to slip him a note that he was needed at the White House. Five minutes into the questioning, he would excuse himself and leave the expert in charge. "Worked every time," he said.

His aides knew to prepare him "to the hilt" when he had to go toe-to-toe with Secretary of State Henry Kissinger. "I remember one briefing at Langley when George excused himself and came out of the conference room embarrassed, confused, and very angry," recalled an assistant. "He brought out his briefing papers, threw them on the table, and demanded that we correct all our mistakes at once."

The staff examined the papers.

"These are all correct, sir," Bush was told.

"Well, why the hell is that goddamn Kissinger yelling at me then?"

"Sir, I think the legends on Mr. Kissinger's maps are incorrect."

George smiled diabolically. He returned to the briefing room, and, as he said later, he "ate Kissinger out."

George's CIA staff played to his animosity toward the Secretary of State by downgrading "Dr." Kissinger to "Mr." Kissinger.

"I learned that one early," said a staffer, who had made the mistake of referring to the Secretary of State respectfully as "Doctor."

" 'The fucker doesn't perform surgery or make house calls, does he?' said George.

" 'No, sir,' I replied . . . After that you can better well believe that it was never Dr. Kissinger again!"

George's facility with "bending" and "stretching" gave him great expertise in keeping secrets, not just for the CIA, but also for his own family. At the time he was running the agency in 1976, his wife, Barbara, was dealing with a serious depression that more than once led her to the brink of suicide. His nephew Prescott S. Bush III was fighting schizophrenia; his uncle James Smith Bush, who had embezzled funds and fled the country, was dying in the Philippines; and George's son George W. Bush, who by his own admission was "drinking and carousing and fumbling around," was arrested that summer for driving under the influence.

George kept all those secrets, even from other members of the family. He had learned to compartmentalize his life so effectively that even within his immediate circle, he operated on a need-to-know basis. He did not tell all of his children the details of their cousin's mental condition. Nor did he give all the sordid details of his Uncle Jim to Jim's children. George did not tell anyone about young George's run-in with the Kennebunkport police when the thirty-year-old had taken his underage sister, Doro, seventeen, out drinking and been arrested driving home drunk. Nor did George tell any of his children about their mother's severe depression.

"George was the only one in the family who knew about it," Barbara said many years later. "He was working such incredible long hours at his job, and I swore to myself I would not burden him."

Barbara was fifty-one years old at the time and in the hormonal throes of menopause. She no longer had children to take care of, and her husband was rarely home. She said she did not like his job at the CIA because he could not tell her the agency's secrets, but in truth she had never played a significant role in George's work, except for his political campaigns. At the time, his confidential assistant, Jennifer Fitzgerald, was privy to all that Barbara was not.

"I was wallowing in self-pity," Barbara admitted. "I almost wondered why he didn't leave me. Sometimes the pain was so great, I felt the urge to drive into a tree or into an oncoming car. Then I would pull over to the side of the road until I felt okay."

George suggested that his wife seek professional help, but she resisted. "I would feel like crying a lot and I really painfully hurt," she recalled. "And I would think bad thoughts, I will tell you. It was not nice . . . I could have gotten help. But I was too sort of proud . . . I didn't tell anyone . . . Not even Andy Stewart, my closest friend.

"I know now that drugs could have helped me but . . . I was ashamed of my depression. My code was, 'You think about other people, stop thinking about yourself' . . . I tried to work myself out of it . . . I know I should have gone to the doctor . . . But I didn't. I gutted it out . . . and it was awful."

In retrospect, the Bushes' Christmas card indicated how Barbara was feeling. The card contained five family pictures: one of George W. and Doro at the Great Wall in China; one of Marvin at the Ming Tombs; one of Neil at the Great Wall; one of George senior at the Summer Palace; and one of Jeb and his wife, Columba, in Houston. There was no picture of the invisible wife and mother.

Years later, when Barbara admitted suffering from depression, she said she had felt totally insignificant as a person. "I went through a sort of difficult time because suddenly women's lib had made me feel that my life had been wasted . . . I felt inadequate and that I hadn't accomplished enough . . . But I got over it, thank heavens."

Some wonder if she ever conquered those feelings because she seemed to harbor real resentment toward the professional women on her husband's staff. "She'd always say to me, 'When are you going to have more children?' " recalled a female lawyer who worked for George Bush. "I only had one child at the time, and Barbara seemed to take it as a personal affront that I hadn't stopped my career then and there to have more."

Barbara snapped defensively at female reporters who asked if she had any regrets about dropping out of college. "If I had regrets," she said, "I would have gone back."

In 1978 she defined herself to *Women's Wear Daily*: "I'm not a feminist. I'm for women's rights, but I haven't those interests. I've been a kept woman for 33 years and very happily. I live in the very large shadow of this man. We're not a team. He should make his own mistakes. Sure, I feed him and get his clothes ready, but I don't discuss the issues with him."

Barbara sounded like Mamie Eisenhower, who once boasted, "Ike runs the country and I turn the lamb chops." As a political wife, Barbara had paid a heavy price to support George's ambitions, but she never admitted the emotional cost. "You have two choices in life," she said. "You can either like what you do or you can dislike it. I have chosen to like my life."

Her choice sometimes required a superhuman effort that could be seen in the clenched teeth of a forced smile or the biting jab of a bitter comment.

Barbara's depression, which lasted most of 1976, began to lift only after the election, when President-elect Jimmy Carter made it clear that he would not consider keeping George on as CIA director. George, who had been giving Carter national security briefings, could not believe that the Georgia peanut farmer was dismissing him. He tried to negotiate. He suggested that by keeping him on, Carter would prove that the CIA was above politics. Carter smiled his half smile. During the campaign he had called the agency a "dumping ground" for failed political candidates. Now he was dumping George.

During their last intelligence briefing one of George's deputies outlined a long-range national security problem due to surface in 1985. Carter waved him off.

"I don't need to worry about that. By then, George will be President and he can take care of it."

George seemed perplexed by the comment. He wrote in his autobiography: "It was an odd statement, coming from Jimmy Carter. I wondered what he meant by that."

The President-elect, who would win the Nobel Peace Prize in 2002, obviously saw George as a rampagingly ambitious man who was not going to rest until he made himself President of the United States, and in that observation Carter was absolutely correct. Even as George watched the 1976 Republican National Convention on television in Kennebunkport that summer, he confided his frustration to his Midland friend John Ashmun: "I think those guys could have relented . . . and at least thrown my name in the hat. I told Ford I wouldn't actively campaign, but I really hoped some of those fellows would say, 'What the heck, let's put his name in the pot.' "

George wrote to his friend Jack Mohler: "I am staying the hell out of politics, but it isn't easy."

He also revealed a melancholic tone when he wrote to Neil Mallon: "I dictate this as the Republican Convention gets under way . . . When I see all my political friends charging around Kansas City, I have a twinge of regret."

When Jimmy Carter beat Jerry Ford for President in 1976, George began making plans to grab the White House for himself in 1980. He decided to return to Texas, join the boards of companies controlled by some of his rich friends, set up a political action committee (Fund for Limited Government), and lay the foundation for his presidential campaign. He told Barbara to head for Houston and find a new house. She felt as if she had regained her life.

"I looked at about thirty houses," she said, "and fell in love with one on Indian Trail." George bought the $325,000 house sight unseen and was dismayed to find out that it needed extensive renovation, but Barbara now had an all-consuming project. He took one room to set up a home office, deducting all the expenses on his 1977 tax returns, right down to the coffeemaker. He identified himself as a "business consultant."

When George learned that President Carter intended to name Kingman Brewster the U.S. Ambassador to the Court of St. James, he wrote to the former Yale president and obtained a job for Jennifer Fitzgerald as special assistant. Conveniently, one of the boards George was on had business that took him to London frequently. "Jennifer only lasted for about a year," said Brewster's biographer Geoffrey Kabaservice. "Kingman was irritated at her frequent absences going to the states to see George . . . Their relationship was no secret to the embassy staff. Everyone knew that she was George's mistress."

During that year, while Jennifer was often absent from her job, George was living in Houston and traveling the country in his first run for the presidency. But he set aside several intervals in which he told aides he would not be reachable. He also said that he could not divulge his whereabouts. He claimed that he was flying to Washington for a secret meeting of former CIA directors. But according to former CIA directors, there were no meetings—secret or otherwise—during that period, and George had no assignments of any kind from the CIA.

"That's a new one on me," said former CIA Director Richard Helms a few months before he died in 2002. "And, as you know, I was at the CIA from the time they opened the doors."

Stansfield Turner, who was CIA director from 1977 to 1981, was equally dubious. "I never knew former directors had meetings and there were none when I was there," he told *The Washington Post*.

Moving back to normalcy in Houston had demoralized George. He felt like a racehorse under wraps. In March 1977 he wrote to his good friend Gerry Bemiss:

> There has [sic] been withdrawal symptoms. I've been tense as a coiled spring hopefully not a shit about it, but up tight . . . I just get bored silly about whose daughter is a Pi Phi or even bored about whose [sic] banging old Joe's wife. I don't want to slip into that 3 or 4 martini late dinner rich social thing . . . I think I want to run or at least be in a position to run in '80—but it seems so overwhelmingly presumptuous and egotistical; yet I'll think some on that.

Barbara, on the other hand, was revitalized to be back home, where Jeb and his wife, Columba, were living with their two young children, George Prescott Bush, age one, and a new baby, Noelle.

Years before, Barbara had interfered with the engagement of her eldest son, supposedly because W.'s fiancée's stepfather was Jewish, but there was nothing she could do when her second son fell in love with a young Mexican woman. Jeb met Columba Garnica Gallo in León, Mexico, in 1971, when he was an exchange student from Andover. He never dated anyone else, and he said he would not be happy until he married her, which he did in 1974 at the Catholic student center at the University of

Texas. He was twenty-one and she was twenty. He gave her a wedding ring that had belonged to Barbara's grandmother Mabel Pierce. He introduced Columba to his parents for the first time on the day of the wedding.

"I'm not going to lie to you and say we were thrilled," Barbara told one writer.

In fact, Barbara was so worried about her son's marriage to a Mexican that she sought advice from her friend the society columnist Ymelda (née Chavez) Dixon.

"I remember Barbara calling me and asking what she should do. She said there were racial problems in Texas and immense discrimination against Mexicans there. Apparently, the only Mexicans in Houston were maids and gardeners. I told Barbara, 'As long as the girl hangs a sign around her neck that says "Bush," she'll be fine.' Barbara was too smart to say she was heartsick about the marriage, but I know she was."

Shortly after his son's wedding George noted in his China diary that he had received "a beautiful letter from Jeb about the problems of Columba adjusting, how much he loves her, how marvelous she is, and what she needs is self-confidence. It was a thoughtful, sensitive piece—an attractive kid who has got it all. I just hope he is fully happy because, knowing him and his sensitivity, he would be deeply hurt if she was ever hurt."

Jeb, who spoke with his wife in fluent Spanish, was spared her further social discomfort in Houston when the Texas Commerce Bank transferred him to Venezuela in 1977 for two years to handle international loans. Jeb had been given the job by his father's good friend Ben Love, who was chairman of the board. The bank had been founded by the family of James A. Baker III, one of George Bush's best friends.

At that time Jeb, twenty-three, looked like the family's standard-bearer for success. He was six feet four, and, with his Phi Beta Kappa key, he seemed to have it all, as his father said. Jeb certainly had more than his reckless older brother, who at the age of thirty was still footloose and foolhardy.

George W. was living in Midland during this period and hustling the gusher fantasies of all oilmen. He spent his days in the courthouse researching titles to mineral rights and negotiating deals to lease them. He lived above a garage in an apartment that was piled so high with dirty clothes that his friends' wives periodically washed them just to keep the public health service at bay. Most of his nights were spent in bars, drinking with buddies in the business.

On his thirty-first birthday, July 6, 1977, he heard that George Mahon was retiring from Congress after forty-three years of representing Midland and Lubbock. He astounded his parents when he told them he was going for the seat. Having been part of his father's campaigns, George, naturally gregarious, was drawn to the political arena. As his cousin Elsie Walker once suggested, he probably knew on some level that winning an election would also win his father's attention and admiration, which were so sorely missing.

George announced his candidacy in July 1977, and two weeks later his friends Joe and Jan O'Neil introduced him to his polar opposite, Laura Welch, thirty, who lived in Austin but happened to be in Midland visiting her parents.

"We were the only two people among our friends who had not yet married," she later joked.

No one expected the introduction to ignite, least of all the O'Neils, but within a week George had arranged to visit Laura in Austin. He left for Kennebunkport in August and called her two or three times a day. Not long after one phone call, he cut short his vacation and returned to Texas.

"I think he called and a man answered in Laura's apartment," said his mother.

Weeks later George brought Laura to meet the family, and Jeb fell down on one knee and flung open his arms: "Brother, did you pop the question, or are we just wasting our time?"

George and Laura married in November 1977, three months after they met, at the First United Methodist Church in Midland. The small ceremony was attended by immediate family, including George's grandmother. When Dorothy Walker Bush asked the bride what she did, Laura replied, "I read."

Barbara later said that Laura's reply was: "I read and I smoke and I admire."

A self-possessed only child, Laura had grown up with the full and undivided attention of doting parents, unlike George, who had had to compete for his father's attention with four siblings and the all-consuming pursuit of politics. As the debutante daughter of a prosperous Midland builder, Laura entered Southern Methodist University in Dallas in 1964, where she joined the top sorority, Kappa Alpha Theta, and majored in education.

"When I started at SMU, girls still wore dresses to school the whole time," Laura said. "It was a fairly conservative campus compared with how it was just a few years after that for the little brothers and sisters of my friends. Even growing up in Midland, they had a different experience than we did. So we weren't wild like that. I mean, people smoked cigarettes—and I did. And they drank beer, and that was sort of the way college kids were wild when I was there."

Laura is remembered by some SMU students for not being as conservative as most. She smoked marijuana, backpacked through Europe after graduation, and supported the antiwar candidate Senator Eugene J. McCarthy when he ran against President Johnson in 1968. Laura enrolled in graduate school at the University of Texas at Austin and received her master's in library science. At the time she met George, she was an elementary-school librarian. She was also a Yellow Dog Democrat who thought that Lady Bird Johnson was the finest First Lady the country had ever known. Laura, who said she became a Republican only by marriage, spent her honeymoon and the first year of her marriage campaigning in West Texas with her husband.

"It was the district both of us had lived in for a lot of our lives," she said. "So we made the drive together every day for a year, driving up and down, campaigning two counties wide, straight up the Panhandle of Texas right on the New Mexico border.

"It was a very nostalgic drive for me. It was a drive I had made many times with my parents when they would drive up to see friends or to go to homecomings at Texas Tech. It was also a time for us to be alone in the car. Newly married—especially after having such a short engagement—it really gave us a chance to know each other. It gave me a chance to see him . . .

"When it was over and he lost, we were disappointed, but I really don't remember it as a huge disappointment. We still felt very optimistic about the things we wanted to do. The way we got to know each other on that race was one of the best parts. He went back to work as an oilman, and I stayed home. He was not so handy around the house. I had to remind myself how great he had been on the campaign trail."

During this time George Herbert Walker Bush told a friend that he was constantly churning, barely able to tolerate the workaday world. He wanted nothing so much as to be back "in the action." Constitutionally incapable of staying at home, he traveled constantly, and campaigned for Republicans, who would then be obligated to do the same for him when he announced for President.

Initially, some of George's friends were taken aback by his presidential presumption, because he had never even won statewide office. John E. Caulkins, a banker in Detroit, recalled his reaction when George phoned him.

"I'm going to run for the presidency."

"Of what?" asked Caulkins.

"The United States."

"Oh, George . . ."

Eventually his friends and associates came to share his belief that he was special and gifted and therefore entitled to aspire to the highest office in the land.

"If Jimmy Carter can be President," George said, "then anybody can be President."

He wrote letters constantly, even excusing himself from family occasions like Thanksgiving and Christmas to fire off notes to friends to set up his political network. The only purpose that engaged him was the pursuit of high office.

In the midst of his presidential sprint he received a disturbing call from his mother, who said that her brother—George's beloved Uncle Herbie—had terminal cancer. George was soon to lose his biggest benefactor. He sat down and wrote another letter:

> *You have shown me how to be a man. You have taught me what loyalty is all about. You have made me understand what it is to make a commitment, "bet on a guy," as you'd say, and then stick with it through thick and thin. Without your friendship and support, I'd never have had the confidence to dream big dreams . . . I'm wit ya, Herby, not just 'cause you handed me the future and made my life sing; but, selfishly, because I need you as my father, my brother, and my best friend. You see, I love you very deeply.*

> *Love, Poppy*

George Herbert "Herbie" Walker Jr., a short, squatty bulldoggish man, idolized his tall, slender nephew, who moved through life with the grace of a gazelle. George Herbert Walker Bush was seven years older than Uncle Herbie's oldest son, George Herbert "Bert" Walker III, but Poppy seemed to have the old man's heart in a way that his two sons never did.

"I can't remember any individual who my father had greater respect and affection for than his nephew, George Bush," said Bert Walker. "Dad never took much enjoyment from his immediate family. If you got him cornered, he would talk more about the Bushes than the Walkers. This . . . made me kind of jealous when we were younger . . . resentful . . . and . . ."

"It made me mad as hell," said Bert's younger brother, Ray Walker.

Uncle Herbie's last act before dying was to call for his checkbook. He wrote a five-thousand-dollar check—the maximum contribution allowed under the law—to George's political action committee, Fund for Limited Government. George Herbert Walker Jr. died on November 29, 1977, at the age of seventy-two. His obituary appeared in *Greenwich Time*, *The New York Times*, the *Portland Press Herald* in Maine, and the *Yale Alumni Magazine*. His funeral at the Second Congregational Church of Greenwich was celebrated by no fewer than three high clergymen. He was buried in the Walker family plot in Kennebunk, Maine.

The homage paid to Uncle Herbie as the financial patriarch of the Bush family dynasty contrasted sharply with the unmentioned death of George's black-sheep uncle Jim the following year. George had been monitoring his uncle's demise from afar, probably hoping that Jim would die before the scandal of his life became public.

FBI files described Jim as "a ladies' man" with "a stormy marital career" who bragged about his extramarital affairs. In an e-mail, his third wife, Lois Niedringhaus Bush, wrote:

> JSB died in 1978 in the Philippines. He was married the day we were divorced and left for Italy [with a woman named Gloria]. He lived there for about six months and then moved alone to the Philippines . . .
>
> I [do] not want to go into the marriage after mine. My life was not beautiful for a while. I never wanted to know Gloria nor do my children.

The Bush family has declined to provide any further details about the life and death of Prescott's younger brother, whose last known address in the United States was Inter-Mundis Capital Service on Broad Street in New York City. The State Department cremated his body and sent the remains to the United States from the Veterans Memorial Medical Center in Quezon City in the Philippines. Under the Freedom of Information Act, the State Department produced a redacted report of the death—not the death certificate—and asserted that all other records for James Smith Bush "no longer exist," including the written consular reports of the Foreign Service officers who visited him regularly and reported back to George Bush. There were no obituaries and no death notices, nothing to draw attention to the family's disgrace. All that remains is a small granite stone tucked in the corner of the Bush family plot in the Putnam Cemetery of Greenwich, Connecticut, and the recollections of two Foreign Service officers who visited Jim Bush during his final days.

"As a consular officer in the Philippines, I would go to visit him," said Charles Stephan. "This was about six to nine months before he passed away. Another consular officer and I would check in on him regularly, and then report back to George senior . . . The Bush family knew where Jim was and that he was poor—destitute really—and blind.

"I knew he was considered the black sheep of the family because of his many marriages, but there was more to it than that . . . Yes, I guess I did know about the embezzlement, but I did not know all the details."

Fred Purdy was acting Consul General of the U.S. Embassy in Manila when he received word that CIA Director George Bush wanted him to look in on his uncle. "I was told that George would be sending money for him that came from his sisters, George's aunts . . . I would pick up the money from the CIA unit and take it to Jim. I first went to visit him when he was living with a Filipino street woman he had met in a bar. She was in her thirties; he was in his seventies. He was almost blind at the time, crippled, and unable to move. He was sleeping on a large piece of woven wicker suspended from two sides, sort of like a hammock. He smoked a lot and had burned the wicker bed in several places. He was drinking as much as he could, but he had problems getting liquor. When the Filipino woman realized he didn't have much money, she started cutting him off . . . Eventually I got him moved into a veterans hospital."

By then James Smith Bush was alone and as poor as a pauper. "He was a man fallen from the top," said Fred Purdy, "and everyone in the family seemed to have shunned him . . . Nobody ever came to see him, and I don't remember him ever having any mail either . . . but he did not complain. He seemed rather resigned to his circumstance, as if he had accepted that it was his fault. He mentioned his brother, Prescott, once, and I think I recall him mentioning one or two wives and several children, but he never heard from any of them . . . He didn't offer to talk about himself or his past. He was eager to find out what was going on in the world, and any news I had about George was a little plum for him.

"I liked him very much. I first went to see him because of the George Bush connection, but then I kept going because he was a nice human being. He was very intelligent and kept up best he could by radio with current events. He was not in much pain when he finally died. Pneumonia had set in, but what really got him was cirrhosis of the liver and lung cancer. Before he died in 1978, he said, 'I think George is going to run for President' . . . and he added, 'He'll make a good one.' "

James Smith Bush died on May 2, 1978, at the age of seventy-seven. A few weeks later George wrote a note to Fred Purdy: "I want to thank you for what you did for my Uncle Jim. He had great ups and terrible downs but you saw him as a human being and I appreciate that."

CHAPTER NINETEEN

George Herbert Walker Bush wanted the White House more than anything else in the world. "I mean, like, hasn't, uh, everybody dreamed about becoming President someday?" he asked a reporter from *Women's Wear Daily*. He had no strong purpose other than his burning desire to become President of the United States. By 1979 he had come to feel he was entitled to the honor, and his wife agreed. So they decided to dedicate themselves to the pursuit. Barbara took her Christmas card list, now up to eighty-five hundred names, and George took his Rolodex from the Republican National Committee, and both hit the road in opposite directions. They rarely saw each other for the next year. George was determined to follow Jimmy Carter's strategy and make himself a household name by winning the first two important primaries in Iowa and New Hampshire. From there, George figured, if he spent every waking hour campaigning, everything else would come his way.

On the road, he was accompanied by one of two aides, either Jeb's young friend David "Batesy" Bates or Cody Shearer, whose mother had grown up across the street from Barbara in Rye, New York.

"Batesy and I were like his adopted sons," said Cody Shearer. "We jogged with the old man, played tennis with him, and carried his briefcase from city to city on that campaign."

In his sprint toward the White House, George raised and spent $22 million ($49.7 million in 2004). He traveled 329 days in one year—1978–79—and covered more than 246,000 miles in forty-two states. He campaigned with indefatigable energy.

"I have covered a lot of political candidates during the last twenty-five years," Roy Reed wrote in *The New York Times*, "but I have never known one—not even Hubert Humphrey—who ran with more zeal and determination."

"Oh, God, George went at it nonstop," recalled Shearer. "He set a pulverizing pace. Sometimes we would hit three or four cities in one day. Of course, we concentrated on New Hampshire and Iowa. That was the strategy: win those two—win the nomination. That's how George was programmed. He spent 1978 traveling to put his organization in place and 1979 traveling to campaign . . . I remember we were in a hotel somewhere. His room was next to mine and there were a bunch of girls in the room on the other side of me raising hell, dancing, pounding the walls, and playing loud music. Around midnight I hear George get up and rip open his door. So I get up to see what's happening. George is standing there in his monogrammed pajamas. He bangs on the girls' door and tells them to pipe down. He's trying to sleep. The girls, of course, don't know who he is. I suggest maybe we join the fun. 'No. No. No,' George says. 'Gotta stay focused. Gotta stay focused. Gotta get up early. Gotta shake hands.' Then he pads back to his room in his monogrammed pj's."

Bush's breathless pace winded even reporters.

"How long are you going to stay out campaigning?" one of them asked.

"Until I run out of underpants," said George.

The men looked perplexed.

"Did he just say . . . underpants?" said the reporter from *The Baltimore Sun*.

David Remnick later wrote in *Esquire*, "[Bush's] problems of style are known among some correspondents as 'the weenie factor.' "

Some reporters wondered why George was banging his wings so furiously for a nomination that seemed to be preordained for Ronald Reagan, the two-term governor of California who had been campaigning since he had lost the 1976 nomination to Jerry Ford. But George considered the sixty-eight-year-old Reagan a doddering old fool. He told an aide: "The age thing is going to get him."

Just to make sure it did, George ran TV spots of himself jogging. The not-so-subliminal message: energetic fifty-five-year-olds don't die in the saddle. His advance team tried to make sure he was always introduced as "a man in his physical prime, a man for the '80s."

George looked at politics through the narrow prism of his own privilege, and sometimes he could not see beyond his sense of entitlement. He
was so blinkered he could not imagine that a Hollywood actor bankrolled
by rich, rabid right-wingers could ever become President of the United
States. Since George did not comprehend that a President's most valuable
asset is his ability to communicate, he missed the gigantic import of
Ronald Reagan. Unlike Bush—who had insider connections, an outsize
sense of his own political destiny, and a blind faith in his own sense of
entitlement—Reagan had a message, and it was one he delivered master-
fully. He also had a devoted following built up from his years on the road
as a spokesman for General Electric.

But George Bush totally dismissed Reagan. Bush believed the man
he had to beat was John Connally, the three-term governor of Texas who
had become a Republican after Nixon made him Secretary of the Treasury. George and his campaign manager, James A. Baker III, made no effort to hide their revulsion when it came to Connally, a poor Texas boy
who had hard-scrabbled his way to millions. Snobbishly, Bush and Baker
looked down on Connally as nouveau riche. They considered the former
governor of Texas not to be of their class and not worthy of their social
consideration.

"They hated him," said David Keene, a political consultant who later
became head of the American Conservative Union.

"You know, the problem with you is that you're pissed because John
got the tennis court and you want it," Keene told George.

"You really don't understand me, do you?" said George.

"What do you mean?"

"None of the clubs that I belong to would accept John Connally."

The most damning indictment of rags to riches is always leveled by
the rich who have never known rags, only monogrammed pajamas.

For those who study the fault line of class in America, the campaign
of 1980 is instructive, because two dynastic sons chose to challenge their
parties' front-runners, and these two presumptive heirs based their candi-
dacies solely on their sense of entitlement. Senator Edward M. Kennedy
of Massachusetts decided to take on the Democratic incumbent without
any idea of what he could bring to the office, beyond his illustrious name.
When Kennedy was asked by Roger Mudd why he wanted to become

President, he could not answer the question. He stammered for many uncomfortable seconds before mumbling something about public service.

George Bush did almost the same thing when he was asked why he should be elected to the highest office in the land.

"It's not a job. It's . . . a . . . a . . . challenge. And I am idealistic. I'm driven . . . I'm driven to contribute something."

Both men portrayed themselves as selfless patricians interested only in serving the public good, far above rank politicians interested only in power. Neither man could articulate his reason for running beyond a visceral dislike of Jimmy Carter. The scions of the Kennedy and Bush family dynasties felt they were more entitled to the White House because of who they were than men of lesser lineage who mirrored the American public.

George so cherished being on the inside that he could not tolerate Carter's pride in being an outsider. "My thesis is that the United States won't ever again elect a person totally unfamiliar with foreign affairs, totally running against Washington and how Washington works," he said in 1979. His son George W. Bush would knock down that proposition in the year 2000.

By January 1980, George's seventeen trips to Iowa had finally paid off as Reagan began faltering in the polls. Reagan had been so sure of winning the state that he hadn't bothered to campaign. George, meanwhile, had assembled one thousand doorbell-ringing volunteers. He and his wife and their five children visited all of Iowa's ninety-nine counties and shook as many hands as they could at least once. On January 21, George surged ahead of everyone's expectations and won the precinct caucuses. The Reagan campaign was reeling, and the political press corps perked up. Suddenly "George Who?" was on the cover of *Newsweek*.

"We've got the momentum," George boasted. "Big Mo is on our side . . . There'll be no stopping me now . . . We've got Big Mo."

Again reporters scratched their heads.

George continued to confound the press with his quirky adolescent phrases such as "tension city," "I'm in deep doo doo now," and "catching the dickens." Other fractured expressions needed a glossary. "It was Vic Damone today" meant victory on the golf course. "Little wiener countries" were small troublemaking nations, "Little Wieners" were his grandsons, and negative campaign ads were "the naughty stuff." He dismissed pesky questions about his gaffes as "No more nit-picking—it's 'Zip-a-Dee-Doo-Dah.' "

As the press struggled to decipher George's fragmented syntax, they tried to comprehend his politics and figure out what he stood for.

"How would you define yourself ideologically? Moderate or conservative?" asked one reporter.

"I don't want to be perceived as either," said George, who wanted to be all things to all people.

"Well, how do you want to be perceived? You can't be both."

"How do you know I can't?"

The reporter persisted.

"Well, would you like to be known as a moderate conservative?"

Bush hesitated. "Yeah," he said. Then he took it back. "No. A conservative moderate is better."

Writing in the *Los Angeles Times*, Barry Bearak said that interviewing George Bush was like dancing without touching.

Finally the press forced George to clarify his positions, most of which contrasted sharply with Ronald Reagan's. Bush said he favored an Equal Rights Amendment, and he opposed an amendment that would overturn *Roe* v. *Wade* and ban abortion. He also opposed licensing and registering firearms.

"Oh, God, did he ever oppose that one," said Cody Shearer. "He must've bitched for three days straight when he had to go down to the District building in Washington to register the guns he kept in his house. 'Outrageous,' he said. 'We don't have to do this in Texas.' "

George crowed about his "Big Mo" for thirty-six days as he sprinted toward the New Hampshire primary. But that state's major newspaper had already taken aim at the man with the "Big Mo." William Loeb, the publisher of the *Manchester Union Leader*, was a fervent Reaganaut, and his editorials scorched Bush as "a spoon-fed little rich kid" and "an incompetent liberal masquerading as a conservative."

The "spoon-fed little rich kid" soon stumbled on his own frugality. When the local newspaper in Nashua agreed to sponsor a one-on-one debate between the two front-runners, Bush and Reagan, the FCC ruled that the newspaper's sponsorship constituted an illegal campaign contribution. Reagan's campaign approached Bush to split the cost, but Bush balked. So Reagan picked up the thirty-five-hundred-dollar tab, and because he was footing the bill, he tried to change the ground rules by inviting the other candidates to participate.

The night of the debate only two chairs were placed on the stage, according to the rules, and George started to take his place when Republican Senator Gordon Humphrey of New Hampshire asked him to meet with the other candidates. George refused.

"Those were not the ground rules," he said.

"Well, they're here now and if you don't come, you're doing a disservice to party unity."

"Don't tell me about unifying the Republican Party," George snapped. "I've done more for the party than you'll ever do. I've worked too hard for this and they're not going to take it away from me."

George pushed his way to the stage and sat down. A half hour of confusion ensued while Ronald Reagan hung back with the other candidates, who argued with the debate officials that they should be allowed to participate. Finally Nancy Reagan forced her husband to go onstage. Reagan walked down the aisle followed by Senator Bob Dole of Kansas, Senator Howard Baker of Tennessee, Representative John Anderson of Illinois, and Representative Phil Crane of Illinois. The unruly crowd of two thousand roared their readiness for a big event.

"Get them chairs," shouted a woman.

Reagan moved toward the mic to explain the situation to the audience.

The moderator, Jon L. Breen, a Bush supporter, screamed at the engineer. "Turn Mr. Reagan's microphone off."

But Reagan grabbed the mic and with it the Republican nomination for President.

"I'm paying for this microphone, Mr. Green," he thundered, mispronouncing the moderator's name.

The crowd, whipped up for gladiators, yelled and stomped their feet in approval as Reagan melodramatically seized the moment. George sat on the stage like a little milquetoast, fidgeting and staring straight ahead as if oblivious to the bedlam engulfing him. "He looked like a small boy who had been delivered to the wrong birthday party," William Loeb wrote. Ronald Reagan concurred. He told an aide that George lacked "spunk."

The moderator insisted that the other candidates leave the stage so the debate could begin. After waving to the crowd, the Nashua Four walked off to hold rump press conferences, in which they all accused Bush of unfairly shutting them out and being afraid to meet them head-on.

The debate that ensued onstage was anticlimactic to Reagan's thundering triumph moments earlier. In contrast, George looked so weak and spineless that his campaign strategists recommended he leave the state early and let them try to salvage the last day of the campaign. Hours later, New Hampshire's television viewers saw Bush jogging in the Texas sun, while the sixty-nine-year-old Reagan stood in the frosty air of New Hampshire, shaking hands with the locals.

George had gone into the New Hampshire primary race neck and neck with Reagan, but on February 25, 1980, Reagan trounced him 49 percent to 23 percent, easily reestablishing himself as the front-runner.

"It was that damn Nashua debate thing, wasn't it?" George asked Pete Teeley, his press secretary.

"The good news is that nobody paid any attention to the debate," said Teeley. "The bad news is that you lost that, too."

But George had enough staying power to win primaries in Massachusetts, Connecticut, Pennsylvania, and Michigan. In each he became more and more critical of Reagan, jabbing at the governor's age and lack of experience. "There may be a better valedictorian out there but not one who has the mix of experience that I do," crowed George. "I feel about 35 years old and am ready to charge." Along the way he captured headlines by declaring that Reagan's proposal to reduce taxes without reducing government spending was "voodoo economics." That phrase provided by Pete Teeley lingered like indigestion. George later denied he had ever said it. Even when shown the videotape from his speech at Carnegie Mellon University in Pittsburgh on April 10, 1980, in which he characterized Reagan's supply-side economics as practicing voodoo, he still denied it.

At every stop, George trumpeted his résumé as if his presidential appointments had imbued him with experience that no one else could match. In fact, those appointments, each lasting only a year or so, merely testified to the kindness of mentors. George was a professional protégé who blacked the King's boots, and whether the King was Nixon or Ford, George was compensated accordingly. His list of appointments sounded so dazzling that no one bothered to question whether he had accomplished anything in his various posts. Just having received the appointments seemed to be enough, but upon examination his résumé was far more impressive than his record. The conservative commentator John Podhoretz dismissed George as nothing more than a glorified clerk.

"He had been an unmemorable UN ambassador, a faceless and powerless ambassador to China, [and] a tentative director of the Central Intelligence Agency," wrote Podhoretz in his book *Hell of a Ride.*

The record shows that as Ambassador to the United Nations, George socialized constantly and made many friends but did nothing substantive in foreign policy, especially with regard to China, the major issue at the time. Nixon and Kissinger made all the important policy decisions and rarely bothered to inform Bush, who admitted he had to read *The New York Times* to find out what was happening.

As chairman of the Republican National Committee, George traveled the country meeting party potentates while supporting the President on Watergate and at the same time trying to get Republicans elected to office. To an extent he succeeded on the former—his support was unwavering until the end, although Watergate eventually brought Nixon down—but he failed woefully on the latter. Shortly after Election Day 1973, George wrote in his diary: "Right now after the November elections there are a wide number of comments that the Republican Party has had it—that we are in for a disaster."

Six weeks after he left the RNC, the Republicans lost forty-eight House seats and four Senate seats in the 1974 elections.

As head of the U.S. mission in Peking, George played a lot of tennis and entertained constantly. "There was nothing for him to do but hold down the fort," said the mission's political counselor. "He went to all the parties hosted by other missions . . . He was great at that kind of thing. Just great."

As director of the Central Intelligence Agency, George was a benign custodian who made no waves, which was a relief to all who worked there. Unlike his predecessor, William Colby, George did not ruffle feathers. For that reason, he received great agency support when he ran for President. "Spooks for Bush" raised thousands of dollars for George in the early primaries.

In May 1980, Texas held its first presidential primary, and the two Republican front-runners debated on television from separate locations, but once again Houston's favorite son folded. "He just melts under pressure," Reagan said of Bush, who suffered a humiliating defeat in the primary. He lost his own state to Reagan, and that was the knockout blow. By then the Bush campaign had run out of money and momentum and Jim Baker wanted to pull the plug, but George was like a punch-drunk boxer. He didn't want to quit.

"Jim Baker was beside himself," recalled Susan King, a former television journalist, now with the Carnegie Corporation of New York. "He and Bush have a complicated relationship because they're such close friends. Baker told him he had to drop out then to have a chance to become Reagan's Vice President. If he didn't drop out, he'd cause so much divisiveness that he'd split the party and probably reelect Jimmy Carter. George wouldn't listen. He wanted to charge ahead into the California primary, which was sheer lunacy, because the campaign was broke, but George was determined, and his wife and kids pushed him hard not to give up. So when Bush was on the road, Baker called a press conference and told all of us that George's time as a presidential candidate was over. Baker folded up the troops and headed them all back home, forcing Bush to concede."

George limped back to Texas and spent the weekend licking his wounds. Then he did the math: he had 400 delegates; Ronald Reagan had more than 1,000; only 998 were needed for the nomination. Reluctantly, Bush approved the concession statement that Baker had drafted, and on Monday morning George agreed to formally withdraw from the race. He sent a telegram of congratulations to Reagan and pledged his "whole-hearted support in a united party this fall to defeat Jimmy Carter."

By the time of the convention in July, George had released his delegates to Reagan and felt that he was entitled to be named as Reagan's running mate. George had been passed over three times since 1968, once by Nixon and twice by Ford, and now he wanted nothing more than to run with Ronald Reagan. "If this doesn't work out," he told the writer Michael Kramer, "I'm gonna be the pissedest-off guy around."

The only problem was that Reagan did not want George as his running mate. He did not like him personally and had no regard for him politically. On top of that, Nancy Reagan could not abide him. But Reagan's polls showed that Bush would help unify the party.

"I remember flying with Reagan from L.A. back to the convention [in

Detroit]," recalled the political consultant Stuart K. Spencer. "We were having a conversation when he brought up George Bush. He was still angry about the stuff Bush had said about him in the primaries. Anyway, I listened and listened and listened, and finally he stopped complaining about Bush and said, 'What do you think?'

"I laughed and said, 'I think you're gonna pick George Bush.' He said, 'Why should I?' And I said, 'Because you're flying back to a convention that's locked you into a lot of right-wing stuff, and this guy has the reputation as a moderate, that's why.'"

Reagan would have far preferred sharing the ticket with former President Jerry Ford, and for a few hours there was a tentative plan in place for such a dream ticket—it was being negotiated in the back rooms by Ed Meese for Reagan and Henry Kissinger for Ford. Ford was demanding everything but the rights to the Lincoln Bedroom and "Hail to the Chief." During the convention Walter Cronkite interviewed Ford about the startling proposal of a former President's running for Vice President. As the interview progressed, Ford described his role as one of equal responsibility in which he would have jurisdiction over the National Security Council and the Office of Management and Budget.

Watching the interview in his suite, Reagan jumped off the couch and pointed to the television.

"Did you hear what he said about his role?" he said to his pollster Richard Wirthlin. "Sounds like he wants to be a co-president." Reagan told Ed Meese to immediately call off the negotiations.

A few hours later, Ford went to Reagan's suite dressed in a navy blue blazer and gray slacks. He and Reagan went into a private room, where they talked: Ford said that he did not think his serving as Vice President would be of value, but he agreed to help in every other way to elect Reagan and defeat Jimmy Carter.

Still Reagan did not want to pick Bush, who also had watched the Cronkite interview and now assumed the worst: a Reagan-Ford ticket. "He was padding around the nineteenth-floor hallway in tan khakis and a red polo shirt," reported Michael Kramer. "He was pulling on a Stroh's beer, and I was his only company . . . The deal had been cut: Ford was going to be 'co-president,' although no one knew what that meant."

"It's the second time Ford has screwed you, isn't it?" Kramer asked. Mellowed by a few beers, George smiled.

"Yeah," he said. "You're right. But you know, it builds character."

Reagan longed to make his good friend Paul Laxalt, the senator from Nevada, his running mate, but Reagan's campaign strategists objected.

"Why can't I pick someone I like?" Reagan asked plaintively. His aides explained that an ideological soul mate would not help the ticket, and Laxalt's ties to casino owners in Las Vegas might be problematic. Bush was the most logical choice, they said, but Reagan resisted, harking back to New Hampshire.

"I'm wary of a man who freezes under pressure," he said. "George froze that night. That haunts me."

He conferred with his pollster, and again the consensus was Bush. Reagan called Stuart Spencer.

"You still feel the same way about Bush?"

"Yeah. Nothing's changed."

Reagan grimaced and nodded toward the phone. The call was placed to Bush's suite; Jim Baker answered and handed George the receiver while Barbara ushered everyone out of the room.

"George, it seems to me that [out of all the other candidates] the fellow who came the closest and got the most votes for president ought to be the logical choice for vice-president," said Reagan. "Will you take it?"

George jumped at the offer.

"He didn't have a moment's hesitation," Reagan wrote in his memoir.

The cartoonist Pat Oliphant captured the essence of the evening by showing Reagan, pompadour piled high on his head, talking to Ford, who was pulling clubs out of his golf bag: "Well," says Reagan, "I guess I'm stuck with him . . . However, he does understand the role of a Vice President."

Splayed on the ground with his arms locked around Reagan's feet and his face scraping the sidewalk is George Bush, panting, "I'll take it. I'll take it."

When Reagan announced his choice to the convention, everyone cheered, with the sole exception of his wife, Nancy, standing next to him at the lectern. She hated the thought of George Bush on her husband's ticket and was unable to hold back her tears. *The Washington Post* reported: "She looked like a little girl who had just lost her favorite Raggedy Ann doll: sad, disappointed, almost crushed."

The next day the Reagans and the Bushes appeared at a press conference, which Mary McGrory described in the *Washington Star* as awkward for everyone. "The new foursome looked like the parents of the bride and bridegroom, who are determined to put a good face on a marriage of convenience."

George berated the press for asking about his past political differences with Reagan. "I'm not going to be nickeled and dimed to death about that sort of thing," he said heatedly. To underscore the point, he dropped his support of the Equal Rights Amendment, vehemently changed his position on abortion, modified his stand on school busing, and proclaimed himself in favor of school prayer, all of which proved he was a man with the soul of a Vice President.

George and Barbara campaigned relentlessly for the ticket, praising the Reagans at every stop.

"I think Nancy is ravishingly beautiful," gushed Barbara. "When we were with them, I could hardly take my eyes off her."

"Ronald Reagan is a man of principle," said George. "He will be a stabilizing force for America."

Even the Bush children fell in line. "Dad likes Reagan," young George W. told the press. "His liking . . . is strong and it amazed me. He [Reagan] is not an uptight guy. He's not paranoid. He's reasonable and he's intelligent."

As Reagan's running mate, Bush blistered Carter for double-digit inflation, a gasoline shortage that reminded Americans of their dependence on foreign oil, and the lingering hostage crisis in Iran, where fifty-two Americans had been held in captivity since November 4, 1979. Bush warned of an ominous "October Surprise," stoking speculation that Carter might strike a deal with Iran to get the hostages home before the election. After the election, the Carter camp accused the Reaganites of making a secret pact with the Iranians not to release the hostages before the election. Carter believed Reagan had promised, in exchange, to resume the sale of U.S. arms to Iran. This "October Surprise" has never been proved, but Carter's former CIA Director Stansfield Turner believed it had transpired.

"No question about it," said Carter's White House press secretary Jody Powell. "My theory is that the Reagan campaign made an overture to Iran regarding the release of the hostages; they cut a deal. I don't know that for a fact, but I would bet my life on it."

By Election Day, November 4, 1980, the hostages had not been released, and Americans had become sick of sitting impotently in front of their television sets watching their flag be set afire by Shiite Muslims.

"I believe that this administration's foreign policy helped create the entire situation," said Reagan. "And I think the fact that the hostages have been held there that long is a humiliation and disgrace to this country."

The American people agreed, and the landslide they gave Reagan was staggering. He carried forty-four of fifty states and received more votes (43,901,812) than Carter (35,483,820) and the Independent, John Anderson (5,719,722), combined. The election was over hours before the polls closed in California, but Reagan was reluctant to declare victory. "I'm too superstitious," he said. In Texas, George Bush was crowing. "The ticket is in like a burglar."

That was the last bit of public boasting George would do for many years. After the election, he made a concerted effort to become the perfect Vice President—loyal, self-effacing, even fawning. It was a natural role for someone who strove to please his benefactors and who had played a similar part frequently in the past. He instructed his staff to follow his lead and never oppose the President's staff. George was so determined to be deferential that he claimed to have deliberately chosen a "weak" staff for the first term so as not to compete with the President's. He also instructed Barbara never to compete with Nancy.

His preoccupation with maintaining secondary status even influenced the way he dressed. When he went into Arthur Adler, a D.C. men's clothing store, before the 1981 inauguration to buy a suit, an Adler salesman recalled, the Vice President–elect looked through the Southwick swatches and mulled over a light brown plaid.

"I don't know about that," George said. "It doesn't look vice-presidential."

"No, it looks presidential," said the salesman.

George dropped the swatch and selected something less prepossessing.

Through Jim Baker, who had been named White House chief of staff because Nancy Reagan was so impressed by his smooth demeanor, Bush was able to negotiate the same prerogatives that Vice President Walter Mondale had held under Jimmy Carter—access to the Oval Office, his own office in the West Wing, intelligence briefings, and a weekly lunch with the President.

"I remember when Bush brought his secretaries over to see their new offices," said Kathleen Lay Ambrose, an aide to Vice President Mondale. "We were agog because each one of them was wearing a mink coat. That was such an eye-opener in 1981. Secretaries in mink coats! Jennifer Fitzgerald had the best of the minks, and we figured that was because she was . . . well . . . you know . . . Bush's mistress . . . How did we know? Well, we didn't 'know' in the French sense of being under the bed, but their relationship was an accepted fact of life among politicos at that time, although it was quiet and discreet and very much under the radar screen."

Jennifer was now very much back with Bush. Jim Baker had threatened not to run the campaign in 1980 if he had to deal with "that impossible woman," so George had kept Jennifer out of the campaign while paying her a salary out of his own pocket. After the election, he insisted that she come back and be part of his vice presidential staff.

"Jennifer was his closest confidante, much to the consternation of many of his closest friends," recalled the political consultant Ed Rollins. "The only guy able to stare Bush down about Jennifer was Jim Baker."

Fitzgerald returned more powerful than ever and soon tangled with Bush's top political aide, Rich Bond, who became so frustrated that he told the Vice President he would have to leave unless she was reined in.

"Jim Baker made me make that choice once before," Bush said, "and I made the wrong choice."

Bond had no option but to resign.

Within weeks the Vice President's extramarital dalliances flashed up on Nancy Reagan's radar screen, and she gleefully related every salacious morsel. When George heard that the President's wife was "rumor mongering," he wrote in his diary: "I always knew Nancy didn't like me very much, but there is nothing we can do about all of that. I feel sorry for her, but the main thing is, I feel sorry for President Reagan."

What came to be known as the story of "George and his girlfriend" occurred the evening of March 18, 1981, when some of the Reagans' closest friends were having dinner at Le Lion d'Or in Washington, D.C. Although no one knew the name of the girlfriend, Nancy was given all the delicious details the next morning.

"Suddenly there was a great commotion as the security men accompanying the Secretary of State [Alexander Haig] and the Attorney General [William French Smith] converged on our table," recalled one of the five dinner guests. "They started jabbering into their walkie-talkies, and then whispered to Haig and Smith, who both jumped up and left the restaurant. The two men returned about forty-five minutes later, laughing their heads off. They said they had had to bail out George Bush, who'd been in a traffic accident with his girlfriend. Bush had not wanted the incident to appear on the D.C. police blotter, so he had his security men contact Haig and Smith. They took care of things for him, and then came back to dinner."

Nancy peddled the gossip about "George and his girlfriend," but only among her closest associates, not enough to stain the public image of the Vice President as the world's nicest guy and a most devoted family man. "If the accident had made the police blotter, we probably would've had to report it," said Michael Kernan, formerly an editor at *The Washington Post*. "But if it was just George Bush with another woman, we wouldn't have touched it—then.

"I remember an occasion after that when Bush was visiting a woman late at night over by the Chinese Embassy on Connecticut Avenue and a fire broke out. The D.C. Fire Department came, but Bush's Secret Service would not let the firemen into the building until they got the Vice President out the back door. We all knew about it at the paper, but nobody wrote about it in those days. There was a conspiracy of silence about politicians and their extramarital affairs until about 1987 when Senator Gary Hart was caught posing with a blonde on his lap, denied he was having an affair, and then dared the press to follow him. That incident changed the press code for political philandering. After that, everyone was fair game. Before that, George, like a lot of others, was able to get away with quite a lot."

Before 1987, George had managed to keep his affairs with other women fairly discreet, and although Jennifer Fitzgerald was a major involvement, she certainly was not the only "other woman" in his life. During his days at the Republican National Committee, there had been a woman in North Dakota who had divorced her husband and moved to Washington to be closer to Bush. During the 1980 campaign he had an intense relationship with an attractive young blond photographer who worked for a photo agency that had assigned her to the campaign. After the election, George offered her a job as his chief photographer, which she declined because of their romance.

In the spring of 1984 the Vice President, accompanied by his "executive assistant," attended nuclear-disarmament talks in Geneva. During the talks the couple registered in separate hotel rooms. One night a lawyer from the Arms Control and Disarmament Agency had to deliver some papers to Jennifer Fitzgerald. The lawyer knocked on Ms. Fitzgerald's door after midnight and was startled when Vice President Bush answered in his pajamas. After the talks, the Vice President and his assistant shared a cottage, Château de Bellerive, on Lake Geneva owned by the son of the Aga Khan, Sadruddin, whom George had met when the Prince was at the UN.

Many years later, Susan B. Trento mentioned the rendezvous in her book *The Power House*, and cited the discomfort of the U.S. Ambassador Louis Fields, who had been asked by the Vice President to make arrangements in April 1984 for his tryst. At the time Barbara Bush was promoting her book on C. Fred, the family dog, and did not accompany her husband to Geneva. Fields, a big Bush supporter and a solid Republican, was stunned by the Vice President's "heavy-handed" request.

"I am not a prude," Fields told one man, "but I know Barbara and I like her."

"He was not out to denigrate Bush," recalled Joe Trento, the author's husband and a former journalist, who had spoken at length with Fields. "He said it was obvious they [Bush and Fitzgerald] were having some sort of relationship by the way it was handled and the way they treated each other . . . He [Fields] feared it could become an issue and put him [Bush] in jeopardy."

Fields died in 1988, and Susan Trento's book was not published until 1992. When reporters tried to ask Bush about the allegations, he refused to answer. "I'm not going to take any sleaze questions," he snapped. "You're perpetuating the sleaze by even asking the question . . . You should be ashamed of yourself . . . dragging down the political process . . . appealing to the prurient interest."

As always, Barbara Bush supported her husband with enough fury for both of them. "It's sick," she said. "It's a lie. It's ugly, and it never happened."

Nancy Reagan always felt she knew better. Perhaps that is why George Bush could never rise in her estimation, despite his undeniable loyalty to Ronald Reagan. As her good friend George F. Will wrote, "The unpleasant sound Bush is emitting as he traipses from one conservative gathering to another is a thin, tinny arf—the sound of a lapdog."

Bush never forgave the bow-tied columnist for his "cheap shot," and told Hugh Sidey that when Will wrote him a note inviting him for lunch, Bush passed. "I've been through about as much as you can go through, ridicule and everything, but I draw the line at personal attacks."

Nancy, who saw the Vice President as weak and sniveling, referred to him as "Whiney" and mimicked his herky-jerky speech patterns. Besides, it was "Ronnie's Presidency" and "Ronnie's White House," and Ronnie's wife was not prepared to share either with someone who had once derided "Ronnie" as an aging Hollywood half-wit. The First Lady never overcame her animus toward the Bushes, and for the duration of her husband's presidency she isolated them like bad bacteria. She invited them to state dinners only because the State Department insisted. She did not invite them to any private White House dinners, including the sparkling affair for the Prince and Princess of Wales. Contrary to all dictates of protocol, Nancy insisted that George Shultz's wife accompany Raisa Gorbachev, the wife of the Soviet premier, on a trip to the National Gallery rather than give the publicity to Barbara Bush. During the Reagans' eight years in the White House, Nancy never once invited the Bushes to dinner in the family quarters, an affront that Barbara never forgave.

"Barbara hated Nancy," recalled Damaris Carroll, Congressman Joel Pritchard's wife. "You could just feel it, especially when we went to the Vice President's residence for a dinner party . . . It was not in anything she ever said; it was in what she wouldn't say that you felt the animosity."

"It was hurtful to Barbara," said Shelley Bush Jansing, the daughter of James Smith Bush. "But she never complained, never once during the White House years . . . It was only after they left that she told us how difficult it really was."

Publicly Barbara tried to be as accommodating as her husband. Both made a concerted effort to avoid publicity and to always cede the limelight to the Reagans.

"I remember they did not want to be put into competition with Nancy's fancy decorating," recalled Dolly Langdon, formerly with *People*.

"The magazine wanted a story about the vice presidential residence and the Bushes didn't want to do it, but they finally agreed . . . Then, of course, they hated what was printed and raised hell. Barbara had worked with the decorator Mark Hampton, but she didn't want that known at the time . . . She's got very, very . . . uh . . . conventional taste, so the house was sort of ladies-club-looking, if you know what I mean . . . Barbara is the type of woman who will wear a circle pin until the day she dies and serve Velveeta cheese on soda crackers, thinking it's the height of good taste."

The Bushes' taste took a drubbing from President Reagan's Pulitzer Prize–winning biographer, Edmund Morris, who was aghast when he saw the present that Barbara and George had given Reagan on his seventy-fifth birthday. The Bushes never understood why the President and his wife had not acknowledged their gift—an elaborate and rather astonishing stool.

"Guess they didn't always thank us," George told the biographer. "Gave him, oh such a neat present for his seventy-fifth birthday, took a whole lot of trouble customizing it to the right measurements, borrowed his boots so it would stand up real pretty . . . Lemme show you. We had a duplicate made."

Bush led Morris to an upstairs bathroom, where the biographer was momentarily struck speechless. He later wrote in his diary:

> It was the single most terrifying piece of kitsch I have ever seen. It would not be out of place at Auschwitz. There, standing booted and spurred, are Dutch's feet and lower legs, supporting, like some flattened dwarfish torso, an embroidered seat, with the presidential seal au centre. While I marvel, as so often before, at the aesthetic perversity of well-born WASPs, Bush shakes his head and says in the same hurt voice, "Not a word of thanks."

Shortly after the *People* article appeared, Barbara opened the Vice President's residence for a nonprofit group from Washington, D.C. "A select number of us had been invited," recalled a designer. "Since I was in the business and Mrs. Bush had just finished working with Mark Hampton, I thought we'd have something to talk about.

"As I went through the receiving line, I shook her hand, said how nice she was to open her home to us. Then I complimented her on the residence. 'I'm a designer, Mrs. Bush, and I think what you and Mark Hampton have done here is lovely,' I said. 'I see a lot of his signature pieces and his chintzes and they're so . . .' Before I could finish, Barbara Bush drew back from me and in my memory looked like a giant gargoyle ready to gnash me to bits.

" 'I beg your pardon,' she said, almost spitting the words into my face like shards of ice. 'I don't know what gives you the impression that Mark Hampton did this house. Why I picked out every piece of furniture in this room. I selected all the fabrics. I chose the paint. In fact, you see that couch over there, well . . .'

"She started pointing to various pieces around the room and hectoring me about what she had done and how dare I suggest otherwise. All I was doing was complimenting her, and she turned into this absolute harridan . . . I stammered and thanked her very much for her generosity and tried to get through the line. My husband, who was behind me, was humiliated and tried to rush me away from her, but Mrs. Bush insisted on grabbing me by the arm and continuing her harangue about her various selections around the room.

"I staggered into the dining room, where my friends were waiting, and I promptly burst into tears. I was so ashamed of being belittled by the Vice President's wife; I didn't know what to do. I was shattered. But when I thought about it later, I started to get mad. How dare she? I'm a taxpayer and I helped pay for the renovation of that house. And why did she lie about Mark Hampton? Pictures of their work had been published in a magazine."

Barbara chafed so much under the yoke of trying to be nice and stay quietly in the background that sometimes the pressure of playing the sweet Second Lady to the formidable First Lady became too much, and the explosion was scalding. Friends of the late Tamara Strickland, the wife of a Washington, D.C., physician, remember how the Vice President's wife lashed out after the 1982 Choral Arts Society's Christmas program at the Kennedy Center.

"Tamara had invited the Bushes to sit in the presidential box that night as the honored guests in the concert hall for a program featuring Leontyne Price," said one of Strickland's friends. "The opera singer sang several carols and some beautiful selections from Handel's *Messiah*. The music critic from *The Washington Post* said the effect of her dazzling voice was an 'experience beyond words.' Everyone was enthralled by the evening. Well, almost everyone . . . except for the Bushes, whose idea of high culture is the Grand Ole Opry.

"The program was being taped for PBS, and, unfortunately, there were a few snafus due to technical problems and several starts and stops as everyone struggled for a perfect performance . . . Leontyne Price was most accommodating about singing her songs over every time she was asked, but the Bushes went crazy. The next day Barbara called Tamara and reamed her out. 'How dare you invite us to something and make us sit through all that awful music and such a dreadful, interminable performance. That was the worst evening of our lives.' Tamara was heartsick. She said later that if you got stung by the business end of Barbara Bush, you'd get yourself a snoot full of hornet venom."

Barbara was as blunt as a battering ram, and her frequent blasts caused a great deal of distress.

"I remember when we went to a book-signing party in 1984 for Barbara and her C. Fred book," said Damaris Carroll, referring to the first book Barbara wrote about the family's dog. "Joel was in front of me and Barbara flung her arms around him and gave him a huge kiss. I was behind him in line, so she started to put her arms around me, too, and give me the same kind of huge hug. But in the middle of the embrace she pulled back. 'I don't know you that well,' she said, and she shoved me away and went on to someone else . . . It was very cutting."

Sometimes Barbara's spontaneity left people speechless. "I remember when I first met her," recalled Aniko Gaal Schott, a public-relations executive in Washington, D.C. "It was while he was Vice President and we were invited to the residence for a reception. We arrived a little early, and Barbara came in and said she'd just been meeting with all the African diplomatic wives. 'I couldn't tell one from the other,' she said. She was quite direct and fresh and unspoiled, but I was a little taken aback. As a diplomatic wife myself who has spent many years in the Foreign Service, I was surprised—shocked, really—that she would be quite so . . . well . . . so undiplomatic about meeting with a group of African women and saying they all looked alike."

Even within her own family Barbara could be extremely abrupt. "She can be a tyrant," said her former daughter-in-law, Sharon Bush, who was married to Neil for twenty-three years until they divorced in 2003. "That's why her boys called her 'The Nutcracker' . . . She is a real stickler for good manners on things like thank-you notes, but she can be unbelievably rude to people, even cruel."

Sharon had never forgotten her wedding day when a photographer from a newsmagazine asked for a family portrait. Barbara, standing next to her husband, rounded up her children. Sharon, described by Barbara in her memoir as "darling," stepped forward in her wedding dress. "I'm sorry," Barbara said to her. "We don't want you in this picture."

Dr. Floretta Dukes McKenzie, the former superintendent of the D.C. public schools, experienced the back of Barbara's hand when she accompanied a group of schoolchildren to the Vice President's house.

"It was just a photo op for Mrs. Bush, who had adopted literacy as her new cause and was trying to get publicity for her association with Reading Is Fundamental, but for the children it was quite an outing and they were excited to go to a mansion and meet the wife of the Vice President of the United States," said McKenzie, one of the nation's leading black educators. "We had been allotted just so much time for Mrs. Bush to read to the children and be photographed . . . We were told when our time was up, and I helped the teachers round up the children and get them back on to their buses. I then returned to the residence to get my purse, but the door had been locked and my purse was left sitting on top of the doorstep."

Shortly before the Bushes moved into the Vice President's mansion, George had sold their home in Houston ($792,017) and used the money to buy Walker's Point in Kennebunkport, which caused a rift on the Walker side of the family.

"Dotty had been working my mother over to sell the big house and all the property to George," said Ray Walker. "After Dad died, my mother considered selling, and she put the house on the open market, but then Dotty started pressuring her. 'Herbie would want it to go to George,' she said. 'Herbie would turn over in his grave if he thought you would sell outside the family . . . George was Herbie's favorite . . . You have to sell to George and keep it in the family . . .' You see, for Dotty, family was church, church family . . . so my mother caved in . . . She sold to George [$780,800] and had to pay a gift tax, but then the Bushes agreed to pay the gift tax . . .

"My brother managed to keep a small piece of property and Dotty, of course, got her house, but my mother sold everything else to George for

practically nothing . . . The whole transaction still bothers me," said Ray
Walker in 2002. "I would have liked my children to have benefited."

To offset the capital gain on his Houston house, George declared
Kennebunkport as his principal place of residence and did not pay taxes
on the declared $596,101 profit from the sale of his Houston home. The
next year the IRS went after the Bushes and claimed that the Vice President's residence, which they lived in for free, was their principal residence
so they owed taxes on the $596,101. George, who had rented an apart-
ment in Houston to keep his voting residence in Texas, threatened to sue
the IRS. He fought the matter for two years, then settled in 1984 by paying the extra tax, $144,128, plus interest, $54,000.

Whenever he blasphemed the IRS, George found his most sympathetic audience with President Reagan. High taxes were the one subject
on which the two men agreed. They sounded like two old pensioners as
they complained to each other about giving up so much of their income
to the government. At the time, Reagan's net worth was $3 million and
Bush's was $2.1 million.

The Reagan presidency nearly ended at 2:35 p.m. on March 30, 1981,
when a deranged gunman shot the President outside the Hilton Hotel in
Washington, D.C. The assailant, John W. Hinckley Jr., who was later
found not guilty by reason of insanity, said he had hoped to kill the President to impress the actress Jodie Foster. He said he had become obsessed
with her after seeing *Taxi Driver*. His brainsick violence almost took the
President's life, wounded a Secret Service man, and severely wounded a
D.C. policeman, who had to be retired on disability. The ricocheting bullets also maimed the White House press secretary, James Brady, who
barely recovered after four and a half hours of brain surgery. He never
walked or worked again, could no longer speak perfectly, and has required
full-time care ever since. He and his wife, Sarah, have devoted themselves
to the Brady Center to Prevent Gun Violence.

At the time of the shooting the Vice President was over Texas in Air
Force Two. He received an in-flight call from Secretary of State Al Haig,
advising him to return to Washington immediately. George arrived at
Andrews Air Force Base at 6:40 p.m. and took a helicopter to the Vice
President's residence on Massachusetts Avenue. The Secret Service had

wanted to chopper him directly to the White House, but he resisted such a dramatic arrival. "Only the President lands on the south lawn," he said.

In the White House situation room, George, who had been told Reagan would recover, left the President's chair empty and sat in his own seat. "The President is still the President," he said. "I'm here to sit in for him while he recuperates. But he's going to call the shots."

His graceful comportment contrasted sharply with that of the Secretary of State, who had raised hackles earlier in the day by dashing to the lectern in the White House pressroom and declaring himself in charge.

Years later the White House physician, Daniel Ruge, admitted that the Twenty-fifth Amendment should have been invoked when the President went into surgery.

"I think we made a mistake in not invoking it," Ruge said. "No doubt about it, because Mr. Reagan could not communicate with the people a President is supposed to communicate with. If ever there was a time to use it that was it . . . But it never occurred to me then."

Those in the White House who had distrusted George Bush as an establishment opportunist came to appreciate his calm demeanor in a time of chaos and confusion.

"I have never been so impressed with Bush as I was that night, the way he instantly took command," the assistant press secretary Larry Speakes wrote in his memoir. He recalled the Vice President saying he would meet with the cabinet and the congressional leadership the next day.

"The more normal things are, the better," said Bush. "If reports about the President's condition are encouraging, we want to make the government function as normally as possible. Everybody has to do his job."

The next morning Bush's considerable calm was jolted when he heard that his son Neil had planned a dinner party at his home that night, barely twenty-four hours after the assassination attempt, for Scott Hinckley, the deranged gunman's brother.

Neil, who worked for Standard Oil Company of Indiana, lived in Denver, where Scott Hinckley was vice president of his father's Colorado-based firm, Vanderbilt Energy Corporation. Scott was dating a friend of Sharon Bush's at the time, and Neil had invited the couple for dinner.

"From what I know and have heard, the Hinckleys are a very nice family . . . and have given a lot of money to the Bush campaign," Sharon said. "I understand that he [John Hinckley Jr.] was just the renegade brother in the family. They must feel awful."

Reporters scurried to uncover what, if any, connection existed between the Vice President's family and the President's assailant. The next day Vice President Bush confirmed that his son was to have hosted Hinckley's brother, but said the dinner had been canceled. The Vice President denied receiving any large campaign contributions from either of the Hinckley brothers or their father, John W. Hinckley Sr. Bush did admit that he had received a modest twenty-dollar donation from the senior Hinckley when he was running for the U.S. Senate in 1970, but added that Hinckley's biggest contributions had gone to John Connally in the last presidential campaign.

Neil told reporters that he first met Scott Hinckley on January 23, 1981, the day after Neil's twenty-sixth birthday. "My wife set up a surprise party for me," he said, "and it was an honor for me at that time to meet Scott Hinckley. He is a good and decent man. I have no regrets whatsoever in saying Scott Hinckley can be considered a friend of mine. To have had one meeting doesn't make the best of friends, but I have no regrets in saying I do know him." Neil added that he had not met the gunman or the gunman's father but would very much like to meet the senior Hinckley. "I'm trying to learn the oil business, and he's in the oil business. I probably could learn something from Mr. Hinckley."

Everyone in the Vice President's office cringed. They scurried to quash any association of the Bush family with the family of the suspected assassin. They worried about conspiracists conjuring dark scenarios about the Vice President's being only a bullet away from the presidency. "It's a bizarre happenstance," said the Vice President's press secretary, "just a weird coincidence."

Another strange confluence was that hours before the shooting on March 30, auditors from the Department of Energy had met with Scott Hinckley in Denver after reviewing Vanderbilt's books. They warned that the Hinckley oil company faced a $2 million fine for overpricing crude oil when price controls had been in effect. This finding raised the question of whether Scott Hinckley had planned to discuss the matter with the Vice President's son that evening over dinner. The FBI investigated the assassination attempt and the connection of the Bush family to the Hinckleys but would not release its findings under a 2002 FOIA request, citing privacy concerns for Scott Hinckley and Neil Bush, both alive at the time.

The governor of Texas, Bill Clements, objected to the news stories of March 30, 1980, that linked Texas to various assassinations. Governor Clements said he felt "horrible" when he heard Hinckley was from Texas, the same state in which Lee Harvey Oswald assassinated President Kennedy; where Mark David Chapman, the killer of former Beatle John Lennon, was born; and where Charles Whitman climbed the Tower at the University of Texas and gunned down more than forty people in one of the worst mass murders in modern history.

"This hasn't got anything to do with Texas," said the governor, "but if the news media works on it long enough it could hurt the state."

Ronald Reagan's popularity soared after the shooting because of the gallant way he had responded. Even with a bullet lodged centimenters from his heart, he walked into the hospital unaided, because he did not want the commander in chief to be shown on television as immobilized. His one-liners to his wife ("Honey, I forgot to duck") and to his surgeons ("I hope you're all Republicans") endeared him to the country. That affection probably cushioned him from the scandal of Iran-contra, which later plagued his administration. The revelation in 1986 that the United States broke its own laws, secretly sold weapons to Iran in exchange for hostages, and then used the revenues from those arms sales to wage a covert war in Nicaragua could have led to impeachment. Few other presidents could have survived such a scandal, but by then the oldest President ever to serve the country had become one of its most beloved.

During Reagan's first term in office, George Bush set a record for vice presidential travel, logging more than 1.25 million air miles to seventy-four countries. He attended so many funerals of foreign dignitaries that he joked, "My motto is: You die, I fly."

For the most part, the office is ceremonial. The Vice President's only prescribed duty in the Constitution is to preside over the Senate, which Bush rarely did except when he was needed. On July 13, 1983, he cast the Senate's tie-breaking vote to save President Reagan's plan to resume production of nerve gas. Dorothy Walker Bush, who had supported the nuclear-freeze proposal introduced by Republican Senator Mark Hatfield of Oregon and Democratic Senator Edward Kennedy of Massachusetts, was horrified.

"But, Mum, I had to do it," George told her. "It was my first tie-breaking vote and the first time in six years that a Vice President has been called upon to cast such a vote . . . I couldn't very well vote against the President."

Dotty Bush was not impressed. She expected her son to uphold humane principles, and she did not consider nerve gas a boon to humanity. Her disapproval bothered George, because there was no one whose good opinion mattered more to him than his mother's. He was almost relieved when the bill was killed in the House of Representatives, but then Reagan insisted it be reintroduced. George, half-jokingly, told the President that he didn't see how he could face his eighty-two-year-old mother if he had to cast another tie-breaking vote in favor of the measure. "If I have to do it, you're going to have to explain to her why her son is in favor of creating a gas that could kill millions," said the Vice President.

Four months later George did what he most dreaded—he displeased his mother. He cast the second tie-breaking vote of his vice presidency on November 8, 1983, which allowed the Senate to pass a bill (47–46) to begin producing nerve gas. That afternoon on Air Force One, as the Reagans were flying to the Far East, the President called Dorothy Bush in Greenwich. He said her son was doing a wonderful job and she could be proud of how he was serving the country as the "best vice president ever." The President then called the Vice President to say that he had made the mommy call.

"The President didn't talk about nerve gas, but I knew what the idea was," Dotty Bush told a reporter. "George knows that I disapprove of it; he knows how I feel. But he said that we have to have it to deter other countries from using it. But George knows I would die if this country would ever use it."

George's vote retained $124 million for production of nerve-gas bombs and artillery shells in a defense appropriations bill. But again it was eventually defeated in the House of Representatives, much to the relief of George's mother.

During the reelection campaign of 1984, her grandson John Ellis, who worked for NBC, kept Dorothy Walker Bush informed of the latest polls. He regularly sent her the state-by-state breakdowns on how the

Reagan-Bush campaign was doing. Ellis, known as the family's media mole, later worked for Fox News and did the same thing for his cousin George W. Bush in the 2000 campaign.

Mrs. Bush said the poll numbers from Ellis showing Reagan with a comfortable margin reassured her, but she cautioned against overconfidence. "Remember the Truman-Dewey race," she said. "We all went to bed thinking it was Dewey, and we woke up and there was Truman in the White House."

George's mother, who offered to work the telephones for the Reagan-Bush ticket, said she felt her son was at a distinct disadvantage having to run against history in the making: Geraldine Ferraro, a former congresswoman from Queens, had been chosen as the first woman to run for national office on a major-party ticket. Her selection by Walter Mondale as his running mate had galvanized many women. Even the elderly Mrs. Bush said she could see herself supporting a woman for Vice President if the woman had the necessary qualifications, which, of course, compared with her son, Ms. Ferraro certainly did not. Seeing the huge, enthusiastic crowds that Ferraro was drawing worried Dorothy, who said she thought her son should not accept Ferraro's challenge to debate. In retrospect, George probably should have listened to his mother.

Three days before the debate Ferraro, whose disclosed net worth was $3.8 million, chided Bush as an example of the Reagan rich who were getting richer at the expense of the poor. Fuming over the criticism, Barbara Bush blasted her husband's opponent in front of reporters. "That $4 million—I can't say it, but it rhymes with rich—can buy George Bush any day."

It was the meanest comment the Vice President's wife had ever made in public, and she suffered from the negative reaction, which made Barbara look like that word that "rhymes with rich." After seeing her comment broadcast on the nightly news, she called George's sister, Nan Ellis. "I just can't believe I did that to your brother," she said. "I've been crying for twenty-four hours and I'll never stop . . . how could I have done it?" She called George in tears, and he told her not to worry. Then she called Geraldine Ferraro. She said she had meant "witch" not "bitch," but she apologized for saying anything.

"At the time, I was annoyed," said Ferraro. "I thought, 'How does a woman act like that?' I felt that it was a terrible put-down—a terrible class put-down . . . I was hurt but I gave her credit for calling as quickly as she did. I told her not to worry about it, that we all say things at times we don't mean. 'Oh, you're such a lady,' she told me. All I could think of when I hung up was: thank God for my convent-school training."

Two days after Barbara Bush's defamation of Geraldine Ferraro, her husband's press secretary, Pete Teeley, delivered his own, calling the congresswoman screechy and scratchy. "She's too bitchy. She's very arrogant. Humility isn't one of her strong points." He refused to apologize. "No reason to," he said. "It has nothing to do with her as a person. On television, she appears bitchy. Her negative numbers are going up because she comes across that way."

Being the first woman to run on a national ticket put enormous pressure on Ferraro, who had to surmount the bigotry and sexism her candidacy unleashed, particularly among men within the media. When George F. Will reported that her husband, John Zaccaro, had not paid taxes, Ferraro proved Will wrong and suggested he publicly apologize. Instead, Will sent her roses with a card, which read: "Has anyone told you you are cute when you're mad?"

The night of the debate, October 11, 1983, Ferraro had been fully prepped. She presented herself as informed and lucid. When attacked, she kept her temper but responded firmly, even sardonically.

"Her opponent, on the other hand, acted much more the hysterical lady," wrote Robin T. Lakoff in her book *Talking Power*. "His voice rose in indignation in both pitch and volume; he waspishly (no pun intended) reiterated the same charges again and again (he didn't listen); he grew visibly upset and overwrought; his face got red, his voice tense and shrill. He went into his lecture mode. This was not the archetypal male in calm control. Yet the next day pollsters declared Bush the 'winner.' No one had much to say about why or how. The answer is that Ferraro lost because she dared to speak up in public against a man."

At one point during the debate Ferraro chided Bush for lecturing her. "Let me just say . . . that I almost resent, Vice President Bush, your patronizing attitude that you have to teach me about foreign policy . . . Secondly, please don't categorize my answers, either. Leave the interpretation of my answers to the American people who are watching this debate."

She missed a chance to clobber Bush when he said that the Reagan administration looked at civil rights "as something like crime in your neighborhood." But she had recovered by the time Bush made his most damning accusation. He said that she and Mondale had claimed the 242 men who had died in the 1983 bombing of the Marine barracks in Lebanon had died in shame. Ferraro immediately corrected him. "No one has ever said that those young men who were killed through the negligence of this administration and others ever died in shame." Mondale labeled Bush's accusation "unpardonable" and said he was "angry as hell" about the untruthful remark. He demanded that Bush issue an apology for his lie, but Bush refused.

The day after the debate the Vice President addressed a rally of longshoremen in Elizabeth, New Jersey, and referred to the previous evening's debate: "I tried to kick a little ass." Hours later his staff showed up on the press plane wearing buttons that said, "We kicked a little ass." Some reporters started calling the Vice President "Kick-Ass George," others wore hats made of jockstraps.

"It set quite a testosterone tone," recalled Julia Malone of Cox Newspapers. "The Bushies didn't understand how offensive it was to women. Later at an 'Ask George Bush' event, the Vice President took questions and kept calling on man after man after man, ignoring the women who had their hands up. Finally he said, 'One last question,' and all the women in the press corps shouted in unison, 'Call on a woman.' He looked so surprised and acted a little put out at being told what to do by a bunch of women, but he finally took one question from a woman."

Bush's attitude raised a great deal of gender tension on his press plane, where he seemed to strut his new "kick-ass" status. "When the debate was over, the women in the press corps stood up and cheered Ferraro," recalled Jeb Bush, who had accompanied his father to the debate. "The whole thing was very difficult. Usually on a press plane, camaraderie develops with the press. But on the Bush plane, things were very difficult."

Female journalists resented Bush's chauvinistic treatment of Ferraro, which showed them something they had not seen before: his discomfort in accepting women as peers. They started to notice that there were no professional women on Bush's staff who held positions comparable to the men. "All the women were either secretaries or gofers," recalled one woman journalist, "and whatever Jennifer Fitzgerald was [her official title was 'executive assistant'] didn't count . . . Maybe Bush's attitude was just part of his generation, but it certainly made you see that even a so-called nice guy can be a male chauvinist pig."

Women reporters also observed there were no women in the Bush family who pursued a career or even held a professional job. Even those wives with college degrees, and in Laura Bush's case a graduate degree, faded into the background of their male-dominated marriages, ceding center stage to their husbands. George W. Bush best expressed the family's male credo when he said, "I have the best wife for the line of work that I'm in: She doesn't try to steal the limelight." He told a Texas writer: "She's not trying to butt in and always, you know, compete. There's nothing worse in the political arena than spouses competing for public accolades or the limelight." As President, one of W.'s first judicial nominations went to James Leon Holmes, who once wrote: "The wife is to subordinate herself to her husband . . . to place herself under the authority of the man." All women who married into the Bush family became housewives and mothers. As Barbara Bush told reporters: "We're all very happy being kept by our husbands."

Garry Trudeau skewered the Vice President's treatment of Gerry Ferraro in a *Doonesbury* strip that showed reporters shouting questions to Bush: "Mr. Bush, in recent weeks, we've heard a lot of vulgar language about Mrs. Ferraro from you, your wife and your campaign manager.

"Was all of this part of a planned manhood strategy, to counter the wimp image that has plagued your political career?"

Trudeau's withering pen has George responding:

"Are you kidding? I've always talked tough! When I said I kicked Mrs. Ferraro's behind that's EXACTLY what I meant! And you can print that!"

"In a family newspaper?"

"Gosh, yes! Heck! It's just an old football term!"

The Pulitzer Prize–winning cartoonist had watched Bush twist himself into a pretzel of reverses on numerous policies—the economy, abortion, the deficit, the Equal Rights Amendment—to become Reagan's man. A few days before the 1984 election Trudeau took deadly aim. He started a week of japes, beginning with a White House correspondent making an announcement on the nightly news: "Good evening. Vice President George Bush's manhood problem surfaced again today as concern over his lack of political courage continued to grow . . .

"Accordingly, in a White House ceremony today, Bush will formally place his embattled manhood in a blind trust.

"It will be restored to him only in times of national emergency."

George became a laughingstock on his own press plane. The next day's strip was even more belittling: "Sir, will your manhood be earning interest?"

"Very little. There's not that much capital."

Humiliated at the sniggering behind his back, George banished the press from his plane and accused Trudeau of "carrying water for the opposition" and "coming out of deep left field, in my view." In his personal diary, Bush referred to the satirist as "the insidious Doonesbury."

Barbara Bush was even more dismissive. "People who saw a man who fought for his country, who built a business and added to the productivity of this country, who never turned down his President when he was asked to serve, nobody thought that," she said. "Only one little cartoonist."

Two weeks later on David Brinkley's Sunday-morning talk show, the Vice President tried to deny his nasty remark about Geraldine Ferraro.

"You said you'd kicked her ass," Sam Donaldson reminded him.

"I didn't say that," Bush snapped.

"What did you say?"

"Well, I've never said it in public."

Donaldson pointed out that he was in public, accompanied by reporters, and his comment was recorded on camera.

"Well, if I'd wanted to say in public the statement that I have never repeated, I would do it."

The positive numbers in the polls had shot up for the Republicans following the debates, but then *The Washington Post* weighed in with an editorial comparing the Vice Presidential candidates. The paper called Ferraro "smart, strong and resourceful," conceding that her lack of foreign policy experience showed up from time to time in her statements. George got hammered:

Something else shows when George Bush speaks—something that threatens to trash whatever esteem his impressive résumé and his private personal grace have earned him. Maybe it is just that he is a rotten campaigner (winning elections, after all, has never been his forte). But he seems to reveal himself as all viewers of "Dallas" will long since have noticed, as the Cliff Barnes of American politics—blustering, opportunistic, craven and hopelessly ineffective all at once. This impression has been so widely remarked in recent weeks by commentators of every political persuasion that it hardly needs elaboration.

On November 6, 1984, Ronald Reagan was resoundingly reelected, winning every state in the Union except for Minnesota and the District of Columbia. The election had been a landslide triumph for the President but a personal defeat for the Vice President, who was so morose about his bad press that, according to close aides, he considered retiring from public life. He sulked for a few days, and then rallied. In a note to Senator Barry Goldwater, George wrote: "It's been tough and ugly this time; but the results are what counts [sic]."

He also wrote to Republican Representative Barber Conable of New York: "I'm glad it's over. It got ugly—you saw vestiges of that ugliness. But worth it? You bet!"

Soon the climate would turn even uglier as the Reagan administration came face-to-face with the scandal of Iran-contra—a shorthand term for the illegalities involved in financing the civil war raging in Nicaragua. President Reagan had pleaded with Congress to aid the contras, whom he referred to as "the moral equal of our Founding Fathers." Congress denied his plea and passed the Boland Amendment, making it illegal to provide funding to overthrow Nicaragua's duly elected Communist government.

By 1986 Americans had become sadly familiar with names such as the Reverend Benjamin Weir, Father Martin Jenco, and Terry Anderson of the Associated Press, who were among the seventeen Americans and seventy-five Westerners kidnapped in Beirut by terrorists and thrown into hellholes around Lebanon. All the captives were brutally tortured, and some left to die like roadkill. These kidnappings were part of a campaign—in retaliation for Israel's 1982 invasion, which had been supported by U.S. warplanes and ships from the U.S. Sixth Fleet—by Islamic Jihad or Hezbollah to rid Lebanon of all Americans.

In a misguided effort to free the hostages and finance Ronald

Reagan's war against the Sandinistas, Lieutenant Colonel Oliver North of the National Security Council devised a complex scheme, which he and others later tried to cover up. Until he was fired in 1986, the Marine lieutenant colonel known as Ollie was the White House official most directly involved in secretly aiding the contras, selling arms to Iran, and diverting proceeds from the Iran arms sales to the contras. The deception by North and others led to joint congressional hearings, a presidential commission, an investigation by the Office of Independent Counsel, court trials, and three convictions. In the end, six participants received presidential pardons.

Throughout it all, Vice President Bush, who had attended most of the planning sessions with Oliver North, would proclaim ignorance about what had happened, maintaining, "I was out of the loop." Yet court documents, congressional reports, transcripts, trial records, and the recollections of others prove otherwise: George Bush knew far more than he ever admitted.

On March 3, 1985, his son Jeb hand-carried to the Vice President's White House office a letter from the Guatemalan physician Dr. Mario Castejon requesting U.S. medical aid for the contras. George penned a note back to the doctor:

> Since the projects you propose seem most interesting, I might suggest, if you are willing, that you consider meeting with Lt. Col. Oliver North of the President's National Security Council staff at a time that would be convenient for you.
>
> My staff has been in contact with Lt. Col. North concerning your projects and I know that he would be most happy to see you. You may feel free to make arrangements to see Lt. Col. North, if you wish, by corresponding directly with him at the White House, or by contacting Mr. Philip Hughes of my staff.

In January 1985, Jeb Bush had met with Felix Rodriguez, the former CIA operative who served as the chief supply officer for North's illegal scheme to supply arms to the contras. Later it was suggested that Jeb was his father's Florida contact in the secret resupply operation.

"That's crap," Jeb told *The Boston Globe*. "I believe the freedom fighters should be supported to the maximum and that their cause is noble and just. But I know the difference between proper and improper behavior because I was brought up well. I would never do anything to jeopardize my dad's career. That would be a dagger in my heart."

The secret Iran-contra skein started unraveling on October 5, 1986, when the Sandinistas in Nicaragua shot down a cargo plane carrying military supplies with three Americans aboard. One American survived—Eugene Hasenfus. He claimed he worked for a CIA man named "Max Gomez," the code name for Felix Rodriguez.

Rodriguez, whose home proudly displayed two autographed pictures of himself with Vice President Bush, called his contact, Donald Gregg, who went to work for George Bush in 1982 as his national security adviser, to report the shot-down plane. Gregg, a former CIA operative, had met Rodriguez in Vietnam about the same time he met Bush.

Upon hearing Rodriguez's report, Bush quickly called a press conference and denied having any connection with the plane that crashed in Nicaragua, although he did admit knowing the man whose code name was Max Gomez.

Several weeks later *The Washington Post* linked Iran's release of three American hostages to American arms sales to Iran. George went on television to defend the administration. He declared that any arms-for-hostages deal was "inconceivable."

The next day Secretary of State George Shultz called the Vice President and reminded him that not only had Bush attended the crucial meeting on January 7, 1986, but he had also supported the plan to sell arms to Iran—the same plan that Shultz and Secretary of Defense Caspar Weinberger had opposed. Shultz could have shown George the notes he had taken during that meeting, which proved his point. He later published them in his book. When Bush realized that Shultz had been taking notes, he was flabbergasted, and he wrote in his diary:

Howard Baker in the presence of the President told me today that George Shultz had kept 700 pages of personal notes, dictated to his staff . . . Notes on personal meetings he had with the President. I found this almost inconceivable. Not only that he kept the notes, but that he'd turned them all over to Congress . . . I would never do it. I would never surrender such documents and I wouldn't keep such detailed notes.

On November 13, 1986, President Reagan announced on national television that he had authorized the sale of arms to Iran, but he denied that it was a trade for hostages.

A few days later Attorney General Ed Meese undertook an investigation to determine how much of a problem the U.S. arms shipment to Iran was going to be for the administration. Within four days Meese found that $10–$30 million from the arms sale to Iran had been diverted to the contras through Swiss bank accounts. The President was forced to fire Oliver North, but he told him, "One day this will make a great movie."

The Iran-contra scandal continued to unfold over the next two years, but the Vice President, who had become adroit at what he called "bending" and "stretching" the truth, ducked and dodged and fenced and hedged. He lied more than once to reporters during press conferences and frequently equivocated. He stonewalled the Office of Independent Counsel, and he withheld all of his personal diaries until after he left government service and was outside the reach of the special prosecutor.

During the 1986 Christmas holiday Donald Gregg and his wife threw a party, which the Vice President and Barbara attended along with Bush's staff lawyer, C. Boyden Gray, and his beautiful new young wife, Carol.

"What has always stuck out about that particular night is the memory of those men, who seemed very playful and a little more tipsy than usual," recalled Carol Gray. "They were kind of huddled together in that good-old-boy sort of way. The Vice President, Boyden, and Donald Gregg were laughing together very smugly.

"Someone had made buttons for them. The buttons were a mustard color with black writing. Printed on the buttons was a question: 'WHO IS MAX GOMEZ?'

"I asked Boyden what it all meant, but he just laughed it off and said it was an inside joke that they had. He never shared with me the exact meaning of the question on the buttons, but I always felt the meaning was part of a serious mission they were involved in . . . They really felt pleased with themselves that evening. They had usurped the powers that were in place. They were above the law. They were going to pull their plan off. They enjoyed the secret they had together. It was a huge rush for them."

CHAPTER TWENTY

To heir is human, even more so in the Bush family.

As Vice President of the United States, George H.W. Bush greatly enhanced his family's fortunes. During those years (1981–89), and the presidential years that followed (1989–93), he enabled his brothers and his sons—women in the Bush family are not breadwinners—to make millions of dollars. It is debatable—at best—whether any of them would have attained their high net worths without George's high office, even though they vigorously assert that they are all self-made men and have never exploited the family name.

"I resent the implication that because George is my brother, I'm getting business," said Jonathan Bush, a Wall Street investor who has run J. Bush and Company since 1980. He was barred from trading with the general public for one year—July 1991 to July 1992—for violating Massachusetts registration laws, fined thirty thousand dollars, and ordered to buy back stocks sold to clients during the preceding forty-three months. Jonathan shrugged it off. One dismayed regulator said: "Anyone who has been notified that he is violating state law and continues to do so certainly exemplifies a cavalier attitude." Jonathan had done the same thing in Connecticut and was fined four thousand dollars in December 1990 for conducting business without registering in the state.

"Being the brother of George Bush . . . is not a financial windfall by any stretch of the imagination," said Bucky Bush, a banker in St. Louis.

George's son Neil said, "We know to say no, and keep to the straight and narrow."

"You avoid sleazeballs, people who have quick-fix solutions, people who want you because your name is Bush," said Neil's brother Marvin, a venture capitalist in Alexandria, Virginia.

A glimpse into the business dealings of the Bush family shows that they acquired their wealth through the intermingling of public policy and private interests. "There's always been a good connection between the political side of our family and the business side," Marvin said.

The family's business transactions, most of which can be described as "international consulting," were frequently conducted in the ethical twilight zone of murky deals and shady dealers. The Bushes usually walked away enriched from these transactions, but they left in their wake the jiggery-pokery of failed banks, fleeced stockholders, bankruptcies, convictions, and lawsuits charging mismanagement, stock manipulation, and fraud. Upon examination, each and every Bush transaction serves as a textbook example of how to exploit the family name lucratively.

"What you've got with George Herbert Walker Bush is absolutely the largest number of siblings and children involved in what looks like a never-ending hustle," said the Republican commentator Kevin Phillips.

When George held the highest and second-highest offices in the land, he allowed his family to take full financial advantage of his high political position. In that sense, he threw open the barnyard door and yelled, "Suey Suey Suey," while his brothers and his sons snuffled up to the trough.

George Bush was certainly not the first man in history whose family cashed in on his high office for personal gain. Richard Nixon's brother Donald tried to start a fast-food chain of "Nixonburgers" and accepted, but never repaid, a $200,000 loan from the billionaire Howard Hughes. Jimmy Carter's brother, Billy, marketed "Billy Beer," wrote a book titled *Redneck Power*, and took $200,000 from the government of Libya to facilitate oil sales at a time the United States had branded Libya a terrorist country. Bill Clinton's half-brother, Roger, accepted $400,000 to lobby for presidential pardons. But George Bush's siblings and sons have surpassed them all, making the errant relatives of other high-office holders look like hummingbirds alongside vultures. (That feathered analogy was inspired by Prescott Bush Jr.'s comment to the *Chicago Tribune* about his various business dealings in Asia: "We aren't a bunch of carrion birds coming to pick the carcass." His choice of words, while unfortunate, proved to be descriptive.)

Shortly after George became Vice President, his older brother, Prescott junior, or P2, left the insurance business (Johnson and Higgins) and started his own firm in New York City, Prescott Bush and Company, described in a court document as a consulting firm that "helped foreign companies invest in the United States and elsewhere." Prescott's foreign clients soon included corporations in China, Japan, Brazil, South Korea, and the Philippines, all hungry to do business with the brother of the Vice President of the United States. In every country he dealt with, Prescott was treated like a head of state. Doors flew open and favors rained down. In the Philippines, President Corazon Aquino gave him a private audience. In South Korea, he met with the speaker of the National Assembly, Kim Chae Soon.

"The tradition in the Far East is for officials to see close linkage between the private business a person is involved in and who his relatives are," said Dennis Simon, an associate professor of international business relations at Tufts University's Fletcher School of Law and Diplomacy. In such circumstances, merely being the brother of a Vice President—a Vice President who might become President—is enough to give one immense consideration by foreign business executives and government officials interested in maintaining good relations with the United States. Consequently, Prescott traveled throughout Asia like a pasha without portfolio. By the time George became President, his brother's business dealings, especially in China, had raised so many problems within the State Department that George finally insisted an official cable be sent to all diplomatic and consular posts, telling them not to give favorable treatment to any members of his family. The cable was meant not to restrain his sons—George would never do that—but to reel in his brother Prescott. "His work in China has always worried me," George wrote in his diary.

The cable had no effect. Embassies treated it as nothing more than a self-protective measure by an American President who needed political cover in case his relatives got caught picking the locks. "It was simply a phony piece of paper that the President could wave in public, saying that he had gone to great lengths to ensure that his family did not use his high office for personal gain," said a Foreign Service officer who worked in the State Department from 1966 to 1996. "There was no way any of our people would not or could not respond to members of the Bush family on their various global plunders . . . Cable or no cable, do you want to be the government employee who bars the door to the President's brother or, God forbid, one of the President's sons?"

Prescott Bush was particularly smooth in circumventing the cable's instructions. On the eve of his trips, he simply wired ahead, alerting the appropriate embassy to his arrival and departure, and insisted that nothing special be done for him during his in-country stay, thereby ensuring that everything—introductions, receptions, arrangements—would be done.

"Prescott knew how to work the system," said Stephen Maitland-Lewis, formerly a consultant with Lazard Frères and a senior vice president of Salomon Brothers in New York. "I met him during the fiasco of AMIFS [Asset Management International Financing and Settlement] . . . His office on Lexington Avenue was close to the offices of Charles Abrams and Albert Shepard, who had combined their companies to form AMIFS. Shepard was instrumental in putting together a highfalutin board that included Admiral Elmo Zumwalt, former Ambassador Maxwell Raab, a few others, and me. But the most important by far was Prescott S. Bush Jr., for the plain and simple reason of who his brother was . . .

"When Prescott started scouting business opportunities in China, he didn't have to drop his brother's name every five minutes, because the Chinese were smart enough to make the connection. Plus, the physical resemblance between the two brothers then was such that you almost thought you were doing business with the Vice President himself.

"Prescott began his China prowls with Charles Abrams, who was close to Prescott's brother Bucky in St. Louis. Charles made a career of assembling prominent figures to lend credibility to his ventures, many of which have failed. He introduced Prescott to Albert Shepard, who lived in Manhattan but also had a home in Greenwich. Shepard was a neighbor of Prescott, but I doubt Prescott ever extended hospitality to Albert . . . He would've been embarrassed if Albert had been sporting his usual collection of diamond rings, flashy gold jewelry, and mink coats . . . Prescott was a thumping snob and a bit tedious . . . I remember sitting next to him at a dinner at the Harvard Club, where he was more boring and pompous than amusing. He was not unpleasant, but it was a long evening, and he was more work than pleasure, if you know what I mean. But that made no difference to Abrams and Shepard . . . They only cared that he was the brother of George Herbert Walker Bush. But for that, Prescott could just as easily have been the janitor."

AMIFS began as a company for counter trade—a brokerage that traded stocks over the counter—for which Prescott was paid to bring in stockholders. As an AMIFS consultant, he also was paid to provide introductions and make connections with foreign clients interested in U.S. investments. When Prescott became a member of AMIFS's senior advisory board and a director of its Asian subsidiary, he negotiated a $5 million deal with Japan's West Tsusho to buy 40 percent of AMIFS. For this, Prescott received a $250,000 finder's fee, plus $250,000 from AMIFS and a renegotiated contract from AMIFS that was to pay him $250,000 a year for three years. If AMIFS failed within five years, Prescott Bush and Company guaranteed one-half of West Tsusho's investment.

"I can assure you that the only reason that West Tsusho sat down with Prescott Bush Jr. was that he was the brother of George Herbert Walker Bush," said Maitland-Lewis. "In the early days Prescott was treated like God. His arrival in the office was akin to the Second Coming of Jesus Christ. Corporate culture was to genuflect before him . . . then much later it became clear that the Japanese group he had brought in was connected to the Japanese Mafia. We found all that out through news stories, but there was some speculation at the time when we saw the kind of people flying into New York City for our board meetings . . . They looked like Sapporo Sopranos, if you will, or Asian GoodFellas . . . definitely not top drawer."

There is no indication that Prescott Bush Jr. deliberately sought to do business with Japan's Mafia. "At first, he was defensive," said Maitland-Lewis. "His embarrassment came later."

Before humiliation set in, Prescott led West Tsusho to invest $3.8 million in Quantum Access, a Houston-based software-development company headed by Draper Kauffman, one of Prescott's nephews on his wife's side. Prescott received another $250,000 for this transaction and joined the board of Quantum Access, for which he was paid additional money. Kauffman claimed that West Tsusho soon seized control of his company, fired the management, and put in their own people. Within two years Quantum Access was forced to file for bankruptcy.

The same thing happened at AMIFS. "The company had a significant burn rate," said Maitland-Lewis. "Corporate salaries were competitive with Wall Street investment banks; rent was high; and, of course, Abrams and Shepard spent money like drunken sailors . . . The company was forced into bankruptcy, most of us who invested lost our shirts, and Prescott, who was unable to bring in the balance of the committed funds, fell out with everyone and became embroiled in several years of litigation with West Tsusho."

The Japanese company sued Prescott Bush and Company for reneging on the $2.5 million repayment Prescott had guaranteed when West Tsusho pledged its initial investment. Prescott dissolved Prescott Bush and Company in April 1991, presumably so West Tsusho could not collect—but West Tsusho sued him personally for the amount. Prescott countersued for $8 million, charging West Tsusho with fraud. West Tsusho argued in court papers that Prescott's allegation of their organized-crime connection was immaterial: "Bush would have signed the guarantee even if these alleged facts had been true and had been disclosed because of Bush's desire to obtain hundreds of thousands of dollars for himself and five million for AMIFS with whom both Bush and his nephew [Draper Kauffman] were associated." After three years of litigation, the court dismissed Prescott's countersuit, and West Tsusho's suit was sent to arbitration. The parties finally settled privately.

Draper Kauffman defended his Uncle Prescott to *The Wall Street Journal*: "They [West Tsusho] set him up as a fall guy and tried to use his name and rip him off. He did make an effort to check these people out and got nothing but favorable reports . . . As a front organization they kept [their crime connections] secret."

The publicity of Prescott's involvement with the Japanese Mafia embarrassed George, who was Vice President at the time, and caused a rift within the family that was never repaired. "I think everyone had a strong feeling of disapproval," said Caroline Bush "Teensie" Cole, the eldest child of James Smith Bush by his first wife. "It was using the Bush name."

"Pres was just so damn stubborn about it," Gerry Bemiss said. "You couldn't even discuss it with him. It was very frustrating for George."

"They were never as close as they had once been," Nancy Bush Ellis said. "Sadly, they probably never will be."

The closeness the two brothers shared in childhood had been sorely tested when Prescott attempted to run for the Senate from Connecticut in 1982 against the incumbent Lowell Weicker. George did not like

Weicker, but as Vice President he was obliged to support him, and Prescott's challenge within the party was an embarrassment. George finally prevailed on his mother to intervene. She called Prescott and asked him to withdraw, which he did.

Prescott resented the charge that his business dealings were an embarrassment. And he did not understand why he should take the brunt of the blame when George's sons had done just as much, and sometimes more, to embarrass their father and shame the family. So despite George's political discomfort, Prescott continued wheeling and dealing.

Despite the bankruptcies of AMIFS and Quantum Access, he continued to operate through Prescott Bush Resources Ltd., a company he had set up for real-estate and development consulting. With this enterprise, he sought to arrange lucrative partnerships with foreign corporations.

His first was with Mitsui, the third-largest exporter of U.S. goods to Japan. He drew up a plan for introducing Mitsui executives to Chinese and American business contacts and later submitted a sizable bill ($500,000) for his work. Mitsui rejected his plan and wanted to reject his bill, but worried about angering the brother of the U.S. Vice President, who looked more and more likely to become the next President.

Prescott also had signed a contract with Aoki Corporation to build an $18 million country club near Shanghai with a golf course designed by Robert Trent Jones for visiting businessmen. Aoki "gave" Prescott a one-third share ($6 million) at no cost. He put up no money for his portion of the investment. When asked about the $6 million gift, an Aoki executive said that Prescott had received the stake for "the good will expected from having him involved." He was to introduce Japanese investors to the Chinese officials participating in the deal.

Soon after George's presidency, Prescott helped start the U.S.-China Chamber of Commerce, whose goal was to promote trade between the two countries. As chairman of the board of directors for several years, Prescott collected fees for recruiting large corporations for membership: United Airlines, American Express, McDonald's, Ford Motor Company, Arthur Andersen, Morgan Stanley Dean Witter, and Archer Daniels Midland.

"From the beginning, Prescott Bush made his relationship to the former president a major part of the Chamber's sales pitch," reported the *Far*

Eastern Economic Review in 2000. Prescott responded: "China has a special place in my heart. I have personally been involved in China for over 15 years. My brother George has been instrumental in the development of U.S. and China relations since 1974."

Flying under the flag of "my brother George," Prescott sailed into several more lucrative contracts, including an agreement in 1999 to be a "counselor" to Wanxiang Group, a large Chinese auto-parts company that exports to the United States. The chairman of Wanxiang Group said: "Inviting Prescott Bush to be the counselor will help expand Wanxiang's operations overseas." A company spokesman elaborated: "The company hired Mr. Bush because of his wide connections. He has many friends." Prescott's yearly retainer was reputed to be $350,000.

Despite the family's discomfort with Prescott's business dealings, there was no denying his vast wealth, and the accumulation of wealth was the first imperative for George Bush's sons, all impatient to become millionaires like their father. "In our family, when you're done in four, you're out the door," said Jeb Bush, meaning that the boys were on their own after their college graduations.

"I'd like to be very wealthy," Jeb told the *Miami News* in 1983. "And I'll be glad to let you know when I think I've reached my goal." By 1998, Jeb had attained a net worth of $2.4 million. He maintained that his success—financial and political—had nothing to do with his family name. "I've always been independent," he said. "I'm a self-made man."

Jeb was ferociously driven to succeed, and he worked constantly, sleeping no more than five hours a night. He completed college at the University of Texas in two and a half years and, like his father, graduated Phi Beta Kappa. He was the first son to marry; the first to have children. He competed with his older brother, George W., but the two were never close; both measured themselves against their father, who had been the dominant, if distant, influence in their lives. At the time, Jeb was the family's golden boy—smart, talented, articulate—the son in whom his parents invested their biggest dreams.

Shortly after his father was sworn in as Vice President, Jeb moved his family out of Houston because the prejudice against his Mexican wife had become too hurtful. "Miami is wide open. It's a frontier town," Jeb said. "It doesn't have a lot of people with Roman numerals behind their names." Columba also wanted to be closer to her mother and her sister, so George H.W. loaned his son twenty thousand dollars to buy a house in Miami, where Jeb had helped his father campaign in the anti-Castro Cuban communities during the Florida Republican presidential primary.

"That's when I caught the bug," Jeb said. "It was perhaps the most rewarding experience of my life . . . I think I grew as a human being. I learned how to deal with people. I learned how to overcome fear: fear of humiliation, fear of embarrassment, fear of not doing as well as you want to do."

"Campaigning for Dad was hardly a paying job," Stephen Pizzo wrote in *Mother Jones*, "but Jeb was about to learn that being one of George Bush's sons means never having to circulate a résumé."

Within weeks of his move, Jeb contacted Armando Codina, a Cuban American developer and a big Bush political supporter who owned a commercial-real-estate development company. Codina was reported to be worth $75 million. He hired Jeb as an agent to lease office space for his development company in Miami, although Jeb had absolutely no real-estate experience. "I learned the business the hard way," Jeb said. "On the job." Codina also offered Jeb a 40 percent share of his company's profits—and Jeb did not have to put one cent of his own money into the firm. Opportunities were also offered to invest in other ventures on the side. Jeb accepted, and the company was renamed Codina-Bush, which gave Codina an instant relationship with the Vice President of the United States.

Within two years Jeb launched himself politically. As his father had done twenty-one years earlier, Jeb sought the top office of his county's Republican Party and he was elected chairman of the Dade County GOP. As someone who played country-club tennis and spoke fluent Spanish, he was uniquely situated to bridge the chasm between Anglos and Cubans within the party. The Anglos were genteel people, much like Jeb's paternal grandparents, who had fled the cold winters up north. The hot-tempered Cubans were brash entrepreneurs who had fled the repressive Castro regime. Each group viewed the other with veiled contempt but revered Ronald Reagan—so the thirty-year-old son of Reagan's Vice President was well and favorably received. This made Jeb a valuable asset to Armando Codina.

Sometimes Codina-Bush clients wanted Jeb to do more than find them office space. They wanted his influence in Washington. Jeb always complied, frequently interceding for thugs and knaves whose blatant criminality defied exaggeration. In every case, the con men who hustled Jeb made contributions to his Dade County coffers before requesting his help. In case after case, Jeb responded as if each were a prince of the realm. As Jefferson Morley of *The Washington Post* wrote: "Political entrepreneurs like Jeb Bush sell access."

In one case Jeb peddled his influence for Miguel Recarey Jr., an international fugitive whose hobby was extortion. Recarey, who boasted of Mafia ties to Santos Trafficante, pulled off one of the biggest Medicare frauds in American history, skimming untold millions from taxpayers. According to law-enforcement officials, he increased his personal net worth from $1 million to $100 million in six years. By the time Recarey met Jeb Bush, the Cuban immigrant had been forced to repay $13 million in improper Medicare payments. He had also been convicted of tax evasion, served time in prison, and was being investigated for hospital embezzlement in connection with his health maintenance organization, International Medical Centers.

In 1984, Recarey made a two-thousand-dollar contribution to Jeb's Dade County coffers. Jeb then acted as a conduit to his father and Oliver North to arrange for IMC to provide free medical treatment for the contras. Afterward, Recarey hired Jeb's personal company, Bush Realty Management, for $250,000 to find IMC an office building. During their conversations, Recarey mentioned that the U.S. Department of Health and Human Services was tightening Medicare rules, which threatened IMC profits. Recarey asked Jeb to call HHS on his behalf. Jeb agreed and made two telephone calls, which he would later deny, asking that Recarey be granted a waiver of the new HHS regulations.

Jeb went right to the top. He called the Secretary of Health and Human Services, Margaret Heckler, and spoke to her chief of staff, C. McClain Haddow. Jeb told Haddow to "discount rumors that were floating around concerning Mr. Recarey . . . He's a good community citizen and a good supporter of the Republican party."

These calls from the son of the Vice President commanded not just attention but action. When Congress later investigated Recarey's Medicare fraud, Haddow testified that Jeb's calls for Recarey had helped IMC receive its waiver, enabling IMC to have more than half its clientele be Medicare recipients. Secretary Heckler's approval of this waiver overruled the decision of a local HHS administrator. Jeb's intervention basically guaranteed that Recarey could continue bilking millions from Medicare, which is exactly what he did for three more years. Recarey paid Jeb seventy-five thousand dollars, which both men claimed was a realty fee, although Jeb never found Recarey any office space. In 1985 and 1986, Recarey also gave more than twenty-five thousand dollars to George Bush's political action committees.

In 1987, when IMC was shut down because of insolvency, more than $200 million in Medicare money was missing. Recarey was indicted for embezzlement, labor racketeering, bribery, obstruction of justice, and wiretapping. He fled to Venezuela, and then to Spain, where he now lives in luxury. To this day he remains on the FBI's list of international fugitives.

In 1985, the year after Jeb intervened with HHS for Recarey, he wrote a letter to the Department of Housing and Urban Development on behalf of another unscrupulous character. Hiram Martinez Jr. had applied for federal loan insurance for an apartment development. The application was stalled because of questions about the value of the land. After Jeb wrote to HUD, Martinez got the loan, but HUD later discovered that Martinez had indeed inflated the value of the land and the cost of the project. He was convicted and served six years in prison for fraud. Jeb said he did not remember writing the letter, but HUD released a copy.

Jeb had interceded for Martinez because he had been hired by Martinez's contractor, Camilo Padreda, another anti-Castro Cuban, who was finance chairman of the Dade County GOP when Jeb was chairman. In 1982, Padreda had been indicted for embezzling $500,000 from the Jefferson Savings and Loan in McAllen, Texas. But the case never went to trial, because the CIA intervened on behalf of Padreda's associate, who was indicted with him. His associate had worked for the CIA during the failed Bay of Pigs invasion. Padreda later pleaded guilty to defrauding the Department of Housing and Urban Development of millions, including the Martinez fraud, but Padreda never went to jail. Instead, he was placed under house arrest and given probation in exchange for cooperating with authorities investigating Dade County corruption.

Jeb, who has claimed that he never lobbied his father's government, petitioned the Justice Department in 1990 in behalf of Orlando Bosch, who was in prison for having entered the United States illegally. The anti-Castro terrorist, who was implicated in the car-bombing assassination of

Orlando Letelier, was notorious for having masterminded the bombing of a Cubana Airlines flight in October 1976, which killed all seventy-three on board, including a group of Cuban athletes returning from the Pan Am Games in Caracas, Venezuela. At that time George Herbert Walker Bush was CIA director. The United States sanctioned terrorism against Cuba and routinely trained commandos to infiltrate the island. Jeb, who planned to run for governor of Florida, represented a rabid anti-Castro constituency, a voting bloc that held his father's anti-Castro actions at the CIA in the highest esteem. Jeb's public support for paroling Bosch further enhanced his standing in the Cuban community, which considered Bosch a patriot in exile and honored him for his murderous bombings around the globe. At his son's behest, George Bush intervened to obtain the release of the Cuban terrorist from prison and later granted Bosch U.S. residency.

By this time Jeb had woven an intricate web of murky business deals with spidery ties to the CIA. He repeatedly profited financially and politically by exploiting his father's high office for personal gain. One of his most egregious deals occurred when he and his business partner, Armando Codina, obtained a loan of $4.56 million from Broward Federal Savings and Loan through a third party, J. Edward Houston. Codina-Bush used the money to buy an office building. When Broward Federal Savings and Loan failed, federal regulators found that the loan to Houston, which had been secured by Codina-Bush, was in default. Rather than force the Vice President's son and his partner to sell the office building to pay off the loan, federal regulators negotiated a settlement in which Jeb and his partner repaid $505,000, retained control of the office building, and passed on to taxpayers the $4.1 million loss. Both men expressed surprise to *The New York Times* that the settlement could be interpreted as the use of taxpayers' money to make good a loan whose proceeds went for their building: "Asked if they were aware that the funds for the repayment of the loan came from the taxpayers, both men said no." Three years later, Jeb and his partner sold the building for $8 million, which Jeb claimed, with a straight face, was just enough to cover their costs and legal fees. "This little episode," observed Christopher Hitchens in *The Nation*, "provides a handy insight into the mental and moral world of people who make money rather than earn it."

By then, Jeb felt he had made enough money to seriously launch his political career. He told his father he wanted to run for the U.S. Senate in 1986, but his father persuaded him to wait. The Vice President said he could not afford "another Pressy deal" just as he was gearing up for his own presidential run. Jeb knew the reference was to his father's brother Prescott's embarrassing candidacy in 1982 for the U.S. Senate seat in Connecticut. Now, George told his son that he needed him in Florida. Jeb, who idolized his father, knew that this was George's last and best chance to become President. No matter whom the Democrats put up, the Vice President to the beloved Ronald Reagan would have an edge. Jeb said he would do anything to help his father get elected.

As chairman of the Dade County GOP, Jeb frequently called his father for political favors, and in 1986 he asked George to come to Florida to campaign for Bob Martinez, the Republican candidate for governor. "The kids were always calling the Vice President's office with requests," said Bush's deputy chief of staff, "but Jeb's calls usually got the old man's best attention . . . I think he trusted Jeb's political instincts."

Jeb's hard-right politics—"I'm a hang-'em-by-the-neck conservative"—and his vociferous support of the contras appealed to his father and boosted Jeb's popularity in the conservative, anti-Communist Hispanic community of Dade County. Jeb's access to fabulously wealthy Cubans made him invaluable to his father's political staff as they prepared their 1988 run for a Bush presidency. Jeb's request for his father to campaign for Martinez was immediately put on the Vice President's schedule, and George made several trips to Florida. When Martinez won, he appointed Jeb to be Florida's secretary of commerce, a job Jeb held for twenty months. It enabled him to travel abroad on trade missions to Latin America and Asia, pursuing further business opportunities for himself and his state. After George was elected President in 1988, he appointed Martinez—who had been defeated in his bid for reelection—"drug czar."

As Florida's secretary of commerce, Jeb awarded a $160,000 state contract to Richard Lawless, a former CIA agent, to promote Florida in the Far East. After Jeb quit his state job, Lawless paid him $528,000 for various real-estate services. Lawless also donated $35,000 to the Republican Party and $5,000 to Jeb's first gubernatorial campaign.

Jeb started a second company with Hank Klein, Bush-Klein Realty, to sell real estate. His new partner wondered if politics would get in the way of business.

"I asked him, 'What does your dad think of your going into business with a liberal Democrat?' " Klein said. "Jeb told me that his father thought about it a minute, then said, 'It's okay—as long as you make money together.'

"I said, 'Spoken like a true Republican.' "

After his father became President, Jeb phoned with more requests—autographed photos, presidential cuff links, and presidential endorsements. When he managed the 1989 congressional campaign of Ileana Ros-Lehtinen in a race against ten other candidates for the congressional seat once held by Representative Claude Pepper, Jeb asked his father to endorse the prominent Cuban American. George agreed and flew to Florida on Air Force One to appear with her during her campaign in Miami. He declared, "I am certain in my heart I will be the first American president to set foot on the soil of a free and independent Cuba."

Ros-Lehtinen won the seat and became the first Cuban-born American and the first Hispanic female to sit in Congress, which further enhanced Jeb and his father in the eyes of the anti-Castro community. Heading an economic mission to Japan a few months later, Jeb attended a seminar at which pamphlets were distributed describing him as "political heir" to the President and as having "the strongest connections to the White House among the members of the Bush family."

Jeb accumulated a great deal of his net worth during his father's presidency. After working in the 1988 presidential campaign, Jeb formed a private partnership, Bush-El, with David Eller of M&W Pump. The two men, who met through the Dade County GOP, sought to sell giant water pumps to poor countries, including Egypt, Indonesia, Malaysia, Mexico, Panama, Taiwan, and Thailand. Perhaps their most lucrative deal occurred in Nigeria, where they pursued a $74 million loan from the Export-Import Bank to finance the sale of pumps for irrigation and flood control.

Two months after his father's inauguration, Jeb walked into the office of Nigerian President Ibrahim Babangida in Lagos and presented him with an autographed copy of President Bush's inaugural address. Jeb and his business partner were visiting Nigeria with their wives for five days, ostensibly for the dedication of a $3.6 million M&W manufacturing plant.

In advance of the trip the President's son had informed the State Department that he was traveling on business and "did not want any special treatment"—shades of his Uncle Prescott. And despite the President's cable to foreign embassies not to accord preferential treatment to his family, Jeb was red-carpeted every step of the way. He told reporters that the meeting with the Nigerian President was a "brief courtesy call" for the President to thank M&W for its investment in Nigeria. The Ambassador's report to the State Department described a longer meeting, which covered human rights in Cuba, the value of close U.S.-Nigeria ties, and President Babangida's desire to visit the United States. After Jeb passed on the Nigerian President's request, a White House state visit was scheduled, although it was postponed at the last minute because of unrest among Nigeria's Muslims.

After Jeb's trip, President Bush sent a handwritten message to the Nigerian President by diplomatic pouch: "I want to thank you for receiving Jeb and Columba Bush and for the hospitality they were shown at all their events in Nigeria. They came back singing the praises of your country and very grateful to you."

On Jeb's second trip to Nigeria, he was accompanied by M&W's Nigerian agent, Al-Haji Mohammed Indimi, who carried a suitcase full of Nigerian cash, which he used to bribe Nigerian officials. Jeb later told the press he knew nothing about the bribes. After Jeb's visit, the Export-Import Bank approved eight direct loans of $74.3 million on Nigeria's pending purchase of pumps from M&W. The U.S. government later accused David Eller of inflating his prices and using the loan money to pay for the bribes and a large commission to Indimi. The business partner of the President's son was not charged with criminal fraud. By the time of the government's investigation, Jeb had departed. Having made $196,000 in commissions from Bush-El, Jeb sold his share of the company to Eller for $452,000. He had worked there for six years.

While the Vice President was discouraging his second son's political ambitions, his third son, known in the family as "Mr. Perfect," was about to bring the Bushes their most public humiliation. His parents had always described Neil Bush as "the ideal child" because in his eagerness to please them he did the unpleasant chores no one else wanted to do. "Neil brings us nothing but happiness," George wrote shortly after his son's birth. He was saying the same thing thirty years later.

"He drove us all crazy, growing up, because he made us look just horrible," Marvin, son number four, told a reporter. Neil said it was his way of making up for his poor grades, which were attributable to his dyslexia. "I always found ways to compensate," he said. "I was nicer. I volunteered to rake the yard when the others were bailing out."

John Claiborne Davis, the former assistant headmaster at St. Albans, said he had the unenviable duty of getting Neil into a good college. "He was a perfectly charming guy," recalled Davis, "but not a spectacular student. Still, I managed to get him into Tulane because of who his father was. Thank God, Barbara Bush didn't press me to get him into Yale. I think she was quite happy that I swung Tulane for him . . . Neil earned a bachelor's degree in international relations and then a master's degree in business . . . How he ever got into graduate school—and finished—I'll never know. At St. Albans we gave out three types of diplomas: one was a diploma with merit, which was for someone at the top of his class. Then there was a diploma with commendation for the B+ students, and, finally, there was a certificate of graduation with no distinction whatsoever . . . That's the certificate that Neil got.

"He had applied to Rice first because he said he wanted to be in Texas, but Rice is a good school with high academic standards, and they turned him down. So I suggested he apply to Tulane in New Orleans . . . I had placed several of our boys there, and I thought I could get him in . . . I remember visiting during the first semester to see how our students were doing. I took Neil and two black boys from St. Albans out to dinner at Commander's Palace. We all ordered lobster, but poor Neil didn't know what to do with his fish fork. When the waitress came, he said, 'How do I eat this thing?' She put the napkin around his neck like a bib on a baby. She cracked the shell of the fish for him, put his fork in, and spoon-fed him his first bite. 'That's how you do it, sonny,' she said. The other boys and I winked at each other; we couldn't believe that Neil had never had lobster before, especially after all those summers at Kennebunkport . . . I guess I had just assumed there was a minimum level of sophistication in the Bush household."

Howard Means, who taught Neil English at St. Albans, did not make that assumption, especially after meeting Neil's parents. "It was probably thirty years after I had taught Neil that I met Barbara and George Bush. He had been out of office for several months, and they were at a party standing all by themselves. No one was paying any attention to them, so I walked over and introduced myself.

" 'Mr. President,' I said, 'I taught Neil at St. Albans. How is his grammar these days?'

" 'Well, he's fine but he still ends a sentence with a proposition.' "

Means waited for Bush to laugh at his gaffe, but the President apparently did not realize he had made one.

Following graduation from Tulane's business school, Neil campaigned as a full-time volunteer for his father in 1980, working in New Hampshire with former Governor Hugh Gregg. There he met Sharon Lee Smith, a schoolteacher. They were married in the summer of 1980 at Kennebunkport and moved to Denver so that Neil, like his father and his brother George, could get into the oil and gas business. Neil started his apprenticeship with Amoco as a lease negotiator for thirty thousand dollars a year. He planned to follow his father's trajectory—make a fortune and go into politics. He had his heart set on becoming governor of Colorado.

"They'd talk about how G.W. was going to run for governor of Texas and Jeb would run for governor of Florida and Neil would run for governor of Colorado," said Douglas Wead, a Bush family friend who served as a special assistant in the first Bush White House. "The family would have bet on Jeb. But if you just observed their personalities, you'd say Neil . . . He's relaxed, he's funny, he's a better speaker than anybody in the family . . . He could easily have been a congressman."

Being the son of the Vice President swung open doors that would have been closed to any other young man without social entrée. Neil and Sharon quickly became part of Denver's social scene. Neil played squash at the exclusive Denver Club, and Sharon did volunteer work at the Children's Hospital, the city's most socially prestigious charity. Both were invited to the very best parties.

Within two years Neil decided to start his own oil business, although the oil boom had peaked in 1981. With James Judd and Evans Nash, he formed JNB Exploration in 1983. Neil and his partners only put up $100 apiece and bankrolled their company with $1 million from two Denver developers, Kenneth Good and Bill Walters. As president of JNB Exploration, Neil paid himself sixty thousand dollars a year. He hung a framed picture of his father on the wall of his office, and on his desk he displayed a nameplate that read "Mr. Bush." Neil told visitors the nameplate had come from the U.S. Senate seat that once belonged to his grandfather Prescott Bush.

Impressed by Neil's lineage, Kenneth Good wanted to further ingratiate himself with the Vice President's son, so he lent Neil $100,000 to invest in commodities. Neil lost the investment, but Good forgave the loan. Walters also lent Neil $100,000, but he held on to the paper. In the spring of 1985 both men introduced Neil to their banker, Michael Wise, the president of Silverado Savings and Loan. Wise asked Neil if he'd like to join Silverado's board of directors.

"I didn't pretend to be an expert on the savings and loan business, but Wise said that was O.K.," Neil recalled. His director's fee was eight thousand dollars a year. "I guess it would be naive to think that the Bush name didn't have something to do with it," he added. Neil said he accepted Wise's offer because he was eager to be respected as a businessman. "I was looking to further establish my roots in this town. I was under the impression then that joining the board of a financial institution is a way to establish one's reputation in the community and to give you exposure to the people who are the players in a community, the people who make a difference."

Ronald Reagan had deregulated the savings-and-loan industry in 1982, which allowed S&Ls to make riskier investments with less government oversight. Neil's only banking experience had been a summer job filling out forms in the trust office of a Dallas bank. He was hardly qualified to provide adequate oversight of Silverado's business practices or to see the questionable deals intended to cover up losses caused by bad loans.

Over the next three years, Neil encouraged Silverado to approve $200 million in loans to Bill Walters and Kenneth Good without fully disclosing to the other directors that both men were part owners of Neil's company, JNB Exploration. Nor did Neil mention that he owed Walters $100,000 for a personal loan and that he had been forgiven another $100,000 loan by Good. When Kenneth Good offered to buy 80 percent of JNB and promised to put $3.1 million into the company by September 1987, Neil leaped. "It was a sweet deal," he said.

Too sweet, thought Evans Nash, who was concerned about Neil's relationship with the high-flying developer. Good lived lavishly, even by big-spending standards, and Neil seemed too dazzled by Good's $10 million home that covered thirty-three thousand square feet and featured an indoor handball court and indoor and outdoor tennis courts. Good sped around Denver in a Maserati and flew to Monte Carlo on a private jet. "He was kind of free with his money," Neil said. "He went for high-risk ventures, which is probably why he was interested in my oil business."

Neil was not at all concerned that Good had persuaded Silverado to forgive $8 million in loans that he could not pay, but Nash was; he wanted out. He sold his interest in JNB Exploration to Neil, who immediately increased his salary to $120,000 a year, plus tax-free bonuses. He also joined the Petroleum Club and refinanced his house with a $300,000 mortgage from Silverado, which gave him a 2 percent break on the interest rate.

Neil, financially dependent on Good, persuaded Silverado to extend a $900,000 line of credit to the developer so that Good could participate in a business deal that JNB Exploration had in Argentina. Neil and his JNB business partner, James Judd, used the money to purchase a 50 percent interest in an oil concession in northern Argentina, but they ran out of money before the drilling started.

"In most circles, people might have sued us because there was a contractual obligation," said James Judd. "To be quite frank, the fact that Neil was involved in this particular deal—I can't help but think there was some preferential consideration."

Rather than sue the son of the Vice President, the Argentine industrialist Santiago Soldati, who owned the other 50 percent interest, took on the full cost of the project. Two years later Soldati was invited as a special guest to George Herbert Walker Bush's inaugural.

Silverado hemorrhaged money throughout 1986 and 1987, because Neil and the other directors approved $200 million in loans to Neil's two partners in JNB, his abysmally unsuccessful oil company. Silverado's failure was due in large part to those two partners, who defaulted on $132 million in loans. This default, plus other Silverado defaults, cost taxpayers almost $1 billion. The order to shut down Silverado did not come until the day after George Bush was elected President in November 1988, suggesting political interference to hold the news until after the election. Had the report been issued earlier, it might have influenced the election because of the involvement of Bush's son. Regulators seized the savings and loan on December 9, 1988, and the Bush family's "Mr. Perfect" became the poster child for bunco banking.

The Office of Thrift Supervision filed three conflict-of-interest charges against Neil and subpoenaed him for a hearing. The Federal Deposit Insurance Corporation filed a $200 million civil suit in Denver against Neil and the other Silverado directors. The House Banking Committee subpoenaed Neil to testify about his role as a director of Silverado Savings and Loan Association.

His mother was irate. "Neilsie is being persecuted," Barbara fumed to the press.

"If it wasn't for me he would not be getting this heat," said his father. The avalanche of negative publicity that hit Neil upset his family.

"The focus would not be on Neil Bush today," said his brother Marvin, "if my dad were not President."

The President became emotionally distraught over the scandal enveloping his son. "I remember being in a luncheon meeting with him and all of his advertising guys for the 1992 campaign," said Bob Gardner of Gardner Communications. "Right in the middle of everything President Bush broke down and started crying over Neil. He said the kid was being unfairly attacked because of who his father is."

After nine months the $200 million civil suit against Neil and the other Silverado directors was settled for $49.5 million, with $26.5 million to come from the pockets of the directors who had allowed Silverado to bleed to death. The directors were all insured, so in the end each one, including Neil, was charged only $50,000 as his share of the penalty. Neil didn't even have to pay that himself or any of his legal fees, which amounted to $200,000. The entire amount—$250,000—was paid by a legal defense fund set up by his father's good friend Lud Ashley, who turned to the Bushes' friends to bail out the Bushes' son. Some wondered why President Bush, with a declared net worth of $4 million at the time, did not pay his son's legal fees himself. Because Neil had named his last child Ashley, in honor of his father's good friend, the honored friend now came to Neil's rescue.

"I did it because I was a friend of the family," said Ashley, the former congressman from Ohio who was head of the Association of Bank Holding Companies when he passed the hat for Neil. At that time Ashley was

supporting legislation submitted by George Bush's White House to deregulate the banking industry. Some bankers in Ashley's association felt uncomfortable with his actions on behalf of his friend's son, because it
created the wrong impression.

By then the savings-and-loan scandal had coiled around Neil's neck
like a noose, but the President's son managed to escape a criminal indictment. In the OTS hearing, he was cited for "an ethical disability, a lack
of skill in seeing ethical issues, he naively violated moral standards. Because he didn't see, he didn't engage in moral weighing . . . [T]he handicap does not absolve [him] of responsibility to depositors, shareholders,
insurers and American taxpayers."

Citing Neil Bush for "an ethical disability" was a public rebuke of
George and Barbara Bush as parents: they had raised a son who either did
not know the difference between right and wrong or was so avaricious that
he deliberately ignored basic moral principles.

"The fact that man knows right from wrong proves his intellectual superiority to other creatures," Mark Twain said. "But the fact that he can do
wrong proves his moral inferiority to any creature that cannot." The judge
in the OTS hearing found Neil lower than a worm. He said Neil had violated "the worst kinds of conflict of interest" and recommended the OTS
issue a cease-and-desist order restraining him from engaging in similar
banking transactions in the future. Neil had to testify before the OTS for
three hours on his own behalf. He was argumentative, uncooperative, and
arrogant. At a later press conference he was even more defiant.

He approached the microphones, adjusted his tie, jammed his hands
in his pockets, and denounced the "inaccurate" media, the "self-serving"
regulators, and the "government bullies." He denounced everything but
his own actions. When a reporter asked him to concede that there was at
least the appearance of a conflict of interest, he erupted.

"I'll say it again," he snapped. "I'm innocent of all charges." Then he
spoke as if the reporters were mutes with a limited understanding of English. Pausing after every word, he glared reprovingly.

"There. Was. No. Conflict. Of. Interest."

The reporters were astounded that in the face of irrefutable evidence,
Neil continued to maintain he was legally and morally in the right. "He
seemed to believe it was his birthright," wrote Steven Wilmsen in *Play-
boy*, "to profit at the nation's expense."

A cease-and-desist order was issued in April 1991, restraining Neil Bush from engaging in bank transactions for the rest of his life. Such an order from the OTS was unprecedented against someone no longer affiliated with a financial institution. For a businessman, the order was the shameful equivalent of a military man's dishonorable discharge. Even so, Neil recovered faster than most from such a wallop.

Months before the hearing he had formed another company, Apex Energy, to prospect for methane gas in Wyoming. He invested $3,000 of his own money and received $2.7 million in capitalization from Louis Marx, a New York financier who had contributed $100,000 to George Bush's campaign. Marx bought 49 percent of Neil's company by using funds he had obtained from a Small Business Administration program designed to help "high risk start-up companies." Neil paid himself $320,000 in salary over two years, plus $150,000 for an oil lease. In the company's first year, it lost $708,000. By the second year, its stock was worthless. When the company defaulted on its SBA loan, Denver's congresswoman Pat Schroeder called for an investigation, but the SBA declined to press the case. In April 1991, Neil resigned as president of the company.

He said the negative publicity had become unbearable. He unlisted his phone and stayed inside his five-bedroom house on the fourth tee of Glenmoor Country Club. "It just exploded into a public nightmare for me," he said later. "I read all the newspaper stories. I worried about what the next leak was going to be. I worried about the impact on Dad and my role in this thing. I gained a little weight. I didn't eat well."

The fancy invitations soon fell off as Denver society jettisoned the young Bushes from the A-list. Barbara Bush flew in to co-host a fund-raising luncheon with Sharon Bush at the home of Bill Daniels, president of TransMedia, a cable-television conglomerate. More than $300,000 was raised for George H.W.'s 1988 campaign, but even the First Lady's cachet did not help her son and daughter-in-law.

The final indignity came when Neil was unceremoniously dumped from the Colorado Tennis Association's Clyde Rogers Memorial Day Open. After Neil and his tennis partner had trounced their opponents in a doubles match, an official protest was lodged, accusing Neil of playing in a bracket below his ability in order to win. Neil said he had not realized he was registered to play a team rated a full point below his U.S. Tennis Association rating of 5.5 (on a 10-point scale). "The bottom line is that it's the player's responsibility," said the organizer, Harold Aarons. "He blew it as far as that goes."

Neil and Sharon decided they had to leave town. Later Neil said, "We were evicted." They put their house, which had been registered in Sharon's name to protect their one and only asset, on the market and made plans to move to Houston, where the Bush name was still socially acceptable. At a going-away party hosted by the Republican National Committeeman Jim Nicholson, Neil apologized for any embarrassment he might have caused the party. He said he realized he'd been in the eye of the storm, and he regretted it. But, he added, he did not feel he had done anything wrong. Nicholson, who would be appointed Ambassador to the Vatican by Neil's brother, agreed.

Democrats, of course, disagreed. At their 2000 national convention Colorado's party chairman introduced his state on national television by announcing, "Colorado is the former home of Neil Bush, the brother of George W. Bush, who fled our state after plundering the hard-earned savings of working families in the Savings and Loan scandal."

Despite his "ethical disability" and the cease-and-desist order, Neil found work through his father's friend Bill Daniels. In 1990 Daniels wrote to the President, asking him to oppose regulation in the cable industry, which the White House subsequently did. A few months later Daniels hired Neil as the director of finance for TransMedia in Houston at sixty thousand dollars a year. Neil had no experience in communications, but Daniels said he "thought Neil deserved a second chance."

Like Fredo in *The Godfather*, Neil is the Bushes' bungling son— weak, superficially sweet, and forever dependent on the family's connections. Those connections paid huge dividends in Houston as his father's friends hired Neil for various "consulting" contracts. After he traveled to Argentina in June 1989 and played tennis with President-elect Carlos Menem, Neil was hired as a consultant by Plains Resources to prepare a bid to buy oil reserves in Argentina. In Beijing in December 2001, Neil dined with Chinese President Jiang Zemin and was hired in the mid-1990s by Thailand's Charoen Pokphand Group to find a U.S. partner for a shopping mall in Shanghai. When the Chinese President's son, Jiang Mianheng, founded a company with Winston Wong, the two men gave Neil a consulting contract in 2002 with Grace Semiconductor that paid him $2 million worth of Grace preferred stock over five years in $400,000 increments. In addition, Neil was put on the board of directors of Grace Semiconductor and paid $10,000 per meeting. Wong told the *Financial Times* that for these munificent fees "Mr. Bush supplied . . . useful guidance about the U.S. economy." Crest Investment Corporation in Houston hired Neil as a $60,000-a-year consultant and made him co-chairman. Neil said he worked only three to four hours a week and described his services as "answering phone calls when Jamail Daniel, the other co-chairman, called and asked for advice."

By this time Neil's father was traveling in a stratosphere of wealth where the air was so thin that only billionaires could breathe. The elder Bush counted among his friends some of the wealthiest men in the world, like Prince Bandar of the Saudi royal family, so close to the Bushes they call him "Bandar Bush"; the Hinduja brothers, who own Gulf Oil, and are among the ten wealthiest people in Britain; the Bass brothers of Texas, whose combined net worth is $8.8 billion; Ali al-Sabah of the ruling family of Kuwait; and Paul Desmarais, the ninth-richest person in Canada.

These financiers—all global-conglomerate giants—were only too happy to help George's dunderheaded son, knowing that in doing so they earned the Bush family's gratitude. A favor done is a favor owed.

Neil had no qualms about approaching any of them for funding when he started an Internet-based software firm called Ignite! to provide an educational tool to students. Instead of books, Neil's company provided cartoons on computers with hip-hop music, which he claimed was the best way to teach children, especially those with dyslexia, attention deficit disorder, and attention deficit/hyperactivity disorder.

His software on early American history contained a jingle to describe the cotton gin to students with learning disabilities:

Cotton was king
Cotton so easy to grow
It was a cash crop, Oh,
Yeah! And it led to a boom in the Southern eee-kon-oh-meee!

Most educators disagreed with Neil's theory that students have different types of intelligences and that traditional schooling (reading, writing, and memorizing) does not work for everyone. But Neil, who suffered from dyslexia, insisted that he had developed an educational tool that helped children with learning disabilities.

Despite resistance from school administrators and criticism from *The Wall Street Journal* and *The Washington Post*, he raised more than $23 million from investors, including his parents, who gave $500,000; Winston Wong of Grace Semiconductor; Hushang Ansary, a former Iranian Ambassador to the United States, a Houston businessman, and a large GOP donor; Canada's Paul Desmarais; and Mohammed Al Sabah of the Ultra Horizon Company in Kuwait.

Neil got a rush of Arab investors after traveling to Jidda, Saudi Arabia, and delivering a speech in which he said that the Arabs' problem in the United States is that their lobby and public-relations machine is not as strong as the Israelis'. In saying that, he fed directly into an article of faith held in the Arab world and by anti-Semites the world over—that America's Middle East policy is driven by the Jewish lobby rather than national interest. Neil simply had repeated the sentiments of his father, who was never perceived as pro-Israel. As President, Bush had complained in a White House press conference about the strength of the Jewish lobby on Capitol Hill. He reminded his critics that the United States gave "Israel the equivalent of $1,000 for every Israeli citizen," a remark that detractors saw as an allusion to the stereotype of Jews as greedy and moneygrubbing. Echoing the President's comments about the Jewish lobby was his Secretary of State James A. Baker, who said, "Fuck the Jews. They don't vote for us anyway."

As his father's son, Neil received red-carpet treatment throughout the Arab world, first in the United Arab Emirates, where he visited the Dubai crown prince, and then in Egypt, where he and his family were entertained by Hamza El Khouli, a close associate of Egyptian President Hosni Mubarak and chairman of the First Arabian Development and Investment Company. Neil returned home with lucrative commitments for Ignite! from Saudi Arabia, Egypt, and the UAE.

Oil was always the family's first priority in the Middle East, not the Arab-Israeli conflict. As George W. Bush said when he was running for Congress: "There's no such thing as being too closely aligned to the oil business in West Texas."

After losing that congressional race in 1978, George W. settled in

Midland and with the rest of his college trust fund (fifteen thousand dollars) started Arbusto (Spanish for "bush"). Pronounced "ar-boo-stow," the company became the first of his failing oil ventures, soon to be pronounced "ar-BUST-oh." George sold 5 percent of his company for fifty thousand dollars to James R. Bath, his buddy from the National Guard, who represented Sheik Khalid bin Mahfouz, the banker for the Saudi Arabian royal family. By always using other people's money, Junior, as W. was called then, managed in ten years to become a millionaire. He started exactly as his father did—by turning to his rich uncle to find wealthy people who were willing to put money into his company and rely on his expertise to strike oil. When W. failed, his investors simply took their investments as tax write-offs, which, in all likelihood, is what they expected to do from the outset.

"I introduced him to clients," said W.'s uncle Jonathan Bush. "I marketed his firm. I think I was probably pretty helpful. It didn't hurt him in the fact that his father had been in the oil business, so he knew a lot of the players. At the time there were big tax advantages in drilling oil wells. In those days, it behooved you to drill. You didn't have to do terribly well in order to do well because you got so many write-offs. So it was an attractive way to invest money and save taxes."

With his list of wealthy clients, Jonathan became for his nephew what Uncle Herbie had been for George H.W.: a financial honeypot. Junior's first investors included his grandmother Dorothy Bush, $25,000; Dorothy's sister-in-law Grace (Mrs. Louis) Walker, $25,000; Dorothy's brother James W. Walker, $25,000; Gerry Bemiss (childhood friend of the elder George and godfather to Marvin Bush), $80,000; George L. Ball (chairman of E. F. Hutton and the boss of Scott Pierce, Barbara's brother), $300,000; financier Lewis Lehrman, $47,500; Celanese CEO John Macomber and William Draper III (both Yale 1950), $172,550.

George set up shop in a cramped three-room office in Midland with his business partner and a secretary. He paid himself a salary of seventy-five thousand dollars a year, and for the next five years he chased what he called "The Liberator," the big oil-spurting gusher that would set him free for life—the dream of every oilman. It never came near him, but George never tired of the hustle. He thrived on chasing the money, meeting investors, and charming them. During that period his uncle corralled ninety-eight people who poured $2,525,000 into Arbusto. Most were eventually forced to write off their investments, and some took exception to the cavalier way the Bushes did business.

"My husband and I were two of the investors that got taken for a ride," said Ina Schnell, a wealthy art patron from Sarasota, Florida. "We invested because Edward, my late husband, went to Yale with Johnny Bush. We lost our money and not happily . . . Edward almost sued Johnny over it . . . Johnny was a little too casual about the loss. The Bushes are . . . well . . . real hustlers is about the nicest way to put it."

The Schnells did not know the joke around Midland: George Bush couldn't find a quart of oil at the 7-Eleven store.

"The first well I ever drilled in which I had a participatory interest was dry," George recalled. "And I'll never forget the feeling. Kind of, 'Oops. This is not quite as easy as we all thought it was going to be.' "

A hard worker, even during his hard-drinking days, George's career is marked by a slash of carelessness. He was careless with other people's money, careless about rules, careless about using the Bush name, and careless with the truth. He, like his brothers, was careless in the way that F. Scott Fitzgerald defined the term in *The Great Gatsby*: "They were careless people . . . they smashed up things and creatures and then retreated back into their money or their vast carelessness, or whatever it was that kept them together, and let other people clean up the mess they had made."

After five years of dry holes and middling wells, George was in trouble. He decided to rename his company to showcase the family name so that he could attract more people to limited partnerships. He wanted to go public, expand his company, and raise $6 million. Hence, Arbusto became Bush Exploration Company, but George failed miserably. He raised only $1.3 million. Worse, he drilled dry holes, and his investors lost 75 percent of their money.

"I really realized that I had made somewhat of a strategic error," he admitted later.

"I was called in to handle the name change," recalled the Midland attorney Robert K. Whitt, "and I jumped at the chance. I wanted to get to know George better. That was in May 1982. He was already throwing around that vice presidential stuff. To really impress us, he'd say: 'When

Dad and the President . . .' or 'When the Vice President and Reagan get together . . .' That was pretty heady stuff in a little Texas town of seventy thousand people.

"After I did the name change for George, he called and asked me to prepare an agreement to sell 10 percent of his company for $1 million to Philip A. Uzielli . . . 'Keep it bland,' he said. 'Phil will bring in the money.' I've never done a deal like that . . . The deal smelled; it really smelled, but it wasn't illegal. Still, I couldn't figure out why someone would spend $1 million to buy 10 percent of a company that was worth only $382,386. In other words, Uzielli paid $1 million for assets that were worth $38,237.

"I became even more suspicious when Uzielli walked in, slid a blank check across the table for $1 million, and said, 'Where do I sign?' He had no attorney. He asked no questions. He requested no information. So strange for a $1 million transaction, even in the high-flying oil and gas business.

" 'Don't you want to read the agreement?' I asked.

" 'It's not my money,' he said. 'I'm not concerned.'

"The stock was issued in the name of a Panamanian corporation named Executive Resources, of which Uzielli was chairman and CEO . . . George didn't want me to include the wording in the legal papers that stated the corporation was organized under the laws of Panama and the sale was consummated with a cash purchase price of $1 million, but I had to."

George, who gave everyone a nickname, called his lawyer "Dim wit." When Robert Whitt, then with the law firm of Cotton, Bledsoe, Tighe, and Dawson, asked George why he was doing business with a Panamanian corporation, he replied: "Dumb question, Dim wit."

Philip A. Uzielli was Jim Baker's best friend at Princeton. He went into business with George L. Ohrstrom of Middleburg, Virginia, who had known the Bush family in Connecticut and went to the Greenwich Country Day School with George Herbert Walker Bush. Earlier the Ohrstroms had invested fifty thousand dollars in Arbusto. Uzielli, who became one of three directors of Bush Exploration, told *The Dallas Morning News* that he had met George in 1979, "after his father was director of the C.I.A." George claimed he did not meet Uzielli until he stepped forward in 1982 with his $1 million. He also claimed he knew nothing of Uzielli's Princeton friendship with Jim Baker.

"Very hard to believe ole George on that," said Whitt, "but I don't know why he would lie. It's as much a mystery to me as why Uzielli would invest a million dollars in a company with no earnings potential, no profit, and very little value. And why a Panamanian partner, I don't know. Some people might use a Panamanian corporation as a way to cover drug money and drug dealers . . . The whole transaction was very odd. No one else in Midland had a Panamanian corporation, but then George was the only one whose father was a former CIA chief serving as Vice President of the United States. That made George such a big deal in Midland that everyone wanted to get close to him. Our law firm even halved his bills." Whitt pointed to a large black leather-bound book. "That represents $50,000–$100,000 worth of work, but George was only billed for half the time. The firm wanted to do business with him, so they kept their bills lower for him than anyone else."

During this time George and Laura had been trying mightily to get pregnant. When her doctor had said that it was unlikely she would be able to conceive, Laura plunged into depression. She became excessively worried because during her childhood her mother had miscarried several times and given birth to a baby who had died in infancy. Laura grew up as an only child and had absorbed her parents' pain. She also spent her childhood always trying to please them to make up for their loss. Now, at the age of thirty-four, she was so unhappy about not being able to get pregnant that she avoided walking down the baby aisle of the supermarket. She also smoked two packs of cigarettes a day, as did George, who half-kiddingly offered his pregnant secretary, Kim Dyches, a hundred dollars if only she would name her son for him. She declined. Finally Laura consulted a fertility specialist in Dallas, and in 1981 she became pregnant with twins.

From the beginning her pregnancy was difficult; in her third trimester she developed toxemia, a malady that can lead to dangerously high blood pressure and edema, sometimes producing life-threatening seizures that require induced labor or a Caesarean delivery. In November 1981, Laura was moved from Midland to Dallas and admitted to Baylor Hospital seven weeks before her due date. She was kept in stirrups so as not to induce early labor, but within two weeks the doctors said they had no choice but to perform a Caesarean and take the babies. Baylor officials called George in Midland and told him to be in Dallas by the next morning: "Your children will be born tomorrow, or your wife's kidneys will fail."

The twin girls were born on November 25, 1981, and George was in the delivery room. "I witnessed it all," he said. "It was beautiful." Photographers and reporters arrived at the hospital to record the birth of the Vice President's fourth and fifth grandchildren. They were named in honor of their grandmothers, Jenna Welch and Barbara Bush.

"A few months later I got into a big hassle with George over hiring an illegal alien, which everyone in Midland did then," said Robert Whitt. "We both were looking for a housekeeper and interviewed a woman named Consuela. We ended up getting her, and George was furious. He called and demanded that we give him and Laura the housekeeper. I told him she did not want to work for him. He was so mad he called my wife back, cussed and swore and chewed her out . . . She got scared and said maybe we should give Consuela up . . . because you couldn't afford to offend the Vice President's son . . . We didn't, because Consuela wouldn't go to the Bushes, but it was not a casual decision.

"George and Laura ran in a much faster and fancier crowd than we did—their friends were all hard-drinking and -drugging. That was part of the oil-business scene then," said Whitt. The lawyer acknowledged that the Bushes' social circle had easy access to "all sorts of recreational enhancements," drugs, which may have occasioned George's frequent all-nighters. Laura, according to one of her friends, spent many nights worrying when or even whether her husband would come home. She had no idea where he was or what he was doing.

"Even though George's business record was bad, and he never really struck oil," continued the lawyer, "he was still considered a success because he was great at raising money from his father's contacts. The Bush name was his gusher. Right after his dad became Vice President, George was made president of the United Way . . . He was put on the board of the United Bank of Midland . . . He ruled Midland."

Taking advantage of his position on the bank board, George borrowed $372,000 for his company, plus $245,000 to buy a house. His equity was his failing oil company and his golden name. Within two years Bush Exploration was broke, but George found a big-money bailout in Spectrum 7, a Cincinnati-based oil company owned by William DeWitt and Mercer Reynolds III.

"The Bush name was definitely the drawing card on that one," said the Midland geologist Paul Rea, who introduced the principals over lunch. "DeWitt had gone to Yale [1963] and Harvard Business School and I thought it would be a good fit with George. They had mutual friends from the Ivy League."

DeWitt did not want Bush Exploration Company, but he needed a business manager for his Texas company, so he proposed a merger that would make Paul Rea president and George chairman and CEO of Spectrum 7. George was paid $75,000 a year in salary, plus $120,000 in consulting fees and 1.1 million shares of stock (worth $530,000), which constituted 16.3 percent of the company.

The merger was completed on February 29, 1984, just as the high prices of oil began to collapse. The next year the rallying cry within the industry was "Stay alive in '85." Spectrum 7 lost $1.6 million. George tried to recoup some of his losses by partnering with Enron Oil and Gas on two projects. Then the bottom dropped out—world oil prices fell from forty dollars a barrel in 1980 to ten dollars a barrel in 1986. Spectrum 7 fell $3.1 million into debt.

The Vice President of the United States was sputtering. "I think it is essential that we talk about stability [in oil prices] and that we not just have a continuing free fall," he said. During a visit to Arab oil-producing nations, Bush asserted that low oil prices represented a threat to national security. Some editorial writers suggested the Vice President was more concerned about the threat to his big political contributors in Texas as well as his two sons in the gas and oil business.

"It's very slow out here—times are tough," Junior told *The New York Times*. "We are using cash to survive." The paper reported there was nothing of the flashy Texas oilman in young George W. He dressed like a Yalie and lived in a modest one-story brick house worth about $200,000. "I'm all name and no money," he said.

Bush and Rea started scrambling. They wanted to merge Spectrum 7 with a bigger company in hopes of surviving the oil crisis, but they had no profits, and the bank was threatening to foreclose. Then they found Harken Energy, a Dallas-based company that was aggressively taking over troubled oil firms.

"One of the reasons Harken was interested was George's name," said Paul Rea. "They wanted to get George on their board."

Harken offered $2 million in stock in exchange for Spectrum 7, even though it was deep into the red. George was personally given stock worth $500,000. He became a director of Harken and was paid an annual consulting fee of $80,000. After his father became President, the fee was raised to $120,000.

The billionaire George Soros also became a stockholder when Harken bought one of his smaller companies. He was not on the board of directors, and he sold his Harken stock in 1989, but he had observed the purchase of Spectrum 7. "We were buying political influence. That was it."

"George was very useful to Harken," said a board member. "He could have been more so if he had had funds, but as far as contacts were concerned, he was terrific . . . It seemed like George . . . knew everybody in the U.S. who was worth knowing."

Even after George moved to Washington, D.C., to help supervise his father's campaign for President in 1987, Harken continued to pay him.

"Hell, that's why he's on the damn board," said a Harken insider. "You say, 'By the way, the President's son sits on our board.' You use that. There's nothing wrong with that."

The presidential connection struck gold when Harken was chosen for an exclusive offshore drilling contract by Bahrain. The tiny oil-rich country, described by *Time* as "unabashed in its desire to foster a warm relationship with the U.S.," chose Harken to drill three exploratory wells at a cost of about $50 million. The project was too big for Harken to handle, so the company partnered with the Bass brothers of Houston, big Republican contributors and close friends of the Bush family.

The founder of Harken, who had sold the company, said George W. Bush was worth every dollar the new owners were paying him. "It's obvious why they kept him," said Phil Kendrick. "Just the fact that he's there gives them credibility. He's worth $120,000 a year to them just for that."

CHAPTER TWENTY-ONE

The Vice President had been defanged. Recovering from what he called "all the Doonesbury dung" of the reelection, he wanted to be a nice guy again. So he called Geraldine Ferraro and invited her to lunch. As the winner, he could afford to be generous. Besides, he did not want a popular woman for an enemy. "George needs to have everyone like him," said his cousin Ray Walker, a psychiatrist. "Otherwise, he's psychically uncomfortable."

Bush's overture to Ferraro was graciously accepted, and lunch was prepared by his Filipino chef, who kept a calendar of nude women on the wall of the Vice President's kitchenette. "We ate in the Executive Office Building," recalled Ferraro years later. "I came with Bob Barnett, the Washington attorney who had prepared me for the debate by playing the part of Bush, and Bush was there with Rep. Lynn Martin [Rep.-IL], who prepped him by playing me. When we told George that Bob had dressed like him for debate practice right down to the pinstripes and preppy watchband, he whipped off one of his striped cloth multicolored watchbands from Brooks Brothers and gave it to Bob as a souvenir.

"It wasn't an easy lunch, sitting there with the guy who had trounced me. But we all did our best and got through it. I do remember something quite bizarre . . . I had mentioned having a house in St. Croix and how I hated changing planes in Puerto Rico because my luggage always got lost. Bush said, 'Oh, I just love lost-luggage jokes.' We sort of looked at him. He said, 'I really do. I just love lost-luggage jokes.' He didn't explain and he didn't tell a lost-luggage joke. It was such a strange thing to say, but maybe lost-luggage jokes are some kind of high WASP humor I don't understand. After lunch Bush pulled open the drawer of his desk to show me where all the vice presidents had carved their initials, and then we had our pictures taken. Bush inscribed mine: 'Let's debate. No, let's be friends. You have a great fan here. George Bush.' "

Geraldine Ferraro was not the only one perplexed by the Vice President's style. President Reagan's White House photographer, Michael Evans, recalled an instance during a Washington blizzard when photographers were waiting to take Reagan's picture walking back to the family quarters. "Serfs had to be called in to salt down the walkway, and we were in the Oval Office waiting for that to happen," Evans said. "The President, the Vice President, Chief of Staff Jim Baker, Michael Deaver, and myself. George started reminiscing about the big blizzard of his childhood. He told a story about the snow falling so hard that his chauffeur, Alec, who was driving him to Greenwich Country Day School, piled off into a snowdrift.

"Poor guy was so out of touch he had no idea of how he sounded to the rest of us who didn't grow up being driven to grade school by the family chauffeur. The looks exchanged between Deaver and Baker were priceless. Both raised their eyes to heaven as if to say, 'Is this guy for real?' In fact, Mike Deaver said afterward, 'With all due respect, Mr. Vice President, I wouldn't tell that story in your next speech.' We all laughed. Heh. Heh. Heh."

George's invitation to Geraldine Ferraro was just a warm-up to the full blasts of ingratiation he would unleash as he revved up for the 1988 presidential race. This was his political currency: being a nice guy, coming from a good family, always being gracious and supportive—as long as victory was already assured. So from his victorious vantage point, George Herbert Walker Bush during the next three years would splash buckets of bonhomie in every direction, but mostly to the far right. Proclaiming himself "born again," he would bootlick evangelicals like Jerry Falwell and Jimmy Swaggart and Jim Bakker, whom he referred to behind their backs as "temple burners." He would toady up to conservatives and shamelessly court right-wingers like Roy Cohn, who told his biographer before he died: "I have to say that Bush has been romancing me for years. He knew I was in with the conservatives, and he wanted my support for '88." George even went on bended knee to extol the memory of William Loeb, the bombastic publisher of New Hampshire's *Manchester Union Leader* who had pilloried him as "a spoon-fed little rich kid" and warned readers: "Republicans should flee the candidacy of George Bush as if it were the Black Plague."

When her brother attended a testimonial dinner in honor of Loeb, Nan Bush Ellis nearly retched. George praised his enemy as "a man of fierce and outspoken loyalty to his friends, his country and his political beliefs," and then praised his widow, Nackey Scripps Loeb, as "his spirited and charming wife who is carrying on his work with tremendous energy." The spirited widow definitely carried on what her husband had started: she vilified George at every turn and endorsed his opponent Pierre "Pete" du Pont for President in 1988.

"I hassled George when he spoke at the Loeb dinner," Nan Bush Ellis admitted. "And, oh, I was so self-righteous here in my beautiful ivory house, and I called up and . . . I said I don't know how he could do this."

What his sister did not understand was that there was almost nothing that her brother would not do to become President of the United States. He devoted the second term of his vice presidency to that pursuit. He began by reshuffling his staff, admitting that for the first four years he had purposely maintained "a weak roster" so as not to compete with or threaten the President's staff. Now there was a fight brewing, so the nice, friendly, supportive Vice President needed hard-nosed professionals who understood political hardball and would do the dirty work needed to make him Ronald Reagan's heir. The succession would not be easy, however, because the King was reluctant to relinquish his crown. When Reagan was asked in February 1985 about endorsing his Vice President for the 1988 nomination, he hedged. "I'll be like Scarlett O'Hara," he said. "I'll think about it tomorrow." Later, at a White House correspondents dinner, he joked, "George Bush has been a wonderful Vice President, but no one is perfect."

Even on July 13, 1985, when the seventy-four-year-old President had to be anesthetized to remove a malignant tumor from his lower intestine, he resisted turning over the powers of the presidency to his Vice President. It was the first time section 3 of the Twenty-fifth Amendment had been invoked. George was in Kennebunkport at the time but flew to Washington when the President entered the hospital. Bush called three friends to join him for tennis at the Vice President's mansion. During the game he lunged for an overhead shot, lost his balance, fell back, smashed his head on the concrete, and knocked himself unconscious. His physician hurried to his side and after a few minutes got him to his feet. He spent the rest of the afternoon resting. George's press secretary, Marlin Fitzwater, who had accompanied him to Washington, withheld the information from the press. It was many years before anyone learned that for an unspecified period of time, the President and the Vice President of the United States had been simultaneously incapacitated.

The next day Fitzwater was asked what the seven hours of the Bush administration had been like. He quipped: "I think I missed it."

Doonesbury immortalized the 474 minutes with a strip that featured the Vice President being interviewed: "How will history judge the Bush hours?"

"I think history will be very high on them, Roland. Remember, not a single country fell to the communists during my watch."

The columnist George Will lamented that the Twenty-fifth Amendment had not transferred power to the First Lady instead of the Vice President, because, as he wrote, the country would have seen how formidable a person in a size-four dress can be. "In George Bush's 8 hours as acting president the deficit increased $200 million. Nancy would never have allowed that."

When President and Mrs. Reagan flew to Honolulu in April 1985, George summoned his family and all his capos and consiglieri to Camp David to discuss the 1988 campaign. "This is my best shot," said the Vice President, "but I am not going to do it if we don't have 100 percent behind me . . . I cannot do this without your support and feeling that you are all with me, because it is going to be a hard thing to do."

George and Barbara, their five children, George's three brothers— Prescott, Jonathan, and Bucky—and his sister, Nancy, sat on one side of a long wooden table in the rustic presidential lodge. Across from them perched the new hard-nosed professionals: Lee Atwater, the campaign manager and a political consultant with Black, Manafort, Stone, and Atwater; Marlin Fitzwater, the VP's press secretary; Bob Teeter, the VP's pollster; Craig Fuller, the VP's new chief of staff.

"They were firing off questions about everything: how we would run the campaign, our loyalty to George Bush, just everything," recalled Marlin Fitzwater. "It struck me then and there that the Bushes were very dif-

ferent from the Kennedys in that they would never have their Ted Soren-
son [speechwriter]. No one outside the family would enter the inner circle."

Two months before that April summit, George Bush had made it
clear that he intended to use his family as a campaign hallmark. He wrote
to his finance chairman, Robert Mosbacher, who was organizing a political action committee for Bush known as Fund for America's Future:

> George and Jeb both want to help on the PAC. George feels that he
> can bring in a lot of young business people from the West coast . . .
> Jeb, as you know, is the County Chairman for the Republican
> Party in Dade County, Florida.
>   . . . I have not talked to Neil in Colorado, Marvin here in
> Washington, or Doro LeBlond in Connecticut. Maybe it would
> make sense to have all 4 boys and Doro on the masthead in order
> to get the Bush name identified with the PAC.

Most participants at the Camp David meeting recalled the fierce in-
terchange between the Vice President's two elder sons and Lee Atwater,
the southern-fried political operative who had worked for the arch segregationist Strom Thurmond. As campaign manager, Atwater ladled out the
facts of political life for the family and what they had to do to drape Reagan's mantle around George's neck. They knew the first priority was raising millions. And Atwater hammered home the importance of Super
Tuesday, the new regional primary in seventeen states—the two biggest
being Florida and Texas—that had been set for March 8, 1988.

"I'm sure you boys will get those wired right for us," Atwater said, nod-
ding toward Jeb and George junior.

George senior found Atwater a little "too brash" for his liking, but
brash as the motormouth was, the family agreed he knew his stuff and
would probably do anything to win. He and his partners had been described in *Esquire* as "outlaws who aren't afraid to bloody their chaps." Jeb
and George W. raised the only reservation: they questioned Atwater's loy-
alties, because they knew his partners would be working for Jack Kemp
and Bob Dole, two of the Vice President's opponents for the GOP nomination.

"How do we know we can trust you?" asked George W.

"What he means is, if someone throws a grenade at our dad, we expect you to jump on it," said Jeb.

"If you're so worried about my loyalty, then why don't one of you come in the office and watch me, and the first time I'm disloyal see to it that I get run off?"

Eventually young George would accept the challenge and move his family to Washington in the spring of 1987. Until then, Ron Kauffman, head of Bush's political action committee, was delegated to ride herd on the hyperkinetic campaign manager.

During the reshaping of the Vice President's staff, everyone watched to see how the reshuffling of top personnel might affect Jennifer Fitzgerald, then the Vice President's executive assistant. Bush had deep-sixed Admiral Daniel J. Murphy as chief of staff and reassigned Pete Teeley to the job of campaign press secretary, but Jennifer was untouchable. When she announced she wanted to transfer from the VP's office in the Old Executive Office Building to the VP's office in the U.S. Capitol, everyone on staff sighed with relief.

"She was a powerful woman in that she could influence the Vice President more than anyone else," recalled a woman on the Vice President's staff, "but she was miserable for morale. She was insecure as far as her intellectual capacity because she did not have a college education. One of the reasons she wanted to transfer was to assert she had substantive knowledge and was not just a secretary/scheduler. In effect that's really all the Veep's congressional office did, but everyone wanted her out of the office, so they conspired to flatter her into thinking she'd be taken much more seriously if she transferred to the Hill. We all encouraged her in that fantasy and it worked . . . But it did not diminish her influence over the Vice President. It only got her out of our hair."

Jennifer became the Vice President's chief lobbyist and contact on Capitol Hill, where she maintained an office with two secretaries. She also kept her access to the VP's office in the West Wing of the White House. She participated in all of Bush's scheduling meetings, oversaw all his arrangements for foreign travel, and accompanied him on trips when he traveled without his wife.

"Barbara couldn't abide Jennifer," said Susan King, the former television journalist who covered the Vice President. "That was clear to everyone during the campaign, even members of the press."

The relationship between the Vice President and his chief lobbyist was accepted by his staff as a fact of life. "I remember talking to Larry Branscum, Bush's Army intelligence officer, when I joined the staff of Vice President Gore," said Anne Woolston. " 'Larry, this stuff about George Bush and Jennifer Fitzgerald. Is it true? That they were having an affair?' Larry said, 'I just know when they traveled we always had to put them in the same corridor.' That practically confirmed it for me," said Woolston, "because when I worked for Gore, staff was never booked on the same floor with the Vice President. Never."

Jennifer catered solely to the boss. "Everyone on staff had run-ins with her, even Marlin, who was very careful around her," said one of Craig Fuller's assistants. "You cannot overestimate her influence on Bush. He went whenever she called. If she wanted him to meet with a senator or a congressman, we had to change his schedule to do it. Those were his orders . . . We all were aware of their relationship—whatever it was. The younger women on staff just couldn't fathom someone who looked as weirdly out of style as Jennifer sleeping with the Vice President. The men couldn't figure it either, but there is no denying the connection between them. I can't explain it, other than to say that Jennifer was a doter. She made George feel that he was God's gift to mankind. She'd bat her eyes and gush all over him. She'd poof her hair, put on lipstick, and spray perfume every time she walked into his office in her high stiletto heels. She was a courtesan, but not that gifted. Still, she was probably a treat from Bar, who is no gusher. Bar would just as soon say, 'George, cut the crap' as 'open the door.' Jennifer was an ego trip for him. She made him feel good about himself. Only reason to think that there might have been something to the alleged affair—and, yes, we all talked about it at one time or other—was that after he became President, Jennifer was shipped off to the State Department so there wouldn't be any questions regarding their relationship. I also think Barbara did not want her in the White House. Whatever, there was a definite decision made that Jennifer would be a target so she had to be moved away from Bush. Jim Baker was the only one who could counterbalance her. So they put her under him because she couldn't do him in with Bush . . . Look what happened to

Rich Bond when he tried to get rid of Jennifer. Bush let him go and kept her . . .

"She catered to the vain and petty side of George Bush in ways that the rest of us would not have done. For example, he wanted his office on the Hill to be redecorated, and so Jennifer brought him decorator boards with color schemes and styles and swatches. I remember he wanted blue draperies and threw a tantrum when the draperies weren't the right shade of blue. I was stunned that the Vice President of the United States was focusing on something so small and incidental, but I guess that's all he really had to do . . . By then he had become so intellectually lazy that he would not spend any time reading the briefs prepared for him. I think he had been a bureaucrat for so long that he simply relied on people to tell him what he needed to know. He did not think for himself. He was verbally inarticulate and could not enunciate a clear concept or formulate ideas. Perhaps he had spent too long in government getting talked to and had lost his ability to think and abstract for himself."

Senate Minority Leader Robert Dole made the same discovery. After meeting with George to discuss political issues, Dole returned to his office fuming. "I couldn't talk to him," Dole said. "He doesn't know enough about the issues to even talk about them. Where has he been for seven years?"

Caring only about becoming President, the Vice President took direction from his new campaign advisers—the hardheads—who polled everything in an effort to make him appear strong and presidential. His pollster pointed out that he needed "shoring up" among southerners, evangelicals, and Jews, three constituencies George had previously ignored. Now he agreed to make a concerted outreach. Since he was scheduled to go to the Middle East in July 1986, he decided to take a film crew for campaign footage of himself in Israel.

The purpose of his stopping in Jerusalem was to meet with Amiram Nir, Israel's deputy on counterterrorism, who was negotiating between the Americans and the Iranians over hostages. Arranged by Oliver North, George's breakfast meeting in the King David Hotel was described first as a briefing on counterterrorism and later as a general review of proposals for rescuing hostages, omitting, of course, any mention of an exchange of arms.

Months later documentary evidence revealed that the meeting was an arms-for-hostages deal. From the statements of Amiram Nir and Craig Fuller, Bush's chief of staff, who accompanied him to the meeting and took notes, the Vice President was told that if the Iranians received weapons, they would arrange the release of two hostages—not all seven of the American hostages being held in 1986, just two. Nir said there was "no real choice" other than to change the all-or-nothing policy of the United States and deliver the arms in hopes of getting the hostages out one at a time. Iran released Father Martin Jenco to encourage the United States to change its policy. The policy was changed, and the weapons were transferred. In November 1986 one more hostage was released: David Jacobsen.

The Vice President later claimed in interviews that he did not know the breakfast meeting's purpose. "The scope of the operation was not clear to me," he said. Then he amended his statement and admitted there was some discussion of arms sales but only as a means to "reach out to moderate elements" in Iran. Within the next year he would practically strangle himself in a cat's cradle of evasions, omissions, and equivocations, repeating over and over, "I was out of the loop . . . out of the loop."

"I still shudder when I think of Bush's trip to Israel," said Roberta Hornig Draper, whose husband was the U.S. Consul General in Jerusalem. "Bush was there to get pictures of himself for the presidential campaign. That was his only purpose as far as I could see. I was with Mrs. [Teddy] Kollek, the wife of the mayor of Jerusalem, and we accompanied the Bushes to the Wailing Wall, where Mrs. Kollek was literally knocked over by all the cameramen crowding in to photograph Bush. He was disgusting to cause such a scene at a holy place. It was so unnecessary. So disrespectful. My husband and I apologized to the Ambassador and his wife and to Mayor Kollek and his wife for the rude behavior of our country's Vice President and his entourage.

"As bad as George Bush was on that trip, Barbara was worse. She was a total bitch. So mean to her staff that it took my breath away. Really nasty, and all because she had dressed inappropriately for visiting the Holocaust Museum. She had worn a blue flowered cotton housedress and open-toed sandals. I couldn't believe it. Here she was the wife of the Vice President of the United States, for God's sakes, and she looked like she was going to a Sears Roebuck picnic. She'd been in public life long enough to know how to dress with decorum, but I guess she was so accustomed to flopping around in tennis shoes and muumuus that she no longer made the effort unless she was forced to . . .

"She barked at me when I showed up in a black suit, pearls, and heels. 'Why are you dressed like that?' she snapped. I told her: I always dress like this when we go to the Holocaust Museum. She was obviously embarrassed. She screamed at her staff and demanded to know why they had not told her how to dress. She sent them to her hotel to get her another outfit."

At the age of sixty-one, Barbara Bush was supremely confident about most things, but, according to those who worked for the Vice President, her one area of vulnerability was her appearance. "Unfortunately, she had no taste in clothes and she was fat," said an assistant. "So every effort was made to make sure there were fewer comparisons between her and Mrs. Reagan so that Bar would not look bad . . . She was always talking about her weight, and she was always on a diet. She said she wished she was smaller, but then she'd eat ten meals. If you tried to compliment her, she came at you like a sledgehammer. For example, at a reception you might say, 'Gee, Mrs. Bush, that's a lovely dress.' The response: 'You don't need to suck up to me. I'm a fat old woman and I look awful and you know it.'

"I don't want to make Mrs. Bush sound like a total harridan, because she can be solicitous and kind and generous, but then in a schizophrenic turn she can lash out and be mean. It's so strange and sudden that you start to wonder if the kind side is just a front. You never know what might provoke the other side—the mean judgmental side. You just know that you don't want to trigger that tiger in her because it's awful.

"I remember someone going through a receiving line with Mrs. Bush and getting the third degree. Barbara challenged her on why she hadn't had any children. 'You're married, right? Don't you want children? Why are you waiting? How many children do you want? What do you mean you don't know? When are you going to get started?' She was very judgmental in that sense. She's secure only with women who have had a lot of children like her. More comfortable with women who are mothers rather than strong professional women."

At a time when half of all American women worked outside the home, Barbara believed they should be inside the home taking care of children. She was skeptical of women who continued to work after having babies.

"She didn't imply that I shouldn't do it," said her chief of staff, Susan Porter Rose, a mother of one. "But . . . women are home with their babies. Period. And that's how you're a mother. And you're not a good mother if you don't do that. But I think our little office and our little staff that had three who were mothers, I think seeing that work was enlightening for her."

The Reagan administration had been accused of insensitivity to the Holocaust when the President decided to visit the little cemetery in Bitburg, West Germany, that held the graves of forty-nine Nazi storm troopers. His decision angered Jewish groups in the United States, Europe, and the Soviet Union, all of whom held public demonstrations. Elie Wiesel, who grew up in the death camps and lost his parents in Auschwitz, pleaded with the President on national television not to lend his presence to a German military cemetery. This provoked further outrage, including two resolutions in the House of Representatives beseeching Reagan not to visit Bitburg, coupled with a similar resolution signed by over half the Senate. The editorial opposition to Bitburg was overwhelming as newspapers throughout the country pleaded with the President to change his mind. Even his wife begged him, but Ronald Reagan would not budge.

He had given his word to West German Chancellor Helmut Kohl, and he said that if he reneged, he would look weak and indecisive. Former President Nixon backed him in his resolve, as did former Secretary of State Henry Kissinger and Vice President Bush, who sent him a secret note, which Reagan later published in his autobiography: "Mr. President, I was very proud of your stand. If I can help absorb some heat, send me into battle—It's not easy, but you are right!!!"

The outcry over Bitburg had convinced the Bush hardnoses that he needed to demonstrate his own sensitivity to the Holocaust. They scheduled a four-day trip to Poland in September 1987 with stops at the concentration camps of Birkenau and Auschwitz, where 4 million people had been exterminated. "There will be a lot of wreaths laid on this trip," said an aide. The trip was so blatantly political that the Polish press accused Bush of using their country to launch his presidential campaign.

He held a press conference in Warsaw, where he seemed to have been endorsed by Lech Walesa, leader of the outlawed union Solidarity. "The next question is, how many relatives does he have in Iowa," said the Vice President. His remark illustrated the obvious reason for his trip.

When he was asked why he had a camera crew accompanying him on what was supposed to be a diplomatic mission, Bush said: "To take good pictures of me in Poland."

At Birkenau he and Barbara stared in disbelief at the gas chambers and ovens that had incinerated ten thousand bodies a day.

"They are big on crematoriums," George said. "There's one over here, one over there."

He asked his guide, a Pole who had survived five years in the camps, if the victims brought by train had suspected their fate.

"Well, they could guess from the fact that the incapacitated were sent to one row, and the rest to another. But they were lied to. The sick were told they were going to the hospital, and the rest to work."

"They must have suspected," said Bush.

"They must have."

"Husbands and wives were separated here?"

"Yes."

"As long as you're alive, you hope," George said.

"That's exactly what I thought," said Barbara.

The Vice President placed a wreath at a stone memorial. The white ribbon crisscrossing the green leaves said: "Never again. The American People."

As George and Barbara toured a cancer ward at a children's hospital, his eyes filled with tears. The memory of losing their three-year-old daughter, Robin, to leukemia seemed as raw as the day she had died in 1953.

Later, as the Bushes approached the gate of Auschwitz, their photographers pushed everyone aside. "Get out of the shot," they yelled. The camera crew wanted a carefully composed picture of the Vice President and his wife, tastefully dressed in a black coat, black hose, and black heels. At the wall of death where twenty-five thousand people had been shot, George placed a wreath inscribed: "Their sacrifice will never be forgotten by the American people." After the Bushes returned to Washington, they produced a glossy campaign pamphlet of colored photos showing George praying at the Wailing Wall, talking with Shimon Peres, visiting a resettlement center for Ethiopian Jews, standing in the Old City overlooking the Temple Mount, and approaching Auschwitz with Barbara. The flyer mailed to Jewish voters in the United States was titled "George Bush. The one candidate who has proven his commitment to the Jewish people." The text quoted him as saying, "I oppose the creation of an independent Palestinian state; its establishment is inimical to the security interests of Israel, Jordan and the U.S."

The former Soviet dissident Natan Sharansky praised George for his efforts on behalf of Soviet Jewry, and the former Israeli Ambassador Meir Rosenne credited him with saving eight hundred Ethiopian Jews. The Ambassador had visited Bush at home to explain that when Ethiopia forbade the practice of Judaism and the teaching of Hebrew in the 1980s, the Israelis launched a secret effort known as Operation Moses to rescue Ethiopian Jews. Once the news of the rescue operation broke, the effort had to be shut down, leaving hundreds of Jews stranded. The Vice President went directly to the CIA and secretly arranged a rescue mission that saved those Ethiopians. The mission was never made public until George's campaign.

In his pamphlet to U.S. Jews, George claimed to be "the first major American political figure to condemn Louis Farrakhan's message of racial and religious hatred." George said he was "the highest ranking U.S. official to have seen firsthand the Nazi death camp at Auschwitz." He said he and his wife "also visited Yad Vashem, the Holocaust memorial in Jerusalem," and that he understood "the lessons of the Holocaust and will fight dangerous hate groups in America." He said he was unequivocal in condemning anti-Semitism and bigotry.

Not all Jews accepted the image of George Herbert Walker Bush as their defender. When Chaim Herzog, former President of Israel and one of the main founders of the Mossad, wrote his memoir, *Living History*, he talked to his editor about what he perceived as Bush's benign anti-Semitism.

"It wasn't an active, blatant anti-Semitism," recalled the editor Peter Gethers. "Herzog felt it was the result of Bush's country-club upbringing. That he radiated superiority. Herzog believed that Bush felt superior to Jews but that he also felt superior to anyone not in his own class and circle. Herzog wasn't bothered by it—he just noted it and felt it was something that had to be dealt with."

The Bush campaign was forced to dismiss seven volunteers who were linked to anti-Semitic organizations, including Jerome A. Brentar of Cleveland, who helped hundreds of Nazis immigrate to the United States after World War II. He was one of the chief financial backers for the defense of John Demjanjuk, who was sentenced to death by an Israeli court. "To appoint this ugly assortment of anti-Semites and racists shows gross insensitivity to the Jewish community and to all those who oppose bigotry," said former Democratic Representative and later Senator of New York Charles E. Schumer, who supported Michael Dukakis. Days after the dismissals *The Washington Post* revealed that Frederic V. Malek, deputy chairman of the RNC and one of Bush's best friends, had carried out a survey in 1971 of Jews in high-ranking jobs in the Bureau of Labor Statistics for President Richard Nixon.

"The moral clock is ticking for the Bush campaign," said Schumer. "Thinking people across the country are waiting to see how quickly he purges his campaign of anti-Semites, hate mongers and those who allowed them to have roles in the race for the White House."

Malek resigned the next day, rather than let the charges against him be used against the Vice President. Bush praised him as a man of honor, and their close friendship remained unchanged. Malek continued raising large sums of money for Bush and was the financier to whom George W. Bush turned when he wanted to buy the Texas Rangers. In later years the Maleks were always invited to accompany the Bushes on their annual cruise of the Greek islands.

The Vice President's glossy campaign pamphlet to American Jews with its impressive quotes and posed pictures seemed of little import on November 25, 1986, when the Iran-contra scandal hit the front pages. The President's admission that the United States had been secretly selling weapons to the Ayatollah Khomeini, whose Iranian fanatics had taken Americans hostage and sponsored terrorism, dumbfounded people. They were further shocked to find out that funds from the arms sales were illegally funneled to the contras in Nicaragua. Both Republicans and Democrats assailed the White House. Former Presidents Gerald Ford and Jimmy Carter were stupefied.

"We've paid ransom, in effect, to the kidnappers of our hostages," said President Carter. "The fact is that every terrorist in the world who reads a newspaper or listens to the radio knows that they've taken American hostages and we've paid them to get the hostages back. This is a very serious mistake in how to handle a kidnapping or hostage-taking."

President Ford said, "Whoever initiated this covert operation and carried it out deserves some condemnation by certain people in Congress, by people on the outside."

Criticism rained down on the President, who suffered the sharpest one-month drop in popularity ever recorded by pollsters measuring presidential job performance. For the first time in his presidency, Reagan's lack of credibility was certified. He appointed a presidential commission to investigate the role of the National Security Council. The commission's role was not to investigate charges but to examine the foreign policy apparatus that had led to the scandal. George suggested that Senator John Tower, his good friend from Texas, head the commission with another Bush friend, retired General Brent Scowcroft, and former Democratic Senator Edmund Muskie of Maine. Attorney General Ed Meese was pressured into transferring the Justice Department's investigation to a special prosecutor, and the morass known as Iran-contra stayed in the news for the next six years with congressional hearings, lawsuits, convictions, and eventually presidential pardons.

Suddenly the Bush campaign had a problem they had not anticipated. Their strategy of riding Reagan's coattails into the White House seemed shaky in the wake of Iran-contra. Ten weeks later their relief was almost palpable when the Tower Commission issued its report, clearing everyone of wrongdoing. The report stated there had been an arms-for-hostages deal and a diversion of funds to the contras, but blamed the State Department for lack of oversight. As Richard Ben Cramer wrote in his campaign book, *What It Takes*, George had convinced the Tower Commission that he was "out of the loop": "Of course, he had that wired with his friend John Tower and his friend Brent Scowcroft as two of the three members . . . but everyone had to admit—right?—he won! He showed he was unaware, not a player—not culpable of knowing anything!"

Throughout the spring of 1987, George fought the taint of Iran-contra and issued a string of denials, claiming he knew nothing about arms for hostages or funding the contras: "I can't recall [when I heard of the sales]. I don't know that I had a specific role in making any determinations of it."

"I wish with clairvoyant hindsight that I had known we were trading arms for hostages."

"Mistakes were made."

"If we erred, the President and I, it was on the side of human life. It was an over concern about freeing Americans."

He wrote to reassure his mother: "Some of our political friends worry about me and what all this will do to me . . . I don't worry—really. I know the President is telling the whole truth. I know I have, too. And I also know that the American people are fair and forgiving."

Dorothy Walker Bush did not believe the President had told the truth. George insisted he did and reiterated that in another letter to her:

> *Loved your post-visit letter; but let me clear up one point. The President did NOT know about the diversion of funds to the Contras. He had stated what his policy was on a limited amount of arms to Iran, but he has stated he did not know about the diversion of funds . . .*
>
> *Don't worry about all this stuff, please . . . the total truth will be out soon, and people will see that the President has told the truth. That's the main thing. Of course there will be differences about arms to Iran, etc., but so be it.*

George's mother had not wanted him to run for President in 1980, because she felt politics had gotten too mean. She did not think George was up to it, but his slashing campaign had proved her wrong. Now she was even more concerned. She told her Hobe Sound friend Dolly Hoffman that George was not cut out to be President.

"Dotty told Aunt Dolly that George wasn't up to the job because he didn't have the killer in him," said Dolly Hoffman's niece. "Dotty said he lacked the necessary toughness to be President. She did not mean he was a weak man, just that he was too genteel and soft to be President."

Within weeks young George W., neither genteel nor soft, was galloping to his father's rescue. "I think [his] coming up here will be very helpful and I think he will be a good insight to me," the Vice President wrote in his diary. "He is very level-headed and so is Jebby. I think some of our political people are thinking, 'Oh, god, here come the Bush boys.' But you know where their loyalty is and they both have excellent judgment and they are both spending a bunch of time on this project."

Marvin, the youngest and least political of George's four sons, had been sidelined with ulcerative colitis. To save his life, doctors had removed his large intestine. The surgery left him with a permanent colostomy bag attached to his abdomen to collect body waste. After several blood transfusions, Marvin later joked about his hospitalization. He said he knew he was dying when two things happened: his father spent the day by his side, and his brother Jeb called to say "I love you."

His mother blamed his inflammatory bowel disease on political stress. "Marvin had his colon taken out because he worried about a lot of things," said Barbara. "A lot of them were related to criticism about his father."

Marvin pooh-poohed politics as the cause for his colitis. "Mom will never be a doctor," he said. "I talked to an eleven-year-old who has it, but her dad didn't run for president." As a spokesman for the Crohn's and Colitis Foundation, Marvin said he wanted to help remove the shame attached to the disease. "The groups I talk to the most are people who aren't married," he said. "They think this ruins all that. It doesn't."

Marvin's wife, Margaret, had been diagnosed with a rare form of ovarian cancer at the age of five. She, too, almost died, and to save her life, doctors removed her ovaries, making it impossible for her to conceive. Shortly after Marvin's hospitalization the couple adopted a baby girl and, four years later, a baby boy. Because of his long convalescence, Marvin dropped out of his father's presidential campaign.

When his brother George W. moved to Washington, he did not want to live in the Vice President's thirty-three-room mansion. Instead, he and Laura and their six-year-old twins rented a town house about a mile away. They had been keeping their distance from the family for several years, passing up the 1980 presidential race, forgoing summers in Kennebunkport, and even skipping the big surprise party in January 1986 that George threw for Barbara on their forty-first wedding anniversary. The Bushes' friends had flown to Washington from all over the country to celebrate, and all the family was on hand, except for W. and Laura. Doro and William LeBlond, who married in 1982, had flown in from Maine; Neil and Sharon from Colorado; Jeb and Columba from Florida; Marvin and Margaret from Virginia; but young George and Laura remained in Texas. "It's a long way," Barbara said later, "and too expensive," reminiscent of her comments after she did not attend her mother's funeral.

She knew that distance and expense had nothing to do with the absence of her firstborn. Family members, including Louise Walker, confirmed that Barbara had stopped speaking to her son for more than a year. At that point George W.'s drinking was out of control, and his drunken outbursts had become a source of unending embarrassment to his wife and to his parents, who no longer wanted to be around him. The last eruption at a family gathering had been W.'s tactless crack to Gerry Bemiss's wife during her fiftieth birthday party. "So, what's sex like after 50, anyway?" George asked. It would be several more months before he finally decided to stop drinking. During that time he began attending a men's Bible class in Midland. He was grappling with the prospect of turning forty on July 6, 1986, and trying to stay afloat in the oil business as prices collapsed. Following his company's merger with Harken, he was paid $80,000 a year as a consultant (translation: for being the Vice President's son), but he had no business to run, no office to manage, no professional responsibilities to uphold.

Once he sobered up, his mother told him he could join his father's campaign, although his father never directly asked for his assistance. "He didn't want me to disrupt my life for him, when in fact, I was looking for, you know, the invitation to come and go to battle with him," said George W. The decision to move to Washington was also one of self-preservation, knowing that the son also rises. "If his father lost, he would be the forgotten son of a Vice President," said his cousin John Ellis. "If his father won, a whole world would open up. His fate would rise and fall with his father's."

Years later George said that the eighteen months he spent in his father's presidential campaign were the best months of his life and reignited his interest in politics. His wife agreed. "I think working with his dad, like George got to do in 1988 . . . if there was any sort of leftover competition with being named George Bush and being the eldest, that it really at that point was resolved."

Junior, as he was called, signed on to the Bush presidential campaign for five thousand dollars a month to be, in his words, "an organizer, handholder and surrogate for my father." He told a reporter: "When your name is George Bush, you don't need a title in the George Bush campaign."

The Vice President's staff called him "the enforcer from hell" and gave him a wide berth. "He was mean, tough, and focused," said the deputy chief of staff. "We treated him the same way we'd treat any hit man."

The dauphin strutted into Bush headquarters in his cowboy boots, chewing tobacco and carrying a Styrofoam cup as his spittoon. "Just call me Maureen," he told the receptionist, taking a swipe at President Reagan's daughter, who was notorious for bossing her father's staff. George bonded immediately with Lee Atwater, also keen, quick, and nasty. George won over the rest of the staff when he said: "Just let me know what I can do to help. All I want to do is get my father elected President." He made few demands, other than to take time out every day to jog. He also took weekends off. On road trips he insisted on spending no more than two nights away from D.C. Part of staying sober depended on maintaining a strict routine. He had fallen off the wagon a few times since his fortieth birthday, but was trying hard to stay sober. So if he was in California for more than forty-eight hours, he insisted the campaign fly him back to Washington for a few days to decompress, then fly him back to California.

Presidential politics—as well as politicans' relationships with the media—changed abruptly that spring, when the Democratic front-runner, Senator Gary Hart of Colorado, lost his candidacy over an extramarital dalliance. Long plagued by rumors of womanizing, Hart, a married man with children, had spent the night with a young model named Donna Rice. She was photographed sitting on his lap aboard a yacht in Bimini ludicrously named *Monkey Business*. Hart denied allegations of their affair published in *The Miami Herald* and challenged reporters to follow him if they did not believe him. Their stakeout of his Washington town house generated massive media frenzy and unleashed a series of investigations into his personal life.

He tried to recoup his standing at a press conference a few days later, but his career was over when he refused to answer a *Washington Post* reporter's question: "Have you ever committed adultery?" Faced with future disclosures of his indiscretions, Hart withdrew from the presidential race on May 8, 1987, in a bitter farewell speech.

That episode shook the timbers of presidential politics. The once-unmentionable subject of a man's personal life was now fair game for reporters. It became a measure of a candidate's character. Every candidate scrambled for cover, including the Republican front-runner. The Bush campaign became particularly concerned when a gossip columnist in the *Chicago Sun-Times* mentioned that several people were working on a story about George Bush that would link "Mr. Boring" to "a prominent east coast socialite and the wife of a close supporter." The exposé never materialized, but it threw Lee Atwater into manic overdrive. He grabbed the phones and peppered reporters. "Whadda ya hear? Whadda ya workin' on? Whadda ya got?"

Over lunch with editors from *Newsweek*, Atwater claimed that his candidate did not have "a pecker problem." The magazine's Howard Fineman called him later for an official denial. Atwater said he would get back to him, and sprinted into young George's office. Together they approached the Vice President. The campaign's press spokesman argued against addressing the rumors, and giving journalists an excuse to broadcast them, and the Vice President agreed, but Atwater and George W. insisted they had to respond. With characteristic bluntness, George asked his father: "Well? You've heard the rumors. What do you say?" The adoring son had no doubt about his father's response.

"They're just not true," said big George.

Junior called Howard Fineman: "The answer to the Big A question is N-O."

Fineman mentioned that supporters of Senator Bob Dole and other Republican presidential contenders were fanning the infidelity rumors.

"They're trying to undermine one of my father's great political strengths—the strength of our family," said George W.

Newsweek ran the story under the headline "Bush and the 'Big A Question.' " "I have no idea what the Bush people were thinking when they came up with that response," Fineman said later. "We wouldn't have run anything at all if the son of the vice president hadn't called us in this really extraordinary fashion."

George W. did not realize then that he had lied for his father, who was angry about the incident. According to an Evans and Novak column, "[The Vice President] expressed the opinion that his son and staff would have been well advised to follow his example and keep silent."

Many reporters felt conflicted about prying into a politician's personal life. Some were revulsed at the prospect of inquiring about extramarital affairs. Others, like William Greider, a *Rolling Stone* columnist and formerly with *The Washington Post*, said the topic was legitimate.

"The press didn't invent the practice of candidates using their families as a selling point. Politicians who use their families to create a public image have no grounds for complaint when the press demonstrates that image is false."

Four months later *Newsweek* dropped a bomb on Bush that nearly obliterated his candidacy. On the eve of his formal announcement for the presidency in October 1987, the magazine ran a cover story titled "Bush Battles the Wimp Factor." George never totally recovered from the fallout of that article, which seemed to ratify the knocks against him as "a lapdog," "an empty suit," and "Ronald Reagan's little echo." The word "wimp," with all its implications of weakness, was a wallop to a politician struggling to be seen as strong and decisive.

George immediately went on the attack but sounded pitiful as he struck back. "It's a lousy cheap shot," he told a crowd in Red Oak, Iowa, "and the American people don't make up their minds over what some elite publication in the East is going to think."

He went on CNN's *Larry King Live* and talked about his exploits during World War II and the death of his child:

> *Nobody on our carrier when I landed there in the water with four depth charges in my plane or after I got back to the ship after being dropped down, said, "Hey, you wimp, I want to talk to you about something." Nobody ever said that when Barbara and I . . . went through a tragedy of seeing our daughter wrenched away from us by cancer, six months sitting at that child's bedside . . . Nobody said that at the CIA when I went out there and said, "Look, we're going to make some changes here and then I'm going to lead you people, I'm going to lift you up and lead you . . ." Here's my heartbeat, here's my pulse right here. Here's what I've done in my life. Now you call me a wimp.*

He ranted against *Newsweek* editors for months and berated Evan Thomas, the magazine's Washington bureau chief. The Bush family rallied and tried to help restore his manhood.

"I'm infuriated," said Barbara Bush. "It was a cheap shot . . . It hurt. It hurt our children, truthfully. It hurt George's mother. It hurt me. I mean it was hurtful . . . I never want to hear that word again."

"My father is a hero," said Marvin Bush.

Nancy Bush Ellis wrote a scathing letter to Katharine Graham, the owner of *Newsweek* and one of Nan's occasional tennis partners. "I felt there were terrible misconceptions," she said. "The whole wimp, elitist, preppy thing."

Neil Bush weighed in. "I get very upset when people try to portray my father as not being a man of character," he said. "There is a four-letter word that begins with a 'w' and ends with i-m-p. It's so outrageous."

No one was more irate than George W. Bush, who unleashed a stream of coarse vulgarities against the magazine and all its writers. To their faces he called them "assholes," and behind their backs he cursed their mothers. He also cut them off from any further access to his father. "I felt responsible, because I had approved the interview," he said. "I was livid, and I let a lot of people know exactly how I felt."

Young George saw the wimp cover as nothing less than a public castration. Like the hotheaded Sonny Corleone in *The Godfather*, he became savage about avenging his father's honor and preserving the family's political fortunes. Profane, abusive, and ugly, he lashed out at reporters whose stories he did not like, sometimes becoming frighteningly confrontational.

When he saw Al Hunt of *The Wall Street Journal* having dinner in a restaurant with his family, Junior blasphemed him in front of Hunt's four-year-old son for an article he had written criticizing the elder Bush. "You [expletive] son of a bitch," Bush yelled. "I saw what you wrote. We're not going to forget this."

George accosted a television correspondent and demanded to know: "Who the hell do you think you are talking about my father that way?" He became so crazed that Lee Atwater limited his press dealings. "I gotta keep the boy caged," Atwater joked. Unfortunately, Atwater was not around when George started bullying female reporters.

"I had a terrifying experience with George W. when I was writing a feature on his mother for *Lear's* magazine," said the Washington journalist Sandra McElwaine. "I was having lunch at the Federal City Club in Washington and saw George W. as I was leaving. So I went over to introduce myself. 'Excuse me for interrupting you but I've been trying to reach you by phone for weeks on a story that . . .' I couldn't even finish my sentence before he started yelling at me. 'That's not true. You have NOT tried to reach me. You're lying.'

" 'No, sir,' I said. 'I've called several times and spoken with your secretary and her name is . . .'

" 'That's a goddamn lie and furthermore who are you to be interrupting my lunch.'

"He got red in the face and pig-eyed and became so hostile I got scared. I should never have interrupted his meal, but I assure you that the reaction I got was an overreaction to what I had done. When he started screaming at me, I backed away and apologized and ran off. He was one of the nastiest people I have ever encountered."

Susan Watters, the Washington correspondent for *Women's Wear Daily*, was equally shaken after her unnerving encounter with the first son. During a White House reception that the press had been invited to cover, Watters approached Doro Bush to get a correct identification for a picture the *WWD* photographer had taken of Doro and her escort.

"George W. raced across the room and started yelling at me for talking to his sister," Watters said. "I was so taken aback . . . by his anger and his offensive language . . . that I didn't know what to say . . . I needed an ID caption . . . He snarled, 'Leave us alone. Why don't you just leave us alone, you so-and-so.'

" 'This is my job,' I said . . . He was scary, really scary."

While George W. was working in the Washington campaign headquarters, his younger brother Neil was working in Iowa as his father's surrogate at forums around the state. When the results of the Ames straw poll arrived and the Vice President finished a humiliating fourth, Neil became petulant.

"Let me just tell you a thing or two," he said. "Iowa isn't the only state that matters. There's New Hampshire and we've got the governor [John Sununu]."

Neil's father reverted to type in explaining his defeat. "A lot of the people that support me . . . were at their daughters' coming-out parties, or teeing up at the golf course for that all-important last round."

After Iowa the Vice President was derided as weak and unelectable. He trailed the Democratic candidate Michael Dukakis by double digits in the polls, and his negative ratings were among the highest of any presidential candidate in history. George was desperate to turn things around. "We got to get me out there," he told his campaign aides. "We got to get more of me out there." He decided the best way to restore his image was to play up his war record, but in the end he overplayed it. He wrote a book with Doug Wead, an evangelical on his campaign staff, titled *Man of Integrity*. Instead of establishing himself as a genuine hero, George created doubts in the minds of many about what actually happened when he bailed out of his plane over Chichi-Jima in World War II. One of the gunners in his unit, Chester Mierzejewski, was so upset by what George told David Frost in an interview in December 1987 that he publicly challenged George and left the impression that he had not fully told the truth about the tragedy that killed his crew.

George had always maintained that he never knew exactly what had happened to his two-man crew. He had repeatedly said that when he finished his bombing run, he flew out to sea and kept his plane aloft long enough for the crew to jump. Only in the Wead book does he imply that he saw what happened to his crew. Contrary to what he had claimed in the past, George now put down in print that he saw his gunner, Lieutenant William G. White, killed by machine-gun fire and his radioman, John Delaney, parachute out. George also claimed that a second parachute, Delaney's, was fired on.

If one accepts contemporaneous accounts in 1944 and official Navy documentation, the story Bush tells in the book he co-wrote with Wead is a fabrication. There were no machine guns, and no dogfights involving machine guns, only anti-aircraft fire. George neither saw nor heard White or Delaney after his plane was hit. No one else saw anyone shoot at the second parachute. Previous accounts of the second parachute indicate simply that it failed to open. There were only American planes around at the time Bush bailed out, and not one person in any of those planes was in a position to say for sure who was wearing the parachute that did not open.

The inescapable conclusion is that George lied about his heroism during World War II for political gain in 1988. In doing so, he violated the report card category at the Greenwich Country Day School: "Claims no more than his fair share of time and attention." In *Man of Integrity*, with its vaunted title and inflated text, George had definitely claimed more than his fair share.

Now that he was a declared candidate for President, George was forced to face tougher scrutiny from the media. In January 1988 he agreed to sit down with Dan Rather of CBS, who was determined to get answers to the unasked questions of Iran-contra.

Craig Fuller warned his boss that he was going to be ambushed.

"No way," said George. "Dan's a friend."

No one could convince the Vice President that reporters were not his friends. He believed that if he was nice to them, they would be nice to him.

"Look," said Fuller. "If Rather really trashes you on Iran Contra, why don't you tell him, 'How would you like to be judged, your whole career on the seven minutes you walked off the set?' "

Fuller was referring to the time Rather left his anchor seat in September 1987 in a fit of pique and let the broadcast go dark.

"Yeah, that's it," said the media consultant Roger Ailes, who had joined the Bush campaign for twenty-five thousand dollars a month. "That's it. Hit Dan with his own crap."

The campaign had insisted on a live interview so the Vice President's answers could not be edited. They had not figured on what Marlin Fitzwater called "a prosecutorial lead-in" about Iran-contra. Rather conducted the interview from his studio in Manhattan, and the Vice President faced the camera in his office on Capitol Hill. Even before Rather asked the first question, Bush heard the lead-in and was ready to blow a gasket.

"Mr. Vice President, we want to talk about the record . . ."

"Let's talk about the whole record . . ."

"One-third of the Republicans in this poll, one-third . . . say that, you know, they rather like you, [but] believe you're hiding something . . . Here's a chance to get it out . . . You have said that if you had known . . . this was an arms-for-hostages swap . . ."

"Yes."

"That you would have opposed it."

"Exactly."

"You also said that you did not know . . ."

"May I answer that?"

"That wasn't a question, it was a statement."

"It was a statement, and I'll answer it."

"Let me ask the question, if I may, first."

454 / KITTY KELLEY

"The President created this program, as testified or stated publicly, he did not think it was arms for hostages."

"That was the President, Mr. Vice President."

"And that's me. Because I went along with it because—you know why, Dan?—because—"

They fenced and sparred for nine minutes as George tried to eat up time. Finally he stopped stonewalling and spat out his calculated response.

"I don't think it's fair to judge a whole career, it's not fair to judge my whole career by a rehash on Iran. How would you like it if I judged your career by those seven minutes when you walked off the set in New York? Would you like that?"

Rather went to a commercial, and George ripped out his earpiece while blasting away at the camera with his mic still on.

"Well, I had my say, Dan . . . That guy makes Lesley Stahl look like a pussy . . . The worst time I've had in twenty years of public life. But it's going to help me, because that bastard didn't lay a glove on me . . . I'm really upset. You can tell your goddamn network that if they want to talk to me they can raise their hands at a press conference. No more 'Mr. Insider' stuff."

Watching the confrontation at the White House, President Reagan nodded with approval. George had finally shown some spunk. Reagan said to an aide, "I didn't see any wimp in that."

The next day George W. roared into campaign headquarters with both fists raised above his head in jubilation. "Macho!" he yelled. "Macho!"

Pete Teeley issued a statement: "What Bush did is show the American people he wasn't going to be pushed around by Dan Rather."

Dan Rather defended himself with his own statement: "Trying to ask honest questions and trying to be persistent about answers is part of a reporter's job."

The columnist Mike Royko shuddered: "It took him only a few grim minutes to turn a rich elitist like George Bush into a sympathetic character for millions of people who work for their paychecks. Think what Rather could do for a guy who doesn't look like his mommie still takes him to tennis camp."

The next day Herblock, the Pulitzer Prize–winning cartoonist for *The*

Washington Post, drew the Vice President as a skinny boxer wearing trunks marked "Iran-Contra Connection." The trunks had fallen to his ankles as he waved a scrawny arm in victory, barely able to hold up the heavy boxing glove. With the other glove he covered his manhood.

Iran-contra continued to dog Bush, and he bristled at reporters who did not accept his declarations of innocence. He became particularly exercised by David Hoffman's coverage in *The Washington Post*. One evening on Air Force Two he asked some reporters to join him for his nightly martinis. "After a couple of silver bullets, he let us know exactly what he thought of Hoffman," recalled Cragg Hines, a *Houston Chronicle* columnist. "Bush said, 'To his face it will always be 'Hi ya, David. How are ya?' Behind his back, it's 'Fuck you, David.' Bush put his hand under the table and gave him the finger."

By then George's niceness had morphed into nastiness, as it always did under political pressure. In Cedar Rapids, Iowa, a high-school student asked him about his changing position on abortion. He saw the student was reading from a pamphlet put out by his rival Republican Representative Jack Kemp of New York.

"I didn't know these things were being passed around," he said. He snatched the flyer and ripped it to shreds.

"Finis," he said, stalking off.

The Vice President fell on his face in the Iowa caucuses and placed an embarrassing third, giving Senator Dole the lead going into New Hampshire. By the time George arrived in Portsmouth, he seemed a chastened man. "I don't always articulate, but I always do feel," he told one crowd. "Here I stand, warts and all." Those who had always admired Bush's decency, his sense of honor and fair play, took heart that the nice guy had returned. Then he thumped Dole for "nearly single-handedly" bringing down the GOP ticket in 1976 and chided him for divorcing his wife who had nursed him back to health after the war. "In my family loyalty is a strength," George said. "It's not a character flaw." He authorized a series of slash ads attacking Dole as "Senator Straddle" for flip-flopping on taxes. Watching his polls rise after the ads ran convinced George that negative trumps positive in the vulture's game, and that was how he decided to play. So much for Mr. Nice Guy. He won the New Hampshire primary with the help of the state's governor, John Sununu, and swept the Super Tuesday primaries, which ensured the GOP nomination. Still, to beat Dukakis he knew that at some point, he would have to stand on the shoulders of the President.

George needed the King's blessing, but the Queen was balking. Nancy Reagan was in no hurry to have her husband anoint his successor. Every time the Bush campaign presented a plan to the President for such a tribute, Mrs. President said no. She had vetoed a dinner in February and a reception in April. She even forced cancellation of her husband's appearance at a Bush rally held within walking distance of the White House. Finally she agreed to a tepid endorsement on May 11, 1988, at a dinner in Washington, D.C., where Reagan was to address three thousand of his staunchest supporters, each of whom paid fifteen hundred dollars to attend. The Bush camp quickly submitted a fulsome endorsement, which Nancy immediately nixed. "No," she said. "It's Ronnie's dinner!"

That evening a black-tie crowd paid homage to the Gipper and watched a dewy twenty-minute film of "great moments in the Reagan years" set to inspirational music with fluttering American flags. Filled with cheerful nostalgia, the film barely mentioned the name George Bush. The President stood to roaring applause and delivered a stirring speech about "morning in America" and "a shining city on a hill." He then ended on a quiet note:

> If I may, I'd like to take a moment to say just a word about my future plans. In doing so, I'll break a silence I've maintained for some time with regard to the Presidential candidates. I intend to campaign, as hard as I can. My candidate is a former member of Congress, Ambassador to China, Ambassador to the United Nations, Director of the CIA, and National Chairman of the Republican Party. I'm going to work as hard as I can to make Vice President Bush the next President of the United States.

There was a round of applause when the President mentioned George by name, although he mispronounced "Bush" to sound like "Blush."

As the crowd waited for a stem-winder endorsement, the President wound down. "Now it's on to New Orleans," he said, "and on to the

White House." He waved good night to the adoring crowd and strode out of the ballroom with the First Lady.

Barbara Bush was furious, and after eight years of knee-cracking service her husband was humiliated. They both cringed when they saw the front-page headline in the next day's *Washington Post*: "Reagan Gives Bush a Terse Endorsement." The subhead said: "Brevity of Remarks at Fund-Raising Dinner Baffles Republican Activists." *The New York Times* noted: "Bush Camp Longs for Signs of More Support by Reagan."

The President's restrained endorsement did nothing to lift the Vice President in the polls. Bush continued to trail Dukakis into the summer. By the time the Democrats gathered in Atlanta for their national convention in July 1988, they had decided that George, as they called him, was some sort of national joke. The keynote speaker, Ann Richards, the Texas state treasurer, brought down the house when she said, "Poor George. He can't help it. He was born with a silver foot in his mouth."

The Texas agriculture commissioner, Jim Hightower, poked fun at Bush as a "toothache of a man, telling us to stay the course and threatening to lead us from tweedledum to tweedledumber."

In his folksy, homespun Texas style, Hightower drawled: "His is an upper-class world in which wealth is given to you at birth. George Bush was born on third base and thinks he hit a triple."

The most blistering attack was delivered by Senator Edward Kennedy, who called George a "hear-nothing, see-nothing, do-nothing" Vice President. With rhetorical flourish Kennedy asked where George was when the Reagan-Bush administration made its biggest mistakes.

"At least Ronald Reagan accepts the blame as well as the credit for the policies of the last eight years," said Kennedy. "But not George Bush, who on question after question keeps burying his head in his hands and hiding from the record."

The senator cited the Iran-contra scandal and the delegates screamed: "Where was George?" He cited the indictment of Panama's Manuel Noriega and drug trafficking in Central America, and the delegates shouted: "Where was George?" He cited the proposed cuts in aid to the elderly, and the delegates yelled: "Where was George?" He decried the administration's veto of a civil rights bill, and the delegates chorused: "Where was George?"

"When those decisions were being made, I think it is fair to ask where was George?" Kennedy said. "George Bush is the man who is never there. And he won't be there after the clock strikes noon on January 20, 1989 [Inauguration Day]."

Wound up to a frenzy, the delegates clapped their hands and stomped their feet as they chanted, "Where was George? Where was George? Where was George?"

Watching in Kennebunkport, Barbara Bush hissed with fury. She called Ann Richards "that woman with all the hair," and she dismissed Senator Kennedy with withering disdain. "That man has no right to even utter my husband's name."

George was spared the Democratic spectacle that touched off his wife's wrath. He had gone fishing in Wyoming with Secretary of the Treasury James A. Baker III, whom he had persuaded to take charge of his faltering campaign. Bush made Baker an offer he could not refuse: "I become President; you become Secretary of State."

Ethnic Americans were reveling in the nomination of Michael Dukakis. As Jeffrey Eugenides wrote in *Middlesex* (published in 2002):

> *This was 1988. Maybe the time had finally come when anyone—or at least not the same old someones—could be President. Behold the banners at the Democratic Convention! Look at the bumper stickers on all the Volvos. "Dukakis." A name with more than two vowels in it running for President! The last time that had happened was Eisenhower (who looked good on a tank). Generally speaking, Americans like their president to have no more than two vowels. Truman. Johnson. Nixon. Clinton. If they have more than two vowels (Reagan), they can have no more than two syllables. Even better is one syllable and one vowel: Bush. Had to do that twice.*

George's election was still far from certain. For weeks he had been running eighteen points behind Dukakis. His problem was summed up by *Time* in its convention-eve cover story: "George Bush—in Search of Stature." His top aides had been urging him for months to develop his ideas and arbitrage the future. "Oh, you mean the vision thing," he said to Lee Atwater, clearly exasperated. George had no inclination to conceptualize and said more than once he did not need to have a vision. No one within his new circle of born-again evangelicals thought to mention a pertinent passage from the Book of Proverbs: "Where there is no vision, the people perish."

By the time of the GOP convention, George had been widely ridiculed as a man without vision and without the ability to communicate one should it come his way. He knew that his acceptance speech was crucial in defining him as a person and as a President. He reached out to Reagan's lyricist, Peggy Noonan, who had composed some of his sweetest music. George asked the speechwriter for her help. "I've got to give people a better idea of myself," he said. She gave him both a voice and a vision.

In the most memorable speech of his career, the sixty-four-year-old Vice President pledged to "complete the mission" begun by Ronald Reagan. George expressed his hope for a "kinder and gentler nation," echoed years later in his son's pledge to be a "compassionate conservative." The Vice President applauded the goodness of people who helped others and said that if everyone embraced volunteerism, the effort would create "a new harmony, like stars, like a thousand points of light in a broad and peaceful sky." He then reassured Americans that he would continue their prosperity, uttering the most famous words he would ever speak: "Read my lips. No new taxes."

Noonan's speech had given the Republican candidate some substance, and George delivered her lines with strength and sincerity. He had been taking lessons for weeks from the speech coach Lilyan Wilder, whose mission was to lower his nasally pitch and slow down his rat-a-tat-tat pace to give him some semblance of statesmanship. She was paid one thousand dollars an hour and deserved one million dollars, so great was her challenge. "I did the best I could with the man," she said wearily, "but it was difficult because . . . of . . . um . . . his busy schedule and . . ."

Her biggest hurdle was George's own resistance. He did not think he needed help with public speaking, despite suggestions to the contrary from campaign aides, friends, and even his family. His brother Jonathan was so frustrated by George's lackluster delivery that he recommended hiring the famous acting coach Stella Adler, but George would not hear of it. "Let the others have charisma," he said. "I've got class."

When he finished his acceptance speech, the hall was transformed into a swirl of balloons and colored streamers. Delegates waved signs that said: "God Is a Republican" and "Mom, Apple Pie and George Bush." His family joined him onstage—his children, his brothers, his sister, and all of his grandchildren. When Jeb and Columba—she had become a U.S. citizen so she could vote for her father-in-law—walked out with their three children, the band broke into a spirited version of Ritchie Valens's song "La Bamba." Earlier, at the Belle Chasse Naval Air Station, George had introduced Jeb and Columba to the Reagans. Pointing toward Jeb and his Mexican wife, Bush said: "That's Jebbie's kids. The little brown ones. Jebbie's the big one in the yellow shirt saying the Pledge of Allegiance tonight." Bush said Jeb's family was his "secret weapon" with Hispanic voters.

"Oh, really," said Nancy Reagan.

Columba Bush, who was to second, in Spanish, her father-in-law's nomination at the convention, was hurt by his reference to her children as "the little brown ones." She later admitted her distress but said, "[I]t turned out to be a great experience. What that made me do was start to promote Mexican art. I wanted Hispanics to be proud of their culture, to not be ashamed of being brown."

The Vice President's polls shot up immediately after his acceptance speech but were dissipated by ongoing criticism of his running mate, Dan Quayle. In selecting the forty-one-year-old senator from Indiana, George thought he could bridge the gender gap by giving female voters someone he said "looked like Robert Redford, only is better looking." That mentality might have accounted for Bush's lack of support among women. Selecting a Robert Redford look-alike certainly did not help. There had been earlier speculation that Bush might select a woman as his running mate, but Pat Schroeder, the Democratic congresswoman from Colorado, quipped it would never happen. "People would say: 'We need a man on the ticket.' "

Quayle was a liability from the beginning. In his first press conference, the young senator stumbled over questions about his military service, why he had served in the National Guard, and whether his family used any undue influence to get him a slot in the Guard. At first he denied influence was used. Later he said he didn't know. Finally he admitted that some phone calls were made. Within hours the headline in *The New Orleans Times-Picayune* threw the convention into a swivet: "Draft-Dodger Questions Dog Quayle." Vietnam remained a raw nerve, especially for veterans, and Bush was bombarded by questions from journalists about Quayle's military service. George ignored their shouted queries as he walked to his hotel suite, but his eldest son stopped to defend Quayle. "The thing that's important is he didn't go to Canada," said George W. Bush, whose own National Guard service would one day come under attack.

Dan Quayle came out of New Orleans as nothing more than a punch line to jokes about how many vice presidents it takes to sink a political campaign. Resisting pleas to remove him from the ticket, George stood by his choice but regretted having made it. At the end of the convention he confided the disaster to his dairy: "It was my decision, and I blew it, but I'm not about to say that I blew it."

Others did it for him. When Quayle went to New York City for a fund-raiser at a golf course, reporters asked the chairman of the state Democratic Committee for a quote. "It's appropriate that Dan Quayle is coming to New York to raise money for Republicans at a golf outing," said John Marino, "since he is George Bush's biggest handicap."

Even George's closest friends were dismayed. "After New Orleans I went to the Bushes for cocktails," said the columnist Charles Bartlett. "As I came in, I said to George, 'How in God's good name did you select Quayle?' A voice at the end of the room said, 'I want to hear this one.' It was Barbara. George told me he'd only met Quayle once or twice, but that Nick Brady played golf with him and Nick told George that Quayle was good on defense issues. George needed someone young and from the Midwest, so Quayle was in . . . That's as much thought as he gave to it."

George later claimed to have considered a long list of candidates, including Senator Robert Dole of Kansas; Secretary of Transportation Elizabeth Hanford Dole; Representative Jack Kemp of New York; Governor Lamar Alexander of Tennessee; Senator Pete Domenici of New Mexico; Senator Alan Simpson of Wyoming; Senator John Danforth of Missouri; Senator Richard Lugar of Indiana; Senator John McCain of Arizona; Senator Bill Armstrong of Colorado; Senator Thad Cochran of Mississippi; Representative Lynn Martin of Illinois; Governor John Sununu of New Hampshire; Governor George Deukmejian of California; Governor John Ashcroft of Missouri; and Governor Kay Orr of Nebraska.

George liked what he saw of himself in Dan Quayle: both came from good (that is, wealthy) families, pledged DKE in college, and played decent golf. He chose his running mate without consulting anyone else, which his campaign manager made clear to reporters in numerous background briefings. "Not my choice," said James Baker. He wanted no part of the young man who kept comparing himself to John F. Kennedy. When Quayle drew the comparison in his debate with Dukakis's running mate, Senator Lloyd Bentsen was ready. Having been prepped by the Democrats' best media and debate coach, Michael Sheehan, the Texas senator demolished Quayle:

QUAYLE: It's not just age; it's accomplishments, it's experience. I have far more experience than many others that sought the office of vice president of this country. I have as much experience in the Congress as Jack Kennedy did when he sought the presidency . . .

BENTSEN: Senator, I served with Jack Kennedy. I knew Jack Kennedy. Jack Kennedy was a friend of mine. Senator, you're no Jack Kennedy.

"As bad a choice as some people thought Dan Quayle was, it could have been a lot worse, I assure you," said French Wallop. "There were a few discreet inquiries made about putting my former husband, Malcolm, on the ticket when he was the senior senator from Wyoming, and that would have been a disaster for family values . . . Malcolm was conservative on all the right issues, but he was too much like George—both were rich, elite Yalies. Then there was another little issue that might have been problematical with the religious right . . . Malcolm liked to dress up in women's clothes."

When Mrs. Wallop discovered her husband's predilection for cross-dressing, she said, she demanded a divorce. She sent engraved announcements to all their friends that said: "French Wallop regrets to inform you that due to a significant indiscretion on the part of her husband of 16 years he may now be reached at the following address . . ."

The Bushes did not seem prudish about the sexual eccentricities of their social set. They counted at least one transvestite, a Los Angeles power broker, among their close friends.

"I think they're much more tolerant than the rest of their right-wing brethren on certain issues," said Cragg Hines, a columnist for the *Houston Chronicle*. "I remember Barbara called reporters in for lunch and talked about their friendship with Stewart McKinney, a Republican congressman from Connecticut, and how angry she was that he had been outed in his obituary for AIDS. She said it was despicable that the cause of his death had to be published and embarrass his wife and children."

The Bushes' sensitivity to the feelings of others was reserved only for personal friends. As the 1988 campaign proved, they did not spare political opponents. In fact, George sank to a new low as he trashed Michael Dukakis with slurs and innuendos about taxes, abortion, pornography, the death penalty, and the Pledge of Allegiance. "Indeed, he has displayed a shameless talent for low blows and big lies," wrote William Greider in *Rolling Stone*, "stunning not only his Democratic opponent but also Bush's old friends."

One old friend was Senator Barry Goldwater, who came out of retirement to tell George to "knock it off and start talking about the issues." No one was more horrified than Bush's eighty-seven-year-old mother. She told a friend she felt like weeping when she saw the inflammatory ads produced by Americans for Bush, one of George's political action committees, that showed Willie Horton, a convicted black murderer who raped a white woman after he was furloughed from prison by then-Governor Dukakis of Massachusetts. Dorothy Bush was offended by the blatant racism of the ad, which ran for twenty-eight days only on cable televison but was reported by the networks. The Willie Horton ad was followed by another, featuring the fiancé of Horton's rape victim, and then another featuring the sister of Horton's murder victim. One particularly racist ad in North Dakota showed the dark visage of the first-degree murderer and told viewers: "Imagine life with Jesse Jackson as secretary of state." Governor Dukakis had never mentioned the possibility.

Three former CIA agents spoke out against George, saying that no former director of the agency should ever be elected President. "Any CIA director carries baggage from having dealt with criminal elements around the world," said John Stockwell, who worked for the CIA in Angola, Vietnam, and the U.S. headquarters in Langley, Virginia. Stockwell quoted from an interview with Manuel Noriega in which the Panamanian strongman said he had information that could be used to blackmail Bush. "There are a hundred Noriegas out there in the world that he has dealt with as CIA director who have similar control over [him]."

Stockwell was joined by two other dissident former agents, Philip

Agee and Phil Roettinger, a retired Marine colonel. All three were touring the country, giving speeches, and urging Bush's defeat. They said their
tour was unconnected with the Dukakis campaign and that they were
paying their own way by holding fund-raising events at various stops.

Philip Agee, who lost his U.S. passport for criticizing the CIA's covert
operations, said that Bush had participated in a secret operation known as
"the supermarket," in which arms were shipped to the contras with funds
raised through the sale of narcotics. Such transactions, of course, violated
U.S. law.

The third former agent, Phil Roettinger, said that the campaign of
"lies and deceit" that Bush was waging reminded him of the psychological-
warfare techniques he taught as a CIA agent. He cited as an example of
character assassination the technique of doctoring a photograph so that
the person targeted is shown with someone unsavory. He said that the
agency usually used Communists to destroy someone's reputation. Bush,
he said, employed the same strategy to discredit Dukakis by using a photograph of Willie Horton.

Donna Brazile, a Dukakis field coordinator, accused the Bush campaign of the basest racism. "They're using the oldest racial symbol imagi-
nable," she said. "A black man raping a white woman while her husband
watches."

George Bush did absolutely nothing to disassociate himself from any
of the Willie Horton ads. Instead, he blamed the media for perpetuating
the charges of racism against him. Even his authorized biographer, Herbert Parmet (*George Bush: The Life of a Lone Star Yankee*), found him
"disingenuous."

Yet three years later Bush continued to deny that the issue was designed to be racially divisive: "The point on Willie Horton was not Willie
Horton himself. The point was, do you believe in a furlough program that
releases people from jail so they can go out and rape, pillage and plunder
again? That's what the issue was." Even Lee Atwater was so ashamed of
the ugliness he had helped perpetuate that he made a public apology before his death in 1991.

By Election Day, Americans had become fed up. The turnout of 88.9
million voters was the lightest since the election of Calvin Coolidge in
1924. Exit polls showed that many of those who did go to the polls were
casting negative votes against either Bush or Dukakis rather than favor-

able votes for either of them. "The American people will vote if they have something to vote about," said Curtis Gans of the Committee for the Study of the American Electorate, a nonpartisan research group. "We had an unprecedented number of voters in 1988 who said they didn't like either candidate."

Still, George Bush received 53 percent of the vote and carried forty states with 426 electoral votes. No new President had ever presided over a more divided government than the one facing Bush, whose coattails were so short that he failed to reduce the opposition's majority in the House or the Senate. He did not seem to be in the least concerned. The day after the election he held his first press conference in Houston and announced James Baker was going to be Secretary of State. The President-elect also mentioned that "George the Ripper" had retired. "The campaign is over," he said. "No more attacks." Proving his angel was the measure of his devil, George sent a silver foot to Ann Richards. After the Democratic convention he had belittled her as "Bessie Bouffant." In a handwritten note, he said: "You've probably received a hundred of these 'feet,' but I want you to have this one from me—a peace offering . . . It's real—just ask the Hunt brothers [a reference to the Texans who attempted to corner the silver market in a financial fiasco]."

Two weeks later he flew to Kennebunkport for Thanksgiving. On the grounds of the family's estate at Walker's Point, he continued to savor his victory. Describing the moment later to a friend, Bush said, "I wondered what my old man would say if he could see his little boy now."

CHAPTER TWENTY-TWO

Never a debutante, Barbara Pierce Bush entered the world of high society at the age of sixty-three when she made her debut as First Lady. Landing on the cover of *Time* as "The Silver Fox," she burst into full bloom as a beloved American icon. When she appeared at her first inaugural luncheon in January 1989, she seized the spotlight and never let it go.

"I want you to watch me all week and remember," she joked. "You may never see it again . . . Notice the hairdo, the makeup, the designer clothes." She whipped open her size-sixteen jacket like a runway model, and the audience erupted with delight, cheering her spoof of herself and her assault on the lacquered image of her predecessor.

"It's so uncalled for," Nancy Reagan complained to a friend after watching Barbara's swipe at her on television. "If it hadn't been for us, they wouldn't even be here." Nancy felt the Bushes had gone out of their way since the election to draw negative contrasts by popping up in churches as well as various restaurants around town, something the Reagans rarely, if ever, did. After showing Barbara through the family quarters on January 11, 1989, Nancy got the stiletto the next morning when she read Barbara's comments: "All those closets—why you just can't believe all the clothes closets Mrs. Reagan has . . . I don't know how I could possibly fill them." Barbara had already bought an $8,000 ermine jacket and a $1,250 Judith Leiber purse for her husband's inauguration, but no one knocked her extravagance the way critics did Nancy Reagan's. Barbara avoided her predecessor's mistakes by withholding news about her Seventh Avenue shopping sprees and the designers who contributed to her inaugural wardrobe. When a reporter asked her at one event whose dress she was wearing, she replied, "Mine."

Throughout that week, she killed the departing First Lady with kindness. She said how much she "admired" Nancy's attention to detail. "She's a perfectionist and I'm not," said Barbara, who did not mention her insistence on pressed sheets, petits fours coated in pastel frosting, and doilies, "not tablecloths," for tea parties. "It doesn't bother me if something isn't perfect," she said. "I'm much more interested in people." Nancy barely saw the velvet glove before the steel fist clobbered her.

Barbara praised the First Lady for redecorating the White House and vowed not to change a thing, "well, except maybe one room." She said she might convert Nancy's beauty salon into a playroom for the Bushes' eleven grandchildren, drawing another galling contrast with the Reagans, whose family was so fractured that few people recalled grandchildren ever visiting them in the White House. "I've got to find someplace for all the children's toys," said Barbara. "Besides I usually do my own hair." Nancy probably did not know her throat was slit until she started bleeding.

She who had pilloried Geraldine Ferraro as something that "rhymes with rich" had perfected her right hook. Battering-Ram Bar had evolved into Bee-Stinging Bar: she now hid hornets in every bouquet she tossed. Reporters saw only her flowers; recipients felt only her sting. "Barbara is like an M-40 sniper rifle," said a military man who worked for George Bush for several years. "She can make a clean kill from a thousand yards away . . . She's got a mouth on her that can maim and destroy . . . scrape her tongue for venom and you could create an antidote for ricin . . . when she delivers the life-taking blow, she does it with a thin-lipped smile . . . Have you ever seen an asp smile?"

An assistant on Vice President Bush's staff once described Barbara as a killer fish. "If you get the look that says, you're trespassing in my waters, you're dead. Crunch. The water fills with blood, and you're holding your head in your hands before some fool can scream: 'Shark attack. Shark attack.' "

Nancy Reagan was renowned as a petticoat President who dominated her husband's White House, hiring and firing his personnel, dictating his schedule, and influencing his policies. Powerful as she was, Mrs. Reagan was a clumsy amateur alongside Barbara Bush, who never left fingerprints. Behind her grandmotherly facade was a pearl-wearing mugger the equal of Ma Barker. Over the years Barbara had become the family's enforcer because her husband, so eager to be liked, was averse to conflict. He left the pistol-whippings to her, and when she needed camouflage, she summoned her firstborn.

"Barbara is the toughie in the family," said Cody Shearer, whose mother grew up with the Pierces. "All the Bush men have bladders near their eyeballs—they all cry all the time. The old man is the worst but not Bar. She sheds few tears."

During inaugural week the matriarch never failed to mention that the entire Bush-Walker clan would be converging on Washington for George's swearing in. "There will be 247 of us," Barbara said, exposing yet another vulnerability of the Reagans, who preached family values but could not practice them, because their family was sundered by dissension.

Barbara excelled at damning with faint praise. During an interview before the inauguration, she was asked about her favorite first ladies. "I wish you wouldn't say Eleanor Roosevelt because I grew up in a household that really detested her," she said. "Let's talk about someone else." She then named Pat Nixon and Betty Ford as two first ladies she particularly admired. She did not mention Nancy Reagan.

By then the week had started to look like a bloody payback for eight years in the shadows as the Second Lady, forced to accept blue as her favorite color because the First Lady had commandeered red. Without uttering a harsh word, Barbara declared her independence by posing for the cover of *Time* in a scarlet suit.

"She never forgave Nancy for treating them like the help," said Edmund Morris, President Reagan's biographer. "It was an open secret in the White House . . . that Nancy and Barbara detested each other."

The final indignity for Nancy Reagan occurred when her alma mater, Smith College, offered Barbara, the First Dropout, an honorary degree. Nancy had chased that accolade for the eight years of her husband's presidency, regularly sending emissaries to the school to plead her case. As a graduate of Smith, she felt more than entitled to an honorary degree and was miffed that it was never forthcoming. Only after she left the White House did the school concede to honor her, but with the proviso that the degree be awarded after Barbara had received hers. Infuriated, Mrs. Reagan declined. Months later she took small consolation in the newspaper photos showing Smith students protesting Barbara's appearance. The students wore T-shirts that had printed photos of both first ladies. The caption beneath Nancy's said, "Smith class of 1943"; the caption beneath Barbara's said, "Left in '44 to marry George." The back of the T-shirts said, "There must be a better way to get a Smithy in the White House."

Throughout inaugural week the media described the new First Lady as warm, likable, natural, down-to-earth, and absolutely genuine, and derided her predecessor as shallow, imperious, and totally obsessed with Hollywood glitz and the fripperies of fashion. Nancy represented the age of avarice; Barbara heralded the age of altruism. Parvenus out; patricians in.

The beleaguered First Lady had not even left town before the press started building up her successor with breathless headlines: "Bye-Bye Glamour," howled USA Today. "Goodbye, First Fashion Plate," chortled the New York Post, "Hello, First Grandmother." "Family, Laughter to Fill White House," proclaimed The Washington Times. "At Last—a First Lady Who's a Real Woman, Wrinkles and All," crowed The Washington Post.

Barbara told The New York Times that she viewed herself as a role model for many American women. "My maid tells me a lot of fat, white-haired, wrinkled ladies are tickled pink," she said.

Even David S. Broder, the premier political columnist of The Washington Post, joined the hallelujah chorus with a column titled "What Makes Barbara Bush So Special." "It may seem exaggerated to suggest that she will be the conscience of this White House, but my guess is that she will be more an example to the country," he wrote. "She comes from a tradition that says that those who are favored with wealth and power thereby acquire reciprocal obligations to those who lack any advantages . . . Her example will now inspire, not just those who have known her in the past, but millions of others who are just discovering what makes Barbara Bush so special."

Within months The Wall Street Journal would praise her as "America's Grandma" and report that she was more popular than her husband: "Barbara Bush Earns Even Higher Ratings Than the President." At the end of four years Vanity Fair would gush: "Barbara Bush stands as close to universal popularity as any figure in America."

Even Democrats were enthralled. "I like her forthright manner, and her no-nonsense ways," said Pamela Peabody, the sister-in-law of the former Democratic governor of Massachusetts Endicott "Chub" Peabody.

"Early on Barbara looked like a great dame," said Bobbie Greene, who later worked for Hillary Rodham Clinton. "I remember how surprised I was when I met her press secretary, Anna Perez, at the beginning of the Bush administration. I said how lucky she was to work for someone who seemed so nice. Anna looked at me, stretched out her arms, and said, 'Yes, and I have all the claw marks to prove it.' I never knew what she meant until many years later."

In the early days, just by not being Nancy, Barbara Bush managed to bridge the gap of age, class, and politics to appeal to a broad segment of the population, particularly women, who had had a bellyful of her anorectic predecessor. Reporters relished the spontaneity of the new First Lady, her frankness, and her quotable humor. "It always helps to have an easy act to follow," noted Calvin Trillin in *The Nation*.

Barbara understood her appeal. "I'm not a threat to anyone," she said. "How could I be? Look at me . . . Nancy wore a size 4. That's the size of one of my legs." Posing for a photographer, she quipped, "Unfortunately, my winning smile makes me look as if I'm being electrocuted. My kids are always looking at pictures of me and saying: 'Look at Mom, she's plugged in again!' " When she was diagnosed with Graves' disease, a thyroid disorder that required radioactive iodine and injections of prednisone, she experienced double vision. When she returned to the White House after a treatment, reporters shouted, "How are your eyes?" She sauntered over to the cameras and playfully crossed her eyes. "They're fine," she said.

Having mastered the art of self-deprecation, Barbara made fun of herself before others could, but she admitted once how much effort it took for her to laugh at the comments about looking so much older than her husband. "That hurt," she said. "Really hurt." When she showed a reporter a picture of George standing between his mother and his wife, she added pointedly, "His mother is the one on the right." Insecure about her looks, Barbara told one photographer she wanted to have her official portrait painted with her wearing a hat. "I'll do anything I can to take the picture off the face."

"Barbara Bush came into the White House with a dexterity at manipulating her image," said Donnie Radcliffe, who covered the Bush White House for *The Washington Post*, "and she wasn't above playing off her own outspoken style against Nancy Reagan's reluctance and often inability to express herself. Media-smart, a less popular political wife might have seemed calculating."

Barbara capitalized on her goodwill with good works. Within weeks of her husband's inauguration, she was photographed cuddling an AIDS baby, an arresting picture in 1989, when many people were so afraid of the disease they avoided the afflicted. Encouraged by the White House physician, Burton Lee, Barbara lent her prestige to the problem in hopes that photographs of her with AIDS babies would help to dispel fears that the disease was transmitted by touching. She felt slighted when Diana, the Princess of Wales, visited New York's Harlem Hospital and made news around the world by cradling a dying AIDS baby. Barbara wanted credit for being in the vanguard. "I visited that clinic a full year before she did," she told reporters. "You just didn't care."

Barbara became a champion of the homeless, the hungry, and the handicapped. People saw her as a humanitarian who might soften her husband's hard stances on abortion and gun control, but she was quick to disabuse them of the notion. "I do not want to dilute what influence I have by talking about things that I was not elected to do anything about," she said. "Besides, I do not lobby my husband." Instead, she spearheaded a drive for literacy, starting the Barbara Bush Foundation for Family Literacy with $500,000 in private contributions. She reached the apogee of her acclaim when she announced that her pedigreed English springer spaniel, Millie, was "getting married." Named for Mildred Kerr, Barbara's best friend in Texas, Millie delivered six puppies in the spring of 1989. Immediately the President's polls shot up.

"Let me give you a little serious political inside advice," he said at his next press conference. "One single word: puppies—worth ten points, believe me."

Months later the First Lady wrote *Millie's Book*, which she dedicated to "George Bush, whom we both love more than life." The First Lady promoted her doggy book around the country and made it a number-one bestseller.

"Millie has made me legitimate," Barbara said. "Who else do you know that wrote a book that made a million dollars for charity and gave it all away? I was feeling a tad guilty by the women's movement until Millie did what she did. And it was all by myself, nobody helped . . . Every word was written by me and Millie."

Again the President took notice. "You have read my tax returns," he told reporters. "You can tell who the breadwinner is in the family. The dog made five times as much as the President of the United States."

Millie followed the First Lady everywhere she went, even sharing the presidential bed. "She gets the middle," Barbara quipped. George said that Millie got better press than anyone in the administration, including Secretary of State James Baker, which the President found amazing, "considering Millie doesn't leak like Jimmy does."

"That dog was a wonderful companion for Barbara," recalled Heather Foley, the wife of the former Speaker of the House of Representatives. "Barbara told me, rather sadly, how essential Millie was to her life in the White House . . . After she said that, I remember thinking how lonely Barbara must have been, which is surprising when you consider that most first ladies see more of their husbands as President than at any other time in their marriage . . . But George Bush was so hyper . . . he was constantly filling their life with other people . . . constant, constant entertaining . . . I guess he never wanted to be alone . . . so while Barbara saw a lot of people all the time, she had no real companionship, except for that dog."

Reporters recalled many occasions when Barbara became exasperated with her husband's impromptu invitations. After a press conference in Paris, the President invited the traveling press corps into the Ambassador's residence for a personal tour. "I don't believe you're doing this," Barbara muttered. She told the reporters they could not come in unless they took off their shoes and washed their feet. (She slapped the same stipulation on Diane Sawyer and Sam Donaldson when they went to the White House to interview the Bushes in the family quarters for *Primetime Live*. Barbara insisted that every member of the ABC-TV technical team—cameramen, light men, soundmen, the makeup artist, the hairdresser, and all the assistant directors—bring a brand-new pair of white sneakers so that they would not soil her new white carpeting.) Another time the President invited a media horde to join him for wine and cheese at Kennebunkport when Barbara would have preferred being alone with him. One journalist walked over to thank her for her hospitality. "Don't thank me," Barbara snapped. "Thank George. He's the one who invited you." She walked off accompanied only by her dog.

The portraitist Herbert E. Abrams realized how much Barbara's dog meant when he sat down to discuss painting the First Lady for her official White House portrait.

"I want Millie to be in the picture with me," Barbara said.

"I'm so sorry, Mrs. Bush, but I don't think that will be possible."

"Mrs. Coolidge had her White House portrait painted with her dog."

"If I put Millie in the picture, she'd be on the floor, and that would reduce the size of you; either that or I'd have to enlarge the painting, which the White House would not accept."

"Well, I can hold Millie on my lap," said Barbara.

"No, Mrs. Bush. That dog is too big to be on your lap."

Barbara looked down at the sad-eyed spaniel sitting at her feet. "I'm sorry, Millie," she said. "I tried."

The First Lady sat for her first session without Millie, but the artist later discussed the problem with his wife, Lois, who had accompanied him to select Mrs. Bush's clothes.

"I had recommended that she wear Bush blue for the sitting," said Lois Abrams, "and Herb decided to paint her seated next to a table with books, because of her interest in literacy, and, of course, the yellow roses of Texas. Then he said there was no reason why he couldn't put a photograph of Millie in the painting . . . He was also doing the President's official portrait, so at their next sitting he had President Bush hold Millie and Herb photographed her. When he painted the First Lady's portrait, he also painted a small portrait of Millie from the photo he had taken, which he then painted into a frame on the table. This was a total surprise to Mrs. Bush, and when she saw it, she was thrilled . . . When Millie died in 1997, Herb sent a sympathy note to Barbara Bush, and she wrote back, thanking him for giving Millie a permanent place in the White House."

Throughout Bush's presidency, the First Lady's polls were so high that reporters dared not show all her feistiness, although she made little effort to hold her tongue with family or friends. Interestingly, for a woman who wrapped her large frame in horizontal stripes and wore more polka dots than Clarabelle the Clown, Barbara considered herself a fashion arbiter and frequently upbraided others for the way they looked and the clothes they wore. She maintained a rigid set of standards, which she expected others to adopt.

"You're too fat," she told her younger brother, Scott Pierce, whenever he gained weight.

"Don't you dare wear that mink coat in public," she instructed her daughter-in-law Sharon Bush. "People will think we're rich."

When she saw C. Boyden Gray's young wife walk into a party wearing a pair of diamond-and-emerald earrings, Barbara demanded to know: "What are you doing with jewels like that?"

She nearly threw the talk-show host Larry King out of the White House when he arrived to interview the President. "I can't believe you would walk into this house without a jacket," she said. In his uniform of pants, shirt, tie, and suspenders, King shrugged and laughed, but Barbara did not smile. "She was seriously offended," recalled a CNN producer.

She railed at her husband's Secretary of Labor, Lynn Martin, for wearing short skirts. "Why do you do that? It looks just awful, awful, awful."

"Because I've got great legs," replied the cabinet member.

When French Wallop arrived for lunch with her hair pulled back in a chic bow, Barbara jumped on her. "When are you going to get rid of that terrible-looking ponytail?"

"Not anytime soon, I hope," said Senator Wallop's wife.

Not even a world-class athlete like Andre Agassi was spared Barbara's snipes. She chastised him for wearing "awful clothes" to play tennis on the White House court, and then hectored him about his ponytail and his earring.

Sometimes Barbara let politics get in the way of good manners. When Jane Fonda visited the White House with her husband, Ted Turner, the First Lady rudely ignored the famous movie star, known to be a liberal Democrat.

"Yes," said Jane Fonda many years later. "Mrs. Bush did refuse to shake my hand. Her husband, however, did. It was not anything dramatic. But I saw that she didn't want to and I didn't push it. Why, after all? It's her right. No big deal far as I'm concerned."

Another time Barbara refused to have her picture taken with Democratic Representative Barney Frank of Massachusetts and his former domestic partner Herb Moses. "I didn't know if it was because I was gay or a Democrat," joked Frank.

"The President posed with us," said Herb Moses, "but then he asked us not to publicize the picture. He didn't say that to any of the heterosexual couples, but we said we would not release the photo because politics is politics and this was a White House Christmas party . . . Barney and I went to the White House every year for the Bushes' parties until I got sick of being the political wife."

Scenes showing Mrs. Bush as less than gracious rarely made the newspapers during her husband's presidency. "Many reporters assumed, without any prompting by her, that her most acid comments [and actions] were off the record," said Paul Bedard, formerly of *The Washington Times*. "Some of us even went out of our way to protect her from herself . . .

"Because I covered Bush, I spent a lot of time at Kennebunkport, and Mrs. Bush always felt more comfortable talking to our reporters than anyone else because we were known as a conservative paper . . . Every summer the President invited the White House press corps to a party at his estate, where he served up hot dogs, beer, and ice cream; rides on his cigarette boat, *Fidelity*; and games of horseshoes. I remember Barbara crapping all over the press for trashing her gardens and stepping on her flowers. Then she started talking to me about D.C. Mayor Marion Barry, who was on crack cocaine, and she crapped all over him, saying how horrible it was for the nation's capital to have such a disgusting lowlife as mayor . . .

"I knew this would be a great story—the President's wife blasting the black mayor of Washington, D.C.—but I didn't use it because I just had a feeling of deference. Part of it was being protective of the First Lady, and part of it was a feeling that there was a trust . . . I doubt she would've talked like that to a reporter from *The Washington Post* . . . I just didn't want to burn her."

For most of her husband's presidency, the First Lady received a deservedly good press. She navigated some rough waters in 1990, when 150 of 600 seniors at Wellesley College protested her invitation to be the commencement speaker. They said her only qualification for the honor was her husband's political success. Barbara agreed, but Mike Barnicle in *The Boston Globe* called them "a pack of whining, unshaven feminists." Even the President was angered by the protest, but the First Lady remained sanguine.

"I chose to live the life I've lived and I think it has been a fabulously exciting, interesting, involved life," she said. "I hope some of them will choose the same . . . In my day, *they* probably would have been considered different. In their day, *I'm* considered different. Vive la différence!"

Barbara made her way to Wellesley accompanied by Raisa Gorbachev, wife of the Soviet President, and won over the protesters, even when she told them, "If you have children, they must come first." She received a standing ovation when she ended: "Who knows? Somewhere out in this audience may even be someone who will one day follow in my footsteps and preside over the White House as the president's spouse, and I wish him well."

By then Barbara Bush had become her husband's greatest asset. She had so endeared herself to the nation that reporters shied away from delving into the persona behind the pile of pearls. No one examined the stagecraft of her carefully constructed image until late into her husband's presidency, when Marjorie Williams wrote a piece for *Vanity Fair* titled "Barbara's Backlash." It laid bare the reality of the First Lady as a "combative politician," so "caustic and judgmental" that she terrified her husband's staff.

Through interviews with friends and employees, the Bushes' marriage emerged as a relationship that was adoring on Barbara's part, but so incidental to her faithless husband that he occasionally forgot she was around. His mother frequently had to remind him to "act" more attentive by letting Barbara exit planes before him. When the Bushes visited the Queen in London, the President left the First Lady in the car until the Queen noticed her absence and sent a footman to open the door. Williams documented Barbara's struggle "to remain as important a part of her husband's life as he has been of hers." The writer described the prickly banter between them as hostile and jabbing. Barbara came across tough as a boot, in contrast to George, who emerged as an absentee father and an inattentive husband. With no display of physical affection, the Bushes acted like two towel-snapping pals who had bonded over their children and their shared investment in George's political ascent. During the 1988 campaign Barbara had made sour comments about the openly affectionate relationship between Michael and Kitty Dukakis as "phony" and "fake." Williams perceptively noted, "Bush often seems to treat Barbara more like a buddy than a wife. In public they present their relationship as a partnership that has transcended sex."

Barbara was irate when she read the profile, which had exposed her greatest vulnerability—her marriage. Instead of taking the high road and ignoring the piece, she railed for weeks. "Granted I was mad as the dickens when I read the article 'cause it was so hurtful," she told the writer Barbara Grizzuti Harrison. "But then I thought: this is so silly, I never met this woman, I don't know her, she's repeating myths. They were just trying to get George. They attack our children, they attack me, but that's not us—that's him. It's too bad; it's so ugly. She didn't even know me to begin with. Anna [the First Lady's press secretary], have I ever met her? No. Never met her. As far as I know, she is just a magazine, not a person . . . just a magazine."

Usually Barbara was too shrewd to flare in public, but she could not contain her anger over the *Vanity Fair* profile. A champion writer as dazzling with her prose as Muhammad Ali with his blows had limned her—and Barbara was reeling. She had memorized all the wounding phrases and was still repeating them weeks later. "I was really offended by [what she wrote about] my relationship with my husband, who I really do love more than life, and who I think loves me and always has. That hurt. 'We've noticed this cooling'—that hurt me a lot. I know I've never met that writer, I couldn't tell you her name now. But it hurt, that article. She said we 'transcended sex.' That just hurt me a lot."

Barbara referred to those she loved by name, beginning with her husband, who was always "George Bush." Those who incurred her wrath were stripped of their identity. Now "just a magazine," Marjorie Williams had joined a list that included Gloria Steinem, whom Barbara baptized as "whatever her name is" after the feminist insulted Richard Nixon; Garry Trudeau was just "a little cartoonist"; Ann Richards remained "that woman with the hair"; Senator Ted Kennedy was the "man [who] has no right to even utter my husband's name"; and after a probing interview, the television journalist Judy Woodruff was reduced to "she."

After the humorist Dave Barry saw that interview, he wrote, "[I]f you think I'm going to say anything bad about [Barbara Bush], you're crazy. She is hugely popular and scary when angered. I saw her get interviewed on TV by Judy Woodruff, who asked some questions that Mrs. Bush didn't like, and Mrs. Bush fired off a glare that left dime-sized burn craters on Judy's forehead. So I'm on the record here as stating that Mrs. Bush's speech was WAY better than the Gettysburg Address, and you better do what she said."

As the family's enforcer, Barbara never forgave and she never forgot. "There were times that people did some things that I think upset my mother," George W. Bush told *The Washington Post*. "Leaks ... especially infuriated her. I would then go talk to them and inform them that they needed to amend their way—and explain to them that if they weren't careful, the wrath of the Silver Fox would fall upon them. Who knows what would happen? It may not happen immediately, it may happen as time would go on."

In a conversation with Canadian Prime Minister Brian Mulroney, Bush alluded to his wife as a grudge keeper. The Prime Minister said his wife was the same way, adding, "Do you think it's because women are less forgiving than men?"

While the President was not as overt as the First Lady, he certainly knew how to drop-kick "kinder and gentler" as well as she did. After he addressed a fund-raiser for Republican Senator Alfonse D'Amato of New York, George Bush became incensed hearing D'Amato rap him a few days later for spending too much time on the golf course. Calling the Republican "an ungrateful son of a bitch," the President sent word to D'Amato that he could forget about any more help from the White House. "George is normally a very even-tempered guy," said his friend Lud Ashley, "but he's also a very loyal guy. And when he doesn't get loyalty in return, that does tick him off."

Ralph Neas, then executive director of the Leadership Conference on Civil Rights, felt the sting of Bush's retaliation after the President vetoed the Civil Rights Act of 1990, which was intended to prohibit discrimination in employment.

"I was very critical of the President for that veto and for calling the bill a quota bill simply to pander to the right wing," said Neas. "I said he was acting beneath the dignity of his office."

Traveling on Air Force One, the President heard Neas describe him on television as the man who had promised during his 1988 campaign to leave "the tired baggage of bigotry behind," and then proceeded to make Willie Horton the most famous black man in America. Despite Bush's rhetoric about voter outreach, he had vetoed passage of a voter-registration program that could have added millions of minority voters to the election rolls, and now he had vetoed a civil rights act passed by overwhelming majorities in both houses of Congress. "The White House is declaring open war on civil rights," said Neas.

The President became so angry at Neas that he momentarily forgot his name and startled reporters by blasting him as "that . . . that . . . white guy who attacked me on this quota bill." Neas became persona non grata at the Bush White House and was barred from all future bill signings.

The former television correspondent Susan King experienced a similar slap after doing a story on the campaign whispers about Bush and other women, including his involvement with Jennifer Fitzgerald.

"He was furious with me," King said. "I didn't say in the piece that he and Jennifer were having an affair, and it's not a story I'd submit for a prize, but it was legitimate to raise the issue because everyone was talking about it at the time. Barbara did not like Jennifer and did not want her around. That was clear to all of us on the campaign . . . George never forgave me for doing the piece . . . A year or so later, when I was doing a story on Dan Quayle and was in the White House to get a shot of Quayle and Bush together in the Oval Office, the President allowed my cameraman in but kept me out."

The same President who called his mother every day, wrote touching notes to strangers in trouble, and constantly extolled the blessings of "family, friends and faith" was spiteful to his adversaries. When House Majority Leader Richard Gephardt criticized the President for his "failure to lead," Bush banned him from several White House events.

Former Connecticut Senator Lowell Weicker experienced one of the meanest rebukes in 1989, when he was turned away from the installation ceremony in the Rose Garden of his friend Justin Dart Jr., who had been named chairman of the President's Committee on Employment of People with Disabilities.

"My assistant, Kim Elliott, and I arrived at the White House for Justin's swearing in, but we never got past the front gate," said Weicker, who had been defeated in 1988 by Joe Lieberman. "The White House guard told me my name had been scratched off the list . . . Vice President Quayle was furious when he found out what happened, and to his credit he called me to apologize . . . He tried to blame John Sununu, the President's chief of staff, rather than the President himself."

Over the years Weicker had worked closely with Justin Dart Jr., who had lost the use of his legs after a bout with polio but continued to fight for the rights of the disabled from his wheelchair. As the senior senator from Connecticut, Weicker had introduced a bill during the 100th Congress that eventually led to landmark civil rights legislation for the disabled. "The legislation was changed substantially after I left the Senate, but nevertheless, no bill ever had more of my stamp or more of my heart in it than the Americans with Disabilities Act."

At the 1988 GOP convention Weicker tried to get a commitment in the Republican platform that the party would support the disabilities act, but he was rebuffed by Sununu, who said Bush did not want the plank. "I think Bush was probably committed," said Weicker, "but he had to take in the bleatings of the hard right."

When the President signed the Americans with Disabilities Act on July 26, 1990, he invited three thousand people to the White House to witness what he said was the major accomplishment of his presidency. Lowell Weicker was not among the honored guests.

"I know there had been some bad blood between the Bushes and Lowell, but it was so petty to keep him away from that bill signing," said Kim Elliott. "We knew it wasn't an oversight, because senators like Harkin, Kennedy, and Dodd lobbied the White House to get Lowell included, but Bush wouldn't do it . . . And Bush didn't even have that much to do with the ADA. The credit for getting it passed goes to Senator Bob Dole on the Republican side and Senator Tom Harkin on the Democratic side."

Try as he might, even the President of the United States could not keep Weicker out of the Bush White House for good. When the President and the First Lady hosted a party for the nation's governors in 1991, they had to invite Weicker because by then he had been elected governor of Connecticut, one of the few people to hold the office of U.S. representative (1969–71), U.S. senator (1971–89), and governor (1991–95).

"I remember when we went to the White House," recalled Weicker's wife, Claudia. "Barbara greeted us by saying, 'Oh, Lowell. You old renegade, you.' "

Tom D'Amore, Weicker's chief of staff, chuckled. "I liked Bar a lot," he said, "because she's Lowell Weicker in a dress. They're both direct and speak their mind."

To the dismay of his aides, President Bush seemed more engaged in planning parties and meeting celebrities in the first months of his term than in dealing with affairs of state or addressing himself to the domestic issues of a faltering economy and burgeoning deficit.

"I covered George senior during the first six months he was President," said Worth Kinlaw, a Navy cameraman assigned to the White House, "and he was like a kid in a candy shop . . . I covered Reagan, Bush, and Clinton—all totally different. Reagan was like your favorite grandfather—funny but you could never get too close. He enjoyed telling great stories, especially about the past. Clinton was the bad boy from high school, always trying to cop a feel. He was totally into babes. Oh, God. When those White House videos finally become public, you'll see what I mean by totally, grossly, and completely into babes. He'll be nailed then like never before. And Bush . . . well, Bush was like your goofy uncle . . .

"I remember when Miss USA came into the Oval Office with her crown and scepter and talked about how she was not just a pretty face but was committed to saving the world. You could see Bush's eyes glazing over. After she left, he said, 'Did ya hear that, fellas? It's all about brains now. I liked it better when it was just bikinis.' Bush is a man's man and has that kind of male humor."

"That's for sure," said Julia Malone of Cox Newspapers. "I went with John Mashek to do an interview in the Oval Office. The first thing the President said was, 'Hey, John. Ya got any jokes to tell?' Then he looked at me. 'I know I can trust you, Mashek, but what about her?' So I agreed to go off the record while the two of them swapped their dirty jokes. It was an awkward moment, but George Bush is a locker-room kind of guy. For all his kindly graciousness, he's really just a towel-snapper at heart."

Mashek admitted there was nothing that President Bush liked more than a dirty joke. "I never heard him tell a racist joke, but he sure did love a good sex joke . . . A far fall from the prudish demeanor of his father, who never swore in front of a woman."

As President, Bush kept a male fertility figure, which he had received from the President of Mozambique, in the Oval Office bathroom. The carved wooden statue, facing the toilet, stood three feet high and was anatomically correct, if somewhat exaggerated. The President kept a roll of toilet paper on the extended male organ. He liked to send young women into the bathroom and watch their reaction when they emerged.

"Alixe Glenn, who was deputy press secretary and about twenty-six years old at the time, told a group of reporters about George Herbert Walker Bush's weird sex thing," recalled one White House correspondent.

"She said the President told her to go into his bathroom and wash her hands. She did as she was told and came out red-faced with embarrassment. The President thought it was killingly funny."

A new President usually gets a "honeymoon" of one hundred days to get the ship of state on an even keel and headed in the right direction. The Bush honeymoon lasted all of two weeks before he was battling the U.S. Senate over his nomination of John Tower to be Secretary of Defense.

The President had been warned by Craig Fuller, Robert Teeter, and Secretary of the Treasury Nick Brady that the former Texas senator would be a divisive nomination. The dictatorial Tower had left few friends in the Senate when he retired, and he had problems with "booze and broads." Bush dismissed the objections: he said he had never seen Tower drunk on all fours in public, and womanizing was a fact of life for all men. Besides, Tower wanted the position at Defense, and Bush wanted to give it to him, especially since Tower's commission had exonerated George from any wrongdoing in Iran-contra. Bush told his aides that a President is rarely denied his choice of cabinet members. Over his aides' objections, he submitted Tower's nomination on January 20, 1989. Bush wrote in his diary: "Not only did I think he would do an outstanding job, I also assumed his nomination would glide through the Hill for two good reasons: he was more than qualified for the job, and Congress is usually kind to its own. I could not have been more wrong."

The President met with the chairman of the Senate Armed Services Committee to plead for Tower, but the Democrat Sam Nunn of Georgia was not persuaded. His committee rejected the President's nomination 11–9 after Nunn announced: "I cannot in good conscience vote to put an individual at the top of the chain of command when his history of excessive drinking is such that he would not be selected to command a missile wing, a SAC [Strategic Air Command] bomber squadron or a Trident missile submarine."

Having nominated Tower over the objections of his advisers, the President would not back down. He stubbornly insisted on taking the nomination to the floor of the Democrat-controlled Senate. "We are not going to paint our tails white and run with the antelopes," he declared. He wrote to his friend the columnist Charles Bartlett: "I am going to stand with Tower all the way, and I am confident he will make it. I have never

Barbara and George Bush arrived in China in October 1974 and left in December 1975. As chief of the U.S. liaison office, Bush carried out the dictates of Secretary of State Henry Kissinger.

ABOVE RIGHT As director of the Central Intelligence Agency from January 30, 1976, to January 20, 1977, George signed his personal letters "Head Spook." He said this appointment was his favorite job in government. He was the only President who had been director of the CIA, and the CIA headquarters in Langley, Virginia, was named in his honor on April 26, 1999.

LEFT MIDDLE President and Mrs. Ronald Reagan with Vice President and Mrs. George H.W. Bush at the Republican National Convention in Dallas on August 23, 1984. The relationship between the two couples was strained; Nancy Reagan called George Bush "whiney" and never forgave him for charging Reagan with "voodoo economics."

LEFT BOTTOM President-elect George Bush and Barbara with Marilyn and Dan Quayle on January 19, 1989, after Bush had confided in his diary (August 21, 1988) he had made a big mistake in choosing the Indiana senator to be his running mate. "It was my decision, and I blew it, but I'm not about to say that I blew it."

ABOVE LEFT George W. Bush, seven years old, with his father and his sister, Robin, in Greenwich, Connecticut, during the summer of 1953. Robin had been diagnosed with leukemia in February of that year and died on October 11, 1953.

ABOVE RIGHT The Bush family in Houston, Texas, in 1959. Seated left to right: Neil, George a.k.a. "Poppy" Bush, holding baby Doro, Marvin, and Barbara. Standing: George W. and Jeb. The family moved from Midland to Houston when Bush's Zapata Offshore and the Liedtke brothers' Zapata Petroleum went their separate ways.

BELOW The Bush family on Inauguration Day, January 20, 1981, in the Vice President's mansion, Washington, D.C. From left: Doro, Marvin, George H.W., Barbara, Jeb, George W., and Neil.

ABOVE The family at the patriarch's seventy-fifth birthday celebration, June 10, 1999, shortly after the elder Bush had parachuted onto the campus of Texas A&M University in College Station. Seated from left: Neil, Governor George W. Bush, President Bush (41), Governor Jeb Bush, Marvin, and Doro. Standing: Sharon, Laura, Barbara, Columba, Margaret, and Bobby Koch.

BELOW The small fraternity of former presidents and their first ladies who gathered on April 16, 1997, in Grand Rapids, Michigan, for the rededication of the Ford Museum. Seated: Lady Bird Johnson, Barbara Bush, Betty Ford, and Rosalynn Carter. Standing: President Bush (1989–93) making rabbit ears behind his wife's head, President Ford (1974–77), and President Carter (1977–81).

ABOVE George Bush meets in his private office at the White House with Jennifer Fitzgerald on May 8, 1989. Fitzgerald became deputy chief of protocol when Bush became President, and remained with him until the end of his public career in 1992.

INSET LEFT Jennifer Fitzgerald at the White House on November 30, 1974, before leaving for China to become George Bush's close personal aide. Known as "the other woman" in Bush's life, Fitzgerald was his personal assistant for fourteen years.

RIGHT Nancy Reagan and Barbara Bush, January 27, 1981, a week after the inaugural. Their relationship was publicly cordial but privately corrosive. During their eight years in the White House, Mrs. Reagan never invited the Bushes to the family quarters. Reagan's biographer Edmund Morris said, "Barbara never forgave Nancy for treating them like the help."

LEFT Vice President and Mrs. Bush aboard Air Force Two on October 25, 1984, a few days after the Vice President's debate with the Democrat Geraldine Ferraro. Barbara Bush described her husband's opponent as a word that "rhymes with rich."

TOP Representative George H.W. Bush (R-TX) is poised to pin a lieutenant bar on his son George W. Bush in 1968 after the son, who never attended Officers' Training School, received a special commission as a second lieutenant in the Texas Air National Guard.

ABOVE LEFT The 1978 campaign poster for George W. Bush with his new bride, Laura Lane Welch, from Midland, Texas. They spent their honeymoon driving around West Texas as George sought to win a seat in the House of Representatives. He lost to his Democratic opponent, Kent Hance, who switched parties years later and supported Bush when he ran for governor.

ABOVE RIGHT George W. Bush at Arlington Stadium in Texas on April 18, 1989, after the American and National League owners approved the sale of the Texas Rangers to a group fronted by Bush and financed by others. The President's son, who invested only $500,000, made $15 million when the team was sold in 1998.

ABOVE LEFT The brothers' sibling rivalry was not evident in 1955 when George W. Bush, nine, posed with his brother John Ellis "Jeb" Bush, two. Growing up, they competed ferociously in sports and later in politics for the approval of their absentee father.

ABOVE RIGHT Florida Governor Jeb Bush embraces his brother, the presumed President-elect, George W. Bush, on election night 2000. Earlier in the evening, when the networks called Florida for Bush's opponent, Al Gore, Jeb was in tears.

RIGHT Florida's Secretary of State Katherine Harris with Governor Jeb Bush on December 18, 2000, after announcing Florida's electoral votes "officially" going to George W. Bush. Harris's decisions assured victory for the governor's brother. In 2002, Harris was elected to the House of Representatives from Florida's thirteenth district. On May 14, 2001, Jeb called a press conference to deny rumors that he had had an affair with Harris.

RIGHT George W. Bush being sworn in as President with his wife, Laura, on January 20, 2001. In his inaugural address Bush said, "Many in our country do not know the pain of poverty, but we can listen to those who do. And I can pledge our nation to a goal: when we see that wounded traveler on the road to Jericho, we will not pass to the other side."

ABOVE George W. Bush speaking at Bob Jones University during the South Carolina primary on February 2, 2000. "We share the same conservative values," he said, "the same conservative principles." Bob Jones University—whose founders were virulently anti-Catholic—opposed integration, banned interracial dating, and condemned homosexuality.

ABOVE President Bush (43) in the rubble of Ground Zero on September 14, 2001, three days after the terrorists' attack on the World Trade Center. Next to the President is Bob Beckwith, a retired firefighter who had just come down to look at the ruins. Accompanied by New York City Mayor Rudolph Giuliani, Bush toured the disaster site on foot.

INSET LEFT The youngest pilot in the U.S. Navy, George H.W. Bush enlisted following his eighteenth birthday after graduating from Phillips Academy at Andover, Massachusetts. He served three years in World War II with the Third and Fifth Fleets in the Pacific. He was awarded a Distinguished Flying Cross for heroism.

LEFT President George W. Bush landing on the USS *Abraham Lincoln* on May 1, 2003, in an S-3B Viking, an antisubmarine aircraft. Behind him, attached to the superstructure of the ship, was a large banner: "Mission Accomplished." The White House reluctantly admitted later that it had not been necessary for Bush to land by plane but that he wanted to. After being photographed in his flight suit, the President changed clothes and announced, "Major combat operations in Iraq have ended."

TOP LEFT The twin daughters of George and Laura Bush: Barbara (Yale 2004) and Jenna (University of Texas 2004) on inaugural night, January 21, 2001. During college, both girls were arrested for underage drinking. They used fake IDs like their father once did. Their grandmother Barbara Bush criticized them privately. Shortly after police in Austin, Texas, cited the twins for violating state alcoholic-beverage laws, Barbara joked that what goes around comes around. Said his mother: "George is getting back some of his own."

BELOW MIDDLE George Prescott Bush with his uncle George Walker Bush. P4, as he's known in the family, the eldest child of Jeb and Columba Bush, was born on April 24, 1976. After graduating from Rice University and teaching high-school history in Florida for a year, he campaigned for his uncle for President before starting law school at the University of Texas. He graduated in 2003, clerked for a federal judge in Dallas, and plans to join the Dallas office of Akin, Gump, Strauss, Hauer, and Feld. The Bush family considers George P. their answer to John F. Kennedy Jr.—handsome, accomplished, and destined for a bright future.

BELOW BOTTOM An Orange County sheriff's deputy escorts Noelle Bush from court in Orlando, Florida, on July 19, 2002, as her brother George P. Bush, far left, looks on. The only daughter of Jeb and Columba, Noelle was born on July 26, 1977, and has been addicted to drugs, and in and out of court and rehab, for several years.

ABOVE Lauren Bush, born June 25, 1984, is the eldest of Neil and Sharon's three children. Enrolled at Princeton (class of 2006), she became a model at the age of sixteen, made her debut at the Crillon Haute Couture Ball in Paris in 2000, and posed for *Vanity Fair*, *Vogue*, and *Town & Country*. Her mother, who enjoys escorting her daughter to social soirees, said, "Bar just hates the fact that Lauren is a model."

seen such a campaign of innuendo, vicious rumor and gossip in my entire life . . . I am not considering alternatives."

On March 9, 1989, the Senate rejected the nomination 53–47, the first time in modern history a former senator had been so rebuffed. The President stood alone in congratulating himself for his loyalty, while others began to question his judgment. Only forty-eight days into his term and his presidency had gone Code Blue; he was forced to call a press conference to announce that his administration was not terminal. "There is no drift," he claimed. "No malaise." Yet the President had saddled himself with a Vice President who was even more gaffe prone than he was. Dan Quayle had addressed the United Negro College Fund, whose slogan is "A mind is a terrible thing to waste," by saying: "You take the United Negro College Fund model that what a waste it is to lose one's mind or not to have a mind is being very wasteful. How true that is."

In addition to his inept Vice President, the President, who said he would not tolerate the appearance of impropriety in his administration, had appointed a White House counsel, C. Boyden Gray, who had not disclosed eighty-seven thousand dollars in deferred income from a family business while he was in government, and a White House chief of staff, John Sununu, whose arrogance was alienating everyone in sight and whose misuse of government planes cost taxpayers $500,000 and would eventually cost him his job.

Compounding the problems within the Bush White House was the President himself. As democracy began bursting forth from the concrete slabs of Communism in Eastern Europe and South America, Bush seemed wary of looking jubilant. "I don't want to do anything dumb," he said.

When Chinese troops fired in Tiananmen Square on June 4, 1989, in a bloody crackdown on the democracy movement, Bush responded lamely: "This is not the time for an emotional response." He did not denounce the violence, the abuse of power, or the loss of lives. He promised to issue an executive order protecting Chinese students in the United States, but he never did, because he did not want to offend his "old friend" Deng Xiaoping, Chairman of the People's Republic of China. Freedom lovers around the world ached for something more inspirational from the President of the United States, but Bush was incapable of giving them the rhetoric they desired. "It would not be prudent," he said. He repeated that phrase so often that it became the signature line for a prissy imitation of Bush by the comedian Dana Carvey on *Saturday Night Live*.

The President performed miserably in July 1989, when he visited Warsaw, which was celebrating the legalization of the Solidarity movement and the restoration of freedom. Lacking the ability to mirror the hope and humanity of the Polish people, the President sounded like a dismal clerk as he emphasized the difficulties of the economic reform that Poland would have to face.

Months later, when Lithuania unilaterally declared its independence from the Soviet Union, the President barely responded. Later he told reporters: "I don't want to make—you know, remember Yogi Berra: 'What happened? Why did you lose the ball game?' He said, 'We made the wrong mistake.' You got to think about that one. And I don't want to make the wrong mistake."

When the Berlin Wall fell in November 1989, Bush's response was so unimaginative as to be a national embarrassment. "I am very pleased with this development," he told the press. Michael Duffy and Dan Goodgame wrote in *Time* that when he appeared before the TV cameras in the Oval Office, he looked as if he had just seen his dog run over by a truck. Even his lyricist felt shortchanged. Years later Peggy Noonan tried to explain what made George Bush so tone-deaf to the harmonics of history.

"Bush had a high character," she said. "What he lacked, however, was a kind of historical imagination—the kind of big-sweep imagination that helps you apprehend and understand the great forces of your time. The day the Berlin Wall fell was a huge moment in history, one of the high points of the twentieth century—Soviet expansionist Communism, the great peace disturber of the twentieth century, was ending. We ended it. Remember what Bush said? Nothing. He told Lesley Stahl [CBS-TV] he didn't want to 'rub it in.' What would Reagan have done? He would have called his speechwriters in and told us to get to work on a speech in which we mark this moment well and indelibly, in which he thanked the people of the West and of America for half a century of blood and treasure that they put toward this day. He would have thanked them. He would have thanked God. He would have told schoolchildren what this day meant, what lessons they could draw from it. He would have captured its meaning. He had a historical imagination. George Bush did not."

The President tried to defend his reticence in an interview with

David Frost. "My restraint, or prudence, if you will, was misunderstood, certainly by some in the Congress. Senator Mitchell, the leading Democrat in the Senate . . . Dick Gephardt, the leader in the House, were saying: 'Our President doesn't get it. He ought to go to Berlin, stand on the Wall, dance with the young people to show the joy that we all feel.' I still feel that would have been the stupidest thing an American president could do because we were very concerned about how the troops would react. We were very concerned about the nationalistic elements in the Soviet Union maybe putting Gorbachev out. I think if we'd have misplayed our hand and had a heavy-handed overkill, you know, gloating, 'We won, Mr. Gorbachev, you've lost, you're out,' I think it could have been a very different ending to this very happy chapter in history when the wall came down."

Whether or not Bush was rationalizing his tepid reaction to a historic convulsion, he showed utter disregard for the emotional component of the presidency and the rapport that binds a leader to his people when he speaks to it in times of joy and tragedy. Yet at the end of his first year the President's popular approval far exceeded that of the Great Communicator himself at the end of Ronald Reagan's first year. In fact, Bush's poll numbers were higher than those of any post–World War II President except John F. Kennedy.

On August 1, 1991, the President visited Kiev and lectured the Ukrainian independence movement on its "suicidal nationalism" in trying to break free from the Soviet Union. He urged them to stay with Moscow. Three weeks later Ukraine declared its independence, and the *New York Times* columnist William Safire needled the President for his "chicken Kiev" speech. Safire accused Bush of being blind to the forces of history. Bush was so incensed he never spoke to the columnist again.

The dramatic developments in the Soviet Union led the President to make an epic decision to reduce the U.S. arsenal of nuclear weapons. He made this titanic announcement in a prime-time speech that was totally devoid of eloquence. His dry recitation buried the historic import of what he was doing to make the world a less dangerous place than ever before in the nuclear age.

On Christmas Day, 1991, the Soviet Union ceased to exist, and Mikhail Gorbachev resigned as Soviet President. President Bush was at Camp David, but he returned to the White House that evening to address the nation from the Oval Office. He announced that the Cold War was over and the Commonwealth of Independent States had emerged from the wreckage of the USSR. He saluted Gorbachev for his revolutionary policies and committed the United States to supporting the liberation of the Russian people. It was a short, serviceable statement, but it lacked the ringing cadence and soaring spirit people wanted from the leader of the free world.

In the beginning of his presidency, Bush seemed timid and unsure of himself on the world stage. "I don't want to make any early term mistakes like Kennedy and the Bay of Pigs," he said. Yet George Bush was as fixated on eliminating Manuel Noriega of Panama as John F. Kennedy had been on eliminating Cuba's Fidel Castro.

Unlike Kennedy, Bush personally knew his nemesis, having met with Noriega twice. Bush had paid him $110,000 a year as a CIA operative, which may have accounted for the strongman's boast "I have Bush by the balls." From February through May 1988, the Reagan administration had tried to find a way to remove Noriega from power without sending in troops. The White House and Noriega negotiated through the papal nuncio in Panama. As Vice President, Bush had objected to these negotiations in favor of force, but, according to Secretary of State George Shultz, President Reagan stood firm. "I'm not giving in," Shultz quoted Reagan as saying. "This deal is better than going in and counting our dead. I just think you [Bush] are wrong as hell on this." Once he became President, Bush took up the cudgels against the drug-dealing dictator. In November 1989 the administration authorized a $3 million plan to topple Noriega by recruiting members of the Panamanian armed forces to stage a coup. But before the coup could be pulled off, the plan became public. The next month Panama declared war on the United States and installed Noriega as the maximum leader. The United States launched Operation Just Cause and invaded Panama on December 20, 1989; twenty-three Americans and five hundred Panamanians lost their lives before Noriega surrendered on January 3, 1990.

"Panamanians, Americans—both have sacrificed much to restore democracy to Panama," said the President in his remarks announcing the surrender of Noriega. "Their sacrifice has been a noble cause and will never be forgotten. A free and prosperous Panama will be an enduring tribute."

Noriega was brought to trial in Miami for eight counts of drug trafficking, racketeering, and money laundering. He was convicted and sentenced to forty years in prison, becoming eligible for parole in 2006. Bush
was presented with the handcuffs used to transport Noriega from Panama
to the United States, which he proudly displayed in his presidential library next to a cardboard target of himself, complete with bullet holes,
that was found in Noriega's quarters.

No President ever needed great speechwriters more than George
Herbert Walker Bush, and yet one of the first things he did upon becoming President was to reduce their importance by revoking their White
House mess privileges, something Ronald Reagan would never have
done. Having deprived his speechwriters of the prized White House
perquisite, the President extended mess privileges to all his children.

"Bush didn't enjoy giving speeches," said Vice President Dan Quayle.
"He tended to prepare for them very quickly, to give his notes a once-over,
and then go out and get them over with."

"Reagan and Bush were so different," said Peggy Noonan. "I was
more in line philosophically with Reagan, and responded in some way to
his personality and character that left me thinking more deeply about him
than anyone else I ever worked with. I thought him such a fine man, and
such a good one . . . He was so emotionally responsive to history, he felt
its tug and force in a personal and imaginative way; and yet to many
around him on a daily basis he was not so responsive. Bush lacked a deep
responsiveness and connection to history, and yet when he spoke of those
he loved, his children and friends and family, his eyes filled with real
tears. They were different men."

The President became extremely emotional in 1989 as he tried to
cope with the public furor over his third son's involvement in the Silverado Savings and Loan scandal. He watched people gather in Lafayette
Park across from the White House waving placards that said, "Jail Neil
Bush." And he railed against them for wrapping the scandals of the S&L
industry around Neil's neck. The First Lady said she could barely contain
her distress as she watched her son "get devoured by the press."

"The thing that's bothered George the most, what he likes least about
politics, is that our children are—I can't think of a bad enough word;
there's no privacy. It's been terrible for our children," Barbara told a writer
for *The New Republic* with tears in her eyes.

"It kills you—just devastates you—the S&L thing. Considering there must have been a hundred thousand outside board of directors, and all Americans know only one—Neil Bush—who happens to be the most honest, decent, fabulous young man, who has really had his whole life changed. Amazing . . . He's gonna be just fine. But it is not easy for him. Nor his wife. Nor his children. They know he's never done anything wrong in his life, so that's OK."

In the beginning, Neil enjoyed going on television and seeing his picture in the paper, but he compounded his problems every time he talked to the press. The family warned him about speaking out, but he claimed he had done nothing wrong so he had nothing to hide.

"When I flew to Denver to interview Neil, a call came in from the White House," said Martin Tolchin of *The New York Times*. "I could only hear Neil's side of the conversation, but when he hung up he said, 'That was my dad. He said I shouldn't be talking to you' . . . He laughed and we went on with the interview."

Soon each of Neil's brothers weighed in on "Project Shut Up," but Neil persisted in proclaiming his innocence. Then George W. called. He told his younger brother that every time he opened his mouth, he harmed his father's presidency and that in turn diminished the family name. Neil finally got the point and stopped giving interviews.

More than anyone else in the family, George W. grasped the value of the Bush brand name. As the son of the Vice President, he had been a star in Midland, Texas, but as the son of the President he was suddenly propelled into another stratosphere. Doors that might have been closed to him now flew open, and multimillionaires stepped forward to invest in any enterprise that carried his name.

Shortly after his father's election, George received a call that the Texas Rangers might be for sale. He immediately moved his family from Washington, D.C., to Dallas, and, as he wrote in his autobiography, "I . . . pursued the purchase like a pit bull on the pant leg of opportunity." He managed to scrape up $500,000 as his initial share of the $86 million price, borrowing the money from the United Bank of Midland, where he had served on the board of directors. On April 21, 1989, despite his minuscule investment, he was made the co–managing partner of the team and paid $200,000 a year to be the front man. "A lifelong baseball fan, I was about to own a baseball team," he wrote in his memoir. "I remember thinking, 'This is as good as it gets. Life cannot be better than this.' "

Each year on opening day, George made sure his father was in Dallas to throw out the first ball. Having the President at the ballpark brought the Texas Rangers international publicity and more than justified Junior as a name, if not a moneyed, owner of the team. At the time the team was sold in 1998, George's share in the sale was 12 percent, which earned him $15 million.

At the same time George W. Bush was living his fantasy of owning a baseball team like his great-uncle Herbie Walker, Jeb Bush received a similar offer in Florida to buy a limited partnership in the Jacksonville Jaguars NFL team. Jeb needed $450,000, so he borrowed the amount from SunBank, where he was on the board of directors. It was not difficult to raise money—or be on a board of directors—if you were a son of the President of the United States.

One of the Bush children definitely not profiting from her father's presidency was thirty-year-old Doro, who was about to bring the family its first—but not last—divorce. Growing up in a family geared to boys, Dorothy Walker Bush almost got lost in the macho shuffle. With her parents constantly traveling, she attended schools in Texas, Washington, D.C., and New York City. Then she was sent to board at Miss Porter's School in Connecticut, the alma mater of her grandmother Dorothy Walker Bush and her aunt Nancy Bush Ellis. Doro graduated from Boston College with a C average and a degree in sociology. She did not have a boyfriend until her sophomore summer, when she met William LeBlond, who attended Boston University. Like Doro, he was the youngest in a large, hard-charging family. Shy and quiet, the couple married after college graduation and moved to Cape Elizabeth, Maine, where they had two children.

"I remember when I worked for Vice President Bush, Doro called him all the time," recalled an aide. "She was much closer to her father than her mother . . . Bush treated her like a little girl. She could get anything she wanted out of him, but she was pathetic, because she was an adult who couldn't make a decision about anything without first calling Daddy. Sad, really. I think Bush was always compensating with her because he wasn't there for her growing up, but then he's the kind of father who acts differently with girl children . . . There were no expectations for her, other than to get married and have kids . . . The family was relieved when she married, but they didn't like her husband. They called him 'the golfer' because that's about all he did."

Doro recognized the problems her husband faced as a Bush in-law. "My family is a hard family to marry into," she said. "I'm sure it can be highly intimidating, especially my brothers — as much as I love them. But it is not easy. They're all power kind of guys."

That she chose someone simple, unambitious, and removed from the turbulence of politics probably spoke to her need for stability. Her husband, who once considered becoming a hockey coach, reconsidered and became a carpenter. He worked for his brother's construction firm, and Doro kept the firm's books. In 1988, she wanted to join the family's campaign for her father, but her father said she needed a skill. She took a secretarial course and learned how to type. She eventually went on the speaking circuit and told audiences that she loved her father "more than life itself," frequently dissolving into racking sobs. Her two-year-old daughter, Ellie, was filmed in a Bush TV ad running into her grandfather's arms.

The campaign changed Doro. "I'm a late bloomer," she said. She lost weight, grew out her short-cropped hair, stopped wearing her father's dungarees, and became a softer-looking version of her mother. Even the family noticed. "She used to be shy," said Barbara Bush, "but now we're all saying, 'Doro, you've gotten positively aggressive.' She's gotten to be a big politician."

By the time of her father's inauguration, Doro had outgrown Billy LeBlond and his pickup truck. She told her mother she wanted a divorce. Barbara begged her to work things out for the sake of the children, but Doro was adamant. Billy moved out of the house, and in August 1989 the Bushes quietly announced their daughter's separation. Two months later her husband was arrested for drunken driving and possession of marijuana in Maynard, Massachusetts. He spent the night in jail. He was convicted of drunk driving, fined $1,280, and prohibited from driving in the state for one year. The marijuana charge was dismissed. That week Doro filed for divorce, citing "irreconcilable marital differences." A mediator in Portland, Maine, handled the divorce. The records, like so many Bush family records, were sealed.

"We're blessed that we love both of them," the President told reporters. "They're having marriage problems, and that comes under the heading of their business. And so we counsel our daughter, and we stay very close to Billy's parents, who are good friends of ours. The last thing Doro and Billy need is pontificating from either of us. But if she needs somebody to hold her hand, well, we're there."

The American press remained silent, but British journalists started snooping. Margaret Hall, from London's *Today* tabloid, flew to Maine to try to interview the couple. Billy LeBlond apologized politely. "I'm sorry. I can't say anything because Doro and I have agreed not to talk about our problems publicly."

He was rewarded with a tabloid headline:

FACE THAT COULD NEVER FIT THE FIRST FAMILY:
SECRET ANGUISH OF GEORGE BUSH'S DAUGHTER,
WED TO A BEER-SWILLING REBEL BRICKLAYER.

When Hall knocked on Doro's door, the housekeeper answered and said that Doro was working at the Maine Tourism Bureau. The housekeeper asked the reporter to step inside while she got the phone number, but Hall remained on the porch. She gave the housekeeper her name and hotel number in case she could not reach Doro at work.

"A few hours later I got a screeching telephone call from Doro Bush: 'How dare you come to my house, invade my privacy, and enter my domain . . . You are the lowest of the low . . .' I stopped her right there," Hall said, "and let her know in no uncertain terms that I could've easily entered her home, taken notes on her untidy kitchen, counted all the empty wine bottles in her bins, and probably nicked a few photographs while I was at it. But I had remained on the front porch because her housekeeper was very sweet and polite and I didn't want to jeopardize her job."

A few months later Doro moved to Washington with her children to be closer to her parents, but her mother would not let them move into the White House. So Doro rented a small house in Bethesda, Maryland, and found a job at the National Rehabilitation Hospital.

"She was very fragile then," recalled Kim Elliott, whose children attended school with Doro's children. "She was going through a tough divorce, but she was devoted to her children. Very hands-on and completely committed to those kids."

Vice President Quayle did not realize how sensitive the White House was about Doro's divorce until he kicked up an ideological firestorm by criticizing the popular TV character Murphy Brown for bearing a child alone and calling it just another lifestyle choice. The headline in the *New York Daily News*: "Quayle to Murphy Brown: You Tramp!"

"Murphy Brown is the second most popular woman in America, next to Barbara Bush," said Mary Matalin, political director of Bush's reelection campaign. The White House staff panicked and pulled away from Quayle.

"You should be supporting me," the Vice President told the chief of staff.

"This thing's a loser."

"It's not a loser. If you handle it right, it's a winner."

"Well, you're a minority of one. Everybody around here is concerned about it. It looks like you're criticizing single mothers . . . They're even worried it looks as if you're indirectly criticizing Doro Bush."

Barbara Bush was more determined than ever to see her daughter remarry. She believed that only through marriage could Doro and her children find their safest haven. To that end Barbara encouraged Doro to date.

"We spent a weekend up at Camp David with the Bushes . . . They had two dogs up there at the time and the divorced daughter," recalled one congressional wife. "Barbara told me she was concerned because Doro had dated Representative David Dreier for a year and he never touched her . . . 'Never laid a hand on her,' said Barbara . . . I think Doro had better luck when she started dating a Democrat."

Doro met Robert Koch, a Democrat, who had worked for House Majority Leader Richard Gephardt and Democratic Representative Tony Coelho of California. Her mother assisted their courtship by inviting them to several White House state dinners. During this time the President dispatched his daughter as the U.S. representative to Paraguay's presidential inauguration; to Morocco for the anniversary of the King's ascension; and to the winter Olympics in Albertville, France. By 1992, Robert Koch had proposed to Doro. The First Lady ordered a mother-of-the-bride dress for herself and a bridal gown for her daughter from their favorite designer, Arnold Scaasi. The family gathered on June 28, 1992, and watched the President walk his only daughter down the aisle of the chapel at Camp David.

"That was one of the happiest days of my presidency," said George Bush. He was still staggering from his unhappiest day two years before, when he had betrayed the most famous words he ever uttered: "Read my lips. No new taxes."

He knew at the time he made the promise that it was a lie, but, as he said, he was prepared to do anything to get elected. His budget director, Richard Darman, convinced him that a tax increase would generate money for domestic spending and be his political salvation. Everyone else said it would be political suicide.

Lee Atwater, whom Bush had made chairman of the Republican National Committee, was flabbergasted. "The guy has no political instincts whatsoever," he told the Republican consultant Roger Stone. "Bush and this crowd are going to screw it up. Bush won't get reelected."

Reneging on his campaign promise to Americans, the President agreed to a tax increase in 1990 as part of the $492 billion deficit-reduction package passed by Congress. He felt compelled to compromise because of the rapidly escalating costs of salvaging the savings-and-loan industry, whose estimated losses exceeded $230 billion. In exchange for agreeing to a tax increase, Bush insisted on cutting the capital-gains tax to benefit those who earned more than $200,000 a year. As a consequence, his poll numbers fell twenty points within twenty days, and he was taunted by newspaper headlines that read: "Waffle," "Retreat," "Blink," "Flip Flop." He admitted later that it was the "biggest mistake" of his presidency. "If I had to do that over, I wouldn't do it."

Democrats applauded him. "It was a profile in courage for George Bush," said Dan Rostenkowski, former chairman of the House Ways and Means Committee. "He laid the economic foundation for the prosperity that Bill Clinton took credit for in the 1990s."

Republicans thought it was a profile in lunacy. "You are going to get killed [in the midterm elections]," Ed Rollins, head of the National Republican Congressional Committee, told Bush's pollster. "This is the most sacred pledge Bush ever made. If you raise taxes in this term, he can kiss his ass away in '92, and he's going to take a bunch of House members with him."

Rollins immediately issued a memo to all House Republicans on the tax pledge: "Do not hesitate to distance yourself from the President." He even went on a morning television show with the Republican consultant Doug Bailey to criticize the President for breaking his campaign promise.

The President, who watched television constantly in the White House, blanched when he saw the show. Demanding blind loyalty no matter what, he insisted that Ed Rollins be fired. "There wasn't anything he could do about me," said Doug Bailey, co-founder of the prestigious Republican consulting firm Bailey/Deardourff and Associates, "but poor Ed lost his job simply because he could not in good conscience tell Republicans running for reelection to fall on the sword of the President's broken promise . . . Bush, of course, didn't see it that way. He is obsessed with loyalty, loyalty, loyalty, which affects the entire family and inevitably leads all of them to their unhealthy preoccupation with enemies: 'If you're not for us, you're against us, and if you're against us, by God, you'll pay.' "

The President laid down the law to House Republican leaders: "I'll never do anything for you guys as long as Rollins is up there." Within months Ed Rollins would resign.

The Vice President was in the shower when CNN reported that the President conceded to the Democrats and would be raising taxes. "I probably should have looked at the drain, because that's where the Republican Party's best issue . . . was headed," said Dan Quayle. To say nothing of his own political career.

On the eve of the midterm elections the President announced his intention to sign the deficit-reduction bill, saying, "I can't say this is the best thing that has happened to us . . . since the elimination of broccoli . . . but it represents a corrective action on a pattern of federal spending gone out of control."

Republicans wished the President had simply backed down on broccoli. Months earlier he had banished the vegetable from the White House menu. "I do not like broccoli," he said. "I haven't liked it since I was a little kid and my mother made me eat it. I'm President of the United States now and I'm not going to eat any more broccoli." The crew of Air Force One put a sign in the galley of a broccoli floret with a red slash through it.

Now Republicans had to contend with bumper stickers that said,

"Nixon lied to me about Watergate, Reagan lied to me about Iran-contra, and now Bush is lying to me about taxes."

Just as Ed Rollins predicted, Republican voters stayed home in droves on November 6, 1990. "It was the lowest Republican off-year turnout since Watergate, and it was all because of Bush's tax increase," Rollins wrote in his rollicking memoir, *Bare Knuckles and Back Rooms*. "We had a net loss of nine seats, but I'm convinced that my memo . . . saved fifteen incumbent seats that otherwise would have gone down the drain."

One Republican disappointment was California's seventeenth congressional district, where the Democrat Calvin Dooley was elected. Dooley made sport of President Bush when, in 1992, after redistricting occurred he was elected to the twentieth district. During the '92 campaign, he regaled constituents about his experience as a first-term congressman in the Bush administration. He told voters in Fresno and Bakersfield how the President showed solidarity with the House of Representatives by coming up to the Hill just like other former House members to use the House gym. The President arrived at the Capitol in his bulletproof limousine accompanied by twenty-six motorcycle police, fourteen Secret Service agents, and enough firepower to arm Paraguay. Amid all this security, Bush worked out, showered, and returned to the White House.

"It's quite an experience to be a lowly freshman congressman in the shower with the President of the United States (pause) and to look over and see (long pause) that the leader of the free world is (longer pause) . . . a . . . well . . . er . . . just an average little guy."

Audiences guffawed each time he told the story, and at one Dooley fund-raiser in California a delegation from Washington, D.C., including the Speaker of the House of Representatives, had to struggle for composure as the congressman described the commander in chief's "little stick."

Determined to recoup his manhood, the President had a plan in place, thanks to the advice of a tough woman. When Saddam Hussein's forces invaded Kuwait on August 2, 1990, the President conferred with British Prime Minister Margaret Thatcher in Aspen, Colorado. "Remember, George," she said. "I was almost to be defeated in England when the Falkland conflict happened. I stayed in office for eight years after that."

Mrs. Thatcher was referring to Argentina's invasion of the Falkland Islands in 1982, when she had dispatched England's armed forces to establish British sovereignty. Known as the Iron Lady, she proved her mettle in that war and emerged victorious. At the time, George Bush characterized her as a "broad with steel balls." Now she would provide the spine he needed to confront Saddam Hussein's invasion of Kuwait. When the President started to waver, she would back up his resolve by saying, "Don't go wobbly on me, George. Don't go wobbly."

Continuing his August vacation at Kennebunkport, the President met with visiting heads of state, including King Hussein of Jordan, who arrived after meeting with Saddam in Iraq. The King argued for negotiations, but Bush demanded immediate withdrawal. Not surprisingly, the President's focus was on the one subject he knew best. "I will not allow this little dictator to control 25 percent of the civilized world's oil," he told Hussein. Queen Noor recalled her husband's describing the meeting as "quite a raw experience." She said the King was shocked by the President's choice of words and his implication that there were only two worlds—the Arab world and "the civilized world."

The President also met with Prince Bandar, the Saudi Arabian Ambassador and a member of the Saudi royal family. Bush told him the Pentagon had satellite photos showing Iraqi troops massing on the Saudi border. This was false. The photos did not show what the President claimed, but Bush felt he needed to exaggerate the danger of an Iraqi invasion to obtain consent to deploy American troops on Saudi soil. Once he had Saudi consent, the President understated the number of troops he intended to deploy in Saudi Arabia. He told Prince Bandar he would send 100,000 troops when he planned to send 250,000. That would be the first phase of the troop buildup known as Desert Shield. The President announced the deployment to the American people on August 8, 1990. But later in a news conference he declined to give any figure at all.

A lifetime of lying to achieve his goals made the President facile in this crisis: he concealed from the American public the massive size and duration of the military deployment; he withheld his plans to defend Saudi Arabia as well as liberate Kuwait; he hid his strategy for all-out war. He made no announcements until after the November elections. As Michael Duffy and Dan Goodgame wrote, "his well-practiced and ruthless use of deception" was crucial in helping win support at home and abroad.

George had already decided that the country's vital interests were at stake. Now he needed to persuade the American people that access to Iraq's oil was a necessity for which it was worth spilling American blood. He careened around for weeks, frantically trying to find high-minded words for committing American troops. He talked about "a mad dictator" who wanted to control "the economic well being of every country in the world." He said, "Our oil-lifeline is threatened." And he said, "It is the national security," and "It is aggression." Grasping for a reason that would resonate, the President said, "If you want to sum it up in one word—it's jobs." He talked about the importance of standing up for the little guy in Kuwait, but people saw only oil-rich emirs riding around in their Mercedeses. "We must restore rulers to Kuwait," said the President, but Americans were unmoved when they learned Kuwait's sixty-four-year-old monarch, Sheik Jaber al-Ahmed al-Sabah, had fled to the Saudi resort town of Taif with five of his forty wives. The President hammered "Iraq's aggression," saying it was a challenge not just to the security of Kuwait "but to the better world we all hope to build in the wake of the cold war . . . We are talking about the price of liberty." Finally he ratcheted up the rhetoric to humanity's greatest fear: annihilation. "Nuclear threat," said the President. "We are determined to knock out Saddam Hussein's nuclear bomb potential."

The rash of excuses—when the simple truth, as he put it to King Hussein, was that it was all about the control of oil—would, of course, be repeated when George W. also invaded Iraq a decade later. Unlike his father, W. claimed his war on Iraq was to get rid of weapons of mass destruction. When no weapons of mass destruction were found, W. said the war was "to make America a more secure country." Bush 43 said the United States must invade Iraq because UN Gulf War cease-fire resolutions had been violated for a decade, allowing Saddam Hussein to amass chemical and biological weapons. Bush 43 said a military campaign was necessary because Saddam "has a connection to Al Qaeda." War was necessary, Bush 43 stressed, "to free the Iraqi people" and "to bring democracy to the Middle East." Playing to the most basic fear of annihilation, he said, "Facing clear evidence of peril, we cannot wait for the final proof— the smoking gun—that could come in the form of a mushroom cloud."

Before George H.W.'s invasion, former President Jimmy Carter wrote to members of the United Nations Security Council and asked them not to support the use of force against Hussein. On November 29, 1990, the UN passed a resolution calling on Iraq to withdraw from Kuwait by January 15, 1991, after which UN member states could use all means necessary "to restore peace and security in the area."

The President knew that waging a war to push the Iraqi army out of Kuwait would cost billions of dollars and require a massive mobilization of the U.S. military. He needed to convince Americans that Saddam Hussein was evil. The second bit of convincing was more difficult: that the oil fiefdom of Kuwait was a struggling young democracy. The CIA describes Kuwait as a "nominal constitutional monarchy," but the emphasis should be on "nominal." The country ruled by the al-Sabah family, personal friends of the Bushes, does not allow political parties, and only 10 percent of its citizens (population 2,183,161) are allowed to vote.

Over the next six months Secretary of State James A. Baker put together a coalition of thirty-four countries to provide ground troops, aircraft, ships, and medics. He also raised $50 million from U.S. allies. The government of Kuwait spent $11.9 million in fees to Hill and Knowlton to mobilize U.S. public opinion against Saddam. The public-relations company conducted opinion polls and audience surveys to take the emotional pulse of the country in order to identify themes that would be most effective in selling the war.

"We found," said Dee Alsop, who helped Hill and Knowlton with the PR campaign, "the theme that struck the deepest emotional chord was the fact that Saddam Hussein was a madman who had committed atrocities even against his own people and had tremendous power to do further damage, and he needed to be stopped."

Bush finally had a rationale he could embrace, which he sold as the struggle between good and evil. Being on the side of the angels gave him renewed confidence as he held forth on the necessity of going to war. He wrote in his diary:

> I know the consequences if we fail, and I know what will happen if . . . we look wimpish, or unwilling to do what we must do . . .
>
> I think of the evil that is this man [Saddam]. He has to not only be checked, but punished, and then we worry about how we handle our relations with the Arab countries.

Time chose the two faces of George Bush—one with foreign policy vision and the other with domestic blindness—as the magazine's "Men of the Year." That mixed honor might have triggered the dream George had about his father:

> *We were driving into some hotel near a golf course, and there was another golf course way over across the fence, though not a very good one. I heard Dad was there, so I went to see him, and he was in a hotel room. We embraced, and I told him I missed him very much. Aren't dreams funny? I could see him very clearly: big, strong, and highly respected.*

The specter of his father as "big, strong, and highly respected" drove the President in his conduct of the impending war. On January 12, 1991, he told his staff: "I have resolved all moral questions in my mind. This is black and white, good and evil."

That day both houses of Congress voted to authorize the use of force against Iraq. In the Senate, the vote was passed through the efforts of Connecticut's Democrat Joe Lieberman and Virginia's Republican John Warner. The ratio of 52–47 was the narrowest ever to vote for war. One newly elected senator who voted against the resolution was Paul Wellstone of Minnesota. On his first trip to the White House, the Democrat had cornered the President and spoken forcefully about the inadvisability of war. Bush shook him off and later asked, "Who is this chickenshit?"

The President felt immense relief when Congress gave him the power to act in accordance with the UN resolution. As he wrote in his diary:

> *I felt the heavy weight that I might be faced with impeachment lifted from my shoulders as I heard the results. In truth, even had Congress not passed the resolutions I would have acted and ordered our troops into combat. I know it would have caused an outcry, but it was the right thing to do. I was comfortable in my own mind that I had the constitutional authority. It had to be done.*

The United States had deployed 540,000 troops to the Persian Gulf by January 16, 1991, when the air war started. The night skies over Baghdad lit up with tracer fire as the first bombs of Operation Desert Storm fell on the capital of Iraq. The world watched the war live on CNN, almost as if it were a video game. The precision of Scud missiles slicing through the skies followed by the swoosh of black bat planes known as stealth bombers became prime-time entertainment. The Saudis were so impressed by the air show they wanted to purchase the same planes, but the United States would not sell them. Instead, the Saudis had to settle for buying the less sophisticated F-15XPs. They purchased seventy-two from the United States at a total cost of $9 billion, including weapons and ground support. Generals with shiny stars on their battle fatigues took to the airwaves to describe the killing efficiency of F-16 Falcons, F-4G Wild Weasels, A-10 Warthogs. The Pentagon had clamped down on press coverage so that viewers saw only what the commanders wanted them to see. The decision to control the news was made early in the strategy sessions. Many in the military believed that they had lost Vietnam because an independent press corps, which had been allowed to travel the countryside unsupervised, reported whatever they saw. The commanders felt the stories had been so negative that Americans turned against the military mission of the war and made it unwinnable. So from the beginning of Desert Storm the generals insisted on a news blackout.

The mesmerizing air war lasted thirty-eight days before the ground war began on February 23, 1991, and carved "a highway of death" through Iraq. The President insisted that Saddam either surrender or face military defeat. "We don't want to have another draw, another Vietnam, a sloppy ending," Bush said. When Saddam agreed to an unconditional withdrawal from Kuwait, the President issued a cease-fire. Within one hundred hours the $61.1 billion war was over.

On February 26, 1991, coalition forces entered Kuwait City and the al-Sabahs, Kuwait's ruling family, promised political reforms. But, to date, they have not been implemented. The monarch with forty wives would not return to his country until March 15, 1991, when he was assured of safety. Upon his arrival, he knelt, his white kaffiyeh flopping on the tarmac, and kissed the ground that had been liberated by 293 U.S. deaths, 100,000 Iraqi deaths, and 300,000 Iraqi wounded.

And so President Bush emerged victorious from the tenth major war America had ever waged. Although it was not a noble war, and proved to be far less pure and antiseptic than presented, Desert Storm reaffirmed

U.S. leadership and demonstrated U.S. technology, which fostered flag-waving patriotism across the country. There were ticker-tape parades in Los Angeles, Washington, D.C., and New York City, where more than 4 million spectators poured out to cheer General Norman Schwarzkopf and the troops who fought in the Persian Gulf. Bush's approval ratings soared to 88 percent, higher than any President ever to hold the office. Polls also showed that a majority of Americans felt frustrated that the coalition had not captured Baghdad and destroyed Saddam and the power structure that supported him. General Schwarzkopf told a TV interviewer that the President did not heed his advice to crush the Iraqi army in "a battle of annihilation." The general later apologized for his "poor choice of words." Assuming that Saddam would be toppled by his own military, the President maintained he had acted in accordance with the mission of a limited war: to have gone further would have destroyed America's standing among its allies. As commander in chief, he was saluted as a hero. Yale presented him with an honorary degree, and, despite facing a barrage of student protesters, George Herbert Walker Bush felt for the first time in his life that he could stand alongside his father as "big, strong, and highly respected."

CHAPTER TWENTY-THREE

In the Rose Garden on March 29, 1991, it was hard to tell which was the President riding the highest polls in history and which was the President smarting under the scandal of Iran-contra. The current President was known to hate standing in his predecessor's shadow. Yet he reflexively surrendered the spotlight, not so much as a gracious host deferring to a distinguished guest, but more like a stand-in bowing to the star.

Still looking robust at the age of eighty, Ronald Reagan had come to Washington to accept an honorary degree from George Washington University. The Doctorate of Public Service was presented to him on the tenth anniversary of the assassination attempt that almost took his life. He had returned to the nation's capital as much to be honored as to honor the medical team that had saved him. At the time of the shooting only his wife and his doctors knew how close to death he had come.

"It was kind of an unspoken agreement that none of us would let the public know how serious it was, how close we came to losing him," said Nancy Reagan, who was honored with a permanent plaque installed in the hospital's emergency room that recognized "her courage, strength and dignity at the side of her gravely wounded husband." The emergency room was renamed the Ronald Reagan Institute for Emergency Medicine.

After accepting his honorary degree, President Reagan delivered a speech that brought the audience of 1,450 to their feet:

> I want to tell all of you here today something that I'm not sure you know. You do know that I'm a member of the NRA. And my position on the right to bear arms is well known. But I want you to

know something else, and I'm going to say it in clear, unmistakable language. I support the Brady bill and I urge the Congress to enact it without delay.

It's just plain common sense that there be a waiting period [seven days] to allow local law enforcement officials to conduct background checks on those who wish to buy a handgun.

The applause was deafening. The former President had just endorsed a bill named in honor of his press secretary James Brady, who was forever disabled by the handgun aimed at the President and his party in 1981. It was a bill that the current President, George H.W. Bush, opposed.

The Bushes did not attend the GWU ceremony only a few blocks away, but had invited the Reagans to the White House after the convocation. President Reagan accepted; Mrs. Reagan declined. She was not about to subject herself to any further abuse from "the Silver Fox." Citing a prior commitment, Nancy attended a tea in her honor to which Barbara Bush pointedly was not invited.

The White House press corps gathered to witness the Rose Garden reunion of the two presidents. When they shouted "Mr. President," George Bush, ever the smiling host, deferred to Ronald Reagan like an acolyte to his more accomplished mentor. Even with two hearing aids, the former President could not understand the first question; as much as the query galled Bush, he repeated it for Reagan.

"On gun control," Bush said, "the Brady Bill."

"I don't think it would be proper for me or any other ex-president to stand and tell an acting president what he should or shouldn't do," Reagan said. But then he added: "I happen to believe in the Brady Bill because we have the same thing in California right now."

Another reporter asked if he was pressuring Mr. Bush to change his stand and endorse the bill.

"I don't put pressure on anybody," said Reagan.

He was asked why he had opposed all gun-control measures while he was President.

He shook his head. "I was against a lot of the ridiculous things that were proposed with regard to gun control."

"Do you think you'll persuade President Bush to change his position?"

"I'm trying to," said the former President.

George Bush quickly ushered his predecessor toward the Oval Office. "I'm going to discuss all this and other weighty subjects with President Reagan right now," he said.

The former President visited the White House telephone operators fabled for their ability to reach anyone in the world, and he was taken to the main house, where the residence staff had gathered in the Diplomatic Reception Room. He was applauded every step of the way.

"Do you miss the White House, Mr. President?"

"We have a standard answer," said Reagan, "and we mean it from the heart. We miss the people."

The Bushes walked the former President to the Colonnade when he was leaving. As they said good-bye, Barbara Bush waved. In a voice loud enough for reporters to hear, she said, "Give Nancy my love."

A few days later the current President confided to a congressman that he wanted to see the former President go down in history as "the man who preceded George Bush."

Many years later, a Bush aide recalled that presidential reunion and shook his head. "It was Nashua, New Hampshire, all over again—only ten times worse," he said, remembering the night in 1981 when Reagan had grabbed the microphone and propelled himself to the presidency, leaving George Bush in the dust.

Anyone else but Ronald Reagan might have been publicly thumped for rudeness. After all, his public support for the Brady Bill had put the current President on the defensive. And Bush scrambled to let it be known that he might be willing to accept a waiting period for handgun purchases if Congress accepted his anticrime legislation. He hoped to glom on to the popularity of the Brady Bill to get a crime bill passed that would get him reelected.

"We are going to win on the three K's," said White House Chief of Staff John Sununu. "Kuwait, quotas, and crime."

The gun lobby had been whip-lashed for years trying to follow the President's flip-flops. As a Texas congressman, Bush voted for a bill that included a limitation on handguns. Yet he opposed licensing and registering his personal firearms as a resident of the District of Columbia. When he ran for President in 1988, he plunked down five hundred dollars to become a "lifetime member" of the National Rifle Association. He then opposed a ban on imports of semiautomatic weapons, for which he received the NRA's endorsement—and their $6 million expenditure for him in the general election. Four weeks into his presidency he changed his position. After five children were mowed down by an assault rifle in a California school yard, he announced that he supported a ban on the importation of semiautomatic weapons. A few weeks later he backed down and said he supported a ban only on imported guns with more than ten bullets in their ammunition clips.

After President Reagan announced his support for the Brady Bill, President Bush seemed to waffle on his opposition, which quickened the hearts of gun-control advocates. In the end, their hopes were dashed. He refused to sign the Brady Bill by itself, despite its overwhelming support in both houses of Congress. He said he would sign it only if it were attached to a crime bill of his liking.

"He had no intention of either signing or vetoing any bill with the Brady measure in it," said Mollie Dickenson, author of *Thumbs Up: The Life and Courageous Comeback of White House Press Secretary Jim Brady*. "Under the Bush administration murders increased more than 25 percent from 8,915 in 1988 to 12,090 in 1991 . . . In defeating the Brady bill . . . Bush . . . probably sold out his principles and contributed to the deaths of innocent people."

The President had held out on the Brady Bill to appease the NRA, but by then he had alienated the powerful gun lobby as well as its opponents. In 1992, all fled from him. The NRA withheld its endorsement, which so angered Bush that he placed a call from Air Force One to Wayne LaPierre, the NRA's executive vice president, to demand the NRA's support. But it was to no avail. The Bradys left the Republican Party and endorsed Bill Clinton, who promised to sign the Brady Bill, which he did in 1993.

George Bush exacted his revenge in May 1995, when he read about an NRA fund-raising letter from LaPierre that described federal agents as "jack-booted thugs" who wore "Nazi bucket helmets and black storm trooper uniforms" to "attack law abiding citizens." Ripping up his NRA membership card, the former President wrote a letter of resignation, which his office made public. He said he was mourning the Oklahoma

City death of a Secret Service agent who had protected the Bush family for years, and he accused the NRA of slandering dedicated officials "who are out there day and night laying their lives on the line for all of us."

Bush's act of principle received national publicity but not national respect. Gun-control advocates were unhappy that he had not resigned from the NRA when he could have made a difference, and the gun lobby dismissed his resignation as an act of pique, nothing more than petty payback. "George Bush has been feuding with the NRA since 1992, when we decided we couldn't back him," said NRA vice president Neal Knox. "He's been biding his time since then, waiting for the right time to kick us in the shins."

The gun issue illustrated the domestic part of the Bush presidency, which was careening like a sailboat in distress, tacking from one side to the other in a stormy sea with an unhinged mainsail flapping dangerously and an inexperienced crew trying to bail before they capsized. When the President's post–Gulf War poll numbers fell, his Triple K strategy for re-election was endangered. Then his political spark plug died.

Lee Atwater's death had been expected for many months. Doctors had diagnosed a malignant brain tumor. In 1990, before he collapsed, the chairman of the Republican National Committee had traveled to Arkansas to lay the groundwork for a political assault against Governor Bill Clinton, whom he saw as the President's most dangerous potential opponent for 1992. With the party apparatus at his disposal, Atwater was gearing up for his biggest mudslinger. Eighteen months later he was dead. His funeral was held on April Fools' Day in Columbia, South Carolina, where the state's senior senator, Strom Thurmond, delivered the eulogy for the forty-year-old bad boy of Republican politics.

"He was loved and admired by his friends and respected and feared by his opponents," said the senator, who introduced the Vice President and many members of the Bush cabinet. "This is the largest number of Cabinet members who've attended a funeral that I am aware of. Why? Because they hold Lee in such high esteem."

Conspicuously missing were the President and the First Lady. The Bushes would not interrupt their vacation to go to the funeral. They were ensconced on Islamorada, a resort in the upper Keys of Florida, where the President went every year to bonefish. On this trip he was accompanied by Treasury Secretary Nicholas Brady, Deputy National Security Adviser Robert M. Gates, and Deputy Chief of Staff Andrew Card.

Not attending the funeral of the man whom many credited with getting him elected President was so uncharacteristically discourteous of George Bush that it shocked many people, including Atwater's widow, Sally, who was particularly hurt. "The President does not go to funerals," said an inept White House aide, "but he will attend the memorial service scheduled later in Washington, D.C., at the National Cathedral." Months later the President would interrupt a campaign trip to fly to Texas to attend the funeral of Betty Lyn Liedtke, the wife of his onetime business partner Pennzoil chairman Hugh Liedtke.

Bush had visited Atwater during his hospitalization and at home during the months he battled inoperable brain cancer. In his final days, Atwater became a born-again Christian and tried to square himself with those he had shamelessly wronged while playing gutter politics. He even expressed regret to Michael Dukakis for the scurrilous campaign he had waged against him in 1988. The Bushes felt Atwater's public apology reflected poorly on them, because they had never disavowed the race-baiting Willie Horton ads. "Lee had nothing to apologize about, ever," Barbara Bush wrote in her memoir, adding, "George Bush truly loved him."

When John Brady, author of *Bad Boy: The Life and Politics of Lee Atwater,* contacted the President for an interview, Brady was told to fax his questions. "I asked President Bush why he did not go to the funeral," he said, "but he did not answer the question."

The President's political meltdown did not start with the death of Lee Atwater—it began with the economic downswing and his inability to do anything about it—but without the frenetic bogeyman by his side, Bush had to work the high wire without a net. Even his mentor Richard Nixon predicted he would fall.

"The White House is in total disarray," Nixon told his policy assistant Monica Crowley, "because it still believes it has a communications problem and if it could just put together a slick photo op, he'll be back to seventy percent approval. The problem is deeper; it's something that Lee Atwater could sense. I knew him. He was a tough southern son of a bitch, and we needed him. Bush will miss him this election. He just doesn't have it without Atwater. Frankly, he's a poor campaigner."

The sixty-six-year-old President had always relied on manic energy to propel him through a campaign, but now he complained to friends of "wearing out and getting older." In May 1991, during a jog on the wooded trails of Camp David, he was stricken with fatigue and shortness of breath. His Secret Service agents assisted him to the infirmary, and from there he was helicoptered to Bethesda Naval Hospital. The White House press secretary announced that the President had suffered atrial fibrillation, also known as an irregular heartbeat.

Suddenly there was a collective national gasp. As *Time* noted: "Public concern about Bush, one of the most popular chief executives in U.S. history, was probably intensified by the fact that his constitutionally designated successor is not highly regarded as a potential President."

A week later the President was diagnosed with Graves' disease, the same thyroid ailment affecting the First Lady. In addition to medications he took for his arthritic hip, ulcer, and hay fever, Bush took heart and anti-stroke pills, plus allergy shots for anaphylactic reaction to bee stings. Now he began thyroid treatments with radioactive iodine, which sapped his energy and made him so tired he required frequent naps. The days of hard tennis and heavy martinis were over.

This was a body blow for a man who had placed his worth in the world of action and believed that constant physical motion demonstrated his manliness. In the White House the hyperactive Bush identified with Theodore Roosevelt, who as an asthmatic boy had willed himself to become the embodiment of energy. Having experienced a childhood illness that kept him out of school for a year, Bush so admired the rugged Rough Rider that he placed a portrait of the Republican Roosevelt in the Cabinet Room. He also put two sculptures of the twenty-sixth President in the Oval Office as reminders of the most intellectual athlete to ever hold the office.

"President Bush never liked to admit to reduced stamina," said his press secretary Marlin Fitzwater, "but to those of us who watched him carefully, the old zip was gone."

With his polls slipping every day, Bush decided to address the U.S. recession by embarking on a twelve-day trip to Australia, Singapore, South Korea, and Japan. He took the chairmen of Ford, General Motors, and Chrysler to make the case for more U.S. auto sales and, in his words, to generate "jobs, jobs, jobs." As he said before his departure in January 1992, "I'll do what I have to do to be re-elected." As always, George H.W. Bush's thoughts were not on ideology. They were on winning.

In Tokyo, Bush sat down for a series of unproductive trade talks, then joined the U.S. Ambassador Michael Armacost in a losing tennis match. That evening the President and the First Lady arrived for Prime Minister Kiichi Miyazawa's state dinner in the dining room of his residence. During a reception before dinner, the President had to quickly excuse himself; he rushed into a nearby bathroom, throwing up on himself on the way in. He changed his shirt and returned in time for the formal dinner, but before the first course was cleared away, he turned to the Prime Minister. "I don't think I'm going to make it," he said, slumping in his chair. His head collapsed on the Prime Minister's shoulder, and before he could turn away, he vomited into Miyazawa's lap. The President's Secret Service agents rushed forward, as did the White House physician. The Prime Minister cradled the President's head as he slipped slowly to the floor. "Why don't you just roll me under the table and let me sleep it off?" Bush said, before losing consciousness.

Dr. Burton Lee dived under the table to loosen the President's tie. A nurse mentioned taking off his belt, but finding none on his tuxedo pants, Lee began to unzip Bush's fly. The President stirred slightly.

"Burt, what the hell are you doing?"

"Just checking out the big boy, Chief," said the White House physician.

The First Lady started laughing, got up from the President's side, and helped clean up the Prime Minister. The President was driven back to the Akasaka Palace and put to bed, while Barbara jocularly addressed the crowd, saying it was all the Ambassador's fault for not playing better tennis. "He and George played the emperor and the crown prince and they were badly beaten. And we Bushes are not used to that."

Some people suspected that George had been drinking heavily before the dinner and Dr. Lee spun a hangover into a case of twenty-four-hour flu. The doctor admitted that he had given the President a flu shot a few months earlier. A television camera left running on the balcony of the dining room had filmed the incident; images of the President of the United States throwing up in the Japanese Prime Minister's lap had been transmitted around the world. The video showed Bush's ashen face as he was being lifted up framed by a floral display on the table, making him look as if he were lying in a wreathed coffin.

The President recovered the next day and held a press conference with the Prime Minister to quash alarms over his health.

> Q: Mr. President, people all around the world yesterday saw some very disturbing video of you collapsing in apparently very severe distress that many of us are not accustomed to when we see people with the flu. Can you describe what you were experiencing there? And also can you say that your doctors have conclusively ruled out anything other than the flu, or will there be further tests?
> A: No further tests. Totally ruled out anything other than the 24-hour flu. I've had an EKG, perfectly normal. I've had blood pressure taken and probing around in all kinds of ways . . . So this is the flu.

The President apologized to the Prime Minister for his "shabby performance" the night before and said he was embarrassed that film of him lying on the floor being attended by aides had been televised.

"George talked about his throwing-up incident constantly after that," recalled former House Speaker Thomas S. Foley. "He and Barbara visited Japan when I was the Ambassador in 1998, and I invited them to lunch. He couldn't stop talking about upchucking at that State Dinner six years before. After lunch, he even called the guy whose lap he had erped in. He just wanted to say hi and see how he was doing."

When the President returned to Washington in January 1992, he flew to New Hampshire, where he was being challenged in the Republican primary by Pat Buchanan, a former Nixon speechwriter and brilliant far-right commentator. At the same time Richard Nixon, appearing on the *Today* show, was asked his opinion of Bush's performance as President. Publicly Nixon supported his former protégé but later confided his concern to his assistant Monica Crowley.

"I hope I sounded all right on Bush," he said. "I'm afraid that I just don't sound credible defending him because I really don't think he's done that great of a job. And his New Hampshire visit is a disaster. He's up there petting cows and raving about God knows what. He just looks so desperate. And you know, he's getting no support from his people; the White House communications people are saying that the New Hampshire trip was triumphant! Oh, boy. They must be dreaming down there."

Sharing this concern was the wife of the White House counsel C. Boyden Gray. "I knew George was going to lose in 1992 because he wasn't focused on winning," said Carol Gray. "How could he be? He was distracted by his own troops and all their skirmishes . . . The infighting around him was so overwhelming you could not believe it, and being an intrinsically weak man, he was unable to keep order in his own office. Remember how he could not fire John Sununu and had to call in his son to do it for him . . . The grown men around the President were fighting like kindergartners, and he could not stop them. He wanted too much to be a pal to everyone, so he didn't step in to stop the wrangling. He did not have the nerve to lay down the law to any of them . . . He had Nick Brady and Jim Baker and Craig Fuller and my husband clawing at each other day and night, trying to get close to him. Their fights sucked all his emotional energy at a time when he needed to run the country. The President is a man too easily distracted. He's got a real attention deficit disorder, and those guys should have protected him. Instead, they fought each other like little boys on the playground trying to be the one closest to the big guy. It was sick, so sick. If not so tragic, it would have been hysterically funny.

"God, I can't tell you the weekends in my marriage that were lost to Boyden stewing over Sununu or Craig Fuller or plotting against Jim Baker. I was so young at the time—Boyden is seventeen years older than I am—but I saw so much being married to him that I knew early on George Bush was never going to be reelected. He was not a strong President like LBJ, who never would have tolerated that kind of interpersonal disarray to dominate the Oval Office. George left the running of his family to Barbara, who was bull-dyke tough . . . He probably should have let her run the country, too, instead of relying on men like Jim Baker and John Sununu and my husband. George might just as well have put the country into the hands of five-year-olds who did nothing but sling Play-Doh at each other as to rely on those men . . .

"To George Bush being President meant dipping into foreign policy and entertaining at the highest level. He loved visiting the Queen of England and meeting heads of state and going to diplomatic parties and hosting State Dinners and playing tennis with Pete Sampras on the White House courts. I hate to say this because I'm a Republican and I loved George Bush . . . He was a great guy. I remember the first time Boyden and I went to Camp David after he was elected President. I felt a little out of my element because I was so young . . . I was walking down the hall to our room and I passed the President's room. He was on the floor. 'C'mon in, Carol,' he said. 'I'm doing my buttocks exercise.' I thought he was great. I loved the way he looked and acted. So friendly, unlike his wife, who was a monster . . . Barbara scared me to death. I blame her in a way for emasculating him to the point that he couldn't delegate and stand up to men like Jim Baker and my husband . . . Those guys were always in fighting mode like cocks ready to claw each other to the death. George couldn't cope with it all . . . I guess his mother was right when she said he was just not cut out to be President because he didn't have a strong stomach."

The President's stamina had been severely tested in July 1991 over his nomination of Clarence Thomas to the Supreme Court. Initially Bush had wanted to make the black lawyer his first nominee to the Court the year before, but Boyden Gray said Thomas, who had been on the D.C. Court of Appeals for seventeen months, was not ready. Gray recommended David H. Souter to fill the first Supreme Court vacancy and Thomas to fill the next one.

Bush wanted credit in the history books for appointing a black justice to the Supreme Court, but he needed to find a conservative who was against abortion to satisfy the demands of right-wing Republicans. Still, the President knew he was in for a confirmation fight when he proposed the inexperienced jurist for the highest court, because when he was confirmed as a federal judge, many senators said they would not confirm him for the Supreme Court. Clarence Thomas opposed affirmative action, the Voting Rights Act, and abortion, but Bush figured that Thomas's race would weigh heavily in his favor and stave off the opposition of civil rights groups. It almost worked.

The National Urban League withheld its opposition, but the board of directors of the NAACP voted 49–1 to oppose; the AFL-CIO Executive Council voted 35–0 to oppose; the NOW officers and convention delegates voted unanimously to oppose; and the black National Bar Association voted to oppose.

Still smarting from the John Tower debacle, the President was determined to have his way on Clarence Thomas. After the American Bar Association had rated Thomas as "qualified" rather than "well qualified" or "not qualified," Bush said, "He is the most qualified person to sit on the court."

"That nomination was a deeply cynical ploy on the part of my husband and the President," said Carol Gray. She said she felt sick watching the machinations of the Bush White House force the Senate to accept a less than stellar conservative jurist for the highest court in the land. "They almost deserved the icky sordid mess they got with Anita Hill."

After Clarence Thomas testified before the Senate Judiciary Committee for five days, the committee deadlocked 7–7 on the nomination and voted to send it to the full Senate without making a recommendation. Days later, Timothy Phelps broke a story in *Newsday* that Anita F. Hill, a University of Oklahoma law professor, had told the FBI that she had been sexually harassed by Clarence Thomas while working for him at the EEOC. The White House dismissed the allegations as "unfounded"; and Clarence Thomas swore in an affidavit that they were not true, but the Senate, embarrassed that the charges were not investigated thoroughly, delayed the vote on Thomas to hold public hearings on the charges.

The debate became rancorous, and the accusations of sexual harassment deeply divided the country, rubbing raw the wounds on both sides of the political spectrum. The television audience exceeded soap-opera ratings as everyone, including the President, watched the men on the Senate Judiciary Committee, all white, interrogate a black female professor and a black male judge about squeamishly intimate details of their personal lives.

Politics had coiled itself around gender and race like a python, crushing decency and decorum from the proceedings. When three Republican senators—Alan Simpson, Arlen Specter, and Orrin Hatch—appeared to be hectoring Anita Hill, women became outraged. The discord between Republicans and Democrats flared like gas flames, and no one emerged from the conflagration unsinged.

The President, who had started it all, wrote to a friend in Lubbock, Texas, complaining about all the groups he saw as being too much in favor of abortion rights and affirmative action that were speaking up against Thomas's nomination:

> *They are trying to destroy this decent man. I do not think they will succeed but they are in frenzy around here. The most liberal of the women's groups are really outrageous; and then you have the smug liberal staffers who leak FBI reports to achieve their ignoble ends. It is sinister and evil, but I doubt the Senate under the control of the one party will do a damn thing about it . . . This is an ugly process and one can see clearly why so many good people elect to stay out of public life.*

A few days later, the President played golf at the Holly Hills Country Club near Camp David and brought a small television so he could watch the Thomas-Hill coverage as he raced from hole to hole. He had been advised more than once not to attack Anita Hill personally for fear of looking insensitive to women, but Bush could not restrain himself. Bristling with anger, he walked toward a group of reporters and described the hearings as "the ultimate in trying to drag someone through the mud and tear down his family . . .

"How come the normal behavior [on the part of Anita Hill] for ten years? How come the last-minute charge brought before the American people? I don't understand that. She didn't have to come forward at the last moment." The President said he and his family "felt kind of unclean watching this."

Three days later Clarence Thomas was confirmed by a hard-fought vote of 52–48, but the fallout had poisoned everyone. Years later Boyden Gray would tell Bob Woodward of *The Washington Post* that it took five years for Clarence Thomas to become a whole person again.

The confirmation process had brought out the worst in everyone, diminishing all those involved in some way: Republican Senator John Danforth of Missouri, who led the bitter fight for Thomas, lost luster among his colleagues for his dogmatic defense. Senators Simpson and Hatch were stung by the fury of their female constituents, who bombarded their offices with letters criticizing them for their treatment of Anita Hill; Senator Arlen Specter barely won reelection in Pennsylvania after his brutal cross-examination of Hill. The handling of her sexual-harassment charges against Justice Thomas had infuriated women across the political spectrum, who realized how little clout they had in a Congress dominated by white men. That fall an unprecedented number of female candidates ran for public office. Five women won seats in the Senate, and forty-seven women won seats in the House of Representatives. Most of the winners were Democrats.

In the end, President Bush got his way with Clarence Thomas, but at enormous cost. The process caused his party great enmity and sacrificed goodwill that he sorely needed. Worst of all, he had soiled his toga. Forsaking the ideal of presidential leadership expressed by Abraham Lincoln, Bush had not strengthened the bonds of affection among people by appealing to their better angels. Rather, he had caused the level of public discourse to be lowered, and the divisive afterclap affected him. He wrote a letter to Senator Alan Simpson, who had berated the press, Democrats, and women's groups while helping to get Clarence Thomas confirmed:

> You were right on all this. You helped a decent man turn the tide. You walked where angels feared to tread by zapping some groups and some press, and, in the process, they climbed all over your ass—but damnit you were right . . . Having said all this I'll confess—there are days when I just hate this job—not many, but some.

Reading the polls after the hearings, the President decided he needed to sign the Civil Rights Act of 1991 in order to get reelected. He had already vetoed the Civil Rights Act of 1990, claiming it was a "quota bill," but in the wake of Clarence Thomas he could not afford another veto. His core beliefs were irrelevant. All that mattered was winning.

Earlier in the year his staff had arranged for him to receive an honorary doctorate from Hampton University, the all-black college in Hampton, Virginia, but the degree did nothing to enhance his standing in the civil rights community. Most of the 1,023 graduates refused to stand for his entrance to "Hail to the Chief." They did not applaud the citation praising him for forty-three years of service to black education, and when he delivered his speech equating prejudice with cowardice, they sat on their hands.

Determined not to veto any more civil rights legislation, the President directed his White House counsel to work with the Senate and House Democrats to reach a bipartisan agreement on the 1991 Civil Rights Act. But those who attended the negotiations said that Boyden Gray consistently stymied the proceedings with contrary proposals. In one meeting, former Transportation Secretary William T. Coleman waved one of Gray's memos.

"The President told us to negotiate in good faith," Coleman said. "Can you believe what Boyden came up with?"

Gray snatched the document from Coleman's hand and ripped it to shreds.

"That's inoperable," said Gray, unable to defend his position.

"I haven't heard that phrase since the Nixon administration," said Coleman, laughing.

During another negotiation with civil rights representatives, including the NAACP Legal Defense and Educational Fund and the Leadership Conference on Civil Rights, Gray tried to establish a rapport with the Latinos and African Americans present by saying that he identified with their plight.

"You know I can understand how you feel, and what it must be like," he said, "because I, too, felt the pain of discrimination when I was at Harvard and I was the only W.A.S.P. on the Crimson."

The room fell silent and people shifted with embarrassment. The White House lawyer did not realize he looked like a dundering fool. "Everyone around that table was thunderstruck at the astonishingly insensitive and inappropriate remark," recalled Ralph Neas, then executive director of the Leadership Conference on Civil Rights. "Here was one of America's scions, an heir to the R. J. Reynolds Tobacco fortune, demonstrating his plantation mentality. This was the type of man George Herbert Walker Bush surrounded himself with as President of the United States. With such a person advising him, there was no danger of Bush ever ascending to the pantheon of presidents where Abraham Lincoln was enshrined."

After a bitter and anguished struggle, a compromise was finally reached, and the Civil Rights Act of 1991 was sent to the President's desk for his signature. On the eve of the bill signing, Boyden Gray again emerged as the hangman. He circulated a presidential order to all federal agencies directing them to comply with provisions that would end a quarter century's worth of affirmative action and hiring guidelines benefiting women and minorities.

The validity of executive orders has been questioned over the years because they are powerful edicts. It is a President's way of avoiding congressional authorization and bulldozing over judicial review. An executive order is a law made by a single individual—the President of the United States—and Boyden Gray's executive order for George Bush sought to overturn decades of civil rights legislation.

When news of the executive order was leaked, the entire Bush administration was turned upside down. Frantic cabinet secretaries called the White House in an uproar, and civil rights leaders denounced the directive as an assault on decades of civil rights progress. Everyone foresaw years of litigation to resolve whether an act of Congress takes precedence over an executive order while those who most needed protection by the law would be stripped of their civil rights. Backed into an uncomfortable corner, the President's press secretary said the executive order, immediately withdrawn, "may have been open to misinterpretation."

The President signed the Civil Rights Act of 1991 on November 21, 1991, in a Rose Garden ceremony that was overshadowed by the intent of Boyden Gray's presidential directive. The President condemned the "evil of discrimination" and reiterated his support for affirmative action, but he got none of the credit he craved. "There is no question that the Bush administration will continue to do everything possible to undermine the Civil Rights Act of 1991," said Ralph Neas at the time, "and undermine the bipartisan enforcement policies of the past quarter century."

Months later the President missed another opportunity to mend racial divisions when rioting broke out after Los Angeles police officers were acquitted in the beating of Rodney King. The verdict was announced on April 29, 1992, as Bush was leaving a state dinner for German President Richard von Weizsäcker. Standing in his tuxedo and black patent-leather dancing slippers, the President made a statement that would be replayed for the next seven days, making him look foppishly cavalier and out of touch with the real world.

"The court system has worked," he said. "What is needed now is calm and respect for the law until the appeals process takes place."

His remark was idiotic because when the defense wins a criminal case, there is no appeal.

What erupted was bloody chaos and the violent deaths of fifty-four people in the most deadly riot in U.S. history. A tornado of destruction whipped through South Los Angeles, turning the area into an incinerator after 4,000 fires, staggering property damage to 1,100 buildings, 2,383 reported injuries, and 13,212 arrests. That evening, television viewers watched in horror as Reginald Denny was dragged from his truck and beaten by a mob. Many people blamed the President of the United States for not immediately stepping forward in a time of national crisis.

"Bush had nothing to say when it counted to address the searing pain, the anger in the soul, that follows a miscarriage of justice of this enormity," wrote Thomas Oliphant in *The Boston Globe*.

The riots continued all day and all night through April 30, when federal troops and the National Guard were sent in to restore order. The President tried to redeem himself with an impassioned speech to the nation on May 1, again calling for calm.

"What you saw and what I saw on the TV video was revolting. I felt anger. I felt pain. I thought: How can I explain this to my grandchildren?"

Whatever ground Bush might have gained with his speech was lost three days later, when his press secretary blamed the riots on the welfare programs enacted by Democrats during Lyndon Johnson's Great Society. "We believe that many of the root problems that have resulted in inner-city difficulties were started in the 60s and 70s," said Marlin Fitzwater, "and that they have failed."

The next day Arkansas Governor Bill Clinton was walking the burned-out streets of South Los Angeles talking to Korean shop owners whose small businesses had been destroyed by looters. Even then the President and the First Lady did not veer from their separate schedules of fund-raising in Massachusetts and Ohio. Only after he saw his Democratic opponent on television meeting with community leaders in Los Angeles did the President realize that he, too, should make an appearance in the nation's second-largest city. He flew to California on May 6, a week after the Rodney King verdict. He arrived on Air Force One and was driven like a potentate in his bulletproof presidential limousine. The crowds jeered, and so did the polls, which showed a drastic fall in his support since the rioting had begun.

"It's hard to believe that the President of the United States was so politically obtuse, but he was," said Professor Susan J. Tolchin of the Institute of Public Policy at George Mason University. "His aides were frantic. I just happened to be included in an informal strategy session one night during the riots that included Bush's campaign manager, Fred Malek, several communications specialists, a couple of journalists, me, and the host, Roy Goodman, a Republican state senator from New York City.

" 'How can we get George Bush reelected?' Malek asked everyone.

"I certainly didn't want to see the guy reelected, but the political scientist in me took over. I had just seen the network news that evening, showing clips of all the black and Korean shopkeepers in tears as they poured out of their blazing liquor stores and groceries. Everything they had worked for was engulfed in flames, every bit of it uninsured.

"I suggested that Malek ask the President to phone his friends in the corporate world and recruit CEOs to each adopt a store, give the owner twenty-five thousand dollars, and put each back in business. Twenty-five thousand dollars to the presidents of Ford, General Motors, and Chrysler for bankrolling a Korean grocer is like twenty-five dollars to me. Republicans would be in the enviable position of rewarding hard work; the GOP could capitalize on its reputation for entrepreneurship; private business could be seen rewarding enterprise, not violence; and the President would position himself in the role of leading the city back to racial peace. It looked like a win-win for everyone. The companies would get great publicity for their good deeds; President Bush would get credit for leadership; and the taxpayer would be off the hook because 'big government' wouldn't have to spend a dime.

"Everyone agreed it was a wonderful idea. A week later I happened to see Fred Malek in the airport. 'What happened to my idea?' I asked. Malek shook his head woefully. 'I couldn't sell it to Bush,' he said. 'I went in to see him the very next morning with your idea . . . He didn't listen to us on anything.'

"I felt then that Bush had blown the domestic-leadership opportunity of his presidency. He missed the chance to reconcile the conflicting angers in South Los Angeles, where people were suffering physical, economic, and emotional damage."

The Bush reelection campaign was in such disarry that Barbara sent up a flare for her firstborn. George W. took a leave of absence from

Harken Energy in June 1992 and began commuting from Dallas to D.C. to ride herd again for his father. Months earlier Junior had warned the White House that Ross Perot was mounting a serious third-party assault on the presidency, but his father refused to take the Texas billionaire seriously. "He's an idiot," said the President. He told his campaign: "I'm not worried about him. You guys get paid to worry about him. If you want to worry about him, go ahead, but what are you going to do anyway?"

After announcing his candidacy in February, Perot bowed out in July but reentered the race in October. George W. told reporters he had named his golf cart "Perot," saying you could just never tell if it was going to run or not.

Whether headhunter or head chopper, George W. made his influence felt throughout his father's White House. Before the inaugural, Junior had chaired the "silent committee" that selected the names for the top federal jobs in the new administration. Ability and experience were irrelevant. Unswerving loyalty to his father was the son's only criterion.

"Let's make Roger Horchow the chairman of the National Endowment for the Arts," Junior said.

The choice of the Dallas catalog king struck one participant as inappropriate.

"Why Horchow?"

"Because he gave money to my father."

A quick cross-check of financial records showed that Horchow also contributed to the Democratic nominee Michael Dukakis.

"It didn't take any more than that," said the participant. "George W. said, 'That's it.' And Horchow ceased to be a candidate."

Documents in the Bush Presidential Library indicate the influence the son wielded in his father's administration. Whether it was a job, an autographed picture, or a personal meeting with the President, the requests George W. forwarded to the White House were honored with dispatch. His memos to C. Boyden Gray resulted in several judgeships. For Rhesa H. Barksdale to the U.S. Court of Appeals for the Fifth Circuit, W. wrote: "Boyden—This guy [is] up for federal judgeship. He is a very good man— Any help would be appreciated. Geo W."

George W.'s memo recommending Ellen Segal Huvelle got her seated as an associate judge for the D.C. Superior Court, and his memo forwarding the recommendation of a fraternity brother, Don Ensenat

(Yale 1968), got Edith Brown "Joy" Clement placed on the federal bench for the Eastern District of Louisiana: "Boyden—Don Ensenat is a very good man and good friend of all Bushes—Please give Joy any consideration you can—Warmly, George."

In December 1991, the President called on his son to fire White House Chief of Staff John Sununu. Sununu had been using government planes for private travel, and young George dutifully delivered the chop. Later W. told *D* magazine in Dallas: "It's just not that often you can do something really meaningful to help the President of the United States."

Unfortunately, the President, who gave full rein to his sense of self-entitlement, did not do much to help himself. Ignoring Ross Perot as a threat, Bush also dismissed Bill Clinton as an "unworthy" opponent. During an Oval Office meeting in 1992, President Bush pointed to his chair and asked, "Can you see Bill Clinton sitting here?" Uproarious laughter all around. Despite polls that showed Clinton beating him, the President told his family and friends that the Arkansas governor did not stand a chance. He could not see a "draft dodger" beating a decorated war hero. Neither could his wife, who went on television to say: "Bill Clinton and I have something in common. Neither of us served in the military. Ha. Ha."

"There were other things as well," said Osborne Day, a Bush family friend. "I'm afraid George was encouraged by what all the Secret Service guys with Clinton told him . . . George told his sister, Nan Ellis, about all the Clintons' rows and Hillary throwing ashtrays at Bill and how they hurled profanities at each other, and fought all the time. 'A guy like that just can't win,' George said. 'A guy like that doesn't deserve to be President.' "

To George H.W. Bush, someone who was not from a family like the Bushes or the Walkers—a "good" family—simply should not be President of the United States. Bush had met the Clintons in September 1989 in Charlottesville, Virginia, at a bipartisan summit of governors that he had convened to write national education goals for the country. The President and Mrs. Clinton got into a heated discussion over education spending and infant-mortality rates. Hillary told friends she was shocked that the President of the United States was so wrong on basic issues affecting America's children and so ill informed. Those friends report she told her husband: "We can take this guy. No question. He knows nothing . . . We have to take him. There's no way the country can survive in his hands."

Having spent 1988 getting his own private tutorial from a Bush strategist on how to run for President, Bill Clinton was more than ready. "I had worked for Bush in 1988 and was very involved with Lee Atwater and Roger Ailes in the anti-Dukakis campaign," said the political consultant Dick Morris. "I had run the campaign that defeated Dukakis for governor of Massachusetts in 1978, so I was kind of the house expert on how to run against the guy . . . Clinton and I talked every day, and I kept him very, very closely informed of what the thinking in the Bush campaign was . . . It was like going to school for Clinton in learning how a presidential campaign worked, how negatives were thrown in, how you retaliate, how you reply . . . We spent a lot of time talking about all of the attacks that Bush was throwing: Willie Horton, the Pledge of Allegiance, ACLU, all that stuff, and Dukakis's failure to respond.

"Clinton had tremendous admiration for Bush's 1988 campaign, an admiration that was more related to Jim Baker as campaign manager, Lee Atwater as political strategist, and Roger Ailes, who did the media. It was an admiration for the operatives, not the candidate. From them Clinton learned a basic lesson: you never let an accusation sleep under the same roof with you. Answer it immediately. He adopted the war-room mentality of rapid response and used it against Bush in 1992 at every turn."

Both sides claimed to have a hands-off policy on using sexual indiscretions against each other during the campaign. "Our guy was more susceptible on that issue," admitted a Clinton aide. "After I went to Arkansas and saw what we were dealing with—lists longer than the phone book— I started doing a little research on the other side and found that Bush also had other women in his life . . . I took my list of Bush women, including one whom he had made an Ambassador, to his campaign operatives. I said I knew we were vulnerable on women, but I wanted to make damn sure they knew they were vulnerable too."

The Clintons had appeared on *60 Minutes* in January 1992 to respond to Gennifer Flowers's story of her twelve-year affair with the governor. With his wife at his side, Clinton acknowledged causing pain in his marriage, and although he did not give a full-throated admission of infidelity, the issue of his womanizing seemed to subside in the polls.

"We knew the Democrats were saying we were negative campaigners and had branded us trash-talkers," said Mary Matalin, political director of the Republican National Committee. "We did not need to reinforce their negative image of us, particularly on an issue like philandering, so we kept out of it. The word went out: nobody will say anything about Clinton's personal life. When the press calls for comment: No comment."

Surprisingly, it was the Bush camp that got walloped next by the issue of philandering. On August 11, 1992, the *New York Post* published a front-page story headlined "The Bush Affair," complete with photos of George Bush and Jennifer Fitzgerald, who some people thought bore an eerie resemblance to Barbara Bush. The story was based on a newly released book by Susan Trento called *The Power House*, which described a Washington lobbyist who had participated in an early effort to cover up "Bush's sexual indiscretions . . . if he ever hoped to be president." A footnote in the book suggested that the late Louis Fields, an ambassador to the nuclear-disarmament talks in Geneva, had arranged for Bush and Ms. Fitzgerald to share a guesthouse in Switzerland when they were together in 1984. A *Post* sidebar with a screeching headline, "New Book: Bush Had Swiss Tryst," carried the details, which quoted Fields as saying, "It became clear to me that the vice-president and Ms. Fitzgerald were romantically involved . . . It made me very uncomfortable."

The morning the story broke, the President was vacationing in Kennebunkport with his family and meeting with Yitzhak Rabin, the newly elected Prime Minister of Israel. After their discussion, the two heads of state planned to hold a press conference.

Reporters were bused from their hotels to the Bush compound and told to queue up behind ropes. As they waited for the press conference to begin, a female aide in the White House press office went up and down the rope line asking which reporter would be asking the President about the *New York Post* story. It seemed to some reporters as if the aide was urging the question to be asked. No one said anything, although all had been discussing the story. On the bus, Brit Hume of ABC-TV said he would not ask the question because it was "intrusive and too personal." Susan Spencer of CBS-TV said she did not want to ask the question, but if no one else did, she would because it was a legitimate inquiry. Mary Tillotson of CNN said the same thing.

Usually, the President of the United States does not have his entire family present at a press conference, but on this particular morning the White House made sure that his white-haired wife of forty-seven years, his children, their spouses, their pets, and all of the grandchildren buttressed Bush. In addition, they even wheeled out the President's mother, who was ninety-one. The most reasonable explanation is that Bush surrounded himself with family as a response to the *Post* story—and in preparation for the inevitable question.

"No reporter really wanted to ask the question in that setting," said Julia Malone of Cox Newspapers, "but it was a major story in that morning's papers and it couldn't be ignored."

From the beginning the press conference was tense and strained. The President called on several people, who side-stepped the question that hung like a cloud. Then he pointed to Mary Tillotson, who had wanted to ask him about Bosnia. But she had told her producer she would ask the infidelity question if she was called on and no one else had asked.

"Mr. Bush, uncomfortable as the subject is, I would think it's one to which you feel the necessity to respond because you've said that family values, character, are likely to be important in the presidential campaign. There is an extensive series of reports in today's *New York Post* alleging that a former U.S. Ambassador, a man now deceased, had told several persons that he arranged for a sexual tryst involving you and one of your female staffers in Geneva in 1984."

The President's face hardened. Grim and thin-lipped with anger, he spat out his response. "I'm not going to take any sleazy questions like that from CNN," snapped the President. "I am very disappointed you would ask such a question of me. I will not respond to it. I haven't responded in the past. I am outraged, but nevertheless in this kind of screwy climate we're in I expect it. But I don't like it and I'm not going to respond other than to say it is a lie."

Sensing her grandfather's fury, one of his granddaughters burst into tears and was led away by her mother.

"It was probably the worst professional day of my life," Tillotson said later. "I so wish someone else had asked the question, but no one did."

Few in the press corps came to her defense. Some felt the question was inappropriate in front of the Israeli Prime Minister. Men seemed to feel it was totally off-limits, because it involved sex; many women saw the sex issue as a matter of hypocrisy and very much within limits. Political science professor Larry J. Sabato of the University of Virginia said that reporters should have a legitimate reason for asking the question. "Politicians who use their family to project a wholesome image are asking for a rude press disclosure if they are not living up to those implied ideals," said Sabato. "A candidate who invites the press into his living room shouldn't be surprised when a skeptical press finds its way to his bedroom. At the same time, in order to convince the public of the truth of any allegation, some proof or evidence ought to be presented with any public accusation of infidelity. Otherwise, there is no end to the published and aired rumors, some true and some false, and there is no way for a good citizen to distinguish among the various allegations. I have a civic-oriented view of press coverage. It should be done not as a game between the pols and the press, but as a means for vital civic education so that informed voters can make wise choices."

The editor and publisher of *The Galveston Daily News* defended the question and praised the questioner. "I've always been proud of my tough, smart sister Mary," wrote Dolph Tillotson in an opinion piece. "But never more so than right now."

Mary Tillotson's question and George Bush's denunciation were broadcast over and over on television. Many thought Tillotson's job might be in jeopardy, especially when one of Marlin Fitzwater's aides threatened to lift her White House press credentials. "Fitzwater and many of those from the White House who were present at the news conference were quite upset," recalled Tom Johnson, former president and CEO of CNN. "He was quoted to me as saying something like, CNN never will get another interview with the President. That includes the Larry King show." (For all of Fitzwater's bluster, CNN did not have to worry. Neither George nor Barbara would ever miss a chance to appear on *Larry King Live*. They even invited the talk-show host to Texas to emcee George's eightieth birthday in 2004.)

The First Lady was incensed that she and her husband had been publicly humiliated. She targeted the *New York Post* with the brunt of her anger by canceling a scheduled interview with Deborah Orin, the paper's White House correspondent. Mrs. Bush condemned the story in an interview with *The Washington Times*, saying it was "an outrage . . . a disgusting lie."

Barbara had no compunctions about taking on the press to protect the family's public image. She upbraided Hearst syndicated columnist Marianne Means for referring to George H.W. Bush's "unhappy experience as Vice President," and writing that "Reagan and Bush had little in common and no history of confidential communication." Means added: "Nancy Reagan was freely quoted expressing her utter scorn for Bush."

In an irate letter, Barbara Bush lectured the prize-winning columnist about her responsibility to her profession and to her readers "to at least present the facts accurately." Despite evidence to the contrary, Mrs. Bush claimed that her husband and President Reagan "became the best of friends." She even criticized the Pulitzer–prize winning biographer Edmund Morris for writing "that terrible book, 'Dutch.'" Mrs. Bush wrote, "George told Nancy Reagan we did not believe one word of it, for which she was very grateful. We also heard from several very close Reagan friends who told us they knew that all the discussion about the hard feelings between the Bushes and Reagans was nonsense."

Marianne Means responded with a polite letter that firmly refuted every point. "I understand your frustration about inaccuracies that appear in the media," wrote the columnist. "We in the press feel the same way about politicians who try to rewrite recorded history for their own purposes."

Unperturbed, Barbara now decided to take on the Cable News Network. At the Republican Convention in Houston, Barbara Bush met with Tom Johnson in the green room before doing a CNN interview with Catherine Crier.

"The quotes I recall are these," said Johnson: "'Tom, I am very disappointed in CNN.' 'CNN used to be the network we respected most.' 'CNN always was fair to us and very responsible.' 'I cannot believe that CNN asked that terrible question of George in Kennebunkport, especially in front of his mother.'"

Mary Tillotson was taken off the White House beat and made anchor and host of CNN and Company, a position left open when Catherine Crier left the network.

"Did the incident affect that decision? I think all of us felt a new assignment would be good for Mary and for CNN," said Johnson. "Frankly, I never would have pulled Mary from the White House beat had the Bush White House pressured me to do so. That would have been caving to political pressure. Doing so would have created major internal problems with our staff and major external problems within our profession."

During the GOP convention Barbara Bush went on CNN to denounce the network. "I think it's disgraceful," she said.

"It's worse, in my opinion, to print a hurtful, harmful story about the president of the United States from a man who's dead, and they're all lies. With no proof, that's disgusting."

She berated the press at every turn and excoriated reporters for pressing the issue with a direct question to the President. "It's sick," she told *The Houston Chronicle*. "It was a lie. It was ugly . . . The mainline press has sunk to an all-time low and CNN gets the top of my list." She also criticized the author Susan Trento. "I don't know the person who wrote that sick book, but they ought to have their mouth washed out with soap and for the press to pick it up is even worse."

The next day Stone Phillips of *Dateline NBC* walked into the Oval Office for a scheduled interview and, despite a warning from the President, repeated the question. He received an angry denial and a lecture about sleazy journalism.

"It was what everyone was talking about," said the NBC spokeswoman Tory Beilinson. "Not to ask the question wouldn't have been right. The question is fair. They're running a campaign where one of the main issues is family values. Marital fidelity has a lot to do with family values."

The British press speculated on "the horizontal jogging" of the two men running for President, pointing out that both Clinton and Bush had alleged paramours with the same first name and both men had put their women on the public payroll. Bill Clinton's Gennifer was paid a mere $17,000 a year in a nonunion low-wage state; George Bush's Jennifer held a high-ranking federal job worth $100,000 a year. The contrasts between the women resided in more than different spellings of the same first name. Gennifer Flowers was a glamorous blond cabaret singer with a preference for low-cut dresses. "Like we say in Arkansas," she told *The New York Times*, " 'if it ain't pretty, don't put it on the front porch.' " She had sold her story to a tabloid, whereas the other Jennifer, also blond but much older and less flamboyant, went into hiding when her story appeared.

Jennifer Fitzgerald refused to respond to press inquiries. She had been stung in the past, particularly in *The Washington Post*, which announced her appointment in January 1989 with a sly lead: "Jennifer Fitzgerald, who has served President-elect George Bush *in a variety of po-*

sitions, most recently running the vice presidential Senate offices, is expected to be named deputy chief of protocol in the new administration."

A year later *The Washington Post* broke the story that she was fined $648 by the U.S. Customs Service for "misdescribing" the value of a fur-lined raincoat ($1,100) and failing to declare a silver-fox cape ($1,300). She had bought them on an official trip to Argentina in July 1989 with the President's brother Jonathan Bush and his wife, Jody. They represented the President in Buenos Aires at the inauguration of President Carlos Menem. After a State Department investigation, Jennifer was suspended for two weeks without pay, but she did not lose her presidential appointment.

Flying to the defense of her sixty-year-old daughter, Frances Patteson-Knight, eighty-six, dismissed rumors of Jennifer's affair with the President as "quite simply and utterly ridiculous." It was the dignified response of a proud woman descended from Russian aristocrats who, she said, became one of the wealthiest families in America before losing millions in the stock-market crashes between the two world wars. Her home in McLean, Virginia, set on twenty acres, was crammed with antiques, pedigreed dogs, and a wide selection of photos of Jennifer and George in silver frames on the piano and adorning the walls of the bathroom, showing them in formal dress as well as casual wear, relaxed and laughing.

"Jennifer is completely tortured by this whole business," said her mother. "She doesn't know what to do. She thinks it is all just horrible, horrible . . . She is very disappointed by Bush's reaction . . . She respects him because he's President, but doesn't think he's acted like a man here. She is very hurt by his lack of support. I don't think he called her. If he did, she would be less desperate."

The only person talking on the Bush side was Barbara. The White House staff remained silent, and the campaign was lip-locked. No one within the inner circle uttered a word. Years later, Carol Taylor Gray said: "Jennifer was a fact of life in George's life. Period. End of discussion. It was what it was. No one knew that better than my husband [C. Boyden Gray], who worked for George Bush for twelve years. We talked about it constantly . . . No one held it against George. Actually, I liked Jennifer — she was petite and attractive, and she made him happy, so I'm glad he had her in his life to give him a little joy . . . I know this is heresy to say because Barbara Bush is adored by the country and looks like such a sweet old grandmother, but the country doesn't know her like I do . . . I don't think she has a good heart . . . she's not a nice woman. To dogs, maybe, but not to people, at least not to women like me . . . I didn't see her after Boyden and I divorced, so I can only speak for what I saw during our marriage."

By the time of the GOP convention in Houston the President was trailing Clinton by thirty points; after Pat Buchanan's fire-breathing speech on prime-time television, the Bushes probably should have started packing. In a remarkable—and, to many moderates, terrifying—tirade, Buchanan laid waste to all but the religious right of the Republican Party. He railed against the agenda "Clinton and Clinton" would impose on America—"abortion on demand, a litmus test for the Supreme Court, homosexual rights, discrimination against religious schools, women in combat units." With the televangelists Pat Robertson and Jerry Falwell beaming down from the VIP skyboxes in the Astrodome, Buchanan, whose speech had been approved by the Bush campaign, repeatedly attacked the morals of the Clintons and all those who accepted abortion as a legal right and considered homosexuals to be human.

"There is a religious war going on in this country for the soul of America. It is a cultural war as critical to the kind of nation we shall be as the Cold War itself. And in that struggle for the soul of America, Clinton and Gore are on the other side and George Bush is on our side."

No one was more shocked by Buchanan's bombast than Barbara Bush, who immediately characterized his rhetoric as "hateful," "mean," and "racist." Not even Ronald Reagan's big-tent speech of love and unity could salvage the damage. Nor could James A. Baker III, who had reluctantly resigned as Secretary of State to run his friend's last campaign. The Republicans limped out of Houston on the defensive and remained there all fall.

Slashing the air, talking too fast, spouting gibberish, flubbing lines, and ad-libbing poorly, the President of the United States campaigned as if English were his second language. He reviled those who said he had no vision. "The vision thing," he said. "Don't want to hear about it." He thrashed his opponents as "crazy." He called Clinton "a bozo." He said, "My dog Millie knows more about foreign policy than that clown." He labeled the Clinton-Gore ticket "Governor Taxes and the Ozone Man." He accused the press of being pro-Clinton. Playing to the public's bias, he waved a bumper sticker that said: "Annoy the media. Elect George Bush President." It was as undignified a campaign as any President had ever run.

By late October the President had sunk in the polls, but he remained defiantly confident. "I don't want to hear the polls," he told Mary Matalin. "I don't care about the polls . . . I know I'm going to win and I know why I'm going to win. It has nothing to do with these numbers."

Iran-contra had started to dog Bush in June, when Caspar Weinberger was indicted for five felonies, including two charges of perjury. One count was thrown out, but on October 30, 1992, a federal grand jury delivered another indictment against Weinberger. This one referenced a note dated January 7, 1986, showing that George Bush had indeed attended the meeting and supported the arms-for-hostages deal that had been opposed by Weinberger and Shultz. For five years Bush had denied that he knew about the plan, claiming repeatedly, "I was out of the loop." Now there was evidence that for five years he had lied.

Campaigning in Wisconsin the day after the indictment, he addressed a crowd that was buzzed by a single-engine plane circling overhead trailing a banner: "Iran-Contra Haunts You." The President nearly snapped his cap.

"Today is Halloween, our opponents' favorite holiday," he cried. "They're trying to scare America. If Governor Taxes and the Ozone Man are elected, every day is going to be Halloween. Fright and Terror. Fright and Terror. Witches and devils everywhere."

When his opponent questioned his honesty, Bush responded like an adolescent. "Being called dishonest by Bill Clinton is like being called ugly by a frog," he said.

He snapped at reporters who tried to interview him about the indictment and his role in Iran-contra. "I think most people concede that the media has been very unfair," he said. "I think the press has been the worst it's ever been, ever!" When confronted by an AIDS activist waving a condom, he remarked, "Oh, look! New press credentials."

Polls that had narrowed in the last few days suddenly showed Clinton pulling ahead again, because a majority of Americans did not believe the President had told the truth about Iran-contra. His biggest deception—withholding his diaries—would not become known until after the election.

The Iran-contra independent counsel, Lawrence E. Walsh, had made his first document request on March 27, 1987, for all of Bush's personal records, including diaries. Rather than issue subpoenas to the White House, Walsh's office relied on written requests because he wanted to avoid taking the executive branch to court. Bush, who kept copious diaries as a matter of habit, ignored the request.

Five years later, on September 24, 1992, his personal secretary, Patty Presock, opened a safe in the residence of the White House and found his long-hidden diary. She recognized that many passages pertained to Iran-contra matters and wondered if it should not be turned over to the independent counsel. When she told the President about her discovery, he said the diary was irrelevant to Walsh's investigation. She disagreed, so he called the White House counsel.

Boyden Gray claimed to be astonished when he first saw the diary—hundreds of pages that were a complete daily record of the last two years of the Reagan presidency, plus the entire Bush presidency up to that point. It is difficult to accept that the lawyer, who worked for Bush for almost twelve years, did not know about Bush's practice of keeping a daily diary by dictating into a tape recorder each night and then having the tapes transcribed. Bush had been doing this for many years, unaware of the legendary Mae West's comment: "Keep a diary and someday it'll keep you."

Boyden Gray's friendship with George Bush stretched back to their fathers, who had played golf together. Now, as White House lawyer, Gray made a calculated decision to withhold the diaries until after the election. He knew the race against Clinton was close, and he worried that if the diaries were suddenly produced after all these years, charges would be made of a cover-up. He went to the President, explained the political problem, and said he planned to tell no one until after the election.

"If that's your judgment, fine," Bush said with no hesitation.

At 3:00 p.m. on Election Day, Tuesday, November 3, 1992, George Bush still believed he would win. His practical wife, who knew better, was already trying to figure out how to get a driver's license, something she had not had to think about for the past twelve years of government cars and drivers. By 10:00 p.m., the President was ready to concede. Clinton won with 43 percent of the vote to 38 percent for Bush and 19 percent for Ross Perot. George Bush had received the lowest popular vote for an incumbent Republican President since William Howard Taft. That night Bush wrote in his diary:

It's hurt, hurt, hurt and I guess it's the pride, too . . . I don't like to see the pundits right; I don't like to see all of those who have written me off right . . . I was wrong and they were right and that hurts a lot.

The hardest blow was yet to come. On November 19, 1992, the President flew to Connecticut to say good-bye to his ninety-one-year-old mother, who was dying. He sat at her bedside with his daughter, Doro, sobbing. Thumbing through the frayed Bible beside her, he found notes that he had written as a young boy at Andover. On her piano in the living room was his official picture as President signed: "For Mummy—I love you very much. Pop." He returned to Washington an hour after he had arrived, and Dotty Bush died the next day. His family remembered that just before he had taken the oath of office on January 20, 1989, he had leaned over to kiss his mother on the platform. "Many of our family are here," he said, "and they all, as does this son, worship the ground you walk on." The night she died he wrote in his diary: "Mum, I hope you know how much we all love you and care. Tonight she is at rest in God's loving arms and with Dad."

Momentarily, the loss of the presidency and the scandal of Iran-contra seemed incidental next to losing the most important person in his life. "It's immaterial when you think of Mother, love, faith, life and death," Bush said. Later, though, in a letter to his brother Jonathan, George wrote about what losing the White House meant to him: "I didn't finish the course, and I will always regret that . . . I also know the press were more hateful than I can ever recall in modern political times. I have to get over my 'hating.' "

George placed most of the blame for his loss on the independent counsel. "Walsh had that phony indictment come out just before the election," he told Marlin Fitzwater. "Probably cost me the election."

The President retaliated a few weeks later and put Lawrence Walsh out of business. The day before Christmas—ten days before Weinberger was to stand trial—Bush exercised his prerogatives as chief executive and pardoned all those who had been indicted and convicted in Iran-contra: Caspar Weinberger, Elliott Abrams, Robert "Bud" McFarlane, and three CIA officials: Clair E. George, Alan D. Fiers Jr., and Duane R. "Dewey" Clarridge.

He confided a slight reservation in his diary: "The pardon of Weinberger will put a tarnish, kind of a downer, on our legacy."

His formal statement accompanying the pardons anticipated the public reaction. After lecturing Lawrence Walsh against "the criminalization of policy differences," he said, "Some may argue that this will prevent full disclosure of some new key facts to the American people. That is not true. The matter has been investigated exhaustively. All have already paid a price— in depleted savings, lost careers, anguished families—grossly disproportionate to any misdeeds or errors of judgment they may have committed."

In a Christmas Day editorial, *The New York Times* called it "Mr. Bush's Unpardonable Act": "Mr. Bush remains implicated in Iran-contra, and in that sense he has shamelessly pardoned himself . . . [He] is beyond the reach of American voters. But he is not beyond the reach of responsible opinion or of history."

Lawrence Walsh nearly flew off his hinges. He announced on television that the President had concealed his diary for five years. "In light of his own misconduct we are gravely concerned by his decision to pardon others." He added, "I think it's the last card in the cover-up. He's played the final card . . . He has shown an arrogant disdain for the rule of law."

The independent counsel took several months to wrap up his report before issuing his findings to the public. In the end he elected not to prosecute the President, although it cost Bush $461,346 to defend himself. Walsh never concealed his disdain for the unindicted commander in chief. "I think President Bush will always have to answer for his pardons," Walsh said. "There was no public purpose served by that."

In the final days of the Bush administration, C. Boyden Gray tried to erase the contents of the White House computers and destroy all National Security Council information, as well as details of the Iran-contra pardons and all evidence of the administration's illegal search of Clinton's passport files during the campaign. But U.S. District Judge Charles R. Richey upheld the law that stipulates presidential records are public property. He ruled Gray's actions unlawful, issued a court order to prevent the threatened destruction, and ordered that the records be turned over to the National Archives. In a late-night meeting, the archivist of the United States, Don W. Wilson, gave Bush exclusive legal control of the computerized records, and then left town to go to work for the George Bush Presidential Library.

As her husband struggled through his final days in the White House, the First Lady was in full bustling mode—making lists and packing boxes to return to Houston. Realizing she would have little need for her ball gowns, Barbara put them on sale. She priced and tagged each one, hung them on a rolling rack, and posted a message to the household staff to come and shop. Many were thrilled to purchase some of the First Lady's hand-me-downs. Others were slightly put off that she would sell clothes that had been given to her or purchased at deep designer discounts. One of the butlers bought a gown for his mother, only to be told several days later that he had to return it. Barbara realized that she had not meant to sell that particular gown, and she wanted it back.

"My mother-in-law has always been cheap cheap cheap," said Sharon Bush. "Embarrassingly cheap."

While the First Lady was turning a tidy little profit upstairs in the White House, her husband was in the Oval Office exacting a little payback of his own. At that point his presidential report card showed he had traveled to 29 foreign countries; hosted 29 state dinners; held 141 press conferences; appointed two Supreme Court justices; vetoed 44 bills; signed 1,239 bills; granted 77 pardons; dispatched two brothers, one sister, and five children on eighteen diplomatic missions; and launched two military operations. On December 4, 1992, he launched his third military operation by sending twenty-five thousand troops into Somalia to help a UN peacekeeping mission.

"This was a very strange thing for a President to be doing in the closing weeks of his administration," said Dick Morris. "Hillary felt and I agreed that this was kind of a trap that Bush had laid for Clinton. She called it 'Bush's parting gift to us.' Clinton withdrew most of the troops Bush sent by June 1993, but in October 1993 more than eighteen soldiers were killed and seventy-eight wounded in a firefight with guerrillas in Mogadishu. The bodies of dead U.S. soldiers were dragged through the streets . . . There was a huge uproar in the U.S., and Clinton had to send in additional troops . . . I think Bush figured Clinton to be an ingenue in foreign policy, which he was, and Bush, the pro, knew he would look good sending troops to Somalia. I think he probably took very seriously the famine going on, but I also think he figured, 'Hey, bozo. This one's for you.' "

CHAPTER TWENTY-FOUR

The family's restoration began as soon as the crown slipped. When George Herbert Walker Bush was forced into retirement, the heir apparent stepped forward to pick up the standard. He had amassed his fortune in business and was eager to pursue public office. His news pumped hope into the old regents, still smarting from the shame of losing the White House. With a new lease on life, the elder Bushes looked forward to rejuvenating the family name through the son whose political gifts had marked him as the anointed one within the family. The news that he would run for governor took the sting out of their crushing defeat.

Three weeks after Bill Clinton's inauguration in 1992, George and Barbara Bush flew to Miami so the former President could play golf with their son Jeb, Arnold Palmer, and Joe DiMaggio at the Deering Bay Yacht and Country Club. Jeb and his partner, Armando Codina, had developed Deering Bay, which had taken a destructive hit when Hurricane Andrew roared through Florida. The celebrity golf game was organized to demonstrate that the course was in excellent playing condition, which, the Bushes hoped, would attract investors for their son. That was the sole purpose of the outing, until a reporter asked Barbara Bush about her plans for retirement. So excited about the family's political future, she burbled the news.

"We're going to play golf, write books, see grandchildren," she said. "But if by chance the most qualified man ran for governor of Florida, I'm coming down to campaign."

Jeb Bush laughed. "Leave it to Mom," he said. "I'm happy to hear about it, but I probably would have preferred [to hear about] it in private. I have every intention to run, it's just that there's a process you have to go through."

Within minutes the wire services transmitted the news that the second son of the former President was going to seek the statehouse in Florida. No one was more interested in that news than the first son in Texas, who had not been apprised of his brother's plans.

The family was accustomed to communicating through the media. When young George announced his interest in running for governor of Texas in 1989, the First Lady summoned reporters to the White House and dispensed her motherly advice. She indicated it would be unseemly for the President's son to run for such a conspicuous public office. "I'm rather hoping he won't," she said, "because everything that happens bad with the administration is going to be young George's fault." She also said that she thought he had an obligation to the seventy investors who had paid $86 million for the Texas Rangers, and she said he should sit on his political ambitions and stick to running the baseball team.

Feeling mommy-whipped, George responded testily through reporters. "For 42 years she has given me her opinion," he said. "I have listened to it—sometimes. I still love my mother, and I appreciate her advice, but that's all it is—advice." He made her wait four months before he announced his decision in *The Houston Chronicle* not to run.

Three years later he toyed with the idea of running for the Senate seat vacated by Lloyd Bentsen, when President Clinton appointed him Treasury Secretary. "I saw young George in Dallas and asked if he was thinking about being a senator or something," said Kent Hance, who had beaten Bush in his first political campaign. "George said, 'I hate Washington.' He told me, 'I like Texas. I might think about governor or something, but I hate Washington.'"

A few weeks later he told *The Houston Chronicle*: "Laura and I seriously considered the Senate race and decided it is best for our family to stay in Texas. Besides, I love my life in baseball." That life consisted in attending games, autographing baseballs for fans, and hanging out with baseball players. Being a public pal of the Hall of Fame pitcher Nolan Ryan was a celebrity-contact high for W., who venerated major-league baseball players. He even printed up baseball cards with his picture, which psychiatrist Justin M. Frank interpreted as "a pathetic effort to erase the fact that he could never be the baseball star his father was." George

attended every home game in the old Stadium in Arlington, a Dallas sub-
urb, sitting in his front-row seat in section 109, row 1, behind the dugout.
With his cowboy boots perched on the rail, he chewed tobacco and
passed out autographed baseball cards of himself to fans. "I want the folks
to see me, sitting in the same kind of seat they sit in, eating the same pop-
corn, peeing in the same urinal," he said.

As the public face of the Texas Rangers' management, George was expected to draw people to the ballpark. "Being the president's son puts you
in the limelight," he said. "While in the limelight, you might as well sell
tickets."

His fraternity brother Roland Betts, an investor in the Texas Rangers,
had told him he needed to do something to step out of his father's shadow.
"Baseball was it," said Betts. "He became our local celebrity. He knew
every usher. He signed autographs. He talked to fans. His presence meant
everything. His eyes were on politics the whole time, but even when he
was speaking at Republican functions, he was always talking about the
Rangers."

Within a year George felt he had earned his spurs as the team's managing partner by pushing a proposal through the legislature for a new
baseball stadium in Arlington. The mayor of the little town was dazzled
to be negotiating with the President's son and turned himself inside out
to make the stadium a reality. The $190 million package, to be financed
mostly by taxpayers, included 270 acres of private land, only 17 of which
were needed to build the stadium; the rest was for development. Determined to make money on a bigger and better baseball team as well as land
speculation, the owners convinced the city that the new stadium would
spur construction of hotels, shops, and office buildings by attracting millions of visitors. Their fanciful plans included an amphitheater, sailboats
skimming across a man-made lake, and gondolas to carry fans to the ballpark. To sell the plan to the working class of Arlington, George mounted
the pulpit of the Mount Olive Baptist Church one Sunday and declared,
"A vote for the tax would be a vote for contracts for African American
businesses."

The plan passed, the stadium was built, and the book value of the
team soared from $86 million to $138 million. The team became valuable—George made a profit of $15 million when the team was sold in
1998—but the commercial development of Arlington never materialized.
A decade later the man-made lake was still a muddy hole and the gondo-

las nothing more than slick sales talk. The landgrab had been all too real for some families, costing them their homes and their farms. The Rangers' management had made them an offer for their property; if they said no, their land was condemned and seized under a legal provision known as eminent domain, which gives the government the power to take private property belonging to its citizens.

"Anybody who was in their way, they just ran them over," said Bucky Fanning, whose ten-acre horse farm became a parking lot for the new ballpark. "I used to be a Rangers fan, but then they stole my property." Ten years after she was driven off her property, Maree Fanning, Bucky's mother, could barely control her anger toward George W. Bush. "If I saw him today, I'd say, 'Bite my ass.' " Her son, Bucky, said, "I don't think he ever cared [about how the land condemnation displaced families and ruined their livelihoods]. All Bush cared about was the money."

Families like the Fannings sued, charging "a group of wealthy and influential people threatened and traded their way into an unprecedented takeover of government power and private property in an awesome display of greed and avarice." The court case lasted seven years, until 1998, when the new owner, Tom Hicks, agreed to pay $11 million in damages, which the families complained was far less than the land was worth. Throughout the proceedings, George publicly claimed he had never heard of the planned land seizures, but Tom Bernstein's deposition—he was one of the partners in the team—proved that George had been fully informed of the strategy from the beginning. Despite the controversy, he pointed with pride to the new stadium. "When all those people in Austin say, 'He ain't never done anything,' well, this is it."

George felt the ballpark at Arlington had given him an accomplishment—something beyond being the namesake son of the President—and he intended to use it to launch himself politically. His brother's announcement to run for governor of Florida had galvanized him into action a little sooner than he had planned, but such was the rivalry between the two that George was not about to be one-upped by his younger brother.

For years George had used Jeb as nothing more than a punching bag. Seven years younger, Jeb was easy to bully. "Then Jebbie grew up to be six foot four and that got complicated," said his cousin John Ellis. "As a kid, George viewed him as a completely unnecessary addition to the family . . . Jebbie was just a pain in the ass. I think that carried on for a long time."

Despite the close and cohesive picture the Bushes presented to the outside world, the family was a complex stew of affiliations and emotions that coalesced best during a political campaign for the elder Bush, when all worked to benefit from the reflected glory of winning. The boys, who idolized their father, grew up in the shadow of his success and competed among themselves to create similar successes of their own. Not so with their sister, Doro, the only girl and the youngest sibling. Little was expected of her, except to get married, which she did—twice. In the Bush dynasty, women have never been expected to succeed in business or politics. Their role is to be useful and supportive adjuncts to their men.

Within a large family, birth order matters, and the firstborn usually gets the lion's share of parents' time and attention, inevitably becoming the most successful of the siblings. For seven years George W. Bush was the only son, and he assumed all the prerogatives of the eldest child. After his sister Robin's death, he became the family clown, a role he used to cheer up his parents. He commanded the spotlight by making everyone laugh. He became closest to his youngest siblings, who did not threaten his dominance. Over the years, his strongest fraternal bond was with his brother Marvin and his sister, Doro, neither of whom was interested in politics or competed with W. in any way.

After the debacle of Silverado, Neil, the dyslexic middle child, was forced to abandon his dreams of public office. He left Colorado and limped back to Texas with his wife and three children to become a ward of the family. His father never stopped blaming himself for Neil's predicament and tried to compensate by helping him get established in business. The President made room for his son in his Houston office, which exposed Neil to a procession of international visitors—heads of state, prime ministers, emirs, and emperors—who came to pay their respects to George. When they did, they also met his son. "It was great for Neil," said his former wife, Sharon. "Just great."

The S&L scandal continued to dog Neil, however, and other scandals followed. After a twenty-three-year marriage he fell in love with a married woman, Maria Andrews, who worked as a volunteer in his mother's office. Neil sued Sharon for divorce, and during the proceedings sordid details of his personal life were made public, including disclosures of an STD he had contracted and his use of prostitutes. It prompted one Texas writer to describe Neil as "the pisswit son of the former president."

Elsie Walker, another cousin, came to know the entire Bush clan well during the family summers in Kennebunkport. Of all the brothers, George was the one with whom she developed her closest bond. She recalled one day when they were all children and were roughhousing. She accidentally broke the Bushes' chandelier. Jeb, the family tattletale, ran to tell his mother, and within minutes Barbara broomed into the room.

"What the hell is going on?" she yelled. "Jebbie tells me that you've . . ."

She saw the chandelier dangling from the ceiling.

Elsie was so terrified of Barbara that she burst into tears.

George stepped forward. "I broke it," he said, staring at his mother defiantly.

The punishment that Barbara meted out to George he later passed on to Jeb, and that was the pattern of their childhood. The two brothers never became good friends growing up. As adults competing for their father's attention and approval, they became even more distant, especially when Jeb emerged as the more successful. He graduated from the University of Texas in three years with a Phi Beta Kappa key just like his father. George W. graduated from Yale at the bottom of his class with nothing more than a keg key.

George had his father's name and his mother's temperament. Taller and better-looking, Jeb got his father's temperament, which made him his mother's favorite. "I must say young George is very much of a different generation," Barbara said in 1994. "With my other governor son, Jeb, you still see the old gentle Bush demeanor. But this George, he's something else entirely." Like his father, Jeb married early, settled down, and began a family while George was still carousing around the oil patch. Jeb carved a political life for himself in Florida, becoming chairman of the Miami–Dade County GOP and state secretary of commerce, whereas George remained in Texas, where the Bush name paved his way. Jeb, known as the most serious in the family, became a sobersided policy wonk; George, a drunken wiseacre. Jeb was the smartest brother; George was the brother with the smartest mouth. Smooth and extremely articulate, Jeb became his parents' pride and joy, while George was their deepest embarrassment. Immune to shame, George operated on the premise that if you can't get rid of the family skeleton, you may as well make it dance. He reveled in his bad-boy status, even introduced himself to Queen Elizabeth at a White House state dinner as "the family's black sheep." By then the differences between the two brothers had become marked: Jeb was the more impressive; George the more amusing.

During the 1994 campaign—when both George and Jeb were running for governor of their states—the brothers seemed to switch personas. Jeb emerged as a hard-edged firebrand, and George came across as a soft generalist who talked about Texas as "a beacon state" and "a place for dreamers." Jeb traveled around Florida in a mobile home/bus named "Dynasty." He told Tom Fiedler of *The Miami Herald*: "I want to be able to look my father in the eye and say, 'I continued the legacy.' " He frightened minority voters in Florida's inner cities by threatening to "blow up" needless state agencies and kill "30-year-old pilot programs that don't work." During a televised debate he was asked what he would do specifically for black people. Jeb's response: "Probably nothing."

"That one statement made by Mr. Bush has truly angered the African-American community," said the Democratic state senator from Fort Lauderdale, Matthew Meadows, "and we're going to show him on Election Day."

Compounding his insensitivity, Jeb later told welfare mothers: "Get your life together and find a husband."

In Texas, George was running against one of the most popular figures in the state—incumbent Governor Ann Richards—so he worked hard not to offend. In a predominantly Republican state, the demographics were in his favor, but he put more stock in his likability. "Looking back on our race [in 1978], I saw that the more people George met, the better he did," said Kent Hance, W.'s Democratic opponent in that early congressional campaign. "People liked him . . . And I've always said that if people like you, there's more potential they'll vote for you. He was so good getting people to like him that I started to worry, until he ran that first ad of himself jogging . . . Then I knew I had him. At that time in West Texas if you were jogging, folks figured you were a bank robber and someone was chasing you or else you were late to work."

When Jeb had announced his plan to challenge Florida's incumbent Governor Lawton Chiles, George decided he had to take on Ann Richards, or, as he called her, "Mrs. Big Hair." His wife and his mother were adamantly opposed. Laura saw the race as nothing more than sibling competition for his father's approval and an effort to stomp someone who had belittled the family name on national television. Laura wanted no part of it. "She's throwing water on it," George complained to friends. His mother felt the same way. Barbara bluntly told her son he did not stand a chance against Ann Richards. "She's too popular," she said. "You'll lose."

His father was not as outspoken, but just as dubious. "George W. was doing very well in business with the Texas Rangers baseball team," President Bush told *Time*'s Hugh Sidey. "It surprised me a little when he decided to run for Governor. I've always felt that people in public life should have done something in the private sector before. But, yes, it was kind of interesting when he told us his plans."

George, who had learned from Lee Atwater to read and rely on polls, hired Karl Rove to test Ann Richards's strength in the state. His early polling showed her with a 58 percent approval rating. She was well liked as a colorful Texas character, but not highly regarded as an effective governor. "They like her hair," said Rove, "but they're not strongly anchored to her." Rove's polls showed Richards's record on crime, education, and welfare reform was spotty. George, on the other hand, had no record to defend, except the success of the Texas Rangers.

"Let's go for it," Rove urged. Described by some as "Bush's brain," although he attended nearly half a dozen colleges but never got a degree, Rove defined himself as "a diehard Nixonite." He had worked with Atwater at the Republican National Committee when the elder Bush was GOP chairman and had met young George in 1973, when he came to Washington to spend Thanksgiving with his parents. Rove had picked him up at the train station, and recalled the meeting for the writer Nicholas Lemann thirty years later, sounding like a breathless schoolgirl describing her first big crush.

"I can literally remember what he was wearing," said Rove. "An Air National Guard flight jacket, cowboy boots, blue-jeans, complete with the—in Texas you see it a lot—one of the back pockets will have a circle worn in the pocket from where you carry your tin of snuff, your tin of tobacco. He was exuding more charisma than any one individual should be allowed to have."

A short, squatty self-made man, Rove was enthralled by the natural assurance of the self-entitled Bushes. He was especially drawn to the magnetism of the first son, whom he saw as the ideal political candidate. "He's the kind of guy political hacks like me wait a lifetime to be associated with," he said. The two stayed in touch over the years, and Rove emerged as Texas's leading Republican political consultant. Over time he became to George W. Bush what Uncle Herbie had been to George H.W. Bush— adoring, worshipful, and absolutely indispensable.

Young George had learned early that there is no education in the second kick of a mule. When he ran for Congress in 1978, he used up a lot of money and energy running in the primary and then the runoff, which depleted his resources for the general election. By the time he lost to Kent Hance, he felt as if he had run three campaigns. He did not want to go through the same ordeal in 1994, so he made sure he had no primary opposition, unlike his brother Jeb, who was facing a five-way primary in Florida. George personally visited each of the three men in Texas who had evinced an interest in running against Ann Richards. He laid out his plans for a full-throated campaign, which would cost $15 million. He made each man understand that the son of the former President of the United States was a formidable opponent with limitless funds and immediate name recognition in a Republican state that revered Bushes. By the end of each meeting the prospective rival had taken himself out of contention. "The wholesale capitulation to George W. Bush had happened with almost perfect precision," wrote his biographer Bill Minutaglio. "It was, old Lone Star pols said admiringly, the only one-day gubernatorial primary in Texas's history."

In 1978, George's mother bankrolled his campaign with her Christmas card list, a roster of 4,738 names of "close family friends" collected during her husband's Yale years, oil years, campaign years, and UN, China, and congressional years. Bar sent a beguiling letter to every name on her list, including Mrs. Douglas MacArthur, former U.S. Ambassador to England Anne Armstrong, and the once and future Secretary of Defense Donald Rumsfeld. On July 8, 1978, Barbara wrote:

I have never done this before, and I feel a little funny about it now, but much more than that, I feel so proud of our George. He is running for the U.S. Congress from the 19th District in West Texas . . . George is bright and is eager to represent this district as they should be represented. He is getting geared up for a big race in the fall . . .

You guessed it—George will need lots of money to run a first class campaign. I hope you will join us in contributing to his campaign. Please forgive a very proud mother for hitting you up for a little (or a lot) of your hard-earned cash for her son.

Barbara's begging bowl collected over $400,000 for her son's campaign, four times what his Democratic opponent raised.

"How could we say no?" said one of the 4,738 "family friends," who felt obliged to send a check. Most responded like Herbert Brownell, former Attorney General in the Eisenhower Administration, who wrote like an investor in a family dynasty: "Doris and I were very pleased to receive your letter and hear about your young George's candidacy. Of course we would like to help in a small way and I am enclosing our check with best wishes for success. If he can do half as good as his grandfather and father, that will suit us fine."

"Our George" lost the race in 1978, principally because his opponent, Kent Hance, denounced him for raising all his money from contributors outside the district. By the time George ran for governor in 1994, his mother concentrated her appeals on the Texas part of her Christmas card list; as a result, only 13 percent of W.'s reported contributions came from out of state.

During the 1978 campaign Mel Turner, a West Texas radio personality and a Republican, said he was leaning toward voting for George but was turned off by his temper. At a candidates' forum in Odessa, Turner had asked him a question about the Trilateral Commission and whether his father was working for one-world government.

"He jumped like he'd been pricked," said Turner. After the forum, Turner stood at the door to say good-bye to the candidates.

"Junior Bush comes up, refused to shake my hand, looked me square in the eye and said, 'You [epithet],'" said Turner. "Then Kent Hance came up and said, 'Mel, I'll see you at the Tech game.'"

Recalling the incident, Turner said of George: "Here's a Republican candidate stepping on the wrong toes. He was an arrogant rich kid, a spoiled brat."

The man who beat George in 1978 became one of his biggest supporters in 1994. "Timing is everything in politics, and Bush's timing in his first campaign was not right," said Kent Hance, who later switched parties and donated ten thousand dollars to George's first campaign for governor. "In our race for the House of Representatives, he was young, just thirty-two years old, and newly married . . . the campaign through West Texas was their honeymoon. There were no issues we really differed on. I was a state senator and a conservative Democrat. He was for a tax cut and so was I. He wanted to cut back on government spending and so did I. Fact, what it came right down to in the end was Yale versus Texas Tech . . . And in the Panhandle, if it's Texas Tech versus Yale, Tech will win every time. Not even a close game . . . I had to hit him with being an outsider and me being a good ole boy."

Nobody "talked Texas" better than Kent Hance, who entertained rural farmers with country jokes, usually at George's expense. For example: "I was on a ranch in Dimmitt during my high-school days, and a guy drove up and asked for directions to the next ranch. I said, 'Go north five miles, turn and go east five miles, then turn again after you pass a cattle guard.' As he turned around, I noticed he had Connecticut license plates. He stopped and said, 'Just one more question. What color uniform will that cattle guard be wearing?' "

The West Texas farmers voted for the down-home guy, who won 53 percent to 47 percent and taught George something he would never forget. "Kent Hance gave me a lesson on country-boy politics," Bush said. "He was a master at it, funny and belittling. I vowed never to get out-countried again." Fifteen years later George was seen on national television sitting behind the Rangers' dugout picking his nose. He was unembarrassed. "Anything that makes me look like the common man is great," he said. "Just great."

During the 1978 campaign he had vehemently opposed abortion rights, gay rights ("I have done nothing to promote homosexuality in our society"), and affirmative action. He called the appointment of Andrew Young, the African American preacher from Atlanta, Georgia, as UN Ambassador "a mistake." Fitting in with the Bush family's view of women, W. said the Equal Rights Amendment was "unnecessary." He also said that Social Security would be bankrupt in ten years unless people were allowed to invest the money themselves. Not exactly the views of a "compassionate conservative," as he later labeled himself. He took the same positions during his 1994 campaign for governor, adding to the political mix two more items key to his agenda: guns and God.

Ever since George had come to Jesus in April 1984, his religion had ruled his life. He became born-again after the bottom dropped out of the oil boom in Midland, Texas. When the National Bank of Midland, the largest independent bank in the nation, failed, fortunes crashed and overnight millionaires tumbled into life-wrecking debt. "What happened in this town was a catastrophe," said Bill Meyers, one of George's friends from Community Bible Study. "Everyone was affected." In a desperate effort to rescue lives and restore morale, some of the church elders invited the evangelist Arthur Blessitt to stage a revival. Among born-agains, Blessitt was known as the man who had wheeled a ninety-six-pound cross of Jesus into sixty countries on six continents, making a place for himself in *The Guinness Book of Records*.

Posters around Midland advertised the meeting as "A Mission of Love and Joy to the Permian Basin." Loudspeakers on flatbed trucks exhorted the populace to gather at the Chaparral Center in the evening "to experience the love of God, the grace of the Lord Jesus Christ, and the fellowship of the Holy Spirit." Residents lined the streets during the day and watched Blessitt roll his twelve-foot-high cross through the boomtown gone bust. Many bowed their heads as he passed. One little boy shouted, "It's the Lord Jesus on wheels!"

"I was speaking during the day all around the city and carrying the cross in the streets," said Blessitt. "It was the focus point of the city of Midland for that week with the meeting being broadcast on the local radio."

George felt uncomfortable about attending the revival, but he listened to the broadcast. On the second day he asked his friend Don Pogue to arrange a meeting with Blessitt. "I want to talk to him about Jesus," George said.

The three men met the next day at the coffee shop in the Best Western hotel. As Blessitt recalled the meeting, George began with a few pleasantries, and then plunged in.

"I want to talk to you about how to know Jesus Christ and how to follow Him."

"I was quite shocked at his direct and sincere approach," said Blessitt. "I slowly leaned forward and lifted the Bible that was in my hand and asked him about his relationship with the Lord . . . 'If you died this moment do you have the assurance you would go to heaven?' "

"No."

"Then let me explain to you how you can have that assurance and know for sure that you are saved."

"I'd like that."

The evangelist read from the Book of Romans. He quoted Mark and John and Luke to the Vice President's son, who held hands with the two men, repented his sins, and proclaimed Jesus Christ as his savior.

"It was an awesome and glorious moment," recalled Blessitt. He later wrote in his diary on April 3, 1984: "A good and powerful day—Led Vice President Bush's son to Jesus—George Bush Jr!! This is great. Glory to God. But I won't speak about it."

That coffee-shop conversion eventually led George to give up tobacco, alcohol, and drugs at the age of forty, illustrating the wisdom of William James, who said "the only radical remedy I know for dipsomania is religiomania."

In his memoir, *A Charge to Keep*, George W. credited his family's good friend the Reverend Billy Graham with planting "a mustard seed in my soul." He did not mention coming to Jesus with the flamboyant Blessitt and his cross on wheels, figuring, perhaps, that Graham was more palatable to churchgoing voters.

George spoke openly about his religious beliefs during his 1994 campaign for governor. He told a reporter from *The Houston Post* that the path to heaven came only from acceptance of Jesus as one's personal savior. He cited the New Testament, which to him represented reality, not metaphor. His comment raised concern among Houston's Jews when *The Jewish Herald-Voice* of November 2, 1994, ran the headline: "Can a Texas Jew Go to Heaven? George W. Bush Says 'No.' "

George had previously debated the issue of who goes to heaven with his mother. He pointed to a passage in his daily Bible readings that said "only Christians had a place in heaven." Barbara disagreed.

"Surely, God will accept others," she said.

"Mom, here's what the New Testament says," insisted George, who read the passage aloud.

Barbara picked up the phone and called Billy Graham.

Graham sided with George. "From a personal perspective, I agree with what George is saying," he said. "The New Testament has been my guide. But I want to caution you both. Don't play God. Who are you two to be God?"

Over the course of their lives Graham and George W. had struggled with negative feelings toward Jews. As a student at Andover, George had played a prank on a Jewish student. Billy Graham had demonstrated raw anti-Semitism in a taped conversation with Richard Nixon on February 1, 1972, in which he characterized "Jewish control" of the American media as a "stranglehold."

"This stranglehold has got to be broken or this country's going down the drain," he told the President. Later in the ninety-minute conversation Graham said, "A lot of the Jews are great friends of mine. They swarm around me and are friendly to me because they know that I'm friendly with Israel. But they don't know how I really feel about what they are do-ing to this country."

When the tapes were released in 2002, the Southern Baptist evangel-ist issued a public apology for his remarks. George, too, was forced to backtrack on his views. He blamed the reporter who quoted him. "It was, of course, picked up and politicized," he told *The New York Times*. "You know, 'Bush to Jews: Go to Hell!' It was very ugly. It hurt my feelings."

Shortly after George won the election in 1994, he met with a group of Jewish leaders in Houston. "I know, really, why you all are here," he said. "You're here to know whether this governor condemns you to hell. I can tell . . . It hurt me. It hurt to think that you think I've condemned you to hell, because I would never do that. That's not my role in life." Yet a few years later, when he announced that he would be making a National Jewish Coalition–sponsored trip to Israel, he was asked what he was going to say to Israeli Jews. Obviously joking, Bush said the first thing he would tell them is that they were "all going to hell." Anti-Defamation League na-tional president Abraham Foxman asked George in a letter to clarify his remarks, and George responded in December 1998: "I am troubled that some people were hurt by the remarks. I never intended to make judg-ments about the faith of others."

In Jerusalem, George had his picture taken wearing a yarmulke and praying at the Wailing Wall, just like his father had done before running for President.

Throughout the 1994 campaign Ann Richards tried to trigger George's volcanic temper. She chided him as "a jerk," "shrub," "little Bush," "Boy George," and "Baby Bush." When he did not respond in kind, she began to look mean-mouthed and slightly desperate. George's cousin Elsie Walker said she cowered behind the bathroom door as she watched their television debate, fully expecting George to blow sky-high each time Richards needled him. When he did not bite her head off and instead smiled amiably, Walker fired off a telegram to Barbara Bush: "What's he on, animal tranquilizers?"

No one in the family denied that George had decided to challenge Ann Richards partly because she had poked fun at his father during the 1988 Democratic National Convention. "Years ago George's emotions related to Ann Richards's statements about my father would have been transparent," said Marvin Bush. "It may have gotten to him. He may have publicly said something that he would regret. By the time the election rolled around in 1994, he was a different guy. He was disciplined. I think he surprised a lot of people who didn't know him."

Demonstrating robotic self-control, George stayed on message, which exasperated the governor, who could not rattle him. Later she said, on *Larry King Live*, "You know, if you said to George, 'What time is it?' he would say, 'We must teach our children to read.' " Karl Rove had stressed four issues that mattered most to Texans—crime, education, welfare reform, and guns, guns, guns. Richards had defied the NRA by vetoing the concealed-weapons legislation, which George promised to sign, saying he supported guns for everyone. He also would sign a bill allowing Texans to carry guns in churches, synagogues, and other houses of worship. As his reward, he received the NRA's endorsement and all their campaign money.

Remembering the effectiveness of his father's Willie Horton ads, George aired a commercial of a man abducting a woman and holding a gun to her head while an announcer intoned that "in the last three years seventy-seven hundred criminals have been released early from prison."

On the opening day of dove season, George shot a songbird known as a killdeer, an endangered species. Ann Richards ripped into him. "Guns don't kill killdeer," she said. "People kill killdeer." George promptly confessed, paid a $130 fine, and opened a press conference that afternoon by saying, "Thank goodness it wasn't deer season. I might have shot a cow." He took so much ribbing for his mistake that he began introducing himself as "killdeer slayer."

With this humorous exception, George kept to Rove's script and never deviated. Polling highest among white males, he played to their visceral dislike of President Clinton, who had raised taxes and admitted gays into the military. Bush painted Ann Richards as an old-fashioned liberal tied to the Democratic administration in Washington. "While I'm going to win on issues that matter to Texans, the Clinton connection and Ann Richards' affection for Clinton is not going to help her at all," George told reporters. Being able to hog-tie both of his father's foes gave the avenging son a powerful one-two punch. Because Ann Richards kept swiping at him as "Daddy's little boy," George banished his father from the campaign and never mentioned him by name. "The minute the other George Bush wades into the process, my message gets totally obscured," he said. When he finally allowed "the old man" to appear with him in public a few days before the election, he introduced the elder Bush by saying, "Mr. President—Dad—we're glad you're here. After two years our country understands how much we miss you." The white male Republican crowd characterized by the Texas writer Molly Ivins as "Clinton-hating, Christian-right, gay-bashing gun toters" gave both Bushes a foot-stomping ovation.

Early on George had become slightly testy when a *Houston Chronicle* reporter asked him whether he had ever used illegal drugs.

"Maybe I did, maybe I didn't," he said. "What's the difference?"

When the story broke, he held a news conference in Lubbock.

"What I did as a kid? I don't think it's relevant. I just don't . . . don't think it matters. I think what matters is my view on prisons, welfare reform and education . . . Did I behave irresponsibly as a kid at times? Sure did. You bet." He had flown to Lubbock on his campaign plane, which he had named *Accountability One*.

When the issue of infidelity surfaced in Florida, Jeb Bush told reporters that the only woman he had ever slept with was his wife. When George heard his brother's declaration, he was shocked. "Jeb said that? Oh, boy. No comment. I mean Jeb is setting a tough standard for the rest of us in that generation."

Even as a married man, George had a whispered past, which almost surfaced during the campaign. A woman appeared in Austin, claiming to have been a call girl from Midland with an intimate knowledge of him during his days in the oil patch. "Supposedly she was 'the other woman' in his life, or one of them," said Peck Young, an Austin political consultant. "She set herself up in a hotel here and was prepared to sell her story to the highest bidder . . . Word got around town, and she claimed she got a visit from some men who made her realize it was better to turn tricks in Midland than to stop breathing. She said she had been approached by what she described as 'intelligence types.' She left town abruptly."

Some people felt that George's past did not seep out and embarrass him and his family because he was protected by a coterie of former CIA men with an allegiance to his father.

"I know for a fact that during the early nineties in Houston there was an outfit we called Rent-A-Spook," said Young. "They were retired Agency guys from NSA [National Security Agency] and CIA, and they were selling their expertise to companies that wanted to avoid corporate espionage. There were some unkind souls in Houston who claimed they would also commit corporate espionage if there were enough money involved . . . I ran into them once working on a political campaign, and they were very real and very professional and very scary . . . George junior has seemed to be protected by some invisible mechanism . . . and the speculation has been for years that that mechanism was Daddy's old retainers from the agency . . . They have made young George bulletproof."

The elder Bush's ties to the Central Intelligence Agency were so strong that when the former President built his presidential library at Texas A&M, the university also established the George Bush School of Government and Public Service next to the library, and installed a CIA career officer to teach and recruit for the CIA on campus. The school was dedicated on September 10, 1997, and the ceremony marked the debut of "The George Bush Presidential March," played by the Texas A&M University band.

"Our cadet code of honor at Texas A&M is 'Aggies do not lie, cheat, or steal, nor tolerate those who do,' " said Zach Leonard (class of 2002), "and that's why the CIA wants to recruit from our corps of cadets. We have a sense of national service and a sense of duty to the country. Jim Olson, who is with the CIA, teaches 'Cold War Intelligence' at the George Bush School and does the CIA recruiting on campus. Allowing the CIA to recruit at Texas A&M is one of the reasons George Bush put his library here . . . He turned down Yale and Rice and the University of Texas to build here at College Station . . . He also made his former CIA director [1991–93] Robert M. Gates president of Texas A&M."

Whether his father's agency contacts insulated George from scrutiny during the 1994 campaign, it looked that way to many in the Richards camp. George appeared particularly invincible to the governor when she tried to make an issue of his insider trades of Harken stock. He had served on the board of Harken from 1986 until 1993, when he resigned to run for office. During those seven years he made four stock transactions for a total of $1 million, none of which was reported to the Securities and Exchange Commission within the legally specified time—the tenth of each month after the sale.

In December 1986, George borrowed $96,000 from Harken to buy 80,000 shares of Harken stock. He used the 212,000 shares of stock he already owned as collateral. He reported the sale to the SEC in April 1987, four months late. He said the SEC lost the original filing.

In June 1989, George borrowed $84,375 from Harken to buy 25,000 shares of Harken stock. He reported the sale to the SEC on October 23, 1989, fifteen weeks late. He blamed the Harken lawyers.

In 1989, Harken instituted a policy that relieved its directors of any personal obligation to repay their loans. This effectively freed up the 212,000 shares that George had used for collateral in 1986 so that he could sell them.

In June 1990, he sold 212,140 shares of Harken stock for $835,000. He reported the sale on March 4, 1991, thirty-four weeks late. One week before he sold the stock, Harken lawyers circulated a memo—one that George definitely saw—stating that Bush and other members of the troubled oil company's board faced possible insider-trading risks if they unloaded their shares.

The reason for the memo was that questions were raised in 1989 as to whether Harken posted an improper profit on the sale of a subsidiary in order to obscure the company's overall losses. The SEC forced them to restate their earnings. In August 1990, Harken announced a $23.2 million loss that was a result of trading in commodity futures and liabilities incurred through its subsidiary Aloha Petroleum. Eight days before this announcement George sold his stock. If he had known about the company's impending loss and sold his shares beforehand because of it, he would have been guilty of profiting illegally from insider information. Businessmen go to prison for such offenses. Because he sat on the directors' audit committee and the restructuring committee, he was assumed to know what was happening to the company's finances and thus able to decide when best to sell his shares.

When confronted, he professed ignorance about the company's loss—such ignorance would not have made him a very effective board member—and blamed the Harken accountants. His only comment on the matter: "All I can tell you is that in the corporate world, sometimes things aren't exactly black and white when it comes to accounting procedures. [It's up to the SEC] to determine whether or not the decision by the auditors was the appropriate decision. And they did look, and they decided that the earnings ought to be restated, and the company did so immediately."

After an article in *The Wall Street Journal*, the SEC investigated George's stock sale but never questioned him personally. "In its investigation the staff reviewed thousands of pages of documents produced by Harken and Bush," said the SEC memorandum. One critical document *not* available to the SEC investigators: the memo from Harken lawyers warning the board that they faced possible insider-trading risks if they sold their shares. Not until the day *after* the SEC closed its investigation of George did his lawyer, Robert Jordan, turn over that memorandum of June 15, 1990, titled "Liability for Insider Trading and Short-Term Swing Profits." By then the SEC had already reached its conclusion. When George became President, he appointed Robert Jordan to be Ambassador to Saudi Arabia.

On August 21, 1991, while President Bush was in Kennebunkport preparing for the arrival of British Prime Minister John Major, the SEC released its report clearing the first son: "In light of the facts uncovered, it would be difficult to establish that, even assuming Bush possessed material nonpublic information, he acted with scienter [deliberately or knowingly] or intent to defraud."

The SEC's finding did not pass the smell test with Governor Richards. During the 1994 campaign she pointed out that the SEC chairman, Richard Breeden, had worked for George Bush when he was Vice President and later when Bush was President before Bush appointed him to the SEC. Breeden had been the principal architect of the President's plan to restructure the savings-and-loan industry, for which Neil Bush had become the poster child. The general counsel of the SEC, James Doty, a big Bush supporter, had helped George W. put together his deal with the Texas Rangers, but Doty said he recused himself from George's SEC investigation. Doty, who later joined James A. Baker's law firm, Baker Botts, explained why the SEC took no action against George for his blatant disregard of reporting regulations: "Half of corporate America was filing those forms late at that time."

Breeden, who lived in Greenwich, Connecticut, and named his first son Prescott, said, "I knew that to protect the integrity of the investigation, I had to leave the investigation up to the career staff. I told them to do it the regular way—which means no holds barred—and I will stand up for you. If anything had been found, it would have been prosecuted. In the end, we didn't bring a case because there was no case there."

The Dallas Morning News reported that the SEC had dropped its case, but said the action "must in no way be construed that he [George W. Bush] has been exonerated."

Toward the end of the campaign Governor Richards ran ads suggesting George was guilty of insider trading when he sold his Harken stock— a criminal act. The Bush campaign responded by rolling out its biggest gun to blast the governor: George's mother.

"It makes me pretty darn mad," said Barbara Bush, "to see these ads that just plain aren't true. [George has] been a good, successful, decent, honest businessman. Why doesn't Ann Richards talk about the issues? That's what George is doing. She should be so lucky as to have a son like George."

The voters agreed with the former First Lady. Despite Richards's popularity—she maintained a 60 percent rating through Election Day— George won by more than 300,000 votes. Exit polls showed his strongest support to be among white Republican males. It was a stunning victory. But the Florida election was even more stunning. Jeb had been expected to win fairly easily, but he lost by 64,000 votes. The incumbent Governor Lawton Chiles defeated W.'s younger brother by fewer than two percentage points in the closest gubernatorial election in the state's history. At home in Houston the elder Bushes were astounded. They had expected the results to be reversed—Jeb to win, George to lose. Having traveled throughout Florida helping Jeb raise over $3 million for his campaign, they were heartsick about his loss.

As George prepared to make his victory speech that night, his father phoned from Houston. After a few minutes, George hung up, dispirited. "It sounds like Dad's only heard that Jeb lost," he told his aunt Nancy. "Not that I've won." George felt even worse when he saw his father interviewed on television. "The joy is in Texas," said the former President. "My heart is in Florida."

The mean streak that once fueled George as a bullyboy playing pig ball at Andover now surfaced to smack his brother. "Jeb would have been a great governor," George told the press. "But such is life in the political world. You cannot go into politics fearing failure." Earlier he had taken a whack at his father. "Bill Clinton drove the agenda against my father," he told *The New York Times*. "My father let Bill Clinton decide what issues the two of them were going to talk about. That was a major mistake, and I wasn't going to let it happen to me this year."

The 1994 election put even greater distance between the two brothers: George sailed on the crest of his success, while Jeb nearly drowned in the undertow of his failure. The campaign almost cost him his family. His marriage was ruptured; his daughter, Noelle, seventeen, was on drugs, and his two sons, Jebby, eleven, and George P., eighteen, were unruly and out of control. His wife blamed him for the wreckage of their lives. Relatives told the writers Peter and Rochelle Schweizer that Columba Bush felt she and the children had paid too high a price for Jeb's political ambition. The Schweizers quote her as saying, "You have ruined my life."

Jeb would spend the next two years like Humpty Dumpty, trying to put himself back together again. Having grown up wanting to be President, he would not give up his political dreams, but he tried to make amends to his family as well as to the minority voters of Florida. He committed to Catholicism so he could share the religion of his wife and children. He attended classes at Informed Families, a drug-prevention agency in Miami. He started a public policy foundation to collect money to keep himself in the public eye. And he joined forces with a leader in the African American community of Miami to start a charter school.

Jeb and his wife attended George's inauguration in January 1995, and the new governor did not let his brother's presence go unremarked. From the podium he nodded toward Jeb. "He's looking happy and proud, but also something else, maybe a little sad, too," George said. "It's a tough moment, tough for me to look at. I love my brother, you see."

That morning Barbara gave George a letter from his father with a set of cuff links that Prescott had given to him when he won his Navy wings in 1943. The former President said the gift was "my most prized possession." George hastily read his father's letter. "At first I didn't think about the continuity, the grandfather part," he recalled. "The main thing I thought was that it was from my dad. He was saying that he was proud of me. But later I reread the letter and thought about it. It ended with, 'Now it's your turn.' It was a powerful moment."

George and Barbara were not just passing out presents. They had rushed into their retirement with both hands out. Within weeks of leaving the White House, they were cashing in on their previous high office by charging stupendous speaking fees. Barbara offered herself for $40,000–$60,000 a speech, and her husband charged even more. For a speech in the States, he charged $80,000 plus first-class expenses, including limousines and hotel suites. For a speech abroad, he charged $100,000. The Bushes had left the White House in 1993 with a net worth of $4 million. Within ten years they were worth in excess of $20 million.

Like all former Presidents, George H.W. Bush received a yearly federal pension ($157,000), plus an additional pension (estimated to be about $100,000) for his government service as congressman (four years), UN Ambassador (two years), liaison to China (one year), CIA director (one year), and Vice President (eight years). He also received a budget for office, staff, travel, and rent ($623,000) and full Secret Service protection for himself and his wife. In addition, the Republican National Committee, unlike the Democratic National Committee, offers its former presidents $150,000 a year for administrative expenses. George Bush did not need his party's offer, so he turned it down, saying that he would not trade on his high office by sitting on corporate boards or lobbying the U.S. government. "I will now try to conduct myself with dignity," he said, "and in a way not to dishonor the office I was so proud to hold." Still, he managed to derive stupendous profit from his presidency, proving that privilege pays.

"You can't believe all the money the Bushes have," said Sharon Bush, Neil's former wife. "Bar doesn't like anyone to think they're rich because then people might not contribute to her sons' political campaigns, but she and Gampy [George Senior] are really, really rich . . . They are paid thousands just to appear at corporate events—they don't even have to speak, but when they do, they get huge fees . . . They have a full-time Secret Service protection—twelve agents all the time . . . they fly all over the world on private planes. They cruise for free on John Latsis's yacht every summer, which has twelve marble bathrooms on board . . . Mr. Latsis only gives his yacht to two people in the world—Prince Charles and George Bush . . . Every time they go to Kuwait or Saudi Arabia or Singapore or Thailand, you can't believe all the money they are paid and the presents they are given."

The Bushes' former daughter-in-law described splendid gifts of diamond-encrusted jewelry, Cartier watches, ruby-inlaid bracelets, emerald necklaces, platinum rings, precious porcelain, silk carpets, leather goods, and 24-karat gold sculptures that she said were worth "hundreds and thousands of dollars, probably millions." She asserted that the gifts collected by President Bush during his three-day trip to Kuwait in April 1993 took his Houston staff four months to catalog.

Sharon Bush saw firsthand how easy it was for her father-in-law to accumulate wealth. In her view, he simply turned on money spigots all over the world, especially in Asia and the Middle East. She witnessed oil-rich potentates lining up to befriend the Bushes at any cost. She watched lucrative contracts and extravagant consulting fees flow into the family coffers as the former President traveled the world, steering foreign business to his sons Neil and Marvin. Seeing the wealth of goods and services that rained down on the family, Sharon Bush could be forgiven for describing their lifestyle as one of "never-ending luxury."

Three months after he left office, George H.W. Bush made his triumphant entry into Kuwait, where he was hailed as "Abu Abdullah," which is Arabic for "Worshipper of God." Kuwait Airways had provided a special plane for the presidential party, which included the elder Bushes; their sons Neil and Marvin and their wives; Laura Bush; former Secretary of State James A. Baker III; former White House Chief of Staff John Sununu; former Treasury Secretary Nicholas Brady; Bush's good friend Lud Ashley; and retired Army Lieutenant General Thomas Kelly, director of operations for the Joint Chiefs of Staff during the 1992 Persian Gulf War.

Having already contributed over $1 million to the George Bush Presidential Library, the Kuwaitis planned a three-day Festival of Gratitude to fete their "liberator," which Kuwaiti newspapers dubbed "Operation Love

Storm." Bush was bathed in adulation from the moment he arrived. He addressed the Kuwaiti parliament and received the nation's highest medal from the Emir, Sheikh Jaber al-Ahmed al-Sabah. Chanting women lined the streets as robed swordsmen danced to the rhythm of beating drums and little children waved banners that read: "Oh dear Bush you are the delight of our smiling eyes."

After the three-day festival, George and Barbara flew home, leaving their entourage to drum up business in the little kingdom. John Sununu, representing Westinghouse, and General Kelly and James Baker, representing Enron, negotiated for contracts to rebuild bomb-damaged Kuwaiti power plants. The rights to rebuild three plants and operate them over twenty years were worth $4 billion. Marvin Bush had been retained by his father's former military aide Admiral Daniel J. Murphy to negotiate bidding for American defense firms. Neil Bush, representing two Houston firms in which he was a partner, tried to get contracts for oil-related ventures from Kuwait's Ministry of Electricity and Water.

Weeks later the Kuwaiti government uncovered an Iraqi plan to assassinate President Bush during his visit. They arrested sixteen people, including eleven Iraqi nationals, and seized 550 pounds of explosives. An attempt on the life of a former President is considered an act of aggression against the United States itself, which forced the Clinton administration to react. After two months of investigation, the United States initiated air strikes against Baghdad and launched twenty-three Tomahawk cruise missiles against Iraq's intelligence agency. In a televised address to the nation on June 26, 1993, President Clinton called Iraq's "attempt at revenge by a tyrant against the leader of the world coalition that defeated him in war . . . particularly loathsome and cowardly."

The former National Security Council chief of counterterrorism Richard Clarke recalled on *60 Minutes*: "We responded by blowing up Iraqi intelligence headquarters and by sending a very clear message through diplomatic channels to the Iraqis, saying if you do any terrorism against the United States again, it won't just be Iraqi intelligence headquarters, it'll be your whole government. It was a very chilling message. And apparently it worked because there's absolutely no evidence of Iraqi terrorism since that day until we invaded [March 19, 2003] them. Now there's Iraqi terrorism against the United States."

Nevertheless, ten years later Saddam Hussein's assassination attempt against his father would provoke George W. Bush to wage an all-out war against Iraq—claiming it was still a threat to the United States and linked to Al Qaeda terrorists—that would bitterly divide the United States and alienate European allies.

During the early months of his retirement the relationship between President Bush and the man who defeated him remained cordial enough so that George returned to the White House on occasion. He joined former presidents Ford and Carter in September 1993 in support of NAFTA. He was so impressed by President Clinton's articulate command of the issue that he said, "Now I know why he's inside looking out and I'm outside looking in." George told *The Washington Times* that Barbara refused to accompany him to the White House because she was uncomfortable socializing with the Clintons. She remained bitter and intractable about losing the election and wanted nothing to do with her husband's successor. Later, as President Clinton became mired in the scandal of his sexual involvement with Monica Lewinsky, a White House intern, George became as vociferous as his wife in his criticism of Clinton.

"I did my job with honor," Bush told an audience at Eckerd College. "I take pride that Barbara and I treated the White House with respect and dignity and we didn't have those scandals in our administration."

While her husband focused disdain on the President, Barbara took aim at the First Lady. When a reporter asked what she thought about Hillary Clinton's plans to run for the U.S. Senate from New York, Barbara looked as if she might regurgitate. "Let her do what she wants," she snapped. "And when she loses, I think she'll feel very badly." Hillary Rodham Clinton was elected to the Senate in November 2000.

"Mrs. Bush would not accept any of Hillary's invitations," recalled a White House social aide. "She wouldn't even come for the White House Endowment Fund dinner, and half the money raised that evening [to establish a fund to replenish the furnishings] was in her name. She came for her portrait dedication [July 1995] and for the two hundredth anniversary of the White House with other first ladies, but that was about it."

The Bushes went into retirement like Salvation Army bell ringers, eager to rake in as much money as fast as they possibly could. George had a library to build, and Barbara wanted to retain the Barbara Bush Foundation staff and office. "Everyone knew that I had never earned any money as I had never seriously worked in the 48 years we had been married," she said. "So besides losing the election, now at 68 years old I was going to have to make some money."

She accepted $2.2 million ("They offered me a sum I couldn't say no to," she told TV's Larry King) to write her autobiography, but the President chose not to write a postpresidential memoir, possibly because of the conflicting stories he had told over the years. He also had an obsession with secrets—personal and political. "I'm not writing a memoir," he stated. "I'd rather let history decide." Instead, he published a book of his letters (*All the Best*) and a book on his foreign policy (*A World Transformed*), which he wrote with retired General Brent Scowcroft.

"I worked as the editorial assistant on *A World Transformed* in 1996," said Leyla Aker, "and I remember the former President insisting he was writing it for his sons. Plural . . . He absolutely considered it his legacy."

The sad irony is that the son who followed him as President seemed not to have read his father's book, which laid out the steps for building the global consensus necessary to pursue U.S. foreign policy in a transformed world. By then, the son had decided that his father, who could not get himself reelected as President, was not a model for success.

In writing her book *Barbara Bush: A Memoir*, George H.W.'s wife achieved the distinction of becoming the only First Lady ever to be sued for libel. Barbara had written that Philip Agee, a former CIA agent, had identified Richard Welch as an agency operative in "a traitorous tell-all book" that caused Welch, the CIA station chief in Athens, to be assassinated in December 1975. Agee denied her allegation and filed a $4 million libel lawsuit against her and her publisher, Lisa Drew Books of Charles Scribner's Sons. Agee proved that he had not identified Welch in his book *Inside the Company: CIA Diary*, and he demanded an apology from Mrs. Bush, plus an immediate retraction in the paperback edition of her book. Barbara refused to apologize for her mistake, but she did make the retraction.

"I did not have to pay the $4 million," she said, "but it was a costly nuisance suit. I will hope not to have to go through that again!"

Two years after the lawsuit, her husband raised the issue in his remarks at the dedication ceremony of CIA headquarters in Langley, Virginia, as the George Bush Center for Intelligence: "[W]e need more protection for the methods we use to gather intelligence and more protection for our sources, particularly our human sources, people that are risking their lives for their country . . . Even though I'm a tranquil guy now at this stage of my life," he said in April 1999, "I have nothing but contempt and anger for those who betray the trust by exposing the name of our sources. They are, in my view, the most insidious of traitors."

Those words would haunt his son four years later, when the conservative columnist Robert Novak, citing two unnamed sources in the George W. Bush administration, identified Valerie Plame, the wife of former U.S. Ambassador to Iraq Joseph Wilson, as a CIA agent. The Ambassador had been asked by the CIA, on orders from Vice President Dick Cheney, to investigate whether Iraq had tried to purchase nuclear materials—a charge that the Bush administration claimed was true and that it gave as a partial reason to justify invading the country and removing Saddam from power. The results of Wilson's investigation, however, challenged Bush's contention. Wilson found the rumors false, and he made his findings public. The Novak column looked like a spiteful attack by the Bush administration to punish the Ambassador for showing that the President had not told the truth in his State of the Union address. The leak to Novak became the subject of a grand jury investigation, which threatened felony charges for Novak's sources, punishable by as long as ten years in prison.

The former President struggled with his enforced retirement. He could not give up wearing his presidential cuff links, his Air Force One windbreaker, or his sweat togs with the Camp David logo. Averse to looking through what physicians call the "retrospectoscope" to examine the mistakes that had led to his defeat, George Bush simply blamed the media. He constantly gave vent to his hostility. "I don't like them and I don't miss them," he said. "As President I defended freedom of the press; now I rejoice in freedom from the press . . . I know I sound bitter but I don't give a damn."

He traveled the world collecting honors and awards, including a knighthood from the Queen in England. Corporations continued paying him $100,000 a speech. Global Crossing, the telecommunications company, paid him in stock that was worth $4.5 million when he sold. His audiences gave him standing ovations, and as he loosened up on the speaking circuit, he revealed a nastiness that he had once tried to conceal.

In a keynote address to a convention of home builders in Las Vegas, he talked about what it was like to be a former President. "One of my major disappointments is that demonstrations are meager now when people protest my appearances," he said. He recalled one of his presidential motorcades in San Francisco, which had drawn a crowd of women's rights activists. "I turned the corner and I saw the ugliest woman I've ever seen. She had a sign that said, 'Stay out of my womb.' And I thought, 'No problem, lady.'"

Each speech was an occasion to reward friends, punish enemies, and castigate the media. George had never recovered from the humiliation of *Newsweek*'s "wimp" cover, which some relatives thought might have prompted his aggressive machismo on the speaking circuit. They speculated it was the need to prove his manhood that led him at the age of seventy-two to take up skydiving. His top aide, Jim McGrath, disagreed: "The reasons behind this are strictly personal . . . It has to do with World War II."

McGrath's remark gave rise to speculation that Bush might have been, as *The Times* of London wrote, "trying to exorcise demons from his earlier jump, the circumstances of which flared up into controversy during his presidential campaign." His 1987 account of what happened during World War II differed from his earlier version, causing some to wonder if he had panicked when his plane was hit by the Japanese and bailed out before trying to save his crew.

Bush admitted that he was still haunted by jumping out of his plane over Chichi-Jima. "I never really dwelled on making another jump," he told Hugh Sidey. "But it was always a thought back in my mind: Do it again and do it right."

To prepare for his first peacetime jump, Bush gave up martinis for a month to get in shape, and he took six hours of flight training. On March 25, 1997, accompanied by two guides from the Army's elite Golden Knights parachute team, George jumped out of a military plane 12,500 feet above the Arizona desert. "I'm a new man," he exclaimed upon landing. Two years later, as part of his seventy-fifth birthday celebration, he decided to sell tickets and make a second jump for charity. More than one hundred members of the media converged in Houston to record that jump on June 9, 1999. Some reporters called it "historic" because no other former President had performed such a stunt. His parachute canopy carried the logo "The University of Texas M.D. Anderson Cancer Center." At the joint birthday party for him and Barbara that followed in the Astrodome with three thousand paying guests, the Bushes raised $10.2 million to establish the George and Barbara Bush Endowment for Innovative Cancer Research at the University of Texas at Houston.

"We do a lot for charity," said Barbara, rightfully proud of her work for good causes. She had joined the board of AmeriCares and the Mayo Clinic. In addition to being president of the Barbara Bush Texas Fund for Family Literacy, she became honorary chairman of the Barbara Bush Foundation for Family Literacy and the Leukemia and Lymphoma Society.

But even in this area, there has been criticism of Barbara's sincerity. "As the longtime honorary national chair of the society, Barbara Bush has made no effort whatsoever to play an active role—no fund-raising, no donations," said someone close to the board of trustees of the Leukemia and Lymphoma Society. "There have been numerous occasions when she might easily have mentioned her role, especially as she and her husband lost a daughter to leukemia, but she has never done so. Yet she had written about her daughter's death and spoken of it on national television at the GOP political convention. The mere mention of that role would have helped gain the society recognition, thus encouraging interest and donations. Not a word has she uttered. No public-service ads, no attendance at major society activities. And I've no knowledge of the family ever encouraging any of their wealthy friends to give money, either."

While the Bushes are not philanthropists, their tax returns—up through 1991, the last year their returns are available—document their commitment to charity. Each year they contributed to Andover, Yale, and Skull and Bones, plus all the schools their children attended. Their checks ranged from ten dollars to one thousand dollars:

YEAR	INCOME	CHARITABLE DEDUCTIONS
1973	$221,577	$9,267
1974	$110,749	$4,000
1975	$72,337	$2,545

1976	$76,868	$7,520
1977	$77,960	$12,901
1978	$67,549	$12,717
1979	$108,043	$1,790
1980	$36,063	$1,850
1981	$260,107	$7,000
1982	$163,531	$7,380
1983	$42,117	$9,000
1984	$87,239	$8,215
1985	$165,821	$10,093.32
1986	$346,344	$12,195
1987	$308,396	$12,225
1988	$287,171	$12,468
1989	$456,780	$37,272
1990	$452,732	$38,667
1991	$1,300,000	$818,803 (includes $780,000 from Millie's book)

"The Bushes are great because if they belong to something, others want to belong, and big money will follow in their wake for a good cause," said Larry Lewin of National Dialogue on Cancer, an umbrella organization of various cancer groups, which the Bushes supported as co-chairmen. "She's a lot smarter than he is . . . George sometimes says silly things that don't make sense or are inappropriate. I remember when the Johns Hopkins report came out that broccoli appeared more effective than antibiotics in fighting peptic ulcers and preventing breast and colon cancer. We were meeting at Kennebunkport and George stood up and said, 'I don't care if broccoli cures cancer, I'm not eating it. No way. No how. I can't stand it. Don't want it. Won't eat it.' He thought he was being funny, but it was a brainless remark and not at all amusing, considering who we were and why we were there. But, of course, we all forced a big belly laugh because of who he is."

After four years of bell ringing around the world, George Bush had raised $83 million to build his limestone-and-marble presidential library on the campus of Texas A&M University. The dedication, on November 6, 1997, showcased the exclusive club of former presidents and first ladies who gathered to honor one of their own. President and Mrs. Clinton arrived on Air Force One to join President and Mrs. Ford, President and Mrs. Carter, Nancy Reagan, and Lady Bird Johnson. Caroline Kennedy Schlossberg represented her parents, and Julie Nixon Eisenhower sat on the dais in the place of her father, who had been Bush's major political mentor.

Jeb Bush acted as master of ceremonies for the event, which featured speeches by all the presidents and the two first ladies who were representing their husbands. As governor of Texas, George W. Bush welcomed the twenty thousand guests, including generals, senators, congressmen, ambassadors, corporate CEOs, university presidents and professors, televangelists, and movie stars such as Arnold Schwarzenegger, Kevin Costner, Chuck Norris, and Bruce Willis. The former leaders of Britain, Canada, Bermuda, the Netherlands, Japan, and Poland also flew in for the occasion.

"It's hard not to notice how white this crowd is," Paul Jennings noted in *The Texas Observer*. "Not just mostly white. Really white. Take away Colin Powell and the A&M grounds crew, and you basically have the whitest group of people that you're likely to run across outside of a gun show."

In his welcoming remarks, the Texas governor bashed bonhomie to smithereens. He praised his father in a way that panned his successor: "I'm here to praise my father as a man who entered the political arena and left with his integrity intact . . . A war hero, a loving husband . . . and a President who brought dignity and character and honor to the White House."

On paper the governor's words looked benign and loving, but spoken by a prideful son at the height of Clinton's personal scandal in front of a predominantly Republican crowd, they sounded biting and censorious. The assault on the President's integrity was not lost on anyone.

"His speech was rude and insulting," said Bobbie Greene, a Clinton aide. "His theme was lack of morality, which was totally inappropriate in that particular setting, especially when President Clinton spoke so warmly and well of his father."

"They [the Bushes] keep believing they can exalt themselves by running down Clinton's character," said George Stephanopoulos, another White House assistant. "But Clinton keeps winning."

Noting the governor's edgy speech, Maureen Dowd wrote in *The New York Times*, "George W. was serving notice on that stage that he would be the instrument of vindicating his father's loss to Bill Clinton."

Barbara Bush, who would not tolerate a negative word about her husband or her children, took exception. "I later heard that some people thought George W. got too close to the line when he spoke about his dad's decency and honesty. That really bothered me, because I remember when I was campaigning for George [in 1992] and would talk about his decency and honesty, reporters would say: 'Do you mean you don't think his opponent is decent or honest?' I would answer, 'Who's talking about him? I'm talking about George Bush.' Well, we were here to talk about George Bush and you can't mention George Bush unless you talk about decency and honor."

The family had never accepted Bill Clinton as a worthy successor, and they delighted in his unfolding scandal. They e-mailed one another ribald jokes about Monica Lewinsky and became as preoccupied as the rest of the country with the prurient coverage of Paula Jones's sexual-harassment suit against Clinton. When it was reported that the plaintiff claimed she could identify a "distinguishing characteristic" of Clinton's anatomy, the former President, once CIA director, did not rest until he discovered exactly what she was talking about. He then e-mailed his sons and several male friends a clinical description of Peyronie's syndrome, which can cause a distinct curvature of the male sexual organ. One man recalled the fillip to Bush's locker-room e-mail: "And, of course, his Johnson curves to the left." Among themselves the Bushes could not get enough of Clinton's humiliation.

By 1998 the family was looking toward its restoration through the presidential candidacy of George W. Bush, whose reelection as governor seemed assured, which would make him the first Texas governor to win back-to-back terms. When asked if George W. would run for President in

2000, his mother told reporters, "If he doesn't, I'll kill him." Barbara Bush already referred to her son as "the Chosen One."

When the television journalist Paula Zahn and her producer interviewed the elder Bush for a CNN profile at Kennebunkport, Mrs. Bush invited them to stay for drinks and dinner with the governor and Laura Bush, who happened to be visiting.

"Part of this story is how Barbara jabs and needles her son," recalled someone familiar with the evening. "They really do go at each other . . . but it's mostly Barbara. That evening George W. was getting antsy because he's impatient, he doesn't drink anymore, and he was hungry. He paced back and forth, making everyone feel uncomfortable. He kept saying, 'C'mon. Let's eat.' The elder Bush was drooling over Paula Zahn's legs, and the younger Bush was yammering to get to the dinner table. Finally Barbara said, 'I guess we'll all have to gulp our drinks to satisfy the Chosen One. C'mon, George, let's get moving. The Chosen One wants his dinner. We dare not keep the Chosen One waiting.' By the time they all sat down, the sun was setting and the last bit of light reflected off the window and framed George W. like a halo. His face was bathed in light as he sat at the table. 'See,' yelled his mother. 'I told you he was the Chosen One.' "

The governor of Texas realized that having his brother as governor of Florida could be an enormous advantage in 2000, so George W. went out of his way to help Jeb win his race. He arranged several fund-raisers for him in Texas, screened his television ads, and dispatched the family to campaign throughout Florida. Both brothers billed themselves as "compassionate conservatives" and tarred their opponents as Clinton Democrats, stopping just short of calling for the President's impeachment. At a debate in Florida, which his mother attended, Jeb said, "The White House is no longer a symbol of righteousness, a symbol of something good, and we need to restore it."

Both brothers were elected resoundingly in November 1998 (Jeb won 56 percent to 44 percent; George won 69 percent to 31 percent), prompting their father to proclaim that Election Day the happiest day of his life. Their mother could barely contain herself. "This means that one out of every eight Americans will now be governed by one of my boys," she said proudly.

Two weeks later the two brothers made their debut at the Republican

Governors Association in New Orleans. Basking in the spotlight, they held a news conference for the national press corps.

"I wanted to introduce my little brother to the Texas press corps," said George W., "but it looks like some others came along."

The two joshed onstage as a horde of reporters peppered them with questions.

"Can I disagree on one thing?" Jeb asked.

"Yeah. Just make sure it's a minor point," said George W., adding, "I've been telling him what to do for 45 years and he hasn't listened yet."

When someone called out "Governor Bush?" they looked at each other and laughed.

A reporter asked about the presidential election in 2000.

"Let me just say this," said George W. "For someone who is running for president, it would be wise for them to knock on Jeb Bush's door. Florida's an important state."

The Texas governor tried to dodge answering the question of whether he would run, although the Florida governor gave him a resounding endorsement.

"Listen, I didn't grow up wanting to be president of the United States," said George W.

Jeb smiled wistfully. "I did," he said.

"Yeah," his brother replied. "You did."

CHAPTER TWENTY-FIVE

"Where is the man that has incontestable evidence of the truth of all that he holds," asked the English philosopher John Locke in 1689, "or of the falsehood of all he condemns?"

Just such a man was sitting in the statehouse in Austin, Texas. Within days of his reelection as governor, George W. Bush was secretly planning to run for President, because, as he said, he felt certain he had been called. He was encouraged in this belief by evangelical friends like Doug Wead and by his mother, who called him "the Chosen One." Anticipating W.'s reelection in 1998, Wead had written a memo encouraging George to run despite his less than promising past. "You have been given a great opportunity, an opportunity that has been denied to many who have sought it. It is a gift that has rarely been extended. It might not ever be extended again."

During the religious service for W.'s second inaugural, the Reverend Mark Craig, pastor of the United Methodist Church of Dallas, preached about a calling for public service. Barbara Bush leaned over and whispered to her son, "He's speaking to you."

By then George had come to believe it himself. Seven months earlier he had not been so sure. At that time Karl Rove had escorted him on his first pilgrimage to the home of former Secretary of State George Shultz on the campus of Stanford University. Shultz was the Jack Steele Parker Professor of International Economics at the Graduate School of Business as well as a fellow at the Hoover Institution. He had gathered a few former Reagan and Bush economists as well as the Stanford provost Condoleezza Rice to take a look at the fifty-two-year-old governor, whom

Republicans were clamoring to make their nominee. Having raised $24 million for his race for governor, George had proved himself a stupendous fund-raiser, and his financial backers now wanted to go the distance for a national race.

His top-ten contributors were:

1. Enron Corporation, Houston, Texas Kenneth and Linda Lay	$312,000
2. Bass Family Enterprises, Fort Worth, Texas Lee and Ed Bass	$221,000
3. Sterling Software, Dallas Charles Wyly Jr. and Sam Wyly	$212,000
4. Arter and Hadden LLP, San Antonio Tom Loeffler	$179,000
5. Denitech Corporation, Austin and Dallas Dennis Berman, CEO	$175,000
6. First National Bank, Dallas Peter O'Donnell	$164,000
7. Sterling Group, Houston William A. McMinn	$164,000
8. Beecherl Investments, Dallas Louis Beecherl Jr. and Louis Beecherl III	$154,000
9. Hicks, Muse, Tate, and Furst, Dallas Tom and R. Steven Hicks	$153,000
10. MBNA America Bank, Wilmington, Delaware Charles Cawley, CEO	$148,358

Knowing that the Palo Alto crowd was looking for someone like Ronald Reagan, George arrived at his first policy salon slightly nervous but charmingly self-effacing.

"You're my professors," he told them. "I'm the Econ 1 student, and I'm taking it again because I didn't do well in it in college." He did not mention his disappointing grades in economics—71 for the first semester and 72 for the second semester—which put him at the bottom of his class at Yale. Instead, he asked the assembled sages what they thought of his plan to reform Social Security by allowing younger workers to invest some of their accumulated revenue in the stock market.

"I'm a little concerned about how much risk is there," George said. "What do you do to prevent people from investing in worm farms?"

The policy discussion lasted several hours, and when George left, he felt a little surer of himself.

"They didn't seem to think I was slobbering on my shoes," he said to Rove.

After that session, George Shultz, then seventy-nine, began making regular trips to Austin to tutor the governor in foreign policy. A long line of GOP elders followed Shultz, practically begging the governor to run. W. was young, attractive, and had a brand name. "It was just one big massive hug around this guy they thought was the most likely to deliver a Republican White House," said the pollster Frank Luntz. Without trying, George was perceived as—and had virtually become—the party's best chance to beat Vice President Al Gore in the 2000 election. Despite an unprecedented period of economic prosperity and world peace during the Clinton-Gore years, the Vice President was considered vulnerable because he would be running in the scandalous wake of the President.

Having spent most of his public life scrambling (in fact, desperate) to become President, George Herbert Walker Bush could not believe what was happening. He was dumbfounded by the presidential groundswell engulfing his son and totally perplexed as he watched his party go down on bended knee to proffer its nomination. He was the last to recognize George's success at retail politics. This was the son he least expected to succeed in anything, let alone national politics. Dizzy with disbelief, George senior sought advice from old friends in Congress about whether George junior should run.

"When he called me, I told him I didn't think the kid was ready," said Dan Rostenkowski, former chairman of the House Ways and Means Committee, who served fifteen months in a federal prison and was fined $100,000 for running petty scams out of his congressional office. "George assured me his boy was ready, so I said, why the hell are you asking me then . . . I like the old man. I think he should've been reelected. George senior went up against the right-wing conservative bastards in his party in 1990 and did the right thing for the country by raising taxes and laying the foundation for the economic growth that took place under Clinton . . . Of course, Clinton took all the bows, but it was George Bush who made it possible . . . When he called to ask me if his kid should go for it, I said that if it's his time, he should grab it because the time only comes around once."

While his father was canvassing friends for a consensus on his son's political future, George W. had already decided. By November 1998 the endearing modesty of the previous April had disappeared, and in its place was something mightily short of the divine right of kings. George W. had come to believe that he had been "called" to the presidency.

"There's a sense of entitlement that all the Bushes have," said Ron Reagan Jr. in 2004. "They feel as if they're entitled to everything that comes their way. I know that the first President Bush felt that he deserved to be President because it was his 'turn' to be President. It was his due. He'd served all the people he was supposed to have served. He'd put in the time. He'd done favors for all the powerful people he needed to do favors for. So in his mind, he deserved to be President . . . His son George W. Bush was 'run' for President. They [the party establishment] came to him and said, 'You've got the name recognition, we can raise the money and run you . . .' I think they looked around at the other potential candidates and thought, 'There's no one else out there we can control.' They found the perfect empty vessel in W. He'll go wherever the wind will go. And 'they're' in charge of the wind. That doesn't mean he's stupid. I don't believe he is. I think he's of average intelligence . . . My sense of him is that he's not ideologically motivated at all. But he's certainly willing to use an ideology to benefit himself. I think George W. Bush's ideology is the ideology of self."

The forty-six-year-old son of President Reagan said he did not share the same sense of entitlement as George W. Bush. "I don't know why I don't have the same feeling," Reagan said. "My father wasn't from old money for one thing. He did most of what he did on his own. He had help; obviously, he didn't do everything by himself. No one gets to be President of the United States without help. But he became President on his own accomplishments . . . Remember when the first President Bush spoke about the vision thing? Well, for my father, vision wasn't a 'thing.'

You can argue with my father's point of view and his policies, which I'm certainly willing to do, but he was a man with a genuine vision. He had very specific beliefs, and he stood by them . . . My father wrote his own speeches. He used to write his own radio addresses. I grew up watching him do that as a child. The Bushes can barely read their own speeches, much less write them . . . I believe the Bush vision—for both H.W. and W.—is probably wrapped up in their family fortunes rather than in anything that has to do with the good of the country."

Despite the pleas of his closest friends and his twin daughters not to seek the presidency, George W. Bush felt that he was the only man who could save the Republican Party. As his close friend and top aide Clay Johnson recalled, it was a "calling, this sense of there's a need [that only] I, George W. Bush, [can] satisfy."

"Very close personal friends of his and Laura's tried to talk him out of this," said Johnson, who went to Andover and Yale with George. "And one woman in particular, a good friend of theirs for many years, just pleaded with him not to run. It would so irrevocably change their lives that she just asked them please not to run. 'Don't do this to yourself.' And his response to her was, 'Look, I share your concern. But if I don't run, who else is there? If not me, who? Who do we want—who are we going to be pleased with as our next President? We—I would love to think that there's somebody else out there that we could all get behind, but I don't know who that person is.' "

The timing was impeccable. Even if George lost, he still remained governor of the second-largest state in the nation. Having become a multimillionaire, he no longer needed to work. He had hit the jackpot in June 1998, when Tom Hicks, one of the Bush family's biggest contributors, bought the Texas Rangers for $260 million. For his 1989 investment of $500,000, George received $15 million. "When all is said and done, I will have made more money than I ever dreamed," he said.

"Who knew that he would be further blessed with an opponent [Al Gore] so wooden and awkward and arch that he would make people overlook Bush's abysmal lack of fitness for the highest office in the land?" said a disgruntled member of the Democratic National Committee several years later.

At the time, Vice President Gore was assumed to be the Democratic nominee for 2000. Ordinarily, his incumbency would have given him an unbeatable advantage, but the Democrats had been damaged by the scandals surrounding President Clinton, who was impeached by the House of Representatives on December 19, 1998, on one count of obstruction of justice and one count of perjury. It was an extraordinarily contentious period in America's political life, but the Senate acquitted Clinton on both charges, permitting the forty-second President to complete the remaining 708 days of his term.

President Clinton had lied under oath—and on television to the American public—about his sexual involvement with a White House intern, Monica Lewinsky. His sex life and his defense of his actions had taken the country on a lascivious loop-de-loop for thirteen months. The Vice President had defended the President against the squalid accusations, but when it became clear that the President had lied to his wife, to his cabinet, and to the country, the Vice President was aghast.

"What he did was inexcusable," Gore said on national television, "and particularly as a father, I felt that it was terribly wrong, obviously."

The Republicans pounced. They saw that their best chance for recapturing the White House resided in the firstborn son of a family universally accepted as good and wholesome. "Family values" became a term of indictment against Bill Clinton. Every time George W. Bush said he was running "to restore dignity to the White House," he subliminally called up the image of a twenty-two-year-old intern from Beverly Hills snapping her thong at the President of the United States. Her seductive trifle had led to a constitutional crisis, following a relationship of oral sex and telephone sex that by turns titillated and revolted all who had become fixated on the saga as it unfolded twenty-four hours a day on television and radio.

At the time Al Gore formally announced his candidacy in June 1999, he did not know how to personally dissociate himself from the man who had made him Vice President and still claim the political advantage of the administration's peace and prosperity. It was a problem that vexed him throughout the campaign, throwing him on the defensive as he teeter-tottered on the Clinton seesaw. The President dominated the primaries of both parties. He was the dog's mess in the middle of the living room; Democrats tried to escape, while Republicans kept dragging them back to rub their noses in it.

"People want to elect a statue," said Oklahoma's Republican Governor Frank Keating. "They want a hero, an unblemished and unvarnished guy in the White House. They don't want to revisit the agony of the past eight years. Bush has to show his character is unvarnished and unblemished."

Karl Rove knew he had to present his candidate as the anti-Clinton: fresh (no inhaling or drugs of any kind, no alcoholism), religious (acceptable to evangelicals), and faithful to his wife (majority of voters: women). Rove wanted no explosive, potentially devastating revelations to emerge that might portray W. and Laura as anything but an ideal and idealized couple.

George W. Bush *wasn't* Bill Clinton, certainly not in terms of sexual excess. But to present him as pure and pristine was hypocritical and untrue. Clinton is not the standard to which George W. should be held. He must be compared to his own declarations on morality and his own carefully crafted public image—the image that the entire Bush family has cultivated for so long.

Both George and Laura used to go down to the island of Tortola in the British Virgin Islands to visit Laura's college roommate Jane Clark and her boyfriend, the former baseball great Sandy Koufax. Elsewhere on the island, the Bushes used to attend and enjoy heavy pot-smoking parties. This was not inconsistent with Laura's past. She graduated from Southern Methodist University in 1968 and had been known in her college days as a go-to girl for dime bags of marijuana. "She not only smoked dope," said public relations executive Robert Nash, an Austin friend of many in Laura's SMU class, "but she sold dope."

Smoking pot was hardly a sin—particularly in the late 1960s—but it did not mesh with the straitlaced image the Bushes were now presenting to the voters.

Because of the anger that Clinton's indiscretions had aroused with voters, W. loudly proclaimed that he had never committed adultery. "Everyone knows, or should know, that I have been faithful to my wife for the past twenty-one years," George told Tucker Carlson of *Talk* magazine.

Potentially more damaging, in some ways, than free-floating rumors of adultery was something that wasn't a mere rumor: George's alcohol-induced behavior toward his wife. In W.'s drinking days, abusive behavior had, several times, driven Laura from their house. Often George would disappear at night, and Laura would not know where he was. Friends recalled a drunken George being bitingly sarcastic and pugnacious. One friend even worried about spousal abuse, but there was no official police report to document the allegation.

In December 1998, the Bush team—Karl Rove, Joe Allbaugh, and Don Evans—began in earnest to tidy up the governor's past. They knew they could rely on Laura's close girlfriends to keep mum and protect her from the hurtful rumors, accusations, and investigations of the abuse. And if there were extramarital affairs, George W. had been discreet. Rove and the others were able to maintain the image. The past, in many ways, had been erased.

George and Laura's marriage had indeed survived all the ups and downs, but the toll was obvious to those close to the couple. Laura developed her own circle of friends, mostly women, with whom she shopped and regularly vacationed. She pursued her interests by herself, going alone to museums, the theater, and the ballet. When they were in the White House, she continued this pattern, taking her annual women-only hiking vacations.

George had declared that he could not tolerate a wife who stole his spotlight, and Laura never did. Even on the national stage, she appeared strangely removed. Some observers wondered if she was on antidepressants because her calm demeanor seemed slightly unnatural. She accompanied her husband to and from the helicopter Marine One on the weekends to fly to Camp David, but there was no public display of affection between them. They rarely held hands. In fact, they were more demonstrative toward their dogs than toward each other. Laura accompanied George to their ranch in Crawford and on some state trips, although she traveled more on her own than she did with him. She even made a few fund-raising trips for him during his drive for reelection, but she remained very much in her own world, not his. She continued her girlfriend outings and spent days and days shopping. Her Secret Service detail was frequently seen on the streets of Georgetown as Laura meandered in and out of antiques shops up and down Wisconsin Avenue.

She embraced literacy as her First Lady cause—causes became a requirement of all presidential wives after the Kennedy administration, when Jacqueline Kennedy made hers the restoration of the White House. To promote reading, Laura dutifully posed for pictures holding a book and reading to schoolchildren, but she never seemed to be actively engaged by making regular trips to schools, traveling to meet with educators and parents and students. She brought none of her mother-in-law's hard-charging energy or commitment to the role of literacy's First Lady. "She excels as an honorary chairman," said a Washington, D.C., woman whose charity has benefited from being able to use Laura's name on its invitations. "But, curiously, she insists on being called Mrs. Laura Bush, not Mrs. George Bush . . . I learned this the hard way when we listed her—properly—on an invitation as Mrs. George W. Bush. The White House called and said I had to have all the invitations redone so that she appeared as Mrs. Laura Bush. I explained that wasn't the proper way to list the President's wife, but her office insisted. 'That's the way Mrs. Bush wants to be presented.' So that's the way we presented her."

As governor's wife, Laura, who loved living in the liberal town of Austin, started the Texas Book Festival. As President's wife, she appeared more reluctant, less involved. She told friends she resented being described as "a fifties throwback," but, in truth, as First Lady she probably most resembled Bess Truman, who frequently left the White House to return to her home in Missouri. To enhance Laura's image as the First Lady of literacy, her husband's promoters portrayed her as a schoolteacher and a librarian devoted to books, although she had stopped working professionally the day she married George Bush in 1977.

In the early years of their marriage, Laura joined her husband in his revels, but after their hard struggle to conceive and her fragile pregnancy, she pulled back from the hell-raising, while he charged on, leaving her behind.

"She was never part of the family scene at Kennebunkport," recalled her former sister-in-law, Sharon Bush. "Laura just sat around on the porch reading and smoking cigarettes. She let the rest of us plan activities for her children and take care of them. She was just in her own world. Not a joiner at all . . . I suppose there were strains in her marriage, just because he's so difficult and high-energy and . . . she isn't, but she never talked about it . . . She really didn't talk much at all. Just read paperbacks and smoked cigarettes."

In 1998 the governor's tidy-up team was not as concerned about Laura as they were about George. Fanning out across the country, they made sure that Andover would not release the governor's personal records as a prep-school student, and they received assurances from Yale and Harvard that his records would be secure unless he gave permission for release. They contacted the Texas Air National Guard to make sure that his service record was "in order."

Retired Guard officer Colonel Bill Burkett is said to have been present during a speakerphone call between Joe Allbaugh of the governor's staff and General Daniel James III during the summer of 1997. Burkett said he overheard Allbaugh tell the general to make sure there were no embarrassments in Bush's Guard record. Both Allbaugh and James deny Burkett's assertions, but another former Guard officer, Dennis Adams of Austin, Texas, said in 2004 that Burkett told him in 1997 about the records cleanup. "I have no doubt he [Burkett] is telling the truth," Adams said. "Bill is one of my heroes. He was trying to take on certain rotten SOBs inside the Guard."

The governor's top aides knew that the long reach of the Bush family worked to their advantage. People naturally want to please, not alienate, those in positions of great power and wealth. The psychological fear of retribution from a family whose patriarch was former director of Central Intelligence automatically worked to silence pesky girlfriends, talkative associates, and grudge-bearing enemies. In Texas especially, the Bushes ruled. Even people who disliked them did not want to run afoul of them socially. "Why disturb a lion that could maim you and eat your young?" said a member of the Houston Country Club.

The first hurdle facing the tidy-up team was to deal with the governor's past drug use. Over the years George had been very careful not to lie about doing or dealing illegal drugs, because he knew there were too many people who could testify to the truth. The steel triumvirate found an honor-among-thieves mentality within the group of those who had been "young and irresponsible" with George. As successful adults, most knew better than to talk about their adolescent use of illegal drugs.

When George had been asked about drugs in the past, he always finessed the question. "When I was young and irresponsible, I was young and irresponsible."

As governor, he required security drug tests for all state employees, so Sam Attlesey of *The Dallas Morning News* asked if he could meet a similar standard. "Could you pass the White House security clearance as it relates to drugs?"

Bush flicked him off. "I've answered that kind of question already."

He later asked one of his aides to get him a copy of the federal guidelines. After reading it, he called the reporter back.

"If you're asking me if I've done drugs in the last seven years," Bush said, "the answer is no."

The next day's headline: "Governor Says He Hasn't Done Drugs in Seven Years." This prompted David Bloom of NBC to ask Bush if he had ever used drugs as a pilot in the National Guard.

"Were you ever high when you were flying the fighter jet?"

The Bush team expected Bloom's question to explode the never-confirmed rumors that George had been grounded by the Guard in 1972 because he had cocaine in his system and knew he would be unable to pass his required physical. Bloom did not get a satisfactory answer to his question and was not permitted to follow up.

Tim Russert, NBC's moderator on *Meet the Press*, tried to engage the governor on the issue of his past drug use, but George dodged the question. "I've said all I'm going to say," he told Russert. "I don't want to provide any excuse for your 14-year-old child to say, 'Hey, maybe if old Governor Bush did something, I think I'm going to try it, that [sic].'"

Watching George bob and weave around the drug question prompted a *Washington Post* reporter to ask, "So why won't you just deny that you've used cocaine?"

"I'm not going to talk about what I did years ago," George said. "This is a game where they float rumors, force a person to fight off a rumor, then they'll float another rumor. And I'm not going to participate. I saw what happened to my dad with rumors in Washington. I made mistakes. I've asked people to not let the rumors get in the way of the fact. I've told people I've learned from my mistakes and I have. And I'm going to leave it at that."

The rumor float he referred to concerned an alleged narcotics arrest in 1972, which supposedly prompted his father to persuade a Texas judge to accept a deal whereby George would perform a certain amount of community service in exchange for getting his record expunged. Although this rumor has never been confirmed, George W. Bush did, in fact, participate in a community-service program right around that time, just before he entered Harvard Business School. The official story is that it was W.'s drinking and driving incident involving his underage brother Marvin that led to their stint of community service. They maintain that this community service—at PULL—was strictly voluntary (or at least dictated by nothing more than parental discipline).

As governor and presidential candidate, George denied he had ever been arrested for dealing drugs; no one ever produced proof of such an arrest, and his father vehemently denied ever trying to obstruct justice on his son's behalf. "It's a lie," said George Herbert Walker Bush. "A vicious lie. And I'll tell you, it's one of the things that makes a lot of people stay out of public service."

As governor of Texas, George took a hard line on drugs. He supported and signed legislation increasing penalties for drug possession in the state. He also signed legislation mandating jail time for people caught with less than a single gram of cocaine. Yet as Sharon Bush's claims show, he could have been subject to jail time himself had he been caught "doing coke" with his brother Marvin and a friend at Camp David during his father's presidency. "There is a long history of biochemical disorders in the family," said Sharon in 2003, in the midst of her unfriendly divorce from Neil. "Schizophrenia, alcoholism, and drug abuse."

The governor's answers to questions about his use of illegal drugs grew so convoluted during the campaign that he became the butt of late-night-comedy jokes. "George Bush has given a half a dozen different answers to this today," Jay Leno said on *The Tonight Show*. "First, he said that he hadn't done drugs in the past fifteen years. Then, later, he changed that. He said, no, no, he hadn't done drugs in the past twenty-five years. Then really, just like an hour ago, what he really meant to say was, he hadn't done drugs since he was twenty-eight. And, then finally, he admitted, he said, 'Look, I'm so high, I don't know what the hell I'm saying.' "

During his first term as governor, George had been summoned for jury duty in Travis County. He filled in the jury questionnaire (number 85009809) but left the following unanswered:

Have you ever been a party to a civil law suit? If yes, what type?

Has your spouse or any child ever sustained an injury requiring medical attention? If yes, describe the injury:

Have you ever served on a jury? Civil? Criminal? Was a verdict
reached?

Have you ever been an accused or a complainant or a witness in
a criminal case?

It was not carelessness that caused him to leave these questions unanswered. There are specific reasons he did not respond to each of the above
queries. Having been a party to a civil lawsuit, George did not want the
matter publicized. Few people knew that in 1994, the caretaker of the
Rainbo Club—an exclusive hideaway in East Texas for Dallas million
aires, in Henderson County—and his wife had accused club members of
conspiring to terminate him out of "spite and ill will" and had sued
George W. and other members. The plaintiffs claimed the caretaker had
been discharged after filing for workmen's compensation after being injured on the job. After two years of litigation, George managed to get his
part of the lawsuit dismissed on summary judgment, but only after the
plaintiff's attorney, Kay Davenport of Tyler, Texas, had deposed him.
George did not want that deposition to surface, because in it he admitted
that the Rainbo Club was "whites only." He had received less than 9 percent of the black vote in his race against Ann Richards, and the rejection
by the black community bothered him. He said it had been the only disappointment in an otherwise ideal campaign. He did not want to further
exacerbate the problem. Nor did he want to draw attention to the tax
write-off he used for his luxury lakeside home. He and the other home
owners in the Rainbo Club had halved their tax liability through a law
that permitted club properties to be designated as recreational, park, and
scenic land. They had formed a private nonprofit corporation, Rainbo
Club Inc., to operate a private hunting and fishing club for eighteen
members. As a result of the loophole, Bush paid only $543.07 in property
taxes in 1998 on a house and guest cottage valued at $101,770. The
Rainbo Club lawsuit cost him enough in lawyer's fees over two years to
make tort reform a major part of his campaign.

On the juror form, the governor also avoided answering the question
about his wife's sustaining any injury that required medical attention. He
did not intend to open a line of inquiry into Laura's painful past. At that

time, not even their fifteen-year-old twins knew about the death their mother had caused when she was a senior at Robert E. Lee High School in Midland. Laura had been driving her parents' car toward the intersection of State Highway 349 and Farm Road. Smoking and talking to her friend Judy Dykes, Laura did not see the stop sign. Flying across the road at fifty-five miles an hour, she smashed her 1963 Chevrolet into the side of a 1962 Corvair. The driver, Michael Douglas, never had a chance. He was dead on arrival at Midland Memorial Hospital. No charges were filed. The police report noted that no one was wearing seat belts, and concluded that there was no indication of drinking, even though no one was tested for alcohol. Laura Lane Welch and her friend were bruised and banged up, but released that evening. Emotionally, they were shattered when they realized that Laura had killed Midland's golden boy, an all-around athlete at their high school who was one of the most popular boys in their class and someone Laura herself had tried to date. She did not return to school for several weeks after the accident and could not bring herself to attend the young man's funeral.

"It was a very, very tragic accident I was involved in when I was 17 years old," she said thirty-seven years later when the story appeared in the *New York Post*. "It was terrible for everyone involved . . . I know this as an adult, and even more as a parent, it was crushing . . . for the family involved and for me as well."

George avoided answering the jury question about being accused in a criminal case because of his arrest in Maine on September 4, 1976, for driving under the influence. His Texas license, suspended at the time, was restored on July 25, 1978. But shortly after he was elected governor in 1995, he applied for a new driver's license with an entirely new number. The new license would make tracing an arrest record through his previous license virtually impossible. Perhaps it was this confidence that emboldened him to lie to Wayne Slater of *The Dallas Morning News* in 1998:

SLATER: Governor, were you ever arrested after 1968?

BUSH: No.

When George first reported for jury duty at the Travis County Courthouse on September 30, 1996, he smiled for the television cameras.

"I'm glad to serve," he said. "I think it's important. It's one of the duties of citizenship . . . I'm just an average guy showing up for jury duty."

Inside the courthouse he found out that he was a potential juror for a drunk-driving case. He summoned his general counsel, Alberto R. Gonzales, to petition the court to exempt him because of the possibility that as governor he might be called upon to pardon the accused. Despite the far-fetched premise, the judge agreed as a courtesy to excuse him from jury duty. Bush would later appoint his lawyer to the Texas Supreme Court.

The Houston Chronicle reported the governor's dismissal as "a development that allowed him to avoid potentially embarrassing questions about whether he had ever climbed behind the wheel after drinking."

When reporters asked George if he had ever been arrested for driving while intoxicated, he said, "I do not have a perfect record as a youth." No one thought to check the arrest records in places where he had lived as a youth—until November 2, 2000. Five days before Election Day, Tom Connolly, a longtime Maine Democrat, stumbled upon the twenty-four-year-old police report that the governor had concealed all his public life. The disclosure cost George more than a modicum of respect, especially since he had been presenting himself as honest and truthful in contrast to the Democrats. His obvious attempt to hide his arrest made reporters skeptical. They used the term "Clintonesque" to describe his squirmy attempts to handle questions about the cover-up. Karl Rove later estimated the revelation had cost Bush about 1 million votes, enough to make him lose the national popular vote.

When the Travis County prosecutor Ken Oden, a Democrat, learned of the governor's arrest record, he felt Bush and his attorney had purposely misled him. "He used his position as governor to avoid having to answer potentially embarrassing questions about his past," Oden told Salon.com. The defense attorney P. David Wahlberg said, "Everybody understood [Bush] just didn't want to answer questions about drinking and drugs and things like that."

Predictably, Barbara Bush rushed to her son's defense. She claimed he had been arrested because he was "driving too slowly." The arresting officer, Calvin Bridges, said he had cited George for "driving erratically and [running] off the road into some hedges."

In her book *Reflections*, Barbara dismissed the arrest as "much ado about nothing." She wrote, "Frankly, I think that instead of the effect that some hoped for, this might have reminded people that George had the discipline to give up drinking and that he was strong."

Those closest to George agreed that the key to his new persona lay in his steely discipline. His sister described him as a fat boy who deprived himself to stay thin. His mother depicted a drinker who denied himself to stay dry. Both acknowledged that the effort to control these appetites was monumental. In order to maintain his rigid discipline, George imposed an inflexible order on his life. Like any addict in recovery, he needed a regular schedule, rising early and retiring early. He prayed daily from his *One-Year Bible*, which was divided into 365 readings, each from the New Testament, the Old Testament, Psalms, and Proverbs. Edgy and impatient, he exercised at least one hour, sometimes two hours, a day. With martinet punctuality, he started and ended meetings exactly on time. He refused to read memos longer than two pages. He thrived on making quick decisions. His religiosity allowed him to live in a black-and-white world of absolutes with no bedeviling in-betweens. His decisiveness sprang from his need to control and to establish order amid chaos. Once he made a decision, he rarely looked back. Reversing himself might be misinterpreted as a sign of weakness, and he dreaded nothing so much as looking wimpish. There would never be a "wimp factor" with George W. Bush.

He swaggered and smirked and seemed to enjoy shocking people with his exaggerated machismo. He cursed constantly, which his father, no stranger to ribald language, said started when he was five years old. In a 1951 letter to a friend, the elder Bush wrote, "Georgie aggravates the hell out of me talking dirty." Years later reporters would be astonished by some of George's obscenities. David Fink, formerly with *The Hartford Courant*, was stunned when he asked George what he and his father talked about. George's response: "Pussy."

"I just couldn't use the word," said Fink years later. "I wrote instead that he had made an unflattering reference to women. I know that he said it on the record, but part of me thought that . . . well, I would not talk that way to a stranger, much less to a reporter on the record . . . so I guess I protected him, because I thought maybe he was trying to be a guy ingratiating himself to another guy."

When Tucker Carlson interviewed the governor for *Talk* magazine, he, too, was surprised by George's vulgarity. Carlson asked about a rumor that the Gore campaign had a photograph of Bush dancing nude on top of a bar.

"They think it's like a high school election," George said, "where if you beat up your opponent enough you can win. They've lost their fucking minds."

When a right-wing friend accused the born-again governor of taking the Lord's name in vain, George exploded. "That's bullshit," he said. "Total bullshit."

Whether talking to reporters, congressmen, or heads of state, George made no effort to curb his trash mouth. He called Adam Clymer of *The New York Times* a "major league asshole." After praising Republican Representative Charles Whitlow Norwood Jr. of Georgia, George said, "So now that I've kissed your ass, what do I have to do to get a deal?" Israel's Prime Minister Ariel Sharon was taken aback to hear, "I said you were a man of peace. I want you to know I took immense crap for that."

George's cock-o'-the-walk manner served him well as governor of Texas. During his six years in the statehouse he allowed 152 executions (150 men and 2 women), a record unmatched by any other governor in modern history. He claimed he reviewed each execution case carefully, but research by *The Atlantic Monthly* suggested that he and his legal counsel, Alberto R. Gonzales, exhibited a shocking lack of attention to the facts of the cases that came before them. Gonzales's memos, which never made specific recommendations to the governor, were found to be cursory summaries lacking crucial specifics about the execution cases. The final page of each summary contained the "Governor's Clemency Decision" with a space for George to check "Deny" or "Grant" and affix his signature. In 152 out of 153 cases Bush checked "Deny." Only once in six years did he intercede with his Board of Pardons and Paroles to stop an execution—that of an alleged serial killer who had been sentenced to die for a murder that two attorneys general concluded he did not commit.

The most famous plea for clemency came from Karla Faye Tucker, who had been convicted of a drug-induced murder of two people with a pickax. During her fourteen-year incarceration, Tucker apparently experienced a religious conversion and became a model prisoner who repented her crimes and asked for forgiveness. She petitioned the governor to stay her execution and commute her sentence to life. Texas had not executed a woman since 1863, and her plea received international attention. Her story was featured on *60 Minutes*, *The 700 Club*, and *Larry King Live* for two consecutive nights. The televangelist Pat Robertson championed her case, as did the human rights activist Bianca Jagger and Pope John Paul II. Governor Bush would not meet with any of them. "If the crime fits the penalty, the penalty is given," he said.

Two weeks before Tucker's scheduled execution by lethal injection, CNN's Larry King traveled to Gatesville, Texas, to interview the condemned prisoner from death row. She broke down and sobbed as she described her crime. She talked about her religious salvation and how she placed her faith in God.

> KING: Do you think . . . politics and everything . . . that politics are involved? That part of the decision [for Governor Bush] is, will it hurt me with the electorate or help me with the electorate, if I decide this? You do think that?
>
> TUCKER: Oh, yes. I am not crazy. I do believe that.
>
> KING: And Texans like capital punishment?
>
> TUCKER: Yes.
>
> KING: So you're in trouble there?
>
> TUCKER: Naturally speaking, it would look like there's no hope but I . . . my hope is in God.

Two nights before the scheduled execution, Jenna Bush, then sixteen years old, told her father over dinner that he should commute the sentence. George refused. "If the crime fits the penalty," he repeated, "the penalty is given." On February 3, 1998, he signed the execution order.

"May God bless Karla Faye Tucker," he said, "and may God bless her victims and their families."

The next day's editorial in the *Austin American-Statesman* sided with Jenna Bush. "[Tucker's execution] was so poignant and unnecessary that it gave all but the most determined death penalty advocates pause," said the paper. "Her death . . . should prompt every judge, jury, and legislator to reconsider the death penalty that Texas indulges with such abandon."

A year later the governor was still smarting from the criticism. Unable or unwilling to hide his mean streak, he spoke sarcastically to a reporter about the execution.

"I didn't meet with Larry King when he came down for it. I watched his interview with [Tucker], though. He asked her real difficult questions, like 'What would you say to Governor Bush?' "

"What was her answer?"

George pursed his lips in mock fear and whimpered, " 'Please, don't kill me.' "

But King never asked her that question and she never gave that answer. Bush's ridicule of the woman executed the previous year seemed exceedingly callous, even cruel.

George would never match his father's graciousness, but he was capable of nice gestures. Ruth Gilson, a realtor with Millicent Chatel, recalled a touching moment during a 1999 fund-raiser at the Willard Hotel in Washington, D.C.

"I had paid one thousand dollars to meet the governor," she said. "I very much wanted to see him because I had voted for his father and I was going to vote for him."

She recalled that she was one of very few women to attend the event. "All the men looked to be lobbyists in expensive suits with huge stomachs. The room filled up fast and we were all squished together. I was at the front of the rope line. A little old lady about eighty-five years old crept in beside me. She said she needed to see the governor. 'I just have to talk to him,' she said."

The elderly woman was frail and wearing clothes that looked worn and dated. Perched on her head was a little hat with a veil. "She looked like a church lady from the 1950s," said Gilson.

George arrived, made a short speech, and then started working the crowd. The little woman stepped forward and asked if she could say something. He reached out and took her hand. She whispered in his ear to please do something about the price of prescription drugs for the elderly. He nodded. "I'll try," he said. Then he stepped back to look at her.

"Did you pay a thousand dollars to come here?"

"Yes, sir, I did."

"Well, I want you to get your money back." He turned to the man with him. "Get her name and address and see that she gets a check for a thousand dollars."

The little old lady shook her veiled head. "No, I want you to have it all, Mr. Bush. I want you to win."

"Well," said George. "I'll tell you what. I'll keep a hundred dollars and you keep nine hundred dollars and we'll both win. That's what we'll do."

She smiled gratefully.

"It was such a sweet gesture on his part," recalled Ruth Gilson. "Others might have seen it as patronizing, but I didn't. In a crowd of fat-cat lobbyists that little woman in her tattered coat looked like someone's poor grandmother, and he responded sensitively."

Much like his father's, however, George W.'s compassion tended to extend only to those who were loyal and helpful to the family. It also extended to those who were in the family's tax bracket.

Even before announcing his candidacy, George had raised $40 million, which anointed him the clear-cut front-runner. Rove's strategy had been to get him crowned before he ascended the throne. "If you are the establishment choice on the Republican side, you are the inevitable nominee," Rove told a group of lobbyists in Austin. "No ifs, ands or buts." By the end of 2000, George had raised more than $193 million to Gore's $133 million, making their race the most expensive presidential campaign in history. *Newsweek* said that George had assembled the greatest fund-raising machine in politics. His single largest financial backer was the credit-card company MBNA, which contributed $240,000 and gave him use of the company plane. The CEO, Charles Cawley, a Bush family friend, was paid $50 million a year by the company he founded. He was a Ranger for Bush, which meant he had to raise over $200,000. He raised $369,156 for the presidential campaign and then personally contributed $100,000 to the Bush inauguration. In 2004, Cawley was forced by his board of directors to retire because of his imperious financial demands.

George made no apologies for aligning himself with the richest men in America. He knew that money was the mother's milk of politics. Addressing an Al Smith Memorial Dinner in New York City, he made sport of his wealthy contributors: "This is an impressive crowd, the haves and the have-mores. Some people call you the elite. I call you my base."

George had become so accustomed to the luxe life of limousines and private jets that he seemed out of touch with those who had to work for a living and rely on buses and trains. Tom Downs, the former head of Amtrak, remembered calling him when Amtrak was canceling the Texas Eagle, the last passenger rail link between Dallas and Houston. Bush was unaware that such a service even existed.

"When we need to get there, we just take one of Herb's planes [Herb Kelleher, head of Southwest Airlines], or drive fast," said the governor. He told Downs to go ahead and drop the service. "No problem."

Downs then called Kay Bailey Hutchison, U.S. senator from Texas, to tell her about the cancellation. She asked about Bush's reaction. Downs phrased the governor's response diplomatically.

"No, tell me what he really said," she insisted.

Downs told her.

"That little shit," said the senator.

George traveled to Cedar Rapids, Iowa, on June 12, 1999, to announce his candidacy. "I am proud to be a compassionate conservative," he said. "I am running so that our party can match a conservative mind with a compassionate heart." He arrived on a chartered jet he had named *Great Expectations*. A reporter asked why he named his plane after a book by Charles Dickens. George looked at him quizzically.

"It started out as 'High Expectations' and I suggested 'Great Expectations,' " he said.

"But the book?"

"If I read it, I can't remember it," said the governor.

When Jim Hightower heard the story, the Texas communicator threw up his hands. "Let's face it," he said. "Gore versus Bush is going to be a race between Dull and Dullard."

In Iowa, George joined a field of eight GOP candidates, most of whom would drop out after he won the caucuses. Staying the course would be Senator John McCain of Arizona, who did not have the money to campaign in Iowa. The underfinanced candidate hoped to beat Bush in New Hampshire, South Carolina, Michigan, and New York before finishing him off in California. A maverick conservative, McCain had beguiled reporters with his refreshing candor, and he excited voters with his honesty and his tough talk about campaign-finance reform. Having been locked in a cage as a prisoner of war for over five years, McCain was revered as a hero. He once joked that he slept more soundly in North Vietnam knowing that George Bush was defending the shores of Texas from invasion. The campaign between the prince and the pauper reflected their contrasting personal styles. Bush flew on luxury jets and carried his own pillow so he would not have to sleep on cheap hotel linen, while McCain traveled on a red, white, and blue bus he had named "The Straight Talk Express."

Days after George made national news with his formal announcement in Iowa, he again hit the front pages—this time as the brother-in-law of Columba Bush, who had been nabbed by U.S. Customs for failing to declare nineteen thousand dollars' worth of clothes and jewelry she had bought in Paris. Claiming she spent only five hundred dollars, the wife of Governor Jeb Bush was stopped, searched, and fined forty-one hundred dollars. At her husband's insistence, she publicly apologized. He said she had lied because she did not want him to know how much she had spent on her five-day shopping trip. "It was a difficult weekend at our house," said the governor.

Columba was so ashamed that she did not want to accompany her husband and children to Kennebunkport for their annual summer vacation with the Bushes. Frightened of her in-laws, she locked herself in the bedroom at the family compound and would not come out until her sister-in-law, Sharon Bush, knocked on the door and invited her for a walk. "I remember [Jeb's] thankfulness and appreciation when I took the time to spend with Columba in Maine," Sharon said.

Jeb later said: "My wife is not a public person. She is uncomfortable with the limelight, which is why I love her. I don't want a political wife—I want someone who when I get home I can have a normal life with."

Normalcy had long since disappeared from their household. In 1994 their eldest son, George Prescott Bush, had a fight with a former girlfriend and her father and drove his SUV into their front yard. He was not arrested, because the girlfriend's parents did not press charges. The next year, Noelle Bush, the governor's daughter, was arrested for shoplifting and paid a $305 fine. As she became more addicted to drugs, she received twelve traffic tickets in six years; including seven tickets for speeding and three for accidents. In October 2000, security guards in a Tallahassee mall parking lot caught sixteen-year-old John "Jebby" Bush with a seventeen-year-old girl, both naked from the waist down except for Jebby's socks. A police report on the governor's son cited "sexual misconduct," but neither was charged with a crime.

"It could have been worse," his uncle George joked to an aide. "The girl could've been a boy." A few seconds later he added, "We might've picked up some gay votes with that one, huh?"

Such jokes made some people wonder if George was genuinely committed to his ferocious public stands or if his proclamations were simply calculated for political gain. With an estimated 4 million gay voters in the United States, as opposed to 15 million social conservatives, a cynical politician could be expected to support the issues favored by the conservative majority. As governor, George had taken a hard line against homosexuality. He said he supported the state's law against sodomy as a "symbolic gesture of traditional values." He opposed hate-crimes legislation that would have protected gays. He also opposed gay adoption and gay marriage. (As President, he came out in favor of a constitutional amendment banning gay marriage.) Yet he approached the former Texas state representative Glen Maxey, an openly gay Democrat, and tried to draw a line between his politics and his personal feelings.

"He pulled me over really close, almost nose to nose, and said, 'Glen, I like you as a person. I respect you as a human being. I want you to know that what I say publicly about gay people doesn't apply to you.' "

Angered by Bush's opposition to gay adoption, Maxey replied, "Governor, when you say that a gay person is not fit to be an adoptive parent, you're talking about me."

During the presidential debates, George pledged that homosexuals "ought to have the same rights" as all other people, but he would not meet with Log Cabin (gay) Republicans. When he was President, his administration decided that homosexuals could be fired from the federal government because of their sexual orientation. In 2004, the Office of Special Counsel ruled that federal employees no longer had recourse if they were fired or demoted simply for being gay.

When Bush proposed the constitutional amendment prohibiting same-sex unions, Calvin Trillin picked up his witty pen to write a poem:

GEORGE W. BUSH SPEAKS OUT ON GAY MARRIAGE

He backs an amendment defining the vow
Of marriage as being a guy and his frau,
Lest civilization sink into a slough—
Which he says could happen. It isn't clear how.

Though he can't explain it, he needn't expand.
We saw this with Poppy. We know what's at hand:
The Jesus battalions demanded this stand.
The yelp of the lap dog is heard in the land.

George's Andover classmate Conway "Doc" Downing, an African American businessman involved in the gaming industry, smiled as he tried to explain his friend's paradox. "I'm in a pariah business—Internet gambling," he said. "When George was governor of Texas, I called Clay Johnson to get Richard Rainwater's address. Rainwater was the big money behind the Texas Rangers. That's all I wanted. No help, no recommendation. Just a personal address. I told Clay I wanted to send Rainwater a proposal about gambling. Clay checked with George and called me back. He gave me the address, but said, 'You didn't get it from us, because the governor is on the record as opposing gambling.'"

As the 2000 presidential campaign heated up, George won the Iowa caucuses, but going into New Hampshire, he fell behind McCain in the polls. Bush's pollsters said that one-fourth of his support came from people who liked his mother and father. "It's powerful," the New Hampshire attorney Tom Rath told *Newsweek*. "People say the acorn doesn't fall very far from the tree." George summoned his family to the state to campaign with him. Jeb arrived and handed out Florida oranges. Barbara appeared in pearls to address the luncheon crowds at Geno's Chowder and Sandwich Shop. "Georgie will keep his promises," she said. "Or else his mother will come get him!" The former President stood on stages with his arm wrapped around his eldest son. "You can trust my boy," he said. "Our son won't let you down . . . Our boy will work to restore respect to the presidency."

Voters in the Granite State were not impressed with the "our boy" argument. They saw the Bush family invasion as a desperate Hail Mary pass by a candidate who had taken them for granted, flying home to Austin every weekend to sleep in his own bed. John Adams, the only President whose son aspired to succeed him—and did—never campaigned for John Quincy Adams. The reason, David McCullough, Adams's biographer, told the columnist Mary McGrory: "It would have been considered 'unseemly.' " In the Adams family, however, the father's redemption was not invested in the political success of his son.

Karl Rove, who had never run a national campaign, predicted an easy victory in New Hampshire. When he saw the early exit polls on primary day, he was astounded. His candidate was down fifty points to thirty-two. He went to the governor's suite.

"We're going to lose and lose badly," he said.

"How bad?" asked Bush.

"Real bad," said Rove. "We're going to lose by eighteen, nineteen, twenty points. There's no good news here."

George did not curse and scream. He sat for a few minutes, watched the Weather Channel, and then drove to a gym in a strip mall and worked out. When he returned, he reassured his troops that no one would be fired, and he braced himself for the call to his father.

"We're going to be whipped," he told him. George later recalled that moment as one of his worst. "It's much harder to be a mother or dad than it is to be the candidate. It was really hard for me to be the son when he was the candidate. And I had to assure them I would be fine. And I will be. I don't rationalize defeat."

He gathered his top aides and questioned them closely. "What the hell happened?" he asked. "Why didn't we know?"

That night, after losing to McCain by eighteen points—49 percent to 31 percent—George called to congratulate his opponent. The senator was as stunned to win as the governor was to lose.

"When he called to concede the primary and offer his congratulations . . . he was quite gracious, and I appreciated it," said McCain. "I told him that I thought we and the people we loved could be proud of the way we had conducted our campaigns. I meant it . . . We said good-bye as friends. We would soon be friends no more."

Later Laura Bush spoke to her husband like a schoolteacher scolding a wayward child for not performing up to his potential. "You let him do this to you," she said. "You let John McCain talk down to you. You've got to fight back."

Laura knew her man. Once he saw the loss as an assault on his manhood, he would jump on his horse and charge. The next day he flew into South Carolina with his youngest brother. As George swept aside the curtain on the plane separating his cabin from the press corps, Marvin said, "The next sound you hear will be the media removing their lips from John McCain's blank, blank, blank." The family felt the media, including reporters covering Bush, had been seduced by McCain.

George made it clear that for the next eighteen days he planned to come from the right on every issue. Within hours he proved, as the New Hampshire attorney Tom Rath had observed, that the acorn truly does not fall far from the tree. He emulated his father's slashing Willie Horton strategy and transformed the South Carolina primary into one of the most vicious campaigns in political history.

George began with a speech at Bob Jones University in Greenville. BJU was an institution that, over the years, had opposed integration, banned interracial dating, and condemned homosexuality and whose founders were vociferously anti-Catholic. In 2000 the university president, Bob Jones III, still referred to Mormonism and Catholicism as "cults which call themselves Christian." The school threatened to arrest any out-of-the-closet gay alumni who dared to return to the school. One political placard on campus read: "Vote Bush Because Gay People Have Too Many Rights." Student-body attendance was compulsory for the governor's speech, and the six thousand Christian-right students turned out to cheer loudly every time George said the word "conservative." *Newsweek* counted twelve cheers in two minutes. George, who had kept a Confederate flag on his wall during his years at Andover, aligned himself with neo-Confederates and questioned McCain's commitment to states' rights—coded rhetoric for the right to be racist.

Not all conservatives applauded George for lending his presence to a citadel of prejudice. "It's one thing to lurch to the right," said Bill Kristol, editor and publisher of *The Weekly Standard*. "It's another thing to lurch back 60 years. You could make the case that 'compassionate conservatism' died February 2 when Bush appeared at Bob Jones U."

The next day George piled on McCain by sponsoring an event with

J. Thomas Burch Jr., the head of a little-known veterans group, who charged that after he came home from Vietnam, McCain "forgot us." After Burch spoke, Bush embraced him.

McCain, who still limped and could not raise his arms as a result of his imprisonment by the North Vietnamese, was livid. He ran an ad comparing George Bush to Bill Clinton, and asked: "Isn't it time we had a president who told the truth?"

Being equated with the man he regarded as reptilian was more than Bush could bear. He retaliated as if McCain had impugned his mother: "Politics is tough, but when John McCain compared me to Bill Clinton and said I was untrustworthy, that's over the line. Disagree with me, fine, but do not challenge my integrity."

"That commercial . . . was the Godzilla judo flip for us," recalled Trey Walker, McCain's national field director. "McCain's momentum had already started to evaporate, and that just stopped him dead."

The two candidates heaped charges upon countercharges as they clawed their bloody way to the conservative high ground on outlawing abortion, gambling, pornography, and homosexuality while supporting guns and God and the Confederate flag.

The Bush team retained the services of Ralph Reed, former director of the Christian Coalition, to run grass roots in the state, and they immediately started attacking with push polls, telephone banks, e-mails, anonymous mailings, automatic dialings of untraceable hate messages, phony front groups, and radio talk-show call-ins to pillory McCain with lies that he was a liberal reprobate who abandoned a crippled wife to father black children by black prostitutes. Preposterous charges of extramarital affairs, abortions, wife beatings, mob ties, venereal diseases, and illegitimate children were flung at him, while his wife, Cindy, was tarred as a wayward woman and drug addict who had stolen to support her habit, his children were vilified as bastards, and his friend and supporter from New Hampshire former U.S. Senator Warren Rudman was subjected to vile anti-Semitism. The poison drip saturated South Carolina for eighteen days and nights of slaughterhouse politics.

"I've seen dirty politics, but I've never seen a rumor campaign like this," said Terry Haskins, the speaker pro tem of the South Carolina House of Representatives and a McCain supporter. "It's a vile attempt to destroy a man's reputation just to win an election, and I know it's organized because none of these rumors existed until the day after New Hampshire."

On February 12, a week before the election, Bush was caught by a C-SPAN camera talking to a state senator. Neither man realized he was being watched.

"You haven't even hit his soft spots," said the senator.

"I know," said Bush. "I'm going to."

"Well, they need to be—somebody does, anyway."

"I agree," said Bush. "I'm not going to do it on TV."

By the time he finished mauling McCain in South Carolina with his anonymous smear campaign, George had almost surpassed his father's vile race-baiting.

"We suspected that Ralph Reed was behind it all," said Mark Salter, McCain's administrative assistant, "but we couldn't prove it, because there was no paper trail . . . They operated under the radar system . . . used political action committees no one ever heard of . . . which gave Bush complete deniability."

Federal Election Commission campaign records would show that Ralph Reed was paid more than half a million dollars by Enron "for ongoing advice and counsel." Karl Rove had recommended the conservative political activist to Enron in 1997, feeding suspicions that Rove wanted to keep Reed's favor for Bush's 2000 presidential campaign.

One aspect of Reed's fiendish operation in South Carolina targeted 140,000 Republicans throughout the state with flyers from the Christian Coalition titled "10 Disturbing Facts About John McCain." A southern female, who identified herself as being with a religious group, followed up with a phone call to these same voters. In a honey-sweet accent, she related horrendous stories about McCain and expressed concern about such a man becoming President. Before hanging up, she said, "You all be sure to listen to the Reverend Robertson this Sunday." When Pat Robertson appeared on one of the morning talk shows, he made a veiled reference to "some of those other things that are in John McCain's background."

Presenting himself as a "reformer with results," George criticized McCain's credentials for espousing campaign-finance reform. "He's the big committee chairman all the lobbyists give their money to . . . He's the

Washington insider." Winding up to clobber McCain as a self-righteous hypocrite, George said, "He can't have it both ways. He can't take the high horse and then claim the low road."

These linguistic gaffes plagued him throughout the campaign, causing great hilarity among the media, which detailed every mental malfunction:

> "What's not fine is, rarely is the question asked, are, is our children learning?" (January 14, 2000)
>
> "You're working hard to put food on your family." (January 27, 2000)
>
> "This is Preservation Month. I appreciate preservation. It's what you do when you run for President. You gotta preserve." (January 28, 2000)
>
> "The most important job is not to be governor, or first lady in my case." (January 30, 2000)
>
> "How do you know if you don't measure if you have a system that simply suckles kids through?" (February 16, 2000)
>
> "I understand small business growth. I was one." (February 19, 2000)
>
> "I don't care what the polls say. I don't. I'm doing what I think what's wrong." (March 15, 2000)
>
> "Laura and I don't realize how bright our children is sometimes until we get an objective analysis." (April 15, 2000)
>
> "Well, I think if you're going to do something and don't do it, that's trustworthiness." (August 30, 2000)
>
> "We cannot let terrorists and rogue nations hold this nation hostile or hold our allies hostile." (September 4, 2000)

Four days before the South Carolina primary, the two GOP candidates met for a nationally televised debate. They were standing awkwardly next to each other in the studio, and McCain turned to his rival.

"George," he said, slowly shaking his head with disgust.

The governor played by *Godfather* rules. "John," he said, "it's politics."

"George, everything isn't politics."

During the debate McCain did not hold back. "You should be

ashamed," he said, castigating George for campaigning with a man who had maligned McCain's commitment to veterans.

Bush shot back with outrage over the ad that had accused him of Clinton-style truth twisting. "Whatever you do, don't equate my integrity and trustworthiness to Bill Clinton," George said. "That's about as low a blow as you can go in the Republican primary . . . Morally, any of us at this table can outperform Bill Clinton."

After the debate the candidates assembled for a group picture. George walked over and grasped both of McCain's hands in his own.

"John," he said. "We've got to start running a better campaign."

McCain was incensed by the hypocrisy. "Don't give me that shit," he snarled, "and take your hands off of me."

By the time voters went to the polls, the two candidates had come to loathe each other. Trouncing McCain 54 to 41 percent, George won South Carolina and reestablished himself as the Republican front-runner over an opponent he described as "self-righteous."

"The reason why I think a few of those people are still angry at me is because we interfered with the coronation," said McCain. "Look, Bush and his people will have to live with the legacy of South Carolina; I don't." In his concession speech, the senator said, "I want the presidency in the best way, not the worst way."

He then charged into Michigan and turned Bush's tactics against him by running a telephone bank that reminded Catholic voters of George's appearance at the virulently anti-Catholic Bob Jones University. George hid behind the skirts of his Mexican sister-in-law.

"Do I support the policy against interracial dating? Of course not. My own brother Jeb, the great governor of Florida, married a girl from Mexico, Columba, a fabulous person . . . plus she's a Catholic." Not even the miscegenation laws in Texas had considered Mexicans a separate race.

McCain questioned how that response excused George's failure to speak out against bigotry. He blasted Bush as "a low-road campaigner" who would stoop to anything, including "character assassination" to win. McCain beat George 50.8 percent to 43 percent in Michigan.

Heading into the New York primary on March 7, 2000, George scrambled to make amends to the state's 7.3 million Catholics for his Bob Jones appearance. With Catholics constituting about 45 percent of the

GOP primary turnout, George wrote a letter to New York's John Cardinal O'Connor saying he regretted not condemning the anti-Catholic policies of the fundamentalist school. He did not apologize, nor did he acknowledge that by accepting the invitation from Bob Jones University he had legitimized the school's bigotry. In an editorial called "Boy George's Bogus Confession," the *New York Daily News* criticized him for pandering. "Bush . . . showed he was willing to sacrifice principles for votes."

The Democratic National Committee printed up T-shirts for reporters covering the Bush campaign that said, "Bob Jones Redemption Tour." Still, George won the New York primary, and by Super Tuesday he and Al Gore had secured their parties' nominations. Their campaigns began in earnest after the political conventions.

George's scorched-earth tactics in South Carolina had enraged his critics, especially Larry Flynt, the publisher of *Hustler* magazine, who felt that Bush's stand on sexual abstinence before marriage was the height of hypocrisy. Bush's pledge to put federal funds into abstinence programs further outraged Flynt, who argued that such programs did not reduce teen sex. Pronouncing Bush a menace to society, the pornographer hired two investigative reporters to explore every aspect of the governor's sexual past. In October 2000, he claimed to have hit pay dirt.

Appearing on CNN's *Crossfire*, Flynt alleged that George W. Bush had impregnated a woman in the 1970s when he was living at the Chateau Dijon in Houston. According to Flynt, George arranged an abortion through a physician, who purportedly performed the procedure at Houston's Twelve Oaks Medical Center.

"When I said that we had the proof, I am referring to knowing who the girl was, knowing who the doctor was that performed the abortion, evidence from girlfriends of hers at the time, who knew about the romance and the subsequent abortion. The young lady does not want to go public, and without her willingness, we don't feel that we're on solid enough legal ground to go with the story . . . One of the things that interested us was that this abortion took place before *Roe* v. *Wade* . . . which made it a crime at the time."

Without confirmation from the woman, who Flynt said had married an FBI agent, the mainstream press would not touch the story. "Walter Isaacson [former editor of *Time*] would not go with it because Larry Flynt was involved," said Brian Doyle, an assistant *Time* editor. "Even though he had four affidavits from the woman's friends." Michael Isikoff of *Newsweek* said, "Certainly, there was a great deal of circumstantial evidence to support it, but without the woman herself coming forward to admit that Bush arranged her abortion, we could not do anything with it." Richard Gooding of *The National Enquirer* said that when he interviewed the woman, she denied having had an abortion. "She admitted they dated exclusively for six months, but said they never had the kind of sex that would get her pregnant."

The story was pursued because of Bush's stand against abortion and his threat to support a "human life amendment" to the Constitution, which would overturn *Roe* v. *Wade*. As governor, he signed eighteen anti-abortion laws, and as a presidential candidate he promised to appoint only pro-life judges.

Following the "our boy" fiasco in New Hampshire, George sidelined his father, who made no further public appearances, lest the public see the patriarch as the puppeteer pulling the wooden puppet's strings. Behind the scenes, however, the elder Bush continued supervising his son's campaign. He was in daily contact with the Austin office. "Sometimes there were four—five—six calls a day," said an aide, "and every night Joe Allbaugh called him with the latest polls, no matter where he was." In Japan the former President announced over dinner that "our boy" was going to sweep Super Tuesday. "He was consumed," admitted his wife. "Absolutely consumed." He had sixteen T1 lines installed in his Kennebunkport estate to accommodate the telephones and computers of campaign aides and advisers flying back and forth from Texas.

At his father's suggestion George appointed former Secretary of Defense Dick Cheney to interview possible running mates. Former Missouri Senator John Danforth, New York Governor George Pataki, Nebraska Senator Chuck Hagel, and Representative John Kasich of Ohio were subjected to the laborious vetting process. George did not want to make the same mistake his father had made in selecting Dan Quayle.

Cheney, then CEO of the huge energy company Halliburton, spent three months on the process, conferring regularly with Bush, visiting him at his ranch in Crawford and at the statehouse in Austin. During the Gulf

War, Cheney had become close to the senior Bush. Toward the end of the vetting process, George H.W. finally recommended Cheney to his son as a running mate when Colin Powell removed himself from consideration. The only concern was Cheney's medical history, which included three heart attacks and a quadruple coronary bypass. His doctors assured the Bushes that Cheney's heart could take the stress, but their assurances proved to be more optimistic than realistic.

George felt comfortable with the balding man who was five years his senior and looked as if he had never missed a meal. Both came from the oil business and shared the same hard-line conservative politics. As Wyoming's only congressman from 1979 to 1990, Cheney had voted against affirmative action, Head Start, the Clean Water Act, and the Equal Rights Amendment. He also voted against freeing Nelson Mandela. Like George, he favored easy access to handguns, and he, too, had been arrested for drunk driving, once in November 1962 and again in July 1963. One of his two daughters, Mary, was an avowed lesbian, which the vehemently antigay Bush accepted as "no problem." Cheney had flunked out of Yale after two years on an academic scholarship, which amused George, who had nothing but disdain for his alma mater. Apparently, Yale and Yalies felt the same way about them. In the general election of 2000 over 84 percent of the Yale student body voted against the Bush-Cheney ticket. They threw their support to Al Gore and Joe Lieberman (Yale 1964; Yale Law School 1967), the first Jew to run for national office.

George announced his running mate by taking another whack at the President. "Dick Cheney is a solid man . . . a man who understands what the definition of 'is' is." The allusion was to Clinton's maddening answer during his 1998 grand jury testimony in the Lewinsky scandal when he said, "It depends on what the definition of 'is' is."

On the eve of the Republican convention, Clinton struck back. Appearing at a Rhode Island fund-raiser, he suggested that Bush was not qualified to hold the highest office in the land. He said Bush's only credential was his highly inflated sense of entitlement. Mimicking him, the President said, "How bad can I be? I've been governor of Texas. My daddy was president. I own a baseball team. Their fraternity had it for eight years, give it to ours for eight years."

The "our boy" contingent in Kennebunkport barked like seals. The next morning Bar and Poppy hit the morning shows. "I'll tell you what I'm going to do," said President Bush on the *Today* show, his voice tight with rage. "I'm going to wait a month and then, you give a call . . . And if he continues that, then I'm going to tell the nation what I think about him as a human being and a person." Barbara followed up on *Good Morning America*, implying that Clinton had brought too much disrespect to the presidency for Al Gore to restore. "It would be very difficult, I think, with some of the things he's done," she said. Lest there be any doubt about restoring the House of Bush, *Newsweek* featured the GOP ticket on its cover as "The Avengers."

Clinton had drawn blood, pushing the candidate's parents to give credence to a poll by the Pew Research Center for the People and the Press that showed 54 percent of those questioned believed that George W. Bush "has relied on family connections to get ahead." That was by far the strongest perception, positive or negative, that applied to either candidate during the election.

The race between Bush and Gore, it was clear to all concerned, was going to be close. From the beginning both parties saw problems in Florida. A high turnout of black voters worried the GOP, because they knew that Jeb's abolishing the state's affirmative-action programs had made him no friends in the African American community.

In September, Jeb, whose positive poll ratings were over 60 percent in the state, met with Florida's Republican leaders. "Please, I'm begging you," he joked. "Don't make me go home to Kennebunkport at Thanksgiving having not carried Florida." He campaigned with George whenever he was in the state, but Jeb toned himself down considerably, because he worried about appearing brighter and more articulate. When George left the state, Jeb did not make speeches for him. He would not go on network talk shows, and he turned down all interview requests from national publications. He did not support his brother as prominently as other Republican governors like John Engler of Michigan, Tommy Thompson of Wisconsin, and Tom Ridge of Pennsylvania. The media noticed.

"Listen, I'm busting my hump," Jeb said, stung by criticism that he was not doing enough. "I've raised a lot of money; I've campaigned when my brother has come to the state . . . I have a different relationship . . . I'm his brother, so I have to be a bit more careful about how I help. Because of the comparisons that might not help George in some cases."

When Al Gore started leading in the polls, the Bush family hit Florida with full force. The former President, who had won the state in 1988 and 1992, exhorted Republicans to support "my boy because he will restore honor and dignity to the White House." Laura Bush read to elementary-school students; Jeb's handsome son, George P. Bush, spoke Spanish to Miami's Hispanics; Columba Bush promoted arts projects in Fort Lauderdale; Barbara Bush visited senior-citizen centers; and George W. Bush promised Cuban exiles that as President he would never lift the sanctions against Fidel Castro until Cuba was free.

The day before the election Bush flew to Bentonville, Arkansas, confident he could humiliate the President by winning his state. When he did, he told his cheering supporters, "They misunderestimated me."

On Election Day, November 7, 2000, the country looked toward Florida as the deciding state for the White House. At 8:00 p.m. the networks called the state for Vice President Gore; by 2:20 a.m. they had reversed themselves for Bush. The Vice President called the governor to concede, only to call back and retract his concession when he found out how close the vote was. Out of 6 million votes cast, the differential was 6,000 votes, and Florida law required a recount for any margin of less than a half percent. By 6:00 a.m. the difference was down to 1,784 votes. Weeks later, the final difference was 537 votes. The official Florida tally was 2,912,790 votes for Bush, 2,912,253 votes for Gore.

All of the canvassing boards in Florida's sixty-seven counties were required by state law to order a recount of the votes cast. What followed was a bewildering procedure that dragged on for thirty-five days as the nation sat on the edge of its seat, breathlessly waiting to see who would become the next President of the United States. Bush immediately assumed the role by publicly setting up a transition office and meeting with staff to discuss the new administration. The family dispatched its consigliere James A. Baker III to Florida to oversee the recount, to insist on counting the overseas military ballots, and to get the votes from the Democratic precincts discarded. Former Secretary of State Warren Christopher tried to fulfill the same role for the Democrats, but he was overmatched by the stealth of Baker, who kept repeating for television cameras, "The vote in Florida was counted . . . The vote in Florida has been recounted . . ." The Democrats never challenged the premise, although it was not true.

Lawyers swarmed into the state from both parties to protect their candidate's rights during the tumultuous process of machine and manual recounts for which the state was ill prepared. Lawsuits flew back and forth as the parties lodged legal challenges against each other, and the nation became embroiled in a numbing discourse on chads—the minuscule squares of paper on punch-out votes. There were descended chads, those that had been properly punched out; dimpled chads, which had been slightly punched; and hanging chads, which had been punched halfway. Weeks later Bush would joke about appointing his brother Governor Jeb Bush of Florida the Ambassador to Chad.

Two weeks into the process, the recount in Miami-Dade, where Al Gore had received a majority of the votes, was shut down by a GOP demonstration that threatened mayhem. In Washington, Doro Bush, disguised in a scarf and dark glasses, joined two hundred protesters to picket the Vice President's mansion, screaming insults. She called her mother that night and said that standing on Massachusetts Avenue shouting at the Gores took care of a lot of her frustrations. The partisan free-for-all in Florida had ignited tempers across the country. The Florida state supreme court had ruled that manual recounts could go forward, but Baker shrewdly appealed the decision to the U.S. Supreme Court. The next day Bush's running mate, Dick Cheney, suffered a heart attack and had to be hospitalized for emergency surgery. Bush appeared on television and denied that Cheney had had a heart attack. He said it was "just a scare." Reporters noticed he was sporting an angry red boil near his eye and they asked if the festering sore was from stress. "Hell, no," Bush snapped.

On December 12, 2000, the U.S. Supreme Court, by a vote of 5–4, stopped the Florida recount, overturning the December 8 decision of the Florida Supreme Court. The majority consisted of five conservative justices, all Republican appointees: William Rehnquist (Nixon); Antonin Scalia (Reagan); Clarence Thomas (George H.W. Bush); Anthony Kennedy (Reagan); Sandra Day O'Connor (Reagan). The minority included Stephen Breyer (Clinton); David Souter (George H.W. Bush);

Ruth Ginsburg (Clinton); John Paul Stevens (Ford). The headline in *The New York Times*:

BUSH PREVAILS

BY SINGLE VOTE, JUSTICES END RECOUNT,

BLOCKING GORE AFTER 5-WEEK STRUGGLE

The final tally showed:

ELECTORAL VOTES

George W. Bush	271
Al Gore	267

NATIONAL POPULAR VOTE

Al Gore	50,996,582
George W. Bush	50,456,062

A fractured Court and a splintered nation awaited the Vice President's concession. The next day, despite winning the popular vote by 540,520 votes, Al Gore ended the national nightmare with the best speech of his political career.

"Just moments ago, I spoke with George W. Bush and congratulated him on becoming the 43rd president of the United States, and I promised him that I wouldn't call him back this time," said the Vice President in his televised address. He quoted Senator Stephen Douglas in his loss to Abraham Lincoln. "Partisan feeling must yield to patriotism. I'm with you, Mr. President, and God bless you." While strongly disagreeing with the decision of the U.S. Supreme Court, the Vice President gracefully accepted the outcome and conceded the election for the sake of national unity.

After the Electoral College certified him as President-elect, George W. Bush resigned as governor of Texas. In a bar near the Austin capitol several legislators hoisted a glass. "Here's to our post turtle," one said. A tourist asked what a post turtle was. The legislator said: "When you're driving down a country road in Texas and you come across a fence post with a turtle balanced on top, that's a post turtle." The tourist looked puzzled. The legislator explained: "You know he didn't get there by himself, he doesn't belong there, he can't get anything done while he's up there, and you just want to help the poor stupid critter get down." They all gulped their drinks.

Later a crowd gathered outside the governor's mansion, where one protester held up a sign: "His Fraudulency."

CHAPTER TWENTY-SIX

For years George Herbert Walker Bush has acted indignant if anyone describes his family as a political dynasty. "That's a bad word you've used," he told a reporter from *Time*, wagging his finger. "Almost taboo . . . I don't like that word 'dynasty' as it relates to the Bushes. Dynasty seems to me to have the connotation of something other than individual achievement."

By the time his son became President, the father's protestations had begun to sound disingenuous. Perhaps he did not want to admit that dynasties have been a fact of life from the time of Moses to Alexander the Great's conquest of Egypt.

Sovereignty, dominion, and lordship had devolved through the ages from the kaisers of Germany, the shahs of Persia, the maharajas of India, the tsars of Russia, China's Great Moguls, Egypt's pharaohs, and the mikados of Japan to a familial line of kings and queens in Britain, Greece, Denmark, Sweden, and Norway.

By the time the word "dynasty" made its way into democracy, the definition had been stripped of its monarchical trappings. The Founding Fathers were adamant when they framed the Constitution: "No title of nobility shall be granted by the United States." Shorn of its crowns and coronets, the word still held allure, and the concept of looking up to a prominent family for leadership became an immediate and accepted verity in America. Dynasties were especially potent in colonial politics: the Winthrops of New England, the Lees of Virginia, the Frelinghuysens of New Jersey, the Carrolls of Maryland, and the Adamses of Massachusetts.

From the beginning, people who believed that all men were created equal also accepted that some men were born more equal than others. Those so fortunate were not only spared resentment at the ballot box but were also frequently rewarded. In a land of opportunity where the electorate yearns to be rich and important, people vote their aspirations. Robert Perrucci, a sociologist at Purdue University, explains this attitude by saying, "People accept inequality if they think there is opportunity." In politics, a dynasty proves to be a positive, not a pejorative.

In 1966, Stephen Hess, a historian with the Brookings Institution, wrote an incisive study of American political dynasties. He defined a dynasty as "any family that has had at least four members, in the same name, elected to federal office." Hess found twenty-two families that qualified under his definition, and he scrutinized fourteen of them in his book *America's Political Dynasties from Adams to Kennedy*. He found that the majority of political dynasties shared certain characteristics: they were well-to-do white Anglo-Saxon Protestants from the Eastern Seaboard with Ivy League educations and advanced degrees in law. Many traced their wealth to advantageous marriages, a few to the grand vision and driving ambition of one self-made man. Some dynasties were highly mobile; others were defined by region. Yet for all the advantages, none escaped its share of insanity, suicide, alcoholism, mental retardation, financial reverses, acts of embezzlement, and sexual scandals.

Since Hess published his book, numerous families have watched their sons and daughters become governors and take their place in the House of Representatives and the Senate. But none has risen as far and as fast as the Bushes. Despite their loud disavowals, they have come to epitomize the American political dynasty. By the year 2000, they had taken an exclusive place in history with the Adamses—the only other family with a father and a son elected President of the United States.

Although Americans are not constitutionally inclined to support royalty, they have historically gravitated to political dynasties like the Roosevelts, the Tafts, the Rockefellers, the Kennedys, and now the Bushes. These dynastic politicians, who have been described as "Democracy's Dukes" and "Princes of Populism," launch their campaigns with a phalanx of relatives, which invigorates the political process as voters identify with the family's trials and triumphs. No institution is more highly prized and praised in our country than the family. People can become so seduced by the image of a good, solid family that they will overlook transgressions that might not be so readily forgiven in someone else, the rationale being "He can't be all that bad, because he comes from such a good family," or "His mother is terrific," or "I so admired his grandfather." As the Pulitzer Prize–winning historian David McCullough said, "If you thought George Bush was just wonderful, you think it's great that his son is coming along. You hope that he'll be as good or maybe even better than his father.

"I think one thing people love about the Bushes is that against all the modern-day odds, they look like this huge happy family that gets together all the time . . . If you're a president who is trying to make a connection with people, the fact that you're at the center of that kind of family goes a long way."

If the foundation of a dynasty is its image as a good, solid family, then its binding elements are marriages that defy divorce or scandal. Frequently, a dynasty draws its strength from merger, or intermarriage between two strong families—the Aldriches and the Rockefellers, the Fitzgeralds and the Kennedys, the Walkers and the Bushes. Here, the dynamic of extended families works to propel the family name into high political office and becomes practically unbeatable.

A dynasty's heaviest burden is carried by its women—the mothers, who produce the progeny and make the presidents. These wives must be as indomitable as the ambitious men they marry. In that sense, Abigail Adams shares much in common with Dorothy Walker Bush. Both sturdy, independent women of intelligence, they were gifted writers with no college educations who did not hesitate to express themselves. Both religious, they cherished their marriages, shared their husbands' careers, and produced sons who adored them.

History shows that most presidents are beloved by their mothers and that these mama's boys grow up having what Freud called "the feeling of a conqueror, that confidence of success that often induces real success."

No political dynasty can survive without strong and enduring mothers like Abigail Adams, Sara Delano Roosevelt, Rose Fitzgerald Kennedy, and Dorothy Walker Bush. It's the women who give such families their ballast and longevity. For a dynasty to survive and thrive, the mothers, daughters, sisters, and wives must be warriors, as tough and battle-tested as the fathers, sons, brothers, and husbands.

Within the Bush family, it's the women, not the men, who elevate the lineage. After studying the bloodlines of American presidents, Gary Boyd Roberts of the New England Historic Genealogical Society found that the Bush men are far less important than the women they marry. "The Bushes' line of royal descent is traced through the females, not the males, as is the family's *Mayflower* lines," he said. He found the Bushes are even "kin of kin" of Pocahontas, the Native American princess: she's said to have saved the life of Captain John Smith by holding his head in her arms to prevent her father's warriors from clubbing him to death.

George Herbert Walker Bush seemed to finally accept his family's place in history when he threw open the doors of his presidential library in College Station, Texas, on March 11, 2002, to an exhibit on the American political dynasty. The display was organized with his blessing, and the highlight of the exposition, titled Fathers and Sons: Two Families, Four Presidents, focused on the dynasties of the Adamses and the Bushes.

The two presidential families span the history of America: John Adams, the second President, was inaugurated in the eighteenth century; his son John Quincy Adams became President in the nineteenth century. The elder Bush assumed the presidency in the twentieth century, and his son George Walker Bush was the first President inaugurated in the twenty-first century.

The dynastic similarities between the Adams family and the Bush family are slight, but those that exist are basic to their political success.

John Adams grew up on a farm in Braintree, Massachusetts, milking cows. George Herbert Walker Bush grew up in Greenwich, Connecticut, playing tennis. Both New Englanders were well educated—Adams went to Harvard, Bush went to Yale—and both shared a respect for writing letters. Several pieces of correspondence in the exhibit at College Station contrasted Adams's elegant cursive with Bush's jerky left-handed scrawl. Adams, a voracious reader, devoured books and studied in Latin and Greek. Bush earned a Phi Beta Kappa key after three years of college, although he read little as an adult. Each man carried the title Ambassador, and each served eight years as Vice President under a beloved President.

Adams chafed at the ceremonial role he had to play for George Washington, but George Bush relished standing in for Ronald Reagan.

As president of the Senate, John Adams frequently lectured the legislators on their responsibilities; in the same position, George H.W. Bush backslapped his way through the corridors of power, eager to be liked and loath to offend.

Both men became President, but when running for reelection, each suffered a crushing defeat. Historians judged both harshly, pronouncing their presidencies failures. Both fathers lived to see their firstborn sons become President, albeit amid extraordinary controversies. John Quincy Adams and George Walker Bush each won the White House while losing the popular vote. Adams's presidency had to be decided by the House of Representatives; Bush's by the Supreme Court. Both men defeated challengers from Tennessee.

David McCullough described John Quincy Adams as "the most intelligent man ever to occupy the Oval Office." Q., as his father called him, was a child prodigy. He traveled to Europe at the age of ten, learned to speak several languages, including fluent French, wrote the Monroe Doctrine, and served as Secretary of State.

Boston University's presidential historian Robert Dallek pronounced W., as George Walker Bush is called, "the stupidest man ever to sit in the Oval Office." A mediocre student, young Bush sailed into Yale on the legacy coattails of his father, his grandfather, his great-great-grandfather, his five uncles, his seven great-uncles, and his five great-great-uncles. Until he became President at the age of fifty-four, W. had never traveled to Europe. As governor of Texas for five years, he learned Spanish *por la calle* (by the street) and dismissed as effete anyone who spoke fluent French.

Despite their many differences, the Adams and Bush families share one dominant characteristic that defines their success. Both are anchored by strong marriages, which enable each to be admired as a good family. Nothing sustains political success more than the image of a good, moral, and happy family—it is a dynasty's pearl and most potent appeal. The electorate is reassured by the picture of supportive parents, hearty children, and scampering grandchildren. The image of a good family is embraced by voters as worthy of admiration and automatically imbues a candidate with the characteristics necessary for leadership.

"What matters is family and I can't emphasize that enough," George Herbert Walker Bush has said on numerous occasions. "Family and faith and friends . . ." To his supporters, the elder Bush embodies the American ideal of a good family man. People bask in the glow of his public image as a faithful husband and faultless father; people want to believe that he and his family have achieved their prominence in American life not because they have spun a shadowy web of oil and money and influence that they sustained through four generations with political muscle but because, as the Bushes have said so often about themselves, they cherish their children, they practice their religion, and they encourage public service. Most important, they exemplify good values.

The politicians in the family—George Herbert Walker Bush and his two sons George and Jeb—have accepted the need for a good family image as an undeniable fact of life. This accounts, in part, for the deceptions of each in presenting his marriage to the electorate as a solid partnership. At various points in their political careers, all three men proclaimed themselves ideal husbands who had been faithful to their wives. Those who knew differently kept a discreet silence, which enabled the Bushes to advance politically and present their dynasty as a moral bulwark.

Still, the word "dynasty" continues to annoy the elder Bush. Even surrounded by dynastic artifacts at his presidential library, he railed against "all this legacy crud" and "dynasty crap." He appeared to be insulted by the unfair advantage implied by the words, especially the sense of entitlement.

"No legacy," he insisted. "No feeling of 'This is a generational thing, we must pass the torch.' No feeling like now the mantle must fall on our grandson George P. Bush." The subject of his grandson—the eldest child of Jeb and Columba Bush—had not been raised, but the former President offered his unsolicited assessment of the young man: "He's a very attractive kid."

Years before, in an unguarded moment, George H.W. Bush had bragged about the dynastic potential of his children over that of the Kennedys. "Just wait until my boys get out there," he said. His mother was appalled by his boastfulness and pounced on him for sounding like "the great I am." Dorothy Walker Bush reminded her adult son that she had not raised him to be a braggart. Abruptly chastened, George deflected any and all comparisons to the Kennedys.

"We're not like them," he told *The New York Times* on January 31, 2000. "We don't do press about everything, and we certainly don't see ourselves as a dynasty. 'D' and 'L'—those words, dynasty and legacy—irritate me. We don't feel entitled to anything."

His son sang the same song. "I don't hate the word dynasty, but it's not really true," George W. Bush told *Time* magazine when he was running for President and his brother Jeb was running for governor of Florida. "Dynasty means something inherited . . . Both Jeb and I know you don't inherit a vote. You have to win a vote. We inherited a good name, but you don't inherit a vote."

Their father had spent his political life trying to camouflage his country-club roots. He had traded tasseled loafers for cowboy boots when he moved from Connecticut to Texas, but it was always a tight squeeze. Figuratively, he could not drop Greenwich lockjaw for a folksy Texas drawl. Now, in 2001, at the age of seventy-seven, with one son in the White House and another the governor of Florida, the former President, whose father had been a U.S. senator, sounded ridiculous as he protested against the word "dynasty." His friends said he was understandably proud of the political success his family had achieved but he was afraid to admit it for fear he might sound arrogant. He had always grappled with the contradictions of being an elitist while trying to look like a man of the people.

Privately, the former President could not hide his delight over the historical connection between the Bushes and the Adamses. When the younger Bush became President, the elder Bush teasingly called him "Quincy." But only within the family. George W. Bush acknowledged his unique position when he hung an imposing portrait of John Quincy Adams in the small dining room off the Oval Office. He later signed a bill to authorize building a memorial on federal land in Washington, D.C., to honor John Adams and his family, which by extension would honor George Bush and his family.

In the summer of 2001 the former President played golf with his son. Both wore baseball caps—one marked "41," the other "43." The following year on the golf course, "43" appeared in a cap that said "El Jefe." By then the dynamic between father and son had changed, and their conflicted relationship was being played out on the international stage with consequences that reached far beyond their own world.

———

Supporters of the former President felt reassured in 2001 as they saw the inexperienced new President surround himself with veterans of his father's administration. The elder Bush had driven his son's decision to choose Richard B. Cheney as Vice President; Cheney had served Bush 41 as Secretary of Defense. The former President also pushed for Colin Powell to be his son's Secretary of Defense. Powell had served the former President as National Security Adviser and chairman of the Joint Chiefs of Staff. But the presidency of Bush 43 was not to be a reprise of Bush 41.

The new President assumed office determined not to repeat his father's mistakes. Unlike the former President, George W. said his first priority was to protect his political base. And that's exactly what he did. Despite his campaign oratory, his core supporters were not "compassionate conservatives." George W. knew that it was the radicalized right who looked upon him as a warrior. So within forty-eight hours of his inaugural, he issued an executive order banning U.S. government aid to international family-planning groups that perform abortions or provide abortion counseling. He also signed a bill requiring that a fetus that showed signs of life following an abortion procedure be considered a person under federal law. He later signed a law prohibiting partial-birth abortion. The measure, which had been vetoed twice by Clinton, was the most significant restriction on abortion rights in years. Federal judges in Nebraska, San Francisco, and New York ruled that the law was unconstitutional, but the President did not care. He had accommodated his evangelical base. His Attorney General, John Ashcroft, another evangelical, announced that to defend the Partial Birth Abortion Ban Act, the Justice Department would subpoena patients' records when doctors sued and argued that the law interfered with necessary life-saving procedures.

By defining a fetus as a person, the President had forced himself into taking a hard line against providing federal funds for embryonic-stem-cell research. His decision will hamper scientific research for decades. Embryonic cells, which give rise to all types of specialized cells in the human body, are said by scientists to hold great promise for the potential treatment of diseases like Alzheimer's, Parkinson's, and juvenile diabetes. But people who oppose abortion abhor the research because the embryo is destroyed in the process of extracting the stem cells.

Former First Lady Nancy Reagan, tending her husband, who was dying of Alzheimer's, urged the President to back stem-cell studies. Instead, he restricted federal funding to only sixty stem-cell lines already in existence. He felt his compromised decision was the perfect political—if not moral—solution. He had satisfied his anti-abortion supporters while giving something to those in his own party who wanted the federal government to advance rather than hinder research into debilitating diseases.

He had alienated Nancy Reagan forever. Ron Reagan Jr. said his mother felt estranged from the Republican Party over the President's opposition to embryonic-stem-cell research. "She distrusts some of these [Bush] people. She gets that they're trouble in all kinds of ways. She doesn't like their religious fervor, their aggression," he said. "Now, ignorance is one thing, ignorance can be cured. But many of the Republican leaders opposing this research know better, people like [Senate Majority Leader] Bill Frist, who's a doctor, for God's sake. People like him are blocking it to pander to the 20 percent of their base who are mouth-breathers. And that's unconscionable—there are lives at stake here. Stem-cell research can revolutionize medicine more than anything since antibiotics."

The new President was not afraid of controversy. Three days into office, he stepped over the constitutional line separating church and state by announcing his intention to make federal funds available to faith-based groups that provided social services. He said, "A compassionate society is one that recognizes the great power of faith." Over $1.1 billion was disbursed by the Bush administration to Christian groups. No Jews or Muslims received funds. The President put no accounting procedures into his faith-based grants, which meant there were no guidelines or restrictions on how the money was to be spent. As a result, the funds rarely reached those who most needed help. Over time W.'s "faith-based initiative" came to look exactly like what it was: a political payoff to church groups to keep them voting Republican.

Bush 43 used the presidency of Bush 41 as a template for what *not* to do. His father had paid no attention to his reelection campaign until it was too late. George W. started running for reelection at the time he took office, and by 2004 he had raised over $200 million to run against Senator John Kerry. Having determined that his father's worst mistake was to raise taxes after promising not to, George W. decided to cut taxes. In the first year he initiated a series of cuts worth $1.35 trillion. When critics closely examined the plan and pointed out that only the wealthiest 1 percent of taxpayers would divvy up 28 percent of the windfall while the poorest 60 percent would split only 8 percent of the benefits, Bush accused them of engaging in "class warfare." The Princeton economist Paul Krugman wrote in *The New York Times* that the nation could not possibly afford these tax cuts if the Bush administration was to keep its promises in such areas as education, health care, and military defense. The *Financial Times* looked at the Bush tax bill and declared, "The lunatics are now in charge of the asylum."

As a presidential candidate, Governor Bush had initiated what he called a "charm offensive" toward the press; as President, he was charmless and defensive. He refused to read newspapers, other than box scores and headlines. "I'm more interested in news [than opinions]," he told Brit Hume of Fox News, "and the best way to get the news is from objective sources. And the most objective sources I have are people on my staff who tell me what's happening in the world."

Even as President, George W. evinced a lifelong pattern: he was not someone who wished to educate himself about life's issues. He wanted only to have his uninformed opinions and beliefs supported and confirmed. This lack of intellectual curiosity combined with dynastic arrogance was to have life-and-death consequences later in his presidency.

Historians especially were appalled by the President's lack of knowledge and his resistance to learning. At a symposium in Raleigh, North Carolina, in 2002, Robert Dallek was seen in conversation with David Herbert Donald. "George W. is the worst President since Warren G. Harding," said Dallek.

The eminent Pulitzer Prize–winning historian shook his head. "Oh, no, Bob," said Donald. "He's the worst since Franklin Pierce."

Neither historian connected the alcoholic, one-term Pierce, fourteenth President of the United States, to George W. Bush, whose mother, Barbara Pierce Bush, was a fourth cousin four times removed.

The President decided early on that press conferences were a waste of his time. He said they served only to let reporters "peacock" (his term for upstaging him on national television) and "play gotcha." During four years, he held only 12 solo press conferences. In the same period of time, his father held 141. As President, George Herbert Walker Bush had cared too much about courting the press; his son did not care at all. W. had never liked reporters. Dealing with the press as his father's enforcer, he frequently responded to their questions by saying, "No comment, ass-hole."

As President, when he does meet with reporters, he is carefully scripted. White House correspondents are asked to submit their questions in advance; the press secretary selects a few, and only those reporters are called on during the press conference. As he plunged the country into war with Iraq, the President demanded that his administration speak with one voice—his. He warned that anyone leaking would be fired. The press was given little access to the White House or the Pentagon. Still, the President was not pleased with the coverage his war received. He complained that it was too negative. "We're making good progress in Iraq," he said in October 2003. "Sometimes it's hard to tell it when you listen to the filter." The "filter" was the national news media, which the President ignored in favor of giving interviews to regional broadcasters. That year he gave no one-on-one interview to any major U.S. newspaper. Instead, he spoke only to *The Sun*, the biggest-selling newspaper in Britain. Roxanne Roberts of *The Washington Post* summed up the Bush administration's attitude toward the press: "They regard us as mosquitoes at a nudist convention. Respect? You must be joking."

The President prohibited any press coverage of the flag-draped coffins being flown back from Iraq, lest people be reminded of the terrible cost of his war. His attitude, reflecting his family's dynastic arrogance, was: "Trust me. I know what's right."

Bush 41 had been so excited when he finally became President in 1989 that for weeks after his inauguration, he greeted tourists at the White House gates. Housekeepers in the family residence fondly recall his bounding around like a friendly Labrador and inviting friends to watch movies, swim, bowl, and play tennis, after which he led them all on personal tours. In contrast, his less gregarious son was like a corgi, a nasty little nipper with a menacing bark. The father, who loved socializing, held twenty-nine state dinners. The son, who insisted on going to bed at 9:30 p.m., has held only four state dinners.

The differences between father and son as President are as marked as the differences between their wives. Barbara Bush was an activist First Lady who enjoyed the limelight as much as her husband. She sought a high profile through her activities on behalf of literacy and courted press coverage for herself by inviting select reporters to private luncheons in the White House family quarters. She also wrote a book in her dog's name, which she promoted widely on television.

More reserved than her formidable mother-in-law, Laura Bush has preferred a lower profile, especially in the wake of her controversial predecessor, Hillary Rodham Clinton. From 2001 to 2004, Laura lent her name to many good causes but gave the country very little sense of who she was, other than a former school librarian who liked to read. Her friends hinted that her political views were "much more liberal" than her husband's, especially on abortion—she was pro-choice—so she avoided speaking out on issues and remained on the periphery of his presidency rather than in its hot center.

The differences between the mother-in-law and the daughter-in-law became pronounced when both first ladies were asked to deliver commencement addresses. Students protested in each instance. At Wellesley, they said Barbara Bush was nothing more than "the college dropout wife" of the President; at UCLA, they objected to Laura Bush's "shallow credentials," saying she had "no merit [beyond] her political celebrity." Unfazed, Barbara bulldozed her way to Wellesley in 1990 and delivered her speech. Laura responded to the protesters in 2002 by declining the invitation from UCLA.

"Laura is a very nice woman who's got a lot of problems and smokes constantly," said a Washington, D.C., interior designer who knows her well. "She spends a great deal of time shopping."

"Everyone likes Laura," said a family friend who knew W. before he was married, "and everyone feels she's good influence on him, but if you're asking, 'Is their marriage a great love affair or some grand passion or whatever it was with the Reagans and the Carters and the Fords,' I'd have to say no, but it's a marriage that works, only because she does all the work . . . He can be quite impossible."

Illustrating what was meant by "impossible," the family friend related W.'s description of meeting Vladimir Putin, the President of Russia. "George said, 'I told Putin that in this country we own our own homes and because we own them we take great pride in them.' Then he told me, 'I don't think the son of a bitch knew what the hell I was talking about.'

"I was speechless," said the friend. "George acted like Putin was the dumb hayseed know-nothing and he, George, was the man of the world. I guess it never occurred to him that Putin, former head of the KGB, had been briefed to the gills on American capitalism . . . It was scary listening to the President of the United States sound so damn stupid and arrogant. I was dumbfounded that George had lectured the President of Russia like a first grader on the basics of home ownership in America . . . I've known George for many, many years, and I've watched him grow more arrogant . . .

"He has no humility whatsoever about being President. He really thinks he deserves the office, that it's his by merit, not default. There's no sense that he's lucky to be there and that if not for a partisan vote by the Supreme Court, he'd still be pumping iron in the governor's mansion in Austin . . . With each job he's gotten worse, more arrogant. Now he's unbearable. But Laura is terrific. Very down-to-earth."

Linden von Eichel, a Canadian who lives in Washington, D.C., met the First Lady at a black-tie dinner at the Library of Congress shortly after Laura returned from Paris, where she had attended ceremonies marking the U.S. return to UNESCO. Traveling without the President, the First Lady had made front-page news when France's President Jacques Chirac kissed her hand.

"Maybe it was because she knew her husband was flirting a little too aggressively that evening," said von Eichel, "but when I met her, she looked like a cardboard cutout with a rictus grin and a glassy-eyed stare. Her face, which looks so pleasant from a distance, up close looked like a Stepford-wife mask, and her handshake . . . well . . . have you ever touched dry ice? But as I say, her husband was coming on strong to my friend [Mrs. John Kluge, the wife of Metromedia's chairman] and also hitting on me . . . Laura reacted like the classic wife of an alcoholic—the police person who is constantly watching and waiting for her husband to screw up."

The First Lady had opened the National Book Festival gala that evening by sharing a poem she said her husband had written to her. "President Bush is a great leader and husband, but I bet you didn't know he is also quite the poet. Upon returning home last night from my long trip, I found a lovely poem waiting for me. Normally, I wouldn't share something so personal, but since we're celebrating great writers, I can't resist." She then read:

Dear Laura,
Roses are red
Violets are blue
Oh, my lump-in-the-bed
How I've missed you.
Roses are redder
Bluer am I
Seeing you kissed by that charming French guy.
The dogs and the cat, they missed you too
Barney's still mad you dropped him, he ate your shoe
The distance, my dear, has been such a barrier
Next time you want an adventure, just land on a carrier.

At the end of the evening, the Kluges said good night to the First Lady, and the President made another beeline for von Eichel.

"That was a pretty funny poem you wrote," she said.

"Ha! Never heard the damn thing before tonight!" said the President. "Didn't write a word of it."

The First Lady admitted a few weeks later on NBC's *Meet the Press* that her husband did not write the poem she read that evening. She did not say who did, or why she had presented it as his, but she left the impression that someone with a sense of public relations might have been trying to make the Bushes' marriage appear more affectionate. "Some woman from across the table said, 'You just don't know how great it is to have a husband who would write a poem for you,'" Laura told Tim Russert.

The family friend who described the Bushes' marriage as workable, thanks to Laura, purposely did not address the issue of the Bushes' indulged twins, Barbara and Jenna. Barbara, who went to Yale, heard much more criticism of her father and his policies at college than Jenna, who went to the University of Texas.

"There is plenty that the Bushes don't ask their daughters to do, that much is clear," Ann Gerhart wrote in her biography of Laura Bush, *The Perfect Wife*. "Jenna and Barbara have not been asked to campaign. They have not been asked to rein in their adolescent rebellions. They have not been asked to appear even nominally interested in any of the pressing issues affecting this world their generation will inhabit . . . These girls have all the *noblesse* with none of the *oblige*."

The girls' various arrests for underage drinking during their father's presidency seemed to mirror their parents' past behavior with alcohol and drugs. One observer quoted Euripides to remind the President that "the gods visit the sins of the fathers upon the children." Pictures of Jenna Bush drunk with a cigarette in her hand and rolling on the floor on top of another woman appeared in a supermarket tabloid. Cited twice for trying to use a false ID to drink, Jenna was fined six hundred dollars and ordered to perform thirty-six hours of community service and to attend sessions where victims of alcohol-related crimes talk. After two convictions, she was put on probation for three months. Soon T-shirts sprouted on campuses around the country with huge letters asking: "WWJD? What Would Jenna Drink?"

Jenna's twin compiled a similar record of misdemeanors. Photos of Barbara dancing suggestively in nightclubs, where she was reported to be partying late into the night in "pot-clouded" rooms, appeared in New York newspapers. Barbara, too, made it into the supermarket tabloids. She was arrested with her sister for using a false ID to buy alcohol in Austin, Texas. She was caught a second time in a bar in New Haven. Both girls made the cover of *People*: "Oops! They Did It Again." Barbara pleaded "no contest," and was ordered to pay a hundred-dollar fine, perform eight hours of community service, and attend six hours of alcohol-awareness class.

As the President coped with the police-blotter publicity of his two daughters, his brother Jeb was dealing with a similar situation in Florida. The governor's daughter, Noelle, was arrested in Tallahassee in January 2002 for trying to fill a false prescription for the anti-anxiety drug Xanax. She was sent to a drug-rehabilitation program in Orlando. Six months later she was jailed for three days in Florida's Orange County Correctional Center for violating the rules of her drug-treatment program. She reportedly had stolen pills from the nurse's office at the rehab center. Her father e-mailed the state's political reporters:

> My family is saddened to share that our daughter Noelle has not abided by the conditions of her drug treatment plan. Unfortunately, this happens to many individuals even as they continue their journey to full recovery. There are consequences for every action we take in our lives, and as her parents, Columba and I wish

we could have prevented our daughter from making the wrong choices.

After her jail time, Noelle returned to the rehab center. On September 9, 2002, one of the rehab patients called 911 to report that staffers had found crack cocaine in Noelle's shoe.

"She does this all the time, and she gets out of it because she's the governor's daughter," the caller told the police. "But we're sick of it here, 'cause we have to do what's right, but she gets treated like some kind of princess . . . We're just trying to get our lives together, and this girl's bringing drugs on [the] property."

Six police cars arrived at the center to investigate the complaint. The staff admitted finding the drug on Noelle but refused to cooperate with the police, and the employee who made the discovery ripped up her written statement to protect Noelle and uphold the center's confidentiality policy. No charges were filed, but a judge sent the governor's daughter to jail for ten days for violating the terms of her treatment.

Jeb and Columba did not appear in court with their daughter. "I just can't believe that they weren't there for Noelle," said Sharon Bush. "My kids are my life, and I know I would be at their side in a courtroom if they were in trouble, no matter how politically embarrassing it might be . . . My former in-laws think it's shameful about all the arrests of George's daughters and Jeb's daughter because it hurts the family's image, . . . but if they practiced the family values they preach all the time, they would've been in that courtroom beside Noelle . . . I feel so sorry for her. She's almost thirty years old."

On the day Noelle was sentenced, her father was raising funds in Florida with his brother George, but neither the governor nor the President appeared in court to stand beside the young woman. Noelle's brother George P. Bush was there, along with their Aunt Dorothy Bush Koch.

The public scrutiny of his family's substance abuse was only part of the new President's problems. By Labor Day 2001, he faced a deteriorating economy, a lopsided federal budget, slumping consumer confidence, and limited political capital to push through his legislative agenda. He confronted an opposition-controlled Senate with controversial proposals that included education reform, a new missile-defense system, a trade bill opposed by labor, an HMO-reform bill, a proposal to restructure Social Security, and an energy bill that contained drilling rights in wilderness areas, which pleased oilmen and angered environmentalists. His approval ratings had dropped below 50 percent, because a majority of Americans felt he was not up to the job of being President.

Then the gates of hell flew open.

At 8:45 a.m. and 9:03 a.m. on September 11, 2001, two hijacked airliners carrying twenty thousand gallons of jet fuel dove into two towers of concrete, steel, and glass in New York City. As the north and south towers of the World Trade Center collapsed in the inferno, sending 2,821 people to their deaths, a similar conflagration shook Washington, D.C.— another hijacked plane hit the west face of the Pentagon, killing 184 people. Less than thirty minutes later a fourth plane aimed for the U.S. Capitol crashed in a field in Shanksville, Pennsylvania, killing all 40 passengers on board, who had overtaken the hijackers, diverted the plane, and saved the lives of many people in the U.S. Senate and House of Representatives. At the end of the day of the worst terror attack the United States had ever endured, a shattered nation faced the loss of 3,000 lives and financial wreckage estimated to be over $27 billion.

At the time of the first attack, the President was sitting on a little wooden stool speaking to second graders at Emma E. Booker Elementary School in Sarasota, Florida. Early on he had dubbed himself "The Education President" after declaring, "The illiteracy level of our children are appalling." He sought to prove his commitment to learning by reading to seven-year-olds, which is what he was doing when his chief of staff, Andrew Card, whispered in his ear that the United States was under attack. The President continued sitting with the children for seven more minutes, reading from their textbook *My Pet Goat* and posing for the cameras. Then he moved to the school library to make a statement.

"Today we've had a national tragedy," he said. "Two airplanes have crashed into the World Trade Center in an apparent terrorist attack on our country." He said that the federal government would "conduct a full-scale investigation to hunt down and to find those folks who committed this act."

After characterizing the terrorists as "folks," the President departed and flew from Sarasota to Barksdale Air Force Base near Shreveport, Louisiana, where he got off Air Force One to make another statement: "I want to reassure the American people that the full resources of the federal government are working to assist local authorities to save lives and to help victims of those attacks. Make no mistake: The United States will hunt down and punish those responsible for these cowardly acts."

He returned to his flying bunker and headed for Offutt Air Force Base near Omaha, Nebraska. He emerged from his plane, which was now guarded by Humvees and soldiers in fatigues gripping machine guns. His motorcade passed through the security gate outside U.S. Strategic Command headquarters, but the President did not go into the command building. Instead, he entered a squared-off structure that looked like the top of an elevator shaft, where he was to receive a briefing from his National Security Council. The White House press corps was left on the plane. When the ABC News anchor Peter Jennings later asked Ann Compton where the President had gone, the White House correspondent replied, "He went down the bunny hole."

While the President was in hiding, his role as commander in chief was shouldered by New York City's Mayor Rudolph Giuliani, who rushed to survey the devastation at Ground Zero. He was on television all day and all night—informative, accessible, and spontaneously human. The death toll, he said, will be "more than we can bear." He was a constant reassuring presence to a frightened nation reeling from the attacks and the searing images of airplanes smashing into buildings and human beings leaping to their deaths to escape incineration. In the absence of presidential leadership, the President's televangelist friends Jerry Falwell and Pat Robertson stepped forward to fan fear and hatred by suggesting the bombings might be God's wrath on homosexuals, lesbians, feminists, and civil libertarians—words that George W. Bush never repudiated.

Breaking through the world's stunned disbelief was Britain's Prime Minister Tony Blair, who reinforced the special relationship between the United Kingdom and the United States by offering the comfort of comradeship. He said that Americans were not alone, that decent people of the world would join them and make common cause against terrorism.

The President's absence from Washington was psychologically jarring for the country. Presidents have always returned to the White House in times of crisis—from Abraham Lincoln during the Civil War to Lyndon Johnson after John F. Kennedy's assassination. No President had been persuaded by security concerns to avoid the U.S. capital since the British burned the White House in 1814. "President Bush made an initial mistake," the historian Robert Dallek told *USA Today*. "The President's place is back in Washington."

The next day Karl Rove, senior adviser to the President and the man frequently called "Bush's brain," read Dallek's comment in the nation's largest newspaper and telephoned the historian.

"The day after the bloodiest attack on U.S. soil and the President's special assistant is wasting his time calling me to say that the President's plane was targeted," recalled Dallek. "I told him that I was not indifferent to the President's security, but the President's place is in the nation's capital . . . I knew then Bush had no brains. Now I knew he had no guts."

Karl Rove's claim that Air Force One was the target of terrorists was not true, but presidential security was the most acceptable excuse for the Bush White House to offer to explain the President's absence from the nation's capital.

Mary McGrory wrote in *The Washington Post*: "Bush said the attack was a test for the country. It was also one for him. He flunked. But he says he believes in education and he has three years to take a makeup exam in leadership."

Overshadowed by Mayor Giuliani, eclipsed by Prime Minister Blair, and dwarfed by the enormous catastrophe, the President of the United States finally returned to the White House on September 11, 2001, at 7 p.m. He addressed the nation at 8:30 p.m., blinking nervously as he read from the teleprompter for five minutes.

"Today our nation saw evil," he said, "the very worst of human nature . . . The search is under way for those who are behind these evil acts . . . We will make no distinction between the terrorists who committed these acts and those who harbor them."

George W. Bush finally stepped into the shoes of a President three days later, September 14, 2001, when he visited Ground Zero. Climbing on top of a crushed fire truck, he draped his arm around the shoulder of the retired firefighter Bob Beckwith and started to speak.

"We can't hear you," someone yelled.

Bush picked up a bullhorn. "I can hear you," he shouted. "The rest of the world hears you! And the people who knocked these buildings down will hear all of us soon!"

At last. The Andover cheerleader had found his voice. His exhortation of strength and resolve roused the bone-weary rescue workers from the white ashes of destruction. Raising hard hats in the air, they cheered their commander in chief. "Bush, Bush, Bush!" they chanted, pumping their fists. "USA. USA. USA."

"It was a simple enough ad lib," Jonathan Alter wrote in *Newsweek*, "but you could almost watch the molecules of presidential leadership being rearranged."

The President told Lionel Chetwynd, a conservative filmmaker who wrote *DC 9/11: Time of Crisis*, that visiting Ground Zero had been visceral for him. "I was lifted up by a wave of vengeance and testosterone and anger. I could feel it." Bush said he was approached by a rescue worker, whom he quoted as saying, "I'm digging for my brother here, and I didn't vote for you, but you find the people who did this, and you take care of business, you hear me?"

The President spent that weekend at Camp David with his national security advisers. When he returned to the White House, he was focused. His mission had crystallized. "The Education President" was now "The War President." George Walker Bush saw himself as the heat-seeking missile of righteousness against "the evil ones" and "the evil doers."

His close friend Don Evans, Secretary of Commerce and a member of Bush's White House Bible group, said that the President felt he had been "called" to lead the country to war.

"This is a crusade," Bush told reporters when he returned from Camp David. The next day the White House apologized for his inept use of the word "crusade," because it suggested the medieval slaughter of thousands of innocent Arabs and Jews. The President had no regrets, and the public responded positively to his zeal and passion. He declared bluntly, "We're at war, there's been a war declared and we will find those who did it. We'll smoke them out of their holes, we'll get them running and we'll bring them to justice." He also demanded the delivery of Osama bin Laden. "We'll take him dead or alive," Bush said. Fearful the remark made him sound hotheaded, his wife gently teased, "Bushie, you gonna git 'im?" The President remained grim. He was determined to launch himself and his country on a "wave of vengeance and testosterone and anger."

Karl Rove, seizing the tragedy of 9/11 for political gain, was immediately set to catch the wave for reelection. "We can go to the country on this issue because they trust the Republican Party to do a better job of protecting and strengthening America's military might and thereby protecting America," he told the Republican National Committee. In what seemed at the time a shrewd move, he recommended the GOP hold its 2004 convention in New York City in September rather than August. The RNC began offering 9/11 commemorative photos of the President on Air Force One. The letter to potential contributors raised over $1.4 million: "Specially commissioned, individually numbered and matted, this limited edition series is yours free for serving as an honorary co-chairman of the 2002 President's Dinner with your gift of $150 or more."

When the President met with congressional leaders after 9/11, he took a direct slap at Clinton when he said, "When I take action, I'm not going to fire a $2 million missile at a $10 empty tent and hit a camel in the butt. It's going to be decisive."

Democrats and Republicans alike were impressed. "We all desperately want him to succeed," said Richard Gephardt, the Democratic Minority Leader of the House of Representatives, "and there is nothing more valuable to a president than that emotion."

Without a single dissenting vote, or even a debate, the Senate passed a resolution authorizing the President to use force. The House approved the resolution 420–1. The single holdout was Representative Barbara Lee, a Democrat from Oakland, California. She knew the resolution would pass with or without her vote, but she opposed as a matter of conscience. She quoted a clergy member who said, "As we act, let us not become the evil that we deplore." Bush's approval ratings soared to 90 percent, the highest ever recorded for a U.S. President since Gallup started polling in 1938, when Franklin D. Roosevelt was in the White House. Until George W. Bush set the record, his father, who hit 89 percent at the end of the first Gulf War, had held the previous high.

Both father and son started wars in the Persian Gulf, and both staked their reelections on the outcome. As Bush 43 prepared to attack Afghanistan, he heeded the advice of Bush 41 to build an international coalition. He began a series of seventy face-to-face meetings with foreign leaders to secure troop commitments from Britain, Germany, France, Italy, the Netherlands, Australia, Canada, the Czech Republic, New Zealand, Japan, Pakistan, and Turkey. After Afghanistan, he fully intended to attack Iraq, determined to change the balance of power in the Middle East once and for all. On September 17, 2001, W. signed a two-

and-a-half-page document marked "TOP SECRET" that outlined the plan for war in Afghanistan and also directed the Pentagon to begin planning military options for an invasion of Iraq. Three days later, during a private dinner with Britain's Prime Minister, the President asked Tony Blair to support the removal of Saddam Hussein from power. Blair, according to Sir Christopher Meyer, the former British Ambassador to Washington who also attended the dinner, told Bush he should not get distracted from the initial goal of dealing with the Taliban and Al Qaeda in Afghanistan.

"I agree with you, Tony," said the President. "We must deal with this first. But when we have dealt with Afghanistan, we must come back to Iraq."

The air strikes against Afghanistan began on October 7, 2001. The original goal, stated clearly and definitively by the President, was to capture Osama bin Laden and destroy his terrorist network. This was a war of revenge. But the goal soon had to be redefined to include replacing the Taliban government that had allowed Al Qaeda to flourish. As bin Laden continued to elude capture, Bush again reconfigured his ultimate goal to justify the tens of billions of dollars spent and the deaths of American service men and women. Then the purpose of the war became rebuilding Afghanistan so the people of that country could enjoy stability and freedom.

To that end, an Afghan coalition government was formed in December 2001, headed by Hamid Karzai, a tribal aristocrat and former Deputy Foreign Minister who had spent the Taliban years in exile in Pakistan. Three years after Karzai became head of state, a large part of Afghanistan still remained under the control of warlords and their private militias—and bin Laden had still not been captured. Farmers had started growing opium again; the practice had been banned under the Taliban, but the United States looked the other way as Afghanistan became a force in the international drug trade.

In April 2003, Secretary of Defense Donald Rumsfeld announced that he was going to meet with Karzai to discuss a date for U.S. withdrawal. In the middle of 2004, there were still twenty thousand U.S. troops in Afghanistan, up from eleven thousand the previous year. The President was not content with one ongoing war; he was obsessed with another one—bloodier and far more costly.

By the end of 2002, it was clear that the President was hell-bent on taking the country to war in Iraq. Yet he responded angrily when pressed on the subject. Speaking to reporters at his ranch in Crawford, Texas, he snapped at one who voiced the assumption.

"You said we're headed to war in Iraq. I don't know why you say that," Bush said. "I'm the person who gets to decide, not you."

Ten weeks later, on March 19, 2003, Bush announced the U.S. invasion of Iraq. Some saw it as his filial trump card: a son going off on his own to surpass his father by finishing off the elder Bush's unfinished business. By now the son had become openly critical of his father's Gulf War. As Bush 43 told Bill Sammon of *The Washington Times* about Bush 41: "Freedom will prevail so long as the United States and allies don't give the people of Iraq mixed signals . . . and that is cut and run early, like what happened in '91."

Others saw the son as the Bush family's spear-carrier, seeking revenge against a despised dictator. "After all," W. told Houston Republicans on September 26, 2003, "this is a guy that tried to kill my dad at one time."

Armchair psychiatrists called the Iraqi war "Oedipus Wrecks."

The President denied any personal animus in his drive to depose Saddam. "The fact that he tried to kill my father and my wife [Laura Bush had accompanied her father-in-law to Kuwait in 1993, when the assassination attempt was aborted] shows the nature of the man," Bush said. "He's cold-blooded. He's a dictator and he's a tyrant. The decision I'm making and have made to disarm Saddam Hussein is based on the security of the American people."

Throughout 2002, Bush built his case against Saddam to Congress and the American people, although much of it later proved to be based on lies, exaggerated intelligence, forged documents, and an insistence that the things George W. wanted to be true must be true. The President had not learned that respecting the truth distinguishes a great statesman from a mere politician. As Winston Churchill said, "Wrongs will be forgiven, sufferings and losses will be forgiven or forgotten . . . but anything like a trick will always rankle."

The President claimed unequivocally that the Iraqi regime possessed weapons of mass destruction, including a possible nuclear capability. He insisted that Saddam had the capacity to develop anthrax and nerve gas. Without proof of any kind—in fact, with proof that just the opposite was true—he linked the 9/11 attacks to Iraq. He declared Saddam a threat to international security, although Saddam had instigated no attacks outside his own borders in a decade. He asserted the U.S. right to act unilaterally and preemptively against any and all terrorist threats. He taunted the UN, saying Saddam had defied all its resolutions for ten years. He demanded total disarmament. He affirmed that a free Iraq would bring democracy to the Middle East, and he promised the Iraqis a new country of prosperity and freedom. "No more poison factories, no more executions of dissidents, no more torture chambers and rape rooms."

The President was obsessed with getting rid of Saddam and determined to make it his country's top priority. In January 2003, he told Senator Peter Fitzgerald of Illinois that if he knew where the dictator was, he would order his assassination. When their conversation became public, the White House hastily affirmed that the executive order forbidding the assassination of foreign leaders was still in place. The President did not retract his words.

By this time, he had come to see himself in the glorious mode of Winston Churchill, who had defied Hitler during World War II. Bush had asked the British embassy in Washington for a bronze bust of the wartime Prime Minister, whose soaring rhetoric had, in the words of John F. Kennedy, "mobilized the English language and sent it into battle." George W. Bush, who mangled the English language, saw Churchill as a kindred spirit. "He really kind of went after it in a way that seemed like a Texan to me," Bush said of Churchill. "He wasn't afraid of public-opinion polls. He charged ahead, and the world is better for it."

White House speechwriters stretched for Churchillian prose when the President announced the beginning of the Iraqi invasion. "We will not waver; we will not tire; we will not falter; and we will not fail," Bush said, borrowing effectively from a famous Churchill speech. The President soon felt the scourge of public opinion as antiwar demonstrations were staged around the world. Several million people took to the streets of Europe on February 15, 2003, in a vast wave of protest against the prospect of a U.S.-led invasion of Iraq. More than 750,000 filled London's Hyde Park for the largest political demonstration in British history. Nearly 1 million people turned out in Rome, and 500,000 demonstrated in Berlin at the biggest rally since the fall of the Wall. The breadth of the global opposition was staggering. From Canberra to Oslo and Cape Town to Damascus, protesters jammed their cities, waving placards that read: "Drop Bush, Not Bombs," "No Blood for Oil," "An Eye for an Eye and the Whole World Goes Blind," "Drunk Frat Boy Drives Country into Ditch."

The former President could not stand any criticism of his son. Three months after W. was sworn into office, George H.W. Bush returned to New Haven for Yale's tercentenary celebration. At the end of his remarks, he begged his audience to give the new President a chance. "He's only been in office 100 days," said the doting father. Speaking in Boston two days after the 9/11 attacks, he said he resented criticism of his son for not returning to Washington sooner. Later, as his son careened away from coalition building to waging his own war, his father again defended him. He told Paula Zahn on CNN, "I hate Saddam Hussein." The elder Bush panned those who did not support his son's war against the dictator. "I read stuff that really burns me up," he said.

The former President smarted each time he heard his son called a warmonger, and he responded as if each rebuke were personal. "They've hurt this loving, proud father very much," he told an audience in Stamford, Connecticut. He protested when the Most Reverend Frank Griswold, presiding Bishop of the U.S. Episcopal Church, said, "I'd like to be able to go somewhere and not have to apologize for being from the United States . . . I am not surprised that we are hated and loathed . . . for indifference to human suffering."

Fighting back tears, the father again sprang to his son's defense. "Should we be loathed for freeing Afghanistan? Or for taking action against a ruthless dictator who has gassed his own people and wants to acquire more deadly weapons? I know this president better than the bishop. He is a man of faith himself."

The President's father was right: W. was a man of faith, and that faith inoculated him against doubt. With absolute certainty that he was right, he announced on March 19, 2003, that he had started the war in Iraq with air strikes designed to kill Saddam and his two sons. Barbara Bush told Diane Sawyer on *Good Morning America* that she would not watch the war coverage on television because "90 percent" of it would be speculative. "Why should we hear about body bags and deaths and how many, what day it's gonna happen? It's not relevant. So why should I waste my beautiful mind on something like that?"

In addition to the United States, which sent 138,000 troops, the only countries making substantial military contributions to the war were Britain—45,000 military personnel—and Australia. Yet the State Department claimed to have forty-nine countries in its "coalition of the willing." When cable television's *The Daily Show* discovered that Morocco's contribution was two hundred monkeys enlisted to set off land mines, the satiric program called it the "coalition of the piddling." Other "coalition" partners, from Latvia to Panama to Uzbekistan, offered only statements of support.

The military conquest seemed simple and inevitable, which at that stage it was. Ground forces entered Iraq from Kuwait, followed by screeching air raids and relentless bombing. In less than a month, U.S. forces were toppling Saddam's statues throughout Baghdad as the city fell and looting broke out.

The biggest decision then facing the White House was how to feature the President claiming victory. His image makers considered putting him before a joint session of Congress or leading a ticker-tape parade through New York City. Finally they devised a dramatic scenario that would make him look more commanding than General George Patton. Their visual of Alamo macho far surpassed even Hollywood's most extravagant *Top Gun* fantasy.

In a snug-fitting olive green flight suit, the President was to take the controls of a Navy S-3B Viking jet on May 1, 2003, and make a tail-hook landing on the USS *Abraham Lincoln* in the Pacific Ocean as the aircraft carrier steamed toward San Diego. According to the orchestrated plan, George W. bounded off the jet like a heroic sky jockey, his helmet tucked under his arm; he strutted along the flight deck, posing for pictures and shaking hands with the crew. He was led to a captain's chair to watch a dazzling air show as thirty-six F-18s of the Naval Carrier Air Wing headed home from duty to their base near Fresno. Three squadrons of Hornets hurtled into the air with a deafening roar; twelve of the jets reappeared in a V formation to fly over the ship in a formal farewell. Then, like Superman, the President disappeared belowdecks to change clothes. He returned in a business suit with an American flag pinned to his lapel and mounted a podium that displayed the presidential seal. Standing under a great banner proclaiming "Mission Accomplished," he announced to five thousand cheering sailors the "end of major combat operations" in Iraq.

With that virtuoso visual, the President of the United States began playing the political equivalent of Texas Hold 'Em poker, a high-stakes game in which the winner takes all. For the next six months, he would gamble his reelection and the continuation of the Bush dynasty on his war, which he saw as visionary and courageous, against those who saw it as reckless and tragic. He was betting on capturing Osama bin Laden and finding weapons of mass destruction in Iraq. He was wagering everything against the mounting death tolls and the scandals of horrific prisoner abuse by U.S. troops. He had calculated the odds that Americans would not desert a President during wartime, even a war that was going to cost at least $200 billion and throw the country into a deficit of more than half a trillion dollars by the end of 2004.

It was a staggering gamble, but the President had no doubts that he would win. His ace in the hole was the House of Bush, which would do anything to ensure his victory and continue the family dynasty. George W. Bush acted like a man who had stacked the deck.

He was so driven to win on Iraq that he would not tolerate dissent. When other heads of state expressed disagreement with his invasion, he treated them like miscreants who deserved to be punished.

When German Chancellor Gerhard Schröder was reelected by opposing the U.S.-led invasion, Bush was incensed, partially because Schröder's Minister of Justice had compared his pressure tactics on Iraq to those of Adolf Hitler. The Justice Minister resigned the day after Schröder's narrow reelection, but Bush refused to pick up the phone and make the customary call of presidential congratulations.

When Mexican President Vicente Fox opposed the U.S. stand on Iraq in the UN Security Council, he, too, got the treatment. "There will be a certain sense of discipline," Bush warned. It sounded like the Mexican President might end up sleeping with the fishes. W. wheeled on Fox, formerly a close friend who had spent time with the Bushes at their ranch in Crawford and had been honored with the first White House state dinner of the Bush presidency. But all of that was forgotten when Fox said that Mexico could not accept Bush's resolution for regime change in Iraq because it would set a precedent that could justify U.S. invasions in any country in the world. Bush stopped speaking to his friend Vicente Fox and made him wait four days before he deigned to return his phone call. Bush's discourtesy to Mexico, the second-largest U.S. trading partner, was personal, petulant, and diplomatically destructive.

Bush canceled a state visit to Canada to show his displeasure with Prime Minister Jean Chrétien's stand against the war, and he turned his back on France when French President Jacques Chirac had opposed him. There was no U.S. participation in the Paris Air Show. The Members' Dining Room in the House of Representatives renamed French fries and started serving Freedom fries. On Air Force One, it was au revoir to French toast and good morning to Freedom toast. President Bush said it was not clear to him that France cared whether U.S. citizens lived in safety and security. With those words, he started an American boycott of all things French.

The bullyboy who played pig ball at Andover had learned to reward his friends and punish his enemies. If you cannot win on merit, you win on might and muscle, but you win—at any price. "Victory," in the words of his hero Winston Churchill, "at all costs, victory in spite of all terror; victory, however long and hard the road may be; for without victory there is no survival."

NOTES

CHAPTER 1

Records: Samuel Prescott Bush Papers, Ohio Historical Society, containing several letters from Flora Bush to Samuel Bush during the summer of 1908; a letter from Harriet Fay Bush (1829–1924), Samuel's mother, to Samuel, also in the summer of 1908; a letter from Samuel's daughter Mary (1897–1992) written to him during the summer of 1908; a letter from his daughter Margie (1899–1993) to Samuel in 1911; letters from Flora to Samuel from the 1911–13 period; five undated letters from Samuel to Flora on the stationery of the Engineers' Club in New York, one of which was written during World War I; a letter from Flora to Samuel, also written while Prescott Bush was in Europe during World War I; poem written by Samuel's daughter Margaret Bush Clement sometime in the late 1930s; a letter from Samuel Bush to his sons, Prescott and Jim, on May 14, 1940; and a letter from Martin J. Gillen to Samuel Bush, Dec. 10, 1942, in which Gillen mentions their first meeting during World War I, when both men served on the War Industries Board. Other records: certificate of Robert S. Bush's death in Milwaukee in 1900, Wisconsin Department of Health and Family Sevices; Prescott S. Bush Oral History, 1966, Columbia University Oral History Research Project, Eisenhower Administration Project; Yale yearbook *History of the Class of 1917* (1917), *Banner and Pot Pourri* (1916–17), and fiftieth-anniversary yearbook, *History of the Class of 1917* (1967), as well as notes on the Silver Dollar Quartet sent by Prescott Bush to Marshall Bartholomew in June 1957 and other documents from the Yale archives concerning Prescott Bush's activities as an alumnus, Manuscripts and Archives, Sterling Memorial Library, Yale University.

Books: Brooks Mather Kelley, *Yale: A History* (New Haven, Conn.: Yale University Press, 1974); Herbert S. Parmet, *George Bush: The Life of a Lone Star Yankee* (New York: Scribner, 1997); Alexandra Robbins, *Secrets of the Tomb* (Boston: Little, Brown, 2002); Grandview Heights/Marble Cliff Historical Society pamphlet, *1998 Tour of Homes*, May 10, 1998.

Articles: Burt Solomon, "A Pair of Dominant Grandfathers Shape a Presidential Persona," *National Journal*, Sept. 7, 1991; "Annual Elections of Senior Societies from Junior Class," *Yale Daily News*, May 19, 1916; "A Call to Undergraduates to Organize a Republican Club of Yale University," *Yale Daily News*, Oct. 6, 1916; Paul McClung, "The Secret of Geronimo's Grave," *Lawton Constitution*, Feb. 18, 1964; Ron Rosenbaum, "I Stole the Head of Prescott Bush! More Scary Skull & Bones Tales," *New York Observer*, July 17, 2000; Tim Giago, "Where Are They Hiding Geronimo's Skull?" *Lakota Nation Journal* (Winter 2000);

"High Military Honors Conferred on Capt. Bush," *Ohio State Journal*, Aug. 8, 1918; "If Prescott Had Read It in a Story-Book When He Was a Kid," cartoon, *Ohio State Journal*, Aug. 9, 1918; "Triple Honor to P. S. Bush, Yale '17," *New Haven Journal-Courier*, Aug. 15, 1918; Flora Sheldon Bush, letter to the editor, *Ohio State Journal*, Sept. 6, 1918, p. 1.

Interviews: Indiana Earl, July 17 and 20, 2001, and Aug. 14, 2001; John G. Doll, Jan. 28, 2003; Stuart Symington Jr., July 3, 2002; James Symington, July 3, 2002; Richard D. Barrett, Dec. 12, 2002; Richard Kimball Jr., Jan. 11, 2003; correspondence with Mark Salter, June 10, 2003.

CHAPTER 2

Records: 1900 U.S. Census record of George W. Walker's household, msn.ancestry.com (April 2004); deeds and plans of Walker's Point, York County Register of Deeds, Alfred, Maine; George H. Walker will, Maine Probate Court, York County; Mary (Carter) Walker Oral History Interview transcript, Greenwich Library Oral History Project, Greenwich Library, Greenwich, Conn.; Veiled Prophet records, St. Louis Public Library; files of *St. Louis Star-Times* and *St. Louis Globe-Democrat*, St. Louis Mercantile Library.

Books: Richard Ben Cramer, *What It Takes* (New York: Vintage Books, 1993); Herbert S. Parmet, *George Bush: The Life of a Lone Star Yankee* (New York: Scribner, 1997); Fitzhugh Green, *George Bush: An Intimate Portrait* (New York: Hippocrene Books, 1989); Julius K. Hunter, *Kingsbury Place: The First Two Hundred Years* (St. Louis: Mosby, 1982); Charles Van Ravenswaay, *St. Louis: An Informal History of the City and Its People, 1764–1865*, ed. Candace O'Connor (St. Louis: Missouri Historical Society Press, 1991); Albert Nelson Marquis, ed., *The Book of St. Louisans* (St. Louis: St. Louis Republic, 1912); William Hyde, *Encyclopedia of the History of St. Louis* (New York: Southern History Company, 1899); *Social Register of St. Louis* (New York: Social Register Association), for the years 1910–26.

Articles: "I'm for Lynch Law and Whipping Post; D. D. Walker Writes," *St. Louis Republican*, July 22, 1914; Jake Tapper, "Judging W's Heart," salon.com, Nov. 1, 2000; Burt Solomon, "A Pair of Dominant Grandfathers Shape a Presidential Persona," *National Journal*, Sept. 7, 1991; "Walker Verdict of 'Unsound Mind' Is Set Aside," *St. Louis Post-Dispatch*, May 13, 1918; "D. D. Walker, Sr., Dies; Founded Dry Goods Firm 40 Years Ago," *St. Louis Globe-Democrat*, Oct. 15, 1918; "D. D. Walker, Sr., Retired Merchant, Dies in East," *St. Louis Republican*, Oct. 15, 1918; "In Memoriam: George Herbert Walker," *Bulletin of the Missouri Historical Society* 10, no. 1 (Oct. 1953); "G. H. Walker & Co. Turns 65," *St. Louis Globe-Democrat*, May 25, 1965; Beth McLeod, "President's Mother Was Captain of Smooth-Sailing Family Ship," *St. Louis Post-Dispatch*, June 30, 1991; "Prophet's Court at Coronation Scene of Beauty," "Veiled Prophet's Queen from Pioneer Family," and "Riot of Color and Iridescence in Gowns Worn at V. P. Ball," *St. Louis Post-Dispatch*, Oct. 8, 1919; *Philadelphia Inquirer* coverage of the first girls' singles national tennis championship, June 19–22, 1918; "Miss Dorothy Walker Weds," *New York Herald Tribune*, Aug. 6, 1921; *New York Journal-American* account of Dorothy Walker's wedding, Aug. 1921; "Mrs. Samuel P. Bush Killed in Auto Accident in Rhode Island," *Columbus Sunday Dispatch*, Sept. 5, 1920; "Investigation Being Made into Watch Hill Accident," *Westerly Sun*, Sept. 7, 1920.

Interviews: Ann Biraben, Oct. 24, 2002; Mary Hall-Ries, Nov. 14, 2002; Robert Duffy, Nov. 13, 2002; correspondence with Robert Duffy, Feb. 21, 2003; Noel C. Holabeck, Nov. 14,

2002; Peggy Adler, Aug. 7, 2001, and Oct. 12, 2001; Christopher Walker, Feb. 10, 2003; James Symington, July 3, 2002; Stuart Symington Jr., July 3, 2002.

RE: *Dorothy Walker's Childhood Home, 12 Hortense Place, St. Louis*
"We have always felt there is a ghost in this house," said Mary Hall-Ries on November 14, 2002. "It's a friendly ghost . . . a woman who smells like violets . . . She's gentle and benign."

Mrs. Hall-Ries described the "weird but wondrous things" that have happened in the old Walker home since she and her husband, Jonathan Ries, bought it several years ago. "Things moved in different places . . . stereos went on in the ballroom at 5 a.m. . . . anytime you changed anything, the ghost would change it back."

The "Georgian, Italianate, Beaux Arts" house, built in 1901, has a sleeping porch ("no air-conditioning in those days"), a ballroom, eight bedrooms, and "a fainting room" (for women in tight corsets). "This was a house built by people who loved entertaining—open rooms for lots of people, all glass so you can see people in every room," said Hall-Ries. "Maybe the ghost is Dorothy's sister, Nancy Walker, who never married and always made her home near her parents."

CHAPTER 3

Records: Prescott S. Bush Oral History, 1966, Columbia University Oral History Research Project, Eisenhower Administration Project; George H. Walker correspondence with Averell Harriman, and other Brown Brothers Harriman business papers, W. Averell Harriman Papers, Library of Congress Manuscript Reading Room; Flora Sheldon Bush will, Franklin County Probate Court, Columbus, Ohio; information on the Bush's Greenwich homes, Greenwich, Conn., Assessor's Office and the Greenwich Town Clerk's Office; James Smith Bush FBI file obtained through Freedom of Information Act.

Books: Peter Arno, "Well, so long. I'll see you at lunch at the Bankers Club," cartoon, in *The New Yorker Twenty-fifth Anniversary Album, 1925–1950* (New York: Harper, 1951); Knight Woolley, *In Retrospect—Very Personal Memoir* (privately printed, 1975); John A. Kouwenhoven, *Partners in Banking* (Garden City, N.Y.: Doubleday, 1968, 1983); Rudy Abramson, *Spanning the Century: The Life of W. Averell Harriman* (New York: William Morrow, 1992); Gail Sheehy, *Characters* (New York: William Morrow, 1988); Herbert S. Parmet, *George Bush: The Life of a Lone Star Yankee* (New York: Scribner, 1997); Fitzhugh Green, *George Bush: An Intimate Portrait* (New York: Hippocrene Books, 1989); Nicholas King, *George Bush: A Biography* (New York: Dodd, Mead, 1980); Joe Hyams, *Flight of the Avenger* (San Diego: Harcourt Brace Jovanovich, 1991); Donnie Radcliffe, *Simply Barbara Bush* (New York: Warner Books, 1989).

Articles: Burt Solomon, "A Pair of Dominant Grandfathers Shape a Presidential Persona," *National Journal*, Sept. 7, 1991; "Big Banking Houses Decide on Merger," *New York Times*, Dec. 12, 1930; George Bush, "A Tribute to a Very Special Mother," *Greenwich Time*, May 12, 1985; Barbara T. Roessner, "Growing Up with George," *Hartford Courant*, Jan. 15, 1989; Barry Bearak, "His Great Gift, to Blend In," *Los Angeles Times*, Nov. 22, 1987; Gail Sheehy, "Is George Bush Too Nice to Be President?" *Vanity Fair*, Feb. 1987, and "Beating Around the Bush," *Vanity Fair*, Sept. 1988; Maureen Dowd, "For Bush, Culture Can Be a Sometime Thing," *New York Times*, Oct. 27, 1988; Garry Wills, "The Ultimate Loyalist," *Time*, Aug. 22, 1988, and "Father Knows Best," *New York Review of Books*, Nov. 5, 1992; cover story, *Nutmegger*, Sept. 1978; Jane Podesta, "Playing to Win," *People*, Aug. 22, 1988; Suzy Kane, "What the Gulf War Reveals About George Bush's Childhood," *Journal of Psychohistory* 20, no. 2

(Fall 1992); George Plimpton, "A Sportsman Born and Bred," *Sports Illustrated*, Dec. 26, 1988; Laura Sessions Stepp, "Nominees' Upbringing and Their Faith," *Washington Post*, Nov. 4, 1988; Dolly Langdon, "However Far George Runs—28 Homes in 35 Years—Barbara Bush Stands by Her Man," *People*, Aug. 4, 1980; Walt Harrington, "Born to Run," *Washington Post Magazine*, Sept. 28, 1986.

Interviews: Ray Walker, May 28, 2003; Osborne Day, Aug. 6, 2002; Coates Redmon, Nov. 2, 2001; Betsy Trippe DeVecchi, July 20, 2003; Robert DeVecchi, July 21, 2003; Charles Kelly, March 12, 2003; Earl Balfour, Aug. 6, 2002; Jenny Lawrence, March 14, 2002; Marne Hornblower, March 7, 2002; Rudy Abramson, Feb. 21, 2001; Gail Sheehy, April 29, 2002, and correspondence, June 24, 2002.

CHAPTER 4

Records: George H. Walker testimony from "Hearings Before a Subcommittee of the Committee on Interstate Commerce, United States Senate, Seventy-fifth Congress, First Session, Pursuant to S. Res. 71 (74th Congress), Part 15, November 10, 12, 17, and 18, 1937, Missouri Pacific Reorganization"; "Additional Report of the Committee on Interstate Commerce Pursuant to S. Res. 71 (74th Congress), Missouri Pacific System: Reorganization, Expansion, and Financing, 1915–1930," printed July 29, 1940; Harry Truman speech in the Senate, "Railroad Finances," *Congressional Record*, Dec. 20, 1937; Samuel Bush to his sons, May 14, 1940, Samuel Prescott Bush Papers, Ohio Historical Society; Samuel Bush correspondence concerning the President's Organization on Unemployment Relief, Herbert Hoover Presidential Library; documents and correspondence concerning Averell Harriman's European business ventures, including letter from Ray Morris to Roland Harriman, Sept. 26, 1941, regarding Silesian-American Corporation, W. Averell Harriman Papers, Library of Congress Manuscript Reading Room; documents created during and after World War II concerning Office of Alien Property vesting orders, National Archives, Record Group 131, Office of Alien Property Custodian in the Office for Emergency Management, especially files for Vesting Order 248 (Union Banking Corp.) and Vesting Order 370 (Silesian-American Corp.); documents concerning Union Banking Corporation from Brown Brothers Harriman and Company Papers, New-York Historical Society, New York City, Manuscript Department; Mary (Carter) Walker and Prescott S. Bush Jr. Oral History Interview transcripts, Greenwich Library Oral History Project, Greenwich Library, Greenwich, Conn.; Jesse R. Nichols, Oral History Project Interview transcript, U.S. Senate Historical Office; Prescott S. Bush Oral History, 1966, Columbia University Oral History Research Project, Eisenhower Administration Project; 1942 *Pot Pourri* (yearbook), Phillips Academy, Andover, archives; Prescott Bush 1942 correspondence concerning USO fund-raising, Franklin D. Roosevelt Presidential Library.

Books: David McCullough, *Truman* (New York: Simon and Schuster, 1992); Charles Higham, *Trading with the Enemy* (New York: Delacorte Press, 1983); Christopher Simpson, *The Splendid Blond Beast: Money, Law, and Genocide in the Twentieth Century* (New York: Grove Press, 1993); Henry Ashby Turner Jr., *German Big Business and the Rise of Hitler* (New York: Oxford University Press, 1985); James Pool and Suzanne Pool, *Who Financed Hitler: The Secret Funding of Hitler's Rise to Power, 1919–1933* (New York: Dial Press, 1978); John Loftus and Mark Aarons, *The Secret War Against the Jews* (New York: St. Martin's Press, 1994); Townsend Hoopes, *The Devil and John Foster Dulles* (Boston: Little, Brown, 1973); Rudy Abramson, *Spanning the Century: The Life of W. Averell Harriman* (New York: William Morrow, 1992); John A. Kouwenhoven, *Partners in Banking* (Garden City, N.Y.: Doubleday, 1968, 1983); Barbara Bush, *Barbara Bush: A Memoir* (New York: St. Martin's Paperbacks,

1995); Donnie Radcliffe, *Simply Barbara Bush* (New York: Warner Books, 1989); Herbert S. Parmet, *George Bush: The Life of a Lone Star Yankee* (New York: Scribner, 1997); Fitzhugh Green, *George Bush: An Intimate Portrait* (New York: Hippocrene Books, 1989); Joe Hyams, *Flight of the Avenger* (San Diego: Harcourt Brace Jovanovich, 1991); Leonard F. James, *Phillips Academy, Andover, in World War Two* (Andover, Mass.: Andover Press, 1948).

Articles: "Senators Assail Railways, Charging Stock Juggling," *New York Times*, Dec. 21, 1937; "Rail Financing Curb Urged in Senate Report," *New York Herald Tribune*, July 28, 1940; "American Capital Pouring into Europe," *New York Times*, July 14, 1929; "Third Plea for Loans to Pay Bonds Denied," *New York Times*, Feb. 5, 1942; M. J. Racusin, "Thyssen Has $3,000,000 Cash in New York Vaults," *New York Herald Tribune*, July 31, 1941; "Thyssen's Role in World Affairs Still a Mystery," *New York Herald Tribune*, July 31, 1941; "No Honey, No Flies," *Time*, March 2, 1942; "Leo the Lion," *Time*, March 23, 1942; Curtis Lang, "Bad Company," *Village Voice*, May 5, 1992; "Author Links Bush Family to Nazis," *Sarasota Herald-Tribune*, Nov. 11, 2000; Martha Pierce on cover of *Vogue*, Aug. 15, 1940; Suzy Kane, "What the Gulf War Reveals About George Bush's Childhood," *Journal of Psychohistory* 20, no. 2 (Fall 1992); Garry Wills, "The Ultimate Loyalist," *Time*, Aug. 22, 1988; Hugh A. Mulligan, " 'I Knew He Was Something Special,' " *St. Louis Post-Dispatch*, Sept. 27, 1988; "Washington Week," *Wallingford Post*, May 26, 1960; Margaret Warner, "Bush Battles the 'Wimp' Factor," *Newsweek*, Oct. 19, 1987; Brock Brower, "Captain Enigma: Can George Bush Lead the Nation?" *Life*, May 1988; Bruce Mohl, "Bush, at Alma Mater, Stresses Values of a Good Education," *Boston Globe*, May 3, 1987; Ernest B. Furgurson, "Bush's War," *Washingtonian*, Aug. 1985; Marjorie Williams, "Barbara's Backlash," *Vanity Fair*, Aug. 1992.

Interviews: Indiana Earl, July 20, 2001, and Aug. 14, 2001; George "Red Dog" Warren, Jan. 8, 2003; William Sloane Coffin, June 15, 2001, and Oct. 11, 2002; correspondence with Patricia Lewis, July 2, 2002; John Loftus, June 13, 2001; correspondence with Ruth Quattlebaum, Phillips Academy, Andover, archives, March 18 and 24, 2003, and Nov. 4, 2003; Christopher Larsen, June 18, 2003, Sept. 25, 2003, and Nov. 12, 2003; Peggy Adler, March 31, 2003; Jesse Nichols, April 15, 2002; Don Ritchie, March 19, 2002.

RE: *Fritz Thyssen*

Fritz Thyssen (1873–1951) was the scion of a powerful German family whose fortune was based on steel manufacturing. He was attracted to right-wing causes and became a financial backer of the Nazis about 1928. Thyssen's connection with the Nazis became public in 1932, when he arranged for Hitler to speak before the Düsseldorf Industry Club. In July 1933, Thyssen became the Nazis' economic czar in Rhineland-Westphalia, Germany's major industrial region; he later was named to the Prussian State Council and became a Reichstag member from Düsseldorf. However, Thyssen broke with Hitler in 1939 and fled Germany. In 1941 he was captured by police in Vichy France as he was preparing to leave for South America, and he spent the remainder of the war imprisoned in a series of concentration camps. After the war, he was fined by a denazification court, and he finally immigrated to Argentina, where he died.

RE: *"Trading with the Enemy"*

There has been a great deal of inaccuracy about Silesian-American Corporation and Union Banking Corporation because of a widespread misunderstanding over the role of the Office of Alien Property. On April 14, 1942, President Franklin Roosevelt signed Executive Order 9142, which, "under the Authority of the Trading with the Enemy Act of 1917 and the First War Powers Act," established the Office of Alien Property Custodian in the Office for Emergency Management and transferred to it all the "functions, personnel, and property of the Alien Property Division, Justice Department." The OAP was empowered to administer $7 billion worth of enemy assets in the United States. Generally, the OAP issued a vesting order, through which the U.S. government took control of a property. The vested property was either returned after the war or liquidated for the benefit of the government. On November 17, 1942, the OAP issued Vesting Order 370, by which it took control of the *German-owned* shares of Silesian-American Corporation. The OAP's action had nothing to do with George H. Walker's earlier efforts on behalf of the *American* shareholders of Silesian-American. Similarly, when the OAP issued Vesting Order 248, by which it acquired control of Union Banking Corporation—which documents show the government had decided in November 1941 to treat as a German-controlled company—the action was not a reflection on the activities of Prescott Bush and the partners of Brown Brothers Harriman; it was a consequence of the Thyssen family's ownership of the Dutch bank that, in turn, owned Union Banking. Documents in the National Archives indicate that Union Banking Corporation was liquidated shortly after the war and that the U.S. government denied legal appeals by the family of Fritz Thyssen's brother, a Hungarian citizen, to compensate them.

CHAPTER 5

Records: George H.W. Bush World War II letters from Chapel Hill and Corpus Christi, Sept. 3 and 27, 1944, Prescott Bush letter to Ann White, Oct. 13, 1944, Marvin Pierce letter to J. G. Kiefaber, March 22, 1948, George Bush Personal Papers, World War II Correspondence, George Bush Presidential Library; Albert Morano Oral History transcripts, Greenwich Library Oral History Project, Greenwich Library, Greenwich, Conn.; National Archives summary, George H.W. Bush Military Personnel Record and James Smith Bush Military Personnel Record obtained through Freedom of Information Act; deck log pages for USS *San Jacinto*, June 19, 1944, and June 24, 1944, and deck log pages for USS *C. K. Bronson*, June 19, 1944, National Archives; "Commander Torpedo Squadron 5, Aircraft Action Report, 8 September 1944," "U.S.S. San Jacinto War Diary, September 1944," "U.S.S. Finback (SS230)—Report of War Patrol Number Ten, 16 August to 4 October 1944," National Archives; translation, "Summary of Combat Results of Allied [Japanese] Forces, 1st Anti-Aircraft (Asahiyama) 9/2/44," received from David Robb; Prescott Bush to Samuel Bemiss, Samuel M. Bemiss Papers, Virginia Historical Society; Prescott Bush to W. Averell Harriman, July 19, 1944, W. Averell Harriman Papers, Library of Congress Manuscript Reading Room.

Books: George Bush letters to Dorothy Bush, undated, from Minneapolis, letter to Dorothy and Prescott Bush, undated, from Chapel Hill, letters to Dorothy and Prescott Bush, April 27, 1944, May 24, 1942, Sept. 3, 1944, Aug. 13, 1944, letter to Prescott Bush, Nov. 1, 1943, in George Bush, *All the Best, George Bush* (New York: Touchstone, 1999); George Bush with Victor Gold, *Looking Forward* (Garden City, N.Y.: Doubleday, 1987); Barbara Bush, *Barbara Bush: A Memoir* (New York: St. Martin's Paperbacks, 1995) and *Reflections* (New York: Scribner, 2003).

Articles: Benjamin C. Bradlee, "Then and Now," *Washington Post*, Sept. 28, 2001; Beth McLeod, "President's Mother Was Captain of Smooth-Sailing Family Ship," *St. Louis Post-Dispatch*, June 30, 1991; "A Son's Restless Journey," *Newsweek*, Aug. 7, 2000; Brock Brower, "Captain Enigma: Can George Bush Lead the Nation?" *Life*, May 1988; Sidney Blumenthal, "War Story: George Bush's Many Versions," *New Republic*, Oct. 12, 1992; Allan Wolper and Al Ellenbert, "The Day Bush Bailed Out," *New York Post*, Aug. 12, 1988; Dan Morgan, "Bush

Released Intelligence Report to Rebut Gunner's Story of 1944 Mission," *Washington Post*, Aug. 14, 1988; Ernest B. Furgurson, "Bush's War," *Washingtonian*, Aug. 1985; "Church Crowded at Bush-Pierce Wedding," *Rye Chronicle*, Jan. 12, 1945; Barbara Grizzuti Harrison, "Lunch with Bar: An Interview with the Ancien Regime," *New Republic*, Nov. 9, 1992.

Interviews: Courtney Callahan, April 17, 2003, and Aug. 29, 2003; Anthony A. Morano, Dec. 5, 2001; correspondence with Jason Morano, Dec. 17, 2001. Interviews by David Robb: Leo Nadeau, April 1991; Wendell Tomes, May 11, 1991; Legare Hole, May 1991; Harold Nunnally, May 11, 1991; James Bryan, May 3, 1991.

CHAPTER 6

Records: Prescott Bush to Charles Seymour and Yale *1948 Class Book*, Manuscripts and Archives, Sterling Memorial Library, Yale University; William F. Buckley Jr. interviewed by Geoffrey Kabaservice, Griswold-Brewster Oral History Project, Manuscripts and Archives, Sterling Memorial Library, Yale University; receipt for 1947 Studebaker, George Bush to his mother, Oct. 28, 1948, and transcript of David Frost interview with George and Barbara Bush, Aug. 25, 1998, George Bush Presidential Library; correspondence with Thomas "Lud" Ashley concerning gifts to RTA 1966 and to Yale 1970, Thomas L. Ashley Papers, Center for Archival Collections, Bowling Green State University; Prescott S. Bush Oral History, 1966, Columbia University Oral History Research Project, Eisenhower Administration Project.

Books: George Bush with Victor Gold, *Looking Forward* (Garden City, N.Y.: Doubleday, 1987); George Bush letter to FitzGerald Bemiss, June 1948, in George Bush, *All the Best, George Bush* (New York: Touchstone, 1999); Barbara Bush, *Barbara Bush: A Memoir* (New York: St. Martin's Paperbacks, 1995); Donnie Radcliffe, *Simply Barbara Bush* (New York: Warner Books, 1989); Alexandra Robbins, *Secrets of the Tomb* (Boston: Little, Brown, 2002); Richard Ben Cramer, *What It Takes* (New York: Vintage Books, 1993); Fitzhugh Green, *George Bush: An Intimate Portrait* (New York: Hippocrene Books, 1989); Gail Sheehy, *Characters* (New York: William Morrow, 1988); Peggy Noonan, *What I Saw at the Revolution* (New York: Random House, 1990); Darwin Payne, *Initiative in Energy* (New York: Simon and Schuster, 1979); H. G. Bissinger, *Friday Night Lights* (Reading, Mass.: Addison-Wesley, 1990).

Articles: "Over 5300 Students Register for Fall Term," *Yale Daily News*, Nov. 2, 1945; Lois Romano, "Joseph Reed, Protector of Propriety; On the Eve of the Floating Summit, Bush's Protocol Chief in the Wings," *Washington Post*, Nov. 28, 1989; "Senior Society Elections," *Yale Daily News*, May 16, 1947; Bob Woodward and Walter Pincus, "Bush Opened Up to Secret Yale Society," *Washington Post*, Aug. 7, 1988; "A Son's Restless Journey," *Newsweek*, Aug. 7, 2000; James Keogh, "Barbara Remembers," *Greenwich*, Dec. 1994; Barbara Matusow, "Mama's Boy," *Washingtonian*, June 2001; "Bush Named New Baseball Captain," *Yale Daily News*, Sept. 22, 1947; Michael P. Keating, "Stan's the Man," *York Weekly*, June 19, 2002; "Stifel Nicolaus Head Glad Bush Turned Down Family Business," *Tulsa World*, Oct. 27, 1988; cover story, *Nutmegger*, Sept. 1978; Barry Bearak, "His Great Gift, to Blend In," *Los Angeles Times*, Nov. 22, 1987; Garry Wills, "Father Knows Best," *New York Review of Books*, Nov. 5, 1992; "Mrs. Bush—U.N. Wife, 'I'd Pay to Have This Job,' " *Washington, D.C., Sunday Star*, Feb. 20, 1972; Bill Minutaglio, "George W.'s Secret Weapon," *Talk*, March 2000; "Auto Crash Kills Publisher's Wife as He Reaches for Spilling Cup," *New York Times*, Sept. 24, 1949; "Mrs. Pierce's Death Shocks Community," *Rye Chronicle*, Sept. 29, 1949; Susan Watters, "Feisty Lady," *W*, Oct. 31, 1988.

TV: "Barbara Bush, First Mom," A&E *Biography*, May 9, 2001.

Interviews: Isolde Chapin, Dec. 19, 2001; Jim Finkenstaedt, June 4, 2002; Harry Finkenstaedt, June 21, 2002; Frank "Junie" O'Brien, April 30, 2003; Betsy Trippe DeVecchi, July 20, 2003; Robert DeVecchi, July 21, 2003; Stephen Thayer, May 2003; correspondence with William R. Massa Jr., Yale Manuscripts and Archives, Feb. 19, 2002; correspondence with Geoffrey Kabaservice, Aug. 16, 2001, and Oct. 9, 2001. Interview by David Robb: Thomas "Lud" Ashley, May 1991.

RE: Skull and Bones Appointments
George H.W. Bush appointed several Bonesmen to federal positions: George H. Pfau Jr. (1940), director of the Securities Investor Protection Corporation; Paul C. Lambert (1950), Ambassador to Ecuador; Victor H. Frank Jr. (1950), director of the Asian Development Bank; David George Ball (1960), Assistant Secretary of Labor; Richard Anthony Moore (1930), Ambassador to Ireland. Moore, a producer for *The McLaughlin Group*, was best known to the public in his capacity as special counsel to President Nixon, 1971–74; in 1973, he had testified for two and a half days before the Senate Watergate Committee and denied that John Dean had informed Nixon about criminal activities involved in the White House cover-up of Watergate. The witness who immediately followed Moore, Alexander Butterfield, revealed that Nixon had taped his conversations; when finally produced, the tapes supported John Dean's version of his conversations with the President.

CHAPTER 7

Records: Elizabeth Hyde Brownell, Prescott S. Bush Jr., Josephine Evaristo, Albert Morano, Charles A. Pirro Jr., John F. Sullivan, Albert F. Varner Jr., Bernard L. Yudain Oral History Interview transcripts, Greenwich Library Oral History Project, Greenwich Library, Greenwich, Conn.; Samuel P. Bush will and Martha Bell Bush will, Franklin County Probate Court, Columbus, Ohio; Prescott S. Bush Oral History, 1966, Columbia University Oral History Research Project, Eisenhower Administration Project; campaign material and newspaper clippings scrapbooks, Prescott S. Bush Papers, Thomas J. Dodd Research Center, University of Connecticut; telegram concerning UN, letter to Richard Nixon, Sept. 4, 1952, and other correspondence, Clare Boothe Luce Papers, Library of Congress Manuscript Reading Room; Prescott S. Bush to Louis Carlisle Walker, June 19, 1950, Louis Carlisle Walker Papers, Bentley Library, University of Michigan; transcript of Drew Pearson radio broadcast, Nov. 5, 1950, and 1947 Planned Parenthood fund-raising letter, Drew Pearson Papers, Lyndon B. Johnson Presidential Library; 1952 presidential campaign material, Brien McMahon Papers, Georgetown University Special Collections; Prescott Bush to Sam Bemiss, Samuel M. Bemiss Papers, Virginia Historical Society; Prescott Bush to A. Whitney Griswold, Manuscripts and Archives, Sterling Memorial Library, Yale University.

Books: David J. Garrow, *Liberty and Sexuality* (New York: Macmillan, 1994); George Bush letter to FitzGerald Bemiss, Jan. 1, 1951, in George Bush, *All the Best, George Bush* (New York: Touchstone, 1999); Alden Hatch, *Ambassador Extraordinary Clare Boothe Luce* (New York: Henry Holt, 1956); Fitzhugh Green, *George Bush: An Intimate Portrait* (New York: Hippocrene Books, 1989).

Articles: "Nancy Bush Bride Saturday of Alexander Ellis, Jr.," *Greenwich Time*, Oct. 28, 1946; "Alexander Ellis Jr. Marries Miss Bush," *New York Sun*, Oct. 26, 1946; Christopher Keating, "Josephine Evaristo Dies at 84," *Greenwich Time*, June 3, 1989; "S. P. Bush, Retired Business,

Civic Leader, Succumbs at 84," *Ohio State Journal*, Feb. 9, 1948; Marquis Childs, "A Nasty Political Rumor," *St. Louis Post-Dispatch*, Aug. 25, 1950; Walt Harrington, "Born to Run," *Washington Post Magazine*, Sept. 28, 1986; "Benton Is Winner, Senate Edge Held," *New York Times*, Nov. 17, 1950; Alexander Cockburn and James Ridgeway, "George Bush," *Rolling Stone*, March 20, 1980; "Bush Believes Gen. Ike Available for '52; Call 'Must Be Compelling,'" *Greenwich Time*, Dec. 3, 1951; "Women Politicos," *Middletown Press*, June 19, 1956; Robert D. Byrnes, "State's Senators Divide on Proposed Equal Rights Constitution Change," *Hartford Courant*, July 7, 1953; "GOPs Boo Bush's Anti-smear Stand," *Hartford Courant*, Oct. 5, 1952; A.H.O., "Connecticut Yankee," *Manchester Herald*, Oct. 7, 1952; "State Political Drive Shows Signs of Warmup," *New Haven Register*, Oct. 14, 1952; "Eisenhower Attacks Rival's 'Fear Campaign,' Scores Democratic 'Drivel' in Speech Here," *Yale Daily News*, Oct. 21, 1952; "Angry Bush Denies 'Smear' Campaign Against Him in Breakfast Address Here," *Greenwich Time*, Oct. 28, 1952; Michael J. Halberstam, "The Campaign," *Harvard Crimson*, Nov. 1, 1952; "McMahon's Death Plays Fateful Role," *Bridgeport Herald*, Nov. 16, 1952; Leonard Schlup, "Prescott Bush and the Foundations of Modern Republicanism," *Research Journal of Philosophy & Social Sciences*, nos. 1 and 2 (1992); "Town Meeting Members Cheer Moderator Bush at Farewell Appearance," *Greenwich Time*, Nov. 7, 1952.

Interviews: Courtney Callahan, Aug. 29, 2003; Robert DeVecchi, July 21, 2003; Mrs. Lawrence J. Evaristo, April 1, 2002; Connie Collins Cain, June 26, 2001; Lowell Weicker, Dec. 5, 2001; Bernie Yudain, Dec. 5, 2001; Joyce Burland, Jan. 9, 2003; Richard Kimball Jr., Jan. 11, 2003; Raymond Price, May 29, 2003, and June 1, 2003; correspondence with David Haight, archivist, Dwight D. Eisenhower Presidential Library, Aug. 16 and 27, 2001.

CHAPTER 8

Records: George Bush to Paul Dorsey, April 8, 1967, George Bush Presidential Library; Mary (Carter) Walker Oral History Interview transcript, Greenwich Library Oral History Project, Greenwich Library, Greenwich, Conn.; James Smith Bush FBI file obtained through Freedom of Information Act.

Books: Gail Sheehy, *Characters* (New York: William Morrow, 1988); Donnie Radcliffe, *Simply Barbara Bush* (New York: Warner Books, 1989); Barbara Bush, *Barbara Bush: A Memoir* (New York: St. Martin's Paperbacks, 1995); George Bush with Victor Gold, *Looking Forward* (Garden City, N.Y.: Doubleday, 1987); Bill Minutaglio, *First Son* (New York: Times Books, 1999).

Articles: Harry Hurt III, "George Bush, Plucky Lad," *Texas Monthly*, June 1983; cover story, *Nutmegger*, Jan. 1970; "J. Hugh Liedtke, 81; Pennzoil Chief Won Suit Against Texaco," *Los Angeles Times*, April 5, 2003; Sidney Blumenthal, "The Sensitive Son," *New Republic*, Oct. 8, 1990; Monica Perin, "Adios, Zapata!" *Houston Business Journal*, April 23, 1999; Amy Cunningham, "Good-Bye to Robin," *Texas Monthly*, Feb. 1988; "Robin Bush Dies; Granddaughter of Sen., Mrs. P. S. Bush," *Greenwich Time*, Oct. 13, 1953; "George Bush's Wife Says He's Terrific," *San Francisco Chronicle*, Aug. 19, 1988; David Maraniss, "The Bush Bunch," *Washington Post Magazine*, Jan. 22, 1989; transcript, *Frontline* interview with Randall Roden, 2000, from pbs.org (Aug. 6, 2001); George Lardner Jr. and Lois Romano, "A Texas Childhood; A Sister Dies, a Family Moves On; Loss Creates Strong Bond Between Mother, Son," *Washington Post*, July 26, 1999.

Interviews: Byron Dobell, March 12, 2003; Stephen Thayer, May 2003; Ray Walker, May 28, 2003; Elizabeth W. Holden, May 28, 2003; Serena Stewart, June 4 and 24, 2002, and July 10,

2002; John Jansing, Oct. 12, 2001; Stuart Symington Jr., July 3, 2002; James Symington, July 3, 2002; Fred Purdy, July 30, 2002; Charles Stephan, July 16, 2002; correspondence with Lois Herbert, July 7 and 25, 2002.

CHAPTER 9

Records: Newspaper clippings scrapbooks, including Dorothy Bush columns, and Prescott Bush Senate office press releases, Prescott S. Bush Papers, Thomas J. Dodd Research Center, University of Connecticut; documents concerning Eisenhower and Burning Tree Club, Dwight D. Eisenhower Presidential Library; Prescott S. Bush Jr. Oral History Interview transcript, Greenwich Library Oral History Project, Greenwich Library, Greenwich, Conn.; Prescott Bush statement in the Senate concerning censure of Senator Joseph McCarthy, *Congressional Record*, Dec. 1, 1954; William Fulbright to Prescott Bush, Dec. 2, 1954, J. William Fulbright Papers, Special Collections, University of Arkansas; Sam Bemiss to Prescott Bush, June 22, 1954, Samuel M. Bemiss Papers, Virginia Historical Society.

Books: Emmet John Hughes, *The Ordeal of Power: A Political Memoir of the Eisenhower Years* (New York: Atheneum, 1963); Randall Bennett Woods, *Fulbright* (New York: Cambridge University Press, 1995); Richard M. Fried, *Men Against McCarthy* (New York: Columbia University Press, 1976); Haynes Johnson and Bernard M. Gwertzman, *Fulbright, the Dissenter* (Garden City, N.Y.: Doubleday, 1968).

Articles: Laura Sessions Stepp, "Nominees' Upbringing and Their Faith," *Washington Post*, Nov. 4, 1988; David Margolick, "Brother Dearest," *Vanity Fair*, July 2001; Michael J. Birkner, "Eisenhower and the Red Menace," *Prologue* 33, no. 3 (Fall 2001); "June 1, 1950: A Declaration of Conscience," www.senate.gov (March 22, 2002); Herblock, "Have a Care, Sir," *Washington Post*, March 4, 1954; "Watered-Down Substitute for M'Carthy Censure Move Offered in Senate," *St. Louis Post-Dispatch*, July 31, 1954; George H. Hall, "Platform Set, Near Unanimous Accord Reached on Civil Rights," *St. Louis Post-Dispatch*, Aug. 20, 1956.

Interviews: Pat Shakow, Aug. 19, 2001; Ellen Proxmire, Oct. 4, 2002; Marian Javits, May 23, 2003; Michael Lynch, Jan. 30, 2002; Harry McPherson, June 7, 2002; Don Ritchie, March 19, 2002; Hamilton Richardson, March 23, 2004; Bobby Wood, Nov. 23, 2002; Frank Valeo, March 14, 2002; William Hildenbrand, March 14, 2002; Pat Holt, March 14, 2002; Betsy Trippe DeVecchi, July 20, 2003; Bernie Yudain, Dec. 5, 2001; Sid Yudain, Dec. 5, 2001; Ray Walker, May 28, 2003; Peter Ribicoff, Feb. 27, 2002; correspondence with Dwight Strandberg, archivist, Dwight D. Eisenhower Presidential Library, July 25, 2003.

CHAPTER 10

Records: Newspaper clippings scrapbooks, 1956 Senate campaign material, and Prescott Bush Senate office press releases, Prescott S. Bush Papers, Thomas J. Dodd Research Center, University of Connecticut; Prescott Bush file, Drew Pearson Papers, Lyndon B. Johnson Presidential Library; Prescott S. Bush Oral History, 1966, Columbia University Oral History Research Project, Eisenhower Administration Project; documents concerning President Eisenhower's schedule, correspondence, including Prescott Bush letter to Sherman Adams, and minutes of cabinet meeting, Feb. 13, 1956, Dwight D. Eisenhower Presidential Library; Paxton Howard testimony from "Hearings Before the Special Committee to Investigate Political Activities, Lobbying, and Campaign Contributions, United States Senate, Eighty-fourth Congress, Second Session, Pursuant to S. Res. 219, May 1, 24, June 14, 15, 21, 28, September 10, 11, 12, October 9, 1956"; Thomas Ashley to George H.W. Bush, July 25, 1956, Thomas L. Ashley Papers, Center for Archival Collections, Bowling Green State University; Prescott S. Bush FBI file obtained through Freedom of Information Act; George H.W. Bush to Paul Dorsey, April 8, 1967, George Bush Presidential Library.

Books: George Bush with Victor Gold, *Looking Forward* (Garden City, N.Y.: Doubleday, 1987); Robert H. Ferrell, ed., *The Eisenhower Diaries* (New York: Norton, 1981); Herbert Brownell and John P. Burke, *Advising Ike* (Lawrence: University Press of Kansas, 1993).

Articles: "Bush Asks Ike to Keep Nixon on Party Ticket," *Hartford Courant*, Sept. 25, 1952; Eric Sandahl, "Wall St. Pals Push $20,000 Bush Fund," *Bridgeport Herald*, Jan. 16, 1955; Drew Pearson, "Another Secret Fund, Nixon Style," *Washington Post*, June 13, 1955; Drew Pearson, "Voter's Stake in Campaign Funds," *Washington Post*, June 15, 1955; "These Senatorial Funds," *St. Louis Post-Dispatch*, June 22, 1955; "Regulation Needed," *Waterbury Republican*, June 23, 1955; Edward F. Woods, "Lawyer Says He Pushed Gas Bill and Got a Bonus," *St. Louis Post-Dispatch*, Oct. 9, 1956.

Interviews: Sydney Soderberg, June 12, 2001; Herman Wolf, May 14, 2002; Sid Yudain, Dec. 5, 2001; Howard Shuman, March 19, 2002; correspondence with Marie Deitch, librarian, *Greenwich Time*, June 14, 2001.

CHAPTER 11
Records: Prescott S. Bush Jr., Albert Morano, Mary (Carter) Walker Oral History transcripts, Greenwich Library Oral History Project, Greenwich Library, Greenwich, Conn.; newspaper clippings scrapbooks, including Dorothy Bush columns, Prescott S. Bush Papers, Thomas J. Dodd Research Center, University of Connecticut; Prescott Bush to Mrs. Allen Dulles, Jan. 29, 1969, posted online at ciajfk.com/images/fbi3.gif (Sept. 5, 2001); memorandum for Barefoot Sanders from George Christian, March 6, 1968, Lyndon B. Johnson Presidential Library; Zapata Offshore Company annual reports, 1955–67; Prescott Bush telegrams to Richard Nixon, Oct. 13, 1960, Oct. 24, 1960, and Nov. 7, 1960, and Prescott Bush letter to Richard Nixon, Nov. 13, 1960, Richard M. Nixon materials, National Archives, Pacific Region (Laguna Niguel); Prescott Bush to John F. Kennedy, Dec. 6, 1960, John F. Kennedy Presidential Library; Prescott Bush telegram to Dwight Eisenhower, Feb. 12, 1962, and Eisenhower reply, Feb. 20, 1962, Dwight D. Eisenhower Presidential Library; Prescott S. Bush Oral History, 1966, Columbia University Oral History Research Project, Eisenhower Administration Project.

Books: George Bush with Victor Gold, *Looking Forward* (Garden City, N.Y.: Doubleday, 1987); Barbara Bush, *Barbara Bush: A Memoir* (New York: St. Martin's Paperbacks, 1995); George Bush letter to Mr. and Mrs. Geza Kapus, Aug. 24, 1959, in George Bush, *All the Best, George Bush* (New York: Touchstone, 1999); Donnie Radcliffe, *Simply Barbara Bush* (New York: Warner Books, 1989); Fay Vincent, *The Last Commissioner* (New York: Simon and Schuster, 2002); Bill Minutaglio, *First Son* (New York: Times Books, 1999); Nicholas King, *George Bush: A Biography* (New York: Dodd, Mead, 1980); Fitzhugh Green, *George Bush: An Intimate Portrait* (New York: Hippocrene Books, 1989); Richard Ben Cramer, *What It Takes* (New York: Vintage Books, 1993); Bill Adler, ed., *The Kennedy Wit* (New York: Bantam Books, 1965).

Articles: Neil Vigdor, "Honoring the Family Patriarch; Bush Family's Political Roots Grow out of Greenwich," *Greenwich Time*, June 15, 2003; "Charity," *Nutmegger*, Sept. 1974; "A

'Joke' About Illegal Aliens Stirs Critics of Prescott Bush," *New York Times*, March 27, 1982; John Robinson, "For Nancy Ellis, a New Role as the President's Sister," *Boston Globe*, Jan. 18, 1989; "Jonathan Bush Would Revive Minstrel Era," *Variety*, July 11, 1962; Louis Funke, "The Theatre: 'Oklahoma!' " *New York Times*, March 8, 1958; Walter Pincus and Bob Woodward, "Doing Well with Help from Family, Friends; They Pointed Bush to Jobs, Investments," *Washington Post*, Aug. 11, 1988; Kenny Kemp, "The Scots Financier, the Bush Oil Dynasty . . . and the Man Who Would Be President," *Glasgow Sunday Herald*, Dec. 10, 2000; David Robb, "Bush's Covenants," *Nation*, Nov. 28, 1987; Margaret Warner, "Bush Battles the 'Wimp' Factor," *Newsweek*, Oct. 19, 1987; Gail Sheehy, "Is George Bush Too Nice to Be President?" *Vanity Fair*, Feb. 1987.

Interviews: Confidential source, Oct. 12, 2002; Isolde Chapin, Dec. 19, 2001; Bernie Yudain, Dec. 5, 2001; Lowell Weicker, Dec. 5, 2001; Kim Elliott, Dec. 10, 2001; Lucie McKinney, Dec. 7, 2001; Ymelda Dixon, Aug. 15, 2003; confidential interview with "Yale roommate," Oct. 2, 2002; Frank Rich, July 2, 2003; correspondence with Edward Albee, April 7, 2003; Ray Walker, May 28, 2003; Stephanie Lilley, Nov. 2001; Herman Wolf, May 14, 2002; Gail Sheehy, April 29, 2002, and correspondence, June 24, 2002. Interview by David Robb: Hoyt Taylor, Jan. 24, 1988.

CHAPTER 12

Records: Issues of *Bush Bulletin* (George Bush 1964 Senate campaign newsletter), John R. Knaggs Papers, John G. Tower Library and Archives, Southwestern University; George Bush to Lud Ashley, Feb. 13, 1963, June 22, 1964, June 8, 1965, and Ashley to Bush, June 19, 1964, Thomas L. Ashley Papers, Center for Archival Collections, Bowling Green State University; Prescott Bush to John Tower, John G. Tower Library and Archives, Southwestern University; newspaper clippings files, William F. Buckley to George Bush, Sept. 17, 1963, George Bush to Richard Nixon, Nov. 12, 1964, George Bush Presidential Library; Prescott Bush to Sam Bemiss, Oct. 17, 1963, July 27, 1964, Nov. 10, 1964, May 13, 1965, Sam Bemiss to Prescott Bush, Nov. 4, 1964, Sam Bemiss to George Bush, Nov. 6, 1963, Samuel M. Bemiss Papers, Virginia Historical Society; FBI memo from Special Agent Graham W. Kitchel, Nov. 22, 1963, concerning George Bush phone call, and documents concerning FBI investigation of James M. Parrott, National Archives, Kennedy Assassination Collection; records concerning George H.W. Bush application for Air Medals, Jan. 27, 1954, obtained from Bureau of Naval Personnel through Freedom of Information Act (by David Robb, 1991); Charles Sargent Caldwell Oral History Project Interview transcript, U.S. Senate Historical Office; telegram from "Seven Democrats Harris County" to the White House, Oct. 27, 1964, Lyndon B. Johnson Presidential Library; Mary (Carter) Walker Oral History Interview transcript, Greenwich Library Oral History Project, Greenwich Library, Greenwich, Conn.; George Bush to Dwight Eisenhower, Jan. 7, 1965, Dwight D. Eisenhower Presidential Library.

Books: George Bush with Victor Gold, *Looking Forward* (Garden City, N.Y.: Doubleday, 1987); Barbara Bush, *Barbara Bush: A Memoir* (New York: St. Martin's Paperbacks, 1995); Herbert S. Parmet, *George Bush: The Life of a Lone Star Yankee* (New York: Scribner, 1997); Richard Ben Cramer, *What It Takes* (New York: Vintage Books, 1993); Theodore H. White, *The Making of the President, 1964* (New York: Atheneum, 1965); John R. Knaggs, *Two-Party Texas* (Austin, Tex.: Eakin Press, 1986); Barry M. Goldwater with Jack Casserly, *Goldwater* (New York: Doubleday, 1988); Michael R. Beschloss, ed., *Taking Charge* (New York: Simon and Schuster, 1997); Bill Minutaglio, *First Son* (New York: Times Books, 1999); Fitzhugh Green, *George Bush: An Intimate Portrait* (New York: Hippocrene Books, 1989).

Articles: "Mrs. Bush Lauds Nixon, Lodge as Team for Times," *Greenwich Time*, Nov. 1, 1960; "Bush Hits Rockefeller Marriage, Hopes He Will Not Be Nominated," *Greenwich Time*, June 7, 1963; Philip Savory, "Bush vs. Rocky," *New York Herald Tribune*, June 8, 1963; "Says Bush 'Defamed' Governor," *New York Journal American*, June 9, 1963; David S. Broder, "Aug. 28, 1963: A Day Guided by Providence," *Washington Post*, Aug. 24, 2003; Jefferson Morley, "Bush and the Blacks: An Unknown Story," *New York Review of Books*, Jan. 16, 1992; Rowland Evans and Robert Novak, "Yarborough Slips in Texas Senate Race," *St. Louis Post-Dispatch*, Oct. 23, 1964; Ed Staats, "George Bush Profile," Associated Press, June 6, 1970; Miguel Acoca, "FBI: 'Bush' Called About JFK Killing," *San Francisco Examiner*, Aug. 25, 1988; "Goldwater's Policies, Kennedy's Style," *Texas Observer*, Oct. 30, 1964; "Cactus-Nasty Campaign," *Time*, Oct. 16, 1964; "This Man George Bush," *Texas Observer*, Oct. 30, 1964; Barry Bearak, "His Great Gift, to Blend In," *Los Angeles Times*, Nov. 22, 1987; Ed Vulliamy, "The President Rides Out," *Observer*, Jan. 26, 2003; "24 Alumni to Appear on Ballots," *Yale Daily News*, Nov. 3, 1964; Helen Thorpe, "Go East, Young Man," *Texas Monthly*, June 1999; Skip Hollandsworth, "Born to Run: What's in a Name? How About the Republican Nomination for Governor," *Texas Monthly*, May 1994; Lois Romano and George Lardner Jr., "Following His Father's Path—Step by Step by Step," *Washington Post*, July 27, 1999; James Adams, "Yale Graduates Survive Elections; Lindsay, Chafee, Murphy Win Big," *Yale Daily News*, Nov. 5, 1964; Mary Rice Brogan, "Yarborough Says Bush Should 'Pack Up, Leave,' " *Houston Chronicle*, Nov. 4, 1964.

Interviews: Aubrey Irby, Sept. 11, 2002; Alex Dickie Jr., July 17, 2002; William Sloane Coffin, June 15, 2001, and Oct. 11, 2002. Interview by David Robb: Legare Hole, May 7, 1991.

CHAPTER 13

Records: 1966 House campaign material and newspaper clippings files, George Bush letter to Paul Dorsey, Jan. 27, 1967, documents concerning William Sloane Coffin's civil disobedience, including Kingman Brewster statement, and George H. Walker Jr. letter to George Bush, Oct. 30, 1967, George Bush letter to David Acheson, Nov. 2, 1967, George Bush letter to Larry V. Moser, Nov. 1, 1967, Howard T. Phelan letter to George Bush, Nov. 20, 1967, R. B. Greene "Open Letter to the President," Dec., 24, 1967, transcript, David Frost interview with George and Barbara Bush, Aug. 29, 1989, documents and statement concerning trip to Vietnam, Jan. 11, 1968, George Bush letter to Richard G. Mack, April 14, 1968, address list for vice presidential bid, July 16, 1968, Louis F. Polk letter to George Bush, July 2, 1968, George Bush letter to Louis F. Polk Jr., July 8, 1968, George Bush letter to Bob Connery, Aug. 20, 1968, George Bush Presidential Library; George Bush to Dwight Eisenhower, June 13, 1966, and note, July 28, 1966, concerning George Bush's requesting a statement endorsing him for Congress, Dwight D. Eisenhower Presidential Library; James A. Baker III interview, David Hoffman Papers, George Bush Presidential Library; Jonathan Bush to Kingman Brewster, Feb. 2, 1968, Manuscripts and Archives, Sterling Memorial Library, Yale University; Prescott S. Bush Oral History, 1966, Columbia University Oral History Research Project, Eisenhower Administration Project; Prescott Bush and George Bush correspondence with Thomas E. Dewey concerning vice presidency in 1968, Thomas E. Dewey Papers, University of Rochester.

Books: Bill Minutaglio, *First Son* (New York: Times Books, 1999); Fitzhugh Green, *George Bush: An Intimate Portrait* (New York: Hippocrene Books, 1989); Herbert S. Parmet, *George Bush: The Life of a Lone Star Yankee* (New York: Scribner, 1997); George Bush with Victor Gold, *Looking Forward* (Garden City, N.Y.: Doubleday, 1987); Barbara Bush, *Barbara Bush: A Memoir* (New York: St. Martin's Paperbacks, 1995); Donnie Radcliffe, *Simply Barbara*

Bush (New York: Warner Books, 1989); William Sloane Coffin, *Once to Every Man* (New York: Atheneum, 1977); George Bush letter to Paul Dorsey, Jan. 27, 1967, letter to Richard Gerstle Mack, Easter Sunday 1968, letter to Charles Untermeyer, April 11, 1968, letter to James Allison Jr., undated, in George Bush, *All the Best, George Bush* (New York: Touchstone, 1999); Gail Sheehy, *Characters* (New York: William Morrow, 1988); George W. Bush, *A Charge to Keep* (New York: William Morrow, 1999).

Articles: "Court Says Texas Must Redistrict," *New York Times*, March 3, 1964; Jefferson Morley, "Bush and the Blacks: An Unknown Story," *New York Review of Books*, Jan. 16, 1992; Lally Weymouth, "The Surprising George Bush," *M*, May 1991; Jake Tapper, "Air War," salon.com, Nov. 22, 1999; Walt Harrington, "Born to Run," *Washington Post Magazine*, Sept. 28, 1986; "Halleck, Bush, Mrs. Reid Get Key House GOP Spots," *Washington Star*, Jan. 26, 1967; Barry Bearak, "His Great Gift, to Blend In," *Los Angeles Times*, Nov. 22, 1987; "Bush Shows Assets Exceeding $1 Million," *Houston Post*, April 28, 1967; "Branding Rite Laid to Yale Fraternity," *New York Times*, Nov. 8, 1967; Jonathan Lear, "No Intervention for Fraternities," *Yale Daily News*, Nov. 7, 1968; David Robb, "Bush's Covenants," *Nation*, Nov. 28, 1987; Maureen Dowd, "Making and Remaking a Political Identity," *New York Times*, Aug. 20, 1992; Carey Cronan, "Bush Opposes Use of Ground Troops," *Bridgeport Post*, May 21, 1954; Sidney Blumenthal, "War Story," *New Republic*, Oct. 12, 1992; William Yardley, "Jeb Bush: His Early Values Shape His Policies," *Miami Herald*, Sept. 22, 2002; Richard A. Serrano, "Bush Received Quick Air Commission," *Los Angeles Times*, July 4, 1999; George Lardner Jr. and Lois Romano, "At Height of Vietnam, Graduate Picks Guard; With Deferment Over, Pilot Training Begins," *Washington Post*, July 28, 1999; "Long Shot," *New Republic*, Feb. 21, 1970; Rowland Evans and Robert Novak, "Young Texas Congressman Bush Gets Nixon Look as Running Mate," *Washington Post*, June 5, 1968; "Rewriting History," *New Yorker*, Oct. 5, 1992; Lois Romano and George Lardner Jr., "Following His Father's Path—Step by Step by Step," *Washington Post*, July 27, 1999; Helen Thorpe, "Hail the Conquering Hero," *New York*, Sept. 20, 1999; "Dedicate Housing in New Haven to Former Senator," *Greenwich Time*, Nov. 7, 1966; Oscar Griffin, "Bush Says 'Poor' Demands Impossible," *Houston Chronicle*, June 10, 1968.

Interviews: Virginia Douglas, Dec. 29, 2003; William Sloane Coffin, June 15, 2001, and Oct. 11, 2002; Kenneth White, March 12, 2003; Mark I. Soler, July 2003 and Nov. 7, 2003; Gail Sheehy, April 29, 2002; Ray Walker, May 28, 2003; Nadine Eckhardt, Aug. 5, 2003, and correspondence, Oct. 10, 2003.

CHAPTER 14

Records: Prescott Bush to Kingman Brewster, Jan. 8, 1968, and *1968 Class Yearbook*, Manuscripts and Archives, Sterling Memorial Library, Yale University; Phillips Academy, Andover, yearbook, *1964 Pot Pourri*.

Books: Mickey Herskowitz, *Duty, Honor, Country* (Nashville: Rutledge Hill Press, 2003); Bill Minutaglio, *First Son* (New York: Times Books, 1999); George W. Bush, *A Charge to Keep* (New York: William Morrow, 1999); Barbara Bush, *Barbara Bush: A Memoir* (New York: St. Martin's Paperbacks, 1995); George Bush letter to his sons, July 23, 1974, in George Bush, *All the Best, George Bush* (New York: Touchstone, 1999).

Articles: Joe Conason, "The Yale Man's Legacy," salon.com, Jan. 16, 2003; "A Son's Restless Journey," *Newsweek*, Aug. 7, 2000; Jane Mayer and Alexandra Robbins, "Debt of Aptitude,"

New Yorker, Nov. 8, 1999; George Lardner Jr. and Lois Romano, "A Texas Childhood; A Sister Dies, a Family Moves On; Loss Creates Strong Bond Between Mother, Son," *Washington Post*, July 26, 1999, and "Following His Father's Path—Step by Step by Step," *Washington Post*, July 27, 1999; David Margolick, "Brother Dearest," *Vanity Fair*, July 2001; Cathy Rampell, "Bush Gives Backseat to Academy Influence," *Phillipian*, Nov. 10, 2000; Helen Thorpe, "Go East, Young Man," *Texas Monthly*, June 1999; transcript, *Frontline* interview with Clay Johnson, 2000, from pbs.org (Aug. 6, 2001); Garry Trudeau, "Card-Carrying Preppy," *Time*, July 2, 2001; transcript, "Class Reunion," ABC News *Nightline*, May 29, 2003; "Marijuana in Spook?" *Yale Daily News*, Oct. 18, 1967; Jake Tapper, "Judging W's Heart," salon.com, Nov. 1, 2000; Geoffrey Kabaservice, "The Birth of a New Institution," *Yale Alumni Magazine*, Dec. 1999; Carter Wiseman, "In the Days of DKE and S.D.S.," *Yale Alumni Magazine*, Feb. 2001; Nicholas Lemann, "The Redemption," *New Yorker*, Jan. 31, 2000; Garry Trudeau, on the Yale '68 reunion, *Doonesbury*, May 26–31, 2003; Janice D'Arcy, "Yale Coaxes Bush Back into the Eli Fold," *Hartford Courant*, May 10, 2001; Leah Garchik, "George Bush Gets It Right," *San Francisco Chronicle*, June 6, 2003; Lloyd Grove, "Boycotting the White House," *Washington Post*, May 9, 2003.

Interviews: Christopher Larsen, June 18, 2003, and Nov. 12, 2003; J. Milburn Jessup, May 21, 2003; correspondence with Timothy Sprattler, Oliver Wendell Holmes Library, Phillips Academy, Andover, Nov. 15, 2001; correspondence with Anthony H. Sgro, director of external relations, Woodberry Forest School, Nov. 14, 2002; correspondence with Ruth Quattlebaum, Phillips Academy, archives, Andover, Nov. 4, 2003, Genevieve Young, Nov. 14, 2003; Torbert Macdonald, July 18, 2003; Sandy Horwitt, May 9 and 14, 2003; Conway Downing, Feb 15, 2002; Eric Wallach, Dec. 30, 2001; correspondence with Randolph W. Hobler, Feb. 21, 2002; Richard Lee Williams, July 2003; Thomas S. Weisser, Nov. 2, 2001; David Roe, Oct. 15, 2002; Christopher Byron, Oct. 14, 2002; Kenneth White, March 12, 2003; Joseph Howerton, July 2003; Cody Shearer, Aug. 21 and 27, 2003, and Oct. 8 and 15, 2003, and correspondence Oct. 16, 2003; George Sullivan, July 2003; Charles Marshall, Nov. 27, 2002; Thomas Wik, July 2003; John Gorman, July 2003; Erica Jong, Feb. 24, 2003; Sharon Bush, April 1, 2003, and May 13, 2004; Thomas B. Wilner, Nov. 30, 2002; Mark I. Soler, July 2003 and Nov. 7, 2003; William Sloane Coffin, June 15, 2001, and Oct. 11, 2002; correspondence with Cathryn Wolfman Young, Nov. 21, 2003, and Jan. 17, 2004.

CHAPTER 15

Records: Barbara Bush to Marvin Pierce, newspaper clippings files, and George Bush diaries for UN years (called "Notes" on finding aid), George Bush Presidential Library; George Bush to Lyndon Johnson, May 29, 1969, with transcript of press conference, May 28, 1969, Tom Johnson memo to Lyndon Johnson, May 28, 1969, George Bush campaign letter, Jan. 23, 1970, and Tom Johnson memo to Lyndon Johnson, Oct. 5, 1970, Lyndon B. Johnson Presidential Library; Dorothy Bush eulogy for Prescott S. Bush, *Observation Post* (Yale class of 1977 newsletter), Manuscripts and Archives, Sterling Memorial Library, Yale University; Prescott S. Bush will, Connecticut Probate Court.

Books: Barbara Bush, *Barbara Bush: A Memoir* (New York: St. Martin's Paperbacks, 1995); George Bush with Victor Gold, *Looking Forward* (Garden City, N.Y.: Doubleday, 1987); Herbert S. Parmet, *George Bush: The Life of a Lone Star Yankee* (New York: Scribner, 1997); Richard Ben Cramer, *What It Takes* (New York: Vintage Books, 1993); George Bush to Carl Warwick, Nov. 8, 1970, in George Bush, *All the Best, George Bush* (New York: Touchstone, 1999); Fitzhugh Green, *George Bush: An Intimate Portrait* (New York: Hippocrene Books, 1989); Donnie Radcliffe, *Simply Barbara Bush* (New York: Warner Books, 1989).

Articles: Jefferson Morley, "Bush and the Blacks: An Unknown Story," *New York Review of Books*, Jan. 16, 1992; "The Nation," *Nutmegger*, Sept. 1978; Gail Sheehy, "Is George Bush Too Nice to Be President?" *Vanity Fair*, Feb. 1987; Robert L. Jackson and Ronald Ostrow, "Bush Got $106,000 in '70 from Secret Nixon Fund," *Los Angeles Times*, Feb. 7, 1980; Walter Pincus and Bob Woodward, "A Public Life Courting the More Powerful; Bush Cultivated LBJ, Sought Nixon's Aid," *Washington Post*, Aug. 8, 1988; Jane Podesta, "Playing to Win," *People*, Aug. 22, 1988; Jerry Tallmer, "Mrs. George Bush," *New York Post*, June 19, 1971; "New Man at the U.N.," *Washington Star*, Dec. 14, 1970; Elaine Sciolino, "Records Dispute Kissinger on His '71 Visit to China," *New York Times*, Feb. 28, 2002; "Bush Assumes Post as U.N. Envoy Today," *New York Times*, March 1, 1971; "Ex-Sen. Bush Dies; Son UN Ambassador," *New Haven Register*, Oct. 9, 1972; Beth McLeod, "President's Mother Was Captain of Smooth-Sailing Family Ship," *St. Louis Post-Dispatch*, June 30, 1991; "Hail and Farewell," *Nutmegger*, Dec. 1972; David E. Rosenbaum, "Bush Easily a Millionaire, but Growth Was Slow," *New York Times*, June 6, 1988.

Interviews: William Millburn, Jan. 30, 2002; John Claiborne Davis, Jan. 24, 2002; Stanley Willis, Jan. 25, 2002; Howard Means, Jan. 17, 2002; Marjorie Perloff, May 21, 2001; Leslie Cockburn, Dec. 12, 2000; Ymelda Dixon, Aug. 15, 2003; Betty Beale, Sept. 12, 2003; William Sloane Coffin, June 15, 2001; James H. Scheuer, April 3, 2002; Franny Taft, Oct. 8, 2002; Harry McPherson, June 6, 2002; Charles Bartlett, Oct. 30, 2003; Sydney M. Cone III, Nov. 29, 2002; Genevieve Young, Nov. 14, 2003; Joyce Burland, Jan. 9, 2003.

CHAPTER 16

Records: George W. Bush Texas Air National Guard records obtained through Freedom of Information Act, 2000; George W. Bush Texas Air National Guard records released by the President, Feb. 2004; documents concerning suspension of dentist's license on Nov. 17, 2003, of Denis A. Peper, D.D.S., Department of Health Professions, Commonwealth of Virginia; George Bush diaries for UN years (called "Notes" on finding aid), April 19, 1971, George Bush Presidential Library; memo to George Bush from John Calhoun, Aug. 16, 1974, Gerald R. Ford Presidential Library.

Books: Molly Ivins and Lou Dubose, *Shrub* (New York: Vintage Books, 2000); Bill Minutaglio, *First Son* (New York: Times Books, 1999).

Articles: Ken Herman, "Barnes Called Guard to Help Bush Get In," *Austin American-Statesman*, Sept. 28, 1999; Cragg Hines, "As Operative for His Father, Loyalty Was the Foremost Watchword," *Houston Chronicle*, May 8, 1994; Skip Hollandsworth, "Younger. Wilder?" *Texas Monthly*, June 1999; George Lardner Jr. and Lois Romano, "At Height of Vietnam, Graduate Picks Guard; With Deferment Over, Pilot Training Begins," *Washington Post*, July 28, 1999; Richard A. Serrano, "Bush Received Quick Air Guard Commission," *Los Angeles Times*, July 4, 1999; Jim Wilkes, "The Pilot in the White House," letter, *Washington Post*, May 23, 2003; John Grizzi, "Launching George W. in Politics," *Human Events*, Jan. 1, 1999; "A Blast from the Past," *New York Daily News*, May 27, 2001; David D. Porter, "Standing Up for Fairness; Blessings Endure from Civil Rights Movement," *Orlando Sentinel*, Aug. 9, 2003; Jill Lawrence, "The Evolution of George W. Bush," *USA Today*, July 28, 2000; Richard T. Cooper, "To the Manner Born, Bush Finds His Own Way," *Los Angeles Times*, July 30, 2000; Rupert Cornwell, "The Bush Clan: The Family That Plays to Win," *London Independent*, Nov. 7, 1998; Julie Hauserman, "Governor Gives Drug Issue Cold Shoulder," *St. Petersburg Times*, Aug. 25, 1999; Greg Palast, "President Top Gun: Affirmatively Missing in Action," gregpalast.com, July 9, 2003; Ralph Blumenthal, "Move to Screen Bush File in '90s Is Reported," *New York Times*, Feb. 12, 2004; Dave Moniz and Jim Drinkard, "Ex-officer: Bush Files Details Cause Concern," *USA Today*, Feb. 12, 2004; "Air National Guard Commanding Officer Alleges Bush Military Records Cleansing," talion.com, Nov. 5, 2000; Jo Thomas, "After Yale, Bush Ambled Amiably into His Future," *New York Times*, July 22, 2000; Glynn Wilson, "George W. Bush's Lost Year in 1972 Alabama," *Progressive Southerner* (southerner.net/blog), Feb. 2, 2004; "Associates Have Differing Memories of Bush's Alabama Stay," *Sarasota Herald-Tribune*, February 12, 2004; Walter V. Robinson, "1-Year Gap In Bush's Guard Duty; No Record of Airman at Drills in 1972–73," *Boston Globe*, May 23, 2000, "Republican Ticket Lets a Military Connection Slip," *Boston Globe*, July 28, 2000, and "Bush Credited for Guard Drills," *Boston Globe*, Feb. 10, 2004; Laurence I. Barrett, "Junior Is His Own Bush Now," *Time*, July 31, 1989; Paul Alexander, "All Hat, No Cattle," *Rolling Stone*, Aug. 5, 1999; "George W. Bush, 1946–," *Harvard Guide*, www.news.harvard.edu/guide (Aug. 18, 2003); "George W.'s B-School Days," *Business Week*, Feb. 15, 2001.

Interviews: Mark I. Soler, July 2003; Robert A. Rogers, Nov. 7, 2003; Christopher Byron, Oct. 14, 2002; Bill Penrose, May 14, 2003; Beverly Jackson, June 11, 2003; close friend of Denis Peper, Nov. 10, 2003; Marylouise Oates, March 18, 2003; Cody Shearer, Aug. 21 and Aug. 27, 2003, Oct. 8 and 15, 2003, and correspondence, Oct. 16, 2003; John Mashek, Aug. 13, 2002; Torbert Macdonald, July 18, 2003; Steve Arbeit, Jan. 14, 2003; Alf Nucifora, Nov. 12, 2003; Yoshi Tsurumi, March 8, 2004.

CHAPTER 17

Records: William J. Clark to George Bush, Jan. 31, 1973, George Bush diaries for RNC years (called "Notes" in finding aid), George Bush Peking diary, transcript of David Frost interview with George and Barbara Bush, Aug. 25, 1998, George Bush Presidential Library; documents concerning 1974 vice presidential search, cable from Henry Kissinger to George Bush, Nov. 1, 1975, and reply, memo from Warren Rustand to Dick Cheney, Nov. 29, 1974, concerning Jennifer Fitzgerald's leaving for China, Gerald R. Ford Presidential Library; George Bush to Lud Ashley, Aug. 21, 1974, Thomas L. Ashley Papers, Center for Archival Collections, Bowling Green State University; State Department Memorandum of Conversation, Peking, Dec. 2, 1975, National Security Archives.

Books: George Bush letter to his sons, July 23, 1974, letters to Richard M. Nixon, Nov. 21, 1972, and Aug. 7, 1974, letter to James A. Baker III, Aug. 24, 1974, and diary entries Aug. 6, 1974, Aug. 22, 1974, Oct. 21, 1974, and July 6, 1975, in George Bush, *All the Best, George Bush* (New York: Touchstone, 1999); Donnie Radcliffe, *Simply Barbara Bush* (New York: Warner Books, 1989); Barbara Bush, *Barbara Bush: A Memoir* (New York: St. Martin's Paperbacks, 1995); Richard Reeves, *President Nixon: Alone in the White House* (New York: Simon and Schuster, 2001); H. R. Haldeman, *The Haldeman Diaries* (New York: G. P. Putnam's, 1994); Nicholas King, *George Bush: A Biography* (New York: Dodd, Mead, 1980); Herbert S. Parmet, *George Bush: The Life of a Lone Star Yankee* (New York: Scribner, 1997); Fitzhugh Green, *George Bush: An Intimate Portrait* (New York: Hippocrene Books, 1989); Lowell Weicker and Barry Sussman, *Maverick* (Boston: Little, Brown, 1995); Richard Nixon, *In the Arena* (New York: Simon and Schuster, 1990); George Bush with Victor Gold, *Looking Forward* (Garden City, N.Y.: Doubleday, 1987); Gail Sheehy, *Characters* (New York: William Morrow, 1988); Richard Ben Cramer, *What It Takes* (New York: Vintage Books, 1993).

Articles: "Mrs. Bush—U.N. Wife, 'I'd Pay to Have This Job,'" *Washington Star*, Feb. 20, 1972; Nicholas Lemann, "Bush and Dole: The Roots of a Feud," *Washington Post*, Feb. 28, 1988; Jules Witcover, "Political Spies Accuse Committee Investigator," *Washington Post*, July 25, 1973; Fred Barnes, "Ervin Brushes Aside Bush's Charge," *Washington Star*, July 25, 1973; Jeff Gerth with Robert Pear, "Files Detail Aid to Bush by Nixon White House," *New York Times*, June 10, 1992; Barry Bearak, "His Great Gift, to Blend In," *Los Angeles Times*, Nov. 22, 1987; Lally Weymouth, "The Surprising George Bush," *M*, May 1991; Christopher Lydon, "President's Instincts Shaped Decision," *New York Times*, Aug. 31, 1974, and "From Watergate Woes to Mission in China," *New York Times*, Sept. 5, 1974; Gail Sheehy, "Is George Bush Too Nice to Be President?" *Vanity Fair*, Feb. 1987.

Interviews: Correspondence with Nicholas Lemann, Nov. 17 and 18, 2003; correspondence with Gore Vidal, July 2001; Lowell Weicker, Dec. 5, 2001; Sam Dash, Jan. 22, 2003; Roy Reed, Jan. 21, 2003; Roy Elson, March 26, 2002; correspondence with Kenneth G. Hafeli, audiovisual archivist, Gerald R. Ford Presidential Library; Nadine Eckhardt, Aug. 5, 2003; Marian Javits, May 23, 2003; Carol Ross Joynt, Oct. 8, 2002, and correspondence, June 11, 2003; Roberta Hornig Draper, Jan. 4, 2003, and Nov. 28, 2003; Phyllis Theroux, Oct. 17, 2001; Gene Theroux, July 17, 2002; confidential source, Aug. 28, 2001; Genevieve Young, Nov. 14, 2003; Gail Sheehy, April 29, 2002, and correspondence, June 24, 2002. Interview by David Robb: Carmine S. Bellino, Sept. 21, 1988.

CHAPTER 18

Records: Documents concerning appointment of George H.W. Bush as CIA director, including Collins and Roth letters and letter from Gerald R. Ford to John C. Stennis, White House memo on Jennifer Fitzgerald, Gerald R. Ford statement, Nov. 3, 1975, on changes in administration personnel and decision of Vice President Nelson Rockefeller not to run for reelection, documents concerning George Bush swearing-in ceremony as CIA Director, documents concerning Justice Department investigation of Richard Helms, Gerald R. Ford Presidential Library; Frank Church statement on George H.W. Bush nomination as CIA director, Nov. 11, 1975, Jacob J. Javits Papers, Special Collections, State University of New York at Stony Brook; "Hearing Before the Committee on Armed Services, United States Senate, Ninety-fourth Congress, First Session, on Nomination of George Bush to Be Director of Central Intelligence, December 15 and 16, 1975"; "Committee on Armed Services Report, Together with Minority Views (to Accompany the Nomination of George Bush)," printed Jan. 6, 1976; newspaper clippings files, Angus Thuermer account of lunch with *Time* editors, Feb. 23, 1976, Christmas card 1976, and Peking diary, George Bush Presidential Library; Lud Ashley to George Bush, Feb. 24, 1976, and George Bush to Lud Ashley, April 14, 1977, Thomas L. Ashley Papers, Center for Archival Collections, Bowling Green State University; George H. and Barbara P. Bush Income Tax Return, 1977; CIA documents concerning George Bush's interest in the John F. Kennedy assassination obtained through Freedom of Information Act (by David Robb, 1991); James Smith Bush FBI file obtained through Freedom of Information Act; divorce decree, Lois K. Bush and James Smith Bush, Dec. 4, 1970, Connecticut Superior Court, New London County; State Department "Consular Report of Death of an American Citizen Abroad" reporting the death of James Smith Bush, May 5, 1978.

Books: Joseph E. Persico, *The Imperial Rockefeller* (New York: Simon and Schuster, 1982); Herbert S. Parmet, *George Bush: The Life of a Lone Star Yankee* (New York: Scribner, 1997); Evan Thomas, *The Man to See* (New York: Simon and Schuster, 1991); Robin W. Winks, *Cloak and Gown* (New Haven, Conn.: Yale University Press, 1987); Fitzhugh Green, *George*

Bush: An Intimate Portrait (New York: Hippocrene Books, 1989); Nicholas King, *George Bush: A Biography* (New York: Dodd, Mead, 1980); Daniel Schorr, *Clearing the Air* (Boston: Houghton Mifflin, 1977); John Dinges and Saul Landau, *Assassination on Embassy Row* (New York: Pantheon Books, 1980); Barbara Bush, *Barbara Bush: A Memoir* (New York: St. Martin's Paperbacks, 1995); Gail Sheehy, *Characters* (New York: William Morrow, 1988); George Bush with Victor Gold, *Looking Forward* (Garden City, N.Y.: Doubleday, 1987); George Bush letter to J. C. Mohler, Aug. 4, 1976, letter to H. Neil Mallon, Aug. 16, 1976, letter to FitzGerald Bemiss, March 9, 1977, and diary entry June 4, 1975, in George Bush, *All the Best, George Bush* (New York: Touchstone, 1999); Bill Minutaglio, *First Son* (New York: Times Books, 1999); Ann Gerhart, *The Perfect Wife* (New York: Simon and Schuster, 2004).

Articles: Bob Woodward and Walter Pincus, "At CIA, a Rebuilder 'Goes with the Flow'; Avoiding Intellectual Debate, Bush Focused on Agency Image," *Washington Post*, Aug. 10, 1988; Norman Kempster, "Bush Urges Secrecy on Reporters List," *Washington Star*, Feb. 10, 1975; "CIA Halting Use of U.S. Reporters as Secret Agents," *Washington Star*, Feb. 12, 1976; Robert Lenzner, "Frank Sinatra Volunteers for a New Role—As CIA Helper," *Boston Globe*, April 15, 1976; David Robb, "Stone Doubts Bush's Faith in Warren Report," *Daily Variety*, Jan. 6, 1992; Scott Armstrong and Jeff Nason, "Company Man," *Mother Jones*, Oct. 1988; Jim Mann, "Bush Tried to Curb Probe of CIA," *Los Angeles Times*, Sept. 30, 1988; Robert Parry, "George H.W. Bush, the CIA, and a Case of State Terrorism," consortiumnews.com, Sept. 23, 2000; "But Who Has His Bag?" Associated Press, Feb. 13, 1976; transcript, *Larry King Weekend*, CNN, June 28, 2003; Kenneth T. Walsh, "The Good Fortune of Being Barbara Bush," *U.S. News & World Report*, May 18, 1990; Susan Watters, "When Push Comes to Shove," *W*, April 28–May 5, 1978; Lally Weymouth, "The Surprising George Bush," *M*, May 1991; Lois Romano and George Lardner Jr., "A Run for the House; Courting a Wife, Then the Voters," *Washington Post*, July 29, 1999; Mary Leonard, "A Dynasty Sign in Bush Sons' Rise," *Boston Globe*, Nov. 18, 1998; Andrew Stephen, "Dog Days at the White House," *Sunday Times Magazine*, July 22, 2001; Laura Bush, "First Person Singular," *Washington Post Magazine*, March 10, 2002; Michael Kranish, "Powerful Alliance Aids Bushes' Rise," *Boston Globe*, April 22, 2001; Jo Anne Davis, "Bush 'Coming Home,'" *St. Louis Post Dispatch*, Oct. 10, 1979; Bob Woodward, "To Bones Men, Bush Is a Solid 'Moderate,'" *Washington Post*, Aug. 7, 1988.

Interviews: Friend of Prescott S. Bush III, Oct. 12, 2002; Elizabeth W. Holden, May 28, 2003; Phyllis Theroux, Aug. 19, 2001; Beverly Sullivan, Nov. 28, 2003; Stephanie Lilley, Nov. 28, 2003; correspondence with Robin W. Winks, June 6, 2002; Roger Molander, Feb. 15, 2002; Osborne Day, Aug. 6, 2002; Robert Lenzner, July 17, 2002; Pat Holt, March 7, 2002; Martha Kessler, Nov. 14, 2001; David Robb, Nov. 14, 2001; Geoffrey Kabaservice, May 24, 2001; Gail Sheehy, April 29, 2002, and correspondence, June 24, 2002; Richard Helms, March 10, 2002; Ymelda Dixon, Aug. 15, 2003; Cody Shearer, Aug. 21 and 27, 2003, and Oct. 8 and 15, 2003, and correspondence, Oct. 16, 2003; correspondence with Lois Herbert, July 7 and 25, 2002; Ray Walker, May 28, 2003; Serena Stewart, June 4, 2002; Charles Stephan, July 16, 2002; Fred Purdy, July 30, 2002.

CHAPTER 19

Records: Press release, April 10, 1989, "Remarks of Ambassador George Bush, Candidate for the Republican Presidential Nomination, Before the Collegiate Press Association at Carnegie Mellon" ("voo-doo economic policy"); George Bush diaries for RNC years (called "Notes" in finding aid), Nov. 30, 1973, George Bush Presidential Library; George H. and Barbara P. Bush Income Tax Return, 1981; George H.W. Bush to Barry Goldwater, Nov. 14, 1984, Barry

M. Goldwater Papers, Arizona Historical Foundation; "Final Report of the Independent Counsel for Iran/Contra Matters, Vol. I, August 4, 1993."

Books: George Bush with Victor Gold, *Looking Forward* (Garden City, N.Y.: Doubleday, 1987); John Podhoretz, *Hell of a Ride* (New York: Simon and Schuster, 1993); Ed Rollins with Tom DeFrank, *Bare Knuckles and Back Rooms* (New York: Broadway Books, 1996); Herbert S. Parmet, *George Bush: The Life of a Lone Star Yankee* (New York: Scribner, 1997); Susan B. Trento, *The Power House* (New York: St. Martin's Press, 1992); Selwa "Lucky" Roosevelt, *Keeper of the Gate* (New York: Simon and Schuster, 1990); Bob Schieffer and Gary Paul Gates, *The Acting President* (New York: E. P. Dutton, 1989); Peter Schweizer and Rochelle Schweizer, *The Bushes* (New York: Doubleday, 2004); Edmund Morris, *Dutch* (New York: Modern Library, 1999); Mollie Dickenson, *Thumbs Up* (New York: William Morrow, 1987); Larry Speakes with Robert Pack, *Speaking Out* (New York: Scribner, 1988); Barbara Bush, *Barbara Bush: A Memoir* (New York: St. Martin's Paperbacks, 1995); Donnie Radcliffe, *Simply Barbara Bush* (New York: Warner Books, 1989); Geraldine A. Ferraro with Linda Bird Francke, *Ferraro, My Story* (New York: Bantam Books, 1985); Peter Goldman and Tony Fuller, *The Quest for the Presidency 1984* (New York: Bantam Books, 1985); Mark Hertsgaard, *On Bended Knee* (New York: Schocken Books, 1989); Jack W. Germond and Jules Witcover, *Wake Us When It's Over* (New York: Macmillan, 1985); Robin T. Lakoff, *Talking Power* (New York: Basic Books, 1990); George Bush letter to Barber Conable, Nov. 8, 1984, in George Bush, *All the Best, George Bush* (New York: Touchstone, 1999); Lou Cannon, *President Reagan: The Role of a Lifetime* (New York: Simon and Schuster, 1991); *The Tower Commission Report* (New York: Bantam Books and Times Books, 1987); George P. Shultz, *Turmoil and Triumph* (New York: Scribner, 1993).

Articles: David Remnick, "Why Is Lee Atwater So Hungry?" *Esquire*, Dec. 1986; Roy Reed, "George Bush on the Move," *New York Times Magazine*, Feb. 10, 1980; Paul Hendrickson, "Marathon with Earnest George Bush," *Washington Post*, May 23, 1979; Susan Watters, "When Push Comes to Shove," *W*, April 28–May 5, 1978; Francis X. Clines, "George Bush—Loyalty to the Cause," *New York Times Magazine*, Oct. 7, 1984; Barry Bearak, "His Great Gift, to Blend In," *Los Angeles Times*, Nov. 22, 1987; Amy Wilentz, "Bygones; Let Us Now Praise Old Enemies," *Time*, Dec. 23, 1985; Lou Cannon, "Bush Wins the Boss' Respect," *Washington Post*, Feb. 1, 1988; James R. Dickenson, "Reagan Has Straight Shot After Bush Concedes," *Washington Star*, May 27, 1980; Michael Kramer, "Inside the Room with George Bush," *New York*, July 28, 1980; Carl M. Cannon, "Reagan and Ford Flirt, but It's Bush," *National Journal*, Aug. 5, 2000; Mary McGrory, "Ford Reached Too Fast for His Inheritance," *Washington Star*, July 19, 1980; Pat Oliphant, "He Does Understand the Role of a Vice President," *Washington Star*, July 25, 1980; Evan Thomas, "George Bush Surprised by Landslide," *Washington Star*, Nov. 5, 1980; "Bush Style," *M*, Jan. 1989; Joe Conason, "He Cheats on His Wife," *Spy*, July/Aug. 1992; Jim Nolan, "Ambassador Who Spilled the Beans," *New York Post*, Aug. 11, 1992; Ian Brodie, "Bush Enraged by 'Sleaze' Claims of Affair with Aide," *Telegraph*, Aug. 13, 1992; Cragg Hines, " 'An Absolute Outrage': Questions About Infidelity Infuriate First Lady," *Houston Chronicle*, Aug. 13, 1992; George F. Will, "George Bush: The Sound of a Lapdog," *Washington Post*, Jan. 30, 1986; Hugh Sidey, "Taking Confidences to the Grave," *Time*, April 18, 1988; Walter Pincus and Bob Woodward, "Doing Well with Help from Family, Friends; They Pointed Bush to Jobs, Investments," *Washington Post*, Aug. 11, 1988; Arthur Wiese and Margaret Downing, "Bush's Son Was to Dine with Suspect's Brother," *Houston Post*, March 31, 1981; Arthur Wiese, "Vice President Confirms His Son Was to Have Hosted Hinckley Brother," *Houston Post*, April 1, 1981; "Hinckleys Reportedly Know Bushes," *Boston Globe*, March 31, 1981; John Mossman,

"Family 'Destroyed' by Assassination Attempt," Associated Press, April 1, 1981; "Hinckley's Father Denies Bid for $5 Million in Legal Move," *New York Times*, Oct. 18, 1993; "Reagan Calls Greenwich to Reassure Bush's Mom," *Greenwich Time*, Nov. 11, 1983; Julie DiMario, "Dorothy Bush Buoyed by Polls, But Wary," *St. Louis Globe-Democrat*, Sept. 29, 1984; "Bush Press Aide Isn't Sorry for Describing Ferraro as 'Bitchy,'" *Seattle Times*, Oct. 12, 1984; transcript, "The Bush-Ferraro Vice Presidential Debate: October 11, 1984," www.debates.org; "Bush Tries to Back Up His Charge That Mondale Said Marines 'Died in Shame,'" *Seattle Times*, Oct. 16, 1984; Susan Watters, "The Real Bush Campaign, Man vs. Politician," *M*, April 1986; Gail Sheehy, "Beating Around the Bush," *Vanity Fair*, Sept. 1988; John Hanchetter, "Laura Welch Bush: Shy No More," *USA Today*, June 13, 2000; Garry Trudeau, *Doonesbury*, on manhood, Oct. 30, 1984, and on Ferraro debate, Nov. 3, 1984; Walter Pincus, "U.S.-Iran Talks Helped Free 3 Hostages, *San Franciso Chronicle*, Nov. 6, 1986, and "How Iran Bluffed U.S. on Captives," *San Francisco Chronicle*, Nov. 12, 1986; "Letter Reveals How Bush Opened Doors for Pro-contra Leader," *Houston Chronicle*, March 15, 1987; "Bush Defends His Letter About North," *San Francisco Chronicle*, March 17, 1987.

Interviews: Cody Shearer, Aug. 21 and 27, 2003, and Oct. 8 and 15, 2003; John Mashek, Dec. 11, 2003; confidential source, Aug. 28, 2001; Susan King, Feb. 21, 2002; Kathleen Lay Ambrose, Feb. 16, 2003; Michael Kernan, Feb. 23, 2002; Robert Fink, Feb. 12, 2002 and April 3, 2002, and correspondence, Feb. 14, 2002 and June 4, 2002; confidential source, Dec. 19, 2003; Demaris Carroll, Dec. 11, 2003; Dolly Langdon Chapin, Feb. 7, 2002; "designer," May 16, 2002; "one of Strickland's friends," Oct. 12, 2001; Aniko Gaal Schott, May 6, 2003; Sharon Bush, April 1, 2003, and May 13, 2004; Floretta Dukes McKenzie, Aug. 4, 2003; Ray Walker, May 28, 2003; correspondence with FBI, June 14, 2002, and phone call, Nov. 15, 2002; Geraldine A. Ferraro, Oct. 22, 2002; Julia Malone, Oct. 9, 2002; Carol Taylor Gray, Oct. 3, 2003, and correspondence, Dec. 1, 2003.

CHAPTER 20

Records: "Stipulation Agreement" between State of Connecticut Department of Banking and J. Bush & Co., Inc., Jan. 20, 1991; "Order Approving Registration upon Conditions" of J. Bush & Co., Inc., July 25, 1991, Commonwealth of Massachusetts Office of the Secretary of State, Securities Division; State Department cable to "All Diplomatic and Consular Posts," Feb. 1989, requiring that they "avoid giving any appearance of preferential treatment . . . to any member of the Bush family," obtained through Freedom of Information Act; documents in the case of *West Tsusho Co., Ltd.* v. *Prescott Bush & Co., Inc.*, and Prescott S. Bush Jr. case no. 92 CIV 3378 (DLC), U.S. District Court, Southern District of New York, National Archives, Central Plains Region, Lee's Summit, Mo.; State Department cables concerning Jeb Bush trips to Nigeria on behalf of M&W Pump, March 1989 and June 1991, as well as proposed trips in May 1990 and October 1990, which were canceled for security reasons, obtained through Freedom of Information Act; "The President's News Conference," Sept. 12, 1991, George Bush Public Papers, bushlibrary.tamu.edu; documents filed with the Securities and Exchange Commission and with the Corporations Division of the Texas Office of the Secretary of State on behalf of Arbusto Energy, Inc., and of Bush Exploration Co.; transcript, "Videotaped Oral Deposition of Neil Mallon Bush, March 4, 2002, in the Matter of the Marriage of Neil Mallon Bush and Sharon Lee Bush"; "Agreement and Plan of Merger" between Spectrum 7 Energy and Harken Oil and Gas, Inc., Sept. 15, 1986.

Books: Peter Schweizer and Rochelle Schweizer, *The Bushes* (New York: Doubleday, 2004); George Bush letter to Marvin Pierce, April 7, 1955, in George Bush, *All the Best, George*

Bush (New York: Touchstone, 1999); Bill Minutaglio, *First Son* (New York: Times Books, 1999); Molly Ivins and Lou Dubose, *Shrub* (New York: Vintage Books, 2000); Ann Gerhart, *The Perfect Wife* (New York: Simon and Schuster, 2004).

Articles: Frank Phillips, "State Fines Bush's Brother in Stock Case," *Boston Globe*, July 26, 1991; " 'Family Values,' " *Treasure State Review*, Autumn 1992; Kenneth T. Walsh, "All the President's Children," *U.S. News & World Report*, Feb. 12, 1990; Michael Isikoff, "As Race Heats Up, So Does Scrutiny of Bush's Family; Relatives' Business Affairs Become Target," *Washington Post*, July 4, 1992; " 'When George Is Ready, I Am,' " *Nutmegger*, Jan. 1985; Debbie Howlett, "President's Uncle Shares Bush Family Ties to China," *USA Today*, Feb. 19, 2002; Jim Mann and Douglas Frantz, "Firm That Employs Bush's Brother Stands to Benefit from China Deal Trade: U.S. Satellite Export Would Aid Communications Venture of New York Firm," *Los Angeles Times*, Dec. 13, 1989; "Bush's Brother Dealt with Japanese Under-world Boss," *Japan Economic Newswire*, June 7, 1991; Leslie Helm, "Bush Brother Was a Consultant to Company Under Scrutiny in Japan," *Los Angeles Times*, June 11, 1991; "Prescott Bush Faces Inquiry on Pay for Arranging Deal," *Wall Street Journal*, Sept. 9, 1992; Stephen Pizzo, "Family Values," *Mother Jones*, Sept./Oct. 1992; David Margolick, "Brother Dearest," *Vanity Fair*, July 2001; Christopher Hitchins, "Minority Report," *Nation*, Nov. 12, 1990; Jeff Gerth, "The Business Dealings of the President's Relatives: What the Record Shows," *New York Times*, April 19, 1992; Alecia Swasy and Robert Triagaux, "Make the Money and Run," and "Commerce Job Led to Overseas Ventures," *St. Petersburg Times*, Sept. 20, 1998; Jefferson Morley, "Dirty Money," *Miami New Times*, Feb. 27, 1991; Mark Hosenball, "The Brothers Bush: Would You Buy a Used Car from These Guys?" *New Republic*, April 3, 1989; "U.S. Switches Gears, Frees Cuban; He Had Become a Cause Celebre for Right-Wing Expatriates," *San Francisco Chronicle*, July 18, 1990; "Choice for High Court May Cast History in a New Light," *St. Petersburg Times*, June 25, 2002; Sharon LaFraniere, "S&L Bailout Involved Jeb Bush Partnership; Federal Government Paid $4 Million on an In-vestment Loan Issued by Florida Thrift," *Washington Post*, Oct. 15, 1990; Pamela Constable, "Bush's Son Gets Political Boost in Miami by Backing Contras," *Boston Globe*, Jan. 14, 1987; Robert A. Liff, "Bush Boosts Martinez Coffers in Top Fund-Raiser," *Orlando Sentinel*, Oct. 10, 1986; David Hoffman, "Bush Boosts Candidate for Pepper's House Seat; Aug. 29 Special Election Contest Marked by Intensifying Racial and Ethnic Overtones," *Washington Post*, Aug. 17, 1989; Thomas Petzinger Jr., "Jeb Bush's Presidential Handle Appears to Prime the Pump Business in World-Wide Markets," *Wall Street Journal*, April 21, 1992; Adam C. Smith, "Some Say Probe Tests Ties to GOP Backer," *St. Petersburg Times*, July 18, 1999, "U.S. Drops Criminal Inquiry of Pump Company," *St. Petersburg Times*, March 16, 2002, and "Ex-part-ner of Jeb Bush Hid Assets Abroad, U.S. Says," *St. Petersburg Times*, April 6, 2002; Jonathan Beaty, "Running with a Bad Crowd," *Time*, Oct. 1, 1990; Bill Hewitt and Gary Clifford, "Neil Bush Fights to Clear His Famous Name," *People*, July 30, 1990; Carl M. Cannon, "Bush Rel-atives Not Always Vigilant to Avoid Conflict," *Greenwich Time*, April 26, 1992; Sharon LaFraniere, "Naivete and the Family Name; Denver Opened Doors to Neophyte Business-man Neil Bush," *Washington Post*, July 29, 1990; Thomas Petzinger Jr. and Edward T. Pound, "Bush Sons Jeb and Neil Have Walked a Fine Line Between Business Career, Ex-ploitation of Name," *Wall Street Journal*, Oct. 23, 1992; Kathleen Day, "Ex-regulator: Silver-ado Closing Was Delayed," *Washington Post*, June 20, 1990; Michael Duffy, " 'I Worried About the Impact on Dad'; Neil Bush Defends His Role in the Silverado Collapse," *Time*, July 23, 1990; George Williamson, "Ethics Expert at Hearing Blasts Neil Bush's Actions with S&L," *San Francisco Chronicle*, Sept. 27, 1990; Steven Wilmsen, "The Corruption of Neil Bush," *Playboy*, June 1991; Joan Lowy, "Neil Bush Cut Sweet Oil Deal Report: Small In-vestment Yielded Big Salary for Bush, but Federal Funding Was Legal," *Rocky Mountain*

News, May 3, 1991; "Tennis Tourney Dumps Neil Bush," *Rocky Mountain News*, May 30, 1991; "Neil Bush Goes Public with House," *Rocky Mountain News*, July 16, 1991; Michelle Schneider, "Neil Bush Tunes into Cable TV Job in Houston," *Rocky Mountain News*, July 17, 1991; Marcy Gordon, "Neil Bush's New Boss Says He Will Continue Fight for Cable Industry," Associated Press, July 18, 1991; Jill Abramson and Peter Truell, "Other Bush Relatives Also Engaged in Various Business Dealings Abroad," *Wall Street Journal*, Dec. 6, 1991; Mimi Schwartz, "Cast Away," *Texas Monthly*, May 2004; Joshua Micha Marshall, "Presidential Brother Watch," salon.com, April 12, 2002; Mure Dickie, "First Big Deal for Grace Semiconductor," *Financial Times*, Dec. 8, 2003; Khalil Hanware and K. S. Ramkumar, "Win American Hearts Through Sustained Lobbying: Neil Bush," *Arab News*, Jan. 23, 2002; "Baker Rejects Clinton Charge of Encouraging Anti-Semitism," *San Francisco Chronicle*, April 2, 1992; Tom Hundley, "Baker Flap Draws Anger from Many in Israel—Alleged Remark Rekindles Anti-Semitism Debate," *Seattle Times*, March 16, 1992; William Safire, "Bureaucratic Elephants Battle over Israeli Policy," *San Francisco Chronicle*, March 20, 1992; Cragg Hines, "As Operative for His Father, Loyalty Was the Foremost Watchword," *Houston Chronicle*, May 8, 1994; Jonathan Beaty, "A Mysterious Mover of Planes and Money," *Time*, Oct. 28, 1991; John Mecklin, "The Tangled Path to a Response," *SF Weekly*, Sept. 19, 2001; Paul Alexander, "All Hat, No Cattle," *Rolling Stone*, Aug. 5, 1999; George Lardner Jr. and Lois Romano, "The Turning Point; After Coming Up Dry, Financial Rescues," *Washington Post*, July 30, 1999; "The Right Price of Oil," *New York Times*, April 11, 1986; Robert Reinhold, "In Troubled Oil Business, It Matters Little If Your Name Is Bush, Sons Find," *New York Times*, April 28, 1986; Richard Behar, "The Wackiest Rig in Texas," *Time*, Oct. 28, 1991.

Interviews: Stephen Maitland-Lewis, July 10, 2001, and correspondence, July 13 and 16, 2001, Jan. 14, 2002, Dec. 17, 2002, and Dec. 28 and 29, 2003; confidential source, March 28, 2003; John Claiborne Davis, Jan. 24, 2002; Howard Means, Jan. 17, 2002; Bob Gardner, June 18, 2003; correspondence with Peter Gethers, Nov. 25, 2001; Robert Whitt, Oct. 3, 9, and 22, 2001; Ina Schnell, Nov. 13, 2003.

CHAPTER 21

Records: "Final Report of the Independent Counsel for Iran/Contra Matters, Vol. I, August 4, 1993"; 1988 campaign pamphlet, "George Bush. The one candidate who has proven his commitment to the Jewish people"; "George H.W. Bush's Acceptance Speech at the Republican National Convention—August 18, 1988," bushlibrary.tamu.edu/research/pdfs/rnc.pdf.

Books: Geraldine A. Ferraro with Linda Bird Francke, *Ferraro, My Story* (New York: Bantam Books, 1985); Sidney Zion, *The Autobiography of Roy Cohn* (Secaucus, N.J.: Lyle Stuart, 1988); Richard Ben Cramer, *What It Takes* (New York: Vintage Books, 1993); Marlin Fitzwater, *Call the Briefing!* (New York: Times Books, 1995); Peter Schweizer and Rochelle Schweizer, *The Bushes* (New York: Doubleday, 2004); Donald T. Regan, *For the Record* (New York: Harcourt Brace Jovanovich, 1988); Bill Minutaglio, *First Son* (New York: Times Books, 1999); John Brady, *Bad Boy* (Reading, Mass.: Addison-Wesley, 1997); George Bush letter to Robert Mosbacher, Feb. 14, 1985, letters to Dorothy Bush, Dec. 16, 1986, and Jan. 11, 1987, in George Bush, *All the Best, George Bush* (New York: Touchstone, 1999); George Bush with Victor Gold, *Looking Forward* (Garden City, N.Y.: Doubleday, 1987); Ronald Reagan, *An American Life* (New York: Simon and Schuster, 1990); Barbara Bush, *Barbara Bush: A Memoir* (New York: St. Martin's Paperbacks, 1995); Donnie Radcliffe, *Simply Barbara Bush* (New York: Warner Books, 1989); George W. Bush, *A Charge to Keep* (New York; William Morrow, 1999); George Bush with Doug Wead, *Man of Integrity* (Eugene, Oreg.: Harvest House Publishers, 1988); Jeffrey Eugenides, *Middlesex* (New York: Farrar, Straus and Giroux, 2002); Herbert S. Parmet, *George Bush: The Life of a Lone Star Yankee* (New York: Scribner, 1997).

Articles: Amy Wilentz, "Bygones; Let Us Now Praise Old Enemies," *Time*, Dec. 23, 1985; Aaron Epstein, "Bush Pays Tribute to Late Rightist Foe, Publisher William Loeb," *Houston Chronicle*, Dec. 15, 1985; John Robinson, "For Nancy Ellis, a New Role as the President's Sister," *Boston Globe*, Jan. 18, 1989; Charles Trueheart, "Bush's Day of Higher Service," *Washington Post*, Jan. 28, 1988; Garry Trudeau, "How will history judge the Bush hours?" *Doonesbury*, Aug. 10, 1985; George de Lama, "Bush's 'Administration' Passed Without a Sound," *Chicago Tribune*, July 16, 1985; David Remnick, "Why Is Lee Atwater So Hungry?" *Esquire*, Dec. 1986; William Greider, "The Bush Question: Is Anybody Home?" *Rolling Stone*, Sept. 22, 1988, and "Bush and Dukakis both Deserve to Lose," *Rolling Stone*, Nov. 3, 1988; Brian Duffy, "Guess Who's in the Loop? New Questions About George Bush's Iran-Contra Story," *U.S. News & World Report*, Oct. 5, 1992; Cragg Hines, "Politics, Poignancy Mix During Bush Auschwitz Visit," *Houston Chronicle*, Sept. 30, 1987, "Bush Battles 'Politics' Label on Europe Trip, but Not Aide," *Houston Chronicle*, Oct. 4, 1987, and "Thorny Issue of Abortion Plagues GOP Politics; Bush Stance Took Sharp Turn in 1980," *Houston Chronicle*, Aug. 10, 1992; Walter V. Robinson, "With Nazi Camp Tour, Bush Ends Polish Trip," *Boston Globe*, Sept. 30, 1987; "Vice President Tours Concentration Camps on Last Day of Visit to Poland," Associated Press, Sept. 30, 1987; "End of 4-Day Trip to Poland; Bush's Emotional Tour of Auschwitz," *San Francisco Chronicle*, Sept. 30, 1987; David Lee Preston, "Fired Bush Backer One of Several with Possible Nazi Link," *Philadelphia Inquirer*, Sept. 10, 1988; Chris Black, "Report Says Emigres with Nazi Ties Form GOP Unit," *Boston Globe*, Sept. 15, 1988; David Hoffman, "Bush Associate Resigns After Disclosure on BLS; Malek Tallied Jews for Nixon Administration," *Washington Post*, Sept. 12, 1988; Paul Alexander, "All Hat, No Cattle," *Rolling Stone*, Aug. 5, 1999; Lois Romano and George Lardner Jr., "Moving Up to the Major Leagues; Father's Campaign, Baseball Provide Foundation for Own Run," *Washington Post*, July 31, 1999, and "A Run for the House; Courting a Wife, Then the Voters," *Washington Post*, July 29, 1999; Michael Duffy and Nancy Gibbs, "The Quiet Dynasty," *Time*, Aug. 7, 2000; transcript, *Frontline* interview with Jim Pinkerton, 2000, from pbs.org (Aug. 6, 2001); Nicholas D. Kristof, "For Bush, Thrill Was in Father's Chase," *New York Times*, Aug. 29, 2000; Margaret Warner, "Bush Battles the 'Wimp' Factor," *Newsweek*, Oct. 19, 1987; Robert Parry, "Bush Family Politics," consortiumnews.com, Oct. 5, 1999; transcript, *Larry King Live*, CNN, Oct. 12, 1987; Bob Minzesheimer, "Bush Strikes Back," *USA Today*, Oct. 27, 1987; Jane Podesta, "Playing to Win," *People*, Aug. 22, 1988; Lori Stahl and Diane Jennings, "Bush Family, Friends Say His Sincerity Outshines Image Honed for Contest," *Dallas Morning News*, Nov. 13, 1994; Sidney Blumenthal, "The Sensitive Son," *New Republic*, Oct. 8, 1990; Maureen Dowd, "Making and Remaking a Political Identity: George Herbert Walker Bush," *New York Times*, Aug. 20, 1992; Allan Wolper and Al Ellenbert, "The Day Bush Bailed Out," *New York Post*, Aug. 12, 1988; Gail Sheehy, "Beating Around the Bush," *Vanity Fair*, Sept. 1988; Lou Cannon, "Bush Wins the Boss' Respect," *Washington Post*, Feb. 1, 1988; Jessica Lee, "Bush Supporters Deny His 'Macho' Stand Was Planned," *USA Today*, Jan. 27, 1988; Herblock and Mike Royko, "Perspectives," *Newsweek*, Feb. 8, 1988; "In Search of Stature," *Time* cover, Aug. 22, 1988; Marjorie Williams, "Reagan, Once Over Lightly for Bush; A Restrained Endorsement at Party Fundraiser," *Washington Post*, May 12, 1988; "Bush Sees Kin as 'the Little Brown Ones,' " *Washington Post*, Aug. 17, 1988; Brock Brower, "Captain Enigma: Can George Bush Lead the Nation?" *Life*, May 1988; David Hoffman, "A Day of Damage Control; Bush Team Hunts Facts, Holds Discipline," *Washington Post*, Aug. 19, 1988; transcript, "The Bentsen-Quayle Vice Presidential Debate," Oct. 5, 1988, www.debates.org; Ken Hoover, "Former

CIA Agents Urge Bush's Defeat," UPI, Nov. 4, 1988; Jonathan Kaufman, "Bush Ads Draw Charges of Racism; Some Say It's Just Politics," *Boston Globe*, Oct. 23, 1988; Jake Tapper, "The Willie Horton Alumni Association," salon.com, Aug. 25, 2000; "Silver-Footed Olive Branch," *Washington Post*, Dec. 4, 1988; Timothy Noah, "Old Bland-Dad: Meet Poppy's Poppa," *New Republic*, April 3, 1989.

Interviews: Geraldine A. Ferraro, Oct. 22, 2002; Michael Evans, July 17, 2002; confidential source, March 8, 2003; Susan King, Feb. 21, 2002; Anne Woolston, May 22, 2003; Roberta Hornig Draper, Jan. 4, 2003, and Nov. 28, 2003; correspondence with Peter Gethers, Nov. 25, 2001; confidential source, Oct. 12, 2001; Sandra McElwaine, April 18, 2001, and Sept. 8, 2003; Susan Watters, Oct. 8, 2002; Cragg Hines, May 22, 2003; Lilyan Wilder, Aug. 1 and 22, 2001; Charles Bartlett, Oct. 30, 2003; French Wallop, Feb. 25, 2003, and May 1, 2003; correspondence with Philip Agee, Dec. 7, 2003, and Jan. 4, 2004; correspondence with Peggy Noonan, Feb. 26, 2002; correspondence with Michael Sheehan, Feb. 1, 2004.

CHAPTER 22

Records: Transcript of David Frost interview with George and Barbara Bush, Aug. 25, 1998, "Gate List for Event: Luncheon—01/21/89," letters dated March 1, 1989, to each of George H.W. Bush's children concerning their White House Staff Mess privileges, Bush Presidential Records, George Bush Presidential Library; George Bush Public Papers, bushlibrary.tamu.edu.

Books: Donnie Radcliffe, *Simply Barbara Bush* (New York: Warner Books, 1989); Barbara Bush, *Barbara Bush: A Memoir* (New York: St. Martin's Paperbacks, 1995); Selwa "Lucky" Roosevelt, *Keeper of the Gate* (New York: Simon and Schuster, 1990); Colin Campbell and Bert A. Rockman, eds., *The Bush Presidency* (Chatham, N.J.: Chatham House Publishers, 1991); Lowell Weicker and Barry Sussman, *Maverick* (Boston: Little, Brown, 1995); Michael Duffy and Dan Goodgame, *Marching in Place* (New York: Simon and Schuster, 1992); John Podhoretz, *Hell of a Ride* (New York: Simon and Schuster, 1993); George Bush letter to Charles Bartlett, Feb. 21, 1989, and diary entry, Dec. 24, 1990, in George Bush, *All the Best, George Bush* (New York: Touchstone, 1999); Dan Quayle, *Standing Firm* (New York: HarperCollins, 1994); George W. Bush, *A Charge to Keep* (New York: William Morrow, 1999); Mary Matalin and James Carville with Peter Knobler, *All's Fair* (New York: Random House, 1994); George P. Shultz, *Turmoil and Triumph* (New York: Scribner, 1993); John Connally with Mickey Herskowitz, *In History's Shadow* (New York: Hyperion, 1993); Queen Noor, *Leap of Faith* (New York: Miramax Books, 2003); Bob Woodward, *The Commanders* (New York: Simon and Schuster, 1991) and *Shadow* (New York: Touchstone, 1999); George Bush and Brent Scowcroft, *A World Transformed* (New York: Vintage Books, 1998); Jim McGrath, ed., *Heartbeat: George Bush in His Own Words* (New York: Scribner, 2001); Robert Baer, *Sleeping with the Devil* (New York: Crown Publishers, 2003); John Brady, *Bad Boy* (Reading, Mass.: Addison-Wesley, 1997); Ed Rollins with Tom DeFrank, *Bare Knuckles and Back Rooms* (New York: Broadway Books, 1996); Jack W. Germond and Jules Witcover, *Mad As Hell* (New York: Warner Books, 1993).

Articles: Margaret Carlson, "The Silver Fox," *Time*, Jan. 23, 1989; Diana Wiest, "For Barbara Bush, This Move's a Joy," *Washington Times*, Jan. 17, 1989; David S. Broder, "What Makes Barbara Bush So Special," *Washington Post*, Jan. 22, 1989; Julia Reed, "The Natural," *Vogue*, Aug. 1989; Donnie Radcliffe, "The Book That's Banned in Kennebunkport," *Washington Post*, Aug. 15, 1989, "First Degree for the First Lady; Smith College Honors Its Undergraduates," *Washington Post*, Sept. 7, 1989, and "The First Daughter's D.C. Option," *Washington Post*, May 15, 1990; Cheryl Lavin, "Barbara Bush: Her Career Has Always Been Her Family, and It Hasn't Been an Easy Career," *Chicago Tribune*, Aug. 14, 1988; Patricia Leigh-Brown, "The First Lady–Elect: What She Is and Isn't," *New York Times*, Dec. 11, 1988; Michel McQueen, "America's Grandma: Barbara Bush Earns Even Higher Ratings Than the President," *Wall Street Journal*, Oct. 9, 1989; Fred Barnes, "CS," *New Republic*, Aug. 7, 1989; Ann McDaniel, "Barbara Bush: The Steel Behind the Smile," *Newsweek*, June 22, 1992; Liz Smith, "Crying Time for 'Evita,' the Movie," *New York Daily News*, Sept. 22, 1989; Marjorie Williams, "Barbara's Backlash," *Vanity Fair*, Aug. 1992; Michael Kilian, "A Lady, Bar None," *Chicago Tribune*, Nov. 8, 1989; Calvin Trillin, "First Lady," *Nation*, July 16–23, 1990; Bill Minutaglio, "George W.'s Secret Weapon," *Talk*, March 2000; Roxanne Roberts, "It's Just a Woof over Their Heads," *Washington Post*, March 19, 1989; Barbara Grizzuti Harrison, "Lunch with Bar: An Interview with the Ancien Regime," *New Republic*, Nov. 9, 1992; Dave Barry, "Barbara Shows She's No Shrinking Violet, and You'd Better Believe It," *Buffalo News*, Aug. 20, 1992; Barbara Matusow, "Mama's Boy," *Washingtonian*, June 2001; Dan Goodgame and Anastasia Toufexis, "What's Wrong with Bush," *Time*, Aug. 10, 1992; Julia Malone, "Bush Hiring Women," *Atlanta Journal-Constitution*, April 22, 1990; George J. Crunch, "Is This Goodbye?" *Time*, March 6, 1989; William Safire, "Media Manipulated!" *New York Times*, Feb. 9, 1989, and "Victory in the Baltics," *New York Times*, Jan. 21, 2002; Michael Kinsley, "Is Bush Nice?" *Time*, July 16, 1990; Kenneth T. Walsh, "The President's Damage Control," *U.S. News & World Report*, Aug. 13, 1990; Bob Woodward, "Origin of the Tax Pledge; In '88 Bush Camp Was Split on 'Read My Lips,' " *Washington Post*, Oct. 4, 1992; Diane McLellan, "First Daughter," *Washingtonian*, Sept. 1990; Landon Y. Jones and Maria Wilhelm, "George Bush," interview, *People*, Dec. 25, 1989; Jean Heller, "Photos Don't Show Buildup," *St. Petersburg Times*, Jan. 6, 1991; John Berry and Dan Koeppel, "A Line in the Sand, Dark Clouds for the Economy," *Adweek's Marketing Week*, Sept. 10, 1990; John Stauber and Sheldon Rampton, "How PR Sold the War in the Persian Gulf," prwatch.org (March 20, 2003); Dan Goodgame, "Men of the Year: The Two George Bushes," *Time*, Jan. 7, 1991; Dane Smith and Patricia Lopez, "A Voice for the 'Little Fellers,' " *Minneapolis Star-Tribune*, Oct. 26, 2002; "George Bush," *People* (Commemorative Issue: Heroes of the War), Summer 1991; Dan Balz, "Bush Seeks Firing of Party Official; White House Turns to Damage Control," *Washington Post*, Oct. 26, 1990.

Interviews: Cody Shearer, Aug. 21 and 27, 2003, October 8 and 15, 2003, and correspondence, Oct. 16, 2003; Bobbie Greene, Aug. 6, 2002; Donnie Radcliffe, Aug. 29, 2003; Heather Foley, Nov. 11, 1989, March 21, 2002, April 18, 2002, and June 24, 2002, and correspondence, May 21, 2002; Herbert E. Abrams, Oct. 8, 2002; Lois Abrams, Oct. 11, 2002; "CNN producer," Oct. 16, 2002; correspondence with confidential source, May 9, 2002; Sharon Bush, April 1, 2003, and May 13, 2004; French Wallop, Feb. 25, 2003, and May 1, 2003; correspondence with Jane Fonda, Nov. 10, 2003; Herb Moses, May 14, 2001; Paul Bedard, Aug. 5, 2002; Judy Woodruff, June 20, 2002; Ralph Neas, June 2, 2003, July 1, 2003, and Aug. 5 and 12, 2003; Susan King, Feb. 21, 2002; Lowell Weicker, Dec. 5, 2001; Claudia Weicker, Dec. 5, 2001; Kim Elliott, Dec. 10, 2001; Tom D'Amore, Dec. 10, 2001; Worth Kinlaw, June 2, 2002; Julia Malone, Oct. 9, 2002; John Mashek, Dec. 11, 2003; correspondence with Peggy Noonan, Feb. 26, 2002; Martin Tolchin, Feb. 10, 2001; Margaret Hall, April 18, 2003; Courtney Callahan, Aug. 29, 2003; Dan Rostenkowski, May 24, 2002; Douglas Bailey, July 12, 2001; Thomas S. Foley, March 19, 2002; confidential source, March 8, 2003.

CHAPTER 23

Records: George Bush Public Papers, bushlibrary.tamu.edu; George W. Bush letter to Boyden Gray on behalf of Rhesa H. Barksdale, July 1989, Case Number 063899cu, George W. Bush letter to Boyden Gray on behalf of Edith Brown Clement, Jan. 1991, Case Number 212251cu, George W. Bush correspondence with White House staff on behalf of Helen Segal Huvelle, April 1990, and others, WHORM: Subj. File, processed Freedom of Information Act request 1998-0044-F, Bush Presidential Papers, George Bush Presidential Library; Barbara Bush letter to Marianne Means, Feb. 1, 2000; Marianne Means letter to Barbara Bush, March 15, 2000; "Final Report of the Independent Counsel for Iran/Contra Matters, Vol. I, August 4, 1993."

Books: John Podhoretz, *Hell of a Ride* (New York: Simon and Schuster, 1993); Sarah Brady with Merrill McLoughlin, *A Good Fight* (New York: Public Affairs, 2002); Donnie Radcliffe, *Simply Barbara Bush* (New York: Warner Books, 1989); Joe Conason and Gene Lyons, *The Hunting of the President* (New York: Thomas Dunne Books, 2000); Michael Duffy and Dan Goodgame, *Marching in Place* (New York: Simon and Schuster, 1992); John Brady, *Bad Boy* (Reading, Mass.: Addison-Wesley, 1997); Barbara Bush, *Barbara Bush: A Memoir* (New York: St. Martin's Paperbacks, 1995); Monica Crowley, *Nixon off the Record* (New York: Random House, 1996); Marlin Fitzwater, *Call the Briefing!* (New York: Times Books, 1995); John Robert Greene, *The Presidency of George Bush* (Lawrence: University Press of Kansas, 2000); Bob Woodward, *Shadow* (New York: Touchstone, 1999), George Bush letter to Robert W. Blake, Oct. 10, 1991, letter to Alan Simpson, Oct. 21, 1991, and diary entries Nov. 4, 1992, and Nov. 19, 1992, in George Bush, *All the Best, George Bush* (New York: Touchstone, 1999); Jack W. Germond and Jules Witcover, *Mad As Hell* (New York: Warner Books, 1993); Susan J. Tolchin, *The Angry American* (Boulder, Colo.: Westview Press, 1999); Mary Matalin and James Carville with Peter Knobler, *All's Fair* (New York: Random House, 1994); Lawrence E. Walsh, *Firewall* (New York: Norton, 1997).

Articles: Donnie Radcliffe, "The First Patient's Return; A Decade After Assassination Attempt, Reagan at GWU," *Washington Post*, March 29, 1991; Frank J. Murray, "Reminiscent Reagan Zaps Bush, Backs Brady Gun Bill," *Washington Times*, March 29, 1991, and "Hampton's Class of '91 Snubs Bush," *Washington Times*, May 13, 1991; Andrew Rosenthal, "In Reagan's Cool Shadow," *New York Times*, March 30, 1991; David Talbot, "Reagan Blasts Bush," salon.com, April 14, 2003; Mollie Dickenson, "Bush's Assassination of the Brady Bill," *Washington Post*, Nov. 2, 1992; Lally Weymouth, "The Surprising George Bush," *M*, May 1991; Michael Kranish, "Outraged Bush Resigns from NRA," *San Francisco Chronicle*, May 11, 1995; Robert Novak, "Get-Even Time for Bush with His Slap at NRA," *Buffalo News*, May 23, 1995; Michael Rezendes, "NRA Says Bush Resignation Tied to '92 Campaign," *Boston Globe*, May 23, 1995; Lee Bandy, "Tributes to Atwater Stress Life," *Columbia State*, April 2, 1991; "Bush Will Attend Services Here for Wife of Ex–Business Partner," *Houston Chronicle*, Oct. 24, 1992; Thomas Sanction, "A Heartbeat from Eternity: Stricken with Fatigue and Shortness of Breath While Running Bush Recovers After Giving the Nation a Little Scare," *Time*, May 13, 1991; Sidney Blumenthal, "Bull Moose: George Bush and Teddy Roosevelt," *New Republic*, Jan. 7, 1991; Michael Duffy, "Mission Impossible," *Time*, Jan. 20, 1992; T. R. Reid, "One Flu Over the State Dinner; Japanese Warm to First Lady's Cool," *Washington Post*, Jan. 9, 1992; Greg McDonald, "Bush Set to Hit the Hustings After Illness; Democrats Get Flu Too, President Says," *Houston Chronicle*, Jan. 10, 1992; "The Clarence Thomas Bandwagon," *Baltimore Sun*, Aug. 12, 1991; Ruth Marcus, "Divided Committee Refuses to Endorse Judge Thomas," *Washington Post*, Sept. 28, 1991;

Timothy M. Phelps, "Ex-staffer Says Thomas Sexually Harassed Her," *Chicago Sun-Times*, Oct. 6, 1991; Walter V. Robinson, "Thomas Vote Delayed a Week; Hearings Set to Air Charge of Harassment," *Boston Globe*, Oct. 9, 1991; Helen Dewar, "Senate Confirms Thomas by 52 to 48 to Succeed Marshall on Supreme Court," *Washington Post*, Oct. 16, 1991; Robert H. Siner, "Women Make Big Inroads in Congress," *International Herald Tribune*, Nov. 5, 1992; "Better Late Than Never," *Time*, Nov. 4, 1991; Phil McCombs, "Counsel's Last Hurrah: The Final Furious Days of C. Boyden Gray," *Washington Post*, Jan. 16, 1993; Ann Devroy, "President Signs Civil Rights Bill; White House Disavows Proposed Directive to End Affirmative Action," *Washington Post*, Nov. 22, 1991; Thomas Oliphant, "Bush Response to L.A. Riots Too Little, Too Late," *Boston Globe*, May 7, 1992; Cragg Hines, "As Operative for His Father, Loyalty Was the Foremost Watchword," *Houston Chronicle*, May 8, 1994; Ruth Miller Fitzgibbons, "George Bush, Too," *D*, April 1992; Jim Nolan, "New Book: Bush Has Swiss Tryst," *New York Post*, Aug. 11, 1992; Dolph Tillotson, "A Sleaze-Monger? Not My Sister," *Galveston Daily News*, Aug. 16, 1992; Ian Brodie, "Bush Enraged by 'Sleaze' Claims of Affair with Aide," *Telegraph*, Aug. 13, 1992; Cragg Hines, " 'An Absolute Outrage'; Questions About Infidelity Infuriate First Lady," *Houston Chronicle*, Aug. 13, 1992; Marianne Means, "Why Dole Won't Get Bush VP Nod," *Houston Chronicle*, Jan. 19, 2002; Jon Swan, "Jennifer," *Columbia Journalism Review*, Nov./Dec. 1992; "Gennifer Flowers Is in Town, and She's Still Singing," *New York Times*, Jan. 25, 2004; Marlee Schwartz, Ann Devroy, and Gwen Ifill, "Bush Office Aide Expected to Get a Protocol Post," *Washington Post*, Jan. 10, 1992; Walter Pincus, "Former Bush Aide Fined for Customs Violations," *Washington Post*, March 18, 1990; Ann Devroy, "State Dept. Charges Longtime Bush Aide," *Washington Post*, Aug. 8, 1990; Gareth Pownall, "Jennifer Is Completely Incapable of Having an Affair," *Daily Mail*, Aug. 14, 1992; Leah Garchik, "President's Pal 'Disappointed' in Him," *San Francisco Chronicle*, Sept. 11, 1992; Janice Castro, "Same to You," *Time*, Aug. 31, 1992; Ann Devroy, "Dorothy Walker Bush Dies at Age 91; President's Mother, 'Righteous Lady,' " *Washington Post*, Nov. 20, 1992; "Mr. Bush's Unpardonable Act," *New York Times*, Dec. 25, 1992; "Was Vice President Bush in the Loop? You Make the Call," *Washington Post*, Jan. 31, 1993; George Lardner Jr., "U.S. Archivist to Quit, Run Bush Library; Wilson Agreed to Give Ex-President Control of White House Computer Records," *Washington Post*, Feb. 13, 1993, and "Archivist Was Sounded Out in December on Library Job," *Washington Post*, March 3, 1993; "Doing Bush a Favor," *Time*, March 1, 1993.

Interviews: Cody Shearer, Aug. 21 and 27, 2003, and Oct. 8 and 15, 2003, and correspondence, Oct. 16, 2003; Mollie Dickenson, May 20, 2002; Anne Pritchard, March 7, 2001; Robert DeVecchi, July 21, 2003; John Brady, May 15, 2001; Thomas S. Foley, March 19, 2002; Carol Taylor Gray, Oct. 3, 2003, and correspondence, Dec. 1, 2003; Ralph Neas, June 2, 2003, July 1, 2003, and Aug. 5 and 12, 2003; Susan J. Tolchin, June 21, 2002; Osborne Day, Aug. 6, 2002; Brian Doyle, Jan. 31, 2001; Dick Morris, Feb. 22, 2003; Julia Malone, Oct. 9, 2002; Mary Tillotson, Feb. 13, 2002; Dolph Tillotson, Feb. 19, 2002; Larry Sabato, May 19, 2004, and correspondence, May 22, 2004; correspondence with Tom Johnson, April 27, 2004; confidential source, Oct. 12, 2001; Sharon Bush, April 1, 2003, and May 13, 2004.

CHAPTER 24

Records: Transcript, "Videotaped Oral Deposition of Neil Mallon Bush, March 4, 2002, in the Matter of the Marriage of Neil Mallon Bush and Sharon Lee Bush"; documents concerning Securities and Exchange Commission investigation of George W. Bush sale of

Harken stock, obtained through Freedom of Information Act; Barbara Bush, July 8, 1978, fund-raising letter, Herbert Brownell Jr., papers, Dwight D. Eisenhower Presidential Library; documents in the case of *Philip Agee v. Barbara Bush et al.*, civil action no. 95-1905 (RCL), U.S. District Court for the District of Columbia; Barbara Bush letter of retraction to Philip Agee, May 9, 1997; "President Bush's Speech 4/26/99," intellnet.org (April 29, 2002); George H. and Barbara P. Bush Income Tax Returns, 1977–86.

Books: Barbara Bush, *Reflections* (New York: Scribner, 2003), *Barbara Bush: A Memoir* (New York: Scribner, 1994), and *Barbara Bush: A Memoir* (New York: St. Martin's Paperbacks, 1995); Peter Schweizer and Rochelle Schweizer, *The Bushes* (New York: Doubleday, 2004); Bill Minutaglio, *First Son* (New York: Times Books, 1999); Molly Ivins and Lou Dubose, *Shrub* (New York: Vintage Books, 2000); Ann Gerhart, *The Perfect Wife* (New York: Simon and Schuster, 2004); George W. Bush, *A Charge to Keep* (New York: William Morrow, 1999).

Articles: Chuck Clark, "Barbara Bush Spills the Beans; Son Jeb Confirms Intention to Enter Race for Governor," *Fort Lauderdale Sun Sentinel*, Feb. 18, 1993; "Mrs. Bush Advises Her Son: Don't Run," *St. Petersburg Times*, April 29, 1989; Cindy Rugeley and Mark Toohey, "Bush's Son Rejects Gubernatorial Bid," *Houston Chronicle*, Aug. 2, 1989; Alan Bernstein and R. G. Ratcliffe, "President's Son Won't Run for Bentsen's Seat," *Houston Chronicle*, Dec. 12, 1992; Paul Alexander, "All Hat, No Cattle," *Rolling Stone*, Aug. 5, 1999; Lois Romano and George Lardner Jr., "Moving Up to the Major Leagues; Laura Miller, "The Inner W.," salon.com, June 16, 2004; Father's Campaign, Baseball Provide Foundation for Own Run," *Washington Post*, July 31, 1999; Nicholas D. Kristof, "Breaking into Baseball; Road to Politics Ran Through a Texas Ballpark," *New York Times*, Sept. 24, 2000, "Governor Bush's Journey: A Master of Bipartisanship with No Taste for Details," *New York Times*, Oct. 16, 2000, "Bush and the Texas Land Grab," *New York Times*, July 16, 2002, and "Learning How to Run: A West Texas Stumble," *New York Times*, July 27, 2000; Dana Milbank, "Dispelling Doubt with the Rangers," *Washington Post*, July 25, 2000; Cragg Hines, "As Operative for His Father, Loyalty Was the Foremost Watchword," *Houston Chronicle*, May 8, 1994; Joe Nick Patoski, "Team Player," *Texas Monthly*, June 1999; Bill Minutaglio and Nancy Beiles, "George W. Bush . . . and the Horse He Rode in On," *Talk*, Nov. 2000; Robert Bryce, "A Home No More," *Talk*, Nov. 2000; Michael O'Keeffe, "Broken Promises Plague Parks; Owners, Mayor Are Texas Two-Faced," *New York Daily News*, Oct. 13, 2002; Charles Lewis, "How George W. Bush Scored Big with the Texas Rangers," public-i.org, Jan. 18, 2001; Skip Hollandsworth, "Born to Run: What's in a Name? How About the Republican Nomination for Governor," *Texas Monthly*, May 1994, "The Many Faces of George W. Bush," *Texas Monthly*, Feb. 1995, and "Younger. Wilder?" *Texas Monthly*, June 1999; Louis Dubose, "O, Brother! Where Art Thou?" *Austin Chronicle*, March 16, 2001; Tom Fiedler, "Bush and Sons," *Miami Herald*, Sept. 5, 1994; Marjorie Williams, "Brothers in Arms," *Talk*, Sept. 2000; Kevin Merida and Anne Day, "Dispatches from Florida GOP Race," *Washington Post*, Aug. 7, 1994; Diane Rado, "Bush Alienates Black Lawmakers," *St. Petersburg Times*, Oct. 28, 1994; "A New Clump of Bushes," *Economist*, Oct. 29, 1994; Jill Lawrence, "Issue May Belong to His Foe, but Jeb Bush Has the Appeal; Revamped Image May Help Candidate Win FLA. Gov's Race," *USA Today*, Oct. 27, 1998; Hugh Sidey, "Dad Says: 'I Don't Miss Politics,' " *Time*, June 21, 1999; Nicholas Lemann, "The Controller," *New Yorker*, May 12, 2003; Michael Duffy and Nancy Gibbs, "The Quiet Dynasty," *Time*, Aug. 7, 2000; Patricia Kilday Hart, "Not So Great in '78," *Texas Monthly*, June 1999; Arthur Blessitt, "The Day I Prayed with George W. Bush to Receive Jesus," www.blessitt.com, May 31, 2003; Ronnie Dugger, "Questions for George W.," *Texas Observer*, May 14, 1998; "Graham Apologizes for Faulting Jews," *Washington Post*, March 2, 2002; Eric Fingerhut, "Bush Tried to Clarify His Stand on

Jews, Heaven," *Washington Jewish Week*, Dec. 17, 1998; Michael Kinsley, "Go to Hell," slate.msn.com, July 24, 1999; Ellen Debenport, "Brothers Ran Different Races," *St. Petersburg Times*, Nov. 10, 1994; Hugh Aynesworth, "Photo Finish Anticipated in Texas," *Washington Times*, Sept. 25, 1994; Barbara Matusow, "Mama's Boy," *Washingtonian*, June 2001; Howard Fineman, "Harkening Back to Texas," *Newsweek*, July 22, 2002; Michael Kranish and Beth Healy, "Board Was Told of Risks Before Bush Stock Sale," *Boston Globe*, Oct. 30, 2002; "Bush's Son Misses Deadline for Reporting 'Inside' Sale," *Wall Street Journal*, April 4, 1991; Dana Milbank, "Bush SEC Delay Called 'Mix-Up'; Under Scrutiny, White House Shifts Blame for '91 Late Filing," *Washington Post*, July 4, 2002; Jules Witcover, "Will President Fall in Dad's Footsteps?" *Baltimore Sun*, July 12, 2002; "Into the Sunset," *Economist*, Jan. 16, 1993; "All the Presidents' Money," *Money*, July 1, 1999; Richard Cohen, "Post–White House Pay Dirt," *Washington Post*, Feb. 1, 2001; Dan Moldea and David Corn, "Influence Peddling, Bush Style," *Nation*, Oct. 5, 2000; "Kuwait, in 'Love Storm,' Welcomes Bush as Hero," *Baltimore Sun*, April 15, 1993; Seymour M. Hersh, "The Spoils of the Gulf War," *New Yorker*, Sept. 6, 1993; "Clinton Awaits Report on Alleged Iraq Plot on Bush," *Boston Globe*, May 9, 1993; Jeffrey Smith and Ann Devroy, "Clinton Says U.S. Action 'Crippled' Iraqi Intelligence; Officials Decline to Release Further Details," *Washington Post*, June 29, 1993; transcript, Richard Clarke interview, *60 Minutes*, March 21, 2004, www.sadlyno.com (March 22, 2004); "Bush Backs Clinton Anew on NAFTA," *Washington Times*, Oct. 21, 1993; Sue Landry, "Pride, Bitterness Fill Bush Speech," *St. Petersburg Times*, Feb. 8, 1995; Bill Minutaglio, "George W.'s Secret Weapon," *Talk*, March 2000; transcript, *Larry King Weekend*, CNN, June 28, 2003; "Ex–CIA Officer Sues Barbara Bush for Libel," *Washington Times*, Sept. 7, 1995; Joseph C. Wilson IV, "What I Didn't Find in Africa," *New York Times*, July 6, 2003; Robert D. Novak, "Mission to Niger," *Washington Post*, July 14, 2003; Mike Allen and Dana Priest, "Bush Administration Is Focus of Inquiry," *Washington Post*, Sept. 28, 2003; James Wolcott, "What If They Gave a War and Nobody Cared," *Vanity Fair*, March 2003; "Bush Sr.'s Profitable Crossing," *Business Week*, Feb. 22, 2002; Linda Rawls, "Home Builders Celebrate Booming Business," *Palm Beach Post*, Jan. 20, 2004; "Bush Made Less Than Reagan, Paid More," *Newsday*, April 23, 1988; Julia Malone, "President's Income, Taxes Drop in 1988," *Austin American-Statesman*, April 13, 1989; "Bush Family Income and Tax Bill Drop Slightly," *Washington Post*, April 16, 1991; Ellen Warren, "As Author, Bush No Match for Dog Millie's Royalties $889,176, the President's $2,718," *Buffalo News*, April 16, 1992; Ted Samply, "George Bush Parachutes Again to Exorcise Demons of Past Betrayal," *U.S. Veteran Dispatch*, March/April/May 1997, www.usvetdsp.com; Hugh Sidey, "Bush's Final Salute," *Time*, April 7, 1997; Jean Seligman, "Presidential High," *Newsweek*, April 7, 1997; Hugh Aynesworth, "Bush Makes Grand Entrance; Former President Parachutes over His Library in Texas," *Washington Times*, June 10, 1999; Cragg Hines, "Day to Remember for Bush; Library Dedicated at Texas A&M," *Houston Chronicle*, Nov. 7, 1997; Paul Jennings, "Planet Bush," *Texas Observer*, Nov. 6, 1997; Maureen Dowd, "Takin' Up for Daddy," *New York Times*, Nov. 8, 1997; Alan Judd, "Bush, MacKay Mince Words," *Sarasota Herald-Tribune*, Oct. 21, 1998; Dan Balz, "The Brothers Bush: One Deadpans, the Other Dances," *Washington Post*, Nov. 19, 1998.

Film: Stephanie Slewka (producer), *Every Head Bowed, Every Eye Closed*, 2004.

TV: Raney Aronsen (writer, producer, director) "The Jesus Factor," PBS *Frontline*, 2004.

Interviews: Kent Hance, May 2003; Peck Young, Aug. 15, 2003; Zach Leonard, June 8, 2002; Bobbie Greene, Aug. 6, 2002; correspondence with Leyla Aker, Sept. 27 and 28, 2001; correspondence with confidential source, March 21, 2004; Larry Lewin, June 21, 2002; correspondence with Philip Agee, Dec. 7, 2003, and Jan. 14, 2004; Lynne Bernabei, Jan. 30, 2004; "someone familiar with the evening," March 22, 2002.

CHAPTER 25

Records: Documents in the case of *John W. Moseley et al. v. Rainbo Club, Inc. et al.*, Henderson County, Tex., District Court, case no. 94A-365; police report on Laura Bush, Nov. 6, 1963, car crash, Office of the City Attorney, Midland, Tex.; Maine Department of Motor Vehicles document and Kennebunkport Police Arrest Record Card concerning George W. Bush DUI, Sept. 4, 1976, Metro Dade Police Department Offense Incident Report concerning George P. Bush, Dec. 31, 1994, and Tallahassee Police Department Offense Reporting Form concerning John Ellis Bush Jr., Oct. 7, 2000, thesmokinggun.com.

Books: Bill Minutaglio, *First Son* (New York: Times Books, 1999); Barbara Bush, *Reflections* (New York: Scribner, 2003); Peter Schweizer and Rochelle Schweizer, *The Bushes* (New York: Doubleday, 2004); Ann Gerhart, *The Perfect Wife* (New York: Simon and Schuster, 2004); James Moore and Wayne Slater, *Bush's Brain* (Hoboken, N.J.: John Wiley and Sons, 2003); Lou Dubose, Jan Reid, and Carl M. Cannon, *Boy Genius* (New York: Public Affairs, 2003); Al Franken, *Lies (and the Lying Liars Who Tell Them)* (New York: Dutton, 2003); George W. Bush, *A Charge to Keep* (New York: William Morrow, 1999); Molly Ivins and Lou Dubose, *Shrub* (New York: Vintage Books, 2000); Dana Milbank, *Smashmouth* (New York: Basic Books, 2001); Stuart Stevens, *The Big Enchilada* (New York: Free Press, 2001); Roger Simon, *Divided We Stand* (New York: Crown Publishers, 2001); John McCain with Mark Salter, *Worth the Fighting For* (New York: Random House, 2002); Jeff Greenfield, *"Oh, Waiter! One Order of Crow!"* (New York: G. P. Putnam's Sons, 2001); Jeffrey Toobin, *Too Close to Call* (New York: Random House, 2001).

Articles: Nicholas D. Kristof, "The Decision; For Bush, His Toughest Call Was the Choice to Run at All," *New York Times*, Oct. 29, 2000; "Pumping Iron, Digging Gold, Pressing Flesh," *Newsweek*, Nov. 20, 2000; "The Governor's Gusher: The Sources of George W. Bush's $41 Million Texas War Chest," tpj.org, Jan. 2000; transcript, *Frontline* interview with Clay Johnson, 2000, from pbs.org (Aug. 6, 2001); Katharine Q. Seelye, "Clinton-Lewinsky Affair 'Inexcusable,' Gore Says," *New York Times*, June 16, 1999; "McCain's Moment," *Time*, Feb. 14, 2000; Tucker Carlson, "Devil May Care," *Talk*, Sept. 1999; Ralph Blumenthal, "Move to Screen Bush File in '90s Is Reported," *New York Times*, Feb. 12, 2004; Dave Moniz and Jim Drinkard, "Ex-officer: Bush Files Details Cause Concern," *USA Today*, Feb. 12, 2004; Michael Rezendes, "Doubts Raised on Bush Accuser," *Boston Globe*, Feb. 13, 2004; Lois Romano and George Lardner Jr., "1986: A Life Changing Year; Epiphany Fueled Candidate's Climb," *Washington Post*, July 25, 1999; Frank Bruni, "Bush Clarifies Views on Abortion; Domestic, Foreign Issues Discussed in TV Interview," *New York Times*, Nov. 22, 1999; Jake Tapper, "Austin, We Have a Problem," salon.com, Aug. 20, 1999, and "Jonesing for Votes," salon.com, Feb. 3, 2000; "Ex-President Stands By His Son," *Houston Chronicle*, Oct. 20, 1999; Robert Bryce, "Prosecutor Says Bush 'Directly Deceived' Him to Avoid Jury Duty," salon.com, Nov. 5, 2000; George Lardner Jr., " 'Tort Reform': Mixed Verdict," *Washington Post*, Feb. 10, 2000; Katie Fairbank, "Bush Uses Tax Law to Cut Costs of Lakeside Retreat," Associated Press, Aug. 24, 1999; Bill Sanderson, "Laura: 'Fatal Crash Was Crushing,' " *New York Post*, March 3, 2000; "Lee High School Senior Dies in Traffic Mishap," *Midland Reporter-Telegram*, Nov. 7, 1963; "A Son's Restless Journey," *Newsweek*, Aug. 7, 2000; Hanna Rosin, "Applying Personal Faith to Public Policy; 'Changed Man' Advocates Church-Based Programs," *Washington Post*, July 24, 2000; Richard T. Cooper, "To the Manner Born, Bush Finds His Own Way," *Los An-*

geles Times, July 30, 2001; Alan Berlow, "The Texas Clemency Memos," *Atlantic Monthly,* July/Aug. 2000; transcript, *Larry King Live,* CNN, Jan. 14, 1998; Marlene Martin and Mike Corwin, "Karla Faye Tucker Executed in Texas," *New Abolitionist,* Feb. 1998; "Bush Donor Profile: Charles M. Cawley," tpj.org, Dec. 31, 2003; Jo Becker, "Bush: Wife Meant to Hide Shopping Spree from Me," *St. Petersburg Times,* June 22, 1999; Mimi Schwartz, "Cast Away," *Texas Monthly,* May 2004; Jim DeFede, "Problem Child," *Radar,* April 2003; "Who Is George W. Bush?" *Advocate,* July 4, 2000; "Bush Allows Gays to Be Fired for Being Gay," mis-leader.org, March 20, 2004; Calvin Trillin, "George W. Bush Speaks Out on Gay Marriage," *Nation,* March 22, 2004; "A Helping Hand from Dad: How Bush the Elder Is Quietly Boosting His Son's Cause," *Newsweek,* Sept. 27, 1999; Martha Brant, "A Little Help from Mom," *Newsweek,* Jan. 31, 2000; Mary McGrory, "New Hampshire's Cold Shoulder," *Washington Post,* Feb. 3, 2000; Andrew Phillips, "McCain's Magic," *Maclean's,* Feb. 14, 2000; Bill Moore and Danielle Vinson, "The South Carolina Republican Primary," byu.edu (Nov. 5, 2002); "Interest Groups Played Key Primary Role," *USA Today,* July 17, 2000; Cragg Hines, John W. Gonzalez, and Clay Robison, "McCain Pulls Attack Ads; Bush Keeps Up Negative Fire," *Houston Chronicle,* Feb. 12, 2000; David Von Drehle, "Lee Atwater, the Specter of South Carolina," *Washington Post,* Feb. 17, 2000; Richard H. Davis, "The Anatomy of a Smear Campaign," *Boston Globe,* March 21, 2004; Pete Yost, "GOP Consultant Named in Enron Ruling," *Washington Post,* March 10, 2003; John Harwood and David Rogers, "McCain and Bush Clash over Negative Tactics in Televised Debate as South Carolina Vote Nears," *Wall Street Journal,* Feb. 16, 2000; William Hershey and Ken Herman, "McCain Sweeps 2 States; Broad-Based Support Gives Him Arizona, Michigan, and Momentum," *Austin American-Statesman,* Feb. 23, 2000; "Boy George's Bogus Confession," *New York Daily News,* Feb. 29, 2000; Dave Gonzo, "Larry Flynt Drops Bombshell on Dubya," americanpolitics.com, Oct. 21, 2000; Ronald Brownstein, "Clinton, Bushes Not Quite Hamilton and Burr," *Los Angeles Times,* Aug. 3, 2000; Howard Fineman, "Ready for Their Close-Up," *Newsweek,* Aug. 7, 2000; Rafael Lorente and Jeremy Milarsky, "Bushes Come A-courtin," *Fort Lauderdale Sun-Sentinel,* Sept. 23, 2000; Glen Johnson, "Cheney Has Surgery After Slight Heart Attack," *Boston Globe,* Nov. 23, 2000; transcript, "Vice President Al Gore Delivers Remarks," cnn.com, Dec. 13, 2000.

Film: Alexandra Pelosi (director and writer), *Journeys with George,* 2002.

Interviews: Dan Rostenkowski, May 24, 2002; Ronald Reagan Jr., Feb. 6, 2004; correspondence with confidential source, June 10, 2003, and Jan. 6, 2004; "Washington, D.C., woman," Oct. 17, 2003; Sharon Bush, April 1, 2003, and May 13, 2004; confidential source, Feb. 7, 2002; David Fink, Oct. 8, 2002; Ruth Gilson, Jan. 21, 2002; Mark Salter, Nov. 4, 2002; correspondence with confidential source about Amtrak, June 10, 2002; Conway Downing, Feb. 15, 2002; Brian Doyle, Aug. 20, 2001; Richard Gooding, June 13, 2003; confidential source, Oct. 30, 2002; Heather Foley, Nov. 11, 1989, March 21, 2002, April 18, 2002, and June 24, 2002, and correspondence, May 21, 2002; Torbert Macdonald, July 18, 2003.

CHAPTER 26

Records: News releases, transcripts of George W. Bush speeches, remarks, and press conferences, and remarks by Mrs. Bush at the National Book Festival, Oct. 3, 2003, whitehouse.gov; George Bush Public Papers, bushlibrary.tamu.edu; statement by Barbara Lee, *Congressional Record,* Sept. 24, 2001.

Books: Gary Boyd Roberts, comp., *Ancestors of American Presidents* (Santa Clarita, Calif.: Carl Boyer 3rd, 1995) and *Notable Kin* (Santa Clarita, Calif.: Carl Boyer 3rd, 1998); Stephen

Hess, introduction to *America's Political Dynasties* (New Brunswick, N.J.: Transaction Publishers, 1997) and *America's Political Dynasties* (Garden City, N.Y.: Doubleday, 1966); Ann Gerhart, *The Perfect Wife* (New York: Simon and Schuster, 2004); Bill Minutaglio, *First Son* (New York: Times Books, 1999).

Articles: Susan Page, "A Dynasty by Any Other Name," *USA Today*, March 5, 2002, and "Crisis Presents Defining Moment for Bush; History Will Remember U.S. Response," *USA Today*, Sept. 12, 2001; David Jackson, "Presidential Library Prepares Exhibit on Bushes, Adamses," *Dallas Morning News*, March 4, 2002; Michael Duffy and Nancy Gibbs, "The Quiet Dynasty," *Time*, Aug. 7, 2000; R. W. Apple Jr., "Dad Was President (but Please, No Dynasty Talk)," *New York Times*, Jan. 31, 2000; Roxanne Roberts, "Like Father Like Sons; The Bushes Have Become the Nation's Most Prominent Political Dynasty," *Washington Post*, Dec. 16, 2000, and "Guess Who's Not Coming to Dinner," *CJR*, Sept./Oct. 2002; Dana Milbank, "Bush Courts Regional Media," *Washington Post*, Oct. 14, 2002; "Sun Beats the World," *Sun*, Nov. 17, 2003; Walter Isaacson, " 'My Heritage Is Part of Who I Am,' " *Time*, Aug. 7, 2000; Jeanne Cummings, "Bush Issues Order to Block Federal Funds for Overseas Groups Involved in Abortion," *Wall Street Journal*, Jan. 23, 2001; Eric Lichtblau, "Ashcroft Defends Subpoenas," *New York Times*, Feb. 13, 2004; Laurie McGinley, "Nancy Reagan Urges GOP to Back Stem-Cell Studies," *Wall Street Journal*, July 12, 2001; Paul Krugman, "Stating the Obvious," *New York Times*, May 27, 2003; Robert Salonga, "Students Protest Bush Speaking at Commencement," *Daily Bruin*, Feb. 20, 2002, and "First Lady Declines Invitation," *Daily Bruin*, Feb. 26, 2002; Cate Doty, "Laura Bush Has Words of Advice for Americans and Her Husband," *New York Times*, Dec. 29, 2003; Jill Smolowe, "Jeb's Daughter Fails Drug Program," cnn.com, July 17, 2002; "Transcript of Call to an Orlando Dispatcher," *Orlando Sentinel*, Sept. 14, 2002; Steve Coldiner, "W's Niece Busted Again," *New York Daily News*, Sept. 11, 2002; David S. Broder, "Now Comes the Hard Part," *Washington Post*, Sept. 2, 2001; Eric Alterman, "9/11/01: Where Was George?" *Newsweek*, Oct. 6, 2003; Jake Tapper, "Bush, Challenged," salon.com, Sept. 11, 2001; Mickey Kaus, "Bush Is No Giuliani; He Shouldn't Even Try," slate.msn.com, Sept. 13, 2001; Mary McGrory, "Leaders in the Breach," *Washington Post*, Sept. 13, 2001; Judy Mann, "Falwell's Insult Compounds Nation's Injury," *Washington Post*, Sept. 21, 2001; Jonathan Alter, "Periscope," *Newsweek*, Dec. 31, 2001–Jan. 7, 2002; Elisabeth Bumiller, "Filmmaker Leans Right, Oval Office Swings Open," *New York Times*, Sept. 8, 2003; Judy Keen, "Strain of Iraq War Showing on Bush, Those Who Know Him Say; He's Said to Be 'Burdened,' Tense, Angry at Media, Second-Guessers," *USA Today*, April 2, 2003, and correction, April 4, 2003; "What a Difference a Year Makes," *People*, Jan. 19, 2002; Thomas B. Edsall, "GOP Touts War as Campaign Issue," *Washington Post*, Jan. 19, 2002; Mike Allen, "GOP Takes in $33 Million at Fundraiser," *Washington Post*, May 15, 2002; Howard Fineman, "A President Finds His True Voice," *Newsweek*, Sept. 24, 2001; Dana Milbank, "A Coalition of the Willing to Visit," *Washington Post*, Dec. 22, 2001; Glenn Kessler, "U.S. Decision on Iraq Has Puzzling Past," *Washington Post*, Jan. 12, 2003; David Rose, "Bush and Blair Made Secret Pact for Iraq War," *Observer*, April 4, 2003; Anton LaGuardia, "Blair 'Restrained Bush From Attacking Iraq After Sept. 11,' " *London Telegraph*, March 21, 2003; interview with Christopher Meyer, March 19, 2003, for "Blair's War," *Frontline*, pbs.org; William Raspberry, "When Did the Target Become the Taliban?" *Washington Post*, Nov. 5, 2001; Marie Cocco, "U.S. Lets Afghanistan Traffic in Opium," *Newsday*, May 18, 2004; Vernon Loeb, "U.S. to Announce End of Afghan Combat," *Washington Post*, April 27, 2003; Eric Krol, "Fitzgerald: Bush Talked of Assassinating Hussein," *Arlington Heights Daily Herald*, Feb. 25, 2003; Richard Wolffe and Stryker McGuire, "A Gathering Storm," *Newsweek*, Jan. 27, 2003; Bill Walsh, "Bush Denies Personal Reasons Involved in Push to Depose Saddam," Newhouse News Service, March 3, 2003;

Eliot A. Cohen, "Air Strikes Shouldn't Raise 'False Hopes,' " *Wall Street Journal*, Oct. 8, 2001; Robert Barr, "Anti-war Protesters Hold Global Rallies," Associated Press, Feb. 15, 2003; Glenn Frankel, "Millions Worldwide Protest Iraq War," *Washington Post*, Feb. 15, 2003; Rebecca Dana, "For Bush Senior, a Return to Yale After Ten Years," *Yale Daily News*, April 25, 2001; transcript, George H.W. Bush interviewed by Paula Zahn, cnn.com, Sept. 9, 2003; "Former President Bush Defends His and Son's Iraqi Policies," Associated Press, Jan. 27, 2003; Les Kinsolving, "Bush Sr. Hammers Episcopal Bishop," worldnetdaily.com, Jan. 28, 2003; Frank Rich, "The Spoils of War Coverage," *New York Times*, April 13, 2003; Mike Allen, " 'Coalition of the Willing,' " *Washington Post*, March 27, 2003; William Douglas, "Bush's 'Great Image,' " *Newsday*, May 2, 2003; Peter Slevin, "U.S. Officials Cold-Shoulder Schröder," *Washington Post*, Sept. 24, 2002; Maureen Dowd, "No More Bratwurst," *New York Times*, Sept. 25, 2002; George E. Condon Jr., "President Hails Arrest, Warns Mexico," *Dover–New Philadelphia (Ohio) Times Reporter*, March 4, 2003; Andres Oppenheimer, "Bush Putting Mexican President on Hold," *Miami Herald*, March 27, 2003; Helen Thomas, "Nothing Sweeter to Bush Than Revenge," *Seattle Post-Intelligencer*, May 30, 2003; "Paris Air Show Opens; U.S. Stays at Home," *New York Times*, June 15, 2003; Lloyd Grove, "Hey France! Here's Spud in Your Eye," *Washington Post*, March 12, 2003.

Speech: David McCullough, National Press Club, June 11, 2001.

TV: Raney Aronsen (writer, producer, director), "The Jesus Factor," PBS *Frontline*, 2004.

Interviews: Susan Page, Jan. 17, 2003; correspondence with Gary Boyd Roberts, Dec. 14, 2002, and Feb. 22, 2003; Robert Dallek, Nov. 19, 2001; confidential source, Oct. 23, 2002; Linden von Eichel, May 17, 2004; Sharon Bush, April 1, 2003, and May 13, 2004.

BIBLIOGRAPHY

Abramson, Rudy. *Spanning the Century: The Life of W. Averell Harriman.* New York: William Morrow, 1992.

Adler, Bill, ed. *The Kennedy Wit.* New York: Bantam Books, 1965.

Amory, Cleveland. *The Last Resorts.* New York: Harper, 1952.

Baer, Robert. *Sleeping with the Devil.* New York: Crown Publishers, 2003.

Bainbridge, John. *The Super-Americans.* Garden City, N.Y.: Doubleday, 1961.

Barrett, Laurence I. *Gambling with History.* New York: Doubleday, 1983.

Beschloss, Michael R., ed. *Taking Charge: The Johnson White House Tapes, 1963–1964.* New York: Simon and Schuster, 1997.

Beschloss, Michael R., and Strobe Talbott. *At the Highest Levels.* Boston: Little, Brown, 1993.

Bissinger, H. G. *Friday Night Lights.* Reading, Mass.: Addison-Wesley, 1990.

Blumenthal, Sidney, and Thomas Byrne Edsall, eds. *The Reagan Legacy.* New York: Knopf, 1988.

Brady, John. *Bad Boy.* Reading, Mass.: Addison-Wesley, 1997.

Brady, Sarah, with Merrill McLoughlin. *A Good Fight.* New York: Public Affairs, 2002.

Briody, Dan. *The Iron Triangle.* Hoboken, N.J.: John Wiley and Sons, 2003.

Brock, David. *Blinded by the Right.* New York: Crown Publishers, 2002.

Brownell, Herbert, and John P. Burke. *Advising Ike.* Lawrence: University Press of Kansas, 1993.

Bruni, Frank. *Ambling into History.* New York: HarperCollins, 2002.

Bush, Barbara. *Barbara Bush: A Memoir.* New York: St. Martin's Paperbacks, 1995.

———. *Reflections.* New York: Scribner, 2003.

Bush, George. *All the Best, George Bush.* New York: Touchstone, 1999.

Bush, George, and Brent Scowcroft. *A World Transformed.* New York: Vintage Books, 1998.

Bush, George, with Doug Wead. *Man of Integrity.* Eugene, Oreg.: Harvest House Publishers, 1988.

Bush, George, with Victor Gold. *Looking Forward.* New York: Doubleday, 1987.

Bush, George W. *A Charge to Keep.* New York: William Morrow, 1999.

Campbell, Colin, and Bert A. Rockman, eds. *The Bush Presidency.* Chatham, N.J.: Chatham House Publishers, 1991.

Cannon, Lou. *President Reagan: The Role of a Lifetime.* New York: Simon and Schuster, 1991.

Carlson, Margaret. *Anyone Can Grow Up.* New York: Simon and Schuster, 2003.

Carlson, Tucker. *Politicians, Partisans, and Parasites.* New York: Warner Books, 2003.

Chester, Lewis, Godfrey Hodgson, and Bruce Page. *An American Melodrama*. New York: Dell, 1969.

Choate, Pat. *Agents of Influence*. New York: Knopf, 1990.

Clarke, Richard A. *Against All Enemies*. New York: Free Press, 2004.

Coffin, Tristram. *Senator Fulbright*. New York: Dutton, 1966.

Coffin, William Sloane, Jr. *Once to Every Man*. New York: Atheneum, 1977.

Conason, Joe, and Gene Lyons. *The Hunting of the President*. New York: Thomas Dunne Books, 2000.

Connally, John, with Mickey Herskowitz. *In History's Shadow*. New York: Hyperion, 1993.

Cramer, Richard Ben. *What It Takes*. New York: Vintage Books, 1993.

Crowley, Monica. *Nixon off the Record*. New York: Random House, 1996.

Dash, Samuel. *Chief Counsel*. New York: Random House, 1976.

Deaver, Michael, with Mickey Herskowitz. *Behind the Scenes*. New York: William Morrow, 1987.

Dickenson, Mollie. *Thumbs Up*. New York: William Morrow, 1987.

Dinges, John, and Saul Landau. *Assassination on Embassy Row*. New York: Pantheon Books, 1980.

Drew, Elizabeth. *Citizen McCain*. New York: Simon and Schuster, 2004.

———. *Election Journal*. New York: William Morrow, 1989.

Dubose, Lou, Jan Reid, and Carl M. Cannon. *Boy Genius*. New York: Public Affairs, 2003.

Duffy, Michael, and Dan Goodgame. *Marching in Place*. New York: Simon and Schuster, 1992.

Ehrlichman, John. *Witness to Power*. New York: Simon and Schuster, 1987.

Ferraro, Geraldine A., with Linda Bird Francke. *Ferraro, My Story*. New York: Bantam Books, 1985.

Ferrell, Robert H., ed. *The Eisenhower Diaries*. New York: Norton, 1981.

Fitzwater, Marlin. *Call the Briefing!* New York: Times Books, 1995.

Franken, Al. *Lies (and the Lying Liars Who Tell Them)*. New York: Dutton, 2003.

Fried, Richard. *Men Against McCarthy*. New York: Columbia University Press, 1976.

Frum, David. *The Right Man*. New York: Random House, 2003.

Garrow, David J. *Liberty and Sexuality*. New York: Macmillan, 1994.

Gerhart, Ann. *The Perfect Wife*. New York: Simon and Schuster, 2004.

Germond, Jack W., and Jules Witcover. *Mad As Hell*. New York: Warner Books, 1993.

———. *Wake Us When It's Over*. New York: Macmillan, 1985.

Goldman, Peter, Thomas M. DeFrank, Mark Miller, Andrew Murr, and Tom Mathews, with Patrick Rogers and Melanie Cooper. *Quest for the Presidency 1992*. College Station: Texas A&M University Press, 1994.

Goldman, Peter, and Tony Fuller. *The Quest for the Presidency 1984*. New York: Bantam Books, 1985.

Goldwater, Barry M., with Jack Casserly. *Goldwater*. New York: Doubleday, 1988.

Gotlieb, Sondra. *Washington Rollercoaster*. Toronto: Doubleday Canada, 1990.

Green, Fitzhugh. *George Bush: An Intimate Portrait*. New York: Hippocrene Books, 1989.

Greene, John Robert. *The Presidency of George Bush*. Lawrence: University Press of Kansas, 2000.

Greenfield, Jeff. *"Oh, Waiter! One Order of Crow!"* New York: G. P. Putnam's Sons, 2001.

Haig, Alexander M., Jr. *Caveat*. New York: Macmillan, 1984.

Haig, Alexander M., Jr., with Charles McCarry. *Inner Circles*. New York: Warner Books, 1992.

Halberstam, David. *The Fifties*. New York: Villard Books, 1993.

Haldeman, H. R. *The Haldeman Diaries*. New York: G. P. Putnam's Sons, 1994.

Hatch, Alden. *Ambassador Extraordinary Clare Boothe Luce.* New York: Henry Holt, 1956.

Helms, Richard, with William Hood. *A Look over My Shoulder.* New York: Random House, 2003.

Herskowitz, Mickey. *Duty, Honor, Country.* Nashville: Rutledge Hill Press, 2003.

Hertsgaard, Mark. *On Bended Knee.* New York: Schocken Books, 1989.

Hess, Stephen. *America's Political Dynasties.* Garden City, N.Y.: Doubleday, 1966.

Higham, Charles. *Trading with the Enemy.* New York: Delacorte Press, 1983.

Holden, Reuben A. *Profiles and Portraits of Yale University Presidents.* Freeport, Maine: Bond Wheelwright Company, 1968.

Hoopes, Townsend. *The Devil and John Foster Dulles.* Boston: Little, Brown, 1973.

Huber, Richard M. *The American Idea of Success.* New York: Pushcart Press, 1971, 1987.

Hughes, Emmet John. *The Ordeal of Power: A Political Memoir of the Eisenhower Years.* New York: Atheneum, 1963.

Hunter, Julius K. *Kingshury Place: The First Two Hundred Years.* St. Louis: Mosby, 1982.

Hyams, Joe. *Flight of the Avenger.* New York: Harcourt Brace Jovanovich, 1981.

Hyde, William. *Encyclopedia of the History of St. Louis.* New York Southern History Company, 1899.

Isaacson, Walter, and Evan Thomas. *The Wise Men.* New York: Touchstone, 1986.

Ivins, Molly, and Lou Dubose. *Bushwhacked.* New York: Random House, 2003.

——. *Shrub.* New York: Vintage Books, 2000.

James, Leonard F. *Phillips Academy, Andover, in World War Two.* Andover, Mass.: Andover Press, 1948.

Johnson, Haynes. *Sleepwalking Through History.* New York: Norton, 1991.

Johnson, Haynes, and Bernard M. Gwertzman. *Fulbright, the Dissenter.* Garden City, N.Y.: Doubleday, 1968.

Judis, John B. *William F. Buckley, Jr.* New York: Simon and Schuster, 1988.

Kelley, Brooks Mather. *Yale: A History.* New Haven, Conn.: Yale University Press, 1974.

Kilian, Pamela. *Barbara Bush.* New York: St. Martin's Press, 1992.

King, Nicholas. *George Bush: A Biography.* New York: Dodd, Mcad, 1980.

Knaggs, John R. *Two-Party Texas.* Austin, Tex.: Eakin Press, 1986.

Kouwenhoven, John A. *Partners in Banking.* New York: Doubleday, 1968, 1983.

Krugman, Paul. *The Great Unraveling.* New York: Norton, 2003.

Lakoff, Robin T. *Talking Power.* New York: Basic Books, 1990.

Lawson, Dorie McCullough. *Posterity: Letters of Great Americans to Their Children.* New York: Random House, 2004.

Lewis, Charles, and the Center for Public Integrity. *The Buying of the President 2000.* New York: Avon Books, 2000.

Loftus, John, and Mark Aarons. *The Secret War Against the Jews.* New York: St. Martin's Press, 1994.

MacPherson, Myra. *Long Time Passing.* New York: Anchor Books, 1993.

Manchester, William. *The Glory and the Dream.* New York: Bantam Books, 1975.

Mares, Bill. *Fishing with the Presidents.* Mechanicsburg, Pa.: Stackpole Books, 1999.

Marquis, Albert Nelson, ed. *The Book of St. Louisans.* St. Louis: St. Louis Republic, 1912.

Marton, Kati. *Hidden Power.* New York: Pantheon, 2001.

Matalin, Mary, and James Carville, with Peter Knobler. *All's Fair.* New York: Random House, 1994.

Mayer, Jane, and Doyle McManus. *Landslide.* Boston: Houghton Mifflin, 1988.

McCain, John, with Mark Salter. *Worth the Fighting For.* New York: Random House, 2002.

McCarthy, Abigail. *Private Faces/Public Places.* New York: Doubleday, 1972.

McCullough, David G. *John Adams.* New York: Simon and Schuster, 2001.

——. *Truman.* New York: Simon and Schuster, 1992.

McGrath, James, ed. *Heartbeat: George Bush in His Own Words.* New York: Scribner, 2001.

McPherson, Harry. *A Political Education.* Boston: Little, Brown, 1972.

Milbank, Dana. *Smashmouth.* New York: Basic Books, 2001.

Miller, Mark Crispin. *The Bush Dyslexicon.* New York: Bantam Books, 2001.

Minutaglio, Bill. *First Son.* New York: Times Books, 1999.

Moore, James, and Wayne Slater. *Bush's Brain.* New York: John Wiley and Sons, 2003.

Morris, Edmund. *Dutch.* New York: Modern Library, 1999.

Newhouse, John. *Imperial America.* New York: Knopf, 2003.

Nixon, Richard. *In the Arena.* New York: Simon and Schuster, 1990.

Noonan, Peggy. *What I Saw at the Revolution.* New York: Random House, 1990.

——. *When Character Was King.* New York: Viking, 2001.

Noor, Queen. *Leap of Faith.* New York: Miramax Books, 2003.

O'Neill, Tip, with William Novak. *Man of the House.* New York: Random House, 1987.

Paley, William S. *As It Happened.* Garden City, N.Y.: Doubleday, 1979.

Parmet, Herbert S. *George Bush: The Life of a Lone Star Yankee.* New York: Scribner, 1997.

Payne, Darwin. *Initiative in Energy.* New York: Simon and Schuster, 1979.

Persico, Joseph E. *The Imperial Rockefeller.* New York: Simon and Schuster, 1982.

Phillips, Kevin. *American Dynasty.* New York: Viking, 2004.

——. *Wealth and Democracy.* New York: Broadway Books, 2002.

Piotrow, Phyllis Tilson. *World Population Crisis.* New York: Praeger, 1973.

Podhoretz, John. *Hell of a Ride.* New York: Simon and Schuster, 1993.

Pool, James, and Suzanne Pool. *Who Financed Hitler: The Secret Funding of Hitler's Rise to Power, 1919–1933.* New York: Dial Press, 1978.

Powers, Thomas. *The Man Who Kept the Secrets.* New York: Knopf, 1979.

Quayle, Dan. *Standing Firm.* New York: HarperCollins, 1994.

Radcliffe, Donnie. *Simply Barbara Bush.* New York: Warner Books, 1989.

Raines, Howell. *Fly Fishing Through the Midlife Crisis.* New York: Anchor Books, 1994.

Ranelagh, John. *The Agency: The Rise and Decline of the CIA.* New York: Touchstone, 1986.

Reagan, Nancy, with William Novak. *My Turn.* New York: Random House, 1989.

Reagan, Ronald. *An American Life.* New York: Simon and Schuster, 1990.

Reeves, Richard. *President Nixon: Alone in the White House.* New York: Simon and Schuster, 2001.

Regan, Ronald T. *For the Record.* New York: Harcourt Brace Jovanovich, 1988.

Robbins, Alexandra. *Secrets of the Tomb.* Boston: Little, Brown, 2002.

Roberts, Gary Boyd, comp. *Ancestors of American Presidents.* Santa Clarita, Calif.: Carl Boyer 3rd, 1995.

——. *Notable Kin.* Santa Clarita, Calif.: Carl Boyer 3rd, 1998.

Rollins, Ed, with Tom DeFrank. *Bare Knuckles and Back Rooms.* New York: Broadway Books, 1996.

Roosevelt, Selwa. *Keeper of the Gate.* New York: Simon and Schuster, 1990.

Scheer, Robert. *With Enough Shovels: Reagan, Bush, and Nuclear War.* New York: Vintage Books, 1983.

Schieffer, Bob, and Gary Paul Gates. *The Acting President.* New York: Dutton, 1989.

Schorr, Daniel. *Clearing the Air.* Boston: Houghton Mifflin, 1977.

——. *Staying Tuned.* New York: Washington Square Press, 2001.

Schweizer, Peter, and Rochelle Schweizer. *The Bushes.* New York: Doubleday, 2004.

Seidman, L. William. *Full Faith and Credit.* New York: Times Books, 1993.

Sheehy, Gail. *Character.* New York: William Morrow, 1988.

Shultz, George P. *Turmoil and Triumph.* New York: Scribner, 1993.

Simon, Roger. *Divided We Stand.* New York: Crown Publishers, 2001.

Simpson, Christopher. *The Splendid Blond Beast: Money, Law, and Genocide in the Twenti-eth Century.* New York: Grove Press, 1993.

Smith, Sally Bedell. *In All His Glory.* New York: Simon and Schuster, 1990.

Speakes, Larry, with Robert Pack. *Speaking Out.* New York: Scribner, 1988.

Stevens, Stuart. *The Big Enchilada.* New York: Free Press, 2001.

Suskind, Ron. *The Price of Loyalty.* New York: Simon and Schuster, 2004.

Talbot, Allan R. *The Mayor's Game: Richard Lee of New Haven and the Politics of Change.* New York: Praeger, 1970.

Thatcher, Margaret. *The Downing Street Years.* New York: HarperCollins, 1993.

Thomas, Evan. *The Man to See.* New York: Simon and Schuster, 1991.

Tifft, Susan E., and Alex S. Jones. *The Trust.* Boston: Little, Brown, 1999.

Tolchin, Susan J. *The Angry American.* Boulder, Colo.: Westview Press, 1999.

Toobin, Jeffrey. *Too Close to Call.* New York: Random House, 2001.

The Tower Commission Report. New York: Bantam Books and Times Books, 1987.

Trento, Susan B. *The Power House.* New York: St. Martin's Press, 1992.

Turner, Henry Ashby, Jr. *German Big Business and the Rise of Hitler.* New York: Oxford University Press, 1985.

Van Ravenswaay, Charles. *St. Louis: An Informal History of the City and Its People, 1764–1865.* Edited by Candace O'Connor. St. Louis: Missouri Historical Society Press, 1991.

Vincent, Fay. *The Last Commissioner.* New York: Simon and Schuster, 2002.

Walsh, Lawrence E. *Firewall.* New York: Norton, 1997.

Wead, Doug. *All the President's Children.* New York: Atria Books, 2003.

Weicker, Lowell, and Barry Sussman. *Maverick.* Boston: Little, Brown, 1995.

Wells, Tom. *Wild Man: The Life and Times of Daniel Ellsberg.* New York: Palgrave, 2001.

White, Theodore H. *The Making of the President, 1964.* New York: Atheneum Publishers, 1965.

——. *The Making of the President, 1968.* New York: Atheneum Publishers, 1969.

Wicker, Tom. *George Herbert Walker Bush.* New York: Viking, 2004.

Wilder, Lilyan. *Talk Your Way to Success.* New York: Eastside Publishing, 1986, 1991.

Wills, Garry. *Reagan's America: Innocents at Home.* New York: Doubleday, 1986.

Wilson, Robert A., ed. *Character Above All.* New York: Simon and Schuster, 1995.

Winks, Robin W. *Cloak and Gown.* New Haven, Conn.: Yale University Press, 1987.

Wistrich, Robert. *Who's Who in Nazi Germany.* New York: Macmillan, 1982.

Woods, Randall Bennett. *Fulbright.* New York: Cambridge University Press, 1995.

Woodward, Bob. *Bush at War.* New York: Simon and Schuster, 2002.

——. *The Commanders.* New York: Scribner, 2001.

——. *Plan of Attack.* New York: Simon and Schuster, 2004.

——. *Shadow.* New York: Touchstone, 1999.

Woolley, Knight. *In Retrospect.* Privately printed, 1975.

Zion, Sidney. *The Autobiography of Roy Cohn.* Secaucus, N.J.: Lyle Stuart, 1988.

ACKNOWLEDGMENTS

The President had declared Friday, September 14, 2001, a National Day of Prayer and Remembrance. He and the First Lady joined former Presidents Clinton, Bush, Carter, and Ford and their wives, as well as members of Congress, the U.S. Senate, the Cabinet, the U.S. Supreme Court, and the Joint Chiefs of Staff at the Washington National Cathedral to honor the memory of the 9/11 victims and the families who had lost so much.

Security was formidable that morning and only those with tickets were allowed inside. I arrived at 10:45 a.m. with a green ticket distributed to family members of the Cathedral Boy and Girl Choristers. My wonderful next-door neighbor Peter Gilchrist, who sang in the choir, had given me one of his tickets, which placed me a few feet away from the pews of the Presidents. Next to me was the Reverend Patricia Johnson, whose son was also a chorister. We sat down together as strangers and departed as friends. She is tall, black, and elegant; I am the opposite, but we had no barriers stronger than our need to feel human and hopeful again after three days of shock and trauma. There were no Republicans or Democrats in the Cathedral that day, only grieving Americans in need of succor.

As the President walked across the marble floor of the main altar to ascend the lectern, Patricia and I instinctively grasped hands, like anxious mothers, hoping for a flawless performance from a child who has frequent pratfalls. The President rose to the occasion and spoke well as he offered the families of 9/11 the nation's sympathy, but he startled many of the three thousand people assembled when he began to mix patriotism with religion and declared that ridding the world of evil was the country's "responsibility to history." As he returned to his seat, he passed the Rev. Billy Graham and affectionately patted the elderly man's shoulder. When Bush sat down, his father, George Herbert Walker Bush, reached over and squeezed his hand as if to say, "You did well."

I tried to remember the President's words about a "responsibility to history" as I researched this book on his family, and I sought the assistance of many people to fulfill that responsibility. I'm indebted to all, especially the librarians, curators, and archivists who helped me in compiling the family's ancestral background and provided access to the unpublished letters, records, documents, and diaries I needed to tell the family's story. I'm extraordinarily grateful for the scholarly research of Ellen Walker, Ruth Quattlebaum, Tana Sherman, Timothy Sprattler, and Lynda V. Diamondis: Phillips Academy, Andover, Massachusetts; Tom Conroy: Yale Public Affairs; William R. Massa Jr. and Diane Kaplan: Manuscripts and Archives, Sterling Memorial Library, Yale University; Angelyn Singer and Christine Baird: Alumni

Records, Yale University; Jessica He, research assistant for Professor Douglas Rae, Yale School of Management; Fred Romanski, Barry L. Zerby, and Pat Anderson: National Archives and Records in College Park, Maryland; Lisa Gezelter, archivist: National Archive in Pacific Region (Laguna Niguel); Research staff: Ohio Historical Society; Barbara Reed: FACT Line, Columbus Public Schools, Ohio; Doug McCabe: Ohio University Library, Athens, Ohio; Donald A. Ritchie, associate historian, and Betty K. Koed: U.S. Senate; Suzanne Callison Dicks: U.S. Capitol Historical Society; American Institute for Economic Research; Ruth Ann Rugg: Sixth Floor Museum, Dallas, Texas; Barbie Selby and Gary Treadway: University of Virginia Law Library, Charlottesville, Virginia; Anthony Sgro: Woodberry Forest School, Orange, Virginia; Kathryn Stallard and John G. Tower, archivists: Southwestern University, Georgetown, Texas; Gregory H. Stoner and Toni M. Carter: Virginia Historical Society, Richmond, Virginia; Jason D. Stratman: Missouri Historical Society, St. Louis; Towana D. Spivey, director: Fort Sill National Historical Landmark, Fort Sill, Oklahoma; Aulene Gibson: Southwest Oklahoma Genealogical Society; Richard Spiers, superintendent: Hope Cemetery, Kennebunkport, Maine; Barbara Barwise: Kennebunkport Historical Society; Betty Austin, archivist: Fulbright Papers, University of Arkansas, Fayetteville, Arkansas; Monica Blank and Amy Fitch, archivists: Rockefeller Archive Center, Sleepy Hollow, New York; Caroline Bradley: Westerly Public Library, Westerly, Rhode Island; Virginia Buchanan: Smith County Historical Society, Tyler, Texas; Richard M. Bulatoff: Hoover Institution Archives, Stanford University; Steve Charter: Center for Archival Collections, Bowling Green State University, Bowling Green, Ohio; Deneen Carter: Franklin County Probate Court, Columbus, Ohio; Mary M. Huth and Sarah DeSanctis: Rush Rhees Library, University of Rochester, New York; John G. Doll: Gilbert Y. Taverner Archives, St. George's School, Newport, Rhode Island; Jules J. Duga: Columbus Jewish Historical Society, Ohio; Megan Hahn Fraser: New-York Historical Society, New York, New York; The Honorable George Mitchell and Ian Graham: Special Collections, Bowdoin University, Brunswick, Maine; Sarah Hartwell: Rauner Special Collections, Dartmouth University, Hanover, New Hampshire; Alexander Sanger, Esther Katz, and Cathy Moran Hajo: Margaret Sanger Papers Project, New York University, New York, New York; Lianne Hartman: Bently Historical Library, University of Michigan, Ann Arbor, Michigan; Cory Hatch and Jared Jackson: Arizona Historical Foundation, Tempe, Arizona; John Neal Hoover, librarian: St. Louis Mercantile Library; Noel C. Hollabeck: St. Louis Public Library; Karen Mason, curator: Iowa Women's Archive, University of Iowa; Kirsten Jensen, archivist: Historical Society of the Town of Greenwich, Connecticut; Kristine Krueger: National Film Information Service, Center for Motion Picture Study, Beverly Hills, California; Bonnie Linck: Connecticut State Library; Barbara Lowden, Assistant Registrar: Vital Statistics, Greenwich, Connecticut; Ryan Hendrickson: Howard Gotlieb Archival Research Center, Boston University, Massachusetts; Kristen J. Nyitray: special collections, State University of New York at Stony Brook; Kathy Ogden: Greenwich Oral History Project, Connecticut; Michael V. Lynch, registrar: vital statistics, New Haven, Connecticut; Mary K. Moore: Bohemian Grove Action Network, Occidental, California; Ken Marder: Silas Bronson Library, Waterbury, Connecticut; Keith Stretcher, City Attorney: City of Midland, Texas; Greg Platts: Alfalfa Club, Washington, D.C.; Marta Ross Dunetz, archivist: St. Albans School, Washington, D.C.

Many presidential archivists contributed to the research and I'm grateful to all: Lynn Smith: Hoover Presidential Library, West Branch, Iowa; Raymond Teichman: FDR Presidential Library, Hyde Park, New York; Dennis E. Bilger: Harry S. Truman Library, Independence, Missouri; David J. Haight, Dwight Strandberg, and Hazel Stitt: Dwight D. Eisenhower Library, Abilene, Kansas; Staff: John F. Kennedy Library, Boston, Massachusetts; Claudia Anderson, Mary K. Knill, and Linda M. Seelke: Lyndon Baines Johnson Library, Austin, Texas; Dimitri K. Simes, president: The Nixon Center, Washington, D.C.; Susan

Naulty, archivist: Richard Nixon Library & Birthplace, Yorba Linda, California; Leigh Dale, Stacy Davis, Geir Gundersen, Kenneth G. Hafeli, and Donna Lehman: Gerald R. Ford Library, Ann Arbor, Michigan; Albert Nason: Jimmy Carter Library, Atlanta, Georgia; Jennifer Sternaman, archivist: Ronald Reagan Library, Simi Valley, California; Laura Spencer, Bonnie Burlbaw, Debbie Carter, R. Matthew Lee, Stephanie Oriabure and Deborah Wheeler: George Bush Presidential Library, College Station, Texas.

My thanks to the newspaper and magazine librarians who helped retrieve what was not available online: Press Association of the U.K.; Joshua Balling, managing editor, *The Inquirer and Mirror*, Nantucket, Massachusetts; Carolyn McClintock, *LA Weekly*; Cam Willis at *D* magazine; Susan Butler, *Portland Press Herald*; Merle Thomason, Fairchild Library, Pasadena, California; Dick Weiss, *St. Louis Post-Dispatch*; Jeanette Dean, *Los Angeles Times*; Marie Deitch, librarian, *Greenwich Time*; Kathy McKula, *Hartford Courant*; Dina Modianot-Fox, *Greenwich Magazine*; and Andrea Murphy, *American Heritage*.

Many people helped me during the four years I worked on this book. While I cannot acknowlege all 937 people I spoke with, I am grateful for their contributions. My thanks to: Rudy Abramson, Herbert and Lois Abrams, David Acheson, Cindy Adams, Peggy Adler, Phillip Agee, Lola Aiken, Miriam Ain, Leyla Aker, Linda Aker, Edward Albee, Marcia Alcorn, Janice and Steve Allen, Margaret Alton and Tom Weisser, Kathleen Ambrose, Robert Sam Anson, Steve Arbeit, Dickie Arbiter, Elizabeth A. Archer, Thomas J. Ashley Jr., Rick Atkinson, Doug Bailey, Pat Bailey, Earl Balfour, Tom Bannon, Mike Barnicle, Richard Barrett, Susan Barron, Anita Bartholomew, Charles Bartlett, Ysaye Maria Barnwell, Roberta Baskin, Patrick Beach, Betty Beale, Barry Bearak, Paul Bedard, Sarah Witham Bednarz, Susan Bennett, Michelle Berman, Lynne Bernabei, Susan Biddle, Sonja Bjelland, Ann Biraben, Alex Mayes Birnbaum, Laura Blaustein, Nathan Blumberg, Sidney Blumenthal, John Bollinger, John Brady, Ralph Braibanti, Richard Breitman, David Brock, Charles Brown, Sally Brown (Mrs. Thatcher III), Bruce Buchanan, Martha Buchanan, Carol Buckland, Cathy Burka, Joyce Burland, Iris Burnett, Elizabeth Burr, Kenneth David Burrows, Sharon Bush, Justin Butcher, Christopher Byron, Connie Collins Cain, Jean Calhoun, Courtney Callahan, Margaret Carlson, Peter Carlson, Robert Caro, Dam Carol, Don Carr, Demaris Carroll, David Challinord, Dolly Langdon Chapin, Isolde Chapin, Bill Chaput, Pat Choate, Michael Cieply, Mary Higgins Clark, Richard Claude, Eleanor Clift, Alexander Cockburn, Andrew Cockburn, Leslie Cockburn, William Sloane Coffin, David Cogan, Lou Colasuonno, Joe Conason, Sydney "Terry" Cone, David Corn, David Crossland, Page Crossland, Julie Currie, Rick Curry, S.J., Robert Dallek, Tom D'Amore, Sam Dash, John Davidson, John Claiborne Davis, Osborne Day, June DeHart, Sally Denton, Stephanie deSibour, Betsy Trippe DeVecchi, Robert DeVecchi, Mary Devlin, Alex Dickie Jr., Mollie Dickenson, Kathleen Dillon, Ymelda Dixon, Byron Dobell, Ariel Dockerty, Jack Doll, Pier Dominquez, Jim Donovan, Michael Dorman, Jenna Dorn, Bob Dotchin, Virginia Douglas, Conway "Doc" Downing, Molly and George Downing, Brian Doyle, Roberta Hornig Draper, Pam Droog, Joseph Duffey, Robert W. Duffy, Indiana Earl, Nadine Eckhardt, Robert J. Edgeworth, Maureen Egan, Sara Ehrman, Daniel and Marina Ein, Albert Eisele, Donna M. Eller, Rayna G. Eller, Dave Elliott, Kim Elliott, Daniel Ellsberg, Roy Elson, Allison Engel, Lionel Epstein, Sally Eskew, Michael Evans, Mrs. Lawrence J. Evaristo, Peter and Pamela Evans, Penny Farthing, Allen Ferguson, Geraldine Ferraro, Robert Fink, Howard Fineman, David Fink, Harry Finkenstaedt, Jim Finkenstaedt, Gerry Fitzgerald, Roland Flamini, Heather Foley, Thomas S. Foley, Bitsey Folger, Jane Fonda, Allan Fotheringham, Barney Frank, Toby Frankel, Roberta Fulbright Foote, Elizabeth Friedsam, Harriet M. Fulbright, Len Funk, Bob Gardner, Ann Geracimos, Ann Gerber, Robin Gerber, Elbridge Gerry, Doug Giebel, Kenneth Gilpin, Ruth Gilson, Todd Gitlin, Vivian Glick, Robert A. Glick, Lynn Goddess, Paul Goldberg, Bonnie Goldstein, Richard Gooding, Suzkie Gookin, John Goerman, Sarah Gorman,

Phillip Grace, Jim Grady, Susan Granger, Ellsworth Grant, Carol Taylor Gray, Bobbie Greene, Wayne Greenhaw, Ralph Grogan, Lloyd Grove, Tammy Haddad, Margaret Hall, Ralph Hallow, Mary Hall-Ries, Kent Hance, Joyce Harris, Richard Hart, Charles Hartman, William Hathaway, Lester Hyman, Richard Helms, Lois Herbert, Seymour Hersh, Stephen Hess, John Hicket, William Hildenbrand, Cragg Hines, Randy Hobler, Elizabeth W. Holden, Tony Holden, Pat Holt, Ellen Horan, Marne Hornblower, Sandy Horwitt, Jay Houston, Janet Howard, Joseph Howerton, Richard M. Huber, Cather Bell Hudson, Edith Hunter, Lester S. Hyman, Aubrey Irby, Michael Isikoff, Molly Ivins, Beverly Jackson, Matt Jacob, John C. Jansing, Marian Javits, Ken Jennings, J. Milburn "Kim" Jessup, Tom Johnson, Erica Jong, Carol Ross Joynt, Geoffrey Kabaservice, Marvin Kalb, Louis J. Kaposta, Steve Katz, Martin Kasindorf, Barbara Kellerman, Charles Kelly, David Hume Kennerly, Michael Kernan, Martha Kessler, Kathy Kiley, James J. Kilpatrick, Richard Kimball Jr., Susan King, Worth Kinlaw, Jill Kirkpatrick, Gerrit Kouwenhoven, Donna Kullberg, Mark Lackritz, Joseph Laitin, Judy Lang, Nelson D. Lankford, Carla Langjahr, Kitty Lansdale, Christopher Larsen, Jim Latimer, Dianne Laughlin, Jenny Lawrence, Jack Leachman, Jay Lefkowitz, Nicholas Lemann, Ann Lenore, Robert Lenzner, Terry Lenzner, Zach Leonard, Larry Lewin, Nancy Lewinsohn, Charles Lewis, Randy and Pat Lewis, R.W.B. Lewis, Stephanie Lilley, Jack Limpert, Aura Lippincott, Juliet Lloyd, Laura Liswood, John Loftus, Joseph Lopez, Claus Lutterbeck, Thomas Lynch, Suzanne Jones Maas, Torbert Macdonald, Ian MacLaughlin, Isabel Maddux, Stephen Maitland-Lewis, Emily Malino, Julia Malone, Charles Marshall, Sheryl Marshall, John Mashek, Kathleen Matthews, Jane Mayer, Bob McAllister, Jerry McCoy, Sandra McElwaine, Kyle McEnearney, Floretta Dukes McKenzie, Phyllis McKenzie, Lucie McKinney, Harry McPherson, William McPherson, Howard Means, Marianne Means, Elizabeth Mehren, Phillip Merrill, Albert S. Messina, Tammy Faye Bakker Messner, Zoe and Abner Mikva, Leslie Milk, William Millburn, John Mintz, George J. Mitchell, Roger Molander, John Monjo, Jonathan A. Moore, Anthony A, Morano, Jason Morano, Jefferson Morley, Barbara and David Morowitz, Celia Morris, Dick Morris, David Mortimer, Herb Moses, Mary Mueller, Bill Moyers, Diego Mulligan, John H. Napier, Robert Nash, Simon Nathan, Kevin Nealon, Ralph Neas, Judy Nelson, David Newscom, Jesse Nichols, Peggy Noonan, Alf Nucifora, Michael Nussbaum, Marylouise Oates, Frank "Junie" O'Brien, Ginny Oler, Deborah Orin, Betsy Osborne, Curtis Owne, Susan Page, William S. Paley Jr., Stephen Pauley, Jan Paulk, Pamela Peabody, Bill Penrose, Ann Peretz, Martin Peretz, Marjorie Perloff, Jost Pollek, Victoria Pope, Jennifer Porter, E. Barrett Prettyman, Raymond Price, Ann Pritchard, Ellen Proxmire, Fred Purdy, Donnie Radcliffe, Douglas Rae, George Ramonas, Dan Rapaport, Marcus Raskin, Ollie Rauh, Sonny Rawls, Coates Redmon, Roy Reed, Deborah B. Reeve, Ken Reigner, Peter Ribicoff, Cindy Rich, Hamilton Richardson, Cam Richey, Jane Rizer, Gary Boyd Roberts, Alexandra Robbins, Randall Roden, Dave Roe, Robert A. "Hawkeye" Rogers, Warren Rogers, Louisa Romano, Marci Rosenberg, Hanna Rosin, Rick Ross, Dan Rostenkowski, Larry J. Sabato, Blair Sabol, Mark Salter, Cindy Samuels, Alexander Sanger, Arnold Scaasi, James Scheuer, Marian Schlesinger, Judith Schiff, Ina Schnell, Daniel Schorr, Aniko Gaal Schott, Dorothy Scott, Bette Seabrook, Elliott Segal, Ruth Osterweis Selig, Carol Seron, Cody Shearer, Riki and Michael Sheehan, Gail Sheehy, Alicia Shepard, Mike Shropshire, Howard E. Shuman, Ellen and Gerry Sigal, Carol Siegal, Ira Silverman, Stephanie Slewka, Mark Smith, Mike Smith, Skip Smith, Terence Smith, Sarakay Smullens, Sydney Soderberg, Mark Soler, Paula Span, Daphne Srinivasan, Dobli and Sheila Srinivasan, Bill Stadiem, Susan Stamberg, Robert Stein, Andrew Stephen, Charles Stephan, Serena Stewart, Juanita Stickney, Karen Street, Elizabeth Streicher, Mickey Stuart, Beverly Sullivan, George Sullivan, Linda Sullivan, Ron Suskind, James W. Symington, Stuart Symington Jr., Franny Taft, Deborah Tannen, Sam Tannenhaus, Erik Tarloff, Steven Thayer, Gene Theroux, Phyllis Theroux, Michael

Thomas, Robert E. Thomason, Elizabeth Thompson, Judy Timberman, Dolph Tillotson, Mary Tillotson, Martin Tolchin, Jeffrey Toobin, Nina Totenberg, Calvin Trillin, Yoshi Tsurumi, Frank Valeo, Robert Van Leeuwen, Gore Vidal, Neil Vigdor, Lindy Von Eichel, Christopher Walker, George M. Walker, Ray Walker, Eric Wallach, George Walldrodt, Mary Wallace, French Wallop, Jeannette Walls, Janice Walsh, Ian Walters, Ellen Warren, George "Red Dog" Warren, Susan Watters, Claudia Weicker, Lowell Weicker, Erika Wenzke, Tim Westmoreland, Bob White, Kenneth White, Robert K. Whitt, Thomas Wik, Lilyan Wilder, Leon Wieseltier, Lee Williams, Majorie Williams, Miyuki Williams, Stanley Willis, Tom Wilner, Mark H. Wilson, Page Wilson, Betsy Winnaker, Ellie Winninghoff, Michael Sean Winters, Herman Wolf, Bobby Wood, Randall "Buck" Wood, Judy Woodruff, Diane Woolley, Anne Woolston, Susan Yerkes, Cathy Wolfman Young, Genevieve "Gene" Young, Peck Young, Bernie Yudain, and Sid Yudain.

Huckleberry Finn had it right. "If I'd a knowed what a trouble it was to make a book," he said, "I wouldn't a tackled it." I wouldn't a tackled this one, either, except for the galvanizing force of John Bennett, a journalist of thirty years who was retired when I started knocking on his door. Since it was January and too cold for golf, he agreed to spend the winter in the Library of Congress, gathering more than five thousand articles on the Bushes. In Connecticut, Diane Stamm did the same thing, poring through the archives of the Connecticut State Library and the Thomas J. Dodd Research Center at the University of Connecticut to assemble the background material on the family. In Greenwich, I was fortunate enough to meet Stephanie S. Gaj, who responded generously to all my requests, and in New York City Marsha Berkowitz retrieved numerous records and documents while researching everything from the files of Brown Brothers Harriman to the Social Register. In Boston, Margo Howard became my beloved leg woman, chasing down everything she could, which blossomed into a mother lode of information. In Washington, D.C., I needed assistance organizing the vast amounts of material pouring in, and was blessed by Sumner MacLeish and Rebecca Hunter. I also received assistance with some of the nearly one thousand interviews conducted for this book. Throughout the process, I also was guided by Patti Pancoc, who has worked on every book I've written. A year into the project Stephanie K. Eller became my full-time assistant, and brought the scholarship of her PhD studies to the detailed research required. She worked tirelessly with no concern for the clock or the calendar, putting in long days and nights, and forgoing vacations until the manuscript was completed. Her commitment has been exemplary and I'm most grateful.

For the last four years, Stephanie and I have been helped every day by Internet retrievals from the California journalist Richard Brenneman. He showed us there is no better resource than a generous journalist, and we also found such a treasure in the investigative reporter David Robb, who sent all of his files on the Bushes, including original taped interviews, which are cited when used. Jefferson Morley from The Washington Post was equally generous with his tapes and notebooks, and Carol Taylor Gray's scrapbooks, complete with pink ribbons, were a colorful addition to our Gray files.

The best part of completing a long project is publicly thanking those who have been loving and long-suffering. My list is long and my heart is full, especially for Margaret Engel, managing editor of the Freedom Forum and director of the Alicia Patterson Foundation; for Colleen Ryan, whose friendship sets the gold standard; for Judy (Demetra) Green, a constant support for over thirty-five years; for Tom and Jean Gilpin, who make Clark County a paradise; for my wonderful book club—writers all, who understand: Linda Cashdan, Patricia O'Brien, Patricia Shakow, Susan Tolchin, Irene Wurtzel, and Catherine Wyler; for the board of directors of the National Women's Health Resource Center, its president, Julie Johnson, and executive director, Amy Niles, who tolerated my absences from meetings; for the Sisters of the Holy Names, who taught me years ago, and who, despite my lapses, continue to send up their prayers; for those who kept life on an even keel while I was in the bunker: James Henderson, Maria DiMartini, Fabiola Molina, Marvin McIntyre, Bob Parr, Steve Weisman, Tracy Noble, Gretchen and Jeremy Zucker, Seymour Zucker, Felice Ross, and Amanda and David Bowker.

My thanks to the Washington Biography Group led by Marc Pachter, who always inspires; to my sister, Mary Cary Coughlan, who honors every publication with a Chicago book party; to Marc E. Miller of McLeod, Watkinson and Miller, who read the manuscript with care, as did Mervin Block and my revered agent, Wayne S. Kabak, co–Chief Operating Officer, in the New York office of William Morris Agency, Inc.

Now comes praise for the magicians who turn a manuscript into a book. I'm ecstatic about the publisher of Doubleday, Steve Rubin, whose enthusiasm is exceeded only by his charm. His choice of Peter Gethers as my editor was the best professional break of my life. I loved every exhilarating moment of working with this wonderful man and I finally understand why F. Scott Fitzgerald worshipped Max Perkins.

It's fair to say that in the course of publishing this book I've fallen in love with everyone at Doubleday: Kathy Trager, general counsel of Random House; Bill Thomas, editor in chief; Rebecca Holland, publishing director; Frieda Duggan, production editor; Ingrid Sterner, copy editor; Katherine Duffy, managing editor; John Fontana, art director; Lorraine Hyland, production manager; Elizabeth Rendfleisch and Gretchen Achilles, designers; Jeff Ward, family tree illustrator; Ada Yonenaka, production editor; Karen Broderick, photo researcher; Claudia Herr, Gethers's assistant; Suzanne Herz and David Drake, publicity; and Janet Renard, proofreader. All have my gratitude.

My deepest thanks to my husband, Jonathan E. Zucker, the dear and glorious physician to whom this book is dedicated. He came into my life twelve years ago and continues to fill my heart with joy.

June 8, 2004

PHOTO CREDITS

George H.W. Bush and Dwight D. Eisenhower © George Bush Presidential Library

George H.W. Bush and President Richard Nixon © George Bush Presidential Library

George H.W. Bush and Henry Kissinger © George Bush Presidential Library

George H.W. Bush, Ambassador to UN © George Bush Presidential Library

George H.W. Bush, chairman RNC © George Bush Presidential Library

George H.W. and Barbara Bush, China © George Bush Presidential Library

George H.W. Bush, CIA director © George Bush Presidential Library

Vice President and Mrs. George H.W. Bush with President and Mrs. Ronald Reagan © AP/Wide World Photos

President and Mrs. George H.W. Bush with Vice President and Mrs. Dan Quayle © George Bush Presidential Library

George H.W. Bush with young George and Robin © George Bush Presidential Library

George H.W. Bush and family, 1959 © George Bush Presidential Library

Vice President George H.W. Bush and family, 1981 © George Bush Presidential Library

George H.W. Bush on his seventy-fifth birthday, with family © George Bush Presidential Library

George H.W. Bush and former presidents and first ladies © AP/Wide World Photos

George H.W. Bush with Jennifer Fitzgerald © George Bush Presidential Library

Jennifer Fitzgerald © Courtesy Gerald R. Ford Library

Barbara Bush and Nancy Reagan © George Bush Presidential Library

Vice President and Mrs. George H.W. Bush aboard Airforce Two © George Bush Presidential Library

George H.W. Bush with George W. in Texas Air National Guard © AP/Wide World Photos

George W. Bush congressional campaign poster © George Bush Presidential Library

George W. Bush with Texas Rangers sign © AP/Wide World Photos

Jeb Bush and George W. Bush, 1955 © George Bush Presidential Library

Governor Jeb Bush and George W. Bush, 2000 © AP/Wide World Photos

Katherine Harris and Governor Jeb Bush © AP/Wide World Photos

President and Mrs. George W. Bush, Inauguration Day, 2001 © WIN McNamee/Reuters

George W. Bush at Bob Jones University © AP/Wide World Photos

George W. Bush at Ground Zero © AP/Wide World Photos

George H.W. Bush in pilot's uniform © George Bush Presidential Library

George W. Bush landing on USS *Abraham Lincoln* © AP/Wide World Photos

Bush twins, Barbara and Jenna, 2001 © Larry Downing/Reuters

Lauren Bush © AP/Wide World Photos

George P. Bush and his uncle George W. Bush © AP/Wide World Photos

Noelle Bush © AP/Wide World Photos

INDEX

campaign, 506, 519–31; report card, 534; socializing during, 480–81, 511–12; Somalia, 534; speechmaking, 487; spitefulness and payback, 478–80, 525; Supreme Court appointments, 512–14; tax hike, 493–95; Tiananmen Square, 483–84; Tower nomination, 482–83; White House mess privileges to family, 487

SPEECHES AND PUBLISHED WRITINGS: *All the Best, George Bush,* xxi–xxii, 560; "kinder and gentler nation/no new taxes" speech, 459, 493; *Looking Forward,* 99, 219; *Man of Integrity,* 452; *A World Transformed,* xxiv, 560

WORLD WAR II: at Andover, 66–67; as cadet and pilot training, 73–75, 78; Chichi-Jima, 80–85, 95–96, 452, 562; combat, 79–83; decorations and heroism, 81, 83, 213–14; enlistment, 67, 70; political influence of service, 77

YALE: Babe Ruth and, 92; class of 1948, 11, 89–98; clubs, 92–93; fraternity, DKE, 106, 461; honors at, 91; "King" of his class, 97; lifelong friends, 94–95; RTA and, 94, 97–98; running for office at, 93; as scholar-athlete, 90–92; Skull and Bones, 82, 92, 94–98; tercentenary celebration, 631; William Sloane Coffin and, 232–36

Bush, George Prescott, 555, 590, 603, 612, 622

Bush, George Walker (43rd President)
BUSINESS, EMPLOYMENT, AND FINANCES: Arlington stadium, 537–38; family money to back ventures, 187; father's political power and business ventures, 421–28, 488–89, 520; Harvard Business School, 308–10, 332, 577; insider trading charges, 552–54; investors, 422; jobs through his father, 300–301, 307; Jonathan Bush as backer, 422; law school turn-down and idleness, 300–301; nomadic years, 303–8, 333, 350; oil companies, 355–56, 421–28; Project PULL, 307–8, 579–80; Rainbo Club home, 581; Saudis and, 422; Texas Rangers ownership, 488–89, 536–37, 542, 573; trust fund, 301; wealth and net worth, 573

CHARACTER, APPEARANCE, AND PERSONALITY: academic mediocrity and lack of intellect, 253–54, 265, 266–67, 271, 294, 309–10, 540, 571, 589, 616;

adolescent-like behavior, 143, 304; alcohol and drug use, xxvi, 25, 259–60, 266, 284, 297, 302–3, 304, 350, 445–46, 550, 575–76, 578–84; arrogance and lack of compassion, 308–9, 585–87, 618–19, 635; bad-boy status, 541; born-again evangelism, 25, 271, 446, 546–47, 584, 631; charisma, 542; credibility and integrity, problems, 223–25, 582–83, 595, 598, 604, 629; discipline and strict regimen, 584; DUI arrest, 350, 582–83; fatalism, 143; hyperactivity, 577; kindness, 587–88; likeability, 300, 308, 541; machismo, 263, 584; mean streak, 555; mother's temperament, 540; narcotics arrest, rumor, 579–80; as prankster and cut-up, 256, 263; privilege, power, sense of entitlement, 187–88, 219, 248–49, 304, 310, 572, 601; sobriety, 445–46, 547; temper and use of profanity, 263–64, 450–51, 540, 548–49, 584–85; Texas good ol' boy persona, 305, 310, 540–41; toughness, 446–47; verbal abusiveness, 25, 575–76; womanizing, 550–51, 599–600

CHILDHOOD AND YOUTH: at Andover, xx–xxi, 252–60, 577; birth, 93; girlfriend and abortion rumors, 599–600; death of sister Robin, 131, 134, 141–42, 253; drug and alcohol use (*see* character and personality); father and, mano a mano incident, 306–7; as "Georgie," 93, 99, 134; Kennedy assassination and, 258–59; Kincaid School, 204; mother and, 134, 142–43, 254; pig ball and stickball, 258, 635; in Scotland, 193; sibling rivalry with Jeb, 538–39, 540; sports and, 257–58

FAMILY AND MARRIAGE: alcohol-induced behavior and marital troubles, 575; birth of daughters, 425–26; as the "Chosen One," 567, 569; infidelity rumors, 575; Laura, marriage and, 576, 620; Laura, meets and marries, 356–57; Laura, political aspirations and, 536, 542, 593–94, 603; lifestyle of wealth and privilege, 427, 589; in Midland, Texas, 422, 426; Rainbo Club, whites only, 581; social circle of, 426; statement on role of wife, 391

MILITARY SERVICE (AIR NATIONAL GUARD): ARFed, 296; commission, 297–98; discharge, 308; excellence as pilot, 299; 147th Fighter Group, 295; preferential treatment, 240–41, 294–95; record